BUSINESS AND INFORMATION SYSTEMS

Robert C. Nickerson

San Francisco State University

ADDISON-WESLEY

An imprint of Addison Wesley Longman, Inc.

Reading, Massachusetts • Menlo Park, California • New York • Harlow, England
Don Mills, Ontario • Sydney • Mexico City • Madrid • Amsterdam

Acquisitions Editor: Michael Roche
Development Editor: Rebecca Johnson
Assistant Editor: Ruth Berry
Production Supervisor: Louis C. Bruno, Jr.
Project Coordination: Electronic Publishing Services Inc., NYC
Text Designer: Electronic Publishing Services Inc., NYC
Electronic Page Makeup: Electronic Publishing Services Inc., NYC
Cover Designer: Gina Hagen
Senior Marketing Manager: Michelle Hudson
Marketing Coordinator: Deanna Storey

For permission to use copyrighted material, grateful acknowledgment is made to the copyright holders in source notes throughout the text, which are hereby made part of this copyright page.

Library of Congress Cataloging-in-Publication Data

Nickerson, Robert C., 1946—
    Business and information systems / Robert C. Nickerson,
       p.   cm.
  Includes index.
  ISBN 0-321-01378-6
    1. Management information systems—Case studies. I. Title.
  HD30.2.N53   1998
  658.4'038—dc21   97-41551
                                                          CIP

Copyright © 1998 by Addison-Wesley Educational Publishers Inc.

All right reserved. No part of this publication may be reproduced, stored in a retrieval system, or transmitted, in any form or by any means, electronic, mechanical, photocopying, recording, or otherwise, without the prior written permission of the publisher. Printed in the United States.

ISBN 0-321-01378-6
2345678910—CRW—01009998

BRIEF CONTENTS

Preface

PART I   **INTRODUCTION**   1

CHAPTER 1   Information Systems in Business   3
CHAPTER 2   Business Fundamentals   29
CHAPTER 3   Information System Fundamentals   59

PART II   **INFORMATION TECHNOLOGY**   87

CHAPTER 4   Information System Hardware   89
CHAPTER 5   Information System Software   125
CHAPTER 6   Information System Networks   157
CHAPTER 7   Information System Data Management   189

PART III   **BUSINESS INFORMATION SYSTEMS**   221

CHAPTER 8   Personal Productivity   223
CHAPTER 9   Group Collaboration   261
CHAPTER 10   Business Operations   291
CHAPTER 11   Management Decision Making   325
CHAPTER 12   Strategic Impact   357

PART IV   **DEVELOPING AND MANAGING INFORMATION SYSTEMS**   381

CHAPTER 13   Problem Solving and Individual Application Development   383
CHAPTER 14   Information System Development   409
CHAPTER 15   Managing Information Systems and Technology   441

Glossary   469
Photo Credits   487
Acknowledgments   489
Index   493

CONTENTS

PREFACE   xvii

Part I Introduction   1

Chapter 1 Information Systems in Business   3

Basic Information System Concepts   5
    What Is an Information System?   5
    Examples of Information Systems   6
Bookmark: *Inventory Control at Guess?*   7
    Information System Functions   9
    Data versus Information   10
Types of Information Systems   12
    Individual Information Systems   12
    Workgroup Information Systems   13
    Organizational Information Systems   15
    Interorganizational Information Systems   17
    International Information Systems   18
Bookmark: *International Information System at Timberland   19*
Information System Users   19
    How Users Use Information Systems   20
    The Ethical Use of Information Systems   20
Connecting Users to Information Technology   21
    Networks   21
    The Internet   21
Benefits of Information Systems   22
    Better Information   22
    Improved Service   23
    Increased Productivity   23
An Approach to the Study of Information Systems   23
Chapter Summary   24
Key Terms   25
Assignment Material   25
Real-world Case: *The Benetton Group, Italy*   27

Chapter 2 Business Fundamentals   29

Purpose of a Business   30
Types of Businesses   31
    Manufacturers   31
    Wholesalers   31
    Retailers   32
    Service Businesses   33
    Not-for-profit Organizations   34
    Government   34

Business Functions   34
  Accounting   34
  Finance   35
  Marketing   35
Bookmark: *Information Systems at American Red Cross and*
    Nature Conservancy   36
  Manufacturing   36
  Human Resource Management   37
  Other Business Functions   37
Organization of a Business   37
Information and Business Operations   39
Information and Business Management   41
Basic Business Information Processing   43
Bookmark: *Custom Jeans Order Entry at Levi Strauss   43*
  Entering Customer Orders   44
  Billing Customers   44
  Collecting Customer Payments   46
  Keeping Track of Inventory   46
  Purchasing Stock and Materials   48
  Paying Bills   50
  Paying Employees   51
  Reporting Financial Information   52
Information Systems and Business   54
Chapter Summary   54
Key Terms   55
Assignment Material   55
Real-world Case: *Daka International   57*

Chapter 3   Information System Fundamentals   59

Components of an Information System   60
  Hardware   60
  Software   60
  Stored Data   61
  Personnel   62
  Procedures   62
Hardware for Information Systems   62
  Input and Output Devices   62
  Primary Storage and the Central Processing Unit   65
  Secondary Storage   66
  Communications Hardware   68
  Computer Systems   68
Bookmark: *Wearable Computers from Carnegie Mellon University   70*
Software for Information Systems   74
  Program Concepts   74
  Types of Software   75
  Sources of Software   77
Bookmark: *Linking Railroads at the Association of American Railroads   77*
Stored Data for Information Systems   78

Personnel for Information Systems   80
Procedures for Information Systems   80
Chapter Summary   80
Key Terms   81
Assignment Material   82
Real-world Case: *Beamscope Canada*   *84*

Part II Information Technology   87

Chapter 4 Information System Hardware   89

The Need for Hardware in Information Systems   90
Input and Output Devices   91
    Keyboards   91
    Pointing Devices   92
    Other Input Devices   92
    Screens   95
Bookmark: *Voice Recognition at Boeing*   *96*
    Printers   97
    Other Output Devices   100
    Terminals   101
    Multimedia Input and Output   101
    Virtual Reality Input and Output   102
Primary Storage   103
    Primary Storage Structure   104
    Data Representation   105
    Primary Storage Organization   106
    Primary Storage Capacity   107
The Central Processing Unit   107
    CPU Structure   108
    CPU Compatibility   108
    CPU Speed   109
    Common CPUs   109
Bookmark: *Supercomputers at Alcoa, AAA, and Best Western*   *111*
Secondary Storage   112
    Magnetic Disk Storage   112
    Optical Disk Storage   116
    Magnetic Tape Storage   117
Chapter Summary   119
Key Terms   120
Assignment Material   121
Real-world Case: *United Parcel Service*   *123*

Chapter 5 Information System Software   125

The Need for Software in Information Systems   126
Application Software   126

Individual Application Software   127
Workgroup Application Software   128
Organizational Application Software   128
Interorganizational Application Software   129
System Software   130
Operating System Concepts   130
Common Operating Systems   135
Bookmark: *Operating System Choices at Gap, LG & E Energy,*
   and Chevron   138
Other System Software   139
Software Development   139
Programming Language Concepts   139
Traditional Programming Languages   143
Object-oriented Programming Languages   146
Internet Programming Languages   148
Bookmark: *Java Internet Application at CERA Bank, Belgium   151*
Chapter Summary   151
Key Terms   152
Assignment Material   153
Real-world Case: *Oakland Housing Authority   155*

Chapter 6   Information System Networks   157

The Need for Networks in Information Systems   158
Communications Hardware   158
Communications Channel Characteristics   159
Communications Channel Media   162
Communications Channel Sources   164
Bookmark: *Wireless Communications at the Internal Revenue Service   165*
Communications Devices   166
Communications Software   169
Personal Computer Communications Software   169
Multiple-user Computer Communications Software   170
Network Communications Software   170
Remote Access   171
Terminal Communications   171
Personal Computer Communications   172
Network Organization   173
Local Area Networks   175
Client-server Computing   176
Wide Area Networks   177
Internetworks   178
The Internet   178
Bookmark: *Internetwork at Scientific-Atlanta   179*
Intranets   181
Chapter Summary   182
Key Terms   183
Assignment Material   184
Real-world Case: *Geffen Records   186*

Chapter 7 Information System Data Management   189

The Need for Data Management in Information   Systems   190
File Processing   190
File Organization   191
File Management   193
Advantages of File Processing   194
Disadvantages of File Processing   194
Database Processing   195
What Is a Database?   196
Database Management   197
Advantages of Database Processing   198
Disadvantages of Database Processing   199
Database Organization   199
Data Relationships   199
Types of Databases   202
Object-oriented Databases   206
Common Database Software   206
Bookmark: *Object-oriented Database at Air France   207*
Personal Computer Database Software   207
Multiple-user Computer Database Software   208
Networked Computer Database Software   208
Using Database Software   209
Query Languages   209
Application Programs   212
Database Use in Information Systems   213
Data Warehouses   214
Bookmark: *Data Warehouse at PacifiCare Health Systems   214*
Database Administration   216
Chapter Summary   216
Key Terms   217
Assignment Material   217
Real-world Case: *Environmental Protection Agency   219*

Part III Business Information Systems   221

Chapter 8 Personal Productivity   223

Improving Personal Productivity   224
Database Management   224
Database Software Functions   226
An Example of Database Management   227
Spreadsheet Analysis   231
Bookmark: *Overcoming Spreadsheet Limitations at MTV   233*
Spreadsheet Concepts   234
Spreadsheet Software Functions   236
An Example of Spreadsheet Analysis   237
Combining Database Management and Spreadsheet Analysis   239

Information Presentation 240
    Word Processing 240
    Graphics 244
    Desktop Publishing 248
    Multimedia 251
Locating Information Using the Internet 251
Bookmark: *Internet Use at Art Anderson Associates and Mobius Computer Corporation 252*
Other Personal Productivity Applications 254
Chapter Summary 256
Key Terms 256
Assignment Material 257
Real-world Case: *Haworth Inc. 259*

Chapter 9 Group Collaboration 261

Encouraging Group Collaboration 262
Characteristics of Group Collaboration 263
    Time and Place of Collaboration 263
    Form of Communication 264
Types of Workgroup Applications 265
    Electronic Messaging 265
    Information Sharing 267
    Document Conferencing 268
Bookmark: *Information Sharing at Jardine Fleming, Hong Kong 270*
    Audio Conferencing 271
    Videoconferencing 273
    Electronic Conferencing 275
    Electronic Meeting Support 276
Bookmark: *Global Electronic Conferencing at Ford 277*
    Group Calendaring and Scheduling 278
    Workflow Management 279
    Summary of Workgroup Applications 280
Office Automation Systems 282
The Virtual Work Environment 283
    Telecommuting 283
    Virtual Offices 284
    Virtual Meetings 284
    Virtual Companies 284
Chapter Summary 285
Key Terms 286
Assignment Material 286
Real-world Case: *Xerox 288*

Chapter 10 Business Operations 291

Increasing Business Operations Efficiency 292
Transaction Processing Systems 293
    Transaction Processing System Structure 293
    Transaction Processing System Functions 294

Controlling Transaction Processing Systems   298
Processing Data in Transaction Processing Systems   299

Basic Business Information Systems   300
Order Entry System   301
Billing System   303
Accounts Receivable System   304
Inventory Control System   305
Purchasing System   306
Accounts Payable System   307

Bookmark: *Accounts Payable at Ademco*   *308*
Payroll System   309
General Ledger System   310

Other Business Information Systems   311
Accounting Information Systems   311
Financial Information Systems   311
Marketing Information Systems   312
Manufacturing Information Systems   312

Bookmark: *Purchasing through the Internet at General Electric*   *313*
Human Resource Information Systems   314

Organizing Information System Functions   315
Centralized Systems   315
Teleprocessing Systems   315
Decentralized Systems   316
Distributed Systems   316

Chapter Summary   319
Key Terms   320
Assignment Material   321
Real-world Case: *Sprint*   *323*

Chapter 11   Management Decision Making   325

Improving Management Decision-Making Effectiveness   326

Management Decisions   327
Levels of Management Decisions   327
Characteristics of Management Decisions   327
Information Needs for Management Decisions   329
Information Systems for Management Support   330

Management Information Systems   331
Management Information System Structure   331
Management Information System Functions   332
Management Information System Software   336

Decision Support Systems   337
Management Decision Support   337

Bookmark: *Decision Support System at Royal Caribbean Cruises*   *338*
Decision Support System Structure   338
Decision Support System Functions   339
Decision Support System Software   340
Group Decision Support Systems   341
Geographic Information Systems   341

Executive Support Systems   342
  Executive Information Needs   342
Bookmark: *Geographic Information System for the City of Scottsdale, Arizona   344*
  Executive Support System Structure   344
  Executive Support System Functions   346
  Executive Support System Software   347
Expert Systems   347
  Expert Advice   347
  Expert System Structure   348
  Expert System Functions   348
  Expert System Software   350
  Other Artificial Intelligence Applications   350
Chapter Summary   351
Key Terms   352
Assignment Material   352
Real-world Case: *Grand & Toy, Canada   354*

Chapter 12   Strategic Impact   357

Providing a Strategic Impact   358
Strategic Information Systems   359
  Characteristics of Strategic Information Systems   359
Bookmark: *Strategic Web Site at National Semiconductor   361*
  Identifying Strategic Information System Opportunities   362
Interorganizational Information Systems   364
  Business Alliances and Interorganizational Systems   364
Bookmark: *Interorganizational System at the National Transportation Exchange   366*
  Characteristics of Interorganizational Systems   366
  Electronic Data Interchange Systems   368
International Information Systems   370
  International Business and International Information Systems   370
  International Business Strategies   371
  Characteristics of International Information Systems   373
Chapter Summary   376
Key Terms   377
Assignment Material   377
Real-world Case: *Levi Strauss   379*

IV Developing and Managing Information Systems   381

Chapter 13 Problem Solving and Individual Application Development   383

End-user Computing   384
Problem Solving   384
  Solution Procedures   384
  Tools for Representing Solution Procedures   385
  Basic Procedure Logic   386
The Problem-solving Process   389
  Problem Definition   390
Bookmark: *Applications Developed by Two Entrepreneurs   391*

Solution Procedure Design   393
Software Implementation   394
Implementation Testing   394
Documentation   396
Computer Applications   396
User Interface   397
Stored Data   397
Business Rules   398
The Individual Application-development Process   398
Bookmark: *Creating a Web Site at Archetype   399*
Application Planning   400
Application Analysis   400
Application Design   400
Application Implementation   401
Application Maintenance   401
An Example of Individual Application Development   402
Application Planning   402
Application Analysis   402
Application Design   403
Application Implementation   404
Chapter Summary   405
Key Terms   405
Assignment Material   406
Real-world Case: *Cigna   407*

Chapter 14   Information System Development   409

People in Information System Development   410
The System Development Process   410
System Planning   411
Bookmark: *System Development Lessons from Time Warner Communications   412*
System Analysis   413
System Design   415
System Implementation   416
System Maintenance   418
System Development Tools   419
Data Flow Diagrams   419
System Flowcharts   422
Entity-relationship Diagrams   423
CASE   424
An Example of Information System Development   425
System Planning   426
Bookmark: *Solving the Year 2000 Problem at The Equitable Life Assurance Society   426*
System Analysis   427
System Design   429
System Implementation   430
System Maintenance   431
Other System Development Approaches   431
Prototyping   431
Rapid Application Development   432
Object-oriented Analysis and Design   432

Business Process Reengineering 433
Chapter Summary 434
Key Terms 435
Assignment Material 436
Real-world Case: *Inland Steel Industries* *438*

Chapter 15 Managing Information Systems and Technology 441

Planning for Information Systems and Technology 442
  Determining the Planning Horizon 442
  Evaluating Risk 443
  Selecting the Application Portfolio 443
Acquiring Information Technology 444
  Hardware 445
  Software 445
Bookmark: *Outsourcing Information Systems at Esprit* *446*
  Network Technology 447
  Data Management Technology 447
  Personnel and Training 448
Organizing Information Systems Activities 448
  Centralization versus Decentralization 448
  Information Systems Organizational Structure 449
Controlling and Securing Information Systems 451
  Information System Controls 451
Bookmark: *Disaster Recovery Plan at Options Clearing Corporation* *453*
  Information System Security 454
Social and Ethical Issues 455
  Privacy 455
  Employment 456
  Crime 458
  Ethics 461
Chapter Summary 463
Key Terms 464
Assignment Material 464
Real-world Case: *Malden Mills* *466*

GLOSSARY 469

PHOTO CREDITS 487

ACKNOWLEDGMENTS 489

INDEX 493

PREFACE

Information systems are essential to the operation and management of businesses today. To become effective business professionals, students must be educated in information systems and technology, and in the integration of information systems into business activities. A student's understanding of business is limited without an understanding of information systems. How can a student understand information systems without *first understanding business?*

This question prompted the writing of this book. *Business and Information Systems* takes a unique approach by covering both business fundamentals and information systems. It views information systems and businesses as intricately intertwined. It presents not only the traditional information systems and technology topics, but also the fundamental business background that students need to know in order to understand the relevance of these topics. It describes how businesses operate and are managed, and shows how information systems support business operations and management. It discusses the importance of competitive advantage to businesses and explains how information systems can help provide that advantage. It covers the technical foundations of information systems and shows how the technology is critical to the success of businesses.

Students taking an information systems course often find the approach followed by other books unsatisfactory. While most books explain information systems and technology adequately, they do not provide a sufficient foundation in business functions so that students can fully understand the importance of the technical topics. As a result, students often go away from the information systems course without knowing how the course material relates to other areas of business, such as accounting, finance, marketing, and production. When they take other business courses, they are not able to use information systems concepts in those courses.

This book overcomes these difficulties by integrating business topics with information systems concepts. For example, the second chapter of the book explains business fundamentals. It describes the functions and organization of a business, explains the flow of information in a business, and examines the use of information in business management. This background serves as a basis for understanding the need for and structure of information systems. This approach is carried through in other chapters. For example, each chapter on information technology (Chapters 4 through 7) begins with a section that explains the need that businesses have for the specific technology. Similarly, each chapter on business information systems (Chapters 8 through 12) begins with a section that discusses the advantages gained by businesses from the systems described in the chapter. These chapters also cover such topics as management decision making and competitive advantage to provide a basis for understanding the role of management information and strategic information systems.

Students taking the information systems course also find that some books provide a narrow view, focusing primarily on personal computers and applications. This book presents a broad view of information systems, showing how systems function at many levels within an organization and between organizations. It describes, in separate chapters, how individuals, workgroups, and organizations as a whole use information systems. It examines systems that operate within a business and between businesses, and that function at local, national, and international levels. All these perspectives, from the individual to the interorganizational and international, are covered completely in the book.

CONTENT AND ORGANIZATION

The importance of information systems to end-users is emphasized throughout the book. Starting with the first chapter, examples show how end-users are involved in information systems.

The book is organized into four parts. Part I introduces business and information systems concepts and examples. Chapter 1 motivates the students by showing that they will be involved with information systems as end-users in their jobs and careers. Chapter 2 covers basic business concepts that students need to know in order to understand information systems. More advanced business concepts appear in later chapters, where they relate to different types of information systems. Chapter 3 presents the basic structure of information systems and introduces the technical foundations for information systems. With the background in Part I, the other parts of the book can be covered in any order.

Part II examines the information technology that forms a foundation for information systems. Chapter 4 covers information system hardware that is relevant to the user. Chapter 5 describes information system software, again emphasizing concepts that are most relevant to the user. Chapter 6 discusses networks used in information systems, including local area networks, wide area networks, and the Internet. Chapter 7 covers data management for information systems, including database organization and processing.

Part III of the book examines information systems in businesses. Chapter 8 discusses the need for improving personal productivity in the workplace and examines the use of common end-user software to solve business problems. Chapter 9 examines the importance of group collaboration in businesses and describes the groupware tools that encourage such collaboration. Chapter 10 covers basic business operations and explains how information systems can increase the efficiency of these operations. Chapter 11 examines management decision making, the information and analysis that can improve the effectiveness of decision making, and the information systems that provide the necessary support. Chapter 12 explains how information systems can have a strategic impact on a business and examines the types of systems that can have such an impact. Numerous examples are used throughout this part of the book to illustrate the information systems that are described.

Part IV of the book discusses the development and management of information systems. Chapter 13 explains how individual applications are developed by end-users. The chapter takes a problem-solving approach to end-user application development. Chapter 14 describes the development of organizational information systems, with an emphasis on end-user involvement in the development process. Chapter 15 discusses the management of organizational information systems and examines social and ethical issues of information systems.

KEY FEATURES

Three fictitious businesses are presented in Chapter 1 and used as examples in various chapters. These businesses—a campus sports shop, an athletic clothing wholesaler, and an athletic shoe manufacturer—were selected because they are easy for students to understand and represent a range of business types. Examples of information systems for these businesses are used in different chapters to illustrate basic concepts.

In addition to fictitious businesses, a wide range of real businesses and organizations are used for examples of information systems in case studies throughout the book. Systems in small, local businesses, those in regional and national companies, and systems in multinational corporations are all presented. Systems in not-for-profit organizations and government agencies are also described. Many of the examples come from businesses and organizations that are based outside the United States, including businesses in Canada, Europe, and Asia.

The use of the Internet and the World Wide Web is covered throughout the book, not just in a single chapter. Chapter 1 introduces these topics and other chapters refer to them when appropriate. A technical description of the Internet is provided in Chapter 6, but students do not need the technical background to use the Internet.

Each chapter in the book begins with a chapter outline and a list of learning objectives. Within each chapter are boxed cases, called Bookmarks, which describe applications and systems in real businesses. These cases, taken from professional publications, show how the topics in the chapter apply in the real world. Each case includes review questions to challenge the students. Each case also includes one or more URLs of relevant Web sites.

Each chapter in the book ends with a chapter summary, a list of key terms introduced in the chapter, review questions, discussion questions, and problem-solving projects. The discussion questions are designed to challenge the students to think more deeply about the chapter's topics. The problem-solving projects, which are designed to encourage the application of the chapter's material, present problems that the students must solve, often using personal computer software such as spreadsheet and database software. Some projects also require the use of the World Wide Web to locate information. Finally, each chapter concludes with a real-world case taken from a professional publication or similar source. The case integrates many of the chapter's topics and includes questions that require the students to apply chapter material in analyzing the case.

INSTRUCTOR SUPPORT MATERIALS

A complete set of instructor support materials is available to adopters of the book. The materials are designed to improve instructor effectiveness and enhance the learning experience for the students. Included in the materials are the following:

- **Instructor's Manual.** A full and complete instructor's manual, written by Robert C. Nickerson and Charles H. Trepper, is available. The manual includes teaching suggestions, lecture notes, answers to review questions, answers to Bookmark and Real-world Case questions, and other items to help the instructor prepare the course.
- **Test Bank.** A complete test bank, prepared by Charles H. Trepper, is available in print form and on CD-ROM with networkable test preparation software. Included in the test bank are multiple-choice, true-false, matching, and short-answer questions.
- **PowerPoint Slides.** A full set of PowerPoint slides is available. Included in the slides are key illustrations from the text as well as new material. The slides are carefully coordinated with the lecture notes found in the Instructor's Manual.
- **Website.** http://hepg.awl.com/nickerson/

- **Videotapes.** Commercially produced videotapes from the Addison Wesley Longman library are available free of charge to qualified adopters. The videotapes can be used to enhance lectures on concepts presented in the book.

WORLD WIDE WEB SITE

A World Wide Web site (http://hepg.awl.com/nickerson/bis/) is available for students to access. The site contains numerous items to enhance the students' learning experiences. Included in the Web site are the following:

- Practice tests
- Web case links
- Updates
- Study break

BUSINESS AND INFORMATION SYSTEMS QUICKBOOKS MANUAL

A separate manual, *Business and Information Systems Using Intuit's QuickBooks* by Charles H. Trepper, is available to support the book. This manual reinforces the business concepts presented in the book by having the students run a small business using Intuit's QuickBooks software. The manual provides complete tutorial instruction on the use of QuickBooks plus a variety of projects related to the operation and management of a business. Included are projects in accounting, finance, marketing, operations, and human resource management. A limited version of QuickBooks is provided with the manual.

SOFTWARE TUTORIALS

Lab manuals for a variety of software packages are available from the Addison Wesley Longman series of books. Included are manuals for common word processing, spreadsheet, database, and presentation graphics software, as well as for operating systems, programming languages, and Internet use. The manuals can be combined in various packages to create customized teaching support systems tailored to individual class requirements.

ACKNOWLEDGMENTS

Writing a book like this one is not done without the help of many people. My developmental editor at Addison Wesley Longman, Becky Johnson, was invaluable in providing advice that greatly improved the book. My acquisitions editor, Mike Roche, was always there to listen to my questions and provide ideas. Michelle Hudson and Ruth Berry, as well as others at Addison, were extremely helpful.

My colleagues and students at San Francisco State University were invaluable. Many of my colleagues provided important input, but Sultan Bhimjee, David Chao, Gary Hammerstrom, Ron Henley, Bonnie Homan, Lutfus Sayeed, and David Whitney stand out. My students' critiques of material for the book that I presented in class were especially useful. Finally, my family provided much support and help during the writing of the book.

REVIEWERS

The following manuscript reviewers did a thorough job, and their comments were especially useful. They provided practical advice on content, depth of coverage, organization, and accessibility to the students. I greatly appreciate their efforts.

Beverly Amer
Northern Arizona University

Gary Armstrong
Shippensburg University

Michael Atherton
Mankato State University

Robert Behling
Bryant College

Eli Cohen
Grand Valley State University

John Eatman
University of North Carolina at Greensboro

Terry Evans
Jackson State Community College

Dan Flynn
Shoreline Community College

Terribeth Gordon-Moore
University of Toledo

Rassule Hadidi
University of Illinois - Springfield

Constanza Hagmann
Kansas State University

Binshan Lin
Louisiana State University - Shreveport

Thom Luce
Ohio University

Gerald F. Mackey
Georgia Institute of Technology

Michael L. Mick
Purdue University - Calumet

John Palipchak
Pennsylvania State University

James Payne
Kellogg Community College

John V. Quigley
East Tennessee State University

David Russell
Western New England College

Janice Sipier
Villanova University

Janet Urlaub
Sinclair Community College

Bruce A. White
Dakota State University

ROBERT C. NICKERSON
San Francisco State University

I

INTRODUCTION

1 Information Systems in Business

Chapter Outline

Basic Information System Concepts   (p. 5)
    What Is an Information System?   (p. 5)
    Examples of Information Systems   (p. 6)
    Information System Functions   (p. 9)
    Data versus Information   (p. 10)
Types of Information Systems   (p. 12)
    Individual Information Systems   (p. 12)
    Workgroup Information Systems   (p. 13)
    Organizational Information Systems   (p. 15)
    Interorganizational Information Systems   (p. 17)
    International Information Systems   (p. 18)
Information System Users   (p. 19)
    How Users Use Information Systems   (p. 20)
    The Ethical Use of Information Systems   (p. 20)
Connecting Users to Information Technology   (p. 21)
    Networks   (p. 21)
    The Internet   (p. 21)
Benefits of Information Systems   (p. 22)
    Better Information   (p. 22)
    Improved Service   (p. 23)
    Increased Productivity   (p. 23)
An Approach to the Study of Information Systems   (p. 23)

Learning Objectives

After completing this chapter, you should be able to:

☐ 1. Explain what an information system is and describe the functions of an information system.
☐ 2. Explain the difference between data and information.
☐ 3. List several types of information systems and give an example of each type.
☐ 4. Explain who information system users are, describe how users use information systems, and explain the importance of using information systems ethically.
☐ 5. Explain how users are connected to information technology locally, nationally, and internationally.
☐ 6. Describe several benefits of information systems.

I magine a business for which you might work in the future, or, if you have a job now, think of the business or organization that you currently work for. What *information* do the employees of that business need? For example, you might work for a supermarket. (See Fig. 1.1.) If you were a checkout clerk in the supermarket, you would need information about prices for certain products, such as produce, to help you check out customers. If you were a supervisor in the supermarket's warehouse, you would need information about how much stock was available on the shelves and

Employees using information in a supermarket

A checkout clerk

A warehouse supervisor

in the warehouse to help you decide when to reorder. If you were an advertising manager for the supermarket, you would need information about which products were selling well and which were selling poorly to help you develop advertising programs and promotions. If you were the supermarket's general manager, you would need information about expenses and revenues to help you evaluate the profitability of the store. No matter what position you had, you would need information related to the business to help you do your job.

How do people working for a business get the information they need? The answer is they use *information systems*. Put simply, an information system provides information to help people operate and manage a business. The checkout clerk in a supermarket uses an information system called a *point-of-sale (POS) system* to find prices of products. The warehouse supervisor uses an information system called an *inventory control system* to keep track of stock availability. The advertising manager uses an information system called a *sales analysis system* to find out how well different products are selling. The supermarket's general manager uses an information system called a *general ledger system* to get reports on the income produced by the store.

This book is about how businesses and other organizations use information and information systems. Since many information systems include computers, part of this book is devoted to computers and related technology. But this is *not* a computer book. It is a book about businesses and their use of information systems. After completing this book, you should understand *why* information systems are important, *how* information systems function and are developed, and *what* your role in information systems is likely to be in the future.

This chapter introduces basic concepts about information systems. It surveys some of the types of information systems and gives examples of each type. It examines the critical role of people—*users*—in information systems and discusses the ethical use of information systems. It explains the importance of connecting users to the technology of information systems. It discusses the benefits of information systems to people and organizations. Finally, it outlines the approach that this book takes to the study of information systems.

Basic Information System Concepts

Throughout this book you will study many topics and learn many ideas about information systems. To get started, however, there are a few basic concepts you need to know.

What Is an Information System?

An information system is not one thing, but a group of things that work together. These things are called *components* of the system, and they include equipment or *hardware* such as computers, instructions or *software* for the computers, facts or *data* stored in the system, *people* to operate the system, and *procedures* for the people to follow. Chapter 3 describes these components of an information system in more detail, but for now it is sufficient just to know that an information system is a group of components. These components work together for the purpose of providing information for an organization. The information is used in the daily operation and in the management of an organization. Put succinctly, an information system or IS is a collection of components that work together to provide information to help in the operation and management of an organization.

An information system may include computers, but it does not have to. People use manual information systems all the time. For example, a name and address book is part of an information system, the purpose of which is to provide information to assist in completing letters and making telephone calls. Many information systems, however, do have computers. Such a system may be called a computer information system or CIS, although usually people just use the term *information system* when they mean one that includes computers. This book uses the terms "information system" and "computer information system" synonymously.

In addition to computers, information systems include other types of technology. Communication links, such as telephone lines and satellites, are commonly part of information systems. Devices such as fax machines, video cameras, and audio speakers are found in information systems. Taken together, the computers and other technology included in information systems are called information technology or IT.

Often you hear the term computer application when someone is referring to an information system. A computer application is a use of a computer. For example, using computers to prepare written documents, to project revenues and expenses, and to keep track of customer names and addresses are computer applications. An information system may involve a single application or it may include several applications. Sometimes the term *application* is used when referring to a *small*, not too complex system and "information system" is used for a *large*, comprehensive system. This book will often use these terms interchangeably.

Examples of Information Systems

This book shows many examples of information systems in different types of businesses. To illustrate some basic ideas in this and other chapters, we use several simplified examples taken from businesses that manufacture, distribute, and sell athletic shoes and clothing. You are probably familiar with manufacturers such as Nike® and Reebok®, and with stores such as Footlocker®. There are many other manufacturers of athletic shoes and clothing, and many other stores that sell athletic wear.

To get started, let's consider three fictitious businesses:

Campus Sport Shop.   An athletic shoe store near a medium-sized university. The store also sells some athletic clothing.

Sportswear Enterprises.   A business that sells and distributes athletic clothing to individual stores. The clothing is purchased from a number of domestic and foreign manufacturers.

Victory Shoes.   A company that manufactures a wide range of athletic shoes domestically and abroad. The company sells shoes to stores and businesses worldwide.

To illustrate the basic information systems concepts presented in this chapter, we take a look at a system in each of these businesses.

An Inventory Control System.   As a first example of an information system, consider an *inventory control system* at Campus Sport Shop, the athletic shoe store. (See Fig. 1.2.) Inventory is the stock of goods that a business has on hand, and in a shoe store, inventory is the stock of shoes that the store has. Each style of shoe that the store stocks is called an *item* in the store's inventory. An inventory control system

Bookmark

Inventory Control at Guess?

Salespeople at 100 specialty apparel retail stores run by Guess? are spending more time with customers, thanks to an automated inventory system.

Before the Back Office PC System was installed, clerks in each Guess? store counted merchandise by hand and kept detailed records on paper. The process was time-consuming and prone to errors. But that's all in the past.

Now, when a box of new merchandise arrives, a clerk picks up a laser scanner and aims it at a bar-code label that was affixed to the shipment by the distribution-center employee who packed it. The scanner reads the label and identifies the contents of the box. Then, the information is transmitted over a local area network to a personal computer in the back of the store. The computers in each store run Microsoft's Windows NT In-Store Processor (ISP) and contain a Sybase database with inventory information.

"This application increases receiving accuracy," said Matthew Gordon, VP of Gateway Data Sciences Corp., the Phoenix systems integrator on the project. "It also makes users more productive by allowing them the freedom to move throughout the store."

Before Guess? delivers a shipment to a store, it electronically sends an Advanced Shipment Notification to the store's computer via the public network. The notification itemizes the contents of the shipment and the date it will arrive. The computer then compares this notification to the box's bar-code information to be sure the two match.

The Back Office PC System even goes a step further. Shipping receipts are relayed, using the public network, from the computers in each store back to a communi-

cations computer at Guess? headquarters in Los Angeles. This computer transfers the file to an IBM AS/400 computer that houses inventory information for the entire company. "A common problem with specialty apparel retailers is they don't have a reliable method to acknowledge receiving a shipment of new merchandise into the store," says Mahlon Book, a manager in the Los Angeles office of Deloitte & Touche LLP, which began designing the system in January 1996.

Deloitte & Touche also has developed an e-mail application as well as applications to process merchandise returns and calculate inventory.

Piper McWhorter, co-manager of the Guess? store in Tucson, Ariz.—which had been one of the test sites for the Back Office PC System—says she and other managers are "pretty excited" about the new system. And who wouldn't be? After all, it means less paperwork and more time with customers.

QUESTIONS

1. What benefits do Guess? stores receive from the use of the Back Office PC System?
2. What benefit does the Guess? headquarters receive from the system?
3. The system described in this article deals with recording inventory that is received at a Guess? store. How do you think a Guess? store could record inventory that is sold?

WEB SITE
Guess?: www.guess.com

Source: Candee Wilde, "Buying More Time," *Information Week*, September 23, 1996, p. 62.

keeps track of information about the items that the business stocks. The quantity of stock that the business has on hand is an example of the information it tracks about each item. Campus Sport records the quantity on hand of each style shoe it stocks in its inventory control system.

Every time Campus Sport removes items from stock, the quantity on hand of the item removed is decreased. Thus, when a pair of shoes is sold, the quantity of that style of shoe is reduced in the inventory control system. Each time Campus Sport adds items to stock, usually because it purchased them from a manufacturer, the quantity is increased. Thus, when a shipment of new shoes is received by the shoe store, the quantity of each style received is increased in the inventory control system.

FIGURE 1.2

Inventory control at an athletic shoe store

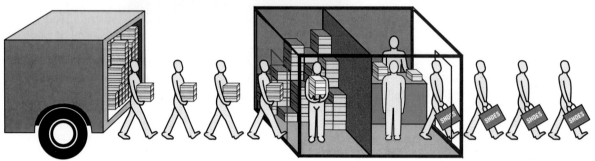

The inventory control system provides information for the daily operation of Campus Sport. For example, a salesperson can check the system to see if shoes of a particular style are available in stock. The system also provides information to help in the management of the store. For example, periodically the system reports on the quantity on hand of each style of shoe. This information helps the store's manager decide whether to increase inventory by ordering more shoes (if stock is low) or to reduce inventory, perhaps by having a sale (if stock is high). Thus, the inventory control system at Campus Sport helps in both the operation and management of the store.

An Order Entry System.   Another example of an information system is an *order entry system* at Sportswear Enterprises, the distributor of athletic clothing. (See Fig. 1.3.) Customers of Sportswear, such as stores like Campus Sport, place orders for clothing. Each order includes the customer's name, the descriptions of the items ordered, and the quantity of each item ordered. This information is entered into an order entry system, which keeps track of the orders from all of Sportswear's customers. The order entry system provides information to Sportswear's warehouse about orders to be filled. If there is adequate stock in the warehouse, the items are shipped immediately to the customers. If the items are not available, Sportswear checks with the manufacturers of the items to determine when they will be delivered. Eventually, when Sportswear receives the items from the manufacturers, it ships them to the customer.

The order entry system helps Sportswear in its daily operation of filling customer orders by providing information about customer orders to the warehouse. This information helps the warehouse ship orders as quickly as possible. The system also provides information to management. For example, management can determine how quickly orders are being filled, and decide whether action, such as using

FIGURE 1.3

Order entry at an athletic clothing distributor

different manufacturers, should be taken. Thus, the order entry system at Sportswear helps in the operation and management of the business.

A Production Scheduling System.   A final example of an information system is a *production scheduling system* at Victory Shoes, the athletic shoe manufacturer. (See Fig. 1.4.) Production scheduling involves determining what items should be produced at what times. One factor that affects the production schedule is the demand for different items, which can vary over time. For example, the demand for basketball shoes increases just before and during basketball season, and the demand for running shoes increases during the Olympic Games. Another factor is the production facility's capacity to manufacture shoes. Only a certain number of shoes can be produced in a period of time.

Victory Shoes enters information about the expected demand for different types of shoes into its production scheduling system. This information includes what types of shoes to produce, what quantities to produce, and when the shoes will be needed. The system uses this information, along with production capacity information, to prepare schedules for the production of different shoes at different times. The production schedules are used by the production facility.

As with the other examples described above, the production scheduling system assists in the operation and management of the business. The system provides information used in the operation of the production facility. This information tells the facility what shoes to produce at what times. The system also helps management plan for production. If, for example, the production facility is not adequate to meet the required production needs, management can determine if new facilities should be built.

Information System Functions

The information system examples described above illustrate the main activities that take place in an information system. Put briefly, an information system accepts facts from outside the system, stores and processes the facts, and produces the results of processing for use outside the system. These activities are performed by four *functions* of an information system: the input function, the storage

FIGURE 1.4

Production scheduling at an athletic shoe manufacturer

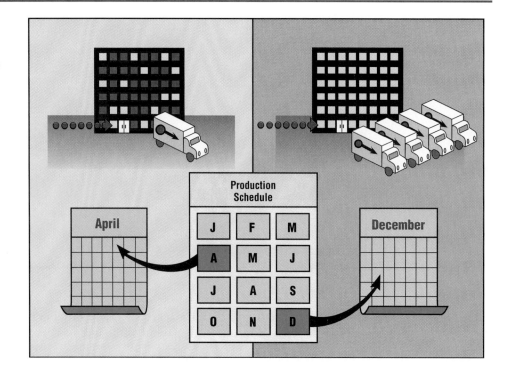

function, the processing function, and the output function. These functions are summarized in Fig. 1.5.

The facts that go into the system are input data. The input function accepts the input data from outside the system. The storage function of the system retains the input data along with other stored data, and retrieves stored data when it is needed by the system. The processing function of the system calculates and in other ways manipulates the input and stored data. Finally, the output function of the system produces the results of processing for use outside the system. These results are called information or output data.

The inventory control system at Campus Sport illustrates these functions. (See Fig. 1.6.) The input data consists of numbers representing changes in inventory—that is, items removed from stock and items added to stock. The input function accepts this input data when it is entered into the system. The storage function keeps track of stored inventory data, including inventory quantities. The processing function adjusts the inventory quantities for changes in inventory. The output function produces information from the system, including the current quantity on hand. This information is used by the salesperson to check inventory availability and by the store's manager to determine if more stock should be ordered or if prices should be reduced.

Data versus Information

Although the terms *data* and *information* have been used almost interchangeably, there is a difference between these terms. Data[1] is a representation of a fact, number,

---

[1] The word *data* is used most correctly as a plural noun. The singular of data is *datum*. A common practice, however, is to use the word data in a singular as well as a plural sense.

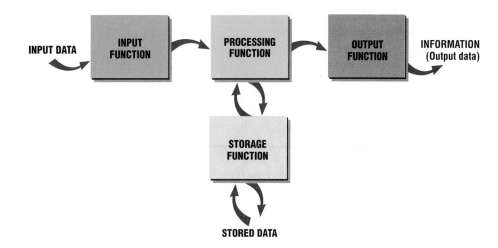

FIGURE 1.5

The functions of an information system

word, image, picture, or sound. For example, the number 10 is data; it might represent the fact that 10 cartons of shoes arrived. Data is entered into the system, stored in the system, and processed by the system. Information, on the other hand, is data that is meaningful or useful to someone. For example, the statement "There are five pairs of running shoes left in inventory" is information. Information comes out of the system, so it is sometimes called output data. Information is used to help operate and manage the organization.

Data for one person may be information for another. For example, if your job is to decide when to buy more shoes for inventory, you need information about the current stock of goods. But you do not need data about which shoes were sold today. On the other hand, a person whose job is to restock store shelves from supplies in a warehouse would need information about the items sold today. Thus, whether something is information or data depends on how it is used.

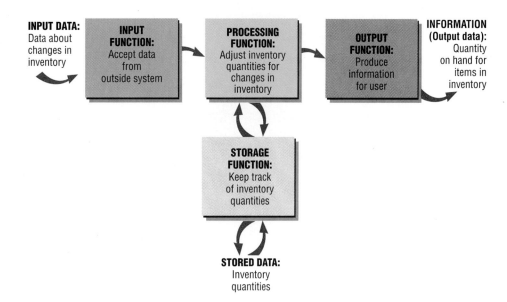

FIGURE 1.6

The functions of an inventory control system

Types of Information Systems

As you will see in later chapters, there are several ways of categorizing information systems. One way is in terms of the number of people whose work is affected by the system. Some systems affect the work of only one individual, some affect several people who work closely in a group, others affect the work of many people throughout an organization or enterprise, and still others affect people in several organizations. Here we look at examples of each of these types of information systems.

Individual Information Systems

Many information systems affect the work of only a single person, so they are called individual or personal information systems. Usually, these types of systems operate on *personal computers* used by one person at a time. (See Fig. 1.7.)

An example of an individual information system is one used to prepare legal documents, such as wills and contracts, in a law office. A legal secretary, under direction of a lawyer, would use a *word processing system*, consisting of a personal computer and *word processing software*, to put together a legal document from standard paragraphs stored in the computer. The secretary would also type new material dictated by the lawyer. After the document is prepared, it could easily be modified or edited before being printed on paper in its final form.

Another example of an individual system is a *financial analysis system* that uses *spreadsheet software* on a personal computer to do financial projections for Campus Sport Shop. A spreadsheet is an arrangement of data into rows and columns. (See Fig. 1.8.) Calculations can be done with the data in the spreadsheet, and the results

FIGURE 1.7

A personal computer

FIGURE 1.8

A spreadsheet

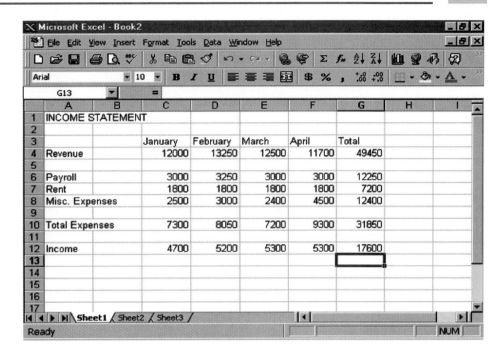

displayed on a screen. A person at Campus Sport Shop could use a spreadsheet to project the store's revenues and expenses for several periods in the future, trying different options for certain items such as advertising expense to see what option is likely to produce the greatest income.

Many individual information systems are used to store and retrieve data on a personal computer using *database software*. A *database* is a collection of related data stored in a computer. For example, a sales representative for Sportswear Enterprises could keep a list of customers in a database on a personal computer. The representative would have an individual *customer database system* that he or she could use to periodically check to see which customers to contact next.

A final example of an individual information system is a *graphics system* used to prepare graphic images, either for including in a document or for showing at a presentation. (See Fig. 1.9.) *Graphics software* is used to create the images on a personal computer, and then word processing software can be used to include the images in a document. A type of graphics software called *presentation graphics software* is used to create images for presentations.

Workgroup Information Systems

Information systems often affect groups of individuals who work together, such as the employees on a team or in a department of a business. Such workgroup or group information systems often operate on nearby personal computers that are connected so that people at different computers can work with each other. This way of organizing computers is called a *local area network* or *LAN*. (See Fig. 1.10.)

FIGURE 1.9

Computer graphics

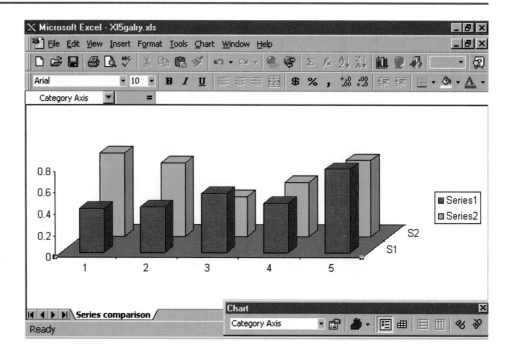

FIGURE 1.10

A local area network or LAN

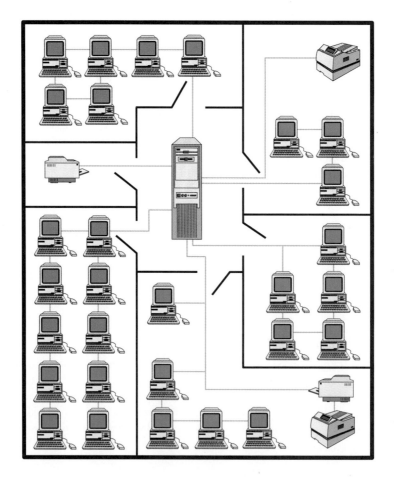

An example of a workgroup information system is one that allows individuals in the group to communicate electronically. This type of system is called an <u>electronic mail</u> or <u>e-mail</u> system. (See Fig. 1.11.) With electronic mail, letters and memos that normally would be sent on paper are transmitted electronically from one computer in the network to another. The sender keys the mail into his or her computer, and then tells the computer to send the mail to one or more other computers in the network. The receiver can read the mail on a computer's screen, and even send a reply with just a few keystrokes.

Another example of a workgroup information system is an *information sharing system* in the sales department of Sportswear Enterprises. Such a system allows employees to share information about projects that they are working on together. For example, employees in the sales department may be working on a brochure. With an information sharing system, group members can view and comment on the brochure through their personal computers connected to a network. (See Fig. 1.12.) Periodically, one person in the group can summarize individual team members' comments and revise the sales brochure.

Organizational Information Systems

An information system that affects many people throughout a business or organization, not just an individual or the people in a group, is called an <u>organizational</u> or <u>enterprise information system</u>. These systems usually operate either on large multiple-user computers, called *mainframe computers* (Fig. 1.13), used by many people at a time, or on groups of computers connected over a long distance to form a *wide area network* or *WAN* (Fig. 1.14).

FIGURE 1.11

Electronic mail or e-mail

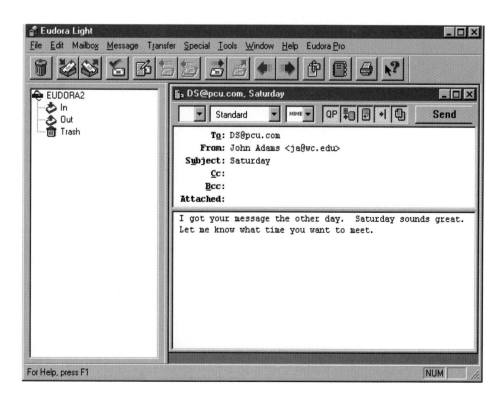

FIGURE 1.12

Information
sharing

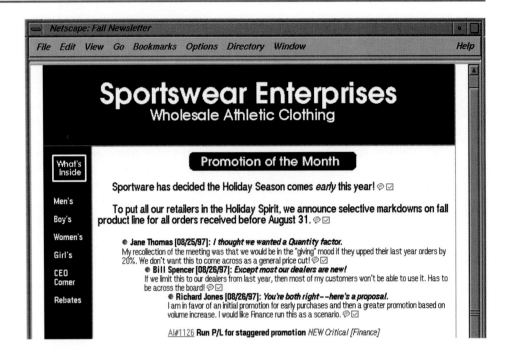

FIGURE 1.12

Information
sharing

One of the most common examples of an organizational information system is a *payroll system.* This system keeps track of when employees work and prepares paychecks periodically for the employees. At Victory Shoes, this system prepares paychecks for employees who get paid by the hour as well as for those who receive a monthly salary. The system also prepares quarterly and annual reports necessary for tax reporting, and other reports used by the business to keep track of expenses.

FIGURE 1.13

A mainframe
computer

FIGURE 1.14

**A wide area
network or WAN**

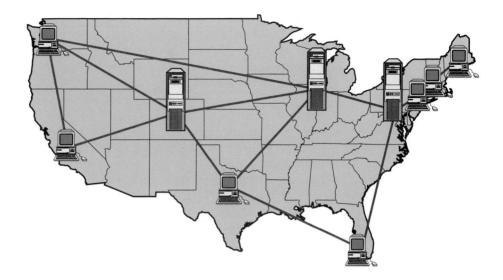

Another example of an organizational information system is an *automated teller machine* or *ATM system*, used by banks. An ATM is a device that allows a person to deposit or withdraw money from a bank account and to perform other banking transactions without the aid of a human teller. (See Fig. 1.15.) An ATM is not a computer by itself but is connected to a computer at the bank's office that performs the tasks requested by the customer using the ATM. The computer looks up the customer's account in its records, keeps track of transactions requested by the customer, and adjusts its records to reflect these transactions. The computer is connected electronically to many ATMs that may be located some distance from the computer. For example, a bank's computer in one city may be connected to many ATMs that the bank has located throughout the state.

Interorganizational Information Systems

The information systems described so far only function within a single business or organization. Some information systems, however, function among several

FIGURE 1.15

**An automated
teller machine**

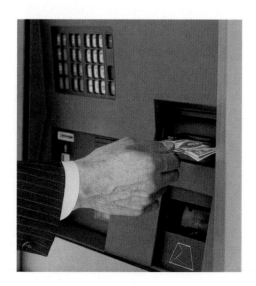

organizations. Such <u>interorganizational information systems</u> operate on groups of computers located in different organizations and connected in an *interorganizational network*. These systems allow the organizations to use computers to transact business among themselves.

An example of an interorganizational information system is an <u>electronic data interchange</u> or <u>EDI</u> system. This type of information system allows businesses to exchange data electronically, such as purchase information and bills. For example, Sportswear Enterprises can electronically place an order to purchase shoes from Victory Shoes. Victory can then, in turn, electronically bill Sportswear for the shoes that are shipped.

Banks and other financial institutions use interorganizational <u>electronic funds transfer</u> or <u>EFT</u> systems. These information systems allow funds to be electronically transferred between financial institutions. For example, when you withdraw cash from an automated teller machine associated with a bank other than your own, your bank will electronically transfer the funds from your bank account to the bank issuing the cash. Another example of an interorganizational EFT system is one that automatically deposits paychecks issued by one bank into employee accounts in other banks.

International Information Systems

If a business only operates within a single country, then its information systems are confined to that country. Many businesses, however, have facilities in more than one country. Such *international businesses* often have information systems that span national borders. These systems are called <u>international</u> or <u>global information systems</u>. Often, international information systems are connected by means of a global wide area network. (See Fig. 1.16.)

An example of an international information system is one used by Victory Shoes. Victory has facilities for manufacturing shoes in several countries. The company uses an international *production scheduling system* to schedule shoe production at different facilities. Production data and schedules are transmitted between Victory's headquarters and different foreign locations using the business's global wide area network.

Interorganizational information systems may also be international. An international EDI system may be used to transmit orders for merchandise to foreign suppliers. An ATM at a bank in one country can be used to withdraw cash in the local currency, deducting the amount from an account at a bank in another country. An international EFT system then transfers the funds electronically between the banks.

FIGURE 1.16

A global wide area network

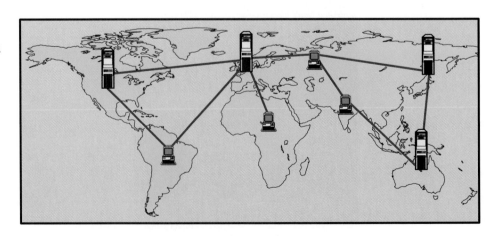

Bookmark

International Information System at Timberland

Going global almost proved disastrous for the Timberland Co., a $655 million manufacturer of footwear and apparel. Timberland had plans to conquer Europe and Asia. There was only one problem: Its shoes weren't selling in those markets.

"One of the first things we noticed when we went into Asia was that footwear skewed to wider and smaller sizes," said Yusef Akyuz, Timberland's VP of information services. But Timberland shoes tended toward the larger and narrower sizes common in the United States. The company had to implement a manufacturing strategy that would allow it to recognize the unique characteristics of each new market, and plan accordingly.

That's why the Stratham, N.H., company turned to software to address this and other issues by buying a full suite of supply-chain management software from Manugistics Inc. Now, instead of using a generic manufacturing profile, Timberland zeroes in on each market and calculates exact consumer demand.

More companies are competing overseas these days, and they're looking for any edge to help them become true global players. Software that functions across multiple borders and multiple languages can be a powerful weapon.

"Not everyone wants to run their business only in English," said Mitch Kramer, consulting editor at the Patricia Seybold Group, a Boston consulting firm. "This is a critical issue to many users."

Timberland plans to implement applications such as demand planning, manufacturing scheduling, and transportation planning in 10 locations worldwide. "The key functions we were looking for are in the Manugistics package," said Akyuz. "The system comes in various languages and, with the next release, we plan to upgrade to a multicurrency version."

Timberland operates in more than 50 countries. With the aid of the software, the company anticipates seamless integration across all areas of its business—from demand forecasting to just-in-time delivery. "This will help to reduce the long lead times of getting the product from cow to customers," said Akyuz, referring to Timberland's popular leather shoes.

How important is this type of software to companies searching for a global solution? "It's certainly valuable for large multinationals," said Henry Morris, an analyst with International Data Corp., an IT research firm in Framingham, Mass. "But at this stage we don't know how ['internationalized' modules] affect buying patterns or whether they are a make-or-break factor."

However, Akyuz is sure his company made the right decision. "Timberland wants to grow as a global business," he said. "That's a major reason we invested in [the software]."

QUESTIONS

1. What problems unique to international business does the Manugistics software address?
2. Without an international information system, how could Timberland determine what unique products to produce for more than 50 countries?

WEB SITE
Shoes on the Net: www.shoesonthenet.com

Source: Tom Stein, "Timberland Gets Global Boost from New Software," *Information Week*, November 4, 1996, p. 72.

Information System Users

Many examples in this chapter and throughout this book illustrate people using information systems. These people are not computer professionals such as computer programmers and operators. Rather, they are noncomputer-oriented people who gain some benefit from using computer information systems in their personal or work lives. These people are called users.

A user performs a task in his or her personal or work life with the aid of a computer information system. For example, a person using an automated teller machine is a user because he or she performs various banking transactions by using an ATM system. Similarly, a person using a computer with word processing software is a user because he or she prepares letters or reports with the help of a word processing system.

Computer professionals also use computers. For example, computer programmers and operators use computers in their technical jobs. We do not think of these people, however, as users as the term has been defined here. In this book, a user is always a person who uses a computer information system to help with some noncomputer activity in his or her personal or work life. Sometimes this type of user is called an <u>end-user</u> to distinguish him or her from computer professionals.

How Users Use Information Systems

A user uses an information system by entering input data and receiving output information. Many users use an information system *directly* by pressing keys on a computer keyboard or by operating a piece of equipment that sends input data to a computer. The computer receives the data and does the required processing. After the computer has completed its processing, it sends output information back to the user, often displaying it on a screen or printing it on paper. A person using spreadsheet software to do financial projections at Campus Sport Shop and a person checking inventory availability on a computer screen at Sportswear Enterprises are examples of direct users.

A user may also use an information system *indirectly*. In this case, the user may have someone else enter the input data and receive the output information, which is then given to the user. A sales manager at Sportswear Enterprises who receives periodic, printed sales reports is an indirect user.

One person may use an information system directly, and another may use the same system indirectly. For example, a sales reporting system could be used directly by some managers, who review sales information on a screen, and indirectly by others, who receive printed sales reports. Sometimes many users use a system at the same time. An automated teller machine system is used by many people doing their banking. Often, however, only one user uses a system at a time. For example, a word processing system is used by only one person at a time.

The Ethical Use of Information Systems

Information systems can be used inappropriately by users. It may be possible for a user to gain access to data not intended for that user, such as personnel data, or to destroy data in the system. Users also may be able to use an information system to steal money from a business. The hardware and software used in an information system also can be stolen or destroyed. Information system security measures, discussed in Chapter 15, are designed to make a system more secure and to minimize the likelihood of these activities. Still, they do occur.

Ultimately, the behavior of the individual determines how secure a system is. *Ethics* are the standards of behavior that people follow. For example, people act ethically when they tell the truth even when lying is not against the law. Information system users must be ethical in their uses of the system. Without such ethical behavior, system security measures would be so strict that only a few people would be able to use information systems.

The ethical use of information systems is related to more than just system security. Ethical issues arise in questions of confidentiality of information, copying of software, use of someone else's computer, and ownership of information. Many ethical questions have no clear answer, but users need to understand and think about them anyway. We will have more to say about ethics in Chapter 15.

Connecting Users to Information Technology

Most users use information systems directly: They enter input data through a keyboard and see output data on a computer screen. In an individual information system, a user uses a personal computer for this interaction. For other types of information systems, the user often uses a personal computer connected to other information technology that is located some distance from the user. Such distant connectivity of users and technology is a critical part of most information systems.

Networks

Typically, users are connected to information technology through a network. In general, a network is a collection of computers and related equipment connected electronically so that they can communicate with each other. Networks can cover a small area such as a building (a local area network), or a large area such as a city, region, country, or several countries (a wide area network).

Users at different computers in a network can use the network to work with others in a group by means of a workgroup information system. Users can use a network to enter input data into and receive output information from an organizational information system. Users can use a network to transact business with other organizations through an interorganizational information system. Finally, users can use a network to process data at locations around the world using an international information system.

The international nature of networks has become increasingly important in recent years. Global connectivity means that businesses are able to operate around the world without concern for where input, processing, storage, and output take place. Business facilities can be separated by considerable distance and many time zones, and still have access to information systems and technology at other business locations. As more businesses globalize their operations, the benefit of global networks will be increasingly important.

The Internet

Users need to be connected to information technology in both their work lives and their personal lives. Businesses provide networks for their employees to use. For personal use, as well as for business use, many users use the Internet to access information technology. Put simply, the Internet is a worldwide collection of interconnected networks. We will have more to say about what the Internet is and how it works in Chapter 6. But you do not need to know technical details to use the Internet.

The Internet can be used for a variety of business and personal activities. One of the most common uses is for transmitting electronic mail. Using the Internet, e-mail can be sent to any computer in the world that is connected to the Internet.

Another important use of the Internet is for locating information from various computer sites around the world. The World Wide Web or WWW, often just called the Web, is a service on the Internet that links together information stored on different computers. By following the links, it is possible to locate information at businesses, universities, libraries, research institutes, government agencies, and so on. (See Fig. 1.17.) The World Wide Web and the Internet are rapidly becoming an essential part of the global connectivity of users and information technology.

FIGURE 1.17

Using the World Wide Web

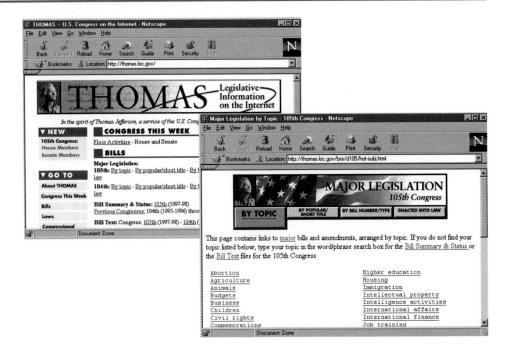

Benefits of Information Systems

Information systems provide several important benefits to an organization. These benefits stem from the system as a whole, not just from the fact that computers are used in the system. Computers are fast and accurate, and they process large volumes of data. Although these characteristics make computer information systems very useful, the real benefits of information systems are much more involved.

Better Information

One of the main benefits of using information systems is *better information*. Information systems store and process data, but they produce information, which is the basis for good decision making. When a business person makes a decision, he or she selects one of several alternative courses of action. Almost always the person is uncertain about what exactly will happen with each alternative. Information helps reduce the person's uncertainty, and with better information a business person is more certain about the outcome of the decision.

   To illustrate this idea, let's look at an example of a personal decision. Assume that you want to buy a new car. You have to make a decision: "Which car should I buy?" You could go to several car dealers, select one car that you like, and buy it. But is it the best car for you? Are there other models with more power, more space, better fuel economy, and more reliability for less money? With more information you might save money and get a better car. So instead of making your decision hastily, you can gather the information you need to help with your decision. For example, you can use a computerized library system to search for articles and reviews of the cars that interest you. You could also use the Internet to find information about cars. With this information, you can make a decision that is more likely to result in selecting a better car.

   Better information is the principal benefit of many information systems in business. For example, a customer database system provides better information to a sales representative for deciding when to contact customers. A sales reporting system provides better information to a sales manager for making decisions to help improve sales. Many other examples throughout this book illustrate the benefit of better information provided by information systems.

Improved Service

Another benefit of information systems is *improved service*. Computer information systems operate at any time of the day or night and process data faster than humans. Thus, organizations and businesses serve their customers and clients more conveniently and efficiently with computer information systems than without.

As a consumer, you see the effect of improved service from information systems whenever you use an automated teller machine system for your banking transactions, or whenever you purchase groceries or merchandise from a store that uses a point-of-sale system to check out customers. These systems provide service that you would otherwise not have. Consequently, you are able to complete your transactions and your shopping conveniently and quickly.

Improved service means that customers may be attracted to a certain business because of its service. In fact, many people have come to expect computerized services, and some types of businesses cannot compete without them. For example, many gas stations have a computerized system that allows customers to pay at the pump with a credit card. Gas stations that do not offer this service may not be as competitive.

Increased Productivity

A third benefit of information systems is *increased productivity*. Productivity has to do with how much people can accomplish in a given time. With computer information systems, people can do more productive work in a period of time than they would be able to do if they did not have such systems.

For example, a typist using a word processing system can revise and print a long document faster than if he or she had to retype the document completely on a typewriter. Hence, the typist's productivity is increased with such a system. A person working in an office with an electronic mail system is more productive because it is easier and quicker for the person to communicate with other workers. Similarly, a clerk using a point-of-sale system instead of a standard cash register can check out more customers, and a bank with an automated teller machine system can handle more customers without increasing the number of human tellers.

Increased productivity means that it costs less for a business to provide its goods and services. These cost savings may be passed on to the customer in reduced prices. Such savings also result in increased profits for the business.

An Approach to the Study of Information Systems

To understand information systems in business, you first need to understand business. You may already have worked in certain types of businesses and have an understanding of how some aspects of a business function. But information systems are found in *all* types of businesses and encompass *all* aspects of a business. To fully understand information systems, you need a broad overview of business and business functions.

This book approaches the study of information systems by first examining businesses and their use of information. In Chapter 2 you will learn what a business does, how a business is organized, and how information is used in business operations and management. You will also examine some of the basic business information processing activities that are common to many types of businesses. With this background you will be well prepared to understand how information systems support the operation and management of a business.

Your actual study of information systems begins in Chapter 3 with an overview of information systems and the technology used in these systems. After completing this chapter you move on to a more in-depth study of different aspects of information systems.

In Part II of the book you will learn about the technology used in information systems. This technology includes the computer hardware and software necessary for information systems. You will also learn how computers are interconnected in networks and how data is organized for storage and processing in information systems.

In Part III you will study common types and examples of information systems found in business. You will learn about information systems that improve personal productivity, encourage group collaboration, increase the efficiency of business operations, improve the effectiveness of management decision making, and provide a strategic impact on the business. The understanding you gain will help you utilize information systems in your job.

Part IV completes your study of information systems by examining their development and management. You will see how individual information systems are developed by users like you. In addition, you will learn how organizational information systems are developed by computer professionals and what role you will play in their development. Furthermore, you will learn how information systems are managed, and examine the social and ethical issues of information system use.

You can use information systems on your job with little understanding of how the systems function. But to be an *effective* user of information systems, you need a more in-depth understanding of information systems. An effective user is one who is able to make the best use of information systems by knowing how and when to use them. The approach taken in this book is designed to provide you with the understanding necessary to be an effective information system user in businesses and other organizations.

Chapter Summary

☐ An **information system** is a collection of components that work together to provide information to help in the operation and management of an organization. The functions of an information system are the **input function**, which accepts data from outside the system; the **storage function**, which stores data in the system until needed; the **processing function**, which manipulates data in the system; and the **output function**, which produces information resulting from processing. (pp. 5–10)

☐ **Data** is a representation of a fact, number, word, image, picture, or sound. **Information** is data that is meaningful or useful to someone. Data for one person may be information for another. (pp. 10–11)

☐ An information system that affects a single person is called an **individual information system**. Examples include a system to prepare written documents using word processing software, a system to do financial projections using spreadsheet software, a system to store and retrieve data using database software, and a system to prepare graphic images using graphics software. An information system that affects a group of individuals who work together is called a **workgroup information system.** Examples are an **electronic mail** or **e-mail** system and an information sharing system. An information system that affects people throughout a business or organization is called an **organizational information system**. Examples include a payroll system and an automatic teller machine (ATM) system. An information system that functions among several organizations is called an **interorganizational information system**. Examples are an **electronic data interchange** (**EDI**) system and an **electronic funds transfer** (**EFT**) system. Finally, an **international information system** is one that spans international borders. An example is an international production scheduling system. (pp. 12–18)

☐ A **user** is a person who gains some benefit from using a **computer information system** in his or her personal or work life. A user enters **input data** into the system and receives output information from the system. Some users use information systems directly by pressing keys on a computer keyboard or operating a piece of equipment that sends data to a computer. Other users use information systems indirectly; they receive output information from the system without operating any computer equipment. Information systems must be used in an ethi-

cal way or their use will be restricted to only a few people. (pp. 19–20)

☐ Users are connected to **information technology** through a **network,** which is a collection of computers and related equipment connected electronically so that they can communicate with each other. A network may cover a small area, such as a building, or a large area, such as a city, region, country, or several countries. The **Internet** is a worldwide collection of interconnected networks that allows users to access information technology. One important use of the Internet is for locating information through the **World Wide Web** (**WWW**). (p. 21)

☐ One benefit of information systems is better information, which helps people make better decisions. Another benefit is improved service, which means customers and clients of businesses and organizations get faster and more convenient service. A third benefit is improved productivity, which means people can accomplish more in a period of time. (p. 22–23)

Key Terms

Computer Application (p. 6)
Computer Information System (CIS) (p. 6)
Data (p. 10)
Electronic Data Interchange (EDI) (p. 18)
Electronic Funds Transfer (EFT) (p. 18)
Electronic Mail (E-mail) (p. 15)
Individual (Personal) Information System (p. 12)
Information (p. 10, 11)

Information System (IS) (p. 5)
Information Technology (IT) (p. 6)
Input Data (p. 10)
Input Function (p. 10)
International (Global) Information System (p. 18)
Internet (p. 21)
Interorganizational Information System (p. 18)
Network (p. 21)

Organizational (Enterprise) Information System (p. 15)
Output Data (p. 10)
Output Function (p. 10)
Processing Function (p. 10)
Storage Function (p. 10)
Stored Data (p. 10)
User (End-User) (p. 19)
Workgroup (Group) Information System (p. 13)
World Wide Web (WWW) (p. 21)

Assignment Material

Review Questions

Fill-in Questions

1. A use of a computer is called a(n) _____.

2. Facts that go into an information system are called _____; the results that come out of a system are called _____ or _____.

3. Data retained in an information system is called _____.

4. Information systems that impact the work of a single person are called _____.

5. The personnel department of a business has an information system to keep track of job applicants. This system is an example of a(n) _____.

6. An information system that affects many people throughout a business or organization is called a(n) _____.

7. EDI and EFT are examples of _____.

8. A noncomputer-oriented person who gains some benefit from using an information system in his or her personal or work life is called a(n) _____.

9. A collection of computers and related equipment connected electronically so that they can communicate with each other is called a(n) _____.

10. A service on the Internet that links together information stored on different computers is called the _____.

Short-answer Questions

1. What is an information system?

2. All information systems use computers. True or false? Explain.

3. What are the four functions of an information system?

4. What is the difference between data and information?

5. Give several examples of individual information systems.

6. Give several examples of organizational information systems.

7. What is the difference between using an information system directly and using one indirectly?

8. How are business and personal users connected to information technology?

9. How do people and businesses benefit from information systems?

10. What does it mean to be an effective information system user?

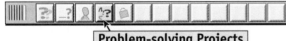

Discussion Questions

1. Think of a business other than a supermarket and list several types of employees in that business. What information does each of the employees you listed need in his or her job?

2. Identify several examples of information systems, other than those described in this chapter, that might be used in Campus Sport Shop, Sportswear Enterprises, and Victory Shoes. For each system, decide whether it is an individual, workgroup, or organizational information system.

3. What interorganizational and international information systems might be used by Campus Sport Shop, Sportswear Enterprises, and Victory Shoes?

4. Think of the outputs produced by your college or university class registration system. For what users of the system (such as students, faculty, advisers, administrators, etc.) are each of these outputs *information,* and not just data?

5. In the global economy, everyone in the world is a user of information systems. Do you agree or disagree with this statement? Why?

6. What are some of the things that could happen if people did not behave ethically in their use of information systems?

Problem-solving Projects

1. Write a description of a manual information system that uses a name and address book to assist in completing letters. What are the input data, stored data, and output information of the system? Briefly describe how the system functions. Use word processing software to prepare your answer.

2. Find an information system not mentioned in this chapter and draw a diagram similar to the one in Fig. 1.6 to describe the system. If available, use graphics software to prepare the diagram.

3. Using word processing software, set up a table with the following headings:

System Name	Users	Inputs	Outputs	Stored Data	Processing

Fill in one row of the table for each system described in this chapter. Under "System Name" give the name of the system (for example, Inventory Control). Under "Users" list the users by job (for example, salesperson, manager). Below "Inputs" list the input data (for example, data about changes in inventory) and below "Outputs" list the output information (for example, quantity on hand for items in inventory). Under "Stored Data" list data stored in the system (for example, inventory quantities). Below "Processing," briefly describe the processing done in the system (for example, adjust inventory quantities for changes in inventory). Complete the table for all the systems discussed in this chapter. As you read about other information systems in other chapters, add entries to the table.

4. Develop a spreadsheet to help you decide which car to buy. The columns should be characteristics of the car that are important to you, such as the safety, mileage, and so on. The rows should be different cars you are considering. If some characteristics can be quantified, use the spreadsheet to find the maximum, minimum, and average of those characteristics for all cars you are considering.

5. Decision making involves selecting among alternatives. The basis for good decision making is information about the alternatives. Select a personal or business decision you need to make and identify three alternatives. For example, if you are trying to decide where to go on vacation, you could select three different destinations. Then use the Internet to gather information about each alternative. Gather information from several sites on the Internet. When you have enough information to make a decision, write a brief summary of your alternatives, the information you gathered about each alternative, and your decision. Justify your decision based on the information you gathered. Use word processing software to prepare your summary.

Real-world Case

The Benetton Group, Italy

The Benetton Group is at home throughout the world. Established in 1965 in Ponzano Veneto, Italy, today it is a worldwide concern which exports not only its own products, ranging from knitwear to clothing and accessories, but also production technology and know-how, which it adapts to each individual environment. Its main brand names, United Colors of Benetton, Sisley, and 012, are internationally renowned.

The Benetton Group consists of a number of companies that design, manufacture, and distribute Benetton products in 120 countries. Benetton sells its goods almost exclusively through 7,000 independently owned shops. To provide the interface between the Group and the shops, Benetton has a sales network consisting of 84 agent offices in 28 countries, each responsible for the shops in a specific geographic area.

Benetton sees information technology as key to its operations. In the Group, each company manages its own processing environment with autonomy in its operations. Group headquarters operate on a large IBM mainframe computer to which more than 800 workstations are connected through a local area network. Typically, other companies in the Group run smaller IBM computers, while agent offices use personal computer configurations.

All the companies involved in design, manufacturing, and distribution of the products that are sold by Benetton shops are connected through a GEISCO Mark III network to the 84 agent offices, which represent the sales organization in the world. The companies use a package called Global (developed and supported centrally) to manage their databases and communications.

The agent offices all run the same application package, in different languages, developed and supported by the central IT staff. This application package manages databases of customers, styles, and prices, and keeps these databases aligned with those of the Group's companies. The functions of the agents' application package include order collection and management, order forwarding to the Group's companies, shops management, and sales analysis.

To place an order for products, an agent sends the order through the network, which forwards it to the appropriate company for production. Orders are received at the Group's companies three times a day and processed during the night to be sure that they are available for production the following day. All production processes, from material requirements to packaging, are managed by computers using sophisticated custom-developed application systems.

The products are packed according to shop orders by an automated packing system. Fifteen thousand boxes per day enter automated warehouses from which, according to the delivery programs managed by the central computer, they are forwarded to shops around the world. EDI messages with the box numbers and their contents are sent through the network to the computers of Benetton agents to keep them updated. Messages are also sent to forwarding agents to prepare custom-clearance documents and to the shops that will receive the goods.

Benetton agents are continuously updated regarding the state of the orders. At any time, they can see, through their computers, what is available in inventory for restocking. If an agent enters an order for restocking, the shop will receive the goods in an average of eight days in Europe and 12 days in the United States. For the shops, an efficient restocking process means improved business in terms of increased sales volumes and profits, with fewer items to be sold off at reduced prices.

Agents are also continuously updated through the network regarding the credit status of each shop. This is made possible by the fact that almost all the payments of the shops around the world are handled using cash management systems based on networks connecting Benetton computers.

The results obtained by applying information technologies to the business are essentially due to the capability to integrate the systems with the overall business purposes, the changing business environment, and the corporate culture and processes of the company.

Questions

1. What type of information system is described in this case? Explain your answer.

2. Who are the users of the information system?

3. What information do the users receive through the information system?

4. How is a network used in the information system?

5. What benefits does Benetton receive from the information system?

Source: "The Benetton Group," www.benetton.com/benetton-web/ benetton/companyintro.html, © copyright 1996 Benetton Group S.p.A. "The Network: Information Technology," www.benetton.com/benetton-web/benetton/it.html, © copyright 1996 Benetton Group S.p.A.

2 Business Fundamentals

Chapter Outline

Purpose of a Business   (p. 30)
Types of Businesses   (p. 31)
    Manufacturers   (p. 31)
    Wholesalers   (p. 31)
    Retailers   (p. 32)
    Service Businesses   (p. 33)
    Not-for-profit Organizations   (p. 34)
    Government   (p. 34)
Business Functions   (p. 34)
    Accounting   (p. 34)
    Finance   (p. 35)
    Marketing   (p. 35)
    Manufacturing   (p. 36)
    Human Resource Management   (p. 37)
    Other Business Functions   (p. 37)
Organization of a Business   (p. 37)
Information and Business Operations   (p. 39)
Information and Business Management   (p. 41)
Basic Business Information Processing   (p. 43)
    Entering Customer Orders   (p. 44)
    Billing Customers   (p. 44)
    Collecting Customer Payments   (p. 46)
    Keeping Track of Inventory   (p. 46)
    Purchasing Stock and Materials   (p. 48)
    Paying Bills   (p. 50)
    Paying Employees   (p. 51)
    Reporting Financial Information   (p. 52)
Information Systems and Business   (p. 54)

Learning Objectives

After completing this chapter, you should be able to:

☐ 1. Explain the purpose of a business and describe the main types of businesses.

☐ 2. Describe the major business functions and explain how a business is organized.

☐ 3. Diagram typical flows of information in business operations.

☐ 4. Explain how information is used in the management of a business.

☐ 5. Describe several basic business information processing activities found in businesses.

☐ 6. Explain how information systems support information needs in all functions of all types of businesses and organizations.

I nformation systems support the operations and management of businesses and other organizations. To understand information systems, you must first understand how businesses and other types of organizations operate and are managed. You also need to understand how information is used to support business operations and management, and how information is processed in common business activities. Although you already may have worked for certain types of businesses and know some things about how they function, you need a broad understanding of business and its use of information to fully comprehend the role of information systems.

This chapter explains what businesses do and describes different types of businesses. It outlines business functions and examines how businesses are organized. It shows how information flows within a business to support business operations, and explains how information helps in the management of a business. It describes several basic business information processing activities. Finally, it explains how information systems support information needs in all aspects of all types of businesses.[1]

Purpose of a Business

The purpose of a business is to provide goods and services for its customers. For example, an athletic shoe store sells running, tennis, basketball, and other types of athletic shoes (goods), and a shoe repair shop repairs shoes (services). In return for the goods and services the customer pays the business. The money received from the customer is the business's *revenue.* To provide the goods and services the business has certain *expenses.* For example, a shoe store must buy shoes to sell, and a repair shop must pay service people to repair shoes. The difference between the revenue and expenses is called the *net income.* If the net income is greater than zero, then the business makes a profit for the owners of the business.[2]

Some businesses sell goods and services to individual customers like you and me, and some businesses sell to other businesses. For example, an athletic shoe manufacturer sells shoes to shoe stores which, in turn, sell shoes to individual customers. It does not matter, however, whether a business sells to individuals or to other businesses. It still receives revenue, has expenses, and makes a profit.

Not all businesses operate for a profit. Some *not-for-profit organizations* do not give any income to the owners but instead use all net income to improve the organization. Examples include hospitals, churches, schools, and community service organizations. Government agencies also are not-for-profit organizations. Although this book mainly uses examples from for-profit businesses, the concepts and principles apply equally well to not-for-profit organizations.

Businesses do not operate in a vacuum, but rather exist within a *business environment* that includes economic, legal, cultural, and competitive factors. Economic factors affect businesses by influencing what and how many goods and services consumers buy. Laws and regulations have an impact on many activities in a business. Cultural and social factors influence the characteristics of the goods and services sold by businesses. Competition affects what products and services a business offers, and the price it charges.

---

[1] If you already have had an introduction to business course or other courses in business, you may find this chapter repeats some of what you know. Still, it would be a good idea to read the chapter for a review and summary.

[2] Some of the net income may be used to improve the business and some of it may be given to the owners of the business.

The business environment is not limited to the effect of these factors in a single country. Many businesses operate on a global scale. These *international businesses* have to be concerned with world economic factors, laws in many countries, cultural differences between countries, and competition from foreign businesses. As more businesses try to produce and sell their goods and offer their services internationally, these factors will become increasingly important.

Types of Businesses

The goods sold by businesses typically flow from raw materials to the final consumer as shown in Fig. 2.1. Raw materials, such as oil and iron, are manufactured into products such as gasoline and automobiles. These products are sold to other businesses at *wholesale*, that is, in large quantities. The products then are resold at *retail*, that is, in small quantities, to the final consumer.

There are three main types of businesses involved in this flow from raw materials to the customer: manufacturers, wholesalers or distributors, and retailers. In addition, service businesses provide services to other businesses or to individual customers. (See Fig. 2.2.)

Manufacturers

A manufacturer produces goods that are sold to other businesses or to individual customers. The goods that are produced may be final products, such as automobiles, or they may be components, such as engines and transmissions, that are used in the manufacturing of the final product. The manufacturer produces goods out of basic materials, such as rubber and steel, or from parts and components purchased from other manufacturers.

Athletic shoe production illustrates the role of manufacturers. A business that manufactures athletic shoes may produce some parts of a shoe from basic materials and purchase other parts from other businesses. For example, a shoe manufacturer may purchase raw fabric and leather from which it makes the upper part of a shoe. It may purchase finished rubber soles from another manufacturer, which it then combines with the other materials to produce the final shoe.

Many businesses manufacture some or all their products, or components for their products, in foreign countries. For example, a shoe manufacturer may manufacture some of its shoes in its own production facility in a foreign country and then ship the finished shoes to other countries where they are sold. A shoe manufacturer may also contract with a foreign manufacturer to produce products to its specifications for sale elsewhere. As another example, some automobiles sold in the United States by U. S. companies are manufactured in other countries. In all these examples of foreign manufacturing, the business is an *importer* of goods to the country where they will be sold. Some manufacturers produce their products domestically and then sell them in other countries. In this case, the manufacturer is an *exporter* of goods.

Wholesalers

Goods produced by a manufacturer may be sold to a wholesaler or distributor. The wholesaler purchases large quantities of the goods and stores them in warehouses. It then sells smaller quantities to retailers (discussed later), and ships or distributes these quantities to the retailers. Sometimes the manufacturer is also a wholesaler/distributor in which case the manufacturer sells and distributes directly to retailers.

FIGURE 2.1

The flow of goods from raw materials to the customer

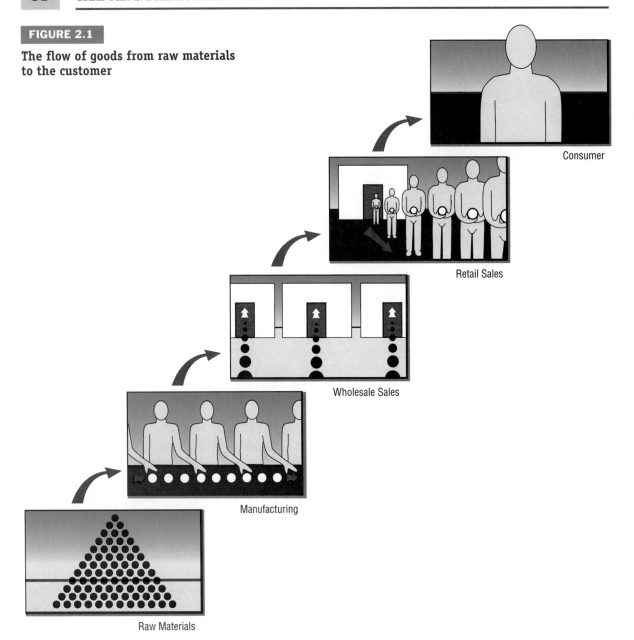

Consumer

Retail Sales

Wholesale Sales

Manufacturing

Raw Materials

Large quantities of athletic clothing may be purchased by a wholesaler from several manufacturers. If the clothing were manufactured in other countries then the wholesaler would also be an importer of clothing. The clothing purchased by the wholesaler would be stored in one or more warehouses until it is sold and distributed to retailers.

Retailers

A <u>retailer</u> purchases quantities of goods from wholesalers or directly from manufacturers. The retailer keeps the goods at a store or other retail location and resells them one at a time or in small quantities to the individual consumer. If the manufacturer is in another country and the retailer purchases goods directly from the

FIGURE 2.2

Types of businesses

Athletic shoe manufacturer

Athletic shoe retailer

Shoe repair service

manufacturer, then the retailer is an importer. Sometimes the retailer purchases large quantities for its own warehouse and then distributes smaller quantities to its retail shops. In this case, the retailer is acting as a distributor. In some instances the retailer is also a manufacturer. For example, some mail-order businesses manufacture their own goods.

An athletic shoe store is a retailer. It purchases from shoe manufacturers several of each type of shoe it plans to sell and keeps these shoes in the store. It also purchases athletic clothing from a clothing wholesaler. Customers come to the store, try on the shoes and clothing, and purchase the items they want.

Service Businesses

A service business is not directly involved in manufacturing, wholesaling, and retailing products but instead provides services needed by other businesses and individual customers. Some businesses provide services related to goods sold by other businesses such as repair and delivery services. Sometimes these services are furnished by manufacturers, wholesalers, and retailers. Other businesses provide services unrelated to such goods. These services include communications (telephone), transportation (airline), utilities (gas and electricity), hospitality (food and lodging), and health (medical and dental) services. Still other businesses furnish financial services such as banking and insurance.

A shoe repair shop is an example of a service business. Another example is a business that replaces worn-out soles on athletic shoes. A business that provides shipping and delivery services for shoe manufacturers and clothing wholesalers is also a service business.

Not-for-profit Organizations

Manufacturers, wholesalers, retailers, and service businesses usually operate for a profit. Not-for-profit organizations, on the other hand, provide goods and services without the intent of making a profit. Most not-for-profit organizations provide services, such as medical care, education, cultural activities, and religious services. Some not-for-profit organizations are involved in manufacturing, wholesaling, or retailing. For example, Goodwill Industries refurbishes goods donated to it and sells them in retail stores.

Used athletic shoes and clothing often end up being donated to not-for-profit organizations. Churches and charitable organizations collect used clothing for distribution to the poor and homeless. Various organizations sell used shoes and clothing donated to them and use the income to provide community services.

Government

Government is a special type of not-for-profit "service business." Government makes laws and regulations that affect businesses and individuals. It also provides some basic services such as police and fire protection. These services are paid for through taxes and fees charged for the services.

An example of the government's effect on athletic shoe and clothing businesses is government regulations regarding product labeling. Other examples are jogging paths, bicycle lanes, and tennis courts built by local governments. These facilities encourage the purchase of athletic clothing and equipment.

Business Functions

To accomplish its purpose, a business or organization must perform certain functions. For example, a business must buy and sell goods, manufacture products, pay employees, and so forth. These functions are grouped into general categories, often called *functional areas*. (See Fig. 2.3.) This section describes the main business functions and discusses how these functions vary for different types of businesses.

Accounting

The accounting function is responsible for recording and reporting financial information about the business. The function records data about the business's assets, which are the items the business owns, such as cash, equipment, and buildings, and its liabilities, which are the debts of the business. It also records data about the business's revenues and expenses. Periodically the function produces reports on the financial state of the business.

All types of businesses require an accounting function. The details, however, may vary somewhat for different types of businesses. For example, manufacturers will

FIGURE 2.3

The main
functional areas
of a business

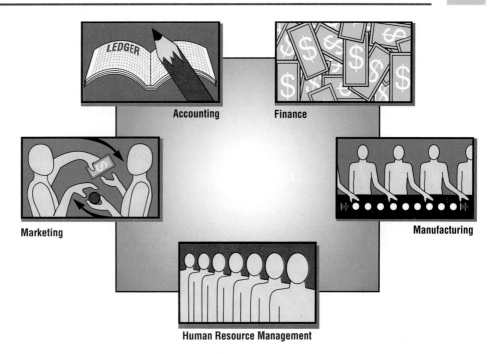

Accounting

Finance

Marketing

Manufacturing

Human Resource Management

have to account for production equipment, but wholesalers, retailers, and service businesses usually will not. A wholesaler, however, may have shipping expenses that a manufacturer does not. A retailer has to account for store space that other types of businesses do not have. Finally, a service business, such as a repair business, may have to account for spare parts expenses, whereas other businesses may not have to.

Finance

The finance function of a business is responsible for obtaining money needed by the business and for planning the use of that money. Money for a business comes from the sale of goods and services, from investments made by the business, and from banks and other institutions that loan money to the business. Once money is obtained it can be used for the day-to-day operations of the business or it can be invested for future use. The finance function plans what money is needed, determines the best way to obtain the money, and decides how the money should be used. The finance function is closely related to the accounting function.

All types of businesses need a finance function. Some businesses, however, do more financial work than others. For example, financial service companies such as banks have extensive finance functions. Other businesses, such as retail stores, may have comparatively small finance functions.

Marketing

The marketing function sells the goods and services of a business. To do so it must determine what products to sell and at what price. Then it must promote the products by advertising and other means. Finally it must make the actual sale and distribute the products that it sells.

All businesses have some form of marketing function although its size varies significantly. Retail and many service businesses have very large marketing functions

Bookmark

Information Systems at American Red Cross and Nature Conservancy

Nonprofit work still involves volunteers, a helping hand, and a cup of coffee, but computer technology now has a major part in the effort.

Information systems staffers at not-for-profit organizations aren't only planning larger and more wide-ranging projects, but they are also working with limited budget and resources.

For example, the Atlanta chapter of the American Red Cross has created a database that runs on an IBM AS/400 computer. The database helped the chapter reduce administrative costs from 24% to 9% of its budget and gives the Red Cross information that lets them contact the right people at the right time when disaster strikes.

"All disasters are run on computer now," said Dee Kellogg, chief information officer at the Atlanta chapter.

Groups such as the Red Cross use computers out of necessity because nonprofits deal with funding cutbacks, diminishing government support, and more competition for donations than ever before.

IS must use special skills to make technology dreams a reality at nonprofits.

"We have to be able to talk about what our mission is and how the donated item will help us provide better service," Kellogg said. "I believe so much in the Red Cross. My passion comes through."

IS dedication is key.

"The drive to deliver on the promise of technology takes on heightened importance for us," said Doug Barker, chief information officer at the Nature Conservancy in Arlington, Va. "If we give our users better ways to pull in all sorts of information and link the data to [geographic information system] tools, it really matters."

Barker has begun a drive to work with technology firms to get the best products available. He says one advantage for the Nature Conservancy is that high-tech companies often support conservation issues. For example, Microsoft Corp. is donating its Office productivity suite to Nature Conservancy offices nationwide.

Another way for the organization to get help is to work out a creative donation deal. Barker worked out an agreement with Learning Tree International, Inc. so Nature Conservancy workers receive donated training on a space-available basis. Thus the group gets much-needed training while filling up Learning Tree's classes.

Major plans, such as the Nature Conservancy's computer technology push or the National Easter Seals Society's linking of its nearly 500 World Wide Web pages, can often take a long time to implement because of the delays in looking for equipment donations.

As a result, these groups may find themselves getting a very early start with new technologies.

"Sometimes I will jump out on the bleeding edge just because it will take me that much longer to get it done as a nonprofit," Kellogg said.

QUESTIONS

1. What benefits did the Atlanta chapter of the American Red Cross receive from its information system?
2. What creative solutions do not-for-profit organizations use to overcome limited funds when setting up information systems?

WEB SITES
American Red Cross: www.redcross.org
Nature Conservancy: www.tnc.org
Easter Seals Society: www.seals.com

Source: Tim Ouellette, "Nonprofits rely on IS innovation," *Computerworld*, December 16, 1996, p. 6.

because they must sell to many customers. Wholesalers also may have fairly large marketing functions because they must sell to many retail businesses. Manufacturers often have comparatively small marketing functions because they may sell to only a few wholesalers.

Manufacturing

The manufacturing function, also called production, is responsible for producing the goods that the business sells. The manufacturing function must acquire the materials or parts that go into the goods being manufactured. It must keep track of the goods as they are manufactured and after they are completed. It must control the manufacturing process to be sure it runs smoothly and cost effectively.

In a manufacturing business, the manufacturing function is very large and important. In other types of businesses, however, this function will usually not exist. Instead there may be a related function, sometimes called operations, that performs various activities. For example, in a wholesale business the operations function would be responsible for running the warehouse where goods are stored. In a service business the operations function would be those activities that provide the services to the customers.

Human Resource Management

The human resource management function, sometimes called *personnel*, is responsible for hiring, training, compensating, and terminating employees. This function must recruit and select employees, assess the skills of employees, and determine the appropriate job for each employee. In addition, it must provide for the continual education and development of employees; determine appropriate compensation, including benefits; and provide procedures for termination due to resignation, retirement, or dismissal.

All types of businesses require human resource management. Businesses that have many employees with specialized skills, such as some manufacturers, need an extensive human resource management function for employee skill assessment and training. Businesses in which many employees perform similar types of work, such as some retail businesses, may not have such an extensive human resource management function.

Other Business Functions

The business functions described above are the most common ones found in businesses. Other functions, however, may be performed in certain businesses. One is the research and development function, which is responsible for developing new products to be manufactured by the business. Another is the information services function, which is responsible for providing computer information systems support for the business. Still other functions may be found in certain types of businesses.

Organization of a Business

The employees of a business are often grouped by the general functions they perform. Within each functional area may be smaller groups of people, often called departments, who have specific responsibilities related to the function. For example, in the marketing area there may be a Sales Department which is responsible for making sales, and an Advertising Department which prepares promotional material. The employees of a department form one or more workgroups to perform specific tasks or activities. For example, several employees in the Sales Department may form a workgroup to sell a particular line of products. In many situations, the entire department forms one workgroup. Workgroups are not, however, restricted to departments but may exist across departmental and functional area boundaries. For example, a product-line workgroup may include several employees from both the Sales Department and the Advertising Department.

Each department is headed by a manager who is in charge of the people working in the department. Thus, the Sales Department has a sales manager and the Advertising Department, an advertising manager. All the managers of the departments in a functional area report to the manager of the area. The functional area managers are often called vice presidents. Thus there would be a vice president of marketing, a vice president of finance, and so forth. (The vice president of accounting is often called the controller.) In smaller businesses, functional areas may be called departments and the person in charge may be called a manager instead of a vice president. In any case, all the functional area managers (vice presidents) report to the manager of the business who is usually the president or chief executive officer (CEO).

This arrangement of people who work for a business is often shown in a diagram called an <u>organization chart</u>. Figure 2.4 shows the organization chart for an athletic-clothing wholesaler. Each box represents a person or a workgroup with several people. The boxes are connected by lines that show who manages what part of the business.

The organizational structure of a business varies for different businesses. For example, a manufacturer would have a manufacturing functional area, but a wholesaler, retailer, or service business would not. Some businesses combine finance and accounting into one area and some have other areas, such as research and development. Other types of organizational structures, not based on business functions, are used by some businesses. For example, some businesses organize employees by product line or by geographic area.

FIGURE 2.4

An organization chart

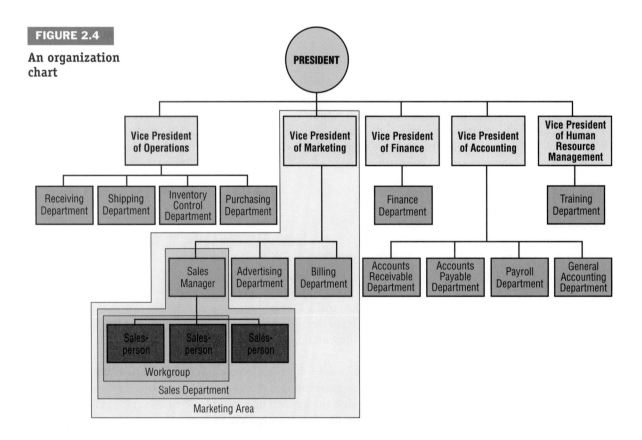

Information and Business Operations

Business operations are those activities that provide the goods and services of the business, and that ensure that the business makes a profit from selling its products. Manufacturing products, processing customer orders, billing customers, keeping track of inventory, purchasing raw materials, and many more activities are all part of business operations. Information is needed for these operations to function efficiently. Information about what products to manufacture, what items have been ordered, how much a customer owes, when inventory is low, and from where raw materials are to be purchased are just a few examples.

The information used in business operations flows between people within a workgroup or a department, and from one workgroup or department to another. The information may be sent by voice, on paper, or by computer. We will discuss several examples of the information flow that might be found in the operations of the athletic-clothing wholesale business whose organization chart is shown in Fig. 2.4.

Figure 2.5 shows how information related to the sale of goods and the payment for the sale flows in a business. When a customer, which in this case is another business, wishes to purchase something, the customer transmits information about what it wants to order. The customer order information is received by a salesperson in the Sales Department, which sends information about what is being sold to the Shipping Department. There the goods are packaged and sent to the customer. The Shipping Department sends information about what was shipped on to the Billing Department, which prepares billing information indicating how much the customer owes. This information is sent to the customer and to the Accounts Receivable Department. When the customer receives the billing information, it sends a payment which is received by the Accounts Receivable Department. This department keeps track of customer bills and payments and sends reminders to customers who have not paid their bills.

The information flow related to inventory control is shown in Fig. 2.6. Recall that inventory is the stock of goods that the business has on hand. The Shipping Department sends information to the Inventory Control Department about what goods were shipped from the inventory in the warehouse. The Receiving Department receives goods sent to the business and stores them in the inventory in the warehouse. It sends information to the Inventory Control Department about what goods were received. The Inventory Control Department keeps track of the inventory, subtracting goods shipped and adding goods received. Periodically it determines what goods should be reordered and sends this information to the Purchasing Department.

Figure 2.7 shows the flow of information related to purchasing goods. The Purchasing Department receives information about what goods should be reordered from the Inventory Control Department. In the Purchasing Department, purchasing information is prepared and sent to the supplier that sells the goods. The purchasing information is also sent to the Accounts Payable Department, which keeps track of bills owed by the business. The supplier sends billing information for the goods purchased to the business. This information is received by the Accounts Payable Department. This department also gets information from the Receiving Department about which goods were received from the supplier. It then sends payment to the supplier for the goods that were billed and received.

The flow of information in business operations described here will be different in other types of businesses. In a manufacturing business, inventory for items the

FIGURE 2.5

The information flow related to sales

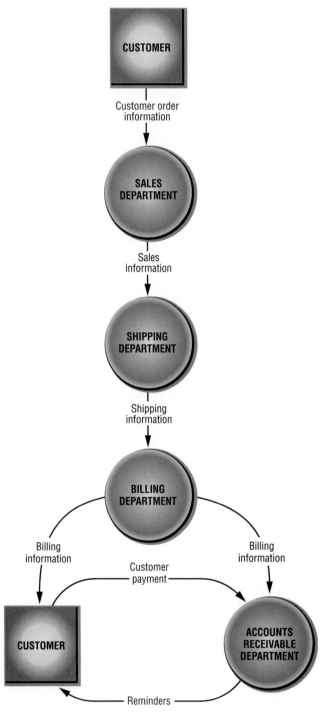

business sells is not replaced by purchasing new stock, but by producing the items. Thus, inventory information would flow to the Production Department to start the manufacturing process. In a retail business, the customer is a person and the customer "order" is a sale which is normally filled immediately, so there is no shipping

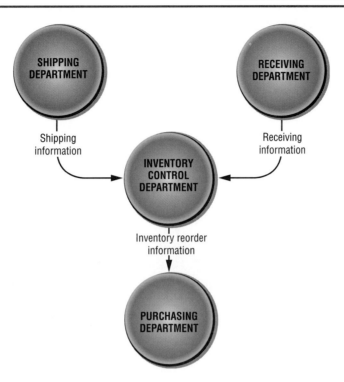

FIGURE 2.6

The information flow related to inventory control

information that flows from the Sales Department to the Shipping Department. Furthermore, billing information is necessary only if the customer charges the purchase. In some service businesses, information is needed to keep track of customer service requests. This information may flow from the customer to the Service Department and on to the Billing Department.

Information and Business Management

In addition to supporting business operations, information is used in the management of the business. Management involves decision making. Managers make day-to-day decisions about who should be allowed to purchase from the business on credit, how much should be ordered for inventory, and which suppliers should be used for purchases. Managers also make longer-term decisions, such as what items should be stocked next season and even whether the business should change to a whole new product line.

A decision involves selecting among different courses of action. For example, in a credit-granting decision, a manager must choose between granting credit and not granting credit to a customer. To make a decision, a manager needs information. Thus, to decide whether to grant credit, the manager needs information about the customer's previous credit history. The information reduces uncertainty for the manager and, as a consequence, reduces risk for the business. Credit-history information reduces uncertainty about whether the customer will pay its bill. With less uncertainty, granting credit is less risky for the business. The information has value to the decision maker and to the business because of the reduction of uncertainty and risk.

FIGURE 2.7

The information flow related to purchasing

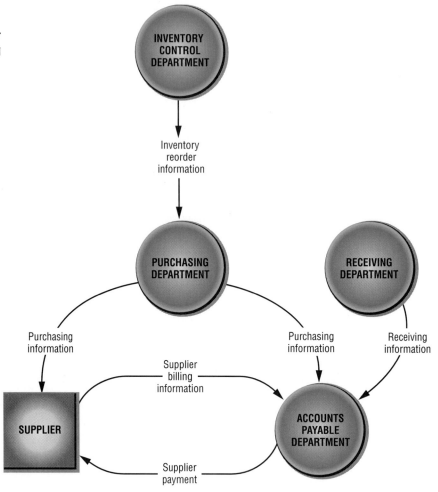

Much of the information that managers need is produced from the information that flows in the business. To illustrate, consider an inventory reordering decision faced by a manager. Figure 2.6 shows that inventory shipping and receiving information flows to the Inventory Control Department. This department keeps track of the quantity of inventory that the business currently has in stock and detects when the inventory level is too low. The Sales Department receives customer order information (Fig. 2.5) and uses this information to help forecast sales. When the manager receives information that the inventory level is low, he or she can use the sales forecast information to help determine how much new stock to reorder. Thus, information flows to the manager so that he or she can make appropriate decisions.

Decisions are made at different levels of a business. The highest-level decisions are made by top managers such as the president or vice president. These decisions affect the business for a long time. For example, deciding whether the business should change to a new product line is a high-level decision. Middle-level decisions are made by departmental managers or workgroup leaders and affect the business for an intermediate period of time. Deciding what items should be stocked next season is an example of this type of decision. The lowest-level decisions are made by individuals at the bottom of the hierarchy, such as credit evaluators, inventory supervisors, and purchasing personnel. These decisions affect the business for a short period of time. The credit-granting decision is an example of this type of decision.

Basic Business Information Processing

The use of information in business operations and management is made possible by various information processing activities. These activities involve people (and computers if the activities are computerized) that receive data for processing, process the data as required, store the data for future processing, and produce information resulting from the processing.

Although many information processing activities are found in businesses, eight basic ones are:

- Entering customer orders
- Billing customers
- Collecting customer payments
- Keeping track of inventory
- Purchasing stock and materials
- Paying bills
- Paying employees
- Reporting financial information

Bookmark

Custom Jeans Order Entry at Levi Strauss

Every woman knows the terror of shopping for jeans. You try on hundreds of pairs, but they're all too short, too tight, too long, too loose, the wrong color . . . There has never been the perfect pair of jeans—until now.

In October 1995, Levi Strauss & Co. bought Custom Clothing Technology Corp., which developed the Personal Pair Program, a system for custom-made women's jeans.

A woman can now walk in to one of 50 Levi store locations that has the Personal Pair Program, decide which color and style she wants, and get measured by a store clerk. Three weeks later, she has a pair of Levi jeans made especially for her.

The clerk enters the information into a personal computer through a proprietary touch screen. That information goes into a Lotus Development Corp. Notes file and is sent via AT&T Network Notes to the factory in Mountain City, Tenn.

Orders are collected at the factory each night. The jeans are bar-coded so they can be tracked through the factory and sent to the correct customer—all for $65 per pair.

The biggest challenge in developing this system was making it very simple to use. "Store people are good at selling clothes, and we don't want to let technology get in the way of them doing their job," said Bethe Palmer, director of retail operations.

This focus on user-friendliness succeeded. "It's easier to use the computer than it is to do the actual measuring," said Amy Sniffen, a clerk at the Natick, Mass., store.

But what about men who share the terror of shopping for jeans? According to Levi, they can expect this technology to be around their waists soon.

QUESTIONS

1. What data is entered for a customer order for a pair of custom jeans?
2. Why is user friendliness important in the information system for custom jeans order entry?
3. What information could Levi Strauss get from the system to help it sell jeans in the future?

WEB SITE
Levi Strauss: www.levi.com

Source: Stefanie McCann, "1996 Computerworld Smithsonian Awards: Business & Related Services," *Computerworld*, June 3, 1996, p. 96.

This section describes the eight activities. The descriptions are general; they do not assume that the activities are done with or without the aid of computers. Each activity is illustrated with an example of how it would be used in an athletic-clothing wholesale business.

Entering Customer Orders

The first business information processing activity is entering customer orders. The purpose of this activity is to accept customer orders for goods or services and to prepare them in a form that can be used by the business. This activity is part of the marketing function and is performed by people in the Sales Department.

The input to this activity is the customer order, which may be received by the business in several forms. A customer may phone in an order to a salesperson who writes the order on a form (Fig. 2.8), or the customer may fill out the order form and mail it to the business. The customer also may order by sending in a purchase order, which is a form prepared in a format that the customer uses. The purchase order may be sent by mail, by fax, or by computer, if an EDI system (discussed in Chapter 1) is used. In any case, the order is received by the Sales Department.

When processing the orders, the business must determine if there is sufficient inventory to fill the order and if credit should be extended to the customer. If both conditions are met, a sales order (Fig. 2.9), which is the output from the system, is prepared. This document, which is also called a shipping order, contains customer information, such as customer name and address, and inventory information, such as the item ordered. It is sent to the Shipping Department to indicate what items should be shipped to the customer.

Billing Customers

The sales order is used by the Shipping Department to determine what items should be shipped to the customer. In some cases the quantity shipped is different from the quantity ordered because of inadequate stock on hand. Therefore, the Shipping Department must mark a copy of the sales order with the actual quantity shipped (Fig. 2.10) and send this copy to the Billing Department. The Billing Department

FIGURE 2.8

A customer order

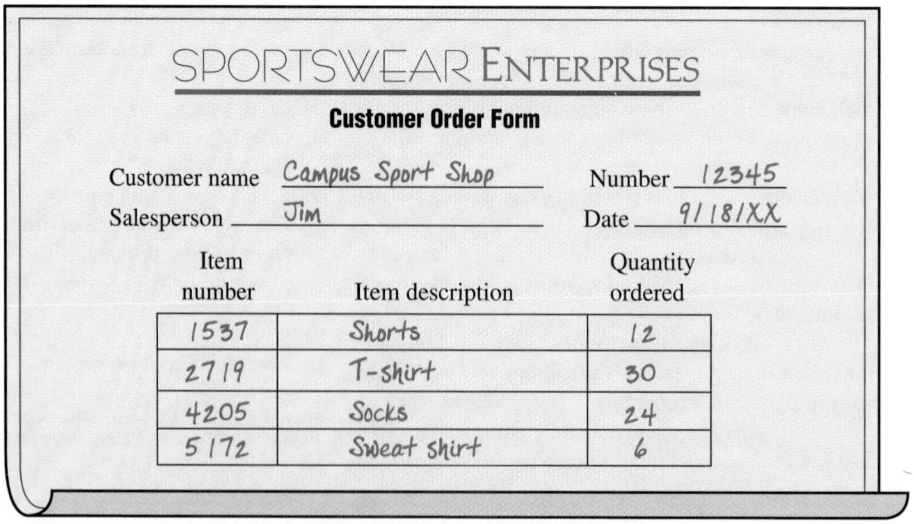

SPORTSWEAR ENTERPRISES

Customer Order Form

Customer name _Campus Sport Shop_   Number _12345_
Salesperson _Jim_   Date _9/18/XX_

Item number	Item description	Quantity ordered
1537	Shorts	12
2719	T-shirt	30
4205	Socks	24
5172	Sweat shirt	6

FIGURE 2.9

A sales order

FIGURE 2.9

A sales order

SPORTSWEAR ENTERPRISES
Sales Order

Customer number   12345   Date   9/20/XX
Customer name   Campus Sport Shop
Shipping address   123 South Avenue
                   Portland, OR 97208

Item number	Item description	Quantity ordered	Quantity shipped
1537	Shorts	12	
2719	T-shirt	30	
4205	Socks	24	
5172	Sweat shirt	6	

uses its copy of the sales order to prepare the customer's bill, which is called the invoice. The Billing Department is usually part of the marketing function but may be part of accounting.

The sales order (Fig. 2.10) is the input to this activity. The output is the invoice (Fig. 2.11), which contains the information about how much the customer owes for the items ordered. To prepare the invoice from the sales order, the customer's billing address must be looked up so it can be included on the invoice. The price of each item shipped also must be looked up and the amount due must be computed by multiplying the quantity shipped by the price. This information is part of the invoice, along with the total due for all items purchased. A copy of the invoice is sent to the customer and another copy is sent to the Accounts Receivable Department.

FIGURE 2.10

The sales order from the Shipping Department

SPORTSWEAR ENTERPRISES
Sales Order

Customer number   12345   Date   9/20/XX
Customer name   Campus Sport Shop
Shipping address   123 South Avenue
                   Portland, OR 97208

Item number	Item description	Quantity ordered	Quantity shipped
1537	Shorts	12	12
2719	T-shirt	30	24
4205	Socks	24	24
5172	Sweat shirt	6	6

FIGURE 2.11

An invoice

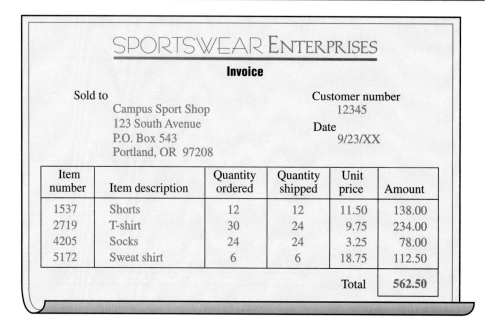

Item number	Item description	Quantity ordered	Quantity shipped	Unit price	Amount
1537	Shorts	12	12	11.50	138.00
2719	T-shirt	30	24	9.75	234.00
4205	Socks	24	24	3.25	78.00
5172	Sweat shirt	6	6	18.75	112.50
				Total	**562.50**

SPORTSWEAR ENTERPRISES — Invoice

Sold to
Campus Sport Shop
123 South Avenue
P.O. Box 543
Portland, OR 97208

Customer number
12345
Date
9/23/XX

Collecting Customer Payments

The copy of the invoice from the Billing Department is used in the Accounts Receivable Department to keep track of money customers owe to the business, which is called *accounts receivable*, and to record customer payments for invoices. In addition, this department sends reminders of overdue invoices to customers, sends summaries of invoice charges and payments to customers, and provides reports of accounts receivable to other business functions. The Accounts Receivable Department is part of the accounting function.

The inputs to this activity are the copy of the invoice received from the Billing Department (Fig. 2.11) and the customer payment. One of the outputs is a statement, which summarizes the invoice charges and payments and gives the current balance due (Fig. 2.12). The statement is prepared once a month and sent to the customer. (Some businesses do not prepare statements.) Another output is overdue notices which are sent to customers who have not paid their invoices. (Sometimes the statement includes a notice for overdue customers.) A final output is an accounts receivable report summarizing charges and payments for the month (Fig. 2.13). This report contains the total invoice charges and total customer payments for all customers. The report is sent to the General Accounting Department.

Processing in this activity involves several tasks. The balance due for each customer must be recorded, along with the current month's invoice and payments. Each month, the new balance due must be computed by adding the customer's previous balance due and the total of the current month's invoices, and subtracting the total of the current month's payments.

Keeping Track of Inventory

To be sure that there is adequate stock on hand to meet customer demand, a business must keep track of its inventory and report when inventory is low so that new stock can be ordered. This information processing activity is performed by the

FIGURE 2.12

A statement

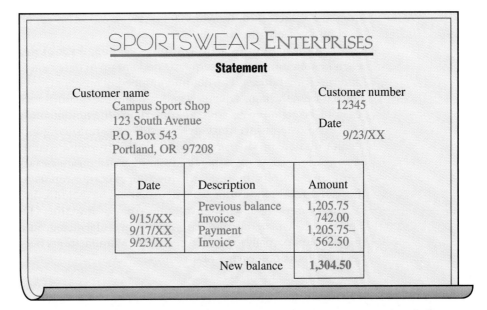

SPORTSWEAR ENTERPRISES

Statement

Customer name   Customer number
  Campus Sport Shop   12345
  123 South Avenue   Date
  P.O. Box 543   9/23/XX
  Portland, OR 97208

Date	Description	Amount
	Previous balance	1,205.75
9/15/XX	Invoice	742.00
9/17/XX	Payment	1,205.75–
9/23/XX	Invoice	562.50
	New balance	**1,304.50**

FIGURE 2.13

An accounts receivable report

\	ACCOUNTS RECEIVABLE REPORT 9 / 30 / XX		

Customer number	Date	Invoice charge	Payment
12345	9/15/XX	742.00	
12345	9/17/XX		1,205.75
12345	9/23/XX	562.50	
48721	9/11/XX		2,135.00
48721	9/15/XX	1,079.25	
93142	9/12/XX	425.00	
93142	9/25/XX		975.25
Total		72,213.50	63,409.00

Inventory Control Department. In some businesses this department is part of the manufacturing or operations function, and in other businesses it is part of marketing or accounting.

The inputs to this activity are the sales order from the Shipping Department indicating the quantity of each item shipped (Fig. 2.10) and the receiving notice from the Receiving Department giving the quantity of items received from vendors or other sources (Fig. 2.14). One output is the inventory reorder report which lists the items that should be reordered because stock is low (Fig. 2.15). This report is sent to the Purchasing Department. Another output is the inventory value report which gives the value of the items in stock (Fig. 2.16). This report goes to the General Accounting Department.

Processing in this activity involves keeping track of the quantity on hand for each item in inventory. This quantity is kept up-to-date from data in the sales orders and receiving notices. The quantity shipped of an item from each sales order is subtracted from the item's quantity on hand and the quantity received for the item from each receiving notice is added to determine the new quantity on hand.

The type of inventory described here is finished goods inventory because it deals with final products ready for sale. This type of inventory is found in manufacturing, wholesaling, retailing, and some service businesses where parts are needed. For manufacturers, however, the inventory reorder report would not be prepared. Instead, a report indicating what items should be manufactured would be produced. Manufacturers usually have two other types of inventory: Raw materials inventory consists of the materials and parts used in manufacturing, and work-in-process inventory involves partially manufactured items. Manufacturers need inventory control systems for these other types of inventory.

Purchasing Stock and Materials

When a business purchases items for inventory, it must first determine the best suppliers of the items and then prepare documents, called purchase orders, which indicate to the suppliers what items are wanted. This activity is done by the Purchasing Department which is usually part of the manufacturing or operations function but may be part of accounting.

FIGURE 2.14

A receiving notice

RECEIVING NOTICE

Date _____ 9 / 17 / XX _____

Item number _____ 4205 _____

Supplier number _____ 62 / 4 _____

Quantity received _____ 180 _____

FIGURE 2.15

An inventory reorder report

INVENTORY REORDER REPORT
9 / 30 / XX

Item number	Item description	Quantity on hand	Reorder point	Quantity to order
2719	T-shirt	0	10	30
3804	Tennis shirt	8	12	25
5173	Sweat pants	18	18	44
6318	Swim suit	12	20	36

FIGURE 2.16

An inventory
value report

INVENTORY VALUE REPORT
11 / 30 / XX

Item number	Item description	Inventory value
1537	Shorts	4,232.00
1609	Jacket	960.00
2719	T-shirt	2,340.00
3512	Tennis shorts	690.00
3804	Tennis shirt	1,904.20
4205	Socks	480.20
.		
.		
.		
5172	Sweat shirt	3,515.75
5173	Sweat pants	4,002.00
5501	Cap	874.00
6318	Swim suit	1,197.00
	Total value	85,352.00

The input to this activity is the inventory reorder report (Fig. 2.15), which comes from the Inventory Control Department. This report indicates what items and what quantity of each item should be reordered. The output is the purchase order (Fig. 2.17) which is sent to the supplier and lists the items the business wants to purchase. A copy of the purchase order is also sent to the Accounts Payable Department.

To produce the purchase order, the preferred supplier for the item to be purchased must be determined. Different suppliers' sales policies and performance information is analyzed to determine the best supplier for each item. The selection of the best supplier may be based not only on price but also on sales terms, delivery time, or other factors that the business considers important. When purchase orders

FIGURE 2.17

A purchase order

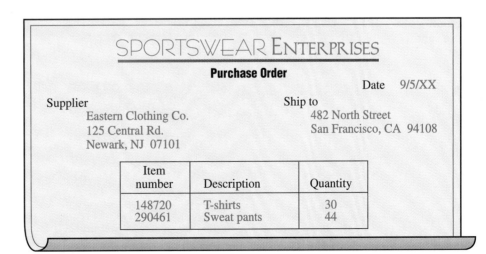

SPORTSWEAR ENTERPRISES

Purchase Order

Date   9/5/XX

Supplier
　　Eastern Clothing Co.
　　125 Central Rd.
　　Newark, NJ 07101

Ship to
　　482 North Street
　　San Francisco, CA 94108

Item number	Description	Quantity
148720	T-shirts	30
290461	Sweat pants	44

are to be prepared, the preferred supplier's name and address must be looked up. This information is included on the purchase order, along with information about the item ordered.

The activity described here is characteristic of purchasing for finished goods inventory in a wholesaling, retailing, or service business. In a manufacturing business, purchasing is necessary for raw materials inventory but not for finished goods inventory. Instead, production scheduling is done to determine, based on inventory needs, what items are to be produced.

Paying Bills

The copy of the purchase order from the Purchasing Department is used in the Accounts Payable Department to keep track of money owed by the business for purchases, which is called *accounts payable*, and to pay suppliers for the items purchased. The Accounts Payable Department is part of the accounting function.

The inputs to this activity are the copy of the purchase order from the Purchasing Department indicating what items were ordered (Fig. 2.17), the invoice from the supplier showing what items the supplier shipped and the charges for the items, and a copy of the receiving notice from the Receiving Department indicating what items were received (Fig. 2.14). The outputs include the supplier payment, which is a check sent to the supplier, and an accounts payable report summarizing the supplier charges and payments for the month (Fig. 2.18). The report contains the total charges and payments for all suppliers and is sent to the General Accounting Department.

Processing in this activity includes several tasks. The purchase order is compared with the supplier's invoice to determine if the items ordered were shipped by the supplier. The supplier's invoice is compared with the receiving notice to see if the items shipped were received. If the supplier's invoice correctly states what items were ordered and received, then a record of the data on the invoice is kept. Included in this data is the due date for the payment of the invoice sent by the supplier. Frequently, perhaps every day, this data is checked to see if any invoice payments are

FIGURE 2.18

An accounts payable report

	ACCOUNTS PAYABLE REPORT 9 / 30 / XX		
Supplier number	Invoice date	Invoice charge	Payment
2147	9/ 3 /XX	10,132.50	10,132.50
2895	9/ 7 /XX	15,911.00	
3245	9/12/XX	780.75	
3513	9/13/XX	9,470.00	9,470.00
7409	9/27/XX	425.00	
7723	9/28/XX	2,630.00	
	Totals	68,425.00	52,095.50

due soon. When a payment is almost due, a check is prepared. Once a month, the accounts payable report is prepared.

Paying Employees

An essential information processing activity in all businesses involves paying employees and providing payroll reports for other business functions. This activity is performed by the Payroll Department. In many businesses this department is part of the accounting function, while in some businesses it is part of the human resource management function.

The input to this activity is the employee work report. For an employee who is paid on an hourly basis, this report is a time sheet that shows how many hours the employee has worked each day (Fig. 2.19). For an employee who is paid a fixed salary, the report indicates whether the employee was present for all workdays, and, if absent, for what reason. The outputs include the paycheck which is given to the employee. Another output is the payroll report listing the gross earnings for each employee, which is the amount earned by the employee, the amount deducted for taxes and for other reasons, and the net pay, which is the difference between the gross earnings and deductions (Fig. 2.20). The report also gives the total of the gross earnings, deductions, and net pay for all employees. This report is sent to the General Accounting Department.

Payroll processing involves using the employee work data and the data about the employee records, such as pay rate or salary, to calculate the pay for each employee. If the employee is paid on an hourly basis, the hours worked from the time sheet is multiplied by the pay rate to calculate the gross earnings. For a salaried employee, the

FIGURE 2.19

A time sheet

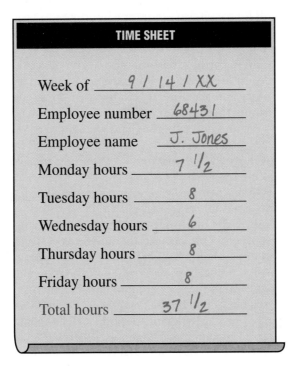

TIME SHEET
Week of ___9 / 14 / XX___
Employee number ___68431___
Employee name ___J. Jones___
Monday hours ___7 ½___
Tuesday hours ___8___
Wednesday hours ___6___
Thursday hours ___8___
Friday hours ___8___
Total hours ___37 ½___

FIGURE 2.20

A payroll report

PAYROLL REPORT 11 / 30 / XX						
Employee number	Employee name	Gross earnings	Federal tax	Soc. Sec. tax	Other deduct.	Net pay
23890	S. Smith	1,305.50	180.83	93.34	.00	1,031.33
25008	M. Andrews	1,162.00	106.80	83.08	15.00	957.12
31942	R. Gonzales	2,443.75	276.56	174.73	7.50	1,984.96
37926	J. Franklin	988.00	80.70	70.64	.00	836.66
		⋮				
87435	L. Wong	1,352.00	229.84	96.69	.00	1,025.47
88207	F. Richardson	872.00	148.24	62.35	18.00	643.41
92371	A. Baker	460.25	78.24	32.91	.00	349.10
	Totals	40,305.00	6,859.50	2,885.03	507.50	33,097.97

gross earnings is the employee's salary unless he or she worked less than a full pay period. In addition, the deductions and net pay are calculated.

Reporting Financial Information

The last business information processing activity we will discuss here is found in all businesses. Its purpose is to provide reports of financial information for the management and owners of the business. To accomplish this activity, a business keeps financial accounts for each form of revenue it receives and each expense that it pays. A business receives revenue from sales and other sources such as investments. It pays expenses for the cost of the goods that it sells and for salaries, rent, advertising, office supplies, and so forth. A business also keeps an account of each of its assets and liabilities. Assets are items the business owns, such as cash, equipment, and buildings. Inventory and accounts receivable are also assets. Liabilities are obligations of the business to pay money, including loans and accounts payable. This activity records revenues and expenses, and changes in assets and liabilities. It prepares reports, called financial statements, that summarize the business's accounts. This activity is performed by the General Accounting Department, which is part of the accounting function.

The inputs to this activity are reports on revenue, expenses, assets, and liabilities. The accounts receivable report (Fig. 2.13) provides information about accounts receivable (an asset). The inventory value report (Fig. 2.16) gives the total value of the inventory (an asset). The accounts payable report (Fig. 2.18) provides information about accounts payable (a liability). The payroll report (Fig. 2.20) gives payroll expense information. Other reports provide information about other accounts.

The outputs from this activity are financial statements; the two most common are the income statement and the balance sheet. The income statement lists all revenues and expenses for a specific time period (such as a month) and the difference between the total revenue and total expenses, which is the net income if positive, or loss if negative. (See Fig. 2.21a.) The balance sheet lists all assets and liabilities and the difference between the total assets and total liabilities, which is called the owner's equity. (See Fig. 2.21b.) Other financial statements may also be produced.

Processing in this activity involves recording data about revenues, expenses, assets, and liabilities. Periodically, the financial statements are prepared from the recorded data.

FIGURE 2.21

Financial statements

SPORTSWEAR ENTERPRISES

Income Statement / September 19XX

Revenue:		
Sales		$232,458
Expenses:		
Cost of goods sold	$88,231	
Salaries	40,305	
Rent	33,250	
Advertising	15,140	
Delivery	13,518	
Supplies	1,519	
Depreciation	12,350	
Total expenses		204,313
Net income:		**$28,145**

(a) Income statement

SPORTSWEAR ENTERPRISES

Balance Sheet / September 30,19XX

Assets:		
Cash	$46,219	
Accounts receivable	52,436	
Inventory	85,352	
Equipment	36,750	
Total assets		**$220,757**
Liabilities:		
Loans payable	$111,500	
Accounts payable	44,216	
Total liabilities		155,716
Owner's equity:		65,041
Total liabilities & owner's equity		**$220,757**

(b) Balance sheet

Information Systems and Business

The preceding three sections of this chapter have shown how information flows in business operations, how managers use information in decision making, and how businesses perform basic information processing. Although the flow, use, and processing of information described in those sections could be accomplished without the aid of computers and related technology, using computer information systems for these activities can greatly increase a business's efficiency and effectiveness.

Information flow in business operations can be controlled by information systems and technology. Computers and networks can be used to transmit data from one department to another. For example, sales information can be sent by computer over a network from the Sales Department to the Shipping Department, then shipping information can be sent on to the Billing Department by computer, and finally billing information can be transmitted over a network to the Accounts Receivable Department. Controlling the flow of information between departments using computers and networks increases the efficiency of the business operations involved.

Information systems and technology also increase the effectiveness of management decision making. Managers use information systems to get information to help in their decision making. For example, when deciding whether to grant credit to a customer, a manager can use an information system to examine the customer's credit history. With relevant and readily available information from computer information systems, managers can make better decisions.

Finally, almost all information processing activities are more efficient and effective when performed by computer information systems. Entering customer orders is faster and more accurate with computers. Preparing customer bills is quicker using a computer information system. Collecting customer payments is more effective with an information system. Keeping track of inventory is more accurate using information technology. All the information processing activities discussed in this chapter, as well as many more, are performed better with the aid of information systems and technology.

Information systems provide the methods and technology to support information needs and processing for every function in all types of businesses. Information systems are used in accounting, finance, marketing, manufacturing, and human resource management. They are found in manufacturers, wholesalers, retailers, service businesses, not-for-profit organizations, and government agencies. No matter what the function or the type of business, information systems play important roles.

Chapter Summary

☐ A business provides goods and services for its customers. A **manufacturer** produces goods that are sold to other businesses or to individual customers. A **wholesaler** purchases large quantities of goods, then sells smaller quantities to retailers, and ships or distributes the goods to the retailers. A **retailer** purchases quantities of goods from wholesalers or manufacturers and resells them, one at a time or in small quantities, to individual customers. A **service business** provides services to other businesses or to individuals. (pp. 30-34)

☐ The **accounting** function of a business records and reports financial information about the business.

The **finance** function obtains money needed by a business and plans the use of that money. The **marketing** function sells the goods and services of the business. The **manufacturing** function produces the goods sold by the business. The **human resource management** function hires, trains, compensates, and terminates employees of the business. A business often is organized into the main functions of the business. Within each function may be **departments** which have specific responsibilities related to the function. Within each department or across departmental lines may be **workgroups** that perform specific tasks or activities. (pp. 34-38)

☐ Information flows between people within a workgroup or a department, and from one workgroup or department to another. The flow of information related to the sale of goods and payment for the sale is diagrammed in Fig. 2.5. The flow of information related to inventory control is diagrammed in Fig. 2.6. The flow of information related to purchasing goods is diagrammed in Fig. 2.7. (pp. 39–41)

☐ Information is used by the management of a business to help in decision making. A decision involves selecting among different courses of action. To make a decision, a manager needs information, which reduces uncertainty for the manager and risk for the business. The information has value to the decision maker and to the business because of the reduction of uncertainty and risk. (pp. 41–43)

☐ Entering customer orders requires accepting customer orders for goods or services, and preparing them in a form that can be used by the business. Billing customers involves preparing customers' bills or invoices. Collecting customer payments requires keeping track of money owed to the business by its customers (accounts receivable) and recording customer payments. Keeping track of a business's inventory is important so that customer demand is met and inventory can be reordered when it is low. Purchasing stock and materials involves determining the best suppliers from which to purchase items and preparing purchase orders. Paying bills requires keeping track of money owed by the business (accounts payable) and paying suppliers for items purchased. Paying employees involves preparing paychecks for employees and providing reports of payroll. Reporting financial information consists of maintaining the business's financial accounts and preparing financial statements. (pp. 43–53)

☐ Information systems provide the methods and technology to support information needs and processing in businesses. Information systems control the flow of information in business operations. They make information readily available to help in management decision making. They improve the efficiency and effectiveness of information processing activities. They can be used in all functions of all types of businesses and organizations. (p. 54)

Key Terms

Accounting (p. 34)
Department (p. 37)
Finance (p. 35)
Human Resource Management (p. 37)
Information Services (p. 37)

Manufacturer (p. 31)
Manufacturing (Production) (p. 36)
Marketing (p. 35)
Operations (p. 37)
Organization Chart (p. 38)

Research and Development (p. 37)
Retailer (p. 32)
Service Business (p. 33)
Wholesaler (Distributor) (p. 31)
Workgroup (p. 37)

Assignment Material

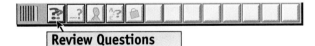

Review Questions

Fill-in Questions

1. Businesses that produce goods are called
   _____.

2. A(n) _____ buys large quantities of goods from a(n) _____ and sells smaller quantities to a(n) _____.

3. A(n) _____ sells goods one at a time or in small quantities to individual consumers.

4. An automobile repair shop is an example of a(n) _____ business.

5. The business function responsible for recording and reporting financial information about the business is_____.

6. The _____ function sells the goods and services of the business.

7. Another name for the manufacturing function of a business is _____.

8. A diagram that shows the arrangement of people who work in a business is called a(n) _____.

9. The information processing activity of _____ prepares sales orders from customer orders.

10. Accounts receivable is money that _____ and accounts payable is money that _____.

11. Purchase orders are prepared for suppliers to indicate _____.

12. Financial information is reported in _____.

Short-answer Questions

1. What is the purpose of a business?
2. Describe the flow of goods from raw materials to the final consumer.
3. What does the finance function of a business do?
4. What is the purpose of the human resource management function of a business?
5. What is a workgroup?
6. How does the shipping department know what goods should be shipped to a customer?
7. What does the accounts receivable department of a business do?
8. What information is needed by the inventory control department to keep track of inventory?

9. How does the purchasing department know when to purchase more goods?
10. What information does the accounts payable department need to make supplier payments?
11. How does the management of a business use information?
12. For what business information processing activities is a sales order an input?
13. What are the outputs from the information processing activity that collects customer payments?
14. Which information processing activity discussed in the chapter affects all employees of a business?

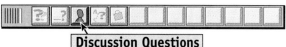

Discussion Questions

1. In some industries, wholesalers are not used; the retailer buys directly from the manufacturer. In other industries, wholesalers are used extensively. Why would a manufacturer want to use a wholesaler to sell and distribute its products instead of selling directly to a retailer? Why would a retailer want to purchase goods from a wholesaler rather than directly from a manufacturer?

2. In which function of a business do you plan to work? What job do you hope to have in that function? What information do you think you will receive in the course of doing that job? What decisions will you have to make in the job? What information will you need to make the decisions?

3. Identify several business information processing activities other than those described in this chapter. What are the inputs and outputs for each activity?

4. To reduce manufacturing costs, many businesses produce their products in foreign countries or purchase their products from foreign manufacturers. Also, many businesses sell their products worldwide. What problems do international production and international marketing create for the various business information processing activities discussed in this chapter?

5. Information can be used in many ways in a business, including unethical ways. What are some unethical uses of information within a business? How can these uses be prevented?

Problem-solving Projects

1. Select a category of consumer products in which you are interested (other than athletic shoes and clothing). Identify several major manufacturers, wholesalers (if used for these products), and retailers. Use the Internet to gather information about these businesses and how products are manufactured, distributed, and sold to the consumer. Write a brief report

summarizing the information you gathered. Use word processing software to prepare your report.

2. Draw an organization chart of a small business or organization with which you are familiar. If available, use graphics software to prepare the chart.

3. Using graphics software, draw a diagram like the one in Figs. 2.5, 2.6, or 2.7 for the flow of informa-

tion related to some activity in a business or organization with which you are familiar.

4. Using spreadsheet software, set up a table in which the columns are the eight business information processing activities discussed in this chapter, and the rows are the various reports and documents that are inputs and outputs for these activities. At the intersection of a row and column, put an "I" if the report or document is an input into the system, put an "O" if it is an output, and put nothing if it is neither an input nor an output.

5. Use the Internet to find financial statements for a company in which you are interested. Then transfer the information from the financial statements to a spreadsheet and compute, using the spreadsheet software, the following:

$$\text{Working capital} = \text{Total current assets} - \text{Total current liabilities}$$

$$\text{Current ratio} = \frac{\text{Total current assets}}{\text{Total current liabilities}}$$

$$\text{Acid-test ratio} = \frac{\text{Cash} + \text{Accounts Receivable}}{\text{Total current liabilities}}$$

$$\text{Rate of return on equity} = \frac{\text{Net income}}{\text{Owner's equity}}$$

$$\text{Earnings per share} = \frac{\text{Net income}}{\text{Shares of stock outstanding}}$$

Real-world Case

Daka International

Daka International is a worldwide diversified food service corporation with a history of reacting nimbly to changes at all levels of its corporate structure. In addition to owning the Daka Restaurants found at many colleges and universities nationwide, the company owns a chain of do-it-yourself hamburger restaurants called Fuddruckers and a string of Midwest restaurants and sports bars called Camps Americana, modeled along similar lines to the Hard Rock Cafe and Planet Hollywood. But operations at Daka—which runs restaurants not only in the United States but also in Canada, Australia, Mexico, and the Middle East—were not always so picked-from-the-farm fresh. Although the lettuce you find on your burgers at Fuddruckers might have been bright and crispy, the networks of communication and budget management were definitely stale.

The problem was located in the incapability to route time-sensitive information to the right place at the right time. The meat for those burgers roasting on Fuddrucker's large, open-flame grills might have been ground that day, the bun pulled from the oven before your eyes, but by the time sales information found its way back to corporate headquarters it was already weeks old—sometimes as many as seven weeks old. For management, seven-week-old data amounted to nothing less than an unappetizing carcass of regional sales information that few top-office managers could really chew on.

The problem was clear, and CEO Bill Baumhauer demanded that corporate-wide action be taken immediately. Daka's IS needed to be modernized, to be placed onto a strategic footing that would make it competitive for the coming century.

Daka's communications infrastructure until just a few years ago still operated on an outdated paper- and mail-based paradigm. The approximately 400 locations were all run independently. Sales data was mailed in on weekly and monthly schedules to corporate headquarters. If a manager at headquarters needed data urgently it was sent overnight at a considerable annual courier expense.

Once the data arrived, already old, it would have to be manually keyed into Digital and Wang computers. The slow turnaround time for critical data and the incapability of management at headquarters to effectively follow and compare individual locations—except via the staggered distance of weekly and monthly reports—resulted in a dangerously uncompetitive, slow response time to the market. This was true on all fronts: locally, nationally, and internationally.

The job to bring Daka's communications infrastructure into the modern age was handed to Chief Information Officer Ted Mountzuris, in Danvers, Mass. Using AT&T's Network Connect, Mountzuris developed a wide area network linking all locations inside the continental United States, not only to headquarters but also to each other. The linking software was XelleNet's RemoteWare package which allowed managers not only to use e-mail for the first time, but to transmit, twice daily, profit and loss data to a central database. Overseas locations were linked via the Internet using RemoteWare.

The point-of-sales solution was enabled through the installation of high-tech NCR cash registers at all locations. These allowed the flexibility of choosing different software solutions for different organizations. So while Fuddruckers used Compris software developed by

Compris Technologies, Champs Americana was given the flexibility to install Aloha software from Ibertech. Both retained full compatibility with RemoteWare and, through this, with each other.

Data sent via RemoteWare is stored on Smart I, an imaging solution from FileMark, that stores all financial reports and sends them out as needed as e-mail reports. One of the many benefits of this system for the corporation is a switch to an almost entirely paperless corporate environment.

"We just don't use paper anymore," Mountzuris says. "Our forms, contracts, reports, and payroll have all become digitized. Only accounting information stays on paper for auditing purposes."

One of the benefits of RemoteWare software is that it allows intensive drilling down and links all three layers of Daka's corporate cake: the field locations, the regional field managers, and the corporate offices.

The drill-downs are viewed through graphical interfaces showing maps that allow managers to click on locations at any level they want to view. A manager can move from a map of the United States to one of Texas right down to the individual restaurants. Locations can be easily compared, and this includes the capability to compare differing kinds of locations: A Fuddruckers in Austin, Texas, can be compared with a Champs Americana in the same city, or a nearby city, or even one clear across the world. Corporate profit and loss data is no longer restricted to the individual organizations within Daka but can be looked at both across these organizations and vertically within each organization. A manager working from any laptop can hook into RemoteWare and dial up the latest profit and loss data within minutes. In short, there are no more seven-week delays.

At all levels, manager response has been enthusiastic. Local managers have found that the system requires no more effort on their part but gives them exciting tools with which to analyze and tackle the challenges of competing locally in a global business environment. At headquarters, no one has been lamenting stale profit and loss data anymore. Daka has moved from being a seller of some of the freshest burgers in the industry to having that same freshness jump off the screens back at headquarters.

Questions

1. Before developing the information system described in the case, how did Daka transmit data? What was the consequence of this method for Daka?

2. What functions of Daka are affected by the information system?

3. What information does Daka get from the information system?

4. The case talks about "drilling down," which means examining data starting with summary data and working down to detailed data. How do Daka managers use drilling down in the information system?

5. What benefits does Daka receive from the information system?

Source: Ranbir Sidhu, "Daka freshens its restaurants' information relay systems," *InfoWorld*, November 25, 1996, p. 63.

3 Information System Fundamentals

Chapter Outline

Components of an Information System   (p. 60)
  Hardware   (p. 60)
  Software   (p. 60)
  Stored Data   (p. 61)
  Personnel   (p. 62)
  Procedures   (p. 62)
Hardware for Information Systems   (p. 62)
  Input and Output Devices   (p. 62)
  Primary Storage and the Central Processing Unit   (p. 65)
  Secondary Storage   (p. 66)
  Communications Hardware   (p. 68)
  Computer Systems   (p. 68)
Software for Information Systems   (p. 74)
  Program Concepts   (p. 74)
  Types of Software   (p. 75)
  Sources of Software   (p. 77)
Stored Data for Information Systems   (p. 78)
Personnel for Information Systems   (p. 80)
Procedures for Information Systems   (p. 80)

Learning Objectives

After completing this chapter, you should be able to:
- [ ] 1. Identify the components of an information system.
- [ ] 2. Describe and give examples of the main components of a computer, and explain the purpose of data communications hardware.
- [ ] 3. Distinguish between the three main types of computer systems.
- [ ] 4. Briefly explain how a computer executes a program.
- [ ] 5. Distinguish between application software and system software, and give an example of each.
- [ ] 6. Describe the way business data is commonly organized in secondary storage in information systems.
- [ ] 7. Identify the personnel in information systems and explain their functions.
- [ ] 8. Describe the types of procedures used in information systems.

Information systems are one type of system. Others include computer systems, educational systems, and transportation systems. In general, a *system* is a collection of parts or *components* that work together for a purpose. For example, an automobile is a system. Its components are an engine, a body, a drive train, and so forth. These components work together for the purpose of providing transportation. As explained in Chapter 1, an *information system* is a collection of components that work together for the purpose of providing information to help in the operation and management of an organization.

The components of an information system are the topic of this chapter. Since these components include information technology, this chapter introduces basic hardware and software technology. Information system components also include data stored in the system, and this chapter examines how stored data is organized. Finally, the components of an information system include human resources, so this chapter explains how people and procedures are involved in information systems.

Components of an Information System

There are five main components of an information system:

- Hardware
- Software
- Stored data
- Personnel
- Procedures

These components are summarized in Fig. 3.1. Hardware and software are the *information technology* in the system, and personnel and procedures are the *human resources*. The stored data ties together the information technology and the human resources.

Hardware

The first component of an information system is hardware, which consists of the computers and related equipment used in a system. Any type of computer, from small to large, can be used in an information system. Many information systems include several types of computers and more than one of each type, often connected together to form a network. For example, a large system may consist of hundreds of interconnected computers. Information systems also include other hardware besides computers. For example, special hardware is needed for communications between computers in a network.

Chapter 1 gave an example of an inventory control information system for an athletic shoe store. This system needs hardware to function. Some hardware accepts input data about stock added to and removed from inventory. Other hardware stores the data about the quantity on hand for each item. Additional hardware calculates values for the new quantities on hand and identifies which items have low or high inventory. Still more hardware produces information in a form understandable to humans. Finally, other hardware provides communication between different parts of the system.

Software

Software is another component of an information system. Software consists of instructions that tell hardware what to do. Computers and computer-controlled hardware cannot function without software; they *must* have instructions to tell them what to do. Many types of software are needed in information systems. Some software

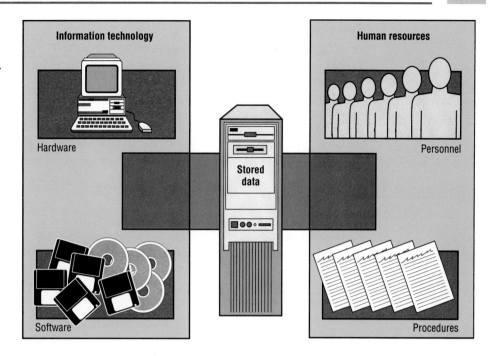

FIGURE 3.1

The components of an information system

tells computers to solve specific business problems, such as computing payroll. Other software manages the computer system to make it usable. Still other software controls communications between computers.

For the athletic shoe store's inventory control system, software is needed for several functions. Some software instructs a computer to accept input data about items that have been added to and removed from stock. Other software tells a computer to make changes in the stored data about the quantity on hand so that this data is up to date. Still other software tells a computer how to produce output with information about which items are low in stock and which are high. Finally, additional software provides instructions to control communication between computers in the system.

Stored Data

The third component of an information system is the data that is retained in the hardware and processed by the software. The stored data component of an information system consists of all the data that is kept in computers in the system and that is used by the software of the system.

In the athletic shoe store's inventory control system, the stored data component includes data about each item that the business stocks. Each item is identified by an item number. This data is stored along with the description of each item, how much each item costs the business to purchase or manufacture, how much the business sells each item for, and the quantity that the business has of each item on hand.

The stored data component of an information system only includes data that is stored in the system, not input and output data. Input data is entered into the system and output data, or information, comes out of the system. In a sense, the input and output flow through the system, but they are not part of the system because they do not contribute to the purpose of the system. Thus, input and output data, while critical for the use of an information system, are not components of the system.

Personnel

An information system does not operate by itself; people are needed to make it run. People have to supply input data to the system, receive the output information from the system, operate the hardware in the system, and run the software that is part of the system. These people, or personnel, are the fourth essential component of an information system.

The inventory control system includes personnel. Some of the personnel are users of the system. These include salespeople, clerical personnel, and the store's manager. Other personnel operate the hardware and software in the system.

Procedures

The final component of an information system is procedures, which are instructions that tell people how to use and operate the system. Just as hardware cannot function without software, people do not know what to do unless they have procedures to follow. The procedures tell the people how to use and operate the system.

The athletic shoe store's inventory control system needs procedures for the personnel to follow. Some procedures describe how to enter input data and what output information to expect from the system. Other procedures describe how to operate the hardware and software.

Hardware for Information Systems

The hardware component of an information system can consist of a number of devices, but central to all of them is the computer. Computers perform the input, storage, processing, and output functions of an information system. But exactly what is a computer? Many devices perform similar functions but we do not call them computers. For example, an abacus, an adding machine, and a pocket calculator all perform computation of some sort, and they could be used in information systems. When we use the word "computer," however, we do not mean one of these devices but, rather, a device that has certain distinguishing characteristics. A computer is a device that (1) is electronic, (2) can store data, and (3) can store and follow a set of instructions, called a program, that tells the computer what to do.

The actual composition of a computer is more complex than this definition implies. A computer consists of several interconnected devices or components as shown in Fig. 3.2. In this diagram, symbols represent the components of the computer, and arrows show the paths taken within the computer by data and program instructions. There are five basic components: the input device, the output device, primary storage, the central processing unit or CPU, and secondary storage.

Input and Output Devices

An input device accepts data from outside the computer and converts it into an electronic form that the computer can understand. The data that is accepted is the input data. For example, if a computer is going to compute the pay for each employee in a business, the input data would include the employees' names, pay rates, and hours worked. An input device would accept this data from the user and transfer it into the computer.

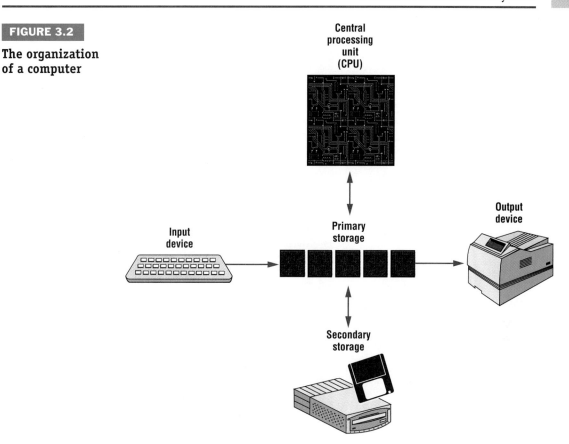

FIGURE 3.2

The organization
of a computer

A common input device is a keyboard (Fig. 3.3a). The user enters input data at the keyboard and the electronic form of the data is sent into the computer. Another common input device is a mouse (Fig. 3.3b). When the user rolls the mouse and presses buttons on the top of the mouse, input is entered into the computer.

An output device performs the opposite function of an input device. It converts data from an electronic form inside the computer to a form that can be used outside the computer. This converted data is the output data or information. For example, the output from a payroll computation would include paychecks with the employees' names and pay. An output device would produce this data in a form understandable to the user.

One common output device is a screen on which the output is displayed as video images (Fig. 3.3c). Another common output device is a printer (Fig. 3.3d), which produces the output as printed symbols on paper.

An input device may be combined with an output device to form a device called a terminal. Typically, a terminal consists of a keyboard and a screen. (See Fig. 3.4.) Terminals are sometimes used as input and output devices with large computers.

Most computers have several input and output, or *I/O*, devices attached at one time. For example, a large computer may have many terminals plus several printers. Many personal computers, however, have only two input devices (a keyboard and a mouse) and two output devices (a screen and a printer).

(a) Keyboard

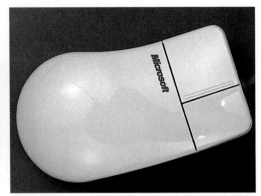

(b) Mouse

(c) Screen

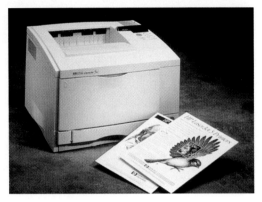

(d) Printer

FIGURE 3.3

Input and output devices

FIGURE 3.4

A terminal

Primary Storage and the Central Processing Unit

Between the input and output devices are two components of the computer that work together to do the computing or processing. These are the primary storage and central processing unit. (See Fig. 3.5.)

The primary storage, also called internal storage, is the "memory" of the computer. An input device converts input data into an electronic form and sends the data to the primary storage, where the data is stored. The data is then used in calculations and for other types of processing. For example, data used in payroll computations, such as employees' pay rates and hours worked, would be stored in the primary storage and used to calculate each employee's pay. After the processing is completed, the results are sent from primary storage to an output device, where the data is converted into the final output. The primary storage also stores instructions in the program currently being performed. For example, in a payroll computation, the instructions necessary to calculate an employee's pay would be stored in the computer's primary storage.

The central processing unit or CPU, which is also called the processor, carries out the instructions in the program.[1] Among other things, the CPU contains electronic circuits that perform arithmetic and logical operations. Data is brought from primary storage to the CPU, where it is processed by these circuits, and the results of processing are sent back to primary storage. The CPU can do the basic arithmetic tasks that a human can do; that is, it can add, subtract, multiply, and divide. The logical operations that a CPU can do usually are limited to comparing two values to determine whether they are equal or whether one is greater than or less than the other. Complex processing is accomplished by long sequences of these basic operations. In a payroll computation, fairly simple arithmetic and logical operations are needed. For example, an employee's pay is computed by multiplying the hours

FIGURE 3.5

Primary storage and the central processing unit

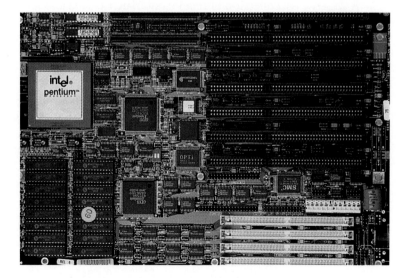

[1] Some people consider primary storage to be part of the central processing unit rather than a separate component. Other people use the terms as they appear in the text.

worked by the pay rate. Logical operations are needed to determine how much income tax should be paid by each employee.

The CPU also contains electronic circuits that control the other parts of the computer. These circuits perform their functions by following the instructions in the program, which is stored in the computer's primary storage. During processing, each instruction in the program is brought one at a time from primary storage to the CPU. The CPU analyzes the instruction and sends signals to the other parts of the computer based on what the instruction tells the computer to do. Performing one instruction may involve actions in any of the other parts of the computer. After one instruction in the programmed sequence is performed, the next is brought from primary storage to the CPU and performed. These steps are repeated until all the instructions in the program have been carried out.

Secondary Storage

The final component of a computer is secondary storage, also called auxiliary storage, which stores data not currently being processed by the computer and programs not currently being performed. Its function differs from that of primary storage, which stores the data and instructions that are currently being processed by the computer. For example, if the computer is currently doing payroll processing, then the employee data and the payroll computation program would be stored in the computer's primary storage. Other data and programs that are not currently being used, such as would be needed for sales analysis, would be stored in secondary storage and brought into primary storage when needed. Primary storage is *temporary storage*, and anything stored in it is lost when the power to the computer is turned off. Secondary storage, however, is *permanent storage*; anything stored in secondary storage remains there until it is changed even if the power is turned off.

Data and programs are stored in secondary storage as files. A file is a collection of related items stored together in secondary storage. There are several types of files. A data file is a collection of related data, such as data about employees in a business. A program file is a collection of instructions that make up a program. Other types of files include *text files*, used in word processing, and *worksheet files*, used in spreadsheet applications. All types of files, however, are stored in secondary storage until they are needed. Then program instructions or data from the required files are transferred to primary storage for processing.

A common type of secondary storage is a magnetic disk, often just called a disk, which is a round platter found in various sizes (Fig. 3.6a). Disks are made of different materials: floppy disks are made of flexible plastic with a metallic coating, and hard disks are made of rigid metal. No matter what type of disk is used, data is recorded on the surface of the disk by patterns of magnetism. A magnetic disk drive, usually just called a disk drive, is a device that records data on magnetic disks and retrieves data from the disks.

Another type of secondary storage is optical disk, which is similar to compact discs (CDs) used for music (Fig. 3.6b). Optical disk is often called *CD-ROM*, which stands for compact disk, read only memory. Data is recorded on the surface of an optical disk using a laser. An optical disk drive is a device that retrieves data from an optical disk.

A third type of secondary storage is magnetic tape, or simply tape, which is much like audio recording tape (Fig. 3.6c). Magnetic tape comes in reels of differ-

FIGURE 3.6

Secondary storage

(a) Magnetic disk and a magnetic disk drive

(b) Optical disk and an optical disk drive

(c) Magnetic tape and a magnetic tape drive

ent sizes and in cartridge form. Data is recorded on the surface of the tape by patterns of magnetism. A <u>magnetic tape drive</u>, or simply <u>tape drive</u>, is a device that records data on magnetic tape and retrieves data from the tape.

Most computers have several secondary storage devices attached to them at one time. For example, a personal computer may have two magnetic disk drives and an optical disk drive; a large computer may have four magnetic disk drives and two magnetic tape drives. Other types of secondary storage also can be used, but magnetic disk, optical disk, and magnetic tape are the most common.

Secondary storage and input and output devices are often called <u>peripheral equipment</u> because they are located outside the central part of the computer, that is, the CPU and primary storage. In fact, the word "computer" is sometimes used just for the CPU and primary storage, and "computer system" is used for the computer with its peripheral equipment.

Communications Hardware

Computers and computer components need ways of communicating with each other. Computer devices are usually connected by electronic cables when they are located near each other. Often, however, computer hardware needs to be connected over some distance. For example, a user at a terminal at one location may need to communicate with a computer at another location. Such distant communication requires <u>communications hardware</u>, which is part of the hardware component of information systems.

If the distance between computer devices is not too great, such as within an office building, it may be possible to connect the devices directly with a long cable. When the distance is beyond a certain limit (such as 1,000 feet), direct connection is not possible. A common method of long-distance communication involves the use of telephone lines. To connect computers to a telephone line, a communications hardware device called a <u>modem</u> is used. (See Fig. 3.7.) Computers connected in this way communicate by sending signals back and forth over the telephone line.

Usually, it is desirable for a number of computers to be connected with each other. As noted in Chapter 1, a configuration of computers connected electronically so they all can communicate with each other is called a *network*. If the network is located in a single building or a group of nearby buildings, it is called a <u>local area network</u> or <u>LAN</u>. A LAN uses a cable to connect all the computers in the LAN, and each computer needs communications hardware to connect to the LAN cable. If the network is spread over a large geographic area, such as a region or a country, it is called a <u>wide area network</u> or <u>WAN</u>. Telephone lines or other methods are used to connect the computers in the WAN. Each computer requires a modem or other communications hardware. The Internet is a worldwide collection of interconnected wide area and local area networks. Communications hardware found in all types of networks is used in the Internet.

In general, any device in a network can communicate with any other device in the same network. One computer can send data to another computer. Several computers can retrieve data from the same disk drive, or print output with the same printer. A terminal can use any computer connected to the network.

Computer Systems

All computers have the basic hardware components shown earlier in Fig. 3.2. Still, computers vary considerably in many ways including storage capacity, speed, and cost. In addition, computers often are linked in networks. All the variations produce three main configurations of computer systems: personal computer systems, multiple-user computer systems, and networked computer systems.

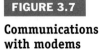

FIGURE 3.7

Communications with modems

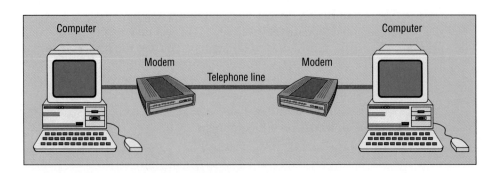

Personal Computer Systems.   A *personal computer system* consists of a single computer used by one person at a time. Most personal computer systems are <u>microcomputers</u>, which are small computers costing a few thousand dollars. They typically have a keyboard and a mouse for input; a screen and a printer for output; and several magnetic disk drives, an optical disk drive, and possibly a magnetic tape drive for secondary storage. (See Fig. 3.8.) Because most microcomputers can only be used by one person at a time, they are *personal* computer systems. In fact, the term <u>personal computer</u> or <u>PC</u> is often used to mean a microcomputer. Individual information systems in all types of organizations and businesses use microcomputers.

The most widely recognized microcomputers follow designs introduced by International Business Machines (IBM) Corporation and Apple Computer, Inc. IBM's first microcomputer was the IBM Personal Computer or PC, and often the term PC is used to refer to any IBM-like microcomputer. IBM microcomputers evolved over time and currently IBM produces several models. Apple's original microcomputer was the Apple II, which is no longer manufactured. Apple currently produces the Macintosh, or "Mac," microcomputer, which comes in several models.

Most microcomputers in use are produced by companies that make computers which act just like IBM personal computers; people call these computers IBM *clones*. Some companies that make IBM clones are Compaq Computer Corporation, Packard Bell, and Dell Computer Corporation, but there are many more such companies. Although Apple sells the majority of Macintosh-type computers, several companies produce Macintosh clones, including Motorola and Power Computing.

Microcomputers that are designed to sit on a desk and not be moved are called <u>desktop computers</u>. Small microcomputers that fold up to the size of a notebook so

(a) IBM personal computer

(b) Apple Macintosh

FIGURE 3.8

Microcomputers

Bookmark

Wearable Computers from Carnegie Mellon University

Aircraft maintenance workers participating in a pilot test at The Boeing Co. were able to throw away the clipboards and pencils that were once necessities when they inspected military tanker planes for defects.

Using prototype "wearable computers" developed by the Engineering Design Research Center at Carnegie Mellon University in Pittsburgh, the workers crawl over the wings and cockpit wearing 4-pound computers that fit into the small of their backs. On their foreheads, they wear transparent monitors that give them a full field of vision but let them call up three-dimensional diagrams of the cockpit or other airplane mechanics, request step-by-step instructions on any procedure, and enter data into a remote database—all with voice commands.

Repair requests are immediately broadcast via radio waves to a Boeing logistics computer server, which then automatically orders the appropriate parts and even schedules the date and time for the repairs.

"It's the next paradigm shift—detaching people completely from the physical constraints of computing," said Dan Siewiorek, director of the Engineering Design Research Center, which created successive generations of the "Vu-man" series of wearable computers, of which the Boeing computer is the latest example. Siewiorek said he sees these types of devices becoming prevalent by the year 2000.

Because workers' hands need to be free, the system uses either voice recognition or a large rotary dial to enable them to move through on-screen lists, enter data, or request additional information. The dial is similar to the old rotary phones.

Devices such as Vu-man 3 will not necessarily be relegated to maintenance, inventory, and similar applications. "Look at the spreadsheet. When it was first introduced, no one had any idea of the size of the market," Siewiorek said. "People thought it would be a specialized tool for accountants and financial analysts."

QUESTIONS
1. What input and output devices are used in the wearable computer developed at Carnegie Mellon University?
2. What are the characteristics of applications that might be good candidates for wearable computers?

WEB SITE
Carnegie Mellon University: www.cmu.edu
Engineering Design Research Center: www.edrc.cmu.edu

Source: Alice LaPlante, "The Ultimate in Portability," *Computerworld Client/Server Journal*, August 1995, p. 36.

they can be easily carried are called <u>notebook computers</u>. (See Fig. 3.9.) Still smaller microcomputers that are designed to be held in a hand are sometimes called <u>personal digital assistants</u> or <u>PDAs</u> because they provide capabilities to assist an individual in his or her work. (See Fig. 3.10.) Very powerful desktop microcomputers are commonly called <u>workstations</u>. Workstations have capabilities beyond those of ordinary micro-

FIGURE 3.9

A notebook computer

FIGURE 3.10

A personal digital assistant

computers, especially in their ability to produce graphic diagrams and pictures on the screen. Examples are computers made by Sun Microsystems, Inc. (See Fig. 3.11.)

Multiple-user Computer Systems.   A *multiple-user computer system* consists of a single computer used by many people at one time. Most microcomputers are not designed to be used by more than one person at a time, so they are not typically used as multiple-user computer systems. Instead, minicomputers, mainframe computers, and supercomputers are used for this purpose. (See Fig. 3.12.)

FIGURE 3.11

A workstation

FIGURE 3.12

Multiple-user computers

(a) Minicomputer

(b) Mainframe computer

(c) Supercomputer

A <u>minicomputer</u> is a medium-size computer, typically costing between $7,500 and $200,000. Minicomputers usually have several terminals for input and output; a printer for output; and one or more magnetic disk drives and sometimes a magnetic tape drive for secondary storage. Because minicomputers can be used by several people simultaneously, they are multiple-user computer systems. Small- to medium-size organizations and businesses sometimes use minicomputers for organizational information systems. Larger businesses may use them for special applications, such as for controlling computerized checkout stands in a supermarket, or for workgroup information systems.

A number of companies, including Digital Equipment Corporation (DEC), Hewlett-Packard Company (HP), and IBM, make minicomputers. These companies make many models of minicomputers that range in size from small systems that are close to being microcomputers to large computers that are almost mainframe computers. Because it is often hard to identify whether a computer is a minicomputer, this type of computer is sometimes called a *mid-range computer.*

A <u>mainframe computer</u> is a large computer usually costing between $100,000 and $10 million. Usually, a mainframe computer has many terminals, several printers, and several magnetic disk and magnetic tape drives. A mainframe computer can be used by many people at one time. Mainframe computers are often used by medium- and large-size organizations and businesses for their organizational information systems. For example, the computer used by a bank to process data from automated teller machines may be a mainframe computer.

IBM makes the most widely known mainframe computers. Some companies make mainframe computers that are similar to IBM's. One such company is Amdahl Corporation. Other companies make mainframe computers different from IBM's, including Unisys Corporation.

The most powerful multiple-user computers are called <u>supercomputers</u> and can cost between $5 million and $20 million. These computers are specifically designed for very fast processing speeds. They may not have as many terminals or as much secondary storage as mainframe computers, but their CPUs can operate much faster. Because they are so fast, supercomputers are mainly used for complex mathematical calculations, such as those needed in scientific research.

Cray Research, Inc., developed the first supercomputers that were commercially successful. Only a few other companies make supercomputers.

Networked Computer Systems.   A *networked computer system* consists of many computers connected in a network used by many users. The network may be a local area network, a wide area network, or a combination of these. Microcomputers, minicomputers, mainframe computers, and supercomputers may all be used in the network. The trend, however, is toward more microcomputers and fewer larger computers.

All sizes of organizations and businesses use networked computer systems for workgroup and organizational information systems. Many businesses are replacing minicomputers and mainframe computers with local and wide area networks. Interorganizational information systems also use wide area networks, as do international information systems.

Networks usually include one or more computers, called <u>servers</u>, that provide services to other computers in the network. (See Fig. 3.13.) For example, a server can

FIGURE 3.13

A server

be used to store data on a large disk drive so that the data is available to all computers in the network. A server can also have a printer attached to it which can be used by any computer in the network to print output. In the Internet, servers are used to store information for all users of the Internet.

Many information systems are designed so that some parts of the system use a server and other parts use personal computers attached to the network. These personal computers, with which users interact directly, are called clients. For example, a server may store a database with data of use to all users. The client computers allow users to retrieve data from the database and display the data on the screen. This approach is called client-server computing, and it is becoming increasingly common in businesses.

Software for Information Systems

The software component of an information system consists of all the computer programs used in the system. A computer can do nothing without a program. For example, to calculate the payroll for a business, the computer must have a program that tells it how to do the calculations. Even to do word processing, a computer needs a program to tell it what to do. Every step that the computer goes through must be given in an instruction in a computer program. The computer will do whatever it is told, even if this leads to an incorrect result.

Program Concepts

To illustrate the idea of a computer program, assume that it is necessary to find the sum of two numbers using a computer. To solve this problem, the computer must go through a sequence of steps. First, the computer must use an input device such as a keyboard to get the two numbers from the user. Then, the computer must add the numbers to find their sum. Finally, it must send the sum to an output device such as a screen so that the user can see the result. Thus, to solve this problem, a computer program would contain three instructions:

1. Get two numbers from the input device.
2. Add the numbers to find the sum.
3. Send the sum to the output device.

To perform or *execute* a computer program, the instructions in the program must be in the computer's primary storage. Before execution, the program is usually stored in secondary storage, for example, on magnetic disk. Thus, to execute the program, it must first be transferred from secondary storage to primary storage, a process called *loading* the program. (See Fig. 3.14.)

Once the program is in primary storage, the computer executes it by going through the instructions in sequence. The computer brings each instruction, one at a time, to the CPU, which analyzes the instruction and sends signals to the other parts of the computer to execute it. For example, execution of the instructions in the example program to find the sum of two numbers would proceed as follows (Fig. 3.15):

1. Get two numbers. The CPU sends a signal to the input device that causes two numbers (input data) to be transferred to primary storage.

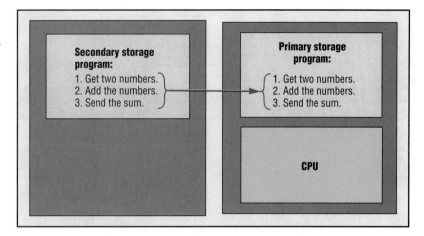

FIGURE 3.14

Loading a program into primary storage

2. Add the numbers. The CPU sends a signal to primary storage that causes the two numbers to be sent to the arithmetic circuit in the CPU. Then the CPU adds the numbers and sends the sum to primary storage.

3. Send the sum. The CPU sends a signal to primary storage to transfer the sum to the output device. Then the output device displays the sum (output data).

This example illustrates two important points. First, primary storage stores both program instructions and data. Instructions in the program are stored in primary storage before the program begins execution. Data is brought into primary storage as the program is executed.

Second, the instructions in the program are executed in the sequence in which they are stored (unless an instruction is included to change the sequence). The sequence must be in a certain order so that, when executed, the problem is correctly solved. For example, if the first two instructions in the previous example were switched, the program would not solve the problem. If the instructions are out of order, the computer cannot figure out what the right sequence should be. The computer would simply follow the instructions in the order in which they are given and produce an incorrect result.

Types of Software

There are two main types of software or programs: application software and system software. Application software or application programs are programs designed for specific computer applications for a business or organization. For example, a program that prepares the payroll for a business is application software. Similarly, a program that analyzes sales and one that keeps track of inventory are examples of application programs. Programs used for word processing and spreadsheet analysis are also application programs. Application software is used in all types of information systems including individual, workgroup, organizational, interorganizational, and international information systems.

System software or system programs are general programs designed to make computers usable. System software does not solve a problem for a specific application, but rather makes it easier to use the necessary application program. System software

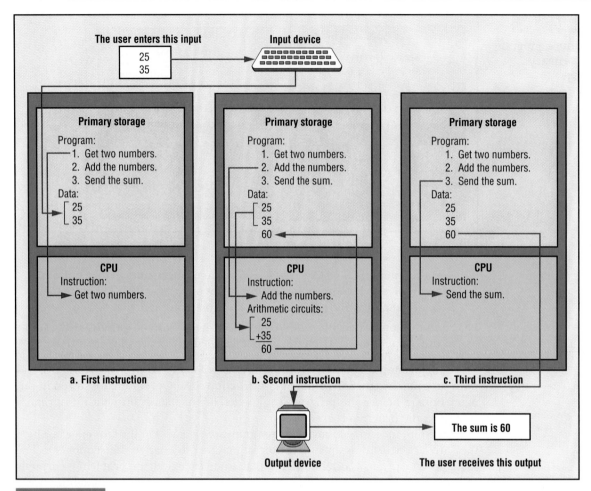

FIGURE 3.15

Executing a program

helps the computer function, whereas application software helps the business or organization function.

An example of system software is an <u>operating system</u>, which is a set of programs that controls the basic operation of the computer. The operating system does many things, such as determining where an application program is stored in the computer's primary storage. The operating system is always in control of the computer when some other program (such as an application program or another system program) is not executing. Examples of operating systems are Windows 95 and MacOS.

Another example of system software is <u>communications software</u>, which is used to provide communications between computers. When a computer is connected to a telephone line using a modem, communications software is needed to control the communications over the line. Similarly, when computers are connected in a local area or wide area network, communications software is necessary.

Sources of Software

If you need software for a particular purpose, you have two main ways of getting it. One is to purchase existing software. You can purchase application software and system software. Purchased programs, which are often called packaged software, are available for personal computer systems, multiple-user computer systems, and networked computer systems.

The other way you can get software is to prepare a new program from scratch. Programs acquired in this way are often called custom software. You can prepare custom software yourself or have someone else do it for you. Custom software can be prepared for all types of computer systems.

Bookmark

Linking Railroads at the Association of American Railroads

Railroads have historically faced a major competitive hurdle: Mergers and acquisitions have left just six major railroads and approximately 500 smaller ones that could have as little as 50 miles of track.

These firms are highly interdependent because most shipments cross multiple territories, requiring two or more rail firms to handle a shipment and claim their share of the revenue from it—a logistic nightmare.

Now, the Association of American Railroads (AAR) in Washington is creating a massive network linking the mainframes of all the major railroads. By distributing information, the AAR hopes to compete better with other transportation industries and settle its internal accounts more effectively.

The AAR is developing three applications, to the tune of $15 million, said Randy Randazzo, the AAR's vice-president of technology services.

An IBM mainframe will act as the host for all three, delivering information via a network to mainframes or PCs at more than 400 railroads in the United States, Canada, and Mexico.

The first application, called the Interline Service Management system, was designed to improve service and shipment reliability across the multiple railroads, according to Randazzo.

The AAR will act as a hub for some 4 million daily electronic-mail messages the major railroads exchange about interline shipments.

The second application, called the Interline Service Settlement system, was designed to help distribute revenue among railroads that cooperate on a single shipment.

With the AAR's mainframe acting as a server in the network to the 12 major railroads' networks, operational and billing information can be shared among the railroads while a shipment is in transit.

Today the railroads rely on paper and electronic data interchange to divvy up customer payments, but the process is extremely inefficient and error-prone. It can take months to settle an account and even longer if disputes occur.

To implement the third major application, the Customer Information File, the AAR is developing a database of 300,000 railroad customers using Dun & Bradstreet Corp.'s abbreviations for corporations as a standard.

Currently, each railroad has a different way to describe the same customer, which makes interline communication extremely confusing.

By standardizing critical processes and creating a national information network, the AAR hopes to increase traffic on the industry's coast-to-coast rail network.

QUESTIONS

1. What types of computers are used in the information systems at AAR?
2. What stored data is used in the Customer Information File system?

WEB SITE
Association of American Railroads: www.aar.org

Source: Candee Wilde, "Working on the Railroad," Computerworld Client/Server Journal, February 1996, p. 40.

System software almost always is purchased, but application software may be purchased or prepared from scratch. Packaged software usually is used for individual and workgroup information systems. For example, for a word processing system on a personal computer you would purchase word processing software. You can also prepare custom software for individual and workgroup information systems, although this is done less often than using packaged software. For organizational, interorganizational, and international information systems, both packaged and custom software are used.

Stored Data for Information Systems

The stored data component of an information system consists of all data used by the system that is stored in secondary storage. Stored data can represent facts, numbers, words, images, pictures, or sounds. In business information systems, stored data most often represents numbers, words, or other written forms. In order for this type of data to be processed easily, it must be properly organized in secondary storage.

Figure 3.16 shows the common way data is organized in information systems. At the most basic level, business data in information systems is composed of characters—that is, letters, digits, and special symbols. A blank space is also a character and is often important in computer data processing.

Although a single character can represent data, groups of characters are used more often. A group of related characters, representing some piece of information, is called a field. For example, a person's name is a field; it is a group of characters that conveys specific information. A social security number is also a field, as are a person's address, pay rate, and age. A field usually contains several characters but can consist of a single character. For example, a one-character code field can be used to represent a person's marital status (*M* stands for *married*, *S* for *single*).

Fields are grouped together to provide information about a single entity such as a person or an event. Such a group of related fields is called a record. For example, all the fields containing payroll information about a single employee (such as the employee's name, address, social security number, and pay rate) form an employee payroll record.

All the records that are used together for one purpose are called a data file, or simply a file.[2] For example, all the employee payroll records for a business make up the employee payroll file. The file contains one record for each employee in the business.

Finally, related groups of data, such as related data files, can be combined to form a database. For example, an employee database may contain employee payroll data, employee job skill data, and employee work history data. All these data are related because they contain information about employees who work for the same business, and therefore they form a database of employee information.

To summarize, data often is composed of characters. A group of related characters is a field. A record is a group of related fields, and a data file is a group of related records. Finally, related groups of data form a database.

Although we have concentrated on data made up of characters, data can also be in other forms such as images, moving pictures, and sound. This type of data often

---

[2] As noted earlier, the term *file* is used to refer to any collection of related items stored in secondary storage. The term *data file* is used for a collection of related data organized into records. Many people, however, commonly use the term *file* when they mean *data file*.

FIGURE 3.16

Data organization for information systems

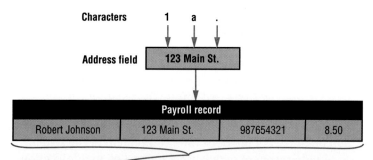

| Characters | 1 | a | . |

Address field   123 Main St.

Payroll record			
Robert Johnson	123 Main St.	987654321	8.50

Payroll file			
Robert Johnson	123 Main St.	987654321	8.50
Mary Jones	876 South St.	135792468	11.00
Susan Andrews	55 First Ave.	564738291	7.25
James Miller	4567 Bay St.	293847560	10.75

Employee database

Payroll data			
Robert Johnson	123 Main St.	987654321	8.50
Mary Jones	876 South St.	135792468	11.00
Susan Andrews	55 First Ave.	564738291	7.25
James Miller	4567 Bay St.	293847560	10.75

Job skill data	
Robert Johnson	Carpenter
Mary Jones	Programmer
Susan Andrews	Driver
James Miller	Operator

Work history data		
Robert Johnson	1 / 23 / XX	Los Angeles
Mary Jones	5 / 19 / XX	Boston
Susan Andrews	11 / 26 / XX	San Francisco
James Miller	8 / 5 / XX	Houston

is referred to as multimedia data because it is in more than one form. For example, a business may store multimedia data consisting of images, pictures, and sounds, along with words and numbers, to describe a new product it has developed. Organizing stored multimedia data requires more complex techniques than those described here.

Personnel for Information Systems

The personnel component of an information system consists of all people who are involved with the system. One such person is the *user*. As you know, users are people who gain some benefit from using the information system. Users supply input data to the system and receive output data from the system. The output provides information that the user needs in his or her job. As discussed in Chapter 1, the user may use the system directly or indirectly. In any case, the user is not separate from the system but is part of the personnel component of the system.

Other types of people who are part of an information system are *operating personnel* who perform technical functions to operate the hardware and execute the software in the system. These people prepare input data received from the user, enter the data into the system, operate computers, run networks, execute programs, and pass the output to the user. If the system is an individual or workgroup information system, the user may operate the computer; but with organizational information systems, specially trained computer operators are needed.

Procedures for Information Systems

The final component of an information system consists of all the procedures that personnel follow to use and operate the system. The procedures are the instructions to the personnel just as the software is the instructions to the hardware.

Included in the procedures are those that tell people how to use and operate the system under normal circumstances. These include procedures for executing programs, entering input data, receiving output, and so on. An example of this type of procedure is one that tells users what to select on a screen with a mouse to begin execution of a program.

Also included in the procedures are those that tell people what to do if the system does not function normally. These include procedures for correcting errors and recovering lost data. An example of this type of procedure is a backup recovery procedure that tells the user how to retrieve stored data from a backup copy of the data.

Procedures need to be written so that personnel can refer to them. This is the purpose of system documentation, which is written instructions on the use and operation of an information system. Personnel must be trained in the procedures so they will know what to do. Thus, when we say personnel is a component of the system, we mean personnel who are trained in the use of the procedures.

Chapter Summary

☐ The components of an information system are **hardware**, which are the computers and other equipment used in the system; **software**, which are the programs in the system; **stored data**, which is the data stored in the system and used by the software; **personnel**, which are the people who use and operate the system; and **procedures**, which are the instructions that tell the people what to do. Hardware and software are the information technology in the system, and personnel and procedures are the human resources. The stored data ties these together. (pp. 60–62)

☐ The main components of a computer are the **input device**, the **output device**, **primary storage**, the **central processing unit** (**CPU**), and **secondary storage**. An input device accepts data from outside the computer and converts it to an electronic form understandable to the computer. A **keyboard** and a **mouse** are examples of input devices. An output device converts data from an electronic form inside the computer to a form that can be used outside the computer. A **screen** and a **printer** are examples of output devices. Primary storage stores data and program instructions currently being processed. The central processing unit carries out instructions in the program. Secondary storage stores data and programs not currently being processed. **Magnetic disk**, **optical disk**, and **magnetic tape** are types of secondary storage. **Communications hardware** is needed to provide communications between computer hardware. An example of communications hardware is a **modem**. (pp. 62–68)

☐ The three main types of computer systems are *personal computer systems*, *multiple-user computer systems*, and *networked computer systems*. A personal computer system consists of a single computer, usually a **microcomputer**, used by one person at a time. A multiple-user computer system consists of a single computer, usually a **minicomputer, mainframe computer,** or **supercomputer**, used by many people at a time. Networked computer systems consist of many computers of any type connected in a network and used by many users. Networks usually include computers, called **servers,** to provide service to other computers, called **clients**, in the network. This approach is called **client-server computing**. (pp. 68–74)

☐ To execute a program, the instructions in the program first must be transferred from secondary storage to primary storage. Then the computer performs the instructions in the sequence in which they are stored. To do so, the computer brings one instruction at a time to the CPU and performs the actions required by that instruction. (pp. 74–75)

☐ **Application software** is any program designed for a specific computer application. An example is a program that prepares payroll for a business. **System software** is any general program designed to make the computer usable. Examples are an **operating system** and **communications software**. (pp. 75–78)

☐ Business data in secondary storage in information systems is composed of **characters**—that is, letters, digits, and special symbols. A group of related characters, representing some piece of information, is called a **field**. A **record** is a group of related fields, and a **data file**, or simply a **file**, is a group of related records. Related groups of data can be combined to form a **database**. (pp. 78–79)

☐ Personnel in an information system include users and operating personnel. Users supply input data to the system and receive output data or information from the system. Operating personnel operate hardware and run software in the system. They prepare input data received from the user, enter the data into the system, operate computers, execute programs, and pass output to users. (p. 80)

☐ Procedures in an information system tell people how to use and operate the system under normal circumstances. These include procedures for executing programs, entering input data, and receiving output. Procedures also tell people what to do if the system does not function normally. These include procedures for correcting errors and recovering lost data. (p. 80)

Key Terms

Application Software (p. 75)
Central Processing Unit (CPU) (p. 65)
Character (p. 78)
Client (p. 74)
Client-server Computing (p. 74)
Communications Hardware (p. 68)
Communications Software (p. 76)
Computer (p. 62)
Custom Software (p. 77)
Database (p. 78)
Data File (p. 66, 78)
Desktop Computer (p. 69)
Disk Drive (p. 66)
Documentation (p. 80)
Field (p. 78)
File (p. 66, 78)
Floppy Disk (p. 66)
Hard Disk (p. 66)
Hardware (p. 60)

Input Device (p. 62)
Keyboard (p. 63)
Local Area Network (LAN) (p. 68)
Magnetic Disk (p. 66)
Magnetic Tape (p. 66)
Mainframe Computer (p. 72)
Microcomputer (p. 69)
Minicomputer (p. 72)
Modem (p. 68)
Mouse (p. 63)
Multimedia (p. 79)
Notebook Computer (p. 70)
Operating System (p. 76)
Optical Disk (p. 66)
Optical Disk Drive (p. 66)
Output Device (p. 63)
Packaged Software (p. 77)
Peripheral Equipment (p. 67)
Personal Computer (PC) (p. 69)
Personal Digital Assistant (PDA) (p. 70)

Personnel (p. 62)
Primary (Internal) Storage (p. 65)
Printer (p. 63)
Procedures (p. 62)
Processor (p. 65)
Program (p. 62)
Program File (p. 66)
Record (p. 78)
Screen (p. 63)
Secondary (Auxiliary) Storage (p. 66)
Server (p. 73)
Software (p. 60)
Stored Data (p. 61)
Supercomputer (p. 73)
System Software (p. 75)
Tape Drive (p. 67)
Terminal (p. 63)
Wide Area Network (WAN) (p. 68)
Workstation (p. 70)

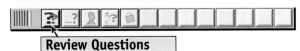

Review Questions

Fill-in Questions

1. Software is instructions for the hardware in an information system; _____ are instructions for the people who use and operate a system.

2. A computer accepts input data with a(n) _____; it produces output with a(n) _____.

3. A device that is a combination of an input and an output device is a(n) _____.

4. The components of a computer that work together to do the actual computing or processing are the _____ and the _____.

5. A collection of related data items stored together in secondary storage is called a(n) _____.

6. Three common forms of secondary storage are _____, _____, and _____.

7. Secondary storage and input and output devices are also called _____ because they are located outside the central part of the computer.

8. A small microcomputer that is designed to be held in a hand is called a(n) _____. A powerful microcomputer with special capabilities for producing graphic diagrams and pictures on the screen is called a(n) _____.

9. Three types of multiple-user computer systems are _____, _____, and _____.

10. A network usually includes a(n) _____ to provide services to other computers in the network.

11. A program must be in _____ storage before it can be executed.

12. A system program that controls the basic operation of the computer is the _____.

13. In terms of stored data organization, a student's grade in a particular course is an example of a(n) _____.

14. Data representing images, moving pictures, and sounds, as well as numbers and words is called _____ data.

Short-answer Questions

1. List the components of an information system.

2. What are the five basic components of a computer?

3. Name two common input devices and two common output devices.

4. What does the central processing unit in a computer do?

5. What is the difference between the functions of primary storage and the functions of secondary storage?

6. What happens to anything stored in primary storage and anything stored in secondary storage when the power to the computer is turned off?

7. Name two types of files stored in secondary storage.

8. What is the purpose of communications hardware?

9. ABC Enterprises has two networks, one that is used in the company headquarters building and one that connects the regional offices with the company headquarters. What types of networks are these?

10. What are the three configurations of computer systems?

11. What happens in the computer during the execution of a program?

12. What is the difference between application software and system software?

13. Explain the differences between fields, records, and data files.

14. Name two types of personnel involved with information systems.

15. What are two general types of procedures needed by personnel in an information system?

16. What is documentation of an information system?

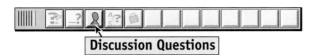

Discussion Questions

1. Think of the course registration system at your college or university. Describe as much as you can of the components of that system.

2. Identify several computational devices that are not computers (e.g., abacus, pocket calculator.) Explain why each is not a computer as defined in the chapter.

3. Why does a computer have two forms of storage, primary storage and secondary storage? Why does it not have just one, large form of storage?

4. A trend in business is to replace multiple-user computer systems with networked computer systems. What reasons can you give for why a business would do this?

5. Computer applications that involve the storage, retrieval, and display of data can use database software. This software, however, will not do any of this without the user first providing special instructions to the software about how the application is to function. Is database software system or application software? Why?

6. Information systems are usually developed by people other than the personnel who use them. What would you do if an information system, developed by someone else, that you use in a business in which you work, requires you to do something that you think is unethical?

Problem-solving Projects

1. Contact a business that will give you information about its information systems. Select one information system for that business and write a brief description of it. Include a summary of the components of that system in your description. Use word processing software to prepare your answer.

2. Visit computer stores and use the Internet to gather information about several personal computers that you might be interested in buying. Develop a spreadsheet in which the columns are the different personal computers and the rows are characteristics of the computers. The characteristics might include, among others, the types of input and output devices, the amount of primary storage (expressed in megabytes), the type of central processing unit, the number and type of secondary storage devices, the software included, and the price.

3. Go to a computer store and look at the software available on the shelves. Write down five different types of software (for example, word processing software) that the store sells. Also write down the name and price of each software package of each type sold. Enter the information into a spreadsheet and use the spreadsheet software to find the mini-

mum, maximum, and average price of each type of software sold by the store. Plot the averages in a graph using the spreadsheet software so you can compare the prices of different types of software.

4. Think of the procedures that you follow when you use an automated teller machine. Write these procedures in a form that would be understandable to someone who has not used the machine. Draw a diagram showing the procedures. Use graphics software to prepare the diagram.

5. Use the Internet to gather historical data on stock prices of a microcomputer manufacturer (e.g., Apple), a minicomputer manufacturer (e.g., DEC), and a mainframe computer manufacturer (e.g., IBM). Since this is a lot of data, just get the closing stock price at the end of each month for the past five years. Enter this data into a spreadsheet and plot, on a single graph, the stock prices of the three companies. Use the spreadsheet to calculate how much your stock would be worth now if you invested $2,500 at the beginning of the five-year period in each of the companies. (Do not consider dividends.) Also use the spreadsheet to calculate the percent increase or decrease in your investment over the five years.

Real-world Case

Beamscope Canada

You can't blame Danny Gurizzan for being a little bit delighted with his company's new computer system, especially when he considers how things used to work. "When I say it was manual, I mean manual," said Gurizzan, director of operational services at Beamscope Canada, Inc., a Scarborough, Ontario, electronics distributor. "When a customer called to place an order, the clerk would scribble it down, run down the hall to the credit check guys, and flip through the files and folders to see if their credit was OK." The clerk would then run to see whether Beamscope actually had the item in stock and then go back to the telephone to confirm the order. "I think we had two PCs in here, and we were doing $93 million [Canadian dollars'] worth of business," he said.

In recent years, though, the company has gone from the *Flintstones* to *Star Trek*, thanks to Gurizzan, Ephram Chaplick (vice-president and general manager), and Jim Jameson (chief operating officer). All three were instrumental in designing Beamscope's new system, which not only takes on order entry but also features a radio frequency bar code system for inventory control, electronic data interchange, and a data warehouse (database) for decision support.

Today, when Beamscope's largest customers call to purchase PCs, printers, software, or the latest Sega Genesis game, they connect over a Datapac line (a toll-free, data-only service), where they can browse 120,000 square feet of shelves holding 8,500 different products in the company's two warehouses. Customers can place orders themselves, check the status of previous orders, and download product literature. If an item is temporarily out of stock, the system will suggest a substitute or put the customer on a list for back orders.

At the heart of the system is Cantoc Business Systems, Inc.'s Censys database, which resides on an IBM AS/400 computer. Beamscope Online, a graphical front end for customers, was jointly developed with Canadian software developer Ironside Technologies.

The database holds data on Beamscope's products, orders, and inventory. By way of a network, it connects to a bank of IBM and Hewlett-Packard Co. servers and warehouses in Toronto and Vancouver, British Columbia.

All incoming shipments are bar coded and scanned. "When a new order comes in," Gurizzan explained, "our runners go out, pick the order, and send it down a conveyor belt and shoot it before and after with the RF gun.

Then the order gets dropped, boxed, and put on the truck." The system is directly tied into United Parcel Service, Inc.'s electronic shipping service.

Under the old system, phone orders were manually routed to the warehouse, where they would sit for at least a week. Plus, it was hard to know what was actually in the warehouse and where it was. Now that orders are placed electronically, they show up at the warehouse every 14 minutes. Warehouse clerks pick up the order ticket, which tells them exactly where the item is, and send the order down to a waiting UPS truck. The RF gun picks up the bar code, which sends an electronic alert to the order processing system and one to UPS with shipping information.

It used to take Beamscope five to seven days to ship an order. "Now we can take an order up to 5 p.m. and it will be delivered to your shop the very next day," Chaplick claims.

Since the system went online, business has soared from $93 million to $300 million (Canadian). "We don't make mistakes with an order anymore, unless it was incorrectly placed to begin with," Gurizzan said.

Customers concur. Beamscope fulfills most of Radio Shack Canada's software inventory, for example, including 450 stores and dealers across Canada. "They're connected to our system right through to the point-of-sale terminals in our stores to replenish our software," said Bob Mayes, vice-president of merchandising at Radio Shack. Thanks to Beamscope, the company carries no software inventory at all in its warehouses. This is very important, Mayes explains, because software titles go out of date quickly.

Products aren't collecting dust at Beamscope's physical warehouse either, thanks to a data warehouse. The warehouse database is an extraction of the Censys database, which is then overlayed with Cognos Corp.'s PowerPlay to enable multidimensional analysis. To make the warehouse manageable, Beamscope pulls out only necessary data, such as information on shipments of individual products or product types, customer buying habits, gross margins, and so forth. Through Microsoft Corp.'s FoxPro and Wall Data, Inc.'s Rumba queries, users can analyze shipments of any product on any given day or can generate charts showing trends by product type.

The success of Beamscope's data warehouse, he said, is its ease of use. "There's a [PC] on our president's desk, and he loves his reports. If the president or CEO of the company is using your product, you're doing something right."

Beamscope's system has become quite a showpiece. From pharmaceutical companies to distributors, reps have been coming in to view the system. Beamscope is working with Ironside Technologies to create an Internet version of the graphical front end.

Questions

1. What is included in the hardware component of the information system described in this case?

2. What is included in the software component?

3. What is included in the stored data component?

4. What procedure is used with the new information system to fill orders in the warehouse?

5. What benefits does Beamscope Canada receive from the information system?

Source: Chris Staiti, "Beamscope Canada, Inc.," *Computerworld Client/Server Journal*, August 1996, pp. 49-50.

II

INFORMATION TECHNOLOGY

4 Information System Hardware

Chapter Outline

The Need for Hardware in Information Systems   (p. 90)
Input and Output Devices   (p. 91)
    Keyboards   (p. 91)
    Pointing Devices   (p. 92)
    Other Input Devices   (p. 92)
    Screens   (p. 95)
    Printers   (p. 97)
    Other Output Devices   (p. 100)
    Terminals   (p. 101)
    Multimedia Input and Output   (p. 101)
    Virtual Reality Input and Output   (p. 102)
Primary Storage   (p. 103)
    Primary Storage Structure   (p. 104)
    Data Representation   (p. 105)
    Primary Storage Organization   (p. 106)
    Primary Storage Capacity   (p. 107)
The Central Processing Unit   (p. 107)
    CPU Structure   (p. 108)
    CPU Compatibility   (p. 108)
    CPU Speed   (p. 109)
    Common CPUs   (p. 109)
Secondary Storage   (p. 112)
    Magnetic Disk Storage   (p. 112)
    Optical Disk Storage   (p. 116)
    Magnetic Tape Storage   (p. 117)

Learning Objectives

After completing this chapter, you should be able to:
☐ 1. Explain why businesses need hardware in information systems.
☐ 2. List common input and output devices.
☐ 3. Explain how data is represented in a computer.
☐ 4. Describe how primary storage is organized.
☐ 5. Describe the structure and functions of the central processing unit.
☐ 6. Explain how data is stored and retrieved using common forms of secondary storage.

T he hardware component of an information system consists of all the equipment used to process, store, and communicate data. For computer information systems, the topic of this book, hardware consists of computers and computer-controlled equipment. Information systems that do not use computers, however, also have "hardware." For example, a manual information system may use a calculator to process data, a file cabinet to store data, and a telephone to communicate data. In a sense, all this equipment is "hardware." It's just not computer hardware. This book, however, focuses on computer-related hardware.

This chapter takes a detailed look at computer hardware used in information systems. This hardware includes hardware for data input and output (input and output devices), data storage (primary and secondary storage), and data processing (the central processing unit). (Refer to Fig. 3.2 in Chapter 3 to review computer hardware organization.) Hardware for data communications is covered later in Chapter 6.

The Need for Hardware in Information Systems

Businesses need hardware in information systems so that the systems can operate quickly and accurately and can handle large amounts of data. *Speed* is important in information systems, and computers provide the speed by processing data and producing information rapidly. Businesses benefit from rapid processing by providing better service at a reduced cost. For example, an automated teller machine system in a bank can process customer withdrawals, deposits, and transfers faster and less expensively than a human teller.

Accuracy also is important in information systems, and computers ensure accuracy by not making mistakes like people do. Without accurate processing, a business's costs would be greater and its information less reliable. For example, a point-of-sale system in a supermarket is more accurate than a human clerk in recording the prices of items purchased by a customer, thus reducing the cost of selling a product at an incorrect price. A point-of-sale system also keeps accurate count of stock and thus provides better information about inventory. You sometimes hear about computer errors, but usually these are the results of mistakes made by humans, not by computers.

Finally, *capacity* is important in information systems, and computers provide the capacity to handle a large amount of data. Businesses benefit from this capability by being able to process volumes of data easily. For example, a sales analysis system in the marketing department of a business can examine data about thousands of sales in order to help a manager draw conclusions about sales trends. A computer can handle such large amounts of data more easily than a human.

All these benefits gained from the use of hardware in information systems allow a business to compete effectively with other businesses. Without the use of computer hardware in information systems, a business would not be able to process data as quickly and accurately, and in the same volume, as its competitors. The business's costs would be greater, its customer service poorer, and the information it needs for decision making less reliable. In the long run, the business may not be able to survive against its competitors who have the appropriate hardware in their information systems.

Sometimes a business can gain an advantage over another business by being the first to use new hardware. For example, the first supermarkets to use point-of-sale hardware gained an advantage over other markets by being able to check out customers quickly and more accurately. The advantage, however, often disappears in a short time as other businesses acquire the hardware. Hardware development proceeds very rapidly, and businesses need to be constantly on the lookout for hardware that will give them a competitive advantage or maintain their competitive position.

Input and Output Devices

The hardware that impacts users of an information system the most is input and output hardware. A user communicates with computers in an information system through input and output devices. The user enters input data into the system through input devices and receives output information through output devices. It is important that a business select the right input and output hardware for its information system so that the hardware will be appropriate for the system and easy for the users to use. This section describes the characteristics of common input and output devices.

Keyboards

The most widely used input device is a keyboard. Keyboards are used for input because most input data consists of letters and numbers. In addition, people are usually familiar with how to use keyboards and with the layout of the keys. Thus, little training is required for users to become familiar with keyboard input.

General-purpose computer keyboards usually have keys in the same basic layout. Many special-purpose keyboards are also used. For example, the keyboard on an ATM machine or on a point-of-sale system usually only consists of the 10 digits and a few special keys such as an Enter key. These keyboards are still input devices, only with limited capabilities.

Extensive use of a keyboard can lead to physical problems called *repetitive strain injuries,* an example of which is a painful condition called *carpal tunnel syndrome.* These problems may occur when the same task is performed over and over again, such as when keying in data repetitively. Taking regular breaks and performing certain exercises may reduce the risk of such injuries.

Special keyboards have been designed to make keying more comfortable. For example, some keyboards are hinged in the middle or curved with keys set at different angles. (See Fig. 4.1.) In general, the study of how to design machines for effective human use is called ergonomics. Ergonomically designed keyboards may improve user comfort and efficiency and reduce the risk of injury. Businesses should consider using these keyboards, although they are more expensive than standard keyboards.

FIGURE 4.1

An ergonomically designed keyboard

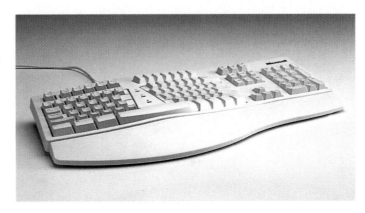

Pointing Devices

After keyboards, the most common input devices are pointing devices such as a mouse. A mouse usually has a ball on the bottom which rolls on a table when the mouse is moved, and one or more buttons on top. Figure 4.2 shows other pointing devices. One is a trackball, which is like an upside-down mouse. A trackball has a ball on the top, which is rolled by a hand or finger, and buttons around the ball. The advantage of a trackball over a mouse is that the user does not need as much table space to use it. Another pointing device is a small stick, sometimes called a *trackpoint*, that protrudes between the letters of the keyboard and that the user moves with a finger. Still another pointer device is a small pad, often called a *touchpad*, over which the user runs a finger. Trackballs, trackpoints, and touchpads are commonly used on notebook computers because they take little space to use.

Pointing devices have two purposes. The first is to move the cursor, which is a mark, arrow, or high-lighted area, on the screen. As the user moves the mouse on a table or rolls the ball on a trackball, the cursor moves to point at different words or symbols on the screen. The second purpose is to select what the computer does next. The user points the cursor at a word or symbol on the screen that indicates what the computer is to do and then presses one of the buttons on the device, a process called "clicking." This action sends a signal to the computer that tells it to perform the task.

A pointing device takes the place of the cursor control (arrow) keys and the function (F1, F2, . . .) keys on a keyboard. The advantage of a pointing device over keys is that using it is like pointing, something that everybody knows how to do. Thus, little training is necessary. Most pointing devices require the user to take a hand off the keyboard, however, which can slow the user down.

Other Input Devices

Keyboards and pointing devices are the input devices most commonly encountered by users. Many other input devices are used, however.

Touch Input Devices.   Several types of devices allow users to enter input by touching something either with a finger or with another device. (See Fig. 4.3.) One common touch input device is a touch screen, which is a screen with the capability of sensing where it is touched by a person's finger. A touch screen is usually used to control the

Trackball

Trackpoint

Touchpad

FIGURE 4.2

Pointing devices

FIGURE 4.3

Touch input devices

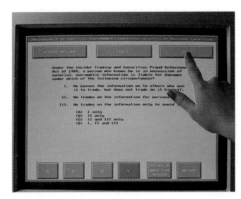

Touch screen

Pen input

functioning of the computer. The screen shows a list of the tasks the computer can do, and the user touches one of the tasks in the list to indicate what is to be done next. One reason businesses use touch screens is they take little or no training to use. Another reason is touch screens work well in places, such as production areas, where there is dirt or contaminants that could cause a keyboard or mouse not to function.

Another touch input device uses a screen that is sensitive to the touch of a special pen, a method called **pen input**. The user can touch points on the screen with the pen to select computer functions. The user can also write on the screen with the pen and the writing becomes input to the computer. With pen input, a keyboard is not necessary for certain types of input data. For example, United Parcel Service uses pen input for entering a customer's signature when deliveries are made.

Other types of touch input devices include a large *touchpad*, which can sense where it is touched by a person's finger; a *light pen*, which is a penlike device that, when touched to the screen, can sense light at its tip; and a *digitizer tablet*, which the user touches with a pen called a stylus. Touch input devices have the advantage of being used by pointing and touching, actions familiar to users. A disadvantage, however, is that the user must take a hand off the keyboard, which can slow down the work.

Optical Scanning Input Devices.   Some input devices recognize data by scanning symbols or codes with light (sometimes with laser light). Because the symbols or codes are "read" much like you read data with your eyes, these devices are called *optical scanning input devices*. (See Fig. 4.4.)

FIGURE 4.4

Optical scanning input devices

Bar code scanner

Scanner

One of the most common optical scanning input devices is a bar code scanner This device recognizes a *bar code*, which is the series of bars of different widths found on grocery and other items. The width and placement of the bars represent a code that identifies the item. The bar code used on grocery merchandise is called the *Universal Product Code*, or UPC, but other bar codes are also used. A bar code scanner, which may be either handheld or fixed, is a device that recognizes the code represented by a bar code and sends the code to the computer.

Businesses use bar code scanners because with them the user does not have to enter the code through a keyboard. As a result, the code is entered into the computer more quickly and more accurately. A disadvantage of these types of devices is that codes must be placed on each item to be scanned.

Another optical scanning input device is simply called a scanner (or, sometimes, an *image scanner* or a *page scanner*). This device uses light to sense an image on paper. Any type of image can be scanned including text, graphics, pictures, and artwork. Color images also can be scanned. Businesses use scanners to transfer documents and images into a computer, where they can be changed, stored for future use, or used in screen or printed output.

Other optical scanning input devices include *optical character recognition* or *OCR* devices, which recognize certain printed characters; and *mark-sense readers*, which sense marks made on forms such as those used to take multiple-choice tests. All scanning input devices sense the input, whether bars, images, characters, or marks, and transfer the input to the computer.

Magnetic Scanning Input Devices.   Another type of scanning input device recognizes magnetic patterns. Data, recorded in a magnetic form, is sensed by a *magnetic scanning input device*. (See Fig. 4.5.)

One example of a magnetic scanning input device is a magnetic strip reader. This device recognizes data recorded in small magnetic strips that are used on credit and ATM cards to store the card number, and on some price tags to store the item's price. The magnetic strip reader senses the data as the strip is passed through the reader or as it is scanned by a wand. Sales clerks sometimes use one magnetic strip reader to scan price tags and another to check customer credit cards. For a business, the advantages of magnetic strip readers are that few errors are made in entering data and the data can be entered very quickly. A disadvantage is that the magnetic strip can be easily damaged.

Another example of magnetic scanning is magnetic ink character recognition or MICR, which is an input technique used in the banking industry to process checks.

FIGURE 4.5

Magnetic scanning input device. This is a magnetic strip reader.

MICR characters are the special characters printed at the bottom of checks. These characters indicate the bank, the check number, and the customer's account number. The amount of the check is printed on the check in MICR characters after it is received by the bank. MICR characters are processed by devices that first magnetize the characters, then read the magnetized characters and send the data to the computer for checking-account processing. Use of this technology in the banking industry is essential because of the high volume of checks that are processed every day.

Voice Input Devices. A type of input that is becoming more common is voice input. In this form of input, the user speaks into a microphone that is attached to the computer. Special computer hardware and software are needed to convert the person's voice into a form that the computer can understand, a process called *voice recognition*.

To use voice input, voice recognition software often must first be *trained* to recognize the user's voice. The training is done by speaking words several times so that the software can learn how the user says the words. Then, when using voice input, the user must be careful to speak each word in a fashion similar to the way in which the software was trained.

Some voice recognition systems are designed to only recognize a few words and do not need to be trained. For example, some telephone systems can recognize a spoken number so that the user does not have to press a key. Other voice recognition systems can recognize thousands of different words and can be used for general input, but require extensive training.

Because voice input is the easiest form of communication for most people, businesses find it very attractive. Even with software that must be trained, however, voice input is not perfectly accurate in recognizing words. Someday, when it is perfected, voice input may be the most common form of input.

Screens

The most widely used output device is a screen. Screens are used for output because they are easily read by most people and what they display can be changed quickly.

Character output is formed on a screen from individual dots, called picture elements or <u>pixels</u>, arranged in the patterns of the characters. For example, Fig. 4.6 shows how pixels can be arranged to form the letter S. Graphic output—diagrams, charts, pictures, and other images—are also formed from pixels arranged in the pattern that represents the image.

The more pixels that are used and the closer they are together, the more the display on the screen looks like a character or a graphic image. The number of

FIGURE 4.6

The letter S formed from pixels

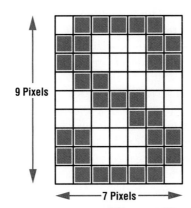

9 Pixels

7 Pixels

Bookmark

Voice Recognition at Boeing

The Boeing Co., the nation's largest exporter, uses voice recognition in its receiving and warehousing operations.

Recently, Boeing polished up a parts check-in system used by 25 employees at two Washington State jetliner factories, said Beverly Stoll, a systems analyst who helped implement the system.

Boeing installed the voice-recognition system to streamline logging, distribution, and payment for the 35,000 parts it received from 1,500 vendors each month. The goal: Eliminate the expense and errors of a two-phase system in which workers handwrote information about incoming parts, and clerks entered that data into a computer.

Boeing chose Talkman, a hardware/software package from Vocollet Inc. in Pittsburgh, which has sold units mostly to warehouses and factories. The units consist of a battery pack and speech module that converts speech to ASCII, and vice versa, as well as a headset with a microphone. The main component is worn on a user's belt.

The Talkman unit is linked by narrow-band radio to a central base radio station connected to a PC running Windows. That PC, in turn, can be "trained" to recognize any number of words and phrases, depending only on memory. Most dialogues, however, require only 50 to 100 words. It takes Talkman users about 15 minutes to train the unit to recognize the user's speech inflections. A user's head cold won't throw off Talkman's accuracy, but changes in speech speed or enunciation will, Stoll said.

Stoll and her colleagues programmed the central terminal with a list of prompts and expected responses. Now, every time workers log in a recently received part, they receive a series of voice prompts: purchase-order number, part number, quantity, unit of measure, ship date, packing-sheet number, and number of boxes. The system echoes each response to make sure it has entered the correct information. Power users can deliver all the information in one long phrase, separating each item with the word "go."

Talkman not only provides greater speed and accuracy, but it also frees workers' hands and lets them concentrate more fully on their work. "Voice recognition is an important part of our operations, and I imagine it will be for a long time to come," Stoll said.

QUESTIONS

1. For what information system does Boeing use voice recognition?
2. Why is training of the voice recognition system not too difficult at Boeing?
3. What does the voice recognition system do to ensure that data is entered correctly?

WEB SITE
The Boeing Company: www.boeing.com

Source: Dan Richman, "Speech replaces point and click," *Information Week,* July 3, 1995, pp. 44,46.

---

pixels that can be displayed at one time is called the **screen resolution**. The higher the resolution, the more the image on the screen looks like the desired output. For example, a screen with 1,280 pixels horizontally by 1,024 pixels vertically has a higher resolution and produces a better image than a screen with a resolution of 640 by 480 pixels.

The most common type of screen uses a **CRT**, which stands for Cathode Ray Tube. A CRT is a tube similar to that used in a television. A CRT designed for computer use is called a **monitor**. Monitors sold today display images in color and vary in size from 14 inches, measured diagonally, to 21 inches. (Some older monitors, called *monochrome monitors*, display images in one color.)

CRTs, although very good for displaying output, have a serious disadvantage: They are bulky. To display the image on the screen, a CRT must be deep. The larger the screen, the deeper the CRT, which makes CRTs big and heavy. Although size is usually not a serious problem with desktop computers, it is a problem with portable computers. To overcome the problem of CRT bulk, flat panel screens, which are thin and lightweight, are used. They are incorporated into portable computers or used in locations where CRTs cannot be used.

The most common type of flat panel screen uses a *liquid crystal display* or *LCD*. (See Fig. 4.7.) LCD screens are thin and lightweight, but they can be harder to read in low light or at an angle than CRT screens. They are also more expensive than CRT screens, but because of their size and weight they are commonly used on portable computers.

As with keyboards, ergonomic considerations are important with the design and use of screens. Screens normally have brightness and contrast controls that provide for adjustment for different light conditions. The surface of a screen may be designed to minimize glare. Monitors often have stands that allow them to be rotated and tilted for the best viewing angle. These and other ergonomic factors may improve user comfort and efficiency, and should be considered by businesses in selecting screens.

Printers

Although screens are the most widely used output device, they do not provide a permanent record of the output. Printers do, however, so they are used when it is important to have a permanent copy of the output on paper.

Many types of printers are used with computers. Some are relatively fast and designed for situations in which a high volume of output is produced, and others are comparatively slow and used when the volume of output is low. Personal computer systems and many networked computer systems use relatively slow, low-volume printers, called *desktop printers*, because they are small enough to fit on the top of a desk or table. Multiple-user computer systems usually use fast, *high-volume printers*

Printer Classifications. Computer printers can be classified in several ways. One is by how they impact the paper. An impact printer makes an image on paper by striking the paper hard with a metal or plastic mechanism. A nonimpact printer makes an image in some way other than by a hard strike on the paper. (An example of a nonimpact printing device is a copier, such as a Xerox machine.) Impact printers tend to be noisier than nonimpact printers, which can be an important consideration in an office environment.

FIGURE 4.7

A liquid crystal display or LCD screen

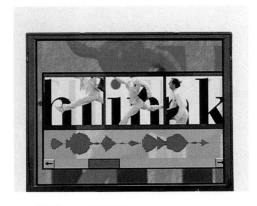

Computer printers also can be classified by how many characters are printed at one time. Printers that print one character at a time are called <u>serial printers</u>. The speed of a serial printer is measured in *characters per second* or *cps*. Printers that print one line at a time are called <u>line printers</u>. Their speed is measured in *lines per minute* or *lpm*. Finally, printers that print an entire page at a time, like a copier, are called <u>page printers</u>. Their speed is measured in *pages per minute* or *ppm*.

A final way of classifying printers is in terms of the quality of the image that the printer produces. The printers that produce the best images are called <u>letter-quality printers</u>. The output from these printers is the quality you would expect in a business letter. At the other extreme are <u>draft-quality printers</u>, which produce output that, although readable, is not of the quality that would normally be acceptable for a business letter. Between these extremes are <u>near-letter-quality printers</u>, which produce output that may be acceptable for business letters in some situations but is not as good as letter-quality output. Letter- or near-letter-quality printers should be used for correspondence or documents that go to individuals or organizations outside the business, but draft quality can be used for documents or reports that are only circulated within a business.

Desktop Printers. The most common types of desktop printers are ink-jet printers, laser printers, and dot-matrix printers. (See Fig. 4.8.)

An <u>ink-jet printer</u> is a nonimpact printer that creates an image by spraying drops of ink on the paper. The drops form characters from dots much like the pixels on a screen form characters. Ink-jet printers are serial printers with typical speeds of 200 to 300 characters per second, although their speed is often stated in pages per minute. The quality of the image of ink-jet printers can be varied from draft-quality to letter-quality output. Many ink-jet printers can print in color.

A <u>laser printer</u> is a nonimpact printer that prints by using technology similar to that of a copier. First, an image of the page to be printed is recorded on the surface of a metal drum by a laser. Then ink called toner is spread on the drum and adheres to the image. Next, the toner is transferred from the drum to paper. Finally, the toner is fixed to the paper using the same technique as a copier. A laser printer prints one page at a time, so it is a page printer. Speeds typically range between four and 24

Laser printer

Ink-jet printer

Dot-matrix printer

FIGURE 4.8

Desktop printers

pages per minute. The image on a laser printer is made up of dots, like an ink-jet printer, but the dots usually produce a slightly better image. Thus, laser printers print letter-quality output. Although they are more expensive than ink-jet printers, a business usually selects a laser printer over an ink-jet printer because the quality of the output is better. Color laser printers are also available, but they are very expensive.

A <u>dot-matrix printer</u> is an impact printer that prints each character by striking a ribbon and the paper with a group of pins that cause dots, arranged in a rectangular pattern or matrix, to be printed on the paper. To form a character, some pins are raised and others are not, so that only certain dots in the matrix are printed. Dot-matrix desktop printers are serial printers with speeds typically ranging from 200 to 300 characters per second. They print draft-quality to near-letter-quality output. The latter is produced by printing more dots in the matrix or by printing each character twice with the dots shifted slightly the second time. Although dot-matrix printers are not as popular as ink-jet and laser printers, they are still used because they are inexpensive and can print on multipart paper, which consists of several sheets of paper with carbon paper between them. They are about the same price as ink-jet printers.

High-volume Printers.   Printers designed for high volumes of output are used mainly with multiple-user computer systems, although they can be found in some networked computer systems. These printers require special training to operate and are almost always operated by computer professionals. The two main types of high-volume printers are line printers and page printers. (See Fig. 4.9.)

Line printers are impact printers that use several techniques to print output. In one common technique, a band containing forms of all the characters moves rapidly past a ribbon and the paper. As characters on the band pass positions to be printed, hammers in the printer strike the band, causing the character to be printed. The band moves so quickly that it appears as if the entire line is printed at one time. Some line printers print as much as 3,600 lines per minute. They produce draft-quality output and can cost as much as $50,000.

FIGURE 4.9

High-volume printers

Line printer

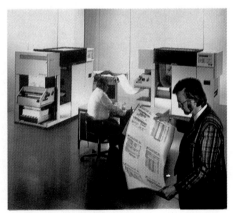

Page printer

High-volume page printers are nonimpact laser printers that use a printing technique similar to desktop laser printers. The difference is that they are much faster and much more expensive than desktop models. High-volume page printers can print over 200 pages per minute and can cost over a hundred thousand dollars. These printers print letter-quality output. Businesses use high-volume page printers when large amounts of printed output are needed, such as in utility companies which print millions of bills each month.

Other Output Devices

The output devices described so far—screens and printers—are most commonly encountered by users. Several other types of output devices are also used.

Plotters. A plotter creates graphic output on paper. (See Fig. 4.10.) Some plotters use one or more ink pens to draw a graphic image, and other plotters spray drops of ink (like an ink-jet printer) in a graphic pattern. Although most printers can create graphic output, plotters produce better-quality graphic images. Some plotters draw with one color (usually black), and other plotters can draw with several colors.

Plotters vary in the size of output they can produce. Small plotters can plot only on letter-size or slightly larger sheets of paper. Large plotters can plot on paper as wide as 50 inches. They are most commonly used for producing engineering and architectural drawings.

Voice Output Devices. In voice output, a human-sounding voice speaks the output to the user through a speaker or earphone. An example of voice output is telephone directory assistance. In this system, a human operator takes the request for a telephone number, but the required number is spoken by a computer-generated voice. Voice output is produced in two ways. One way is for the computer to play recorded words stored in secondary storage. The second way is to create the voice with special computer circuitry, a process called *speech synthesis.*

FIGURE 4.10

A plotter

The advantage of voice output over other forms of output is that it is in a form with which people are most familiar. Voice output, however, is not permanent, as is paper output. Generally, voice output is best for small amounts of output.

Sound Output Devices.   Computers often have speakers to produce sound output, which could be recorded voices, music, or simple beeps and tones. The speakers are attached to special circuits in the computer that supply the electronic impulses for the sounds to the speakers. Often the speakers require separate power to amplify the sound so that it can be heard.

Terminals

A terminal is a combination input/output device. Normally, terminals are used with multiple-user computer systems which are often some distance from the terminal. The most common type of terminal is a video display terminal or VDT, which consists of a keyboard and a screen. Some VDTs (called *dumb terminals*) can only send input to the computer and receive output from the computer, but others (called *intelligent terminals*) can also perform some basic data processing such as identifying errors in input data.

Microcomputers can also be used as video display terminals. To do so requires data communication technology discussed in Chapter 6. The result, however, is that the microcomputer can do much of the data processing normally done by the larger computer, plus act as a terminal for the other computer. Because of these advantages, microcomputers have replaced terminals in many businesses.

Numerous other devices are also terminals. For example, an automated teller machine is a terminal connected to a distant computer run by the bank. An ATM has several input and output devices. For input it has a magnetic strip reader to sense the magnetic strip on the back of the ATM card, a keyboard, and sometimes a touch screen. For output it has a printer to print receipts, a screen, and a money dispenser.

Multimedia Input and Output

Multimedia input and output consists of data in more than one form. Multimedia input can include still pictures, moving images, and sound. Multimedia output can include graphic images which can be still or moving pictures or animation, and sound which can be voice, music, or any other sound. In the future, multimedia input and output may include other forms such as that sensed through touch or smell.

Multimedia output is often used in highly interactive presentations to users. The user can select what he or she wishes to see or hear, and can move through the presentation in sequence or jump from one point in the presentation to another. Because of its characteristics, multimedia is useful in education and training, in product presentations to customers, in reference works such as encyclopedias, and in entertainment.

To produce multimedia output, appropriate output devices must be available, including a high-resolution screen and speakers or headphones. Because multimedia is interactive, printers are not normally needed unless certain output can be printed.

Input devices for multimedia depend on whether the presentation is to be used or created. To *use* multimedia, a keyboard and a pointing device such as a mouse are necessary so that the user can interact with the presentation. A touch screen may also be used and some multimedia "kiosks" in public locations such as shopping centers are entirely used through a touch screen. (See Fig. 4.11.)

FIGURE 4.11

A multimedia kiosk

To *create* a multimedia presentation, however, additional input devices are necessary. These include video input devices that can take still images or moving pictures and convert them to a form that can be stored in the computer. This process is called *digitizing* because the image is converted to the digits 1 and 0. To accomplish this, video cameras and videocassette recorders are used along with special digitizing circuits. Sound input devices also are needed. These include microphones, tape recorders, music keyboards, and other audio devices. These devices must be connected to special digitizing circuits to convert the sound input into a form that can be stored in the computer.

Virtual Reality Input and Output

Virtual reality is the use of a computer to produce realistic images and sounds in such a way that the user senses that he or she is a part of the scene. (See Fig. 4.12.) In effect, virtual reality creates a nonreal, or *virtual*, world and puts the user in the world through sight and sound.

Special input and output devices are needed to use virtual reality. (See Fig. 4.13.) The user usually wears a headset connected to a computer. The headset contains two small screens, one for each eye, to project three-dimensional images for the user. The headset also contains headphones for sound output.

FIGURE 4.12

Virtual reality output

FIGURE 4.13

Virtual reality input and output devices

The headset is not only an output device but also an input device. As the user moves his or her head, the movement is sensed and the image is adjusted to where the user is "looking." Another input device that may be used is a special glove which senses hand movement so that the user can point to things in the virtual world. Instead of a glove, some virtual reality systems use a joystick, which is a stick that can be moved in any direction to control the virtual world.

Virtual reality has many uses. An obvious one is for entertainment. Users can experience fantasy worlds and play games using virtual reality. Another important use is to train doctors in sophisticated medical procedures. Virtual reality is also used in architecture and design to allow the user to "walk" through a building or room to see how it will look after it has been constructed.

Primary Storage

Input data is stored in primary storage (memory) after it is received from an input device, and output data is stored in primary storage before it is sent to an output device. Data from secondary storage and programs that are executing are also stored in primary storage. It is important that a computer used in an information system have adequate primary storage so that it can store the data and program instructions needed for current processing. Without enough primary storage, it may not be possible to execute certain programs or use certain data. Even if there is enough primary storage, more storage may result in faster processing. Thus, businesses need to select computers with adequate primary storage to meet their needs. This section describes the structure and function of primary storage.

Primary Storage Structure

Primary storage is composed of silicon chips (integrated circuits) containing millions of electronic circuits. Silicon, a substance found in sand, is formed into pieces about ¼-inch square into which electronic circuits are etched. (See Fig. 4.14.) A computer's primary storage usually consists of a number of memory chips.

Each circuit on a chip can be in only one of two states: on or off. In a way, a circuit is like a lightbulb, which can be only on or off. You can think of primary storage as being composed of millions of lightbulbs—each of which is either on or off. The computer stores data in primary storage by turning some circuits on and others off in a pattern that represents the data. For example, Fig. 4.15 uses the lightbulb analogy to show a pattern that represents a person's name. Later you will see the types of patterns that computers use to represent data.

Once data is stored in primary storage, it stays there until the computer changes it. To change the data, the computer changes the pattern in the circuits by turning some circuits on and others off. When the computer changes the data, the original data is destroyed and replaced by the new data. To retrieve data from primary storage, the computer senses the on–off pattern in the circuits. It can transfer this pattern to another part of the computer such as the CPU, an output device, or secondary storage. When data is retrieved, the old data is *not* destroyed; it remains in primary storage and can be retrieved again.

Primary storage circuits, like lightbulbs, need electricity to stay on. If the power to the computer is turned off, all the circuits will turn off, and all data in primary storage will be lost. When the computer is turned back on, the data will not reappear; the data is lost forever (unless it is stored in some other form). Because of this characteristic, primary storage is called volatile storage.

The type of primary storage described so far is called random access memory or RAM. *Random access* simply mean that data in any part of the primary storage can be retrieved (accessed) in any order (that is, randomly). RAM is the main type of primary storage used with computers and, as you know, it is volatile. Computers also have a type of primary storage called read only memory or ROM. ROM is nonvolatile storage, which means that when the power to the computer is turned off, anything stored in ROM is not lost. ROM, however, can store only preset programs and data put in ROM by the computer manufacturer. Programs and data in ROM can be

FIGURE 4.14

A chip

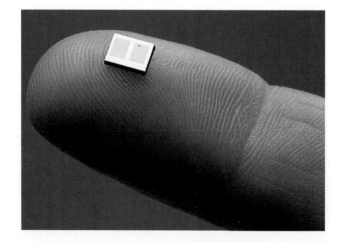

FIGURE 4.15

Storing a name in
primary storage:
the lightbulb
analogy

retrieved (read) as many times as needed, but new programs and data cannot be
stored in ROM. ROM is used to store special programs and data needed for the basic
operation of the computer.

Data Representation

Data appears in several forms, including graphic images, pictures, and sound. Most
common data, however, is made up of characters. People represent data by using a
group of characters, such as a group of letters for a name, or a group of digits for a
quantity. Computers, however, cannot represent this data in the same form that
people use.

There are over one hundred common characters, such as letters, digits, and
symbols like periods and commas. If a computer circuit were used to represent any
character, that circuit would need over one hundred states, one for each character.
But as you have seen, each computer circuit has only two states: on and off. Thus, it
is not possible to represent any character with a single circuit.

Computers represent data by using different patterns of on–off states in a
series of electronic circuits. A computer stores data by converting the data to this two-
state representation, which is called *binary representation*. To show data in binary representation on paper, people use the digit 1 for the "on" state and the digit 0 for the
"off" state. The digits 1 and 0 are called binary digits or bits. For example, the bits
that represent the data in Fig. 4.15 are:

0100000101001100

All data is stored in the computer as patterns of bits.

Characters are stored in a binary representation by using a code for each character. Although over the years many codes have been developed, two common
codes—ASCII and EBCDIC—are used today.

The name ASCII is pronounced "as-key" and stands for *American Standard Code
for Information Interchange*. An industry group composed of many computer manufacturers developed this code as a standard code to be used in all computers. In
ASCII, each character is represented by seven bits, and because there are 128 combinations of seven bits, 128 characters can be represented in the code. For example,
the name JOHN in ASCII is:

J	O	H	N
1001010	1001111	1001000	1001110

Notice that 28 bits are needed for the name, seven for each character. Although ASCII
is a seven-bit code, computers normally use an eight-bit version of ASCII which allows

for 256 characters. ASCII is used in all microcomputers, including those made by IBM and Apple, and in many minicomputers, mainframe computers, and supercomputers.

Although ASCII is an industry standard code, it is not used in all computers. IBM mainframe computers, and some mainframe computers that are similar to IBMs, use the EBCDIC code. The name of this code is pronounced "eb-si-dick" and stands for *Extended Binary Coded Decimal Interchange Code*. It was developed by IBM for use in its computers. In EBCDIC, each character is represented by eight bits. Because there are 256 combinations of eight bits, 256 characters can be represented in EBCDIC. The name JOHN in EBCDIC is:

$$\underbrace{11010001}_{J} \quad \underbrace{11010110}_{O} \quad \underbrace{11001000}_{H} \quad \underbrace{11010101}_{N}$$

Notice that 32 bits are needed for the name, eight for each character.

When computers use different codes to represent data, a problem arises if the computers need to communicate with each other. For example, a microcomputer, using ASCII, cannot communicate with an IBM mainframe, which uses EBCDIC, without special hardware or software to convert between the codes. Although the necessary hardware and software is readily available, businesses must be aware of this problem so they can acquire what is needed.

As computers are used for more and more international information systems, limitations in the ASCII and EBCDIC codes become evident. These codes can represent only 256 characters, but there are many more characters found in the alphabets and writing systems used around the world. For example, the Russian alphabet has 31 characters and the Greek alphabet has 24. In addition, systems such as those used in China and Japan have thousands of characters. An eight-bit code such as ASCII or EBCDIC is not adequate to represent all possible characters.

In an effort to create a single code for all characters, a 16-bit code called *Unicode*, for Universal Code, has been developed. With 16 bits, there are 65,536 combinations, enough for all the characters used in all the alphabets and writing systems in the world. Although not widely used yet, it may some day be the standard code on all computers.

Primary Storage Organization

Recall that each circuit in primary storage can be either on or off and hence each circuit can store one bit. The bits in primary storage must be organized so that they can be used to store data and so that the stored data can be retrieved. This organization is accomplished by arranging the bits into groups called storage locations.

The number of bits in each storage location depends on the type of computer being used. Most computers have eight or nine bits per storage location. Computers with eight- or nine-bit storage locations use either eight-bit ASCII or EBCDIC and store one character in each location. In addition, computers often add a ninth bit, called a parity bit, which is used to check if there are any errors in the other bits. A group of bits that are used to store one character is called a byte. Usually, a byte is eight or nine bits. Computers organize primary storage so that each storage location is one byte.

The computer keeps track of storage locations by giving each location a unique number called an address. A simple analogy is that of post office box addresses. Think of primary storage as being organized into boxes just like the boxes in a post office. For example, Fig. 4.16 shows part of primary storage organized into 12

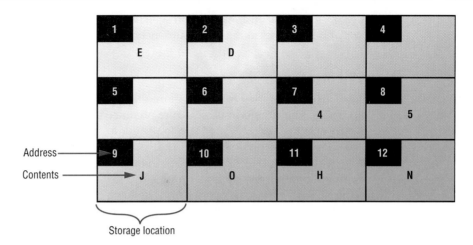

FIGURE 4.16

Primary storage organization

Address

Contents

Storage location

boxes—that is, storage locations. Each storage location in primary storage, like each post office box, has an address to identify it. The contents of each storage location in the computer is data just like the contents of each post office box is mail. To locate a specific post office box, you search through the boxes until you locate the one with the desired address. You can store mail in the box or retrieve mail from the box. Similarly, the computer locates a specific storage location by its address and stores data in or retrieves data from that location.

Primary Storage Capacity

A computer's storage capacity is measured in terms of the number of bytes in primary storage. In older computers, the capacity is stated in kilobytes or K bytes (KB). One kilobyte is 1,024 bytes (2^{10} bytes), but most people round this number off to 1,000 bytes. The primary storage of most current computers is measured in terms of megabytes or M bytes (MB). One megabyte is 1,048,576 bytes (2^{20} bytes), but again, people round this number off to one million bytes. Thus, 32 M bytes of primary storage would be about 32 million bytes. An even larger measure than megabytes is gigabyte or G byte (GB), which is approximately one billion bytes (2^{30} bytes). Some mainframe computers have gigabyte primary storage capacity. A still larger capacity is terabyte, which is about one trillion bytes (2^{40} bytes). Someday, computers may have terabyte capacity.

The Central Processing Unit

Once data is in primary storage, it can be processed by the central processing unit (CPU). The CPU does arithmetic and makes logical decisions using data from primary storage. In addition, the CPU controls the computer by following instructions in a program, sending signals to other parts of the computer to tell them what to do.

From a business's point of view, the CPU is important because it determines to a large extent the speed at which processing is done. Businesses need to be aware of this fact when purchasing computers so that processing will be completed at an acceptable rate. In addition, not all CPUs are the same, so that programs for some computers will not work on other computers. This compatibility problem must also be considered by businesses when selecting computers. This section describes how the CPU functions, and explains the speed and compatibility characteristics of CPUs.

CPU Structure

The CPU is composed of one or more silicon chips containing millions of electronic circuits. The circuits in the CPU are organized into two main units, called the <u>arithmetic-logic unit</u>, or <u>ALU</u>, and the <u>control unit</u>. (See Fig. 4.17.)

The ALU contains circuits that perform arithmetic and logical operations. The arithmetic circuits can add, subtract, multiply, and divide two numbers. More complex operations, such as finding the square root of a number, are done by sequences of these basic operations. The logic circuits in the ALU can compare two values to determine if they are equal or if one is greater than or less than the other.

To perform a calculation or logical operation, numbers are transferred from primary storage to the ALU. These numbers are then sent to the appropriate arithmetic or logic circuit for processing. Finally, the result is sent back to primary storage.

The control unit contains circuits that analyze and execute instructions. Instructions in the program are brought one at a time from primary storage to the control unit. In the control unit, circuits analyze the instruction to determine what type of instruction it is. Then the control unit sends signals to the ALU, primary storage, I/O devices, and secondary storage, that cause the actions required by the instructions to be performed. These steps are repeated for each instruction in the program until all instructions have been executed.

CPU Compatibility

The CPU functions by executing instructions in a program. The instructions are in a very basic form called <u>machine language</u>. Each instruction in a machine language program consists of a code that indicates the operation to perform (e.g., add, subtract, etc.) and the location of the data on which to perform the operation. The instructions are in a binary form (sequences of 1s and 0s).

Different CPUs use different machine language instructions for their programs. Each type of CPU has its own set of instructions, which may be different from that of other CPUs. The instruction sets may differ in the types of operations that can be performed, which codes are used for each operation, and how the location of the data to be processed is identified in an instruction. This incompatibility means that a machine language program for one CPU may not be executed on a different CPU.

FIGURE 4.17

The structure of the central processing unit

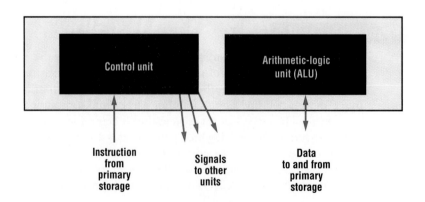

Two different CPUs are *compatible* if the machine language instructions for one are identical to those of the other. Thus, a machine language program for one compatible CPU can be executed on the other and vice versa.

CPU Speed

The way a CPU is designed affects its speed. One factor is the number of bits that can be processed in the CPU at one time. Early CPUs could only process eight or 16 bits at a time (one or two bytes), while current CPUs process 32, 64, and even 128 bits at a time. In general, the more bits that can be processed in the CPU, the faster the computer will be.

Another factor is the amount of data that can be transferred between the CPU and primary storage at one time. Data is transferred between these and other components of the computer over a set of wires called a *bus*. Older computers could transfer only eight or 16 bits (one or two bytes) at a time, but current computers can transfer 32 bits (four bytes) or 64 bits (eight bytes) at a time. In general, the more data that can be transferred between the CPU and primary storage at a time, the faster the computer will be.

The speed at which a computer can transfer data is measured in fractions of a second. The first computers could transfer data to and from primary storage in milliseconds. One millisecond is one-thousandth of a second. Later computers stored and retrieved data in microseconds. One microsecond is one-millionth of a second. Today's computers transfer data between primary storage and the CPU in nanoseconds. One nanosecond is one-billionth of a second.

Another factor that affects CPU speed is *clock speed*. CPUs are synchronized to run at the speed of an internal clock. With each tick of the clock, the CPU performs one step in executing an instruction. If the clock ticks faster, then the CPU runs faster. Clock speed is measured in megahertz or MHz. One megahertz is one million cycles (ticks) per second. For example, the CPU in the original IBM PC ran at 4.77 MHz, or 4,770,000 cycles per second. The CPUs in some microcomputers today run at over 200 MHz, which means that many more operations can be performed in a second on these computers than on early IBM PCs.

In recent years, new types of CPUs have been developed that are designed to be faster and much less expensive than older ones. These types are called *RISC* processors. RISC stands for *Reduced Instruction Set Computer*. A RISC processor has a smaller set of instructions than an older type of processor, which makes it less expensive, but it can execute its instructions very rapidly.

Common CPUs

CPUs in all computers have basically the same structure: a control unit and an arithmetic-logic unit. CPUs differ, however, in the machine language instructions they can execute and in characteristics that determine their speed.

Microcomputer CPUs. A microcomputer uses a single-chip CPU, called a microprocessor. (See Fig. 4.18.) The first microprocessor was developed by Intel Corporation in the early 1970s and was called the Intel 4004. It was a slow processor used in calculators. Over the years, Intel developed faster and better microprocessors, including the 8088, which was used as the CPU in the original IBM PC; the 8086; the 80286, usually just called the 286; the 80386, or simply the 386; and the 80486, or 486. After the 486, Intel changed the way it named processors, and called the next model

FIGURE 4.18

A microprocessor

the Pentium. Then came the Pentium Pro, the Pentium MMX, and the Pentium II. All the Intel microprocessors use the same machine language instructions so they are compatible. Each new model, however, is faster and more powerful than the previous one. They are used on IBM microcomputers and IBM clones.

The original Apple Macintosh used a microprocessor for its CPU developed by Motorola, Inc., called the 68000. This microprocessor is not compatible with the Intel microprocessors. Faster Motorola microprocessors—called the 68020, 68030, and 68040—wcrc used in later models of the Apple Macintosh. Even faster is the most recent Motorola microprocessor, called the PowerPC, which was developed jointly by Motorola, Apple, and IBM. It is used in current Apple Macintosh models and clones.

As you can see, microcomputer companies, such as IBM and Apple, use microprocessors developed by other companies, such as Intel and Motorola. Different microcomputers may use the same microprocessor and thus the computers are compatible with one another. For example, all IBM clones using the Intel Pentium are compatible. A microcomputer that uses a different microprocessor, however, is not compatible. Thus an Apple Macintosh using a PowerPC is not compatible with an IBM clone.

Each year, new microprocessors are developed by Intel, Motorola, and other companies. These new microprocessors are faster than previous ones, and may offer improved capabilities such as multimedia processing. You can expect this trend to continue. In a few years, all the microprocessors in use today will be obsolete.

Minicomputer and Mainframe Computer CPUs. Minicomputers and mainframe computers often use CPUs developed by the computer manufacturer. The CPUs developed by one company often are not compatible with those of another company. Within a line of computers manufactured by a company, however, the CPUs usually are compatible. For example, the DEC Alpha line of minicomputers uses CPUs developed by DEC that are compatible throughout all models in the line. Similarly, all IBM System/390 mainframe computers use compatible CPUs developed by IBM. IBM mainframe computers, however, are not compatible with DEC minicomputers. Thus, a machine language program for an IBM System/390 computer cannot be executed on a DEC Alpha.

Supercomputer CPUs. Like minicomputer and mainframe computer CPUs, supercomputer CPUs are often developed by the computer manufacturer. As a result, the CPU used in one supercomputer usually is not compatible with that of other supercomputers.

To obtain great processing speeds, supercomputers often use CPUs that can process 64 or 128 bits at a time. In addition, special chips that are designed for high-speed processing are used. For example, supercomputers often use special high-speed chips for arithmetic calculations. Another technique used to increase speed is

Bookmark

Supercomputers at Alcoa, AAA, and Best Western

Walter Wahnsiedler has a dream. The technical specialist for process and design smelting at the Aluminum Co. of America's (Alcoa) technical center in New Kensington, Pa., would like to cut the time needed to simulate the modeling process for new aluminum castings to just one hour from as long as three weeks.

For Wahnsiedler and thousands of others, the search for fast prototyping has led to the supercomputer. More than a decade ago, Wahnsiedler spent $500,000 on a Convex C1 supercomputer. Now, he's upgrading to an eight-processor Hewlett-Packard Convex Exemplar SPP1000/CD, which provides 96 times the performance of his original Convex C1.

At Alcoa and elsewhere, high-performance computing is mainstream. Gone are the days when supercomputing was restricted to seismic explorations or code-breaking. Now, the demand for computer time includes everything from automobile modeling to mining of huge databases that bring companies closer to their customers.

The appeal of supercomputing has expanded the use of the technology for competitive business processes. Alcoa's Wahnsiedler, for instance, wanted a machine that would provide faster design to bring products to market more quickly. "The crucial issue is turnaround time," Wahnsiedler said. "If it took months to translate [a] design into a product, we'd be too late."

Neal Duff, staff director at the American Automobile Association in Orlando, Fla., was desperate to provide hotel, recreation, and travel information to AAA agents. Duff wanted some 1,000 agents nationwide to have access to travel information in two seconds or less, at least 95 percent of the time.

Duff and his technicians chose a $1 million, 20-processor CS6400 departmental supercomputer from Cray Research Inc. in Eagan, Minn., which had the right scalability and price/performance for AAA's needs. Moreover, it performed the queries on a single machine.

The machine supports 600 AAA travel counselors nationwide on a 24-hour, seven-day schedule. Eventually, the CS6400—which can scale as high as 64 processors—will support the scheduled maximum of 1,000 users at AAA field offices.

Best Western International Inc. in Phoenix uses Digital AlphaServer 8400 TurboLaser servers with Digital PC front ends for nearly 1,000 reservations and travel agents. The 3,500-location hotel chain expects a doubling of reservations traffic by 1999.

Best Western spent $15 million on the Digital technology. Early users trained six hours per day for 10 days to learn the sales, geography, and general business components of the system.

"This definitely puts us on the leading edge of corporate supercomputing environments," said Mary Swenson, Best Western's worldwide vice-president of reservations sales.

Swenson also believes that the system provides the right amount of flexibility to incorporate even larger amounts of traffic. "We want to react quickly [with] development time and cost [at] a minimum," Swenson said. "Now we're in a much better position to bend with the marketplace."

Not all companies spend $15 million on high-performance systems. But the Best Western scenario—along with the experiences at Alcoa and AAA—proves that there are business trailblazers firmly on the supercomputing path. "There's no doubt supercomputing is working its way into the mainstream," said Alcoa's Wahnsiedler. "I like the excitement of being on the leading edge."

QUESTIONS

1. For what does Alcoa use a supercomputer?
2. What benefits does AAA receive from a supercomputer?
3. Why did Best Western decide to get a supercomputer?

WEB SITES

American Automobile Association: www.aaa.com
Best Western International:
   www.travelweb.com/bw.html

Source: Willie Schatz, "More Power, Lower Cost," *Information Week*, February 26, 1996, pp. 48, 52.

<u>multiprocessing</u>, which involves using several CPUs in the computer. For example, a supercomputer may have eight CPUs, which means eight operations can be performed at one time, making the computer eight times as fast as one that has only a single CPU. (This technique of multiprocessing is also used in some less powerful computers, including some microcomputers.)

Some supercomputers do not use specially developed CPUs but instead use many standard CPUs such as those made by Intel. These supercomputers may have several hundred to several thousand CPUs, allowing hundreds to thousands of operations to be performed simultaneously. This approach is called <u>massively parallel processing</u> and it may be the direction that most supercomputers go in the future.

Secondary Storage

A computer in an information system not only stores data and programs currently being processed but also data and programs for future processing. Primary storage, as you know, stores data and programs currently needed by the computer. Data and programs that are not being processed, but that may be needed in the future, cannot be stored in primary storage because primary storage is volatile. Secondary storage, on the other hand, is nonvolatile, and so it is used to store data and programs needed in the future.

Secondary storage has several characteristics that impact information systems in businesses. One characteristic is the capacity of secondary storage for storing data and programs. Different types of secondary storage have different maximum capacities. Another characteristic is the speed at which data can be retrieved from secondary storage. Different forms of secondary storage can retrieve data at different rates. Businesses need to be aware of these characteristics when selecting secondary storage for computers used in information systems.

Magnetic Disk Storage

The most widely used form of secondary storage is magnetic disk. Magnetic disk storage is used on all types of computers from microcomputers to supercomputers.

Magnetic Disk.   A magnetic disk is a flat, round platter made of metal or plastic and covered with a metallic coating, which can be magnetized at different spots. You probably remember that a magnet has a north end and a south end. When a spot on a disk is magnetized, imagine that a magnet is placed there. The magnet may be aligned with the north end up or with the south end up. To store data on the disk, let one way of aligning the magnet (north end up) represent the digit 1 and the other way (south end up) represent the digit 0. Thus, each spot of magnetism represents a binary digit or bit on the surface of the disk.

Millions of bits (magnets) can be recorded on the disk. The bits are organized into concentric circles called <u>tracks</u>. (See Fig. 4.19.) The number of tracks on the surfaces of disks vary with different types of disks; some have as few as 40 while others have more than 500 tracks.

The bits along tracks are grouped to form bytes in the same way that the bits in primary storage form bytes. Each byte stores the code for one character of data in either ASCII or EBCDIC, depending on the code used in primary storage.

The capacity of a disk depends on the number of bytes per track and the number of tracks. Some older disks can store only a few hundred thousand bytes. The floppy disk used with the original IBM personal computer could store only 360 kilobytes.

FIGURE 4.19

Tracks on a magnetic disk

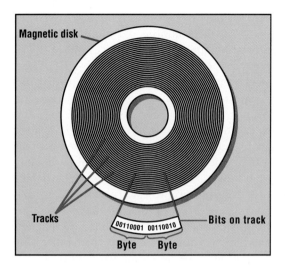

Current disks can store millions, billions, and even trillions of bytes. For example, the most common floppy disk stores about 1.4 megabytes and the hard disk on many microcomputers can store several gigabytes. Minicomputers and mainframe computers have hard disks that can store hundreds of gigabytes or even several terabytes.

Because data is stored magnetically on a disk, the data remains on the disk even when the power to the computer is turned off. This characteristic explains why data is permanent on a disk, unlike data in primary storage. The data may be changed, however, by realigning the magnetic spots.

Disks come in various forms and sizes. The most common floppy disk is 3½ inches in diameter. Hard disks range in size from less than 2 inches to 14 inches across. Sometimes a single hard disk is used, and at other times several disks are stacked on top of each other with space between the disks. This latter arrangement is called a disk pack. Because both sides of a disk are used to record data, a disk pack with three disks, for example, has six surfaces on which data can be recorded.

Magnetic Disk Drives.   A magnetic disk is the media on which data is stored. To use the disk, it must be in a magnetic disk drive. (See Fig. 4.20.) This device stores data

FIGURE 4.20

A magnetic disk drive

on a disk and retrieves data from a disk. The disk drive rotates the disk at a speed ranging from 300 to 7,000 revolutions per minute, depending on the type of disk. While the disk is rotating, an access arm comes out of the side of the disk drive; at the end of the arm is a read/write head. (See Fig. 4.21.) The access arm can position the read/write head over any track on the disk. As the disk rotates, data can be stored on the track by sending electronic signals to the read/write head. That is, the read/write head can *write* data on the disk. Similarly, as the disk rotates, the data stored on a track can be retrieved by the read/write head. That is, the read/write head can *read* data from the disk. When data is written on a disk, any data in the same place is destroyed but when data is read from a disk, the data is not destroyed.

A disk drive has one access arm and read/write head for each side of a disk. Thus, a floppy disk drive has two access arms and a hard disk drive for a disk pack with three disks has six access arms. All arms move back and forth in unison.

The speed at which data can be retrieved from a magnetic disk depends on how fast the disk rotates and how quickly the access arm moves. Floppy disk drives are the slowest. The average time to retrieve data from a floppy disk and transfer it to primary storage can be as slow as a third of a second. A hard disk drive is much faster. The average time to retrieve data from a hard disk and transfer it to primary storage can be as fast as a hundredth of a second.

Floppy disks can always be removed from the disk drive, but hard disks may be removable or nonremovable. An advantage of removable disks is that they allow unlimited storage capacity; if you use all the space on a disk, you just remove it and insert another disk. Nonremovable disks have the advantages of being more reliable, faster at transferring data, and greater in storage capacity.

Some disk systems include many disks or disk packs on which data is stored. These systems, called <u>RAID</u> for *redundant array of inexpensive disks*, allow data to be duplicated on other disks or spread across a number of disks. The advantage of this approach is that if any disk or disk pack fails, the data can be recovered from the other disks. Thus, RAID systems provide a high level of reliability for storing important business data.

Magnetic Disk Access. Recall from Chapter 3 that data in secondary storage is stored in files. A file consists of many records, each record has many fields, and each field consists of one or more characters. On magnetic disk, each byte on a track stores one character. (See Fig. 4.22.) The bytes are grouped to form fields, and all the fields

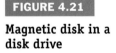

FIGURE 4.21

Magnetic disk in a disk drive

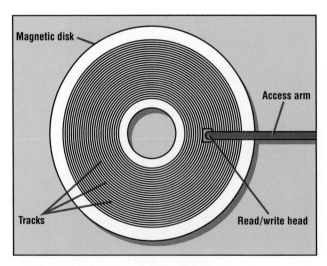

FIGURE 4.22

Magnetic disk data organization

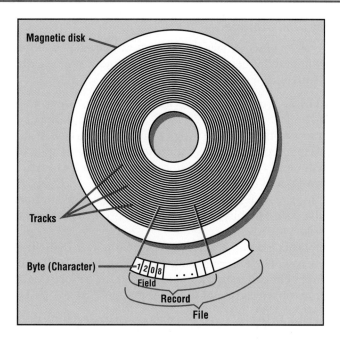

in a record are grouped together on a track. One record is stored after another along a track, and each track can usually hold several records. When a track is full, another track is used. A file may occupy many tracks.

Data is read or written on a disk one record at a time. To write a record on a disk, instructions in a computer program tell the computer to send the data for the record from primary storage to the disk drive, which then writes the data on the disk. Any data in the space where the record is written is destroyed when new data is written on the disk. To read a record from a disk, program instructions tell the computer to bring the data in the record from the disk into primary storage. When data in a record is read, the original data in that record on the disk is not destroyed.

When the disk drive reads or writes a record in a file, the drive can position the read/write head at the first track of the file and read or write the data in sequence, one record at a time, moving the read/write head from track to track. This method is called <u>sequential access</u> because the disk drive goes through the records in the file in sequence. It is also possible for the disk drive to move the read/write head to any track in a file, and read or write a specific record on that track without going through other records in the file. This method is called <u>random access</u> or <u>direct access</u>. The records in the file are read or written in random order by moving the read/write head forward and backward to any track in the file.

Magnetic Disk Usage.   Magnetic disk is the main form of secondary storage on most computers because it enables large volumes of data to be stored or retrieved rapidly. In addition, data may be accessed randomly or sequentially. Because of these characteristics many computers use magnetic disk as their sole form of secondary storage.

Microcomputers usually have one or two floppy disk drives and a nonremovable hard disk. Larger computers usually have one or more removable hard disks. Some mainframe computers have dozens of hard disk drives. Some minicomputers and mainframe computers also have nonremovable hard disks.

Optical Disk Storage

Another form of secondary storage that was developed more recently than magnetic disk but that has become extremely common is optical disk storage. Optical disk is used with all types of computers.

Optical Disk.   An optical disk is a round metal platter on which small holes or pits are used to store data. (See Fig. 4.23.) A pit represents the binary digit 1; the absence of a pit represents the binary digit 0. Thus, the surface of an optical disk is covered with pits that represent data in the same way that magnetic spots on a magnetic disk represent data. This system of storing data is similar to that used for storing music on compact discs (CDs).

Data is recorded on an optical disk along a single track that spirals into the center of the disk. The bits along a track are grouped to form bytes, just as on a magnetic disk.

Optical disks come in several sizes, from over 12 inches in diameter to about 5 inches across. The latter are called compact disks or CDs. Because the bits can be placed very close together, a single CD can store more than 600 megabytes of data. This large capacity is one of the main reasons CDs are used.

Optical Disk Drives.   To record data on an optical disk, the disk is put into an optical disk drive which rotates the disk. In the drive, a high-powered laser burns pits into the disk's surface as the disk turns. Data can be recorded only once because there is no way of erasing the pits after they are burned into the disk. To retrieve data from the disk, a low-powered laser is used to sense the pits on the disk's surface. The data can be retrieved as many times as needed. The speed at which data can be retrieved from an optical disk falls between that of a floppy disk and a hard disk.

Most optical disk drives for compact disks can only retrieve, that is read, data from disks. This type is called a CD-ROM drive, which stands for *Compact Disk- Read Only Memory*. The disks used for CD-ROM must be purchased with prerecorded data. This system can be used to gain access to generally available data such as a computerized encyclopedia or census data. CD-ROM is used mainly with microcomputers.

Optical disk storage

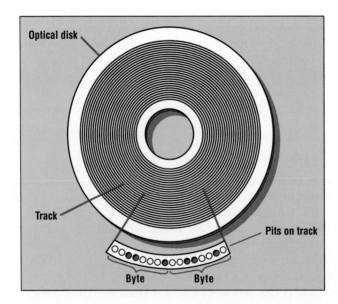

Some optical disk drives can store or *write* data once and read the data many times. This type is called a *WORM* drive, which stands for *Write Once, Read Many*. This system can be used to store data that is not likely to change in the future, such as old business records. Once the data is stored, it can be retrieved repeatedly. WORM drives are found on all sizes of computers.

Optical Disk Access.   Data on optical disks can be accessed sequentially or randomly. Sequential access is accomplished by using the laser to read data in sequence along the track on the disk. In random access, the laser is moved to the part of the disk where the data is stored. Then, as the disk rotates, data is retrieved from that part of the disk.

Optical Disk Usage.   Optical disks have several common uses. One is for storing large amounts of prerecorded information sold to consumers, which is the common use of CD-ROM. Encyclopedias, dictionaries, cookbooks, and other reference works are available on CD-ROM. Works of literature, such as the complete works of Shakespeare, are also available. Many computer programs and games are sold on CD-ROM.

Another use of optical disk is for recording multimedia material. Because optical disk uses the same technology that is used in music disks and video disks, optical disks can store music, pictures, and video, as well as words and diagrams, which makes them ideal for storing multimedia presentations. Many multimedia titles are available on CD-ROM.

Optical disk is also used to store data for *archival* purposes. Data appropriate for such storage is not normally changed in the future, such as old tax records for a business and transcripts of students who have graduated from a college. Data storage requires a writable optical disk drive such as a WORM drive. Because archival data normally is not changed in the future, the fact that the data cannot be erased is not important.

Erasable Optical Disk.   Another type of optical disk, called erasable optical disk, is also available. An erasable optical disk actually stores data in a magnetic form, like a magnetic disk. Consequently, the data can be erased and changed.

To record data, an erasable optical disk drive uses a laser beam and a magnet. The laser beam heats the spot on the disk where a bit is to be recorded, which makes the spot easier to magnetize. The magnet then magnetizes the spot in a 1 or 0 pattern. Any spot can be changed to a different pattern by repeating the process. To retrieve data from the disk, another laser beam is reflected off the spot. The pattern of light that is reflected depends on whether the spot is a 1 or a 0. Because erasable optical disk uses both magnetic and laser (optical) techniques, it is sometimes called *magneto-optical* or *MO disk*.

Magnetic Tape Storage

The last common form of secondary storage is magnetic tape. Developed before magnetic or optical disk, magnetic tape currently is not as common as the other forms of storage. Although tape can be used on all types of computers including microcomputers, it is most commonly found on minicomputers and mainframe computers.

Magnetic Tape.   Magnetic tape is made of a plastic material covered with a metallic coating, which can be magnetized at different spots. The spots of magnetism are like those on a magnetic disk and represent bits on the surface of the tape.

Several approaches are used to record data on a tape. In one, the bits on a tape are recorded along parallel tracks. (See Fig. 4.24.) The number of tracks on different types of tapes varies, but one type uses nine tracks. Bytes are stored on the tape

FIGURE 4.24

Tracks on a magnetic tape

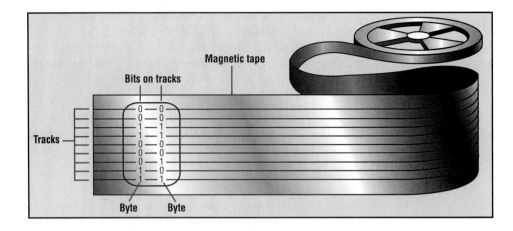

by recording one bit of the byte in each track across the tape. Each byte stores the code for one character in either ASCII or EBCDIC, depending upon the computer. The ninth bit is for a parity bit. The capacity of a tape is measured in terms of the number of bytes that can be stored. Tapes have capacities of 200 megabytes to over 40 gigabytes.

As with magnetic disk, data stored on a tape remains there when the power to the computer is turned off, because the data is stored magnetically. The data can be changed, however, by changing the magnetic spots on the tape and thus changing the bits that are stored.

Tapes come in various forms and sizes. One form is open reel tape, which is ½-inch wide and usually comes on reels that are 10 ½ inches in diameter. Another form is cartridge tape, which is ½-inch or ¼-inch wide.

Magnetic Tape Drives. Data is stored on and retrieved from a magnetic tape using a tape drive. (See Fig. 4.25.) In the tape drive, the tape is fed past a read/write head. Data can be stored (written) on the tape by sending electronic signals to the read/write head. Similarly, data stored on the tape can be retrieved (read) by the

FIGURE 4.25

A magnetic tape drive

read/write head. As with magnetic disks, writing data destroys existing data, but reading data does not.

Magnetic tape can always be removed from the tape drive. Thus, tape provides unlimited storage capacity. When a tape is full, it can be removed and replaced by another tape. Some organizations have thousands of tapes in a *tape library*.

Magnetic Tape Access.   Data on magnetic tape can only be accessed sequentially. When reading or writing data on a tape, the tape drive starts at the beginning of the tape and reads or writes the data in sequence. It is not possible to go forward without reading or writing data along the way, and it is not possible to go backward. Thus, unlike magnetic and optical disks, data on a tape cannot be accessed in random order.

The speed at which data can be retrieved from a magnetic tape depends on where the data is located. If the data is at the beginning of the tape, it can be retrieved quickly, maybe as fast as retrieving data from a floppy disk. On the other hand, if the data is in the middle or end of a tape, it can take minutes or even hours to retrieve the data.

Magnetic Tape Usage.   Magnetic tape is not often used as the main form of secondary storage on a computer because tape data can only be accessed sequentially, and usually an information system needs to access some data randomly. Normally, tape is used along with magnetic disk on a computer. Tape is much less expensive, however, than disk, so when data needs only to be accessed sequentially, tape may be used. Tape is most often used for storing copies of disk data, called backup copies, in case the original data is lost or destroyed.

Chapter Summary

☐ Businesses need hardware in information systems so that the systems operate quickly and accurately, and can handle large volumes of data. Computers provide speed by processing data and producing information rapidly. Businesses benefit from rapid processing by providing better service at a reduced cost. Computers ensure accuracy by not making mistakes like people do. Without accurate processing, a business's costs would be greater and its information less reliable. Computers provide the capacity to handle a large amount of data. Businesses benefit from this capacity by being able to process volumes of data. All these benefits gained from the use of hardware allow a business to compete effectively with other businesses. (pp. 90–91)

☐ Common input devices are keyboards, which can be general or special purpose, and pointing devices such as a mouse, **trackball**, trackpoint, and touchpad. Other types of input devices are touch input devices (**touch screens**, **pen input** devices, large touchpads, light pens, and digitizer tablets), optical scanning input devices (**bar code scanners**, image or page **scanners**, optical character recognition (OCR)

devices, and mark-sense readers), magnetic scanning input devices (**magnetic strip readers** and **MICR** devices), and voice input devices. Common output devices are screens and printers. Screens may be either **CRT monitors** or **flat panel screens**. Printers may be **impact** or **nonimpact printers**; **serial**, **line**, or **page printers**; **letter-quality**, **draft-quality**, or **near-letter-quality printers**. Desktop printers include **ink-jet**, **laser**, and **dot-matrix printers**. High-volume printers include line printers and page printers. Other types of output devices are **plotters**, voice output devices, and sound output devices. A **video display terminal** (**VDT**) consists of a keyboard and a screen. Input and output devices used for multimedia presentation include keyboards, pointing devices, high-resolution screens, and speakers or headphones. **Virtual reality** input and output devices include headsets and special gloves that sense hand movement. (pp. 91–103)

☐ Data is stored in primary storage in binary representation, that is, as patterns of **binary digits** or **bits**, which are the digits 1 and 0. Characters are represented by using a code for each character. The common codes are **ASCII** and **EBCDIC**. Computers using different codes cannot communicate with each other without special hardware or software to convert between the codes. (pp. 103–106)

☐ Primary storage consists of many electronic circuits, each capable of storing one bit. The bits are organized into groups called **storage locations**. On most computers each storage locations is a **byte**, which is a group of bits capable of storing one character of data. The storage capacity of computers is measured in terms of **kilobytes** (thousands of bytes), **megabytes** (millions of bytes), **gigabytes** (billions of bytes), and **terabytes** (trillions of bytes). It is important that a computer have enough primary storage to store data and programs needed for current processing. (pp. 106–107)

☐ The central processing unit consists of the **arithmetic-logic unit** (**ALU**) and the **control unit**. The ALU performs arithmetic operations and makes logical comparisons. The control unit analyzes and executes instructions in a program. The instructions are in a basic form called **machine language**. Different computers use different types of machine language instructions, and so machine language programs for different computers may be incompatible. (pp. 107–112)

☐ Data is recorded on a magnetic disk by spots of magnetism representing bits along concentric circles on the disk's surface called **tracks**. A magnetic disk drive stores data on a disk by moving the read/write head at the end of the access arm to the appropriate track, and writing the data on the track as the disk rotates. A magnetic disk drive retrieves data from a disk by moving the read/write head to the appropriate track and reading the data recorded there as the disk rotates. Data can be retrieved in sequence from a series of tracks, which is called **sequential access**, or from a specific track not in sequence, which is called **random access**. Data is recorded on optical disk by small pits that represent bits recorded along a track on the disk's surface. The pits are created by a high-powered laser in an optical disk drive. Once the data is recorded, it cannot be changed because the pits cannot be erased. The data can be retrieved by sensing the pits with a low-powered laser in an optical disk drive. Data can be accessed sequentially or randomly on an optical disk. Data is recorded on magnetic tape by spots of magnetism representing bits recorded along tracks on the tape's surface. A magnetic tape drive stores data on a tape by moving the tape past a read/write head and writing the data on the tape. A tape drive retrieves data from a tape by moving the tape past a read/write head and reading the data recorded on the tape. Data can only be accessed sequentially on magnetic tape. (pp. 112–119)

Key Terms

Address (p. 106)
Arithmetic-Logic Unit (ALU) (p. 108)
ASCII (p. 105)
Backup Copy (p. 119)
Bar Code Scanner (p. 94)
Binary Digit (Bit) (p. 105)
Byte (p. 106)
CD-ROM (p. 116)
Chip (p. 104)
Compact Disk (CD) (p. 116)
Control Unit (p. 108)
CRT (p. 96)
Cursor (p.92)
Disk Pack (p. 113)
Dot-Matrix Printer (p. 99)
Draft-Quality Printer (p. 98)
EBCDIC (p. 105)
Erasable Optical Disk (p. 117)
Ergonomics (p. 91)
Flat Panel Screen (p. 97)
Gigabyte (G byte, GB) (p. 107)
Impact Printer (p. 97)

Ink-Jet Printer (p. 98)
Kilobyte (K byte, KB) (p. 107)
Laser Printer (p. 98)
Letter-Quality Printer (p. 98)
Line Printer (p. 98)
Machine Language (p. 108)
Magnetic Ink Character Recognition (MICR) (p. 94)
Magnetic Strip Reader (p. 94)
Massively Parallel Processing (p. 112)
Megabyte (M byte, MB) (p. 107)
Megahertz (MHz) (p. 109)
Microprocessor (p. 109)
Microsecond (p. 109)
Millisecond (p. 109)
Monitor (p. 96)
Multimedia (p. 101)
Multiprocessing (p. 112)
Nanosecond (p. 109)
Near-Letter-Quality Printer (p. 98)
Nonimpact Printer (p. 97)
Nonvolatile Storage (p. 104)

Page Printer (p. 98)
Parity Bit (p. 106)
Pen Input (p. 93)
Pixel (p. 95)
Plotter (p. 100)
RAID (p. 114)
Random Access Memory (RAM) (p. 104)
Random (Direct) Access (p. 115)
Read Only Memory (ROM) (p. 104)
Scanner (p. 94)
Screen Resolution (p. 96)
Sequential Access (p. 115)
Serial Printer (p. 98)
Storage Location (p. 106)
Terabyte (p. 107)
Touch Screen (p. 92)
Track (p. 112)
Trackball (p. 92)
Video Display Terminal (VDT) (p. 101)
Virtual Reality (p. 102)
Volatile Storage (p. 104)

Assignment Material

Review Questions

Fill-in Questions

1. Some keyboards are designed using principles from _____ to improve user comfort and reduce the risk of injury.
2. An alternative to a mouse is a(n) _____.
3. A device for recognizing the Universal Product Code or UPC on grocery merchandise is a(n) _____.
4. The technique used by banks to process checks is _____.
5. Character and graphic output are formed by patterns of _____ on a screen.
6. Two types of screens are _____ and _____.
7. The speed of serial printers is measured in _____. The speed of line printers is measured in _____. The speed of page printers is measured in _____.
8. A type of desktop page printer is a(n) _____.
9. A(n) _____ is a device for drawing graphic output on paper.
10. A piece of silicon containing electronic circuits is commonly called a(n) _____.
11. A bit is represented by a(n) _____ or a(n) _____.
12. An industry standard code for representing characters is _____. It uses _____

bits for each character. A code developed by IBM is _____. It uses _____ bits for each character.
13. A group of bits used to store one character is a(n) _____.
14. Each storage location in the computer's primary storage is identified by a unique number called a(n) _____.
15. A kilobyte is about _____ bytes. A megabyte is about _____ bytes. A gigabyte is about _____ bytes. A terabyte is about _____ bytes.
16. The basic language of a computer is _____.
17. A millisecond is _____ of a second. A microsecond is _____ of a second. A nanosecond is _____ of a second.
18. Concentric circles of bits on a magnetic disk are called _____.
19. Several magnetic disks stacked on top of each other with space between them is a(n) _____.
20. Data on a magnetic disk can be accessed _____ or _____.
21. A type of secondary storage on which data is stored and retrieved using a laser is _____.
22. Data on a magnetic tape can only be accessed _____.

Short-answer Questions

1. Explain why businesses need hardware in information systems.
2. What are two purposes of a pointing device?
3. Name two touch input devices.
4. What is meant by screen resolution?
5. Explain the difference between impact and nonimpact printers.
6. What are the three types of desktop printers in order from poorest- to best-quality print?
7. What are the two main types of high-volume printers?
8. What is a video display terminal, and what is it used for?
9. What special I/O devices are used for virtual reality?
10. Explain the difference between volatile and nonvolatile storage.
11. Explain the difference between RAM and ROM.
12. What do we mean when we say data is stored in binary representation in a computer?
13. What are the main units in the CPU, and what does each do?
14. What do we mean when we say two CPUs are compatible?

15. A computer salesperson tells you that one micro-computer has a 133 MHz CPU and another has a 200 MHz CPU. What does this mean?

16. What is parallel processing, and why is it used?

17. How is data recorded on a magnetic disk?

18. How does a magnetic disk drive store and retrieve data on a magnetic disk?

19. Explain the difference between sequential access and random access.

20. Can data on an optical disk be changed? Explain.

21. How is data recorded on a magnetic tape?

22. How does a tape drive store and retrieve data on a magnetic tape?

Discussion Questions

1. Many colleges and universities use a telephone system for course registration. What input and output devices does a student use with this system? What input and output devices does the college's or university's administration use?

2. Computer speed and storage capacity increase with each new model. Why do you think this is true?

3. How do the components other than the CPU affect the speed of a computer?

4. Why do computers often have several different forms of secondary storage?

5. An international business has decided to purchase the same IBM clones for all its offices around the world. What problems could this decision create?

6. Assume that the business you work for has decided not to get ergonomically designed keyboards for its data entry clerks who use a keyboard up to eight hours per day. Instead, the business has decided to pay medical bills for those employees who suffer repetitive strain injuries, arguing that this approach will be less expensive. What ethical issues does this decision raise?

Problem-solving Projects

1. If you are using a computer for a class or have access to one, find out everything you can about it. What input and output devices does it have? How much primary storage capacity does it have? What CPU does it use? What forms of secondary storage does it have? Write a brief description of the computer. Use word processing software to prepare your answer.

2. The total cost of a printer includes not only the purchase price but also the cost of operation. Operating costs include the cost of paper, ribbons, ink, and so on. Set up a spreadsheet to determine the total cost and the cost per printed page of an ink-jet, laser, and dot-matrix printer. Include in your spreadsheet the purchase price and the operating costs. Assume that the printer will have a useful life of three years and that you can sell it for 25 percent of its purchase price after three years. Assume that you print an average of 5,000 pages per year. Use the following data in the spreadsheet or get real data for printers from a computer store.

	Ink-jet	Laser	Dot-matrix
Purchase price	$220	$450	$180
Paper	$2/500 pages	$2/500 pages	$15/2500 pages
Ribbon/Ink	$30/1000 pages	$80/3000 pages	$12/2500 pages

3. New models of microprocessors are introduced regularly. Using spreadsheet or word processing software, set up a table giving information about microprocessors. Have columns for the manufacturer, model, clock speed, computers in which the microprocessor is used, and any other information you wish to include. Use the Internet to research current microprocessors and include information in your table about them. As new models are introduced, add information about them to your table.

4. Use the Internet to get information about the computers produced by several minicomputer and mainframe computer manufacturers. Try to find information from non-U.S. companies as well as U.S. companies. Write a report, using word processing software, summarizing what you found.

5. Personal computers sold at retail stores need to have characteristics that appeal to consumers. Market research is often used to gather information about consumer preference. Some questions that might be asked in a questionnaire about consumer taste in computers are:

- Do you prefer computers that are putty (light beige) or black in color?
- Do you prefer a standard keyboard or an ergonomic keyboard?
- Do you prefer a mouse or a trackball?
- Do you prefer speakers that are attached to the monitor or separate from the monitor?
- Do you prefer a monitor that is separate from the CPU box or combined with the CPU box?

Prepare a questionnaire based on these questions and others that you think of using a word processing software. Include a no preference answer for each question. Give the questionnaire to at least 15 people. (You might want to have everyone in your class complete the questionnaire.) Then use a spreadsheet to analyze the results. Enter the response from the questionnaires into the spreadsheet. For each question, compute and plot on a graph the response percentages. For example, for the first question, compute and graph the percent of people who prefer putty, the percent who prefer black, and the percent who have no preference.

Real-world Case

United Parcel Service

United Stationer Inc., an office products wholesaler, ships thousands of goods to its 20,000 dealers and their customers nationwide. But the wholesaler's dealers can be a jittery lot. Hundreds of them call United Stationers every day to see if clients received their shipments.

That's why United Stationers has put in place an automated shipping tool, UPS OnLine—from United Parcel Service—to help calm dealers' nerves. UPS OnLine allows customers like United Stationers to ask for pickups and track their shipments. It also helps UPS clients customize record-keeping and reports, print bar-coded address labels, review rate tables, and order supplies.

The new technology—part of a broad customer-automation initiative at UPS—provides customers with advanced shipment notification, daily shipment summaries, customer-to-UPS e-mail services, and automatic customs documentation for overseas deliveries. Eventually, it will permit UPS, the world's largest shipper, to bill customers automatically. "Carriers today are expected not only to pick up shipments, but also to provide information on those shipments," said Ed Brockwell, vice-president of strategic accounts for UPS in Atlanta.

UPS OnLine rivals Federal Express' Powership, a customer-automation system unveiled in 1987. Ongoing efforts by UPS, FedEx, DHL Worldwide Express, and Airborne Express, among others, represent a shift in the highly competitive package-delivery business from merely shipping goods to also providing information about these shipments.

For instance, until United Stationers installed UPS OnLine, customer representatives needed hours to verify the receipt of a shipment. The wholesaler was among the first to use the service. Eventually, Dudley Land, vice-president of customer automation and information at UPS, says data on about 85 percent of the parcels the company handles daily will be captured electronically.

UPS plans to rely on a public network to establish links with customers, but the system may use the Internet as its communications medium.

Since 1994, UPS has spent $100 million annually on customer-automation projects, primarily UPS OnLine. It expects to spend the same amount over the next few years. UPS OnLine lets customers tap into UPS's IBM DB2 databases to pull down shipment information in 30 seconds or less from several IBM and Hitachi Data Systems mainframes through an advanced communications protocol using IBM AS/400 front-end computers. A custom-built customer-message server routes the data to the appropriate database.

Eventually, UPS OnLine will be available for three types of customer front ends—smart phones, PCs, and mainframes. The PC front end uses Microsoft Windows and a Gupta SQLBase relational database management system. UPS plans to supply key large-volume customers with a free turnkey system—a preconfigured PC, laser printer, modem, and package scale. UPS will make a free software-only system available to lower-volume customers.

At United Stationers, UPS OnLine links with the wholesaler's own order-entry system, which operates on an Amdahl mainframe. The integrated system lets workers using United Stationers' dumb terminals or PCs access United Stationers' invoice numbers, which can be cross-referenced with UPS tracking numbers. "From our standpoint, both [our and UPS's] systems have become one," said Steve Schwarz, and executive vice-president at United Stationers.

UPS also developed UPS OnLine for Philips Electronics and Forval smart phones. Both types of smart phones use Intel-compatible microprocessors. UPS OnLine software is embedded in a PC Card, which allows memory to be retained when power to the phone is turned off.

To run the UPS OnLine systems, UPS dedicates two mainframes, one each at data centers in Mahwah, N.J., and Alpharetta, Ga., that back each other up in the event of a failure. Also, UPS plans to more than double its 3.5 terabytes of network storage capacity, adding 4.5 terabytes of storage.

UPS anticipates that the system will produce a deluge of customer data traffic. "The amount of customer access in the next five years will be the equivalent of all network activity that exists right now," said R.J. Montouro, manager of telecommunications application support at UPS.

There's little doubt that the entire shipping industry is pushing automation for its customers. The move is fueled because so many enterprises want just-in-time delivery and little or no inventory. "Some customers won't accept a package until they're pre-alerted of its arrival," said UPS's Land.

Adds James Cook, an editor at *Traffic Management*, a logistics trade publication in Newton, Mass.: "It's most important to deliver the right product at the right time to the right customer. That's why UPS and FedEx are pouring big bucks into information technology."

In a business where customer information is becoming almost as critical as delivery itself, investments of hundreds of millions of dollars on customer automation systems are becoming a competitive necessity.

Questions

1. What type of computers are used by UPS OnLine?

2. How can customers connect to UPS OnLine?

3. What computer hardware is used by United Stationers to link with UPS OnLine? What input and output devices are used by users at United Stationers?

4. How much secondary storage capacity will UPS eventually have with OnLine?

5. What information does OnLine provide to UPS customers?

Source: Eric R. Chabrow, "Data is Part of the Package," *Information Week*, December 25, 1995, pp. 43-44.

5 Information System Software

Chapter Outline

The Need for Software in Information Systems   (p. 126)
Application Software   (p. 126)
    Individual Application Software   (p. 127)
    Workgroup Application Software   (p. 128)
    Organizational Application Software   (p. 128)
    Interorganizational Application Software   (p. 129)
System Software   (p. 130)
    Operating System Concepts   (p. 130)
    Common Operating Systems   (p. 135)
    Other System Software   (p. 139)
Software Development   (p. 139)
    Programming Language Concepts   (p. 139)
    Traditional Programming Languages   (p. 143)
    Object-oriented Programming Languages   (p. 146)
    Internet Programming Languages   (p. 148)

Learning Objectives

After completing this chapter, you should be able to:

☐ 1. Explain why businesses need software in information systems.

☐ 2. Identify the common application software used in information systems.

☐ 3. Describe some ways that users can tell an operating system what to do.

☐ 4. Describe some of the characteristics that distinguish operating systems.

☐ 5. Explain the main differences between the five types or generations of programming languages.

☐ 6. Explain the difference between object-oriented programming and traditional programming, and identify one traditional and one object-oriented programming language.

☐ 7. Identify languages that are used to create pages and applications on the World Wide Web of the Internet.

T he software component of an information system consists of all the programs used in the system. Software is needed because hardware cannot function without it; computers and computer-controlled equipment must have programs to tell them what to do. Information system software tells the hardware in the system how to perform the functions required of the system.

This chapter examines computer software that is used in information systems, including application software and system software. This chapter also looks at how software is developed.

The Need for Software in Information Systems

Businesses need both application software and system software in information systems. They need *application software* to provide specific system functions. Recall from Chapter 1 that an information system has four main functions: the *input function*, the *storage function*, the *processing function*, and the *output function*. (Refer to Fig. 1.5 for a review of information system functions.) The input function accepts data from outside the system; the storage function stores and retrieves data in the system; the processing function manipulates data within the system; and the output function produces the results of processing for use outside the system. The application software of an information system tells the hardware how to perform these functions.

Businesses also need *system software* in information systems so that computers will be easy to use. Recall from Chapter 3 that system software is the basic software that makes computers usable. An example of system software is an *operating system*, which controls the basic operation of computer hardware. An operating system is needed because without it the computer would require very complex procedures to perform even simple tasks. Other system software besides an operating system is also needed, including communications software and software to help develop programs.

The operating system software together with the hardware creates the environment, or platform, upon which the application software of an information system runs. For example, a personal computer with a specific operating system is one platform, and a network of computers with their operating systems is a different platform. The application software for these two platforms would be different because the hardware and the operating systems are different.

A business needs to select the platform to be used for its information systems. Personal computers with their operating systems, multiple-user computers with their operating systems, and networked computers with their operating systems are all different platforms with different characteristics. The choice of platform and the specific hardware and system software selected affects the form that the application software takes and the functioning of the information system.

Application Software

Application software is the software that performs the functions of an information system. The user interacts with the application software when entering input into an application program and receiving output from the program. The application program also performs the processing and storage functions required by the information system.

Since most of this book is devoted to information systems and the application software used in these systems, this section just summarizes the common application software. Figure 5.1 lists some of the common application software used in businesses.

Individual Application Software

The application software with which many users are most familiar is individual or personal application software, that is, software used by a single person for an individual purpose. This type of software is usually used on a personal computer system, which may or may not be connected to a network.

Word processing software is probably the most widely used individual application software. With word processing software, a user can enter the text of a document—such as a letter or report—into the computer, make changes in the document, and print one or more copies of the document. The user can save the document in secondary storage and return to it in the future, perhaps to make changes and print another copy.

After word processing software, spreadsheet software is perhaps the most widely used individual application software. With spreadsheet software, the user can create an *electronic spreadsheet*, which is a computerized arrangement, in rows and columns, of data and formulas for calculating spreadsheet values. The electronic spreadsheet can be used to analyze data such as budgets and income projections. The

FIGURE 5.1

Common application software

INDIVIDUAL APPLICATION SOFTWARE
Word processing software
Spreadsheet software
Database software
Browser

WORKGROUP APPLICATION SOFTWARE
Electronic messaging software
Information sharing software
Electronic conferencing software

ORGANIZATIONAL APPLICATION SOFTWARE
Business operations support software
Management decision support software

INTERORGANIZATIONAL APPLICATION SOFTWARE
Electronic data interchange software

user can change values or formulas in the spreadsheet to see the effect of the change, and can print copies of the spreadsheet for presentation to others.

Database software is another common type of individual application software. With database software, the user can store large amounts of data in a database in secondary storage, change data in the database when necessary, and retrieve data from the database to find useful information. For example, a salesperson can store customer data in a database; modify the data when information about a customer, such as the phone number, changes; and retrieve data about a customer, such as when the last sales contact was made and what was purchased.

Another common type of software used for individual applications is a browser. With a browser, a user can view screens called pages on the World Wide Web of the Internet, and go from one page to another. This capability allows a user easy access to information on the Web.

Although there are other types of individual application software, word processing, spreadsheet, database, and browser software are the most common. The principal benefit of individual application software is that it helps people improve their productivity. Chapter 8 discusses personal productivity and individual application software in detail.

Workgroup Application Software

Users often work in groups and use workgroup application software called groupware. This type of software allows users to collaborate with each other without having to be in the same place at the same time. Groupware is used on networked computer systems.

The most widely used form of groupware is e-mail software, which allows a user to send letters and memos electronically to other users. E-mail software is a type of electronic messaging software. In general, electronic messaging software provides e-mail capabilities plus other capabilities such as the ability to send work assignments or reminder notes to others.

Another type of groupware is information sharing software. With this type of software, users in a group can share ideas by putting notes and comments in a common database that can be viewed by other users. This approach is not the same as using e-mail, in which a message is sent from one person to another, but is more like using a bulletin board which all users can view.

A third type of groupware is electronic conferencing software, which lets users talk to and see each other while also viewing a common document on a computer screen. (See Fig. 5.2.) This type of software requires a computer with a microphone, speakers, and a video camera, as well as special software. Electronic conferencing is very useful when group members are located some distance apart.

There are a number of other types of groupware but, in general, all workgroup application software is designed to encourage collaboration between group members. Chapter 9 discusses group collaboration and workgroup application software in detail.

Organizational Application Software

Much application software used in a business is designed to provide applications that affect more than an individual or a workgroup. The most all-encompassing information systems in a business use such organizational application software. This type of software is used on networked computer systems or multiple-user computer systems.

FIGURE 5.2

Electronic
conferencing

Some organizational application software is designed to support the day-to-day operations of a business. This type of software, which usually processes basic business transactions such as the sale of products or the purchase of items for inventory, increases the efficiency of business operations. Chapter 10 discusses business operations and the organizational application software used in basic operations.

Other organizational application software supports management decision making in a business. This type of software supplies information to managers to help in decision making. It can also provide ways of analyzing data used in decision making, special support for the highest level of decision making in a business, and expert advice to decision makers. Chapter 11 discusses management decision making and the organizational application software used in decision making.

Interorganizational Application Software

Transactions between two businesses can often be done electronically using interorganizational application software. This type of software, which allows one business's computer to transmit data to another business's computer, is used on networks that operate between two or more businesses.

An example of interorganizational application software is *electronic data interchange* or *EDI* software. This type of software lets businesses electronically exchange data about business transactions, such as a request to purchase items or a bill for items purchased. The business does not have to send a paper copy of the request or bill to another business; computers and networks, with the necessary interorganizational application software, provide all the capabilities needed.

Interorganizational application software can give a business an advantage over another business by reducing costs and increasing transaction speed. Other types of application software, including those used in organizational and international applications, can impact a business in a similar way. Chapter 12 discusses the types of application software that can have such an impact, including interorganizational application software.

System Software

Application software, which performs the functions of the information system needed by the user, will not work without system software. System software provides capabilities that make computers usable.

The most important system software is the operating system because without it computers would be extremely difficult to use. This section takes a look at operating systems in detail and describes other types of system software.

Operating System Concepts

An operating system is a group of programs that manages the operation of the computer. The operating system controls the computer whenever another program, such as another system program or an application program, is not executing. As soon as one program stops executing, the operating system takes control of the computer. It then begins execution of the next program. During the execution of a program, parts of the operating system may be used by the program to perform certain functions.

Figure 5.3 illustrates the role of the operating system in a series of layers. The inner layer is the hardware. Around this layer is the operating system, which communicates with the hardware and manages its operation. If the operating system is in control of the computer, the user can communicate directly with it to perform various functions, as shown in the top half of Fig. 5.3. For example, if the user wishes to display the contents of a disk, the user gives the operating system an instruction to do so. Then the operating system tells the hardware what to do to display the disk contents. If an application program is executing, the user communicates with that program, as shown in the bottom half of Fig. 5.3. The application program may use parts of the operating system to perform certain functions. For example, if the user wants an application program to print certain output, the user tells the program to do so. Then the program gives the operating system an instruction to print, which in turn tells the hardware what to do to print the output.

FIGURE 5.3

The role of an operating system

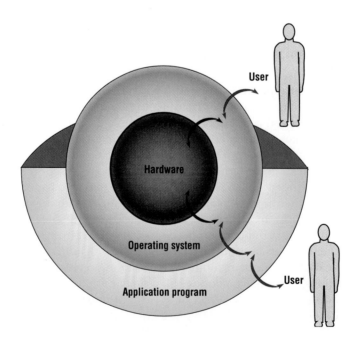

Functions of an Operating System.   An operating system has three main functions: process management, resource management, and data management. To understand the first function, *process management*, think of the execution of a program as a process that the computer performs. The operating system keeps track of all processes—that is, all program executions. It schedules programs for execution, starts the execution of programs when needed, and monitors the execution of a program in case any errors occur.

The second main function of an operating system is *resource management*. A computer has many resources, including primary storage, input and output devices, and secondary storage. The operating system assigns the required resources to each process. The operating system determines where in primary storage programs and data will be stored, what input and output devices will be used by the program, and where in secondary storage program and data files will be stored.

The final main function of an operating system is *data management*. The operating system handles the movement of data between the main components of the computer. Any time input data is entered or output data is produced, a part of the operating system controls the transfer of the data between primary storage and the appropriate input or output device. Any transfer of data between primary storage and a data file in secondary storage is handled by another part of the operating system.

Organization of an Operating System.   An operating system is usually made up of several programs. One program in the operating system is stored in a section of primary storage whenever the computer is running. Depending on the operating system, this program is called the *supervisor, monitor, executive, kernel,* or *command processor.* It is the part of the operating system that controls the computer when another program (such as an application program) is not executing.

The part of primary storage not occupied by the supervisor is used to store one or more other programs. To start the execution of a program, the supervisor passes the control of the computer to the program in primary storage. (See Fig. 5.4a.) When the program finishes executing, it returns control of the computer to the supervisor. Then the supervisor can start the execution of another program by passing the control of the computer to that program. (See Fig. 5.4b.) This process continues for all the programs to be executed.

The supervisor brings programs into primary storage when they are needed. Usually, nonexecuting programs are stored in secondary storage. When a program is needed, the supervisor *loads* it into primary storage. Once the supervisor has loaded the program, it can start the execution of the program.

FIGURE 5.4

Operating system control of the execution of programs

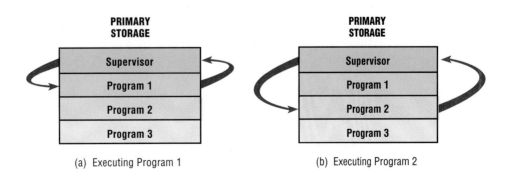

(a) Executing Program 1   (b) Executing Program 2

An operating system contains other programs besides the supervisor. These programs are stored in secondary storage and loaded into primary storage by the supervisor when they are needed. They perform functions that are used less frequently than those of the supervisor. An example is a program that copies the contents of one disk to another disk. Because this program is not often used, it is stored in secondary storage and loaded only when it is needed.

Using an Operating System.   Although the supervisor is in primary storage whenever the computer is running, it, as well as everything else in primary storage, is lost when the computer is turned off. Thus, when the computer is turned on again there is nothing in primary storage, including a program to load the supervisor. How, then, does the supervisor get into primary storage when the computer is turned on?

The process of loading the supervisor into primary storage is called booting; someone "boots the computer" or the computer "boots up." The supervisor is stored permanently in secondary storage. A special program for loading the supervisor into primary storage is stored in ROM, which as you know from Chapter 4 is nonvolatile, read-only memory. When the switch for the computer is turned on, a circuit is activated that causes the program in ROM to execute. This program then loads the supervisor into primary storage and transfers control of the computer to it.

A user can use a personal computer's operating system right after the computer has been started. With multiple-user computers, however, a user normally has to go through a process called *logging in* before using the operating system. This process, which connects the user's terminal to the operating system, is needed because large computers are used by more than one person at a time, and the operating system must have a way of distinguishing the users. After using the computer, the user must disconnect his or her terminal by following a procedure called *logging out*. With networks, a procedure similar to logging in may be necessary to connect a computer to the network.

When using an operating system, the user needs to be able to tell it what to do. The way this is accomplished depends on the user interface, which is the link between the user and the software. (See Fig. 5.5.) Some operating systems have a user interface in which the user keys in words or phrases called commands after a prompt on the screen, which is a word or symbol indicating that the software is ready for the next input. Many operating systems have a user interface in which the user selects a command from a list or menu shown on the screen by pointing at it with a mouse and then clicking the mouse. The user interface of most operating systems shows some commands on the screen by using small pictures called icons, which the user selects by pointing at an icon with a mouse and then clicking the mouse. Icons or other symbols enclosed in shapes that look like keys on a keyboard are often called buttons. In all cases, the supervisor interprets the command and performs the requested function for the user.

Operating systems, as well as other software, that use buttons, icons, menus, and other features are said to have a graphical user interface or GUI. (See Fig. 5.6) The user uses the system through the GUI by selecting icons and menu options, and by providing input requested by the system in small boxes called dialog boxes. A GUI is also divided into sections, surrounded by borders, called windows within which different functions can be performed. The user can change the size and position of windows, and create (open) new windows and delete (close) old ones. Using windows allows the user to customize the graphical user interface.

Characteristics of Operating Systems.   Not all operating systems are alike. Some of the characteristics that distinguish operating systems are discussed here.

FIGURE 5.5

Operating system user interfaces

Prompt

Buttons

Menu

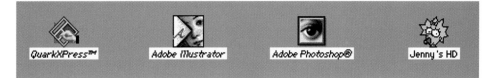

Icons

FIGURE 5.6

A graphical user interface

Single- versus Multitasking.　　Some operating systems allow only one program to be executed at a time. The operating system will not begin the execution of the next program until the current program is finished. You can think of this process as *single-tasking* because only one task (program) is done at a time. With a single-tasking operating system only one program (and the supervisor) is in primary storage. (See Fig. 5.7a.)

Other operating systems allow __multitasking__, which means that more than one program can execute at a time. With these operating systems all programs being executed are in primary storage. (See Fig. 5.7b.) (If the operating system uses virtual memory, which is discussed below, this may not be entirely true.) Although the CPU can execute instructions from only one program at a time, the operating system can jump from one program to the next without waiting for the first program to finish. Thus, the computer can execute a few instructions in the first program, then a few instructions in the second program, then some in the third program, and so forth.

One reason that multitasking is used is that a user often wants to go from one program to another without losing the work done by the first program. A user may begin executing one program, then decide to execute another program, and later go back to the first program. Multitasking is accomplished in this situation by letting the user interrupt the execution of a program whenever he or she wants to execute another program, usually by pressing certain keys on the keyboard or by selecting the other program with the mouse. The operating system remembers where the first program was interrupted so that the user can go back to where he or she left off in that program and continue execution.

Another reason multitasking is used is that programs often have to wait for some other process to take place in the computer. For example, a program may have to wait for a user to enter input data or for output to be printed. During the wait, another program can be executing. Multitasking in this case is accomplished by giving each program a priority level. When a program with a higher priority has to wait for some other process such as input or output, the operating system executes a lower-priority program. When the higher-priority program needs to execute, however, the operating system interrupts the lower-priority program and gives control back to the higher-priority program.

Single- versus Multiple-user.　　Some operating systems allow only one user to use the computer at a time; they are *single-user operating systems.* A user can decide which program he or she wants to execute, and no other users can execute a program at the same time. These operating systems may allow the user to execute only one program at a time or may be multitasking systems so the user can have several programs executing simultaneously.

Other operating systems allow more than one user to use the computer at a time; they are *multiple-user operating systems.* These operating systems are multitasking

FIGURE 5.7

Single-tasking versus multitasking

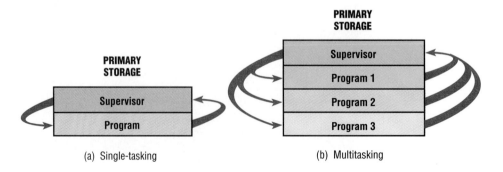

(a) Single-tasking

(b) Multitasking

because each user could be executing a different program. A technique that is used with multiple-user operating systems is called time-sharing. With this technique the operating system allows each user a small amount of time to execute his or her program before going on to the next user. After all users have had a small amount of time to execute, the computer returns to the first user. This process is accomplished so fast, however, that the user probably never knows that his or her program was not executing for a period of time.

Batch versus Interactive.   Early operating systems were *batch operating systems*, which meant that a program and its data had to be prepared in a batch before it could be processed on the computer. The computer executed the first program and processed all its data in a batch, then went to the next program and processed its data, and so on. These operating systems did not allow the user to enter data as the program executed.

Current systems are *interactive operating systems*, which means they allow interaction with the users as programs execute. A user can enter input data and get the results of processing that data before going on to the next input. Interactive operating systems also allow programs and data to be prepared in a batch and processed without user interaction. Thus, current operating systems provide both interactive and batch processing.

When an operating system interacts with multiple users, each user sometimes has to wait a few seconds for a response. Some systems, called *real-time operating systems*, respond immediately to high-priority requests for processing. The "users" of these operating systems usually are machines or equipment that must get a response immediately—that is, in "real time." For example, an operating system for a computer that controls equipment monitoring patients in an intensive-care unit of a hospital must respond immediately to any abnormal change in a patient's condition.

Real versus Virtual Memory.   One of the limitations of computers is the amount of primary storage available for storing programs. A program may be too large for primary storage, or several programs that need to be in primary storage at one time may require more space than is available. Some operating systems can only execute programs that can fit into the available primary storage or *real memory*. Other operating systems, however, can execute programs that are too big for primary storage by using secondary storage to make the computer appear as if it has more memory than the real memory. The memory the computer appears to have with these operating systems is called virtual memory. For example, a computer may have real memory of 32 megabytes and virtual memory of 128 megabytes. Thus, programs larger than 32 megabytes can be executed. If the operating system is multitasking, several programs that together require more than 32 megabytes can be executed.

A virtual-memory operating system executes large programs by dividing the program into parts in secondary storage and loading into primary storage only one part at a time. (See Fig. 5.8.) When a part of the program that is not in primary storage is needed, the operating system loads it from secondary storage, replacing another part of the program already in primary storage. This process is handled automatically by the operating system without the user knowing it is going on. The disadvantage of virtual memory is that execution of the program will be slower because parts of the program must be loaded into primary storage when they are needed.

Common Operating Systems

Many operating systems are currently in use. For some computers, only one operating system is available, but for many computers several different operating systems can be used.

FIGURE 5.8

Virtual memory

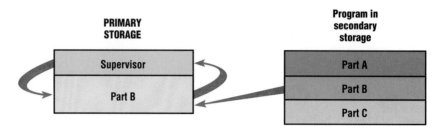

Load and execute Part A of program

Load and execute Part B of program

Personal Computer Operating Systems. Several common operating systems for personal computer systems are available. Because personal computers are used by one person at a time, they are all single-user operating systems. Other characteristics of these operating systems vary, however.

Windows. Windows refers to one of several programs from Microsoft for IBM personal computers and clones. The first versions of Windows (up to version 3.1) were not operating systems, but rather <u>operating environments</u>, which are programs that provide a special interface between the user and the operating system. These versions of Windows required an older operating system called DOS. DOS was a single-tasking, real-memory operating system which the user controlled by entering commands after a prompt. Thus, it was difficult to use. The first versions of Windows provided a graphical user interface for DOS so that the operating system was easier to use. They also made available a simple form of multitasking, not available with DOS, that allowed the user to switch between programs.

The most recent version of Windows, called Windows 95, is a complete operating system and does not require DOS. It has a different graphical user interface than previous versions of Windows. It also provides a more sophisticated form of multitasking than was available previously, but it is still a real-memory operating system.

Another version of Windows is called Windows NT Workstation. It is a sophisticated operating system designed for powerful microcomputers connected in a network. It provides multitasking and virtual-memory capabilities. Windows NT is not normally used on stand-alone personal computers, that is, those not connected to a network.

OS/2. OS/2 is an operating system from IBM for IBM personal computers and clones. It has an operating environment that provides a graphical user interface like

Windows. OS/2 has multitasking capabilities and is a virtual-memory operating system. Some large businesses that have IBM mainframe computers use OS/2 for their personal computers.

Mac OS. The operating system for the Apple Macintosh is sometimes called System followed by a number, such as System 7, but it is also referred to as Mac OS. The operating system provides a graphical user interface like Windows. It has a simple form of multitasking so that a user can switch from one program to another. It also provides virtual-memory capability.

UNIX. Some powerful microcomputers use an operating system called UNIX. This operating system was developed for minicomputers in the early 1970s by Bell Laboratories. Since its original development, it has undergone many revisions. Today, versions of UNIX are available for some microcomputers.

UNIX is a sophisticated multitasking, virtual-memory operating system. It also is a multiple-user operating system, although on personal computers it is only used by a single user. The user can, however, have multiple programs executing at the same time and can execute programs larger than primary storage. UNIX has a number of special features, but some people find it difficult to use.

Multiple-user Computer Operating Systems. The first operating systems for large computers were single-tasking, batch, real-memory systems. As computers became more powerful, their operating systems became more sophisticated. Today, multiple-user computers such as minicomputers and mainframe computers use operating systems that are multitasking, time-sharing, interactive, virtual-memory systems. These operating systems have many more features than personal computer operating systems have. For example, they often have complex security features to prevent unauthorized use of the computer. They are also more complex to use than personal computer operating systems. Two examples are MVS (Multiple Virtual Storage) for IBM mainframe computers and VMS (Virtual-Memory System) for DEC minicomputers.

Most operating systems for minicomputers and mainframe computers, such as those listed in the previous paragraph, are designed to be used on a specific computer. For example, MVS can be used only on IBM mainframe computers. Versions of UNIX, however, are available for many minicomputers and mainframe computers. As discussed earlier, UNIX is also available for some microcomputers. It is a multiple-user, multitasking, virtual-memory operating system.

Networked Computer Operating Systems. Computers connected to a network require special operating systems to handle communications between them. Recall from Chapter 3 that in a network, computers used by end-users are called *clients* and computers that provide service to many clients in the network are called *servers*. Client computers can use any of the personal computer operating systems discussed previously: Windows 95, Windows NT Workstation, OS/2, Mac OS, and UNIX.

Server computers, however, require special operating systems to manage multiple clients and to provide communication between clients and server computers. Often, this type of operating system is called a network operating system or NOS. An example is Windows NT Server, which is like Windows NT Workstation except it has the necessary features for a server. Another example is NetWare from Novell. UNIX is also used as the operating system on a server. In general, network operating systems provide capabilities for handling significant software malfunctions and security features to prevent unauthorized use of the network.

Operating System Choices at Gap, LG&E Energy, and Chevron

There is no one obvious choice for the operating systems used on computers in a network. Gap, LG&E Energy, and Chevron took three different approaches.

WINDOWS NT WORKSTATION DESKTOPS, UNIX SERVERS

For Phil Wilkerson, director of technical architecture at Gap, Inc., in San Bruno, Calif., choosing when to use NT or UNIX is almost a "no-brainer," he said. "The industry's already stood up and decided which way they're going to go," he said. "It's a forced march."

For the retailer's 2,500 desktop PCs, the march is from OS/2 to Windows NT Workstation. "Vendors . . . are going toward the [newer] Windows world" on the client, Wilkerson said.

Wilkerson said he chose NT Workstation over Windows 95 because it suffers fewer time-wasting system crashes. "Our commitment to our business partners is that we have stable machines," he said. In addition, he gets the Windows 95 interface with the current version of NT.

On the application server side, Gap is on another forced march—to UNIX. "We have a fairly large, multiple-gigabyte database . . . ," Wilkerson said. "UNIX was an attractive option because its scalability and performance were proven."

Again, key server-side vendors drove the choice. Those vendors "have more experience in the UNIX environment," Wilkerson said.

WINDOWS NT WORKSTATION DESKTOPS, WINDOWS NT SERVERS

Ray Palazzo, a member of the Advanced Technology Group at LG&E Energy Corp. in Louisville, Ky., said there are plenty of holes in Windows NT.

On the client side, "we're waiting for NT to deliver some basic features" already in Windows 95, Palazzo said. On the server, NT still lacks features now offered by Novell's NetWare, he said.

So what is LG&E choosing for its long-term operating system? Windows NT, for virtually all its 1,600 clients and 80 servers.

Palazzo said he has faith that Microsoft will eventually fix NT's problems.

But "the biggest driving factor for it being our strategic direction is the sheer momentum" of support for NT from application and tool vendors, Palazzo said.

More than 90 percent of LG&E's desktops still run Windows 95. The utility will move to NT Workstations during the next few years as Microsoft adds to it the features Palazzo needs. LG&E is further along the migration on the server, with 55 of 90 servers running Windows NT.

"NT is very cost-effective" because, for most applications the utility needs, NT can run on comparatively low-cost Intel-based servers, Palazzo said.

WINDOWS 95 CLIENTS, WINDOWS NT SERVERS

The IS arm of Chevron Corp. is trying to cut costs and improve service to its 44,000 internal customers. With that many users and 1,500 servers to support, this means sticking to standards.

On the client, Chevron is going with Windows 95 instead of NT because of Windows 95's compatibility with older DOS and Windows applications, said Michael Wolfe, a network software engineer at Chevron Information Technology Co., in San Ramon, Calif.

Although NT Workstation was a tempting choice, "there's probably not enough time to go through all the application integration and certification issues [we would] have to face with Windows NT," Wolfe said.

As part of its long-term strategy, Chevron chose Windows NT Server as its network operating system over NetWare. Although very close, the decision tipped to NT because of "intangibles," such as market momentum. UNIX wasn't considered for low-end application servers because of its higher hardware and software cost, Wolfe said.

QUESTIONS

1. What technical reasons influenced Gap in the selection of operating systems?
2. What external factor influenced LG&E in the selection of operating systems?
3. What factors influenced Chevron in the selection of operating systems?

WEB SITES

Gap: www.gap.com

LG&E: www.lgeenergy.com

Chevron: www.chevron.com

Source: Robert L. Scheier, "How does Windows NT fit in to your company?", *Computerworld*, March 24, 1997, p. 82.

Other System Software

Operating systems are just one type of system software. Several other types are also used. One type is <u>utility programs</u>, which perform common functions. Examples are a *sort utility*, which rearranges data in a file into a specified order, and a *merge utility*, which merges two files into one. Other utility programs are a *print utility* for printing the contents of a file and a *copy utility* for copying data from one device to another, such as from a disk to a tape. Sometimes utility programs are included with the operating system. Businesses use utility programs because these programs make it easy to perform common processing functions on a computer.

Other system software includes *communication software*, which is used for communication between computers (discussed in Chapter 6), and *database management systems*, which are used for managing databases (described in Chapter 7). Finally, some system software is used to help develop programs. This software is discussed in the next section.

Software Development

Software is developed by people called <u>programmers</u> who prepare the instructions in computer programs. The process they go through, called <u>programming</u>, involves a number of steps, including writing the instructions in a form that a computer can understand. The form that the instructions take depends on the <u>programming language</u>, which is a set of rules for preparing a computer program. This section takes a look at common programming languages used to develop application and system software.

Programming Language Concepts

What is a programming language? Why are there many programming languages? How do you select a programming language? What are the types of programming languages? These are common questions about programming languages which we answer here.

What Is a Programming Language?   English is a natural language. It has words, symbols, and a set of grammatical rules for combining the words and symbols into sentences. When you form a grammatically correct sentence, it means something. You can make grammatical errors in a sentence however, and a person still may be able to understand it.

A programming language is like a natural language in many ways. It has words, symbols, and rules of grammar. The grammatical rules are called the *syntax* of the language. A programmer forms an instruction by combining the words and symbols according to the syntax rules. The instruction formed by the programmer has some meaning; that is, it tells the computer to do something.

Unlike a natural language, if a programmer makes an error in writing an instruction in a programming language, the instruction will not mean anything; the computer will not be able to understand it. To write a program, a programmer must know the syntax rules of the language he or she is using. If the programmer does not abide by these rules, the program will have errors and the computer will not be able to execute it.

Each programming language has a different set of syntax rules. When a new language is invented, the designer of the language determines its syntax rules and the meaning of each instruction. To use a new language, a programmer must learn the syntax and meaning of each instruction.

Why Are There Many Programming Languages?   There are two answers to this question. First, programming languages have evolved over time as researchers have found better ways of designing them. The first languages were developed in the 1950s and, by today's standards, were poorly designed. Today, researchers know much more about what makes a good language, so current languages are quite a bit different from the early languages.

Second, different programming languages are designed for different types of programs. Some languages are designed for writing system programs and some for application programs. In addition, there are two major types of application programs: business application programs, which are used in information systems for business data processing, and scientific application programs, which are used to solve problems in science and engineering. Some languages are designed for business application programs and some for scientific application programs. Because a computer can be used for many types of programs, there are many programming languages.

How Does a Person Select a Programming Language?   Several factors must be considered when selecting a programming language for a particular program. One factor is whether the language is designed for the type of program that needs to be written. Different languages are appropriate for different types of programs. Another factor is the availability of languages on the computer being used. Not all languages can be used on all computers. A third factor is the availability of trained programmers to write and maintain the programs using the language. Some languages, although excellent for certain programs, are known by so few programmers that it may be very difficult to find someone qualified to write or modify the program. Another factor to consider is the ease of writing programs in the language. Writing programs in some languages is easier and takes less time than in others. The last factor in selecting a programming language is the efficiency of the program written in the language. Some languages produce programs that are faster and take less primary storage space than programs in other languages.

What Are the Types of Programming Languages?   Programming languages have evolved over time. As a result, languages fall into five generations.

Machine Languages (first generation).   Chapter 4 discussed machine language, which is the basic language of a computer. When computers were first invented, this was the only type of language available for them. Hence, machine language forms the first generation of programming languages.

A machine language instruction consists of an *operation code* for operations such as addition and subtraction, and one or more *operands* that identify data to be processed. Instructions are represented in a binary form, so they appear as strings of 1s and 0s. For example, Fig. 5.9 shows a machine language instruction to add one number to another number.

Each type of computer has its own machine language that may be different from the machine language of other types of computers. Hence, programs written

FIGURE 5.9

A machine language instruction

01011010 0001000011110011101100010

Binary operation code

Binary operand

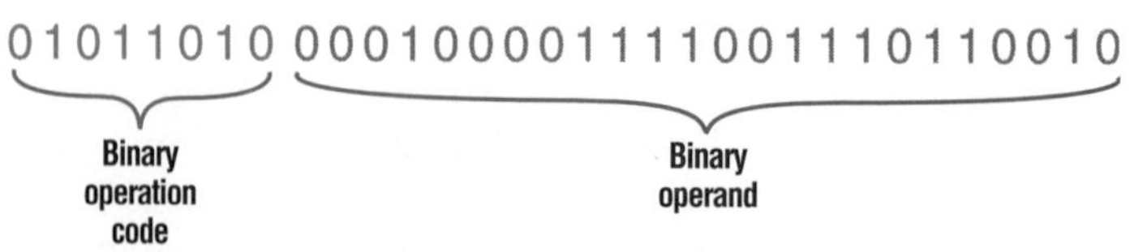

for one computer may not be compatible with another computer; we say machine language is *machine dependent*. Machine language is the only language a computer can understand. Any program for a computer must either be written in the machine language of the computer or written in some other language and then translated into machine language, a process that will be discussed below.

With machine language the programmer has control over everything the computer can do and so can write very efficient programs. Writing programs in machine language is very difficult, however, because the programmer must remember binary codes and numbers. Hence, machine languages are not normally used today.

Assembly Languages (second generation). Early in the history of computers, computer professionals thought there must be an easier way of writing programs than by using machine language. Their idea was to replace instructions represented in a binary form with words and symbols. Binary operation codes were replaced by symbolic codes that stood for the operation. Thus, instead of using the binary operation code 01011010 for the addition operation, the word ADD was used. In addition, instead of using a binary operand, a symbol such as X was used to stand for the data to be processed by the instruction. Thus, an instruction to add one number to another number would be written as in Fig. 5.10 instead of the form shown in Fig. 5.9. Languages using this form became the second generation of programming languages.

Since programs written this way are not in machine language, they have to be translated into machine language before they are executed. The translation process involves converting each symbol into its equivalent binary form. This translation process is called *assembly*, and these languages are called assembly languages. In the assembly language process, each assembly language instruction is translated into one machine language instruction.

Originally, assembly was done by hand; a person would manually translate each assembly language instruction into its equivalent machine language instruction. Then, computer professionals realized that since the translation process was largely mechanical, a computer could do it. People wrote computer programs in machine language to translate assembly language programs into equivalent machine language programs. An assembly language translation program is a system program called an assembler.

Because each type of computer has its own machine language, each has its own assembly language, which may be incompatible with the assembly language of other computers. Hence, assembly language is machine dependent. In addition, each type of computer needs its own assembler program to translate its assembly language into its machine language.

As with machine language, the programmer has control over everything the computer can do with assembly language and programs written in assembly language usually are as efficient as those in machine language. Programming in assembly language is easier than it is in machine language, however, because symbolic codes are easier to remember than binary codes. Still, assembly language is not used much

FIGURE 5.10	ADD	X
An assembly language instruction	Symbolic operation code	Symbolic operand

because other languages are even easier to use. Only in certain situations, such as when the program has to control special parts of the computer, is assembly language used to write system and other types of programs.

Third-generation Languages. Although assembly language is easier to use than machine language, it is not very close to human language because each assembly language instruction is equivalent to one machine language instruction. So, in the mid-1950s computer professionals started to develop languages that were closer to human language, in which each instruction was equivalent to several machine language instructions. Hence, fewer instructions were required in programs written in these languages than in assembly languages. They became the third generation of languages.

The first third-generation languages were similar to simple mathematical notation. Later third-generation languages were closer to English. Still later languages were closer to other notations, such as those used in advanced mathematics. Figure 5.11 shows examples of instructions in FORTRAN, COBOL, and C, which are common third-generation languages.

Programs written in third-generation languages have to be translated into machine language before they can be executed. There are several processes that are used for the translation. One process is called *compilation*, and it is done by a machine language system program called a compiler. Sometimes third-generation languages are called *compiler languages*. In the compilation process each third-generation language instruction is translated into several machine language instructions.

An alternative to compilation is *interpretation*, which is done by a system program called an interpreter. The difference is that in compilation the entire program is translated into machine language before any instruction is executed whereas in interpretation each instruction is translated and executed before going on to the next instruction.

Third-generation languages are not tied to particular computers as are assembly and machine languages; we say they are *machine independent*. If a programmer wants to use a third-generation language on a different computer, he or she just needs a compiler or interpreter to translate the language into the machine language of the computer.

With third-generation languages, the programmer has less control over what the computer can do than with assembly or machine languages, and third-generation lan-

---

FIGURE 5.11

Third-generation language instructions

$X = Y - Z$

FORTRAN

SUBTRACT TAX FROM GROSS-PAY GIVING NET-PAY

COBOL

$x = y - z$

C

guage programs usually are less efficient than assembly or machine language programs. Third-generation languages, however, are easier to learn and have features that make writing programs easier than in assembly or machine language. Many people are familiar with one or more third-generation languages. Many common third-generation languages are in use including C, C++, COBOL, Visual Basic, and FORTRAN.

Fourth-generation Languages.   The fourth generation of programming languages is not so clearly defined as the earlier generations. Most people feel that a <u>fourth-generation language</u>, commonly referred to as a <u>4GL</u>, is a high-level language that requires significantly fewer instructions to accomplish a particular task than a third-generation language requires. Thus, a programmer should be able to write a program faster in a fourth-generation language than in a third-generation language.

Many 4GLs are used to retrieve information from files and databases. These 4GLs contain a *query language,* which is used to answer queries with data from a database. For example, Fig. 5.12 shows an instruction in SQL, a common query language. (Query languages are discussed further in Chapter 7.) Some 4GLs include special *report generators* that make it easy to produce complex printed reports. Other 4GLs include *forms designers*, which are used for creating forms for data input and output on screens. Still other 4GLs have *application generators* that produce entire systems of programs for computer applications. The programmer specifies the queries, reports, and forms needed, and the application generator creates the necessary program.

Fourth-generation languages are mostly machine independent; usually they can be used on more than one type of computer. Some 4GLs are designed to be learned easily and used by end-users. With these languages, the user can create programs without the aid of a programmer.

Fifth-generation Languages.   What is the fifth generation of computer languages? There is no clear answer to this question right now. Some people feel that human languages, that is, *natural languages*, are fifth-generation languages. There have been some attempts to create computer programs that understand natural languages such as English. These programs, however, are very limited in their capabilities. Someday we will probably have programs that can understand natural languages. When that happens, we might be able to say what fifth-generation languages are.

Traditional Programming Languages

There are hundreds, perhaps thousands, of programming languages. Only a few, however, are commonly used. The most widely used languages are third-generation languages, although some fourth-generation languages are being used more often. Third-generation languages fall into two groups: traditional programming languages and object-oriented programming languages. This section takes a look at some of the common traditional programming languages. The next section examines object-oriented programming languages.

FIGURE 5.12

A fourth-generation (query) language instruction

```
SELECT ADDRESS
FROM PERSONNEL
WHERE NAME = "JONES"
```

FORTRAN.   The first widely used third-generation language was <u>FORTRAN</u>, which stands for FORmula TRANslation. It was developed by researchers at IBM Corporation in the mid-1950s and has undergone a number of modifications and improvements since that time. As its name implies, FORTRAN is designed to make it easy to write programs that include many mathematical formulas. Because scientific application programs have numerous formulas, FORTRAN is commonly used for these types of programs. In fact, FORTRAN may be the most common third-generation language used today by scientists and engineers. Figure 5.13 shows an example of a simple FORTRAN program.

COBOL.   The second widely used third-generation language was <u>COBOL</u>. It was developed by a group of computer professionals in 1959 and has evolved through a number of versions since then. COBOL stands for COmmon Business Oriented Language. As the name implies, the language is designed to be *common* to many different computers. In addition, it is used most effectively for *business* application programs, not for scientific programs. Today COBOL is one of the most widely used third-generation language for business data processing

COBOL is available on almost all computers including personal computers. It is most often used, however, on mainframe and minicomputers, although COBOL programs are often developed on personal computers for later execution on larger computers. Many businesses use it as the only language for business application program development. Figure 5.14 shows an example of part of a simple COBOL program.

BASIC.   <u>BASIC</u>, which stands for Beginner's All-purpose Symbolic Instruction Code, was developed in the mid-1960s at Dartmouth College. At that time, the main languages (FORTRAN and COBOL) were used for programs that processed batches of data; it was not easy to write programs in these languages that interacted with the user. The designers of BASIC wanted a simple language for students to write programs with which they could interact through terminals.

BASIC, like FORTRAN and COBOL, has evolved through a number of versions over the years. On IBM personal computers, common versions are *QBasic* and *QuickBASIC*. Another version, called *Visual Basic*, which is an object-oriented pro-

FIGURE 5.13

A FORTRAN program

```
C   TEST SCORE AVERAGING PROGRAM
        CHARACTER*18 NAME
        REAL SCORE1,SCORE2,SCORE3,TOTAL,AVE
        PRINT *, 'ENTER STUDENT NAME OR TYPE END TO STOP:'
        READ (*,300) NAME
100  IF (NAME .EQ. 'END') GO TO 200
        PRINT *, 'ENTER THREE TEST SCORES:;'
        READ *,SCORE1,SCORE2,SCORE3
        TOTAL = SCORE1 + SCORE2 + SCORE3
        AVE = TOTAL / 3.0
        PRINT *
        PRINT *, 'STUDENT NAME ',NAME
        PRINT *,'TOTAL SCORE ',TOTAL
        PRINT *,'AVERAGE SCORE ',AVE
        PRINT *
        PRINT *, 'ENTER STUDENT NAME OR TYPE END TO STOP:'
        READ (*,300) NAME
        GO TO 100
200  STOP
300  FORMAT (A18)
        END
```

FIGURE 5.14

Part of a COBOL program

```
PROCEDURE DIVISION.
*
A000-MAIN-CONTROL.
    OPEN INPUT STUDENT-FILE
        OUTPUT REPORT-FILE.
    PERFORM B010-WRITE-HEADING.
    MOVE "N" TO WS-EOF-FLAG.
    PERFORM B020-READ-INPUT.
    PERFORM B030-PRODUCE-REPORT-BODY
        UNTIL WS-EOF-FLAG IS EQUAL TO "Y".
    CLOSE STUDENT-FILE, REPORT-FILE.
    STOP RUN.
*
B010-WRITE-HEADING.
    WRITE REPORT-DATA FROM HEADING-LINE
        AFTER ADVANCING PAGE.
    MOVE SPACES TO REPORT-DATA.
    WRITE REPORT-DATA
        AFTER ADVANCING 1 LINE.
*
B020-READ-INPUT.
    READ STUDENT-FILE INTO STUDENT-RECORD
        AT END MOVE "Y" TO WS-EOF-FLAG.
*
B030-PRODUCE-REPORT-BODY.
    PERFORM C010-CALCULATE-TOTAL-AVERAGE.
    PERFORM C020-WRITE-DETAIL-OUTPUT.
    PERFORM B020-READ-INPUT.
*
C010-CALCULATE-TOTAL-AVERAGE.
    ADD ST-SCORE1, ST-SCORE2, ST-SCORE3
        GIVING WS-TOTAL.
    DIVIDE WS-TOTAL BY 3
        GIVING WS-AVERAGE ROUNDED.
*
C020-WRITE-DETAIL-OUTPUT.
    MOVE ST-NAME TO DL-NAME.
    MOVE WS-TOTAL TO DL-TOTAL.
    MOVE WS-AVERAGE TO DL-AVERAGE.
    WRITE REPORT-DATA FROM DETAIL-LINE
        AFTER ADVANCING 1 LINE.
```

gramming language, is discussed later. Most versions of BASIC are good for writing quick programs to solve simple problems, although Visual Basic is used for writing sophisticated programs with complex graphical interfaces. Figure 5.15 shows an example of a simple program in QBasic.

FIGURE 5.15

A QBasic program

```
REM - TEST SCORE AVERAGING PROGRAM
INPUT "ENTER STUDENT NAME OR TYPE END TO STOP: ", StuName$
DO WHILE StuName$ <> "END"
    INPUT "ENTER THREE TEST SCORES: ", Score1, Score2, Score3
    LET Total = Score1 + Score2 + Score3
    LET Ave = Total / 3
    PRINT
    PRINT "STUDENT NAME "; StuName$
    PRINT "TOTAL SCORE"; Total
    PRINT "AVERAGE SCORE"; Ave
    PRINT
    INPUT "ENTER STUDENT NAME OR TYPE END TO STOP: ", StuName$
LOOP
END
```

RPG.   RPG, which stands for Report Program Generator, was designed in the mid-1960s by IBM for writing programs that produce business reports from data in secondary storage files, a typical situation for many business application programs. It is used most frequently on IBM minicomputers, although versions are available for other computers. Some small and medium-size businesses use it as their only language for business application programs.

In RPG, a programmer does not write instructions as in other languages. Instead, he or she fills out special forms to describe the files, inputs, calculations, and outputs for the program. Figure 5.16 shows part of a simple RPG program written on these forms.

C.   C was developed by Bell Laboratories in the early 1970s. It includes features that provide the control and efficiency of assembly language (second generation) but at the same time has third-generation language features. C is used extensively for system programs. For example, the UNIX operating system, discussed earlier, is written in C. Many personal computer application programs, such as word processing, spreadsheet, and database programs, are also written in C. C is used for complex system and application programs that require control of the computer and that must execute rapidly and use primary storage efficiently. Figure 5.17 shows an example of a simple C program.

Object-oriented Programming Languages

Programs written in traditional programming languages consist of sequences of instructions that tell the computer how to process data. The data processed by the program is separate from the program, perhaps stored in a file or a database. Another approach to programming uses languages in which the instructions for processing the data and the data are not separate, but instead combined to form an object. This approach, called object-oriented programming, has become common in recent years.

To illustrate the idea of object-oriented programming, consider data consisting of a bank customer's account number and balance, and instructions for adding to the account balance (depositing), subtracting from the account balance (withdrawing), and displaying the account balance. In traditional programming, the customer number and account balance would be stored in a customer account file and the instructions for depositing, withdrawing, and displaying the balance would be in a program separate from the data. (See Fig. 5.18a.) In object-oriented programming, a customer account object would be created with the customer number and account balance, along with the instructions for the different forms of processing. (See Fig. 5.18b.)

The advantage of object-oriented programming is that once an object has been created, it can be reused in many programs. Thus the customer account object just described could be used in a checking account program and in any other program that uses the same data and procedures. As a result, object-oriented programs can be easier to develop than traditional programs. Objects are especially good for storing sound, pictures, and video, and object-oriented programs are commonly used for processing this type of data.

A number of object-oriented programming languages have been developed over the years. One of the first was *Smalltalk*, which was developed in the mid-1970s by Xerox Corporation. It is still in use today on some computers. The most widely used object-oriented programming language is C++, which is a version of C with additional features

RPG INPUT SPECIFICATIONS

Date _____
Program _____
Programmer _____

Punching Instruction — Graphic / Punch

Page [1][2]

Program Identification [75 76 77 78 79 80]

Line	Form Type	Filename	Sequence	Number (1-4) Option (0)	Record Identifying Indicator or **	Record Identification Codes — Position 1 / Not (N) / C/Z/D / Character	Position 2	Not (N) / C/Z/D / Character	Position 3	Not (N) / C/Z/D / Character	Stacker Select	Field Location — From	To	Decimal Positions	Field Name	Control Level (L1-L9)	Matching Fields or Chaining Fields	Field Record Relation	Field Indicators — Plus	Minus	Zero or Blank	Starting Sign Position
01	O	STUDENT	AA	01																		
02	O											1	18		NAME							
03	O											19	21	0	SCORE1							
04	O											22	24	0	SCORE2							
05	O											25	27	0	SCORE3							
06																						
07																						

RPG CALCULATION SPECIFICATIONS

Date _____
Program _____
Programmer _____

Punching Instruction — Graphic / Punch

Page [1][2]

Program Identification [75 76 77 78 79 80]

Line	Form Type	Control Level (L0-L9, LR, SR)	Indicators — And / And	Factor 1 / Position	Operation	Factor 2	Result Field	Field Length	Decimal Positions Half Adjust (H)	Resulting Indicators	Comments
01	O	c	01	SCORE1	ADD	SCORE1	TOTAL	30			
02	O	c	01	TOTAL	ADD	SCORE3	TOTAL				
03	O	c	01	TOTAL	DIV	3	AVE	41H			
04		c									
05		c									

RPG OUTPUT - FORMAT SPECIFICATIONS

Date _____
Program _____
Programmer _____

Punching Instruction — Graphic / Punch

Page [1][2]

Program Identification [75 76 77 78 79 80]

Edit Codes:

Commas	Zero Balances to Print	No Sign	CR	–	X = Remove Plus Sign / Y = Date Field Edit / Z = Zero Suppress
Yes	Yes	1	A	J	
Yes	No	2	B	K	
No	Yes	3	C	L	
No	No	4	D	M	

Constant or Edit Word

Line	Form Type	Filename	Type (H/D/T/E) Stack or Select Fetch Overflow (F)	Space — Before / After	Skip — Before / After	Output Indicators — Not / And / And	Field Name	Edit Codes / Blank After (B)	End Position in Output Record	B = Binary	Constant or Edit Word	Sterling Sign Position
1 O	REPORT	H	201			1P						
2 O									15		'STUDENT'	
3 O									26		'TOTAL'	
4 O									36		'AVERAGE'	
5 O		D	1			01						
6 O							NAME		18			
7 O							TOTAL		25		' 0'	
8 O							AVE		35		' 0. '	
9												
0												

FIGURE 5.16

Part of an RPG program

FIGURE 5.17

A C program

```
main ()    /*Test score averaging program*/
{
        char name[19];
        float score1,score2,score3,total,ave;
        printf ("Enter student name or type end to stop: ");
        scanf ("%s",name);
        while (strcmp (name,"end") != 0)
        {
                printf ("Enter three test scores: ");
                scanf ("%f%f%f",&score1,&score2,&score3);
                total = score1 + score2 + score3;
                ave = total / 3;
                printf ("\n");
                printf ("Student name $s\n",name);
                printf ("Total score %4.0f\n",total);
                printf ("Average score %5.1f\n",ave);
                printf ("\n");
                printf ("Enter student name or type end to stop: ");
                scanf ("%s",name);
        }
}
```

for object-oriented programming. It is widely used today for developing system and application software. Figure 5.19 shows an example of a simple C++ program.

Some object-oriented languages provide the ability to easily develop graphical user interfaces. Items displayed in a graphical user interface such as icons, menus, and windows are representations of objects. Languages for developing such interfaces are sometimes called *visual programming languages* because the programmer develops a program in the language using a mouse and a screen that displays graphical images for icons, menus, windows, and so forth. (See Fig. 5.20.) An example of such a language is *Visual Basic*. The use of object-oriented and visual programming languages will increase in the future.

Internet Programming Languages

Special programming languages are used with the Internet to create the pages seen on the World Wide Web. The main language used for this purpose is HTML, which stands for Hypertext Markup Language. With HTML, a World Wide Web page developer can lay out the form of a page with text and graphics and provide connections called *hyperlinks* to other pages. The developer does this by putting brief codes called *tags* in the page to indicate how the page should be formatted. (See Fig. 5.21.) When viewed with a browser, the page appears in its formatted form without the tags. Software is available for developing Web pages without having to use HTML. This type of software automatically puts the necessary tags in the page.

Another language used with World Wide Web pages is Java. Java is an object-oriented programming language similar to C++ that allows a page developer to create programs for applications (sometimes called *applets*) that can be used through a browser. For example, a Web page for a bank could have a Java program that calculates mortgage payments from input entered by the user. Using Java, developers can create Web pages that do more than just display words and images.

As use of the Internet and the World Wide Web increases, more applications will be written in HTML, Java, and similar languages. Someday, the majority of applications may be developed in Internet programming languages.

Customer account data

Customer account program

(a) Traditional programming

Customer account object

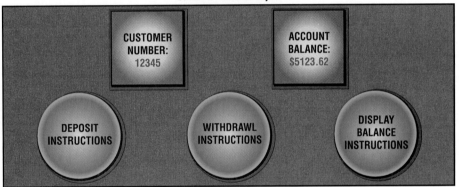

(b) Object-oriented programming

FIGURE 5.18

Traditional versus object-oriented programming

FIGURE 5.19

A C++ program

```
// Filename: acctmain.cpp
#include "account.h"
#include <iostream.h>
int main()
{
    cout << endl;
    cout << "Starting project";
    Account myAccount;
    myAccount.deposit(199.99);
    cout << endl;
    cout << "My Account has &" << myAccount.retrieveBalance();
    cout << endl;
    cout << "Ending project";
    return 0;
}
```

FIGURE 5.20

A visual
programming
language screen

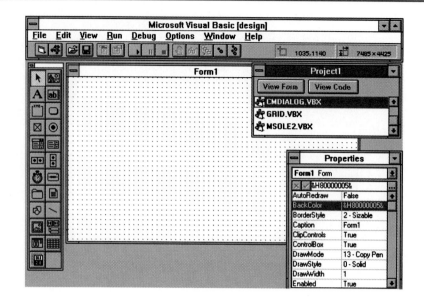

FIGURE 5.21

**HTML for a World
Wide Web page**

```html
<HTML>
    <HEAD>
        <TITLE>Addison Wesley Longman * Higher Education
        Division* Information Systems</TITLE>
    </HEAD>
    <BODY BGCOLOR="#FFFFFF">
        <P ALIGN = CENTER>
        <IMG SRC="images/ISbanner.gif">
        <BR>
        <A HREF="maps/ISmainNavi.gif.map"><IMG
        SRC="images/ISmainNavi.gif" ALT="Information
        Systems Masthead" ISMAP BORDER=0></A>
        <BR>
        <BR>
        <!--What's New-->
        <A HREF = "whatsnew/whatsnew.html">|What's New|</A>
        <!--Book Info-->
        <A HREF = "bookinfo/bookinfo.html">|Catalog|</A>
        <!--Instructor Forum-->
        <A HREF = "instructors/instructors.html">|Instructor
        Forum|</A>
        <!--Student Forum-->
        <A HREF = "students/students.html">|Student Forum|</A>
        <!--Feedback-->
        <A HREF = "feedback/feedback.html">|Comments &amp;
        Questions|</A>
        <!--Ordering-->
        |<A HREF = "ordering/ordering.html">Ordering</A>|
        <a href="reviewing/reviewing.html">|Review|</a><a
        href="submission/submission.html">|Write for Us|</a>
        <P ALIGN = CENTER>
        <IMG SRC="images/brule.gif">
        <P><blockquote>
        <P>If you're looking for the latest in information
        systems textbooks, educational multimedia tools,
        innovative software, and outstanding service, then
        you've come to the right place!
```

Bookmark

Java Internet Application at CERA Bank, Belgium

In the first of what IBM hopes will be a torrent of joint Web projects with its customers, a large Belgian bank in partnership with IBM has built a Java-based application designed to streamline operations and expose the bank to new on-line business possibilities.

CERA, in Louvain, Belgium, with the help of IBM's Network Computing Projects business unit, created an application in Java that lets users view CERA's mortgage rates and then calculate the loan amount based on several criteria, such as fixed mortgage rate and duration.

Users can estimate their loan payments over the Internet from anywhere in the world by downloading the application from CERA's home page. (See Web site listed below.)

While this application benefits the bank, the CERA project also represents a big win for IBM's Network Computing Projects group, because it is the first deal the division has struck to co-build Java applications with customers.

CERA's application, running on OS/2 Warp Server, was developed in response to business and technical dilemmas, said Rudi Peeters, the bank's electronic banking officer.

"We've been doing electronic banking for eight years, and the cost of shipping new versions of the software and installing the software with each new release was becoming a problem," Peeters said. "I wanted to get rid of that but also give our customers enough functionality, not just a dumb application."

In addition to advertising the bank's services, the Java application will help streamline operations. Consumers can go into a branch, negotiate a preferred rate, then use the application later to simulate mortgage scenarios that could help them to make a decision.

"The other reason we did the application was to get some experience with Java," Peeters said. "Until now,

we'd been building our applications with HTML and JavaScript only, and we wanted to see if Java can do what they say it can."

Enter IBM's Network Computing Projects division, which dedicated some of its top Java developers to CERA's application. This new group's charter is to work hand-in-glove with an IS department's programmers to determine the best solution to a business problem and then jointly craft the best Java code.

The applet, made up of several objects, lets user do their calculations and loan simulations offline, and Java's international features let the bank roll out the program in three languages simultaneously.

For the future, CERA is training developers in Java programming, so they can maintain the existing application and create new ones.

Deciding to go with this application was a no-brainer, Peeters said, particularly with IBM's support. "The time to market was short, and the financial investment was really low," Peeters said.

"Deals like this show that Java can be used for more than just building Web pages," said John Soyring, director of technical projects for IBM's Personal Software Products division, in Austin, Texas. "It can be used for building mission-critical applications."

QUESTIONS

1. For what application was Java used at CERA?
2. Why did CERA decide to develop this application?

WEB SITE
CERA: www.cera.be

Source: Martin LaMonica, "Java's on the job at Belgian bank," *InfoWorld,* March 10, 1997, p. 37.

Chapter Summary

☐ Businesses need application software in information systems to provide the input, storage, processing, and output functions of the system. They need system software, such as an operating system, so that computers will be easy to use. The operating system together with the hardware create the **platform** upon which the application software of an information system runs. (p. 126)

☐ Individual application software is used by a single per-

son for an individual purpose. In includes **word processing software, spreadsheet software**, **database software**, and World Wide Web **browsers**. Workgroup application software, or **groupware**, is used by members of a workgroup to collaborate with each other. It includes **electronic messaging software**, **information sharing software**, and **electronic conferencing software**. Organizational application software provides applications that encompass much of the business, not just an individual or workgroup. It can be used to support day-to-day business operations and management decision making. Interorganizational application software allows one business's computer to transmit data to another business's computer. (pp. 126–129)

☐ Some operating systems are told what to do by keying in instructions called **commands** following **prompts** displayed by the operating system. Other operating systems allow the user to select commands, using a mouse, from a **menu** displayed on the screen. Many operating systems display available commands as **icons** or **buttons**, which the user selects with a mouse. Operating systems that display icons, menus, **dialog boxes**, and **windows** are said to have a **graphical user interface** or **GUI**. (pp. 129–132)

☐ Some operating systems can execute only one program at a time, and others are **multitasking**, which means they can execute more than one program at a time. Some systems can be used by only one user at a time, and others can be used by multiple users simultaneously. Early systems were batch operating systems, which meant that all data had to be prepared in advance in a batch. Current operating systems are interactive, which means they allow interaction with the users as programs execute, but they also provide for batch processing. Finally, some operating systems are capable of executing only programs as large as the actual primary storage or real memory of the computer, and other operating systems allow programs to be larger than real memory by using secondary storage to store parts of programs. With these operating systems the computer has **virtual memory** that is larger than the real memory. (pp. 132–139)

☐ Machine languages (first generation) have instructions with operation codes and operands in a binary form. **Assembly languages** (second generation) use symbolic operation codes and operands, but each instruction still is equivalent to one machine language instruction. In third-generation languages, each instruction is equivalent to several machine language instructions. Programs in these languages require fewer instructions than are needed in assembly language programs. Programs in **fourth-generation languages** or **4GLs** require even fewer instructions than third-generation language programs. Thus, a programmer can write a program faster in a 4GL than in a third-generation language. Fifth-generation languages may turn out to be natural languages like English. (pp. 139–143)

☐ In traditional programming the data processed by the program is separate from the program instructions. In **object-oriented programming** the data and the instructions for processing the data are combined to form an **object**. **FORTRAN**, **COBOL**, **BASIC**, **RPG**, and **C** are traditional programming languages. Smalltalk and **C++** are object-oriented programming languages. (pp. 143–148)

☐ **HTML,** which stands for Hypertext Markup Language, is used to create pages on the World Wide Web. Using HTML, a page developer puts codes, or tags, in the page to indicate how the page should be formatted. **Java** is an object-oriented programming language that allows page developers to create programs for applications that can be used through a browser. (p. 148)

Key Terms

Assembler (p. 141)
Assembly Language (p. 141)
BASIC (p. 144)
Booting (p. 132)
Browser (p. 128)
Button (p. 132)
C (p. 146)
C++ (p. 146)
COBOL (p. 144)
Command (p. 132)
Compiler (p. 142)
Database Software (p. 128)
Dialog Box (p. 132)
Electronic Conferencing Software (p. 128)
Electronic Messaging Software (p. 128)

FORTRAN (p. 144)
Fourth-Generation Language (4GL) (p. 143)
Graphical User Interface (GUI) (p. 132)
Groupware (p. 128)
HTML (p. 148)
Icon (p. 132)
Information Sharing Software (p. 128)
Interpreter (p. 142)
Java (p. 148)
Menu (p. 132)
Multitasking (p. 134)
Network Operating System (NOS) (p. 137)
Object (p. 146)

Object-Oriented Programming (p. 146)
Operating Environment (p. 136)
Page (p. 128)
Platform (p. 126)
Programmer (p. 139)
Programming (p. 139)
Programming Language (p. 139)
Prompt (p. 132)
RPG (p. 146)
Spreadsheet Software (p. 127)
Time-Sharing (p. 135)
User Interface (p. 132)
Utility Program (p. 139)
Virtual Memory (p. 135)
Window (p. 132)
Word Processing Software (p. 127)

Assignment Material

Review Questions

Fill-in Questions

1. The operating system software together with the hardware forms the _____ upon which the application software of an information system runs.

2. Individual application software that lets a user manage large amounts of data stored in secondary storage is called _____.

3. A(n) _____ is used to locate information on the World Wide Web.

4. EDI software is an example of _____ application software.

5. Loading the supervisor is called _____.

6. Before you can use a multiple-user computer you must _____. After you have finished you must _____.

7. A word or phrase entered at a keyboard that tells a program to perform a function is called a(n) _____.

8. Small pictures displayed on a screen that represent functions a program can perform are called _____.

9. A technique used by some operating systems that allows multiple programs to be executing at one time is called _____.

10. Some operating systems allow programs to be larger than primary storage by creating _____ that is greater than the primary storage.

11. Machine languages are _____-generation languages.

12. A programming language that can be used on only one type of computer is called _____, whereas one that can be used on several types of computers is called _____.

13. Second-generation languages are _____ languages.

14. Third-generation language programs are translated into machine language by a(n) _____.

15. The first widely used third-generation language was _____.

16. A widely used third-generation language for business data processing is _____.

17. A third-generation language used for system and general application programs is _____.

18. Pages on the World Wide Web are created using _____.

Short-answer Questions

1. What is workgroup application software called, and what is an example of this type of software?

2. Organizational application software only supports the day-to-day operations of a business. True or false? Explain your answer.

3. Why do businesses need application and system software in information systems?

4. What are the three main functions of an operating system?

5. What does the supervisor of an operating system do?

6. Why do users use multitasking?

7. Name some common personal computer operating systems.

8. What operating system can be used on some personal computers as well as on some multiple-user computers?

9. What is a graphical user interface?

10. Why is there not just one programming language that can be used for all programs?

11. List several factors that should be considered in selecting a programming language.

12. What is the difference between assembly and machine language?

13. What must be done to a third-generation language program before it can be executed?

14. What is a fourth-generation language or 4GL?

15. What is an object?

16. What languages are used for object-oriented programming?

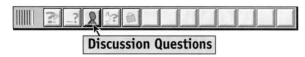

Discussion Questions

1. Sometimes it is hard to decide whether a program is application software or system software. For example, some application programs, such as spreadsheet programs, are not capable of solving a business problem until they are customized, and some operating systems come with applications such as simple word processing and graphics capabilities. Is it important to distinguish between application and system software?

2. Many people complain that graphical user interfaces, although easier to use than other interfaces, are still difficult to use. In what ways do you think a user interface can be improved to make it easier to use?

3. Describe an application in which multitasking would be useful on a personal computer.

4. Why is there not just one operating system for all computers?

5. Think of a computer application in a business with which you are familiar. What programming language would you select for that application? Why?

6. Many people feel that third-generation programming languages are no longer needed because of fourth-generation languages. On the other hand, languages such as C, COBOL, and FORTRAN are still used extensively. What do you think is the future of third-generation languages?

7. What problems besides natural language differences do software companies have in developing application and system software for sale around the world?

8. Software, especially that used on personal computers, is easily copied. Most software, however, is copyrighted, so it is usually illegal to copy software without the developer's permission. What would you do if a coworker gave you a copy of a program and asked you to "try it out" to see if you liked it?

Problem-solving Projects

1. Analyze the graphical user interface of several software packages. Identify the elements found in each user interface (e.g., menus, icons, buttons, etc.) and determine what they are used for. If possible, print copies of sample screens. Prepare a report, using word processing software, in which you summarize the results of your analysis and comment on the ease of use of each interface. Conclude your report by outlining the characteristics that you feel are the most important in a user interface.

2. Using spreadsheet or word processing software, set up a table giving information about different personal computer operating systems. Have columns for the name of the operating system, the company that developed it, the current version, the price, the characteristics of the operating system (e.g., single vs. multitasking, real vs. virtual memory), and any other information you wish to include. Fill in the table with information about the operating systems listed in the chapter. You will have to research some information, such as the current version and price. Identify several other operating systems not listed in the chapter and add information about them to your table. As new operating systems or new versions of existing operating systems become available, update your table.

3. Set up a table giving information about programming languages. List the name of the language, the generation, whether it is machine dependent or machine independent, and the types of programs for which it is used. Include machine language, assembly language, all the third-generation languages listed in the chapter, and fourth-generation languages. Find several other third-generation languages not listed in the chapter to include in your table. Use spreadsheet or word processing software to prepare your table.

4. Interview a programmer and find out what programming languages he or she uses. Find out what the programmer likes and dislikes about the languages. Write a summary of your interview. Use word processing software to prepare your summary.

5. Use the Internet to investigate the legal requirements for copyrighting software in the United States. Start at the Web site for the U.S. Copyright Office. Also use a search engine to explore other sites that have information. Using word processing software, prepare a brief summary of what a business must do to copyright a program it has developed.

Real-world Case

Oakland Housing Authority

Like a car buff who's attached to a vintage vehicle, Curt Beckman, IS director of the Oakland Housing Authority (OHA), in Oakland, Calif., spent several years nursing an aging minicomputer system while the rest of the world embraced sportier, faster networks and PCs. The system, a 1980s-vintage NCR Corp. minicomputer running the proprietary Applied Digital Data System (ADDS), did something that none of the client/server, open systems-based alternatives could do: run the entire housing agency in a way that nearly 200 users were familiar with.

Sure, it was painfully slow, forcing users to plan 24 hours ahead which reports they wanted to be run overnight. It was expensive; parts and software were difficult to find. For newcomers to the agency, the Pick operating system was a startling return to an earlier era of computing. The minicomputer simply couldn't communicate with either the new PCs and LANs or the systems being used by other agencies.

But, like the car buff who finally stores away or sells the old clunker, Beckman decided to move his agency off the minicomputer. What happened? The software the employees so depend on was ported to UNIX. Now, reports are being produced in minutes instead of hours, employees can use familiar ADDS screens as well as popular applications, and Beckman is eyeing a list of new applications that his new computing infrastructure will support.

The Oakland Housing Authority is responsible for helping low-income residents of the city of Oakland find housing. It places applicants in housing from both the private sector and its own properties.

The computer system is used for the entire rental process, from applications keyed in by data entry clerks to follow-up letters to applicants and reports on vacancies. Each time the OHA rents an apartment, it takes on the duties of landlord and the computer system tracks rent payments, work orders for fixing up structures, and a variety of social services that the OHA provides.

In addition, the system has to provide daily reports on properties and applicants to its main funder, the Department of Housing and Urban Development.

With maintenance costs rising and the minicomputer's capacity diminishing, the agency had to do something about its computing system. Beckman created a strategic task force to develop a requirements list and study the agency's options. At that point, the issue of whether to stick with the ADDS software or switch to something else came up.

"We talked to people about going out to the marketplace to look for a new application," Beckman says. "The answer was no. They knew what the pains were and didn't want to do that."

That limited the options to ADDS for UNIX.

"We got a nice migration path and did not have a major interruption in our business. Yet we got the advantage of an open environment in UNIX," Beckman says.

The task force came up with a total of 12 recommendations ranging from upgrading the infrastructure of the computing system to providing new applications and even constructing an Internet strategy.

In addition, the agency was under a mandate from HUD to improve its telecommunications links; HUD is switching to SprintMail as its vehicle for collecting daily reports from housing authorities, and the old system simply could not have supported such a link, Beckman says.

The OHA put out a request for proposals, specifying what the new system should provide. After evaluating all the proposals, the OHA selected Edge Information Systems, in San Jose, Calif., to provide systems integration, programming, and installation of the new network.

The new network uses a Hewlett-Packard Co. HP 9000 UNIX database server running the Unidata database system (from Unidata Inc., in Denver), as well as Novell Inc.'s WordPerfect word processing software for UNIX and Lotus Development Corp.'s 1-2-3 spreadsheet software for UNIX. Three Pentium-based servers run the network operating system.

The 175 clients on the system are sitting at a variety of terminals and systems. In fact, about half of the users at the OHA are still in front of dumb terminals.

These workers, mostly clerical, take advantage of the UNIX version of WordPerfect to create form letters and property maintenance tickets, Beckman says. The PCs, used by analysts and executives, handle both word processing and data analysis.

All told, the new system cost about $750,000. Was it worth it? Beckman says absolutely. First of all, the network has reduced Beckman's overall support and maintenance costs. Supporting the network is vastly easier than supporting LANs, stand-alone PCs, and the aging minicomputer system.

"There has been a tremendous downward curve in maintenance costs. They are a fraction of what they were on the ADDS," Beckman says. "But that isn't really the payback. That is in the productivity angle."

"I'm particularly pleased with response times from the HP," Beckman says. "We have one application that used to take six hours just to do the processing; it takes nine minutes on the HP." Now, instead of having to schedule reports to print at night at a central location, managers and case workers do all their printing locally on one of the HP printers. "Users now don't have to plan ahead just to get a report," Beckman says.

Switching to WordPerfect for UNIX from the combination of packaged and proprietary word processing applications has yielded two benefits. First of all, new employees are able to get up to speed much more quickly, Beckman says. And because files are stored centrally, his shop has been able to create standardized form letters, providing consistency among all the different departments.

Now that he has replaced his old jalopy with a brand-new network, Beckman is able to move on to some of the other recommendations his task force compiled, including a data warehouse, imaging, and e-mail. And communications have risen to the top of the OHA's to-do list, thanks in part to the flexibility of the new system.

Questions

1. What problems did OHA have with its old minicomputer system?

2. What organizational application software is used in the OHA system?

3. What individual application software is used in the new OHA system?

4. What operating system is used with the network?

5. What benefits does OHA receive from the new system?

Source: Rachel Parker, "Client/server system puts housing agency into overdrive," *InfoWorld*, January 8, 1996, p. 58.

6 Information System Networks

Chapter Outline

The Need for Networks in Information Systems   (p. 158)
Communications Hardware   (p. 158)
    Communications Channel Characteristics   (p. 159)
    Communications Channel Media   (p. 162)
    Communications Channel Sources   (p. 164)
    Communications Devices   (p. 166)
Communications Software   (p. 169)
    Personal Computer Communications Software   (p. 169)
    Multiple-user Computer Communications Software   (p. 170)
    Network Communications Software   (p. 170)
Remote Access   (p. 171)
    Terminal Communications   (p. 171)
    Personal Computer Communications   (p. 172)
Network Organization   (p. 173)
Local Area Networks   (p. 175)
    Client-server Computing   (p. 176)
Wide Area Networks   (p. 177)
Internetworks   (p. 178)
    The Internet   (p. 178)
    Intranets   (p. 181)

Learning Objectives

After completing this chapter, you should be able to:

☐ 1. State four reasons why businesses need networks in information systems.
☐ 2. Describe the main characteristics of communications channels.
☐ 3. Describe the function of a modem and list several other communications devices.
☐ 4. Describe the main functions of communications software.
☐ 5. Identify the communications hardware and software needs for personal computer access to a remote computer.
☐ 6. Explain how local area networks are organized and list the special hardware and software found in LANs.
☐ 7. Describe the organization of wide area networks.
☐ 8. Explain how and why networks are interconnected and explain what the Internet and intranets are.

Networks in information systems provide communication between computers and related devices. The communication may be over a short distance using a local area network (LAN) or over a long distance with a wide area network (WAN). To make communication possible, networks use special *telecommunications* or *data communications*[1] hardware and software. This chapter covers communications hardware and software, and explains how this hardware and software is used in networks that function within and between businesses.

The Need for Networks in Information Systems

[handwritten: Reasons for Networks]

[handwritten: 1) remote access]

[handwritten: 2) info. sharing]

[handwritten: 3) resource sharing]

[handwritten: 4) interorg. communic.]

Businesses need networks in information systems for four main reasons. The first is for *remote access* to information and processing. Often a user with a personal computer or terminal at one location needs to use computer hardware or software at another, remote location to store and process data. To access the storage and processing capabilities of the remote computer, the user's computer or terminal and the remote computer must be connected in a network so that they can communicate with each other. The network provides the capabilities for the remote access.

A second reason businesses need networks is for *information sharing*. Users in an organization often need to share information related to the operation and management of the business. The information may be shared by using electronic mail; by transmitting documents, spreadsheets, data, images, sound, and so forth; and by accessing common files and databases. Networks provide the capabilities for sharing such information.

The third reason businesses need networks is for *resource sharing*. Often businesses have certain expensive computer resources such as high-volume printers, large-capacity disk drives, high-speed computers, and special software. These resources may need to be available to many users for specialized processing. By including them in a network, users can easily share them.

A final reason businesses need networks is for *interorganizational communication*. Computers in different businesses need to communicate with one another in order for interorganizational systems to function. Electronic data interchange and electronic funds transfer systems are examples of systems that require interorganizational communication. Interorganizational networks provide the capabilities needed for such communication.

Communications Hardware

[handwritten: 2 Types of ↗]

[handwritten: 1) comm. channel]

[handwritten: 2) comm. device]

Before examining networks in detail, you need to know something about communications hardware and software. This section describes communications hardware and the next section looks at communications software.

Communications hardware allows computer devices to communicate over distances. Two main types of communications hardware are needed. (See Fig. 6.1.) The first type is a <u>communications channel</u>, which is the link over which data is sent. An

---

[1] Sometimes the term *telecommunications* is used to refer to all forms of electronic communication, including telephone and fax, and the term *data communications* is used just to refer to transmission of data. Often, however, these terms are used interchangeably.

FIGURE 6.1

Communications hardware

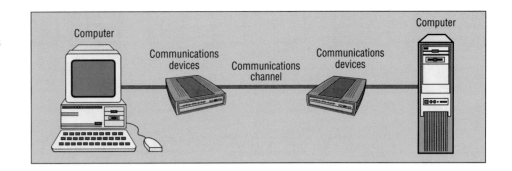

example of a medium that is used for a communications channel is a telephone line, but there are other media used for channels. The second type of communications hardware is <u>communications devices</u>, which provide communications processing capabilities between the computer and the channel. An example of a communications device is a modem, but there are other types of communications devices.

Communications Channel Characteristics

A communications channel is the link over which data is transmitted when using data communications. Data is transmitted over a channel as bits; one bit is sent after the other over the channel. (See Fig. 6.2.) The bits are grouped to form bytes that represent characters using ASCII, EBCDIC, or some other code. The way in which the bits are sent determines four characteristics of the channel: signal type, data rate, data flow, and transmission method.

Digital vs. Analog

Signal Type.   Bits can be sent over a channel as either a <u>digital signal</u> or an <u>analog signal</u>. (See Fig. 6.3.) A digital signal is one that transmits bits as high and low pulses. In a digital signal, a high pulse represents a 1 bit and a low pulse represents a 0 bit. An analog signal, however, transmits data by a wave pattern that varies continuously. A human voice is an analog signal because it varies continuously from high to low. In an analog channel, different wave patterns represent bits.

Some channels can transmit digital signals, and some can transmit analog signals. A computer uses digital signals to send data between its components. Thus, a computer can transmit data over a digital channel without changing the signal type. The wire line from most telephones is an analog channel, so to transmit computer data over a telephone line, the data usually must be converted from a digital to an analog form, a process that will be discussed below.

Data Rate.   Data rate has to do with how fast the bits can be sent over the channel. The rate is measured in *bits per second* or *bps*. Each type of channel has a maximum data rate varying from a low of 300 bps for very slow-speed channels to over

FIGURE 6.2

Sending bits over a communications channel

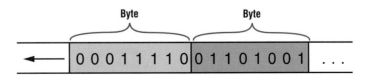

Communications channel

FIGURE 6.3

Signal types

Digital signal

Analog signal

50,000,000 bps for high-speed channels. It is always possible to transmit at a slower rate than the maximum allowed by the channel.

Sometimes the term baud rate is used to express the data rate. For example, someone might say he or she is transmitting at "9600 baud," meaning 9600 bps. This term is not exactly correct, however. Baud rate refers to the number of times per second that the signal on a channel changes—for example, in changing from a high to a low pulse. Depending on the channel, each signal change can represent one, two, or more bits. If the channel is such that each signal change represents one bit, the baud rate and bps are the same. But if the channel is such that each signal change represents more than one bit, then the baud rate will be less than the bps. Hence, baud rate and bps may or may not be the same. To be safe, the data rate should always be stated in bps.

Because data is transmitted on a channel in a code, each character requires a certain number of bits (seven or eight bits for ASCII, eight bits for EBCDIC). As you will see below when we discuss transmission method, other bits are sent with the code for each character. As a rough rule of thumb, you can assume that each character requires 10 bits. Hence, you can estimate the data rate in characters per second by dividing the bits per second by 10. For example, a 28,800 bps channel can transmit approximately 2,880 characters per second, which is the number of characters in almost one and one-half screens.

The term bandwidth is also used when discussing data rate. Bandwidth has to do with how much data can be transmitted over a channel. "Higher bandwidth" means more data can be transmitted. The technical definition of bandwidth is not important here, only the concept that higher bandwidth means more data can be sent. Bandwidth becomes especially important when transmitting graphics, sound, video, and other nontext data because this type of data requires large numbers of bits.

Data Flow. The direction that data can flow in a channel can vary. (See Fig. 6.4.) With simplex transmission, data can flow only in one direction. In half-duplex transmission, data can flow in both directions but in only one direction at a time. With full-duplex transmission, data can flow in both directions simultaneously.

Simplex transmission is rarely used in data communications today. An example of its use is for transmission to a stock-quotation terminal that only receives data. Half- and full-duplex transmissions are used for most data communications. In some situations full-duplex is faster than half-duplex. When a person is communicating with a remote computer through a personal computer or a terminal, however, the

FIGURE 6.4

Data flow in channels

Simplex transmission

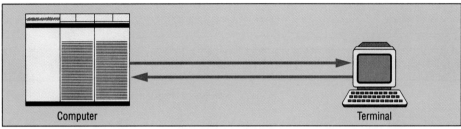

Half-duplex transmission

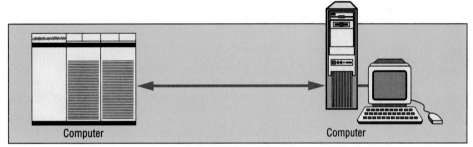

Full-duplex transmission

difference between half- and full-duplex is not significant. For transferring large volumes of data between computers, full-duplex can be better.

async vs. sync.

Transmission Method.   Two methods are used to transmit characters on a channel: asynchronous transmission and synchronous transmission. (See Fig. 6.5.) In asynchronous transmission, one character is sent at a time. A solid stream of 1 bits is sent between characters. When a character is going to be transmitted, a 0 start bit is sent. Then, the bits in the code for the character are sent, followed by a 1 or 0 parity bit, which is used to check for transmission errors. Following this bit comes a 1 stop bit to signal the end of the character transmission and the beginning of the stream of 1 bits between characters.

In synchronous transmission, the codes for several hundred characters are sent together in a block, rather than one character at a time as in asynchronous transmission. In addition, start, stop, or parity bits are not provided for each character. Instead, a group of start bytes are sent before the block, a group of error-checking bits follows the characters in the block, and a group of stop bytes comes at the end.

Asynchronous transmission requires less expensive equipment than synchronous transmission. The latter, however, is faster for sending large amounts of data.

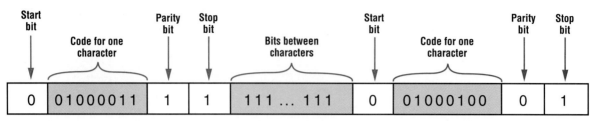

Asynchronous transmission

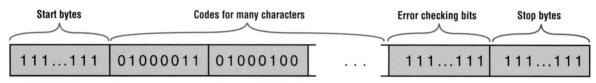

Synchronous transmission

FIGURE 6.5

Transmission methods

For communications where a user is entering input and receiving output, which usually involves only small amounts of data, the asynchronous method is less expensive and usually satisfactory. For communications that involve transferring large amounts of data, however, the synchronous method is the preferred technique.

Communications Channel Media

Different media can be used for communications channels. In fact, a channel may consist of several different media connected in sequence. The choice of the media affects the speed and the cost of communications.

Wire Cables. Wire cables are the oldest media used for electronic communications. They have been used since the first telegraph machines in the 1800s. Data is transmitted over a wire cable by sending an electrical signal along the wire. Data may be sent in an analog or digital form over a wire cable. Today, two main forms of wire cables are used for data communications: twisted-pair wiring and coaxial cable. (See Fig. 6.6.)

Twisted-pair wiring consists of two wires twisted together. Most telephone lines use this medium for local voice communications, but it can also be used for data communications. It is relatively inexpensive, but its data transmission rate is slow compared to other media. *Coaxial cable* consists of copper wire heavily insulated with rubber and plaster. It is the type of cable used with cable television systems and is more expensive than twisted-pair wiring, but can transmit data at a greater rate.

Fiber-optic Cables. An alternative to wire cable is *fiber-optic cable.* (See Fig. 6.7.) A fiber-optic cable consists of bundles of glass or plastic fibers. Each fiber is 1/2000 inch thick—about the size of a human hair. Data is transmitted by a laser that pulses light through the fiber. Each pulse represents a bit, so data is transmitted in a digital form. The laser can pulse more than one billion times per second, meaning data can be transmitted at more than one billion bps, a very fast rate. For long-distance communications, fiber-optic cables are preferred over wire cables.

FIGURE 6.6

Wire cables

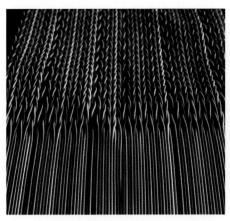

Twisted-pair wiring

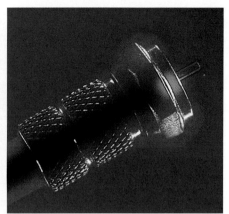

Coaxial cable

Most telephone companies use fiber-optic cables for some voice communications. Because a voice is an analog signal, the voice must be converted to digital form (bits) for transmission over a fiber-optic cable and then converted back to analog form at the receiving end. (This conversion is done by a device called a *codec*, which stands for coder-decoder.) Computer communication using fiber optics, however, does not require conversion because computer signals are already in digital form.

Microwave Systems.   *Microwaves* are special types of radio signals that are sent from one microwave antenna to the next. Microwave transmission is "line-of-sight," which means that there must be nothing between the antennas. (Microwaves cannot bend around objects.) Both voice and data can be transmitted by microwaves, and the signal can be in analog or digital form. Microwave systems are very expensive, but they do not require direct cables, and they can transmit data very rapidly.

Two types of microwave systems are used. (See Fig. 6.8.) The first is a land-based system, in which data is sent from one microwave antenna to the next. Because microwave transmission is line-of-sight and because of the curvature of the earth, land-based microwave antennas must be no more than about 30 miles apart. The second

FIGURE 6.7

Fiber-optic cable

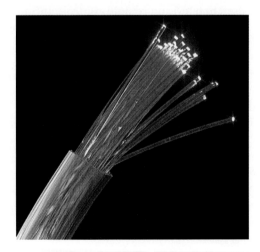

FIGURE 6.8

Microwave systems

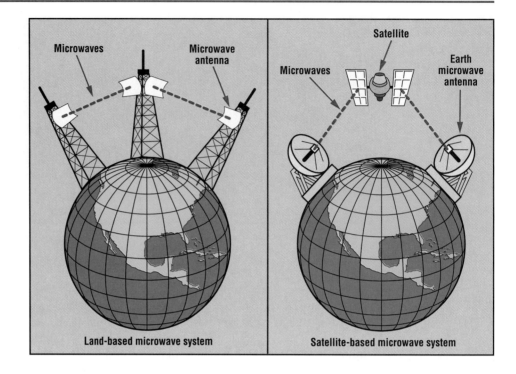

Land-based microwave system   Satellite-based microwave system

type of microwave system is satellite-based. In this system, data is sent from an earth microwave antenna up to a satellite and then down to another earth antenna. The satellite is about 22,300 miles in space. At that altitude, the satellite revolves around the earth at the same velocity as the earth rotates, so it appears to be in a fixed position in the sky. Satellite-based microwave systems can transmit data over a much greater distance than land-based systems.

Wireless Systems.   Microwaves are a form of wireless transmission that is used for long-distance communication such as in wide area networks. For short-distance communication, such as in local area networks, two other wireless systems are used. One uses radio waves similar to those used in cordless telephones. These radio waves have a range limited to a few hundred feet. Another wireless system uses infrared beams, which are like those used in television remote controls. Infrared is line-of-sight transmission so infrared systems must be placed such that the beam cannot be broken. Infrared transmission is limited to about 100 feet.

Wireless systems are sometimes used for wireless LANs, which are local area networks that communicate without wires. Wireless LANs are used in situations where it is difficult to connect computers directly with wires. For example, a wireless LAN might be used in a production area where wiring a LAN would be difficult, or in a situation where portable computers are used and are frequently moved to different locations.

Communications Channel Sources

Communications channels are provided in two main ways. One is by purchasing and installing the necessary hardware, which forms a *private communications system*. The other is by purchasing time on hardware owned by another company, which is called a *public communications system*.

Bookmark

Wireless Communications at the Internal Revenue Service

In the battle against tax fraud, one Internal Revenue Service division has decided to use wireless mobile communications as a weapon in the arsenal of field agents.

The IRS's diesel fuel program has implemented a wireless mobile computing system nationwide for agents who track diesel fuel tax fraud.

The IRS implementation is part of a general trend in which mainstream corporate functions such as sales are increasingly using wireless communications.

Until recently, most wireless mobile programs were relegated to specific functions such as field service, warehouse inventory tracking, and transportation.

"Wireless is still targeted at the vertical applications, but we are definitely seeing more uses such as general field sales, consulting, and real estate," said Dan Merriman, an analyst at Giga Information Group, Inc. in Norwell, Mass. "We are still not talking about general-purpose mobile professionals. But mobile professionals who place a high value on speed of communications are using wireless."

Using Oracle Mobile Agents software from Oracle Corp. in Redwood Shores, Calif., and a wireless mobile system designed by Aris Corp. in Seattle, about 150 IRS agents use laptops from Compaq Corp. in Houston and handhelds from Hewlett-Packard Co. in Palo Alto, Calif., to log discrepancies and complaints, settle fines, and access the IRS's main database.

All diesel vehicles and diesel fuel stations are subject to inspection by IRS compliance officers. The inspectors check vehicles for untaxed gas at weigh stations or at truck stops—and they check the pumps, too.

Prior to the implementation of the program, field agents lugged extensive files and data on the road, according to Roy Lively, an excise program analyst at the IRS. The agents—who inspect stations that sell diesel fuel and the vehicles that use it to ensure that the proper taxes are being paid—had to sort through paperwork while making inspections and then mail in information.

Lively couldn't give a total cost of the project. But he said, "We definitely think it was worth it, and in the end we will save money." The users also have cellular hookups to the laptops for wireless access to file reports and to access the Oracle Mobile Agent on the data server. The handheld computers are used to record site locations, license plate numbers, and other information.

QUESTIONS

1. What types of applications have wireless communications been used for in the past and what types is it moving into?
2. Why did the IRS decide to use wireless communications for their diesel fuel program?

WEB SITE
Internal Revenue Service: www.irs.ustreas.gov

Source: Mindy Blodgett, "IRS goes wireless to fight diesel fuel tax fraud," *Computerworld*, February 10, 1997, pp. 47–48.

Any organization can purchase the necessary hardware to set up a private communications system. This approach is common when the communication is limited to a small geographic area. Private systems are rare, however, for long-distance communications. Stringing long-distance wire or fiber-optic cables, setting up a system of microwave antennas, or launching a satellite is very expensive. Such expense is warranted only when the organization has significant communication needs.

Most organizations use public communications systems for long-distance communications. These systems are called *public* because anyone who is willing to pay the fee can use them. The main public system is the telephone network, which is owned by many companies called *common carriers*. In the United States, local telephone companies, such as Pacific Bell in California, handle short-distance communications and other companies, such as AT&T, Sprint, and MCI, handle long-distance communications. In many other countries, telephone communication is handled by government-owned systems.

Telephone networks from common carriers most often send analog signals over wire cable to and from a customer's telephone. Between telephones, the analog signal may be converted to a digital signal for transmission over a fiber-optic cable. An alternative approach that is becoming increasingly common is to use a system called ISDN, which stands for Integrated Services Digital Network. With ISDN, the signal from the telephone is in digital form. (A special telephone is needed to use ISDN.) The advantage of ISDN is that both voice and data can be sent over the telephone line at the same time. In addition, data can be transmitted at a greater speed than with an analog telephone line. The main disadvantage of ISDN is that it is more expensive than standard telephone communication.

Communications Devices

A computer cannot be connected directly to a channel. Instead, special devices are needed between the channel and the computer. These communications devices provide various functions so that data can be sent and received over the channel.

Modems. Computers transmit data using digital signals. If a communications channel is a digital channel, the computer can send data over the channel without changing its signal type. If an analog channel is used, however, the digital signals from the computer must be converted to analog form for transmission, a process called *modulation*. The analog data, when it reaches the other end of the channel, must be converted back to digital form, which is called *demodulation*. Modulation and demodulation are performed by a communications device called a modem, which means MOdulator-DEModulator. There must be a modem at each end of the channel—one to modulate the signal and one to demodulate it. (See Fig. 6.9.) Because the most common source of analog communications channels is the telephone network, most modems are designed to connect computer devices to telephone lines and to modulate and demodulate signals sent over those lines.

In addition to providing conversion between digital and analog signals for a channel, modems determine other characteristics of the channel. First, the modem sets the data rate of the transmission. Modems can be purchased with different data rates. For example, 28,800 bps and 33,600 bps modems are common and even higher rates are available. In general, the faster the modem, the more expensive it is. The speed of the modem must be less than or equal to the maximum speed allowed by the channel. Second, the modem determines the data flow: half-duplex or full-duplex. (Simplex is rare.) Most modems can be switched between half-duplex and full-duplex by special software. Finally, the modem determines whether the trans-

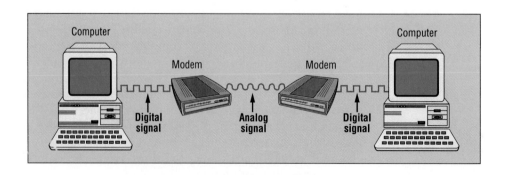

FIGURE 6.9

Use of modems

mission is asynchronous or synchronous. Modems can be purchased for either method; usually synchronous modems are more expensive than asynchronous modems. Note that the characteristics of the modems at both ends of the channel must match; that is, they must both use the same data rate (which can be adjusted automatically by most modems), data flow, and transmission method.

Most modems plug into the main circuit board of the computer which connects the modem to the other components of the computer. The telephone line then plugs into a jack in the modem. These modems are called *internal modems* because they are inside the computer. Sometimes *external modems* are used which are outside the computer, connected to it by a cable. Many modems also include facsimile, or fax, capability, which allows the computer to send and receive faxes using the modem. These modems are often called *fax modems*.

ISDN Terminal Adapters.   Modems are used to connect computers to analog telephone lines. To connect a computer to a digital ISDN telephone line, an ISDN terminal adapter is needed. Because the channel is digital, an ISDN adapter does not do modulation and demodulation as does a modem. Instead, the adapter adjusts the form of the digital signal from the computer to the form required by the ISDN line. Just as with a modem, an ISDN adapter must be at each end of the channel to provide the connections between the ISDN channel and computers. ISDN provides faster communication than modems and analog telephone lines. Data rates up to 128,000 bps are possible with ISDN.

Communications Control Units.   Two computer devices may be connected over a channel with no other devices sharing the channel. In this simple situation, usually only modems, ISDN terminal adapters, or similar units for connecting the computer to the channel are needed. An alternative is to have several computer devices share a channel. When this situation occurs, special communications control units are needed. These units control the communications traffic over channels much like traffic police control auto traffic on city streets. For example, when several terminals share a channel, a device is needed to keep the communications from getting mixed up.

There are several types of communications control units. One is a *multiplexer*, which takes the signal from several slow-speed computer devices and combines them for transmission over a high-speed channel. At the other end of the channel another multiplexer breaks the high-speed signal from the channel into the separate signals from each device. Another type of communications control unit is a *controller*. This unit allows several computer devices to communicate over a channel by storing signals from each device and forwarding them when appropriate.

Many computer systems have a separate computer, often a minicomputer, that handles communications control. This computer is called a *front-end processor* because it operates between the channel and the main computer. It performs all communications functions for the main computer, thus reducing the workload of that computer.

Figure 6.10 shows how communications control units may be used for data communications. In this figure, several terminals at the user's local site are managed by a controller. This controller and other terminals send signals to a multiplexer, which combines the signals and forwards them to a modem. The modem modulates the signal from the multiplexer for transmission over a high-speed communications channel. At the remote site, where the main computer is located, another modem demodulates the signal and sends it to the front-end processor. Also at the remote site, the front-end processor receives signals directly from other terminals and from

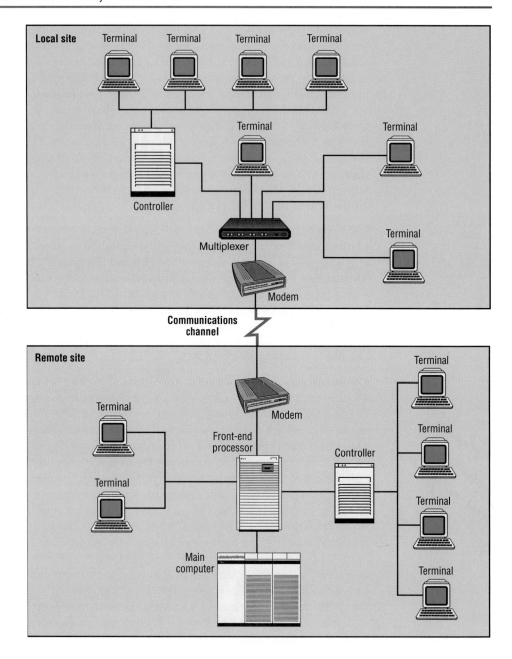

FIGURE 6.10

Use of communications control units

another controller. The front-end processor sends signals from all sources to the main computer, which is sometimes called the *host computer*. To send signals back to the terminals from the computer, this process is reversed.

Protocol Converters.   When people talk with each other, they follow unstated rules about how to communicate. For example, they agree to talk in the same language, they say "hello" when they meet and "good-bye" when they part, and when one person talks the other person is quiet. These rules are necessary to ensure proper communication.

When computer devices communicate, they also must follow rules. These rules are called <u>protocols</u>. The protocols state what language the communication will be in (ASCII or EBCDIC), what signal will start the communication and what signal will end it, and how one device will know whether the other is communicating so that it does not try to communicate at the same time.

Unfortunately, not all computer systems use the same protocols. Often, computer devices manufactured by different companies use different protocols. If two devices with incompatible protocols are to communicate, some way of converting the protocols of one device to those of the other device is needed. This function is performed by a communications device called a protocol converter. The converter connects one device with the channel that goes to the other device. With the appropriate type of protocol converter, a computer device manufactured by one company can communicate with one that uses different protocols manufactured by another company.

Data Encryption Devices. One problem with data communications is the need for security of the data transmitted over a channel. It is sometimes possible to tap into a communications channel and intercept data sent over it. One way of solving this problem is to code the data in an unintelligible form before it is transmitted. This process is called data encryption and it can be done by a special data encryption device. The data is coded by the device and then sent over the channel. At the other end of the channel, a similar device is used to decode the data after it is received. The coding and decoding requires the use of a special *key*, which is a number entered into the data encryption device at each end of the channel. If the channel is tapped and the key is not known, the coded data cannot be interpreted correctly.

LAN Adapters. When computers communicate using local area networks, special communications devices are needed to connect the computers to the channel that forms the network. These devices, called LAN adapters, allow a computer to send data to and receive data from other computers in the local area network. Each computer needs a LAN adapter which plugs into the computer's main circuit board. The LAN channel then plugs into a connector in the LAN adapter.

Communications Software

In addition to communications hardware, communications software is needed to control communications between computers. Each computer must have communications software. This software receives data from communications devices connected to the channel and passes the data on to other programs in the computer for processing. The communications software also gets the results of processing from programs in the computer and sends this data to communications devices for transmission over the channel.

Personal Computer Communications Software

Communications software in personal computers provides two main functions: terminal emulation and file transfer. Terminal emulation makes the personal computer act like a terminal, which is necessary because computers expect a terminal at the other end of the channel, not another computer. The communications software in the personal computer makes the other computer "think" it is communicating with a terminal. A user then can use the personal computer exactly as if he or she were using a terminal connected directly to the other computer. Because different types of terminals have different characteristics, personal computer communications software allows the user to select which type of terminal he or she wants the software to emulate.

The other function provided by personal computer communications software is file transfer, which involves sending data from a file at the personal computer to the other computer and vice versa. When data is sent from a personal computer to a remote computer, the process is called uploading. When data is sent from a remote computer to a personal computer, the process is called downloading. (See Fig. 6.11.) Personal computer communications software allows a user to both upload and download files with another computer.

File transfer is accomplished by following certain rules called file-transfer protocols. The protocols specify how data will be transferred and how errors will be checked. There are several file-transfer protocols in use, and the same protocol must be used by the communications software at both ends of the channel. Most personal computer communications programs allow a user to select the desired protocol.

Multiple-user Computer Communications Software

Multiple-user computer communications software provides the ability for minicomputers and mainframe computers to communicate with many terminals. This type of software, which is sometimes called a *telecommunications monitor*, keeps track of which terminal sent which data and decides to which terminal the results of processing should be sent. The telecommunications monitor also provides security. When the user logs in, it checks to see if the user's identification number and password are valid. The telecommunications monitor or other software in the computer may provide certain functions sometimes done by hardware including protocol conversion, code conversion (i.e., conversion between ASCII and EBCDIC), and data encryption. If the system has a front-end processor, the telecommunications monitor runs to that computer so that the main computer does not have to do communications processing.

Network Communications Software

With a local area network, software is needed on server and client computers to provide communications over the network. On servers, this software is the *network operating system* or *NOS*, which was discussed in Chapter 5. On clients, network communications capabilities must be provided with or added to the operating system. Network communications software allows the computers in a network to send and receive data through the LAN adapter connected to the LAN channel.

Wide area networks use a variety of communications software, including telecommunications monitors on multiple-user computers. The communications software transmits data between distant computers, sometimes selecting alternate routes to speed communication. It also provides for communications with users at terminals or personal computers.

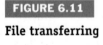

FIGURE 6.11

File transferring

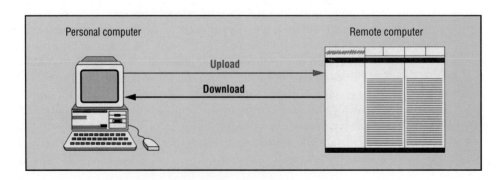

Remote Access

Data communication can take several forms, the simplest of which is communication between a user and a remote computer. The user may have a terminal or a personal computer. The channel used is usually a telephone line. The remote computer may be a multiple-user computer, such as a minicomputer or a mainframe computer, that does processing required by the user, or a server computer in a network that provides access to the network for the user. Communication between the user and the remote computer is needed so that the user can access the capabilities of the remote computer or the network.

Terminal Communications

Figure 6.12 shows the communications hardware and software needed for terminal communications with a remote computer. At the terminal end, the user must have hardware to connect the terminal to the communications channel. At a minimum, a modem (or ISDN terminal adapter) is required. The modem at the terminal must have the same characteristics as the modem at the computer's end of the channel. Thus, the data rate (bits per second), data flow (half-duplex or full-duplex), and transmission method (asynchronous or synchronous) must be the same for both modems. In addition to a modem, a protocol converter and various communications control units may be needed. A protocol converter is required if the terminal's protocol is not compatible with that of the computer. The communications control units are not usually the user's concern, although they may be present to help with the communications. Finally, a data encryption device is needed if data encryption is used.

At the remote computer's end, communications hardware is needed to connect the computer to the channel. In addition to a modem, various communications control units may be used. A protocol converter may be needed unless protocol conversion is provided at the terminal end. A data encryption device is needed if data encryption is used.

Communications software is not needed with the user's terminal because a terminal is not a computer. The remote computer, however, needs a telecommunications

Terminal vs. P.C.

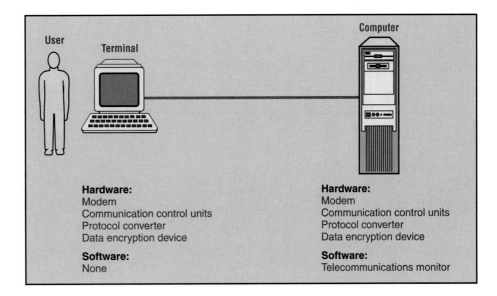

FIGURE 6.12

Communications hardware and software needs for terminal communications

User   Terminal   Computer

Hardware: **Hardware:**
Modem   Modem
Communication control units   Communication control units
Protocol converter   Protocol converter
Data encryption device   Data encryption device

Software: **Software:**
None   Telecommunications monitor

monitor to manage communication with the terminal. With terminal communication to a remote computer, the user can use the terminal exactly as if it were connected directly to the computer.

Personal Computer Communications

Figure 6.13 summarizes the hardware and software needs for personal computer communications with a remote computer. A modem (or ISDN terminal adapter) is needed at the personal computer end of the channel and at the remote computer end. The characteristics (rate, flow, and method) of these modems must match. Also at the remote computer end may be various communications control units. A protocol converter may be needed at the personal computer end or the remote computer end. Data encryption devices may be needed at both ends if data encryption is used.

Both computers in personal computer communications need communications software. The remote computer needs a telecommunications monitor, and the personal computer needs a communications program to provide terminal emulation and file-transferring capabilities.

When a personal computer communicates with a multiple-user computer, the user can use the personal computer as a terminal exactly as in terminal communications. In addition, the user can transfer files to and from the remote computer. If a personal computer communicates with a server in a network, the user can use the personal computer as if it were part of the network. Businesses allow users to use personal computers to communicate with the company's computers and networks so that the user can use the remote system's capabilities, including processing and storage of data. In addition, such communication lets users transfer data between their personal computers and the company's computers and networks.

Another use of personal computer communications is to access a computer system at an information utility. This is a company such as CompuServe, America Online, and Prodigy, which has computers that store information of interest to a variety of users. Some information utilities store information for the general public, such as stock prices, airline flight schedules, and recent news. Other utilities store information useful to certain types of businesses, such as legal data used by law firms.

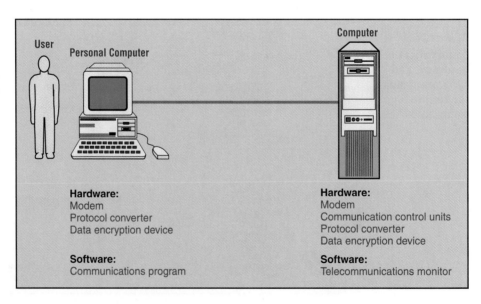

FIGURE 6.13

Communications hardware and software needs for personal computer communications

Information utilities also provide services such as e-mail and access to the World Wide Web on the Internet. If a user only wants e-mail and Internet access, and not other services provided by an information utility, the user can access an Internet service provider or ISP, which is a company offering only these services.

Network Organization

Network communications involves the transmission of data between users, and between users and servers connected to a network. To accomplish network communications, the network must be organized in a logical way. Each computer or other device connected to a network is called a *node* in the network. One way of organizing the nodes in a network is for each node to be connected to all other nodes in the network, an arrangement sometimes called a *mesh*. (See Fig. 6.14.) The problem with this arrangement is that as more nodes are added to the network, many more connections are needed. (With 5 nodes, 10 connections are needed; with 6 nodes, 15 connections are needed; with 7 nodes, 21 connections are needed, and so forth.) To solve this problem, several common organizations are used for networks. (See Fig. 6.15.)

In a star network each node is connected to a central computer node. For two nodes to communicate, data must be sent from one node to the central computer, and then the central computer sends the data on to the other node. The primary advantage of this approach is that the "distance" that data has to travel is short; data has to travel only through the central computer to get from one node to another. The main disadvantage is that if the central computer fails the entire network cannot function.

A hierarchical network consists of nodes organized like a family tree. The top node is a central computer that is connected to several other nodes, which may also be computers. Each of these nodes may be connected to several other nodes, and

FIGURE 6.14

Network organization with each node connected to all other nodes

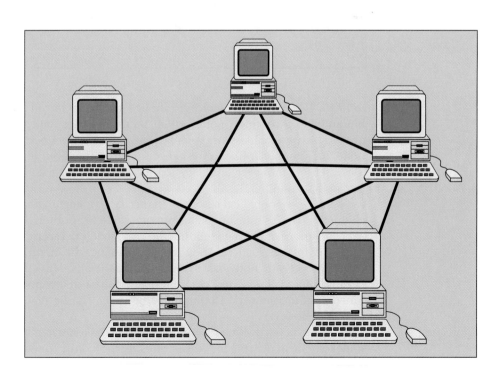

FIGURE 6.15

Network organizations

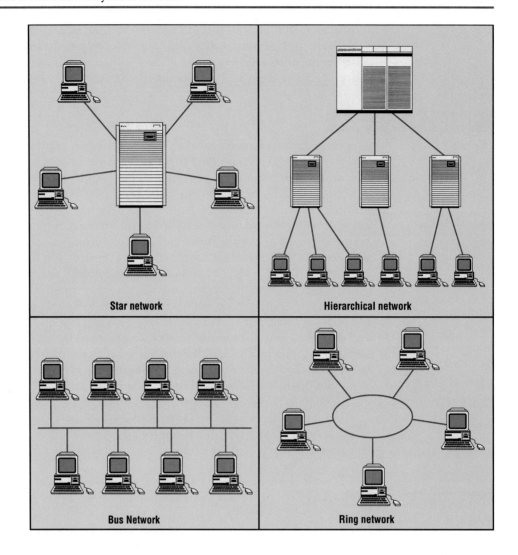

Star network

Hierarchical network

Bus Network

Ring network

so forth. Two nodes can communicate by sending data from the first node "up" the hierarchy to a common node, which then sends the data "down" to the second node. This approach is more reliable than a star network because failure of any one node does not mean the entire network cannot function. It is more complex than a star network, however, and data may have to travel a greater "distance" to get from one node to another.

In a bus network, each node is connected to a single, common communications channel or *bus*. To transmit data from one node to another, the first node sends the data and information that identifies the node that is to receive the data in both directions over the bus. Each node on the bus examines the identifying information and, if it is the receiving node, takes the data from the bus. This approach is very reliable because there is no central computer, and failure of any node does not affect the function of the network. Communication speed can be slower than other types of networks, however.

A ring network consists of nodes connected to form a loop. Data travels from node to node in the ring, usually in one direction only. To send data from one node to another, the first node sends the data and information about which node is to receive the data to the next node in the ring. This node either keeps the data if it is the receiving node or forwards the data on to the next node. This process continues until the data reaches the receiving node. Most ring networks are as reliable as bus networks because if a node fails the data usually can be sent past the failed node and hence the function of the network is not affected. Like a bus network, communication can be slower on a ring network than on other types of networks.

Finally, many networks are hybrid networks, which means they are combinations of the network organizations described so far. Thus, a network may have some nodes connected in no particular pattern, others connected in a star or a hierarchy, and still others that form a bus or a ring. A hybrid network provides the greatest versatility in network organization.

Local Area Networks

As you know, a *local area network* or *LAN* is a network located in a single building or in several nearby buildings. LANs usually are organized as bus or ring networks using coaxial cable, twisted-pair wiring, or fiber-optic cable as a communications channel medium. LANs may also use radio waves or infrared beams for wireless communications. Local area bus networks are usually a type of network called an *Ethernet*, which is an approach developed by Xerox Corporation. Ring networks, on the other hand, are often a type of network called a *Token Ring*, which is an approach developed by IBM.

Users most often use a LAN through personal computers, which are clients that communicate with server computers. Figure 6.16 summarizes the hardware and software needed for LAN communications. Each client personal computer is connected to the channel by a LAN adapter in the computer. The LAN cable or wire plugs into the adapter. Each personal computer also needs a network communication capability in its operating system to allow the computer to send and receive data over the network's channel. A server is also connected to the LAN by a LAN adapter. A server needs a network operating system to provide communication with client computers.

A LAN may contain several servers with resources that can be used by any of the client computers. A print server is a server with a printer that can be used for printing by other computers connected to the LAN. A file server is a server with a secondary storage device, usually a large hard disk drive, that can be used for file storage by other computers in the LAN. (Often one server is used as both a print server and a file server.) A database server is a server with secondary storage that can be used for database processing by other LAN computers.

With a LAN, a user can use any of the resources in the LAN. For example, when the user needs to print output, he or she can transmit the data to the print server. To store or retrieve common data, the user can communicate with the file or database server. The user can use any of the shared resources in the LAN by transmitting data over the LAN.

A LAN also provides convenient information sharing. Data can be stored on a file or database server where it is available to all users. Spreadsheets, graphic images, and other items can also be stored on a file server for access by different users. LANs usually have an e-mail system that stores electronic messages on a file server. All these techniques make LANs very useful for sharing information.

FIGURE 6.16

**Communications
hardware and
software needs for
local area network
communications**

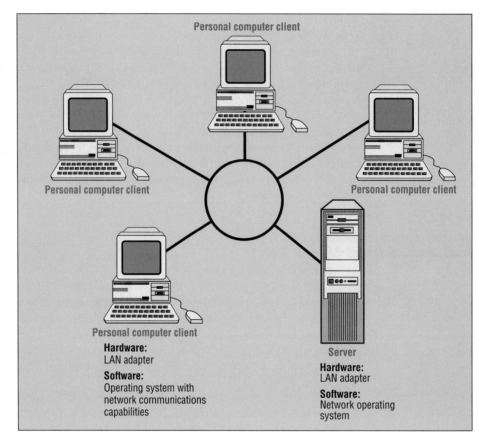

Personal computer client

Personal computer client

Personal computer client

Personal computer client

Server

Hardware:
LAN adapter
Software:
Operating system with
network communications
capabilities

Hardware:
LAN adapter
Software:
Network operating
system

Client-server Computing

Local area networks are often used for <u>client-server computing</u>. (See Fig. 6.17.) In this approach, a server computer stores databases for use by many clients. The server has database software for storing and accessing data on the server. The client computers are usually the users' personal computers with application software that processes data and provides a user interface.

Client-server computing might be used as follows: A user enters a request for data processing through the user interface on the client computer. The client determines what data is needed and sends a request for the data over the LAN to the server computer. The server then locates the requested data and sends it back to the client over the LAN. The client processes the data and presents the results of processing through the user interface to the user.

Client-server computing is used extensively in information systems. For example, a business may do inventory control using client-server computing. The inventory database would be on the server in the network and the client computers in the network would have access to the inventory data, processing it and presenting the results to the user.

There are several advantages of client-server computing over multiple-user computer processing. One advantage is that the shared server computer only does database management, not data processing or user interface control. With multiple-user computer processing, however, the central computer must do database management, data

Advantages of Client/server

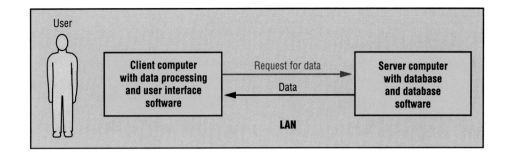

FIGURE 6.17

Client-server computing

processing, and user interface control, which requires a much larger computer than a database server. Another advantage to client-server computing is that it is relatively easy to add capabilities for more users. More client personal computers with the required software can easily be added to the network without changing the server. With multiple-user computer processing, however, it is often necessary to acquire a new main computer in order to add more users. Because of these advantages, networks using client-server computing are replacing multiple-user computers in many businesses.

Wide Area Networks

A *wide area network* or *WAN* covers a large geographic area. Some WANs just cover a city, in which case they may be called *metropolitan area networks (MAN)*. Other WANs cover a part of a country or an entire country. Still other WANs are international, extending into several countries.

WANs consist of nodes that sometimes are organized as star or hierarchical networks, but more often are organized as hybrid networks. Computers in a WAN communicate over public or private communications systems. WANs may use any channel media, including fiber-optic cable and microwaves, for communication. Often, the channel is a combination of media. For example, a channel may start off as a twisted-pair wire which connects to a fiber-optic cable, which then connects to a land-based microwave system, and eventually connects to a satellite system.

WANs often include many different types of computers from personal computers to supercomputers. Users use a WAN through a terminal or personal computer. The user's device may be connected to the WAN using the communications devices described earlier, such as modems and communications control units. Multiple-user computers found in WANs also need various communications devices. All computers in WANs require communications software.

Wide area networks are used by many businesses that have offices and other facilities at distant locations. For example, airlines use WANs for their reservation systems so that reservation clerks at airports and travel agents in their offices can communicate with central computers. Another example is banks, which use WANs to connect automated teller machines (ATMs) with the bank's computers.

WANs provide long-distance remote access to information and processing. When data is stored on a computer in the WAN, it can be accessed by any other computer connected to the WAN. Processing can be done at remote computers in the WAN by signaling the computer to execute a particular program.

As with LANs, information can be easily shared with WANs. Data stored in a computer in the WAN is available to any other WAN computer. Many organizations use WANs for sending and receiving e-mail over long distances.

Finally, WANs make it easy to share resources. A WAN may contain special computers, printers, storage devices, software, and other resources that can be shared among all WAN users. For example, a business may have a supercomputer connected to a WAN that can be used by anyone in the business. WANs provide such resource sharing over long distances.

WANs make global connectivity a reality for businesses. Through international WANs, global businesses are able to keep track of distant operations. For example, a business with headquarters in San Francisco can communicate with its operations in South America, Europe, and Asia, and share information with offices in New York and London. Such international communication is made possible by wide area networks.

Internetworks

One of the major trends in communications is toward interconnecting different networks to create an _internetwork_. For example, a business may have LANs in each office which are connected to a national WAN which in turn is connected to an international WAN. Internetworks provide the ability for any user connected to any network in the business to share information and resources, or have access to remote information or processing throughout all the networks in the business.

Internetworks use various devices to connect different networks. A _bridge_ is a hardware device that is used to connect two similar networks, such as two similar LANs. A _gateway_ is a device used to connect two different types of networks, such as a LAN with a WAN. A _router_ is a device that routes messages through various networks. Sophisticated communications software is required with these and other devices to interconnect networks.

Internetworks are often used in organizational information systems that span significant distances. For example, a business may have a customer order system in which orders are entered at computers connected to LANs in several distant locations. The remote LANs are then connected by a WAN to another network at a central location where access to customer and product databases is provided. The network may even cross national borders so that different parts of it are in different countries, in which case it would be an _international network_. The customer order system would then be an international information system. The order system functions smoothly because of the ability to interconnect the different networks.

Internetworks are also used for interorganizational information systems. These systems, which were introduced in Chapter 1, allow organizations to use computers to transact business among themselves. Examples of interorganizational information systems are electronic data interchange (EDI) systems that allow businesses to exchange data such as purchase orders and bills, and electronic funds transfer (EFT) systems that allow funds to be transferred electronically between financial institutions. These systems require networks in different businesses to be interconnected in _interorganizational networks_ so that information can be electronically exchanged between the businesses.

The Internet

Perhaps the most well-known internetwork is the _Internet_. The Internet is the name of a public, international collection of interconnected wide area and local area networks. The Internet grew out of several military, academic, and research networks. Today its exact size is unknown but it includes over a million computers and many millions of users around the world. The Internet is part of the _information superhighway_, which is a concept for allowing any computer to be connected to a national or international network, just as any telephone can be connected to a telephone network.

Internetwork at Scientific-Atlanta

Scientific-Atlanta Inc., a $1.2 billion cable and satellite communication equipment supplier, has an internetworking strategy that links 10 worldwide sites to and within its Atlanta headquarters.

Creating this new network meant abandoning a mix of equipment from eight different networking companies over a three-year period. Networks in Hong Kong, Rome, Shanghai, and other locations evolved separately at each site without a centralized, internetworking plan. Together, the mix of equipment proved too unreliable to sustain the communication links required by Scientific-Atlanta's growing global operations.

"We are Atlanta-based but becoming international in a big way; it's the fastest-growing market for us," said Kamalesh Dwivedi, vice-president of IT for Scientific-Atlanta.

Based in Atlanta for more than 40 years, Scientific-Atlanta's 4,600 employees provide business services through 16 worldwide offices with representatives in more than 70 countries. Customers of the firm's networks include cable operators, broadcasters, telephone and utility companies, governments, and corporations worldwide.

While Scientific-Atlanta is probably best known as a supplier of cable television set-top terminals, its alliances with other companies position the company to take advantage of telecommunications deregulation. At the same time, competition is becoming more fierce as new competitors enter the market.

With deregulation at hand and the new network installation the firm is better prepared to react to market changes. "Now, our salespeople can get information instantaneously instead of biweekly updates," said Jim Gurr, manager of worldwide networks for Scientific-Atlanta. "If they need to check on a customer's credit rating, they can get it on-line in real time."

By 1993, Scientific-Atlanta found itself with several disparate networks on four continents and unreliable communications links. To address the inadequacies in its growing network, Scientific-Atlanta opted to centralize its network administration and design. Using routers and other equipment from Bay Networks Inc., of Santa Clara, Calif., the multinational company installed a fiber-optic backbone at its Atlanta headquarters. The backbone connects all of Scientific-Atlanta's metro sites within a 100-mile stretch, all within a 20-mile radius of Atlanta.

The Atlanta operations are powered by three of Bay Network's BCN routers. Five smaller BLN routers feed traffic onto the BCNs. Additionally, hundreds of ASN routers reside at remote locations in Atlanta and around the globe, sending traffic from Canada, Mexico, Australia, England, Italy, Hong Kong, and China. The result is a robust internetwork that makes worldwide communications commonplace.

"Worldwide, we can communicate much easier, and the productivity of the employees has grown because of highly reduced downtime," said Dwivedi.

Applications now accessible to all its offices include the firm's own KnowledgeNet program that includes information on Scientific-Atlanta's customers, suppliers, and competitors, as well as the industry. KnowledgeNet gathers real-time information from external sources and makes this available on a company intranet.

"Now our users can get the information they need to operate instantaneously," said Gurr.

QUESTIONS

1. What problems did Scientific-Atlanta have that prompted the company to install an internetwork?
2. How is the internetwork connected at Scientific-Atlanta?
3. What benefits does Scientific-Atlanta receive from the internetwork?

WEB SITE
Scientific-Atlanta: www.sciatl.com

Source: Kristina B. Sullivan, "Networking around the globe," *PC WEEK*, May 13, 1996, pp. N17, N20.

The Internet is not one network but many networks connected together. The networks are connected to high-speed communications channels, called *backbones*, that are used to transmit data between networks. Routers are used to route data from one location to another.

In order for the Internet to function, computers in the network must use the same rules or protocols for communications. The Internet uses two protocols: Transmission Control Protocol (TCP) and Internet Protocol (IP). Together these are referred to as TCP/IP. Using these protocols, any computer connected to the Internet can communicate with any other computer.

Servers:

- print

- file

- database

- web

The Internet provides a number of services, the most widely used of which is the World Wide Web or WWW. The World Wide Web provides easy access to many types of information found on the Internet. The Web is a *hypertext* system, which means that information is linked together so that the user can easily go from one piece of information to another, related piece. Through the Web the user can access many types of information from universities, businesses, libraries, research institutes, government agencies, and so on. Web information includes not only text but also graphic images, pictures, video, and sound.

Businesses use the World Wide Web for providing information about their products and services. This information is given in screens or *pages*. All the pages for a business are stored on a computer, called a Web server, that is connected to the Internet. A consumer can use a Web *browser* to look up a business's *home page* on the Web, which is the beginning page for information provided by the business. (See Fig. 6.18.) From there, the user can select options with the mouse to see details about products available from the business. The user can often request additional information about the product to be sent by regular mail and can sometimes order the product itself. Many businesses list information about their services on the Web. For example, many airlines provide flight schedules on the Web. Banks also provide electronic banking through the Web. The use of the World Wide Web by businesses is increasing very rapidly. In general, the use of the Web and related technology to promote and sell products is called electronic commerce.

The Internet includes a number of other services besides the World Wide Web:

- *E-mail.* The Internet provides electronic mail service between users of the network.
- *Telnet.* This is a service for connecting one computer in the Internet to another computer in the Internet.

FIGURE 6.18

A home page

- *FTP (File Transfer Protocol).* This is a service for transferring a file from one computer to another.
- *Gopher.* This is a menu-driven service that provides easy access to information on the Internet.
- *Usenet or NetNews.* This service allows users to share information about a wide range of topics.

The Internet is truly an international network. Any Internet information service almost anywhere in the world is available to almost any computer anywhere else in the world. Such easy access to Internet information and services has been part of the reason for its very rapid rise in popularity.

Intranets

The popularity and ease of use of the Internet has resulted in businesses establishing Internet-type networks entirely within the business. Such a network, which uses the TCP/IP protocol, is called an <u>intranet</u>. An intranet is used in the same way as the Internet: Users within the business view pages with a browser.

Users outside a business cannot access the business's intranet. To prevent such access, a hardware and software system called a <u>firewall</u> is used. (See Fig. 6.19.) Users from outside the business have access to the public information, such as pages with descriptions of products and services, but are prevented by the firewall from getting to private company data.

Firewall

FIGURE 6.19

An intranet with a firewall

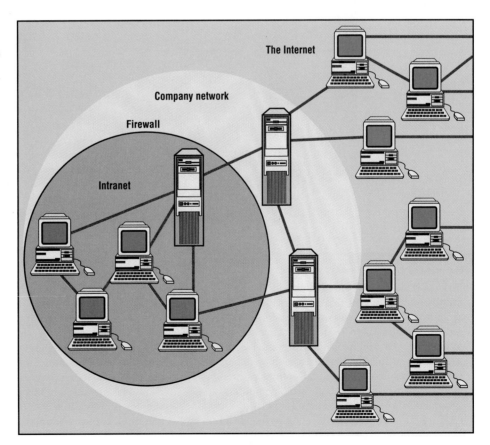

Some businesses have set up intranets that they let certain companies or individuals outside the business access. For example, a business may have an intranet with inventory data that a supplier can use to check inventory levels for automatic restocking. Connection to the intranet is allowed by means of codes and passwords so that only certain companies or individuals have access. This type of externally accessible intranet is called an <u>extranet</u>.

In general, users do not need sophisticated personal computers to use intranets or the Internet. All that is needed is a computer that can run a browser and has the necessary communications capability. A computer with capabilities limited to intranet and Internet access is called a <u>network computer</u>. (See Fig. 6.20.) Network computers sell for one-third to one-half the price of other personal computers. Some businesses are eliminating many of their personal computers and replacing them with network computers, resulting in a considerable cost savings.

The use of intranets is likely to increase in the future. Businesses are finding that intranets, along with extranets and the Internet, provide a common network system that can handle many of their needs. Someday, businesses may use intranets, extranets, and the Internet for most of their networks.

FIGURE 6.20

A network computer

Chapter Summary

☐ Businesses need networks in information systems for four main reasons. The first is to provide remote access to information and processing for users. The second is to allow users to share information related to the operation and management of the business. The third reason is to allow users to share expensive computer resources such as high-volume printers, large-capacity disk drives, high-speed computers, and special software. The final reason is to provide interorganizational communication so that different businesses can communicate with each other. (p. 158)

☐ The main characteristics of **communications channels** are signal type, data rate, data flow, and transmission method. A channel may transmit data using a **digital signal**, which is a series of pulses, or an **analog signal**, which is a wave pattern. The data rate of a channel is measured in **bits per second** or **bps**. With **simplex transmission**, data flows in one direction; in **half-duplex transmission**, data flows in both directions but only in one direction at a time; with **full-duplex transmission**, data flows in both directions simultaneously. In **asynchronous transmission**, one character is transmitted at a time over the channel. In **synchronous transmission**, a block of characters is transmitted over the channel. (pp. 158–166)

☐ A **modem** converts digital signals to analog signals (modulation) and converts analog signals to digital signals (demodulation). Other communications devices include **ISDN terminal adapters**, **communications control units**, **protocol converters**, **data encryption** devices, and **LAN adapters**. (pp. 166–169)

☐ **Communications software** controls communications between computers. Personal computer communications software provides **terminal emulation**, which makes a personal computer act like a terminal, and **file transfer**, which allows data from a file to be sent between computers. On multiple-user computers, communications software keeps track of which terminal sent which data and where to send the results of processing. Communications software on a local area network includes a network operating system on server computers and communication capabilities in client computer operating systems. With a wide area network, communications software transmits data between distant computers. (pp. 169–170)

☐ For personal computer communications, the personal computer needs a modem (or ISDN terminal adapter), possibly a protocol converter and a data encryption device, and a communications program. The remote computer must have a modem and possibly various communications control units, a data encryption device, and a protocol converter. In addi-

tion, the remote computer must have a telecommunications monitor. (pp. 171–173)

☐ Local area networks are usually organized as **bus** or **ring networks**. Each computer in a local area network must have a LAN adapter. A LAN may contain several servers, including **print servers**, **file servers**, and **database servers.** Each computer in a local area network must also have network communications software. (pp. 173–177)

☐ Wide area networks are sometimes organized as **star** or **hierarchical networks**, but more often as **hybrid networks**. All types of computers are found in WANs, from personal computers to supercomputers. Various communications devices are needed in WANs, including modems and communications control units. All computers in WANs require communications software. (pp. 177–178)

☐ Networks are interconnected to form **internetworks** by using communications devices such as bridges, gateways, and routers, along with special communications software. Internetworks allow businesses to connect different networks within the business to support organizational information systems. They are also used for interorganizational information systems such as electronic data interchange and electronic funds transfer systems. The **Internet** is a public, international collection of interconnected wide area and local area networks that provides a number of special services, including the **World Wide Web**. An **intranet** is an Internet-type network that is contained entirely within a business. (pp. 178–182)

Key Terms

Analog Signal (p. 159)
Asynchronous Transmission (p. 161)
Bandwidth (p. 160)
Baud Rate (p. 160)
Bus Network (p. 174)
Client-Server Computing (p. 176)
Communications Channel (p. 158)
Communications Control Unit (p. 167)
Communications Device (p. 159)
Communications Software (p. 169)
Database Server (p. 175)
Data Encryption (p. 169)
Digital Signal (p. 159)
Downloading (p. 170)
Electronic Commerce (p. 180)
Extranet (p. 182)

File Server (p. 175)
File Transfer (p. 170)
File-Transfer Protocol (p. 170)
Firewall (p. 181)
Full-Duplex Transmission (p. 160)
Half-Duplex Transmission (p. 160)
Hierarchical Network (p. 173)
Hybrid Network (p. 175)
Information Superhighway (p. 178)
Information Utility (p. 172)
Internet (p. 178)
Internet Service Provider (ISP) (p. 173)
Internetwork (p. 178)
Intranet (p. 181)
ISDN (p. 166)
ISDN Terminal Adapter (p. 167)

LAN Adapter (p. 169)
Modem (p. 166)
Network Computer (p. 182)
Print Server (p. 175)
Protocol Converter (p. 169)
Protocols (p. 168)
Ring Network (p. 174)
Simplex Transmission (p. 160)
Star Network (p. 173)
Synchronous Transmission (p. 161)
Terminal Emulation (p. 169)
Uploading (p. 170)
Web Server (p. 180)
Wireless LAN (p. 164)
World Wide Web (WWW) (p. 180)

Assignment Material

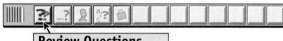

Review Questions

Fill-in Questions

1. A data communications link between computers is called a(n) _____.

2. The data rate over a communications channel is measured in _____.

3. Data flow in only one direction in a channel is called _____. Data flow in two directions in a channel but in only one direction at a time is called _____. Data flow in two directions simultaneously in a channel is called _____.

4. Transmission of one character at a time in a channel is called _____, whereas transmission of a block of characters together in a channel is called _____.

5. Local area networks that use radio waves or infrared beams are called _____.

6. The rules that describe how computer devices communicate are called _____.

7. Changing data to a form that is unintelligible unless a special key is known is called _____.

8. A(n) _____ is used to connect a personal computer to the channel of a local area network.

9. Two functions provided by personal computer communications software are _____ and _____.

10. Transferring data from a local computer to a remote computer is called _____. Transferring data from a remote computer to a local computer is called _____.

11. A network in which each node is connected to a central computer node is a(n) _____ network. A network that consists of nodes organized like a family tree is a(n) _____ network. A network in which each node is connected to a single, common communications channel is a(n) _____ network. A network in which the nodes are connected to form a loop is a(n) _____ network.

12. A(n) _____ has a printer that can be used for printing by other computers in a network. A(n) _____ uses a hard disk drive for file storage by other computers in a network. A(n) _____ has a hard disk drive that can be used for database processing by other computers in a network.

13. A collection of interconnected networks is called a(n) _____.

14. An Internet service that provides easy access to many types of information through hypertext is the _____.

15. An Internet-type network only accessible from within an organization is called a(n) _____. Access to such a network is prevented by a(n) _____.

16. A(n) _____ is an inexpensive computer with capabilities limited to Internet access.

Short-answer Questions

1. Give three reasons why businesses need networks in information systems.

2. What is the difference between a digital signal and an analog signal?

3. What is meant by *baud rate* and is it the same as bps?

4. List several common media used for communications channels.

5. What does a modem do? What is used instead of a modem in ISDN communication?

6. List several devices other than modems that are communications devices.

7. What communications hardware and software are needed with a terminal so that it can communicate with a remote computer?

8. What communications hardware and software are needed with a personal computer so that it can communicate with a remote computer?

9. How are local area networks usually organized?

10. What communications hardware and software are needed with a personal computer so that it can use a local area network?

11. What is client-server computing?

12. What communications hardware and software are used in a wide area network?

13. What is the Internet?

14. What is an extranet?

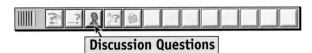

Discussion Questions

1. Other than the four reasons given in the chapter, why else might a business want to have a network?

2. What communications methods do businesses use other than computer networks?

3. With notebook computers and personal computer communications, it is possible to do some types of work almost anywhere. What advantages and disadvantages does this provide a business?

4. Imagine a college or university with no desktop computers for students to use. Instead, the school would be wired with a large local area network. Jacks to plug into the network would be provided almost everywhere—in the library, in all classrooms, in the student lounge, in dorm rooms, everywhere students can go—and wireless access to the network would also be provided. Each student would have a notebook computer that could be plugged into the network at anytime. How would this system change the educational process?

5. The Internet is an international network. Why would an international business want to have its own international wide area network instead of using the Internet?

6. Networks, and especially the Internet, make access to information very easy. Businesses and governments often want to limit access to certain information, however. Assume that you work for a business and found some information that one of your company's products has a defect. Would you ask to have that information put on the company's Web site?

Problem-solving Projects

1. If you are using a local area network or have access to one, find out everything you can about the network. What type of network is it? How is the network organized? What medium is used for the network channel? At what rate is data sent over the channel? What computers and other devices are connected to the network? Write a summary of what you found out. Use word processing software to prepare your summary.

2. Contact several information utilities (e.g., CompuServe, America Online, or Prodigy), and find out what services they provide and how much they charge. Prepare a spreadsheet, using appropriate software, that summarizes the services provided by the utility and how much it costs. Most utilities have several rate plans. Some charge a flat monthly fee, and some charge a fee plus a variable amount depending on use. Include formulas in your spreadsheet to compute the total monthly cost of using each utility with each of its different rate plans. Try several different scenarios for monthly use to see how much each utility would cost to use. Plot the results using the graphics capabilities of the spreadsheet software.

3. Use the World Wide Web to find information about jobs and careers in your field of interest. Locate an announcement for a job that you might be interested in applying for someday. Keep track of how you found the information, such as what Web sites you visited. Write a summary, using word processing software, of how you found the information and what you found out.

4. The World Wide Web is used for a number of things in marketing. It can be used for advertising by displaying promotional material for products and services. It can be used to gather information about consumer preferences by collecting responses to a questionnaire. It can also be used for selling products by providing customer order entry forms. Find Web sites that include each of these uses. (Try to find one site that has all three uses.) Write an assessment of how effective this approach is for marketing products compared to traditional forms of marketing.

Real-world Case

Geffen Records

Guns n' Roses. Sonic Youth. Elastica. Garbage. Urge Overkill. White Zombie. Lisa Loeb. Weezer. It's probably safe to say that the names of these rock acts don't immediately turn a young person's mind to thoughts of client/server computing, cyberspace, and Windows 95. Unless, of course, you're Jim Griffin, enthusiastic Internet surfer, Web cruiser, and director of technology for Geffen Records, the influential recording company that produces these and many other acts at the center of today's music scene.

To support the 225 employees who parlay these musicians into a $500-million operation, Griffin and his IS staff at Los Angeles–based Geffen have created a company intranet that uses existing technology and solutions from an information environment that boasts Internet and other cyberspace solutions.

What Griffin envisioned was a fully networked, multimedia environment that would bring together the kinds of data Geffen's employees need to do their jobs, including the music and videos of artists they represent and the financial data residing on mainframes and midrange computers at MCA, Geffen's parent corporation.

In the process, Geffen deployed Windows 95 in a corporate enterprise setting. The results, said Griffin, show that a combination of simple and inexpensive Windows 95 and HTML tools can be the basis of a highly flexible and robust enterprise information system, boasting communications and connectivity that rival more traditional—and, in many cases, far more expensive—approaches.

The impetus for the new system was the realization that Geffen's information infrastructure was woefully fragmented and inefficient. The company needed a more coherent strategy to take advantage of the benefits offered by the latest technologies. Griffin sat down with his IS staff and brainstormed about ways to create a new information environment for their company.

"We were thinking client/server and realized pretty quickly we needed a cross-platform solution," Griffin says, citing the mix of 60 Macintoshes and 170 IBM-type PCs used by Geffen's employees.

"That meant [Powersoft Corp.'s] PowerBuilder and [Microsoft's] Visual Basic weren't good choices, because at the time they weren't there for the Mac," Griffin says.

Griffin recognized the potential of the World Wide Web and Web browsers to solve the cross-platform information-sharing problems within Geffen that had already been successfully dispensed with on a global scale by the World Wide Web and the Internet.

"The best part is that [companies] like Netscape have already developed these solutions, and they already worked on all Macs and PCs," Griffin says.

The decision to build a Geffen intranet marked the inception of what Griffin and his colleagues came to call Geffen World, the company data crossroads that blends internal and external data resources under a single umbrella.

"There's a lot of information that everyone in the company needs to access," Griffin says.

Data could be generated either internally, as with Geffen's album release dates, or externally, as with radio airplay statistics collected by a separate company that studies the entire music industry and makes its data available on-line via modem.

"In the past, people would go to their computer and dial up various services by modem several times a day," Griffin says.

Now, users need only click on a button in Windows 95 and the Geffen World system accesses the information without requiring the user to know whether it resides on a company server, on the Internet, or wherever.

Less flashy but equally important data, such as phone and e-mail lists, are maintained by various users in each department, who need only learn the not terribly daunting HTML to modify the database, Griffin says.

One other thing: The Geffen World intranet cost only about $10,000, he says. Hardware costs were minimal because Griffin was able to conscript unused Pentium boxes running Microsoft's Windows NT that Geffen had already purchased.

Geffen's IT staff was drawn to Windows 95 largely because of their remote computing demands.

"Remote access is real important to us," explains network systems engineer Chris Bradfield.

About 40 of the 225 PC users in the company are permanently remote, scattered around the country in regional sales and promotion offices," Bradfield says.

Additionally, about a third of Geffen's employees have home computers or laptops that they can use to access the computer resources on Geffen's network—and through that, the Web.

"One click and you're in, and from that point on, it's just like you're at your desktop," Griffin says.

The Geffen World intranet does much more than support the information needs of the company's employees. Using the internal Web pages also gives them expertise in the most important new realm of Geffen: cyberspace.

As the on-line multimedia marketplace hungers for new content, Griffin also sees a marketing advantage in providing Geffen's employees with Web and Internet skills. Because Geffen records—like any music publisher—is an intellectual-property company, says Griffin, employees using their internal computing tools also gain expertise in the very environment that the company may one day do much of its business. Ultimately, Geffen hopes to advertise in cyberspace, as well as create and sell music and other media content over the Internet.

"Why develop two different skill sets?" Griffin asks rhetorically. "A year from now, people in this company are going to be way ahead in their knowledge of these tools. The way I see it, the duty of a CIO [chief information officer] or IT director should be to educate the constituency of users."

Questions

1. Why did Geffen Records decide to set up an intranet instead of a client/server system?
2. What do Geffen employees use the intranet for?
3. Why is remote access important at Geffen?
4. What benefits does Geffen receive from the intranet?

Source: Paul Karon, "Intranet solution makes Geffen shake, rattle, and roll," *InfoWorld*, February 12, 1996, p. 65.

7 Information System Data Management

Chapter Outline

The Need for Data Management in Information Systems   (p. 190)
File Processing   (p. 190)
    File Organization   (p. 191)
    File Management   (p. 193)
    Advantages of File Processing   (p. 194)
    Disadvantages of File Processing   (p. 194)
Database Processing   (p. 195)
    What Is a Database?   (p. 196)
    Database Management   (p. 197)
    Advantages of Database Processing   (p. 198)
    Disadvantages of Database Processing   (p. 199)
Database Organization   (p. 199)
    Data Relationships   (p. 199)
    Types of Databases   (p. 202)
    Object-oriented Databases   (p. 206)
Common Database Software   (p. 206)
    Personal Computer Database Software   (p. 207)
    Multiple-user Computer Database Software   (p. 208)
    Networked Computer Database Software   (p. 208)
Using Database Software   (p. 209)
    Query Languages   (p. 209)
    Application Programs   (p. 212)
Database Use in Information Systems   (p.213)
Data Warehouses   (p. 214)
Database Administration   (p. 216)

Learning Objectives

After completing this chapter, you should be able to:
- [ ] 1. Explain why businesses need to manage data in their information systems.
- [ ] 2. List the advantages and disadvantages of file processing.
- [ ] 3. Explain what a database is.
- [ ] 4. List advantages and disadvantages of database processing.
- [ ] 5. Identify the main types of relationships in database processing.
- [ ] 6. Outline the characteristics of the main types of databases.
- [ ] 7. Describe the main differences between database software for personal computers, multiple-user computers, and networked computers.
- [ ] 8. Describe several ways of using database software.
- [ ] 9. Describe the use of databases in different types of information systems.
- [ ] 10. Explain what a data warehouse is.

T he stored data component in an information system consists of all data stored in the system's hardware and processed by its software. This data must be managed so that it will be usable by the system. Data management involves making the data available, keeping the data current, checking the data for accuracy, and insuring the security of the data. This chapter examines data management in information systems. Because stored data in information systems is usually organized as data files and databases, this chapter concentrates on file and database processing.

The Need for Data Management in Information Systems

Businesses need to manage the data in their information systems for four main reasons. The first is to be sure that the data is *available* for processing by the system. To make the data available, it must be organized in such a way that the required data can be easily located and retrieved. Data can be organized as data files, databases, or other ways. In all cases, the data organization must be carefully planned. Good data management includes organizing the data so that the needed data will be available for processing.

The second reason businesses need to manage data in their information systems is to make sure the data is *current*. Stored data reflects the state of a business, such as how many items are in inventory or how much money is available for paying bills. The state of the business changes constantly, however; for example, inventory items are sold and money is paid out. The stored data needs to be updated regularly so that it correctly reflects the current state of the business. Proper data management includes ensuring that the data is current.

A third reason data needs to be managed in information systems is to ensure that the data is *accurate*. Data cannot simply be stored in secondary storage; it must be checked for errors and inconsistencies before it is stored. A well-known acronym in information systems is GIGO, which stands for "garbage in, garbage out." This means that if you put bad data (garbage) into the system, you will get bad data (garbage) out of the system. Proper data management involves ensuring the accuracy of the data stored in the system.

The last reason businesses need to manage data in their information systems is to be sure the data is *secure*. Stored business data includes much information about the organization. If the data is lost, destroyed, or stolen, the business can be severely affected. For example, many businesses are dependent on financial data which they store in a computer. If the data is accidentally destroyed, the business may be ruined. If the data is acquired by another business, it may help the other business compete. Good data management includes guaranteeing the security of the stored data.

File Processing

The simplest way to manage data in an information system is to store the data as a *data file*. Recall from Chapter 3 that a data file, or simple *file*, consists of a group of related *records*. Each record in the file contains a group of related *fields* and each field consists of one or more related *characters*.

To illustrate the idea of a file, Fig. 7.1 shows a file of inventory data in an athletic-clothing wholesale business. Each row in this figure represents a record in the inventory file. Each record contains fields with data about one item stocked in inventory. The fields are the columns in the figure. The first field is the item number, the

FIGURE 7.1

An inventory file

Item number field	Item description field	Unit price field	Quantity on hand field
1537	SHORTS	11.50	136
1609	JACKET	24.85	40
2719	T-SHIRT	9.75	24
3512	TENNIS SHORTS	18.90	35
3804	TENNIS SHIRT	17.45	118
4205	SOCKS	3.25	160
5172	SWEATSHIRT	18.75	225
5173	SWEATPANTS	14.70	322
5501	CAP	7.20	90
6318	SWIMSUIT	21.50	52

Inventory records

second field is the item description, the third field is the unit price (how much the business sells one item for), and the last field is the quantity of the item on hand.

The records in a file should be identified in some way, usually by including a field that uniquely determines the record. Such a field is called a key field, or simply a key. In the inventory records, the key field is the item number. Each record in the inventory file has a different value in its key field. Then, if the value of the key field is given, the corresponding record can be located in the file.

Key fields are usually code fields consisting of numbers or combinations of numbers and letters. Thus, item number, customer number, social security number, and similar fields are used as key fields. The reason codes and not names or descriptions are used for key fields is that codes can be assigned that are unique. Name and description fields, although easier to remember, are often duplicated in a file and thus cannot be used as key fields.

File Organization

A file can be organized in several ways and its organization determines how a key field is used to locate a record in a file. (See Fig. 7.2.) In a sequential file, the records are organized in sequence, one after the other in the order in which they are placed in the file. For example, Fig. 7.2a shows the inventory file stored as a sequential file, with one record coming immediately after the previous one in the order in which they were put in the file. (Records in this figure are numbered in the order in which they appear in the file.) The records in a sequential file can be retrieved only in the order in which they are stored. The computer must first retrieve record number 1, then record number 2, and so on. Recall from Chapter 4 that this approach is called *sequential access*. A sequential file can only be accessed sequentially. A sequential file can be stored on any type of secondary storage—magnetic disk, optical disk, or magnetic tape.

The key field in the records in a sequential file identifies which record was retrieved. When the computer retrieves a record, it simply gets the next record in sequence, not a record with a particular key field value. Once a record has been

FIGURE 7.2

File organizations

Record number				
1	1537	SHORTS	11.50	136
2	1609	JACKET	24.85	40
3	2719	T-SHIRT	9.75	24
4	3512	TENNIS SHORTS	18.90	35
5	3804	TENNIS SHIRT	17.45	118
6	4205	SOCKS	3.25	160
7	5172	SWEATSHIRT	18.75	225
8	5173	SWEATPANTS	14.70	322
9	5501	CAP	7.20	90
10	6318	SWIMSUIT	21.50	52

(a) A sequential inventory file

Record number				
1	5501	CAP	7.20	90
2				
3				
4	3804	TENNIS SHIRT	17.45	118
5	4205	SOCKS	3.25	160
6				
7				
8				
9	1609	JACKET	24.85	40
10				

(b) A direct inventory file

Index file

Key field	Record number
1537	1
1609	2
2719	3
3512	4
3804	5
4205	6
5172	7
5173	8
5501	9
6318	10

Data file

Record number				
1	1537	SHORTS	11.50	136
2	1609	JACKET	24.85	40
3	2719	T-SHIRT	9.75	24
4	3512	TENNIS SHORTS	18.90	35
5	3804	TENNIS SHIRT	17.45	118
6	4205	SOCKS	3.25	160
7	5172	SWEATSHIRT	18.75	225
8	5173	SWEATPANTS	14.70	322
9	5501	CAP	7.20	90
10	6318	SWIMSUIT	21.50	52

(c) An indexed inventory file

retrieved, the computer can examine the value of the key field in that record to see exactly which record it is.

In a <u>direct file</u>, which is also called a <u>random file</u>, the records are not necessarily stored in sequence. For example, Fig. 7.2b shows part of the inventory file stored as a direct file. Notice that the records are in random order and that there are spaces in the file with no data. Where a record is stored in a direct file is determined directly from the value of the record's key field. Several different methods are used to determine where a record is stored. For the direct inventory file, the computer uses the last two digits of the item number (the key field) as the record number where the item's record is stored. Thus, the record for item 1609 is stored as record number 9, the record for item 3804 is stored as record number 4, and so on. Notice that this approach can waste storage space in the file and can lead to conflicts when two records have the same last two digits in their key fields.

A computer can retrieve records in a direct file in any order. Recall from Chapter 4 that this approach is called *random access*. Given the value of the key field, the computer can find the corresponding record. For example, to retrieve the data for item 1609 from the direct inventory file, the computer would determine from the last two digits of the key field that the data is found at record number 9. Then, the computer would retrieve that record directly without going through the other records in the file in sequence. Because a direct file can be accessed randomly, it can only be stored on secondary storage devices that provide random access, such as magnetic disk and optical disk. It cannot be stored on magnetic tape.

An <u>indexed file</u>, which is also called an <u>indexed sequential file</u>, is actually two files: a data file and an index file. The *data file* is organized as a sequential file with records in increasing order by key field. The *index file*, or simply the *index*, is a file that has one record for each record in the data file. Each index record contains the value of the key field of a record in the data file and the location of that record in the file. Figure 7.2c illustrates the idea of an indexed file. The inventory file is stored as a sequential file, with its records in increasing order by key field, which is the item number. The index contains the key field and the number of the corresponding record for each record in the data file.

The records in an indexed file can be accessed either sequentially or randomly. For sequential access, the computer retrieves the records in the data file one at a time in the order in which they are stored. To access the records randomly, the computer locates the key field of the desired record in the index, which can be done faster than searching the data file for the record because the index is much smaller than the file. After the key field is found, the corresponding record number in the index indicates where the record is stored in the data file. The computer retrieves the record directly without retrieving any other records in the data file. (This process is like using an index of a book to locate a subject without reading the book in sequence.) Like direct files, an indexed file can only be stored on a random access device such as magnetic disk or optical disk, but never on magnetic tape.

File Management

Recall from the beginning of this chapter that businesses need data management for four main reasons: to make data available, to keep data current, to guarantee that data is accurate, and to ensure that data is secure. With file processing, data is made available by organizing the data in one of the three ways described here. A computer program can then access the data. If the file is a sequential file, then the program accesses the data sequentially. For a direct file, the program accesses the data randomly. If the file is an indexed file, the program can access the data either sequentially or randomly.

File data is kept current by updating it regularly. Updating can involve any of three activities: *adding* records to a file, *deleting* records from a file, or *changing* data in records in a file. A computer program does the updating. If the data is organized as a sequential file, the program creates an entirely new updated file because it is normally not possible to change an existing sequential file. If the data is organized as a direct or indexed file, however, a program can update the file itself; it is not necessary to create a new file.

To ensure the accuracy of data in a file, the data to be stored in the file must be checked as it is entered into the system. This process is called data validation and it is done by a computer program. This program accepts the data from outside the system (usually the data is entered at a terminal or personal computer) and checks the data for errors. Examples of the data validation checks include checking to be sure that the correct type of data has been entered (e.g., that only letters and no numbers have been entered for a person's name), that acceptable values have been entered (e.g., that only an M or an F has been entered for a person's sex), and that the data is within reasonable limits (e.g., that a person's pay rate is less than $50 per hour). If a record contains any data that has errors, the record is not stored in the data file. Only records that pass all data validation checks are included in the file.

Data security in file processing involves ensuring against loss or destruction of the data and unauthorized access or updating of the data. Loss or destruction of the data is secured by a procedure for backing up the data on a regular basis. Backup copies of all data files should be made periodically. The copies normally are kept in a special fireproof vault or at a separate location. Another procedure is needed for recovering the data from the backup copy if the original data is damaged. Security against unauthorized access or updating of the data involves procedures that prevent the data files from being removed from the business and that prevent programs that process the data from being executed by unauthorized personnel.

Advantages of File Processing

Data files are used in information systems because they are simple to use. Many information systems do not need anything more complex because they use only a single file of data. For example, an inventory control system may only need a single inventory file to store all data. In situations such as this, a data file is the easiest way to organize the data.

Because of their ease of use, data files are used extensively in information systems. Sequential files are used in simple situations where only sequential access is needed. Direct or indexed files are used where random access is needed. Direct files are more complex to use than indexed files, so they are not as common.

Disadvantages of File Processing

The main disadvantages of file processing appear when it is necessary to process data in more than one related file. For example, assume that the athletic-clothing wholesale business needs to do inventory control, order entry, and customer billing. With file processing, the business would need three files to store the data: an inventory file, an order file, and a billing file. (See Fig. 7.3.) Application programs for inventory control would access the inventory file, programs to enter customer orders would access the order file, and programs to bill customers would access the billing file.

FIGURE 7.3

File processing

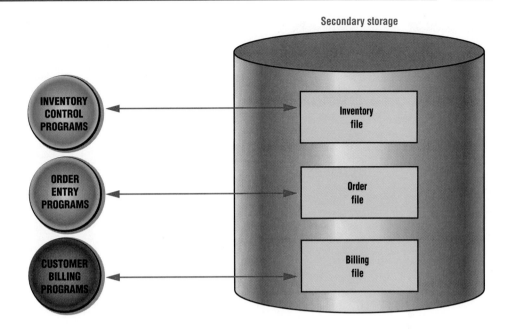

One of the main problems with this situation is that some data may be dupli-cated in several files. For example, the customer's name and address may appear in both the order file and the billing file. Duplicated data requires extra storage space. More significantly, if duplicated data changes, someone must make sure it is updat-ed every place it is stored. Thus, if a customer moves, his or her address must be updated in all files in which the address is stored. Ensuring that all duplicated data is updated can be a difficult task.

Another problem in this situation is that it is difficult to access data from more than one file at a time. If, for example, the order entry program needs to process data in both the inventory file and the order file, complex programming is required. If a program needs to access three files, the programming is even more complicated.

A final problem with file processing is that there is a dependency between pro-grams and data. Each program must have instructions that tell it how the data in the files it processes are organized. Each program must identify what fields are in the records of each file and how the files are organized. If the fields in the records or file organization are changed, every program that processes that file must be modified. Such modification can be time-consuming and expensive.

Database Processing

To overcome some of the disadvantages of file processing, database processing is used. In database processing, related data is not stored as separate files. Instead, all data is stored together in a *database*. In our athletic-clothing wholesale business example, the database would contain inventory, order, and billing data. (See Fig. 7.4.) To process the data in the database, special database software is needed. This software is called a database management system or DBMS. The DBMS pro-vides capabilities for creating, accessing, and updating data in a database. In fact, the DBMS handles all interaction with the database. If a user or an application

FIGURE 7.4

Database processing

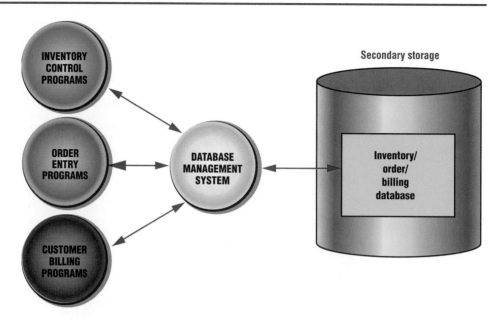

program, such as an order entry program, needs to process data in the database, the program sends instructions to the DBMS, which then carries out the actions requested by the program.

What Is a Database?

To understand database processing, you first need to know exactly what a database is. In Chapter 3 you learned that related data are sometimes grouped to form a database. This definition is adequate for a basic understanding of databases, but you need a complete definition for a thorough knowledge of database processing.

A <u>database</u> is a collection of *data* and *relationships* between the data stored in secondary storage. The data in a database may be stored in several separate files or in one large file. The actual way the data is stored depends on the database software. To the user, however, the database is viewed as a single set of stored data. The data in the database is arranged into related groups, similar to records, each containing several fields. Groups of data are related to other groups of data, meaning that the groups have something in common. The ways in which the groups of data are related are called <u>relationships</u>, and they are part of the database.

To illustrate the idea of a database, consider how data used for inventory control, order entry, and customer billing in an athletic-clothing wholesale business can be stored in a database. Figure 7.5 shows a database with the required data. Notice that inventory data, order data, and billing data are grouped separately in the database. The relationships between the data are shown by lines connecting the groups of data. There is a relationship between inventory data and order data if an item in inventory has been ordered. An inventory item can be ordered one or more times or not at all. There is a relationship between billing data and order data if a customer needs to be billed for items ordered. Each customer can order one or more items.

Databases are not stored the same way as are data files. A database not only must store data but also the relationships between the data. Consequently, special storage organizations are used for databases, although techniques similar to those

Inventory / order / billing database

Inventory data

Item number	Item description	Unit price	Quantity on hand
1537	SHORTS	11.50	136
1609	JACKET	24.85	40
2719	T-SHIRT	9.75	24
3512	TENNIS SHORTS	18.90	35
3804	TENNIS SHIRT	17.45	118
4205	SOCKS	3.25	160
5172	SWEATSHIRT	18.75	225
5173	SWEATPANTS	14.70	322
5501	CAP	7.20	90
6318	SWIMSUIT	21.50	52

Order data

Customer number	Item number	Quantity ordered
48721	2719	8
48721	5501	6
29636	3804	5
12345	1537	10
12345	2719	12
12345	3804	18
51387	2719	2
51387	5501	4

Billing data

Customer number	Customer name	Total due
12345	CAMPUS SPORT SHOP	546.10
29636	CITY SPORTS	87.25
34074	SMITH'S SPORT SHOP	.00
48721	JOE'S SPORTS	121.20
51387	ABC SPORTING GOODS	48.30

Inventory/order relationship — *Billing/order relationship*

FIGURE 7.5

A database

used in direct file organization and indexed file organization are often found in database storage. How the data and relationships are stored depends on which of several database organizations is used, a topic that will be covered later in this chapter.

Database Management

With database management, data is made available by accessing the data in the database with the database software. Accessing may involve retrieving data from a single group of data or from several related groups of data. For example, in the database shown in Fig. 7.5, inventory data could be retrieved alone or inventory and order data could be retrieved together. To retrieve inventory and order data together, the relationship between the data is used by the database software. Thus, to answer the question "What are the descriptions of the items ordered by customer number 48721?", the database software uses the relationship that links together the order data containing the customer number with the related inventory data to get the item descriptions.

Database data is kept current by updating the data in the database. The database software handles the updating, which may involve *adding* data or relationships, *deleting* data or relationships, or *changing* data or relationships. A single group of data can be updating or several related groups of data can be updated. For example, assume that the database in Fig. 7.5 needs to be updated when a customer orders another item. That customer's order must be added to the order data, a relationship to the item in the inventory data must be established, and the total due in the billing data must be changed. All this updating is handled by the database software.

The accuracy of the data in a database is guaranteed by data validation, as with file processing. In database processing, however, the database software often does the validation. Thus, it is not necessary to have a special computer program to validate the data. The database software not only checks the data for errors, but also checks the relationships to be sure they are valid.

Data security in databases is handled in a manner similar to that in file processing. Security from data loss or destruction is accomplished by a procedure for regularly backing up the database and keeping the backup copy in a safe location. If the database is damaged, a recovery procedure is followed to restore the data from the backup. Securing against unauthorized access or updating of the data usually is handled by the database software. Often, the software can be set to require special passwords or codes before data can be accessed or changed. The software may also be set so that different users have different privileges. For example, some users may be able to access the data but may not be able to update it, and other users may be able to both access and update the data.

Advantages of Database Processing

Database processing has important advantages over file processing. First, duplication of data is reduced. Most data values need to be stored only once in the database because the data is treated as one collection of data rather than as separate files. Thus, in our athletic-clothing wholesale business example, each customer's address needs to be stored only once in the database. This characteristic means that extra storage space is not required for duplicate data. More importantly, the updating of data needs to be done only once, thus improving the likelihood that the data is correct.

A second advantage of database processing is that it makes it easier to process different groups of data—that is, data that in file processing would be stored in separate files. Because the data in a database is stored as one collection of data, the DBMS can process any data in the database with minimal difficulty. Thus, if, in our example, a program needs to process inventory data and order data, it sends instructions to the database software to tell it what to do and the software handles all details of processing the data.

A final advantage of database processing is that programs are not dependent on the organization of the data in the database. The database can be changed without changing every program that uses the database. For example, if fields or records are added to the database, it is necessary only to change those programs that use those fields or records. All other programs can be left unchanged. This characteristic results from the fact that the database software handles all database interaction. Because programs do not have to be changed as much, less time and expense is required for programming.

Disadvantages of Database Processing

There are several disadvantages of database processing. First, it can be expensive. One source of expense is the cost of the database software. On personal computers this software typically costs $100 to $500, but on multiple-user computers and networks the database software can cost $25,000 to over $100,000. Another source of expense is that usually a faster computer with more primary and secondary storage is needed for database processing to get the same performance as in file processing. Such a computer is more expensive than one needed for file processing. Finally, programmers' salaries are usually higher with database processing because the programmers are more skilled than those who know only file processing.

Another disadvantage of database processing is that data is more vulnerable than it is in file processing. If several files are used in file processing, each file can be stored on a different disk. If one disk is accidentally destroyed, the files on other disks are not damaged. In database processing, however, all data must be stored on the same disk. Damage to that disk means all data is lost.

A final disadvantage of database processing is that information systems that use this approach can be complex to develop. Such systems often involve several applications, all using the same database. The development of these information systems usually requires more careful planning and is more time-consuming than file processing systems.

You can see from this discussion that database processing has advantages and disadvantages over file processing. In general, file processing should be used for simpler systems that involve few programs and a single file. Database processing is best for systems that have numerous programs and that use multiple files. In between are many information systems in which the best approach may be either file processing or database processing.

Database Organization

A database is a collection of data *and* relationships between the data. The data is organized much like data in a file: Characters are grouped to form fields and fields are grouped to form records (although the terms "field" and "record" may not be used). The key to database organization, however, is not the data but the relationships between the data. Different types of relationships can be used in databases and using them results in different types of databases.

Data Relationships

There are three main types of relationships in databases: one-to-one relationships, one-to-many relationships, and many-to-many relationships. In a <u>one-to-one relationship</u>, one group of data is related to only one other group of data, and vice versa. For example, assume that a database contains records of customer data, each with the customer's number and name, and accounts receivable data, each with the balance due owed by the customer and the date due. There is one customer record for each customer and one accounts receivable record for each customer. Then, each customer record is related to one accounts receivable record, and vice versa. Thus, there is a one-to-one relationship between customer records and accounts receivable records.

Figure 7.6 shows a one-to-one relationship between two records. Part *a* of this figure shows the *structure* of the records and the relationship between the records. The record structures are shown by the long boxes with smaller boxes for the fields in each record. The relationship structure is indicated by the line connecting the records. This line means that there is a one-to-one relationship between the records. Part *b* of the figure shows data for the fields in two records. These records are connected by a line, meaning they are related. This diagram gives an *occurrence* of the records and the relationship between them. In this occurrence, customer number 12345 has a balance due of $1789.60.

The second type of relationship is called a <u>one-to-many relationship</u>. In this type, one group of data is related to one or more other groups of data, but not vice versa. For example, assume that a database contains customer records and invoice records, each with an invoice date and amount. Each customer can have any number of invoices, but each invoice can be associated with only one customer. Thus, the relationship between customer records and invoice records is one-to-many.

Figure 7.7a shows the structure of the customer and invoice records and the one-to-many relationship between them. As before, the record structures are shown by boxes and the relationship structure is indicated by a line connecting the records. The line, however, spreads out at one end (sometimes called a "crow's foot"). The spread-out part of the line points to the "many" record and the other end of the line points to the "one" record. Thus, the relationship is one-to-many. Figure 7.7b gives an occurrence of these records and the relationship between them. In this occurrence, customer number 12345 has three invoices.

The last type of relationship is a <u>many-to-many relationship</u>. In this relationship, one or more groups of data are related to one or more other groups, and vice versa. For example, assume that a database contains supplier records, each with a supplier's number and name, and inventory records, each with an item number, an item

---

FIGURE 7.6

A one-to-one relationship

Customer record

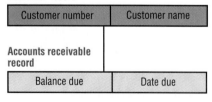

(a) Structure

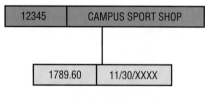

(b) Occurrence

FIGURE 7.7

A one-to-many relationship

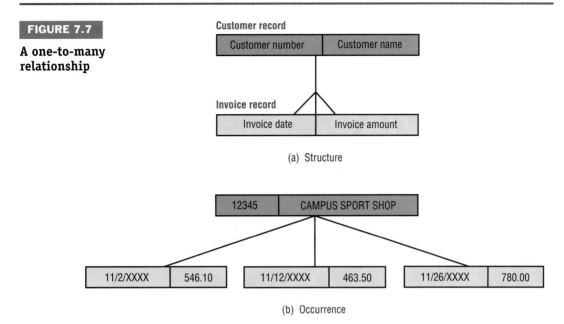

(a) Structure

(b) Occurrence

description, a unit price, and a quantity on hand. Each supplier can supply several inventory items, and each item can be supplied by several suppliers. Thus, the relationship between supplier records and inventory records is many-to-many.

Figure 7.8a shows the structure of the inventory and supplier records and the many-to-many relationship between them. In this figure, the boxes for the records are connected by a line that spreads out at each end, signifying a many-to-many relationship between the records. Figure 7.8b gives an occurrence of these records and the relationship between them. Notice in this occurrence that supplier number

FIGURE 7.8

A many-to-many relationship

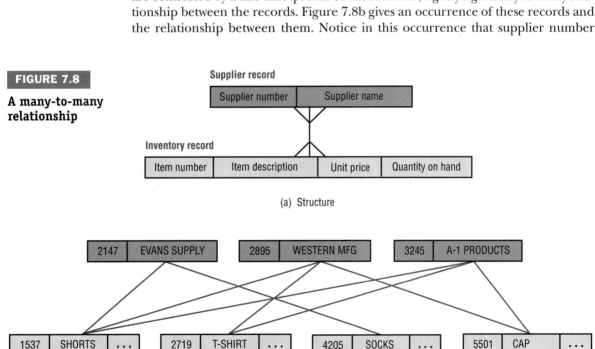

(a) Structure

(b) Occurrence

2147 can supply items number 1537 and 4205, and that item number 1537 can be supplied by all three suppliers.

Types of Databases

The data in a database is organized in a way that is easy for people to understand. Most databases use one of three approaches for arranging data in a database, resulting in three types of databases: hierarchical databases, network databases, and relational databases. Some DBMSs store data as hierarchical databases and some as network databases, but most store data as relational databases. A fourth approach, called an object-oriented database, is also used by some database management systems.

Hierarchical Databases. In a <u>hierarchical database</u>, all relationships between groups of data are one-to-one or one-to-many, but no group of data can be on the "many" side of more than one relationship. Figure 7.9 shows an example of a hierarchical database. Notice that only one-to-many relationships are used in this database and that all the relationships "go in the same direction." (One-to-one relationships could also be used, but many-to-many relationships cannot.) The meaning of the database is that each salesperson has any number of customers and that each customer can place any number of orders.

FIGURE 7.9

A hierarchical database

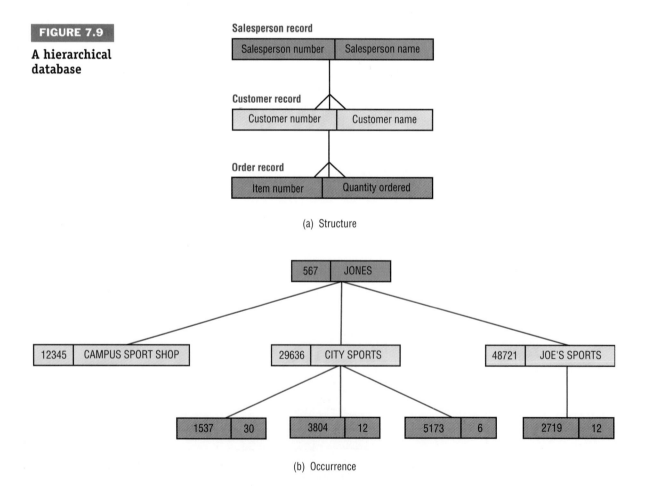

(a) Structure

(b) Occurrence

Network Databases.   In a <u>network database</u>, all types of relationships are allowed without restriction. Thus, one-to-one, one-to-many, and many-to-many relationships are permitted. Figure 7.10 shows an example of a network database. This database has one many-to-many relationship, which is interpreted as meaning that each supplier can supply many inventory items and that each item can be supplied by many suppliers. The database also has one one-to-many relationship, which is interpreted as meaning that each warehouse can store any number of inventory items, but that each item can be stored in only one warehouse.

Relational Databases.   A <u>relational database</u> takes an approach to organizing data that is different from that used by hierarchical and network databases. In a relational database, data is arranged in tables that have rows and columns. For example, Fig. 7.11 shows a table with 10 rows and four columns. To be absolutely correct, a table in a relational database is called a *relation* (not to be confused with a *relationship*), a row is called a *tuple* (which rhymes with *couple*), and a column is called an *attribute*. These terms are not commonly used, however. Instead, relational databases usually use the terms *table*, *row*, and *column*, or the terms *file*, *record*, and *field*, or a combination of these. This book will use the terms *table*, *row*, and *column*.

FIGURE 7.10

A network database

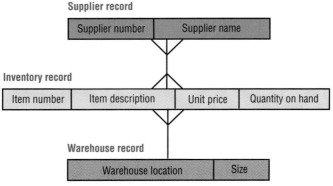

(a) Structure

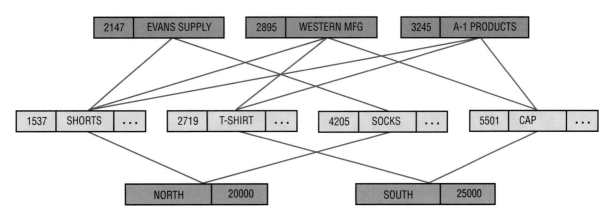

(b) Occurrence

Columns

1537	SHORTS	11.50	136
1609	JACKET	24.85	40
2719	T-SHIRT	9.75	24
3512	TENNIS SHORTS	18.90	35
3804	TENNIS SHIRT	17.45	118
4205	SOCKS	3.25	160
5172	SWEATSHIRT	18.75	225
5173	SWEATPANTS	14.70	322
5501	CAP	7.20	90
6318	SWIMSUIT	21.50	52

Table — Rows

FIGURE 7.11

A table in a relational database

A relational database is a group of related tables. Figure 7.12 shows an example of a relational database with three tables. The structure of the database is indicated by identifying the tables and their columns. A name is given to each table and to each column in each table. These names are listed at the top of the tables in Fig. 7.12.

Each table in a relational database must have a column or combination of columns, called the **primary key**, that uniquely identifies the row in the table. The primary key is similar to the key field in the records of a file. Given the value of the primary key of a table, the corresponding row can be located in the table. In Fig. 7.12, the primary key of the Inventory table is ItemNumber and the primary key of the Billing table is CustNumber. In both of these tables, the primary key is a single column. The primary key can also be the combination of several columns. Thus, in the Order table the primary key is the combination of two columns, the CustNumber and the ItemNumber, because it is necessary to have both of these to uniquely identify a row in the table.

Relationships in relational databases exist for a reason different from that of relationships in hierarchical and network databases. In hierarchical and network databases, relationships exist because connections between records are stored as part of the database. (In other words, the lines in Figs. 7.9b and 7.10b between records are actually part of the database, although they are stored in a special way.) In a relational database, however, relationships are *not* stored this way. Instead, a relationship exists between two tables because there is a *common column* in the tables. The common column normally is the primary key of one of the tables. For example, there is a relationship between the Inventory table and the Order table in Fig. 7.12 because the ItemNumber column, which is the primary key of the Inventory table, is also in the Order table. Similarly, there is a relationship between the Billing table and the Order table because the CustNumber column, the primary key of the Order table, appears in both tables. Any type of relationship—one-to-one, one-to-many, and many-

FIGURE 7.12

A relational database

Inventory Table

ItemNumber	ItemDesc	UnitPrice	QtyOnHand
1537	SHORTS	11.50	136
1609	JACKET	24.85	40
2719	T-SHIRT	9.75	24
3512	TENNIS SHORTS	18.90	35
3804	TENNIS SHIRT	17.45	118
4205	SOCKS	3.25	160
5172	SWEATSHIRT	18.75	225
5173	SWEATPANTS	14.70	322
5501	CAP	7.20	90
6318	SWIMSUIT	21.50	52

Order Table

CustNumber	ItemNumber	QtyOrdered
48721	2719	8
48721	5501	6
29636	3804	5
12345	1537	10
12345	2719	12
12345	3804	18
51387	2719	2
51387	5501	4

Billing Table

CustNumber	CustName	TotalDue
12345	CAMPUS SPORT SHOP	546.10
29636	CITY SPORTS	87.25
34074	SMITH'S SPORT SHOP	.00
48721	JOE'S SPORTS	121.20
51387	ABC SPORTING GOODS	48.30

to-many—can be represented in a relational database, although the details of how each is represented are beyond the scope of this book.

Comparison of Databases. DBMSs for hierarchical databases, called *hierarchical database management systems,* were developed first, in the 1960s. This type of database is very good for data that is naturally organized in a hierarchical manner, like a family tree. For example, data about products and the parts used in the assembly of the products is organized hierarchically: Each product is made up of several main parts, each main part is made up of many subparts, and so on. A hierarchical database would be appropriate for storing this data. Hierarchical databases, however, are not good when data is not organized in a hierarchical way, such as when many-to-many relationships are needed.

DBMSs for network databases, called *network database management systems*, were developed in the 1970s. A network database is good for complex data that is not naturally organized in a hierarchical way. For example, data about students, courses, and faculty is complex: Each student takes many courses, each course is taken by many students, each faculty member teaches many courses, and each course can be taught by many faculty members. A network database would be appropriate for storing this data.

The relational approach was first proposed in 1970, but DBMSs for relational databases, called *relational database management systems*, did not become widespread until the 1980s. This type of database is considered to be the easiest for users to understand because all data is presented in tables, which are easy to comprehend. In addition, processing data in tables is relatively simple. A relational database can be used for any type of data, including the product/parts data and the student/course/faculty data described in the previous two paragraphs. Because of its advantages, most newly developed databases today are relational, although older hierarchical and network databases are still used.

Object-oriented Databases

Hierarchical, network, and relational databases all store only data (and relationships) in the database. Instructions for processing the data are stored separately from the database in the application program. Another approach to database organization is to store the data and instructions together in the database. Such a combination of data and instructions is called an *object* and databases organized around objects are called object-oriented databases. They are manipulated through an *object-oriented database management systems*.

Object-oriented databases are based on object-oriented programming concepts described in Chapter 5. In both object-oriented databases and object-oriented programming, objects are the basic elements used for representing data and instructions. (See Fig. 5.18.) The difference is that with object-oriented programming, the objects are only present while the program is executing (we say they are "transient") whereas with object-oriented databases, the objects are stored between executions of a program (we say the objects are "persistent"). Thus, the objects in an object-oriented program cannot be used to store data permanently, whereas the objects in an object-oriented database do store data permanently.

Although object-oriented databases have attracted a lot of attention, they are not in widespread use; there are only a few object-oriented DBMSs. Most databases in use are relational, although many older ones are hierarchical or network databases. Recently, however, object-oriented capabilities have been incorporated into relational databases to create hybrid object-relational databases. This approach to databases may become common in the future because it combines the best features of the relational and object-oriented approaches.

Common Database Software

As you know, a database management system or DBMS is a program that provides capabilities for manipulating data in a database. The DBMS handles all interaction between the user or application program and the database. It provides capabilities for storing

Bookmark

Object-oriented Database at Air France

Air France is taking off on a project that shuttles key pieces of its mainframe-based reservation system to a server running an object database—a maneuver that it hopes will lead directly to a 1% revenue boost.

The Paris-based airline has annual sales of more than $7 billion at current exchange rates, so an additional 1% would translate into $70 million in new business. "That's quite a large amount of money for us," said Pierre Gandois, who is managing the project at Air France.

Air France is one of the first companies outside the telecommunications and financial industries to use an object database in a core transaction application, said Liz Barnett, an analyst at Giga Information Group in Cambridge, Mass. But that doesn't mean object databases will soon be widely infiltrating data centers. "It's definitely still a niche kind of thing," she said.

Even Air France is going only so far with the technology. Airlines as a whole still depend on mainframe databases for their transaction-gobbling reservation systems, and Air France plans to leave all ticket processing on its Unisys Corp. mainframe, Gandois said.

The server handles the airline's revenue and yield management applications.

By leaning on the object database, Air France hopes to get a real-time system that can help better fill planes with higher-paying customers, Gandois said.

The airline's revenue managers can now track only individual segments, which means that filling up a Paris-to-New York flight could prevent it from selling more expensive tickets to passengers who want to start elsewhere and connect to that flight. The new system will track "a combination of flights rather than looking at each flight as a single unit," Gandois said.

Parameters for ticket availability and discounts will be set by an Oracle Corp. relational database running on a Sun Microsystems, Inc. server that gets nightly batch feeds from the mainframe. As flights start filling up, ticket requests will be fed through another Sun server with Versant Object Technology Corp.'s object database, which will approve or deny bookings. Approved requests will then be processed at the mainframe.

About 20% of the airline's 500 daily flights are expected to be controlled by the Versant-based system, Gandois said.

The application was written by Sabre Decision Technologies, the software development arm of AMR Corp. in Fort Worth, Texas. Sabre is marketing the design to other airlines, but many "are scared to go into an object database" because the technology is unproven for transaction processing, said Vic Nilson, Sabre's Air France project director.

QUESTIONS

1. What type of database does Air France use for its reservation system?
2. What use is Air France making of its object database?
3. What financial benefit does Air France hope to receive from the use of its object database?

WEB SITE:
Air France: www.airfrance.fr

Source: Craig Stedman, "Object project flies," *Computerworld,* February 10, 1997, p. 20.

data in the database, retrieving data from the database, and updating data in the database. Without the DBMS, the manipulation of a database would be very complex.

Each DBMS is based on one of the database approaches described previously. Thus, a DBMS may be a hierarchical, network, relational, or object-oriented DBMS. The first DBMSs were developed for mainframe computers in the late 1960s. In the 1970s, DBMSs were developed for minicomputers, and in the 1980s personal computer DBMSs appeared. In the 1990s, DBMSs for networked computer systems became common.

Personal Computer Database Software

Personal computer database software is the simplest form of DBMS. This software is designed to be used by one person at a time. Almost all common personal computer database programs use the relational approach. Most of the programs not only provide the ability to create, access, and update databases, but also allow the user to print reports based on data in the database, design forms for input and output of data on the screen, and develop entire computer applications around a database. Most also include a programming language for developing complex applications. Some personal computer database programs for IBM clones are Access, FoxPro, Paradox, and dBASE. Fourth Dimension is a database program for the Apple Macintosh. Database programs for personal computers usually cost between $100 and $500.

Multiple-user Computer Database Software

Database management systems for multiple-user computers are large, complex programs that are designed to be used by multiple users at one time. They are expensive, typically costing $25,000 to over $100,000. Because of their complexity, specially trained computer professionals are usually needed to utilize them. Most multiple-user computer DBMSs in use are relational, but some hierarchical DBMSs and network DBMSs are still used. A few of the more widely used mainframe and minicomputer DBMSs are IMS (hierarchical) for IBM mainframe computers; IDMS (network) for IBM and some other mainframe computers and some minicomputers; DB2 (relational) for IBM mainframe computers; and Oracle (relational) for a wide range of mainframe and minicomputers.

Networked Computer Database Software

Networked computer systems use database software that runs on a database server, manipulating data in a database stored on the server. The software for data processing and the user interface, on the other hand, runs on client computers in the network. This is the idea of client-server computing discussed in Chapter 6. (See Fig. 6.17.) The database software handles the creation, access, and updating of the data in the database. It receives instructions from the client computer over the network and sends the results of database processing to the client.

Examples of database programs for networked computer systems are Oracle, Sybase, and Informix. These programs are all relational DBMSs for use on database servers. The client computers use other software for data processing and user interface control. An example of the software used for these purposes on client computers is Powerbuilder. The cost of database and client software depends on how many computers are in the network but can be as expensive as multiple-user computer database software. Object-oriented database management systems are also designed for use on server computers in networks. Examples are GemStone, ObjectStore, and Versant ODBMS.

Networked computer systems also allow the creation of a distributed database. In this approach, the database is divided into parts and each part is stored on a different computer in a network. The database is manipulated through a *distributed database management system*. Each computer in the network has a copy of the distributed DBMS. Using the distributed DBMS, a user at any computer can access data from any part of the database, no matter where it is stored. The user, however, is unaware of where the data is stored. The advantage of distributed databases is that each user has control over the part of the database stored on his or her computer, but all users may have access to all parts of the database.

Using Database Software

Two main ways of manipulating a database using database software are summarized in Fig. 7.13. In the first approach, the user interacts directly with the DBMS by using a special language called a *query language*. In the second approach, an application program sends instructions to the DBMS, which carries out the actions requested by the program. The user interacts with the application program by supplying input and receiving output.

Query Languages

A query language is a language that allows the user to *query* a database—that is, to retrieve data from a database. This type of language also allows the user to update the database. The user uses a query language by entering an instruction, usually called a *command*, at the keyboard. The instruction goes directly to the DBMS, which reviews it and performs the requested processing. Depending on the command, the DBMS may display data on the screen or perform an update. Thus, with a query language, the user interacts directly with the database software to process the data in the database.

One of the most widely used query languages is SQL, which stands for Structured Query Language. SQL is used with relational database management systems. Recall that a relational database consists of tables with rows and columns. In SQL, a user can retrieve selected rows and columns from a single table or several related tables in a database. A user can also update data in one or more tables.

In a relational database, each table and each column has a name. To query a table, the user gives the name of the table, a condition that indicates the rows to be displayed from the table, and the names of the columns the user wants to display from those rows. The form of a query in SQL is:

SELECT column names
FROM table name
WHERE condition

FIGURE 7.13

Using database software

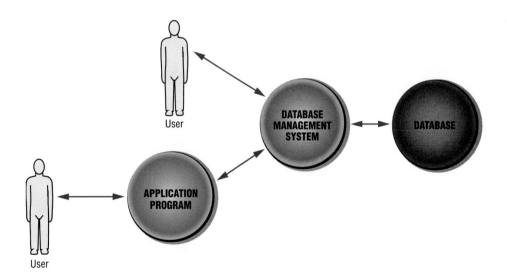

As an example, assume that a user wishes to query the inventory/order/billing relational database shown in Fig. 7.12. If the user wants to know the item number and description of all items in inventory with a quantity on hand of less than 100, he or she would use the following query in SQL:

SELECT ItemNumber, ItemDesc
FROM Inventory
WHERE QtyOnHand < 100

Figure 7.14 shows the screen display after executing this command. Notice that several lines are displayed because several items in the Inventory table in Fig. 7.12 satisfy the condition that the quantity on hand is less than 100.

As another example, assume that a user wants to know the names of the customers who ordered item 2719 and the quantity that each customer ordered. The item number and the quantity ordered are in the Order table and the names of the customers are in the Billing table. The two tables are linked together by the customer number, which is in both the Order table and the Billing table. Hence there is a relationship between these tables. The following SQL command accomplishes what the user wants:

SELECT Billing.CustName, Order.QtyOrdered
FROM Billing, Order
WHERE Billing.CustNumber = Order.CustNumber
        AND Order.ItemNumber = 2719

This command retrieves the CustName column from the Billing table (Billing.CustName) and the QtyOrdered column from the Order table (Order.QtyOrdered), where CustNumber in the Billing table is the same as CustNumber in the Order table, and ItemNumber in the Order table is 2719. Figure 7.15 shows the screen display after executing this command. The operation performed by this query is called a *join* because it brings together data from two tables based on a relationship. It is the main way of using relationships between data in a relational database.

FIGURE 7.14

Executing an SQL command

SELECT ItemNumber, ItemDesc
FROM Inventory
WHERE QtyOnHand < 100

SQL command

ItemNumber	ItemDesc
1609	JACKET
2719	T-SHIRT
3512	TENNIS SHORTS
5501	CAP
6318	SWIMSUIT

Screen display

FIGURE 7.15

Executing an SQL command

SELECT Billing.CustName, Order.QtyOrdered
FROM Billing, Order
WHERE Billing.CustNumber = Order.CustNumber
    AND Order.ItemNumber = 2719

SQL command

CustName	QtyOrdered
CAMPUS SPORT SHOP	12
JOE'S SPORTS	8
ABC SPORTING GOODS	2

Screen display

The examples given here show how SQL can be used to query a relational database. SQL also has commands to update a relational database. With these commands a user can add rows to a table, delete rows from a table, and change data rows in a table.

SQL is used with most relational database management systems. In fact, it has become the standard query language for relational databases. Some relational database software also uses a graphical approach called *query-by-example* or *QBE*. (See Fig. 7.16.) In this approach, the user makes entries into a grid pattern, indicating the columns he or she wishes to display and the conditions that determine which rows are to be displayed. Neither SQL nor QBE are used with hierarchical and network DBMSs. These types of database management systems have unique query languages.

FIGURE 7.16

A query-by-example

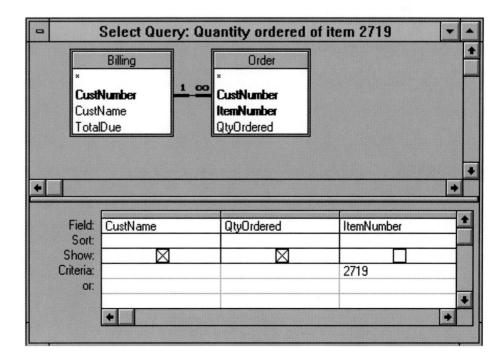

Application Programs

An application program can be developed by writing the program in a programming language or by using special software to develop the program. A host language is a programming language for writing application programs containing commands from a query language. A host language may be a general-purpose programming language that is used for other types of data processing. For example, COBOL and C are commonly used host languages in business. When a programmer uses a host language for database processing, commands from a query language, such as SQL, are placed within a program written in the host language. For example, Fig. 7.17 shows part of a COBOL program containing an SQL query. Usually, a programmer can use a host language with several different database management systems. Thus, a programmer can query several databases using the query languages of different DBMSs. To use a general-purpose programming language as a host language requires special training in computer programming and is only done by computer professionals.

A host language may also be a special-purpose programming language that can be used only with a particular database management system. In this case, queries are contained within the host language program, but the program can be used only with the DBMS for which it is designed. This is the most common approach used with personal computer database software.

An application generator is a special software system that makes it easy to develop a computer application. With an application generator the user does not write a program in programming language but, rather, specifies input and output form layouts, report formats, menus, and calculations. The user also specifies the database queries needed to complete the forms and reports, and do the calculations. Then the application generator prepares an application program that accomplishes the required processing. The application program may be in a general-purpose programming language such as COBOL or C, in a special-purpose language, or in some other form. After the program has been prepared it can be executed on the computer to perform the required processing. Application generators are a type of 4GL, discussed in Chapter 5.

Application generators are very convenient for developing computer applications. They are included in most personal computer database software and are used by professional computer personnel and end-users. They have limits, however, because not all types of processing that can be done with a host language can be done with an application generator. Still, their ease of use makes them very popular.

FIGURE 7.17

Part of a COBOL program with an SQL query

```
DISPLAY "ENTER CUSTOMER NUMBER".
ACCEPT REQUESTED-CUST-NUMBER.
EXEC SQL
    SELECT CUSTNAME, TOTALDUE
    INTO :INPUT-CUST-NAME, :INPUT-TOTAL-DUE      ⎫
    FROM BILLING                                 ⎬  SQL query
    WHERE CUSTNUMBER = :REQUESTED-CUST-NUMBER    ⎭
END-EXEC.
MOVE INPUT-CUST-NAME TO OUTPUT-CUST-NAME.
MOVE INPUT-TOTAL-DUE TO OUTPUT-TOTAL-DUE.
DISPLAY OUTPUT-LINE.
```

Database Use in Information Systems

Databases used in individual information systems are often called personal databases because they are used only by one person. Usually, these databases are stored on a personal computer and processed with personal computer database software. Typically, they are simple databases, with a relatively small amount of data, and are used for only one application. An example is a database of customer and sales data used by only one salesperson. The salesperson creates the database, updates data in it as needed, and accesses data in it to help make sales. It is a personal database for that salesperson.

Workgroup, organizational, and other multiple-user information systems often require large, complex databases. These databases are used by many users at one time, so they are called shared databases. Such databases are stored on multiple-user computer systems or servers in networked computer systems. Networks with shared databases may be local area or wide area networks, and even interorganizational networks. Usually, shared databases are used for several applications. For example, the inventory/order/billing database described earlier could be used for inventory control, order entry, and billing.

Often, with a shared database, each user needs only a part of the database. For example, in processing the inventory/order/billing database, one user may need only inventory and order data and another may need only order and billing data. To prevent users from processing data that they do not need, the database is divided into views, which are parts of the database. (See Fig. 7.18.) Each user is given access only to his or her view of the database. A user with one view cannot process data in another view.

Sometimes a user with a personal database on a personal computer needs data from a large, shared database on another computer. To get the data, the user can use data communications techniques (discussed in Chapter 6) to communicate with the other computer either by remote access or through a network. Then, the user can use the communications software to download the needed data from the large database to his or her personal database.

FIGURE 7.18

User views of a database

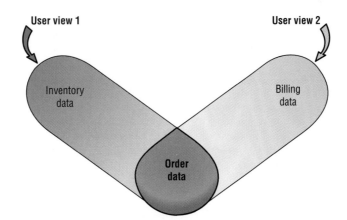

Data Warehouses

Most databases are used to store current data about a business. For example, the inventory/order/billing database shown in Fig. 7.12 contains data about current orders, bills due now, and items presently in inventory. Once an order is filled, a bill is paid, or an item is dropped from stock, data about the order, bill, or item is deleted from the database. Sometimes, it is useful to be able to analyze old, historical data. For example, a business could look at older orders to see what items were ordered, in what quantities, and by which customers. Most databases, however, are not designed to retain historical data.

Bookmark

Data Warehouse at PacifiCare Health Systems

PacifiCare Health Systems, one of the nation's largest managed care providers, has learned there is no managed care without managed information. But until the provider built a data warehouse, it was difficult to get the information it needed to hold down health care costs.

Managed care providers sign up customers, such as large employers, by saying they will keep a grip on rising health care costs. But PacifiCare doesn't supply health care services. It reimburses doctors, medical groups, and hospitals for their expenses.

With the data warehouse, PacifiCare analysts can track provider performance and confront them on rising costs.

A pharmaceutical company's sales force, for example, will promote a medicine that reduces side effects, even though it costs twice as much as a similar generic drug. "We'll say to the doctor, 'It only reduces side effects from 6% of the population to 4%. Why not reserve it for the patients who suffer side effects?'" said Ed Feaver, vice president of PacifiCare's Prescription Solutions subsidiary.

PacifiCare's first application for the data warehouse drew a bead on pharmaceutical claims, a well-defined area for which historical data already existed. The application produces regular reports on the expense norms for given drug treatments. The application also compares the use of generic vs. more expensive, formulary drugs.

In some cases, Feaver said, the use of expensive drugs is justified. In others, doctors prescribe drugs without realizing a less-expensive generic drug is available.

PacifiCare's reports on such issues go out to providers and become debated topics. Medical groups don't like being labeled as high-cost providers and often argue with PacifiCare's analysis.

"We get into these discussions all the time," Feaver said. "It lends credibility to have data" from the warehouse, he noted.

Jerry Silva and his data warehouse development team built the pharmacy claims analysis system to replace a decision-support system that had been running as a PC application in the Prescription Solutions unit. The amount of data needed had overwhelmed the PC database software, Feaver said.

Silva consolidated 16G bytes of data from pharmaceutical suppliers and PacifiCare's PC and relational databases into a data warehouse built on Oracle 7.1. To make the data more accessible, he put Holos, a front-end tool from Holistic Systems, Inc., on top of the Oracle Corp. database. Data from suppliers and claims processing continues to pour in, and the data warehouse has grown to 70G bytes.

The next challenge is to build warehouse systems that shed light on clinical care, not just pharmaceuticals, Feaver said. In some cases, the two sets of information need to be correlated. A doctor might show up as a low-cost prescriber of drugs for diabetes patients, but his patients might spend more time than necessary in the hospital due to lack of proper drug therapies, which is bad for overall costs, he said.

QUESTIONS

1. How does PacifiCare control pharmaceutical claims costs using a data warehouse?
2. Why does PacifiCare use a data warehouse instead of a database for pharmaceutical claims?

WEB SITE
PacifiCare Health Systems: www.phs.com

Source: Charles Babcock, "Data 'carehouse'," *Computerworld*, November 4, 1996, pp. 53,57.

Data in one database, whether current or historical, may be related to data in another database. For example, customer data in a customer database is related to order data in the inventory/order/billing database because customers place orders. Supplier data in a supplier database is related to inventory data in the inventory/order/billing database because different suppliers provide different inventory items. Accessing data from different but related databases can be useful. For example, accessing inventory and supplier data from different databases can help a business decide from which supplier to purchase certain inventory items. Most databases, however, are not designed to be accessed along with other databases.

To make historical data and data from multiple databases available, many businesses use a <u>data warehouse</u>. A data warehouse is a collection of data drawn from other databases used by the business. The data warehouse contains data extracted over time from other databases so that historical data is included in the warehouse. The data warehouse includes data taken from multiple databases within the organization. The idea is to bring together data from all sources within the business. The data in the data warehouse is analyzed to provide users with information to help in the management of the business. (See Fig. 7.19.)

A data warehouse can contain vast quantities of data, so much data that users have difficulty analyzing it. To solve this problem, data related to specific areas can be separated from the data warehouse and made available to specific users. The specific data from the data warehouse is called a <u>data mart</u>. For example, data only used in human resource management can be put in one data mart, data used in production can be put in another data mart, and data used in marketing can be put in a different data mart. This approach makes it easier for users in separate areas to have access to just the data they need.

FIGURE 7.19

Creating and using a data warehouse

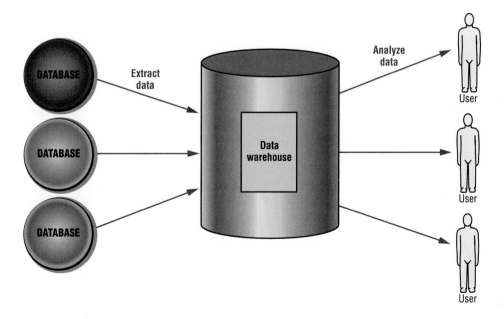

Database Administration

Data is an important resource of an organization. With the right data available at the right time, an organization can operate better. To accomplish this goal, organizational data must be managed just like people and money are managed. As data increases in volume and complexity, the management of the data becomes more difficult. With large, complicated databases, the problem of data management is the most severe.

To solve this problem, an organization with large databases often has a person called a database administrator or DBA who is responsible for managing the organization's databases. Some organizations have several database administrators or people with other titles performing the database administration function. As the number, size, and complexity of databases increases, the number of people needed to manage the databases increases.

The database administrator is responsible for the databases. The DBA designs the databases based on the needs of the users. If necessary, he or she changes the databases to meet new requirements. The DBA selects the database management system to process each database. He or she controls the use of the database by giving permission only to specific users to access data in the databases. These tasks and others are performed by the database administrator to manage the database.

Chapter Summary

☐ Businesses need to manage data in their information systems for four main reasons. The first reason is to be sure the data is available for processing by the system. The second reason is to make sure the data is current. The third reason is to ensure that the data is accurate. The last reason is to be sure that the data is secure. (p. 190)

☐ The main advantage of file processing is that it is simple to use. Many information systems do not need anything more complex. Disadvantages appear when it is necessary to process data in more than one related file. One disadvantage in this situation is that data may be duplicated in several files, making it difficult to ensure that changed data is updated every place it is stored. Another disadvantage is that it is difficult to access data from more than one file at a time. A final disadvantage with file processing is that there is a dependency between programs and data, which means that programs may have to be modified if a file's organization is changed. (pp. 190–195)

☐ A **database** is a collection of data and relationships between data. A **relationship** is a way in which one group of data in a database relates to another group. With file processing, separate files are needed to store the data for each application. In database processing, however, all data is stored together in a database. A **database management system**, or **DBMS**, is a program that provides capabilities for creating, accessing, and updating a database. (pp. 195–198)

☐ One advantage of database processing over file processing is that duplication of data is reduced. Another advantage is that with database processing, it is easier to process different groups of data than with file processing. A third advantage is that programs that perform database processing are not dependent on the organization of the data in the database. One disadvantage of database processing is that certain costs are greater than with file processing. Another disadvantage is that data is more vulnerable with database processing than with file processing. A third disadvantage is that information systems that use database processing can be more complex to develop than those that use file processing. (pp. 198–199)

☐ Relationships are important in database processing because related data are processed through relationships. The three main types of relationships are **one-to-one relationships**, in which one group of data is related to only one other group of data and vice versa; **one-to-many relationships**, in which one group of data is related to many other groups of data but not vice versa; and **many-to-many relationships**, in which many groups of data are related to many other groups of data, and vice versa. (pp. 199–202)

☐ In a **hierarchical database**, all relationships are one-to-one or one-to-many, but no group of data can be on the "many" side of more than one relationship. In a **network database**, any type of relationship is allowed. In a **relational database**, data is arranged into tables with rows and columns. A relationship exists between two tables when there are common columns in the table. Some database management systems store data as hierarchical databases and some as network databases, but most store data as relational databases. Some other database management systems store objects, which consist of data and instructions for processing the data, in an **object-oriented database**. (pp. 202–206)

☐ Database software for personal computers is the simplest form of DBMS and is designed to be used by one person at a time. Almost all personal computer database programs are relational. Database management systems for multiple-user computers are large, complex programs designed to be used by multiple users at a time. A few multiple-user DBMSs are hierarchical or network, but most are relational. Database software for networked computers runs on database servers and communicates with client computers in the network. Most DBMSs for networked computers are relational, but some are object-oriented. (pp. 206–208)

☐ Database software can be used through a **query language**, which allows the user to query a database—that is, to retrieve data from a database. Database software can also be used through an application program written in a **host language**, which is a program-

ming language containing commands in a query language. A host language may be a general-purpose programming language that can be used with several database management systems, or it can be a special-purpose programming language that can be used only with one database management system. (pp. 209–212)

☐ Databases used in individual information systems are often called **personal databases**. These databases usually are stored on personal computers and used by only one person. Databases used in workgroup, organizational, and other multiple-user information systems are called **shared databases**. These databases are stored on multiple-user computer systems or networks. Often, with a shared database, each user needs only a part of the database, called a **view**. Sometimes a user with a personal database needs to use data communications techniques to transfer data from a shared database. (p. 213)

☐ A **data warehouse** is a collection of data drawn from other databases used by the business. The data warehouse contains historical data extracted over time from another database. It also contains data taken from multiple databases within the organization. To use a data warehouse, data related to specific areas of a business may be put in smaller **data marts** and made available to certain users. (pp. 214–215)

Key Terms

Application Generator (p. 212)
Database (p. 196)
Database Administrator (DBA) (p. 216)
Database Management System (DBMS) (p. 195)
Data Mart (p. 215)
Data Validation (p. 194)
Data Warehouse (p. 215)
Direct (Random) File (p. 193)
Distributed Database (p. 208)

Hierarchical Database (p. 202)
Host Language (p. 212)
Indexed (Indexed Sequential) File (p. 193)
Key Field (p. 191)
Many-to-Many Relationship (p. 200)
Network Database (p. 203)
Object-Oriented Database (p. 206)
Object-Relational Database (p. 206)
One-to-Many Relationship (p. 200)
One-to-One Relationship (p. 199)

Personal Database (p. 213)
Primary Key (p. 204)
Query Language (p. 209)
Relational Database (p. 203)
Relationship (p. 196)
Sequential File (p. 191)
Shared Database (p. 213)
SQL (p. 209)
View (p. 213)

Assignment Material

Review Questions

Fill-in Questions

1. A field that uniquely identifies a record in a data file is called a(n) _____.

2. A type of file organization used when only sequential access is needed is _____.

3. A type of file organization used when only random access is needed is _____.

4. A type of file organization used when records need to be accessed sequentially and randomly is _____.

5. The process of checking for errors in data entered into a system is called _____.

6. A database is a collection of data and _____ between the data stored in secondary storage.

7. A(n) _____ is a program used to create, access, and update a database.

8. If each student can have at most one car, and each car can be owned by only one student, then the relationship between students and cars is _____.

9. If each adviser has many students, and each student has only one adviser, then the relationship between advisers and students is _____.

10. If each student can belong to several clubs, and each club can have many student members, then the relationship between students and clubs is _____.

11. Each table in a relational database must have a(n) _____ to uniquely identify the row in the table.

12. A(n) _____ database is one that is divided into parts, and each part is stored on a different computer in a network.

13. A(n) _____ is a language that allows the user to retrieve data from a database. An example is _____.

14. A(n) _____ is a programming language for preparing application programs in which commands from a query language are embedded.

15. A software system that can be used to develop a computer application by specifying screen layouts, report formats, menus, calculations, and database queries is called a(n) _____.

16. An individual user would use a(n) _____ database, but multiple users would use a(n) _____ database.

17. A(n) _____ is a collection of current and historical data extracted from databases used by an organization.

18. The person responsible for managing the databases of an organization is called a(n) _____.

Short-answer Questions

1. Give four reasons why businesses need to manage the data in their information systems.

2. Why are key fields usually code fields rather than names or descriptions?

3. Explain the differences in the organization of a sequential file, a direct file, and an indexed file.

4. What three activities are involved in updating a data file? a database?

5. How is data in a file or database secured against loss or destruction?

6. Explain the difference between file processing and database processing.

7. Give several advantages of database processing.

8. Give several disadvantages of database processing.

9. Why are relationships important in database processing?

10. Explain the difference between a hierarchical database and a network database.

11. What is a relational database?

12. What type of database is considered to be the easiest for users to use?

13. What is an object-oriented database?

14. How does database software function in a network?

15. Describe two ways that a user can use a database.

16. What is a view of a database?

Discussion Questions

1. Will file processing eventually be entirely replaced by database processing? Why or why not?

2. Think of a computer application in a business with which you are familiar. Would this application be better using file processing or database processing? Why?

3. Select several relationships at your college or university and determine if each is a one-to-one, one-to-many, or many-to-many relationship. Some relationships you could consider are student/professor, professor/class, student/major, professor/department, and student/dorm.

4. Sometimes a relationship is supposed to be one type but in reality is another type. For example, at a college or university a student is supposed to have one adviser but may, in fact, talk to several advisers. Identify several relationships in your experience that you think might be like this.

5. Many people who work in a business need to access data in a database. Should they all have to learn a query language such as SQL to do this?

6. Views are used to keep users from accessing data that they are not supposed to see in a database. To access data in a view, a user needs a special password or code. Assume that one of your coworkers has access to a view that contains personnel data that you are not supposed to see. Your coworker is very busy one day and asks you if you would retrieve some personnel data from his view. He says he will give you his password so you can see the data in his view. What would you do in this situation?

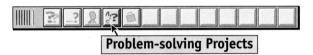

Problem-solving Projects

1. Find out how an organization or business to which you have access uses data files or databases. What data files or databases does the organization have? For what information systems is each data file or database used? Which data files or databases are used by single users and which by multiple users? Write a summary of your findings. Use word processing software to prepare your summary.

2. Think of the database that would be used for class registration at your college or university. What data and relationships do you think would be in the database? Draw a diagram like Fig. 7.9 or 7.10 of how you think the database is organized. If available, use graphics software to draw your diagram.

3. Using spreadsheet or word processing software, set up a table giving information about different personal computer database software. Have columns for the name of the software, the current version, the price, what type of computer the software runs on, and characteristics of the software such as whether it uses SQL, has a programming language, or can generate complete applications. Fill in the table with information about software listed in the chapter as well as other software. Use the World Wide Web to find more information to complete your table. As new software or new versions of existing software become available, update your table.

4. Using personal computer database software, set up the inventory/order/billing database discussed in the chapter with the data shown in Fig. 7.12. Then use the software to complete the queries shown in Figs. 7.14 and 7.15. Finally, use the software to answer the following queries:

   a. What are the names of the customers who owe more than $100?

   b. What are the descriptions, prices, and quantities ordered of all items ordered by customer 12345?

5. Human resource management information systems often include a personnel database. The data in such a database usually includes employee data (name, address, social security number, pay rate, etc.), skills data (skill, training, years of experience, etc.), and work history (previous positions, dates, pay rates, etc.). Each employee can have one or more skills and can have any number of previous positions. Set up a personnel database with these and other data that you think would be appropriate. Enter data for 10 to 20 fictitious employees in the database. Then design queries that you think would be useful to a personnel manager. Test your queries to be sure they work correctly.

Real-world Case

Environmental Protection Agency

How do you give thousands of users easy access to five mainframe databases? One way is to build them a data warehouse and make it accessible by Web browser over the Internet.

That's exactly what the Environmental Protection Agency has done. Its Envirofacts data warehouse lets EPA staffers and the public access five databases containing information on air and water pollution, hazardous-waste sites, and environmental programs.

Since Envirofact's launch, the public has gained access over the Internet via Web browsers, while EPAers have accessed Envirofacts using a proprietary interface called Gateway. Now the EPA is rolling out a Web-browser front end for its employees; Gateway will be phased out. "We used to be a bunch of gofers getting data for people," says Patrick Garvey, Envirofacts' director, of the EPA's IS department. "Now we can spend more time thinking about tools."

Using a Web front end to access legacy data is catching on in corporate IS as well. "It gives companies platform independence, and browsers are easy to update," says John Robb, an analyst at Forrester Research Inc. in Cambridge, Mass.

The EPA runs seven major mainframe databases, each with its own password and log-on procedure. Two are written in Adabas, two in Focus, and one each in Oracle, System 2000, and DB2.

Before Envirofacts, IS staffers were deluged by information requests from EPA employees and the public. In 1986, Congress passed the Community Right to Know Act, requiring the EPA to share the information in its databases with the public. With Envirofacts, the data warehouse is automatically updated every month from the EPA databases by scripts (programs) written in the native database languages.

The EPA's IS operations were getting bogged down with work on Gateway, Garvey says. At the same time, Internet technology was advancing rapidly. When the EPA bought a site license for Netscape Navigator, Garvey decided browser technology was ready. Garvey says he's letting Gateway die by attrition—features added to Envirofacts in the future will be accessible only by browser. But the EPA won't yank Gateway off users' desktops. The agency has 24,000 PCs, and no one knows exactly how many run Gateway.

Envirofacts runs in Oracle 7.1 on two Data General Aviion servers at the EPA's data centers in Research Triangle Park, N.C. An Aviion 9500 with 12 CPUs handles requests from the public; an Aviion 8500 with six CPUs handles requests from EPA staff.

The Aviion servers share a Data General Clariion RAID (redundant array of independent disks) with a capacity of 180 Gbytes of memory. The Aviions are linked to one another and to an IBM ES/9000 mainframe through TCP/IP over Ethernet. This mainframe runs the EPA's seven major databases—including the five accessed by Envirofacts.

Remote offices and state agencies link to the EPA's data center through a WAN. EPA employees use a high-speed line for Internet access and access to Envirofacts. The public accesses Envirofacts through dial-up Internet connections (www.epa.gov/enviro).

Envirofacts has been a boon to the EPA's IS department and local branches. Missouri's environmental officers, for example, no longer have to ask the IS department for help to find out what types of activities are going on at a given facility, says Ann Peton, geographical information system (GIS) coordinator at Missouri's division of environmental quality. Instead, they use Netscape Navigator to troll the data warehouse.

Providing Internet access to the public also has eased the burden. "It used to be, 'I don't know if there are any Superfund sites in my neighborhood; how can I access information from them?'" says Karen Schneider, director of the EPA's regional library in New York. "But now when we describe our services, people say, 'We already researched that from home over the Internet.'"

The EPA's Web site, Garvey says, has 80,000 pages. It receives 100,000 hits a month from the public and "a couple thousand a month" from EPA staffers, he adds.

The EPA's IS staff now has time for more creative work. Already, the group has developed a system that lets users access maps from the EPA's ArcInfo GIS database.

But Envirofacts still has a long way to go, says Warren Muir, president of environmental scientific and engineering consulting company Hampshire Research Institute Inc. in Alexandria, Va. "A large part of the data consists of information submitted as parts of things like permit applications and emergency notifications. It's unstructured and very difficult to piece together," Muir says.

Also, a lot of EPA information is stored on inaccessible databases, and there's no uniformity in the way data is classified. For example, one form may be from General Motor's corporate headquarters, while others are from the Cadillac division or individual plants, Muir says. "There's nothing inappropriate in that," he adds, "but it does make data analysis difficult."

Garvey is well aware of these problems. He plans to plug more databases into Envirofacts. The Safe Drinking Water database is going online; Garvey is working on adding databases on water-quality and air-quality monitoring. Also, the EPA has launched the Key Identifiers initiative, which proposes to standardize the way applicants are identified.

Another project in the works will provide hot links to the Web sites of other government agencies and universities that provide environmental information. The goal: to get users into Envirofacts and, by providing all the information they need, keep them there.

Questions

1. How many major databases does the EPA have and how many supply data to the Envirofacts data warehouse?

2. What type of data is contained in the Envirofacts data warehouse?

3. What types of user interfaces can be used to access Envirofacts?

4. Why is Internet access to Envirofacts beneficial to the EPA?

5. What data is planned to be added to Envirofacts in the future?

Source: Richard Adhikari, "Saved by the Web," *InformationWeek*, March 17, 1997, pp. 95, 96.

III

BUSINESS
INFORMATION
SYSTEMS

8 PERSONAL PRODUCTIVITY

Chapter Outline

Improving Personal Productivity   (p. 224)
Database Management   (p. 224)
    Database Software Functions   (p. 226)
    An Example of Database Management   (p. 227)
Spreadsheet Analysis   (p. 231)
    Spreadsheet Concepts   (p. 234)
    Spreadsheet Software Functions   (p. 236)
    An Example of Spreadsheet Analysis   (p. 237)
    Combining Database Management and Spreadsheet Analysis   (p. 239)
Information Presentation   (p. 240)
    Word Processing   (p. 240)
    Graphics   (p. 244)
    Desktop Publishing   (p. 248)
    Multimedia   (p. 251)
Locating Information Using the Internet   (p. 251)
Other Personal Productivity Applications   (p. 254)

Learning Objectives

After completing this chapter, you should be able to:
- [ ] 1. Explain how individual information systems can improve personal productivity.
- [ ] 2. Explain the main functions that users can perform with database software.
- [ ] 3. Describe the types of situations in which spreadsheet analysis is used and explain why spreadsheet software makes the analysis easy.
- [ ] 4. Explain the main functions that users can perform with spreadsheet software.
- [ ] 5. Describe the software used to prepare information for presentation to others.
- [ ] 6. Explain how database management, spreadsheet analysis, word processing, and graphics applications can be combined.
- [ ] 7. Explain how the Internet can be used to locate information.

I ndividuals in a business use a variety of information systems, including word processing, spreadsheet analysis, and personal database systems. These systems do not affect a workgroup or an entire business, only individuals in an organization. As you learned in Chapter 1, a system that impacts the work of a single person is an *individual information system.* This chapter examines the common computer applications found in individual information systems, and shows how these applications affect personal productivity in businesses.

Improving Personal Productivity

Businesses use individual information systems to improve personal productivity. Productivity has to do with how much a person contributes to a business. For example, if a salesperson can make six sales calls in a day instead of five, with just as good a chance of making a sale on each call, then that salesperson is more productive than one who makes only five calls. If a person can write a new advertising brochure in three weeks instead of four, with the new brochure being just as effective, then the person is more productive.

Businesses are always looking for ways to improve the productivity of employees. The more an individual contributes to the business, the greater will be the business's revenues or the less will be its expenses. Thus, improving personal productivity can impact the profitability of the business. Individual information systems are one way of improving personal productivity.

Individual information systems provide applications that assist individuals in locating, storing, analyzing, and presenting information. These systems, which typically use personal computers, include database software to manage stored data, spreadsheet software to analyze data, and word processing and graphics software to present information. They also include browser software to locate information on the Internet. An individual information system may use just one of these types of software or it may use several types, with data being transferred between programs. By using an individual information system, a person can be more productive because information that the person uses in his or her job is easier to locate, manage, analyze, and present.

Database Management

Individual information systems often involve organizing and processing data that is stored in secondary storage. As you know, data can be stored in secondary storage in *data files* or *databases.* With the proper software, the user can store data in a data file or a database, access the stored data, and update the data. These tasks are needed in many individual information systems.

How software for managing data functions depends on whether data is stored in a data file or a database. Recall that a data file consists of a group of *records,* each record contains several *fields,* and each field has several *characters.* A database, on the other hand, consists of groups of related data. Each group of data is like a data file organized into records and fields, but between the groups are *relationships* that indicate how the data is related.

Data stored in a data file is managed by a file manager, which is also called a *flat-file manager.* (See Fig. 8.1a.) With this type of software, a user can process the data in only one file at a time, even though several files may be stored in secondary storage.

Examples of personal computer file managers are FileMaker Pro and Q&A. On the other hand, data stored in a database is managed by database software. (See Fig. 8.1b.) Recall from Chapter 7 that with this type of software, which is also called a *database management system* or *DBMS*, the user can simultaneously process related data from different groups of data in a database. Examples of personal computer database software are Access, FoxPro, Paradox, dBASE, and Fourth Dimension. All these are relational database management systems in which the data is organized into tables consisting of rows and columns.

Although the difference between file managers and database software may seem small, it is significant. In fact, file managers usually are much less complex and less expensive than database programs. Unfortunately, there is much confusion in the terminology used to describe these programs, and often, software that is only a file manager is called a database program.

The basic capabilities of file managers and database software are similar, with the exception, just mentioned, that database programs can process related data in a database. When only a single file needs to be processed, either a file manager or a database program can be used. If a database program is used in this situation, the database consists of the data from a single file. When data from several related files must be manipulated simultaneously, database software must be used.

Although file managers are used occasionally, database programs are more common. The remainder of this section shows how database software is used in individual information systems. Many of the concepts, however, also apply to file managers.

FIGURE 8.1

File manager versus database software

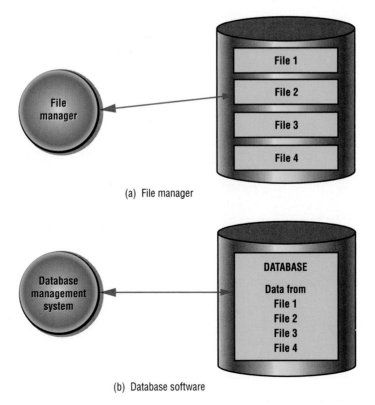

(a) File manager

(b) Database software

Database Software Functions

There are three main functions that the user can perform with database software: create a database, access a database, and update a database. (See Fig. 8.2.)

Creating a Database. Before a database can be used, it must be *created*, using the database software, a process that involves two steps. First, the user must enter a description of the structure of the data and relationships in the database. The data-

FIGURE 8.2

Database software functions

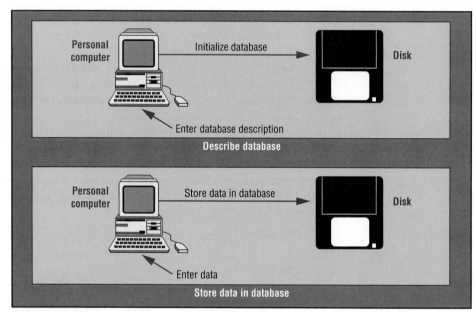

Creating a database

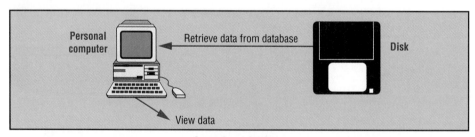

Accessing a database

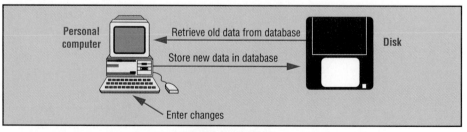

Updating a database

base software must be told what fields are in each record, what type of data is in each field, what records are in the database, and what types of relationships exist between the records. With this information the database software initializes the database in secondary storage, which means it reserves space for the data and stores the description of the database in this space. Second, the user must enter data for the database. Data for each field in each record must be entered. (Sometimes users say that they "populate" the database with data.) The data entered is stored in secondary storage by the database software.

Accessing a Database.   After a database has been created, a user can use the database software to *access* data in a database. Accessing data means to bring the data from secondary storage into primary storage. The user may retrieve all the data in a database, or he or she may retrieve only certain data. With database software, the user can use relationships to access data from several related records simultaneously. After the data has been brought into primary storage, it can be displayed on the screen, printed on paper, or used in some other way.

Updating a Database.   The third main function a user can perform with database software is to *update* data in a database. Updating includes three tasks. One is to *add* new data to a database, which usually involves adding one or more records. Another task is to *delete* old data in a database, which normally involves deleting one or more records. A final task is to *modify* the data in the fields of the records.

When a database is updated in any of these ways, changes are made in the data stored in secondary storage. The updating process usually involves three steps. First, the user enters information about what changes he or she wishes to make. Then the database software retrieves the old data, that is, the record that is to be changed. Finally, the software makes changes in the old data and stores the new data in secondary storage. (If new records are to be added or old records deleted, the process is slightly different.)

An Example of Database Management

To illustrate database management in individual information systems, assume that you are the national sales manager of an athletic clothing wholesaler. As part of your job, you need to keep track of data about each salesperson you manage. You must be able to look up quickly the month's sales for any salesperson, the region in which the person works, and the person's address. Every month, you have to update each salesperson's sales and, occasionally, you have to change a salesperson's address because the person has moved. Also, sometimes you have to delete all information about a salesperson because the person has left the company, and occasionally you must add information about a new salesperson who has been hired.

You could keep the information for all the salespeople on paper. If there are many salespeople, however, looking up information can be time-consuming, and updating data can involve much erasing and rewriting. You decide to develop an individual information system with a database containing the data about all salespeople. The system will allow you to retrieve the required information and do the necessary updating more easily than you could using a paper system. Thus, you will be more productive in your job.

Your first step is to determine what data is to be stored in the database and how the database is to be organized. You have decided to use Access, a personal computer relational database management system. In Access, data is stored in tables. Each row in a table is called a record and each column is called a field. You have to determine what fields and records make up the tables in the database. You decide that you will need the following fields for each salesperson:

Salesperson number
Salesperson name
Salesperson address
Region name
Salesperson sales

Because all these fields apply to a salesperson, they can be in the same record. Hence, you decide that the database will have one record for each salesperson with these five fields. The records for all salespeople can be in one table.

Because you have only one table of data, you could store it in a single file and use a file manager. You think, however, that you may want to add other related data later, so you decide to use a database program.

First, you must create the database. You select the software function to create a new table in a new database. For each field in the records in the table, you must give a field name and the type of data in the field (number, text, currency, date, etc.). You call the salesperson number field Slspers Number and you indicate that this field contains numbers. You call the salesperson name field Slspers Name and indicate that this field contains text. You enter similar information for the salesperson address field (Slspers Address), the region name field (Region Name), and the salesperson sales field (Slspers Sales). This last field contains currency data. When you are finishcd, you give the table a name, calling it Salesperson. Figure 8.3 shows the screen after all the required information is entered. The database software uses this information to initialize the database in secondary storage.

With information about the fields and records in a table in the database specified, you can store data in the records. You enter the data for each field in each record. Figure 8.4 shows the screen after the data for several records have been entered. After you enter the data for each record, the database software stores the record in the table, which is in secondary storage. After all the data has been entered and stored in secondary storage, the database creation process is complete.

Sometime after creating the database, you need to access data in it to help you with your job. First, you want a complete list of all the data in the database. You select an option that causes the software to retrieve all the data in the Salesperson table and to display it on the screen. You also print a copy of this list. Figure 8.5 shows the printed output. Notice that the data is displayed in rows and columns.

FIGURE 8.3

Creating a database: describing the fields in the records of the Salesperson table

Field Name	Data Type	Description
Slspers Number	Number	
Slspers Name	Text	
Slspers Address	Text	
Region Name	Text	
Slspers Sales	Currency	

Table: Salesperson

FIGURE 8.4

Creating a database: storing data in the records of the Salesperson table

SlspersNumber	Slspers Name	Slspers Address	Region Name	Slspers Sales
10421	John Smith	San Francisco, CA	Western	$29,500
12307	Alan Wood	Atlanta, GA	Southern	$1,050
15096	Susan Jenson	Cincinnati, OH	Northern	$42,800
17228	Frank Fuller	Flint, MI	Northern	$12,050

Table: Salesperson

FIGURE 8.5

A list of the data in the Salesperson table

Slspers Number	Slspers Name	Slspers Address	Region Name	Slspers Sales
10421	John Smith	San Francisco, CA	Western	$29,500
12307	Alan Wood	Atlanta, GA	Southern	$1,050
15096	Susan Jenson	Cincinnati, OH	Northern	$42,800
17228	Frank Fuller	Flint, MI	Northern	$12,050
22751	Joyce McAdams	Newark, NJ	Eastern	$10,250
23105	James Bennett	Eugene, OR	Western	$18,050
28625	Francis Benton	Birmingham, AL	Southern	$3,675
28733	Andrew Lee	New York, NY	Eastern	$14,700
31970	Mary Wong	Seattle, WA	Western	$37,025
34582	Fred Parks	Philadelphia, PA	Eastern	$14,800
39377	Robert Marshall	Minneapolis, MN	Northern	$31,500
46068	Susan Brown	Boston, MA	Eastern	$8,525
47216	Paul Napier	New Orleans, LA	Southern	$12,100
51927	Olivia Lock	Chicago, IL	Northern	$40,550
58114	Jose Sanchez	Miami, FL	Southern	$21,415
63725	Martha Young	Indianapolis, IN	Northern	$25,900

Each row is a record in the table, and each column is a field. The name of the field is displayed above its column.

Next, you want to analyze the sales for each of the four sales regions that you manage. You create a *query* that retrieves just the records for the salespeople in the northern region and lists the salesperson number, name, and sales from these records. Figure 8.6 shows the output displayed on the screen. Notice that only five rows are displayed because only five salespeople work in the northern region. From this display you can see who are the best salespeople in the northern region and who are not doing well. You do the same thing for the southern, eastern, and western regions.

FIGURE 8.6

A query of selected data from the Salesperson table

Select Query: Northern region sales

Slspers Number	Slspers Name	Slspers Sales
15096	Susan Jenson	$42,800
17228	Frank Fuller	$12,050
39377	Robert Marshall	$31,500
51927	Olivia Lock	$40,550
63725	Martha Young	$25,900

Periodically you have to update data in the Salesperson table. When a new salesperson is hired, you have to add a record for that salesperson. You enter the data for the salesperson in the same way that you entered data when creating the database, and the database software stores the new record in the table. If a salesperson leaves the business, that person's record must be deleted from the table, which can be done easily with the software. At the end of each month, you have to change the sales figure in each record in the table to reflect the current month's sales. You enter the new sales figure for each record, and the database software modifies the records. Also, you sometimes have to change a salesperson's address in the table because the person has moved. All updating involves making changes in data stored in secondary storage.

After you have used the Salesperson table for a while, you decide you would like to create another table to keep track of data about each region. You will need the following fields for each region:

Region name
Region total sales
Number of salespeople in region

You could create a Region table by describing these fields and entering data into the table. An easier approach, however, is to use a series of operations to retrieve data from the Salesperson table, compute each region's total sales, count the number of salespeople in each region, and store the required data in a Region table. Figure 8.7 shows a printed list of the data in the Region table after these operations have been performed.

You now have two tables: the Salesperson table and the Region table. Because each table contains a field for the region name, there is a *relationship* between these tables. Hence, you have a *database* consisting of two related tables.

Now you can retrieve related data from the tables at the same time. You decide that you need a list of the salesperson name and sales data for each salesperson from the Salesperson table along with all the data for the region in which the salesperson works from the Region table. You create a query to retrieve the required data. The database software retrieves each salesperson's record and related region record, and displays the required data on the screen. Figure 8.8 shows the screen output. With this information you can determine, among other things, how much each salesperson is contributing to the region's total sales.

At the end of each month, you need to update the database with each region's total sales. After changing each salesperson's sales in the Salesperson table, you perform a series of operations to modify the data in the Region table using the new data in the Salesperson table. Then you print a *report* from the data in the Region table giving the total sales for each region and the total sales for all regions. (See Fig. 8.9.)

FIGURE 8.7

A list of the data in the Region table

Region Name	Region Total Sales	Number of Salespeople
Eastern	$48,275	4
Northern	$152,800	5
Southern	$38,240	4
Western	$84,575	3

FIGURE 8.8

A query of related data from the Salesperson and Region tables

Slspers Name	Slspers Sales	Region Name	Region Total Sales	Number of Salespeople
John Smith	$29,500	Western	$84,575	3
Alan Wood	$1,050	Southern	$38,240	4
Susan Jenson	$42,800	Northern	$152,800	5
Frank Fuller	$12,050	Northern	$152,800	5
Joyce McAdams	$10,250	Eastern	$48,275	4
James Bennett	$18,050	Western	$84,575	3
Francis Benton	$3,675	Southern	$38,240	4
Andrew Lee	$14,700	Eastern	$48,275	4
Mary Wong	$37,025	Western	$84,575	3
Fred Parks	$14,800	Eastern	$48,275	4
Robert Marshall	$31,500	Northern	$152,800	5
Susan Brown	$8,525	Eastern	$48,275	4
Paul Napier	$12,100	Southern	$38,240	4
Olivia Lock	$40,550	Northern	$152,800	5
Jose Sanchez	$21,415	Southern	$38,240	4
Martha Young	$25,900	Northern	$152,800	5

Select Query: Salesperson/Region

FIGURE 8.9

A report of data from the Region table

Sales by Region

Region Name	Region Total Sales	Number of Salespeople
Eastern	$48,275	4
Northern	$152,800	5
Southern	$38,240	4
Western	$84,575	3
	$323,890	16

Notice in this example how you have taken advantage of the database program's ability to store, retrieve, and change data. These capabilities allow you to manipulate data in a database more easily than if you kept the same data on paper. The advantages are especially great when there is a large amount of related data in a database.

Spreadsheet Analysis

Many individual information systems involve analyzing data in a spreadsheet, which is an arrangement of data into rows and columns. Figure 8.10 shows an example of a hand-prepared spreadsheet that gives the projected revenue and expenses for a business over several years. The spreadsheet also shows the projected total expenses for each year, which is the sum of the individual expenses, and the projected net

FIGURE 8.10

A hand-prepared spreadsheet

PROJECTED NET INCOME

	Year 1	Year 2	Year 3
Revenue	2784500 -	3062950 -	3369245 -
Expenses			
Cost of goods sold	1058700 -	1164570 -	1281027 -
Salaries	483600 -	531960 -	585156 -
Rent	399000 -	438900 -	482790 -
Advertising	181000 -	199100 -	219010 -
Delivery	162200 -	178420 -	196262 -
Supplies	18300 -	20130 -	22143 -
Depreciation	148200 -	163020 -	179322 -
Total expenses	2451000 -	2696100 -	2965710 -
Net Income	333500 -	366850 -	403535 -

income, which is the difference between the total expenses and the revenue. A businessperson would use this spreadsheet to analyze projected figures from one year to the next, and to present the results of the analysis to another person (such as a manager).

The results of a spreadsheet analysis are often used to help in decision making. For example, the spreadsheet in Fig. 8.10 could be used to help in a decision about purchasing a building by showing whether there is likely to be sufficient revenue each year to cover the expense of the building.

A hand-prepared spreadsheet may be satisfactory if the figures in the spreadsheet do not change. Often, however, spreadsheet figures change, and whenever they do, other figures must be recalculated. For example, certain revenue or expense figures in the spreadsheet in Fig. 8.10 may have to be changed because of new projections. Then, the person using the spreadsheet would have to recalculate all total expense and net income figures that are affected. Recalculations can be time-consuming if changes occur often.

Overcoming Spreadsheet Limitations at MTV

When Jeff Polner came aboard MTV Networks as director of the financial planning department, he encountered a system for handling financial consolidations that was so unwieldy it actually interfered with the heart of the department's job: budget analysis. On only his second day of work, he spoke up at a staff meeting to push for TM1 Perspectives, from TM1 Software, in Warren, N.J. It is an online analytical processing (OLAP) product that he had worked with in two previous positions. He knew that it would revolutionize the department.

MTV Networks' financial planning department oversees costs in operating areas, specifically at the channel level. MTV Networks, based in New York, operates nine cable channels both domestically and internationally, including Nickelodeon, MTV Latino, and VH-1. As director of financial planning, Polner maintains the consolidation reporting model used to pull together the budget and quarterly projection numbers for comparison with actual results. The department essentially lends its expertise to the nonbusiness-minded people who run other departments, making sure that they operate within their approved financial limits.

The department, which prefers to do its reporting with Microsoft Excel spreadsheet software, was handling consolidations through a series of linked spreadsheets. It was a very manual, time-consuming process because there was no way to get the general-ledger data, which was on an IBM AS/400 computer, into Excel. All the data was being keyed in manually off the accounting profit and loss statements. Every time there was a change in data, it had to wait for the updated results, and financial planners were spending a significant portion of their time just maintaining the system.

Although the general-ledger application had some reporting capabilities built into it, it didn't lend itself to creating a fully consolidated package straight out of the system, let alone have the capability to do the variance analysis MTV desired.

"We needed to be able to spin and slice and dice and mix and match and compare with flexibility and ease so we weren't generating spreadsheets and Excel Workbooks up to our eyeballs," Polner says.

Polner wanted a system that would, in short, allow the department to do cross-dimensional analysis across

MTV Networks' channels and augment Excel's analytical flexibility with better storage, manipulation, and organization of data.

One of the main benefits of TM1 Perspectives is that instead of numbers being typed into a spreadsheet, analyses are created by pulling data from tables.

Sixty-five users work with TM1 Perspectives, which resides on a mixed family of IBM PCs. These are connected via a LAN to the TM1 table server on an IBM server. TM1 Spreadsheet Connector resides on the database server. Users are in turn connected to MTV Networks' regional offices in Miami and Orlando, Fla., via a WAN.

Although the users had the initial trepidation and skepticism that often accompanies new technology, the transition to TM1 was eased with its familiar Excel setting.

"Because it was an add-in to Excel, and Excel was everybody's bible, it wasn't really disrupting their normal operating environment," Polner says. Training was therefore minimal.

In essence, TM1 has given MTV's financial planners their jobs back.

"As financial planning people, we should spend the bulk of our time explaining what the numbers mean rather than spending it making sure that the numbers tie in and add up. That's monkey work," Polner says.

Good rock 'n' roll is innovative by nature, and the free spirit of MTV's rock videos spills into its corporate environment.

"MTV Networks is progressive," Polner says. "It's not a very uptight, button-down, conservative company. I'm on the job two days, and they listened to what I had to say and said, 'Hey, you think you've got a good idea, let's see what you've got.'"

QUESTIONS
1. What problems did MTV have in using Excel spreadsheets for budget consolidation?
2. Why was TM1 easy for users to use?

WEB SITE
MTV: here.mtv.com

Source: Grant Faulkner, "MTV rocks on again with TM1 Perspectives," *InfoWorld*, December 16, 1996, p. 67.

One reason for making changes in figures in a spreadsheet is to see what would happen to other figures when the changes are made. This technique is called what-if analysis because someone usually asks a question that begins with the words *what if*. For example, using the spreadsheet in Fig. 8.10, a person might ask, "What if revenue increases 10 percent each year and salaries increase 15 percent?" Answering this question involves using new numbers in the spreadsheet and recalculating the total expenses and net income for each year. This recalculation can be a lot of work for a large spreadsheet and would be especially tedious if someone decides to ask several "what-if" questions.

Individual information systems for spreadsheet analysis use spreadsheet software with which a user creates the equivalent of a spreadsheet in the computer. The user includes with the spreadsheet not only the data but also the rules that describe how totals and other figures are calculated in the spreadsheet. For example, the spreadsheet in Fig. 8.10 would include data for the revenue and expenses, and rules that specify how the total expenses and net income are to be calculated. The result is an *electronic spreadsheet* which is called a worksheet. Once the worksheet is created, the user can easily change data in it, and the computer will automatically recalculate those values determined by the rules. Thus, if a user has an electronic form of the spreadsheet in Fig. 8.10, he or she could change any revenue or expense figure and the computer would calculate the new total expenses and net income automatically. Common spreadsheet programs for personal computers are Excel, Lotus 1-2-3, and Quattro Pro.

Spreadsheet software is useful in many situations, including income projection, budgeting, sales forecasting, and investment analysis. Almost any problem in which data is put into rows and columns and used in calculations, as well as many other problems, can be solved using spreadsheet software.

Spreadsheet Concepts

Spreadsheet software creates a worksheet consisting of rows and columns in the primary storage of the computer. The rows are numbered (1, 2, 3,. . .) and the columns are identified by letters (A, B, C,. . .) with double letters (AA, AB, AC,. . .) used beyond the twenty-sixth column. (See Fig. 8.11.) The maximum number of rows and columns depends on the spreadsheet software, but one common program has 16,384 rows and 256 columns. Because of the size of a screen, the software can display only part of a worksheet at one time. In other words, the screen is like a "window" through which the user looks at part of the worksheet.

The intersection of a row and column is called a cell. A cell is identified by a cell reference or cell address, which consists of the column letter followed by the row number. For example, Fig. 8.11 shows the cell with cell reference B5.

A user can enter three types of information into a cell in a worksheet. One is a *number*; any number can be entered into any cell. Another is *text*, which is used to provide headings and other descriptions in a worksheet. For example, Fig. 8.12 shows part of the worksheet for the spreadsheet given in Fig. 8.10. Text has been entered for the column headings and row labels, and numbers have been entered for the revenues and expenses.

The third type of information that can be entered into a cell is a formula, which describes how the value in the cell is to be computed. In a formula, the user uses cell references to identify the data in the computation and mathematical symbols, such as + and -, to specify what type of computation is to be performed. For example, to

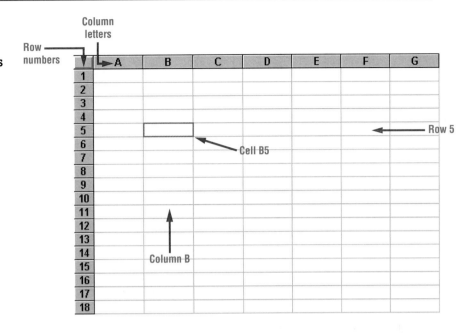

FIGURE 8.11

Worksheet rows, columns, and cells

FIGURE 8.12

A partial worksheet with text and numbers

	A	B	C	D	E	F	G
1		PROJECTED NET INCOME					
2							
3		Year 1	Year 2	Year 3			
4							
5	Revenue	$ 2,784,500	$ 3,062,950	$ 3,369,245			
6							
7	Expenses						
8	Cost of goods sold	$ 1,058,700	$ 1,164,570	$ 1,281,027			
9	Salaries	483,600	531,960	585,156			
10	Rent	399,000	438,900	482,790			
11	Advertising	181,000	199,100	219,010			
12	Delivery	162,200	178,420	196,262			
13	Supplies	18,300	20,130	22,143			
14	Depreciation	148,200	163,020	179,322			
15	Total expenses						
16							
17	Net Income						
18							

find the total expenses for Year 1 in the worksheet in Fig. 8.12, the user would use the formula =B8+B9+B10+B11+B12+B13+B14.[1] This formula means add the values of cells B8, B9, B10, B11, B12, B13, and B14. The user would enter this formula into cell B15, which is where the total expenses are to appear. After entering the formula, it would *not* appear on the screen in the cell. Instead, the computer would compute the value of the formula and display this value in the cell. As another example, cell B17 (the net income for Year 1) would contain the formula =B5-B15, which

---

[1]A shorthand way of writing this formula is to use the SUM *function*. The result is =SUM(B8:B14).

means subtract the value of cell B15 from the value of cell B5. Figure 8.13 shows the complete worksheet for the spreadsheet in Fig. 8.10 after the total expenses and net income formulas have been entered for all years. Notice that the values for each year are correctly calculated and displayed in the worksheet.

Formulas provide a user with the capability to easily specify how to recalculate values in a worksheet. Each time a number in a cell is changed in a worksheet, all formulas that use that cell's address are recalculated and the new values are displayed. Thus, in the worksheet shown in Fig. 8.13, the user can change any of the revenue or expense figures, and the corresponding total expenses and net income will be recalculated because these values are computed using formulas. This capability is one reason spreadsheets are so useful for analyzing data.

Spreadsheet Software Functions

A user can perform three main functions with spreadsheet software: create a worksheet, change a worksheet, and print a worksheet. (See Fig. 8.14.)

Creating a Worksheet. To use spreadsheet software to analyze a worksheet, the user must first create the worksheet. When the spreadsheet software is first loaded, a blank worksheet appears on the screen. To create a worksheet, the user enters the numbers, text, and formulas into the cells that make up the worksheet. After the worksheet is complete, it should be *saved* in secondary storage. This step is necessary because the worksheet is created in primary storage and would be lost when a new worksheet was entered or the computer was turned off.

Changing a Worksheet. After a worksheet has been created, it can be changed using spreadsheet software. First, the worksheet must be *retrieved* from secondary storage if it is not already in primary storage. Then, the user can change any number, text, or formula. The changes appear in the worksheet immediately, and any affected formulas are recalculated. Changes are made because of changes in data and in how calculations are done, and to do what-if analysis. If the changes are to be kept permanently, the revised worksheet must be *saved* in secondary storage. When the user saves a revised worksheet the old worksheet in secondary storage is replaced.

FIGURE 8.13

A complete worksheet after the formulas are entered

	A	B	C	D	E	F	G
1		PROJECTED NET INCOME					
2							
3		Year 1	Year 2	Year 3			
4							
5	Revenue	$ 2,784,500	$ 3,062,950	$ 3,369,245			
6							
7	Expenses						
8	Cost of goods sold	$ 1,058,700	$ 1,164,570	$ 1,281,027			
9	Salaries	483,600	531,960	585,156			
10	Rent	399,000	438,900	482,790			
11	Advertising	181,000	199,100	219,010			
12	Delivery	162,200	178,420	196,262			
13	Supplies	18,300	20,130	22,143			
14	Depreciation	148,200	163,020	179,322			
15	Total expenses	$ 2,451,000	$ 2,696,100	$ 2,965,710			
16							
17	Net Income	$ 333,500	$ 366,850	$ 403,535			
18							

FIGURE 8.14

Spreadsheet
software functions

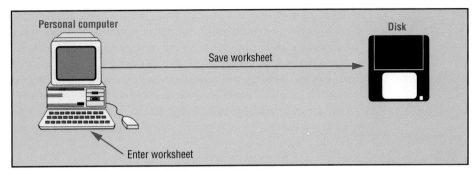

Creating a worksheet

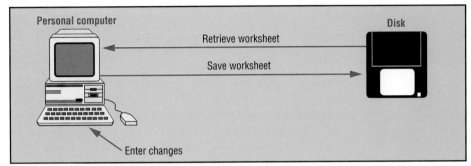

Changing a worksheet

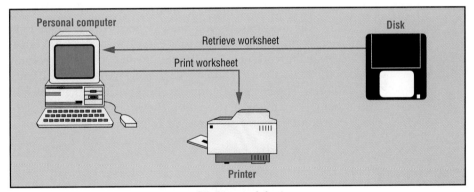

Printing a worksheet

Printing a Worksheet. At any time, a user can use the spreadsheet software to print the worksheet. If it is not already in primary storage, the worksheet must be *retrieved* from secondary storage before it can be printed. All or part of the worksheet can be printed. For example, the user could print all three years in the worksheet shown earlier in Fig. 8.13, or he or she could print just the information for one year. When a worksheet is printed, the row numbers and column letters are not normally printed; just the information in the worksheet is printed.

An Example of Spreadsheet Analysis

To illustrate the use of spreadsheet software, assume, as in the database management example given earlier, that you are the national sales manager of an athletic clothing wholesaler. You want to do an analysis each month of the sales in the four regions that you manage. You are interested in how the sales for the current month compare with the sales for the previous month, and you would like to know the percentage increase or decrease in sales for each region and for the total sales of all four regions. You could calculate the values by hand, but you plan to do the analysis each month. Therefore, you decide to develop an individual information system that uses spreadsheet software to do the analysis for you in a worksheet. Because the software will do the analysis more easily than you could by hand, you will be more productive in your job.

Your first step is to enter the numbers, text, and formulas needed for your analysis into a worksheet. You have decided to use Excel as your spreadsheet software. You start by entering the text for the column headings and row labels. Next, you enter numbers for the sales data for each region. You enter the data for last month and for this month, but you do not enter the totals or percentages because these values will be calculated by the spreadsheet software. After the headings, labels, and sales data have been entered, the screen will look like the one shown in Fig. 8.15.

The final step is to enter the formulas. For the total sales last month you enter the formula =B6+B7+B8+B9 into cell B11. This formula finds the sum of the values of the cells from B6 through B9. For the sales this month you enter a similar formula in cell C11 that finds the sum of the values of the cells from C6 through C9. Then you enter formulas for the percent changes—one for each region in cells D6 through D9, and one for the total in cell D11. For example, the formula in cell D6 is =(C6-B6)/B6.[2] As each formula is entered, its value is calculated and displayed in the worksheet. Figure 8.16 shows the final worksheet with all values calculated. At this point you save your worksheet in secondary storage. You also print the worksheet so that you can refer to it later.

The next month, you need to perform the same analysis with new data. You start by retrieving the previous month's worksheet from secondary storage. You change the worksheet by copying the sales data in the column labeled "This Month" to the "Last Month" column. Then you enter new sales figures for the "This Month" column. The formulas automatically recalculate the totals and the percentages as the changes are made. The result is shown in Fig. 8.17. You save the revised worksheet in secondary storage and print a copy for use later.

FIGURE 8.15

The sales analysis worksheet after the headings, labels, and sales data are entered

	A	B	C	D	E
1			SALES ANALYSIS		
2					
3		Last Month	This Month	Pct Change	
4					
5	Region:				
6	Eastern	$ 48,275	$ 121,400		
7	Northern	152,800	72,325		
8	Southern	38,240	39,500		
9	Western	84,575	85,525		
10					
11	Total:				
12					

[2]The percent changes have been given percentage formats. Consequently, the result of this formula is converted to percentage form (i.e., it is multiplied by 100).

FIGURE 8.16

The sales analysis
worksheet after
the formulas are
entered

	A	B	C	D	E
1			SALES ANALYSIS		
2					
3		Last Month	This Month	Pct Change	
4					
5	Region:				
6	Eastern	$ 48,275	$ 121,400	151.48%	
7	Northern	152,800	72,325	-52.67%	
8	Southern	38,240	39,500	3.29%	
9	Western	84,575	85,525	1.12%	
10					
11	Total:	$ 323,890	$ 318,750	-1.59%	
12					

FIGURE 8.17

The sales analysis
worksheet after
the sales data is
changed for the
next month

	A	B	C	D	E
1			SALES ANALYSIS		
2					
3		Last Month	This Month	Pct Change	
4					
5	Region:				
6	Eastern	$ 121,400	$ 103,500	-14.74%	
7	Northern	72,325	94,550	30.73%	
8	Southern	39,500	42,725	8.16%	
9	Western	85,525	96,730	13.10%	
10					
11	Total:	$ 318,750	$ 337,505	5.88%	
12					

Notice in this example how you have taken advantage of the fact that the worksheet already contains the text, formulas, and some of the numbers you needed. Although setting up the worksheet in the first month can be time-consuming, using the worksheet each of the following months makes the analysis much easier.

Combining Database Management and Spreadsheet Analysis

It is often possible to use the results of one application in another application. Essentially, this means that an *output* from one application becomes an *input* to another. With the proper software, data can be transferred from a database to a spreadsheet or vice versa, thus saving the effort of having to key in input.

To illustrate this approach, consider the database management and spreadsheet analysis examples. One of the results of the database example was the total sales for each region, which was recomputed from salesperson sales data entered into the database each month (Fig. 8.7). The region totals are used in the spreadsheet analysis (Fig. 8.16). Using the software, you can transfer the region total sales from the database to the worksheet.

Transferring data between applications reduces the time needed to complete the work. Thus, productivity is improved. Accuracy is also improved because no keying mistakes will be made in entering the data. When developing an individual information system, you should always consider how applications could fit together and whether data can be transferred between applications. We will show other examples of this in the next section.

Information Presentation

One of the most common tasks performed by individuals in a business is to prepare information for presentation to others. The information may be presented in a text form such as a memo, letter, or report; in a graphical form such as a diagram or chart; in a published form that includes text and graphics such as a pamphlet or brochure; or in a multimedia form that includes pictures and sound such as a sales presentation. Individual information systems often present information in one or more of these forms. This section examines each of these forms and shows how they can be part of an individual information system.

Word Processing

Information is prepared for presentation in a text form using word processing, which is the use of a computer to prepare documents containing text. Documents such as memos, letters, and reports are often used to present information to others, and word processing makes the preparation of such documents easier and faster. Sometimes, short documents that are used only once, such as a brief memo or letter, can be prepared just as easily with a typewriter, and forms are often easier to complete using a typewriter. But for long reports and documents that may require changes in the future, word processing is much more efficient. The principle advantage of word processing is that a person's productivity is improved. Most organizations no longer use typewriters but instead use computers for preparing all memos, letters, reports, and other documents.

A word processing system consists of a personal computer and word processing software. The word processing software provides the functions needed to accomplish word processing with the computer. Examples of word processing programs are Word, WordPerfect, and Word Pro.

Word Processing Software Functions. When a user uses word processing software, he or she manipulates a document that consists of text—that is, characters, words, paragraphs, and so on. The user can perform three main functions with a document using word processing software: enter the text of a document, change or edit the text of a document, and print a document in different formats. (See Fig. 8.18.)

When a user enters the text of a document using word processing software, he or she keys in the text's characters, which are displayed on the screen and stored in the computer's primary storage. As the user keys in the text, he or she can correct keying errors, select the type style or *font* for the text, look up synonyms for words, check the spelling of the document at any time, and perform many other functions with the word processing software.

After entering the text of the document, the user must *save* the document in secondary storage. This step is required because the text is stored in primary storage when it is entered. If the user does not save the document, it will be lost when a new document is started or when the computer is turned off. At any time when text is being entered or afterwards, changes can be made in it. *Editing* is the process of making changes or corrections in data. With word processing software, a user can easily edit the text of a document without having to completely rekey it. Before the text of a document can be edited, however, it must be in primary storage. If the text has just been entered, then it is still in primary storage, but if the document was previously saved in secondary storage, the user must *retrieve* it first. (Sometimes this is called *opening* the document.)

FIGURE 8.18

**Word processing
software functions**

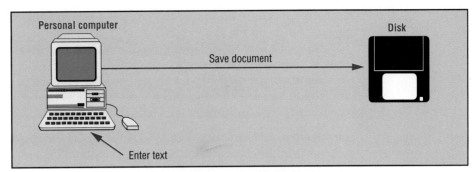

Entering the text of a document

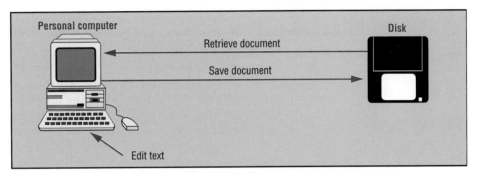

Editing the text of a document

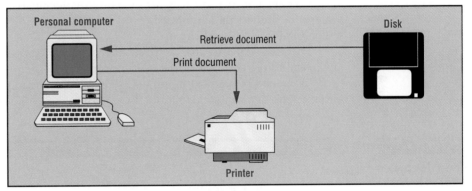

Printing a document

When a user edits the text of a document, he or she makes changes only in the text in primary storage. If the document is retrieved from secondary storage, the original unedited version would appear. Thus, if the user is not satisfied with any changes made, he or she can retrieve the document again and start over. If the editing is satisfactory, however, the user must save the new version of the document in secondary storage.

Before printing a document, a user needs to put it into the format in which it will appear on paper. The user must specify how wide the margins should be, how the lines should be spaced (single-spaced, double-spaced, and so on), whether headings should be printed on each page, whether the page numbers should be at the top or at the bottom of the page or omitted altogether, and other characteristics of the output.

After the user has entered, edited, and formatted the document, he or she can print it. If the document is not currently in primary storage, it must be *retrieved* from secondary storage before it can be printed. The user can print a single copy or several copies. Because the document is saved in secondary storage, additional copies can be printed at any time in the future.

An Example of Word Processing.　To illustrate the use of word processing software, assume as in the database and spreadsheet examples given earlier that you are the national sales manager of an athletic clothing wholesaler. Each month you have to send a memo to the vice president of marketing summarizing the company's sales for the month. You could type a new sales memo each month, but with word processing you can reduce the amount of typing required and save time. The first month's memo will take you about the same amount of time using word processing as it would take using a typewriter, but the memo for each subsequent month will take less time.

At the end of your first month—November—you need to enter the text for your sales memo. You have decided to use Word as your word processing software. You start by keying in the text of the sales memo. Figure 8.19 shows how the memo looks on the screen after the keying is completed.

After keying in the memo, you read it on the screen and decide to make several changes. First, instead of using "VP" in the "TO" line, you decide to use "Vice President." You delete the letters "VP" and enter the words "Vice President." Next, you notice that the word "sales" is misspelled in the first paragraph. You delete the word and type it correctly. (You could have used the spell-checking feature of the software to locate and correct the error.) Finally, you decide to add another sentence at the end of the last paragraph. After this editing is completed, the memo on the screen will look like Fig. 8.20.

The next step is to save the text of the memo in secondary storage. Then the memo can be printed. The output will appear just as it did on the screen (Fig. 8.20).

At the end of the next month—December—you need to send a similar memo with the sales figures for that month. Instead of rekeying the entire sales memo, you

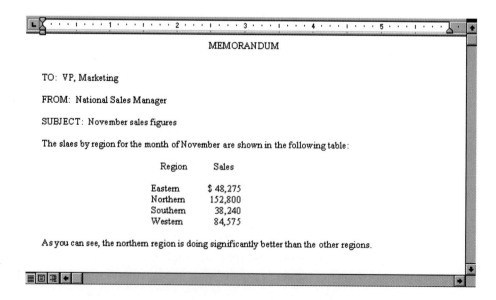

FIGURE 8.19

The sales memo after it is first entered

MEMORANDUM

TO: VP, Marketing

FROM: National Sales Manager

SUBJECT: November sales figures

The slaes by region for the month of November are shown in the following table:

Region	Sales
Eastern	$ 48,275
Northern	152,800
Southern	38,240
Western	84,575

As you can see, the northern region is doing significantly better than the other regions.

FIGURE 8.20

The sales memo
after it is edited

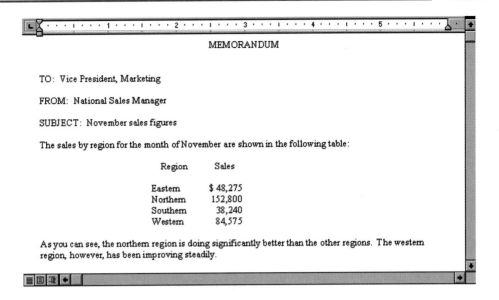

decide to edit the current one. You start by retrieving the document with the previous month's memo from secondary storage. At this point the memo on the screen will be the same as the one in Fig. 8.20. You change the month in the "SUBJECT" line from November to December. You do the same with the month in the first paragraph. Next, you key in new figures for the sales for the four regions. Then you decide that you need an entirely new final paragraph, so you delete the existing paragraph and enter a new one. After making these changes, the memo on the screen will look like Fig. 8.21. After reading it over to be sure there are no errors and checking the spelling, you save the document in secondary storage. Finally, you print the new sales memo.

Notice in this example how you have taken advantage of the editing capabilities of the word processing software. These capabilities let you reuse work that you have done previously instead of redoing everything from scratch. By reusing previous work, you can greatly increase your productivity in preparing memos, letters, reports, and other documents.

FIGURE 8.21

The sales memo
after it is edited
for the next
month

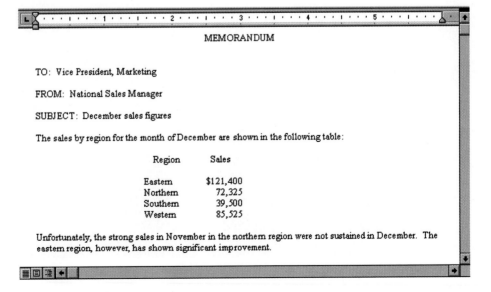

Combining Other Applications with Word Processing. The results produced by other applications such as database management and spreadsheet analysis are often used in documents prepared by word processing. Sometimes it is necessary to key the results of the other applications into a word processing document. It may be possible, however, to transfer the results without rekeying them. For example, consider the spreadsheet analysis example discussed previously. With the proper software, the total sales for each region can be transferred from the sales analysis worksheet (Fig. 8.16) directly to the sales memo (Fig. 8.20). This process would save time in preparing the sales memo and reduce the chances of making an error.

Graphics

Information is prepared for presentation in a pictorial or graphical form using computer graphics. With computer graphics the user can create a variety of types of images. (See Fig. 8.22.) One is *charts* or *graphs*, which are often used by business-

FIGURE 8.22

Computer graphics

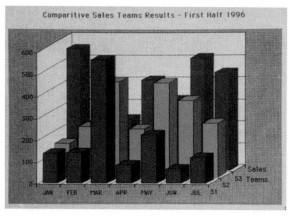

Chart or graph

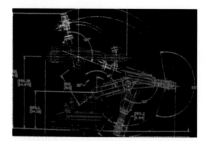

Diagram

Graphic design

Computer art

Realistic image

people, scientists, and others to summarize data in an easily understood form. Another is *diagrams* showing outlines or designs of objects. These are used by architects and engineers when designing buildings, automobiles, and other objects. *Graphic designs* are another type of computer graphics. These are used in advertisements in magazines and on television, and often include movement or animation. Another type of computer graphics is a *realistic image* of an object, such as a car or an airplane. One use of this type of image, which may be three dimensional and include movement, is in machines that simulate real-world situations, such as airplane simulators. A final type of computer graphics is *computer art*. Many artists use computers to create unique works of art.

Graphics Software. Computer graphic output is produced by graphics software. With this type of software the user can create charts, graphs, diagrams, designs, images, art, and other forms of graphic output on a screen or on paper. Some graphics software is very specialized and is used only by certain types of people such as graphic designers and artists. Other graphics software is more general and can be used by almost anyone.

Charting software is used to create charts and graphs that summarize business data. Figure 8.23 shows some of the forms of charts and graphs that can be produced by charting software. Data must be supplied to the charting program so it can create the chart or graph. The data can come from several sources. One is a worksheet; data from rows and columns in a worksheet created by a spreadsheet program can be plotted in a chart or graph. Another source of data is a data file or database created by a file manager or database program. Finally, the user can enter data directly into a charting program, which can use the data to plot the output. To use a charting program, a user must specify the source of the data and what type of chart or graph he or she wants created. The software uses the data to figure out how the chart or graph should appear and then produces the output. Spreadsheet programs such as Excel, Lotus 1-2-3, and Quattro Pro have the ability to produce charts and graphs from data in a worksheet. Charting programs such as Corel Chart can produce charts and graphs from other sources.

Drawing software allows the user to draw pictures and diagrams on the screen. This type of software usually provides the user with many standard shapes and symbols that can be used to create the output. Boxes, circles, and other shapes may be provided. To use this type of graphics software, the user selects a shape, positions the shape on the screen, changes its size, rotates it, and fills it in with shades and colors. By repeating this process for other shapes and symbols and by drawing other lines on the screen with a mouse, the user can create complex pictures and diagrams. Examples of drawing programs are Visio and Corel Draw.

Graphic output is often used in presentations given to groups of people. To create high-quality graphic output for such presentations, presentation graphics software is used. (See Figure 8.24.) This type of software is usually a combination of a charting program and a drawing program but with additional capabilities. Added capabilities include the ability to prepare different border and background designs, to enter and edit text, and to use graphic images from special files.

The output produced by a presentation graphics program can be produced in several forms suitable for presentations. Often, the graphics are displayed on a large computer screen or projected, using special hardware, on a film screen for viewing by an audience. A laser printer can produce presentation graphics output on transparency sheets, which can be projected on a film screen during a presentation. Special hardware is available that records graphic output on photographic film. Slides made

FIGURE 8.23

Charting software: common forms of charts and graphs

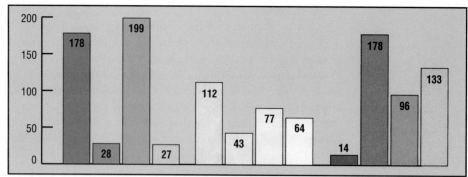

Bar graph

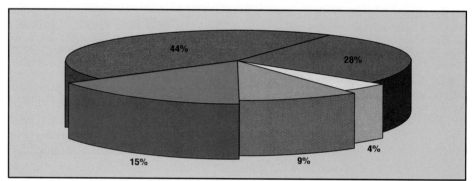

Pie chart

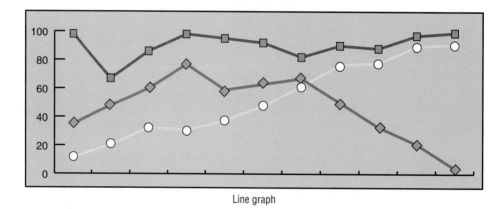

Line graph

from the film can then be used to display the graphic output. These techniques and others make graphics effective in conveying information in a presentation.

Any of the charting programs and drawing programs discussed earlier can be used to prepare presentation graphs, but their capabilities are limited. More powerful presentation graphics programs include PowerPoint and Harvard Graphics.

Graphics software used for designing objects such as buildings and machines is called computer-aided design (CAD) software. Using CAD software, a specially trained person can draw the design of an object with a computer, modify the design, try different designs, and perform other design functions. For example, an automotive engineer can use CAD software to design an automobile. Using the graphics

FIGURE 8.24

Presentation
graphics software

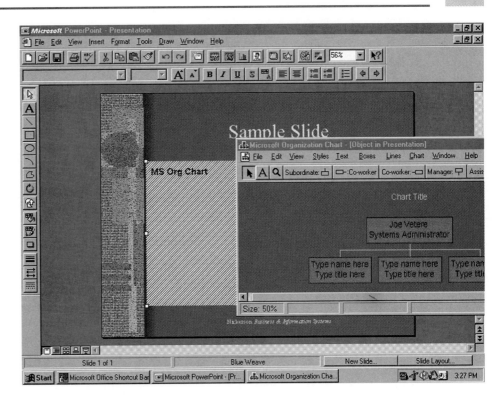

capability of the software, the engineer draws a car on the screen. Then he or she uses the computer to analyze characteristics of the design. The engineer can change the design easily and analyze the new design. Once a design is finalized, it can be drawn on paper with a plotter. Other people who use CAD are aircraft engineers, computer circuit designers, ship builders, and architects. AutoCAD is an example of a CAD program.

An Example of Graphics Preparation. To illustrate the use of graphics software, assume as before that you are the national sales manager of an athletic clothing wholesaler. Each month you analyze the sales in the four regions that you manage using spreadsheet software (Fig. 8.16.) You decide that you would like to graph the sales last month and the sales this month for each region. Such a graph will help you analyze the sales when you prepare your sales memo. The data for the graph will come from the sales analysis worksheet you created earlier and so you decide to use spreadsheet software to create the graph. You start by retrieving the worksheet from secondary storage using your spreadsheet program. Then you select the data in the worksheet to be graphed. For this example, you want to graph the sales in each region for both last month and this month. You decide to display the output in a bar graph and you indicate this to the software. Finally, you enter titles and legends to make the graphic output easier to read. When these tasks have been done, you display the sales analysis graph on the screen and print a copy. Figure 8.25 shows the graphic output that is produced by the spreadsheet program.

Combining Other Applications with Graphics Preparation. In the previous example you used the data that already existed in the worksheet to produce the graphic

FIGURE 8.25

The sales analysis graph

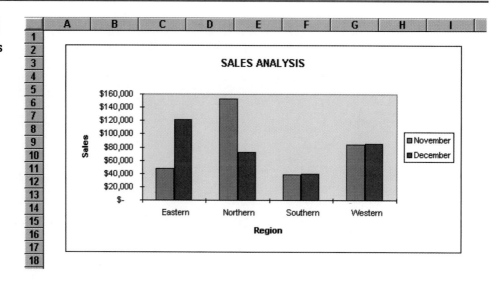

output. You did not have to enter the data again. You only needed to specify what type of graph is to be produced and what data in the worksheet is to be used. The graphics capability of the spreadsheet software determined how the graph should appear.

You can also incorporate your graph into your sales memo (Fig. 8.21). Most word processing programs have the ability to include diagrams, charts, and other graphic images in a document. You can transfer the sales analysis graph from the worksheet to the sales memo document, edit the document, and print the document with the graph. Figure 8.26 shows how the sales memo will look with the graph included.

Combining applications can greatly improve productivity and reduce errors. The database, spreadsheet, word processing, and graphics examples in this chapter illustrate how applications can be combined. (See Fig. 8.27.) In the database example, individual salesperson sales are entered into the Salesperson table and totaled for each region in the Region table (Fig. 8.7). Then the region total sales are transferred from the database to the sales analysis worksheet (Fig. 8.16) and used to analyze changes in sales. The sales data in the worksheet is also used to produce the sales analysis graph (Fig. 8.25). Next, the region total sales are transferred from the worksheet to the sales memo. Finally, the sales analysis graph is transferred to the sales memo (Fig. 8.26). All these applications can be combined in an individual information system that provides capabilities for managing data, analyzing data, and presenting information.

Desktop Publishing

Information can be prepared for presentation in a high-quality printed form similar to that produced by a printing company using <u>desktop publishing</u>. With desktop publishing, professional-looking reports, newsletters, pamphlets, and other printed materials can be prepared directly by the user.

To do desktop publishing, a user must have <u>desktop publishing software</u> designed specifically for this use. This type of software has many word processing capabilities. More importantly, it has the ability to incorporate complex design features, such as graphic images, various type styles, and different column widths, into the printed output. Examples of desktop publishing programs are Pagemaker and Microsoft Publisher.

FIGURE 8.26

The sales memo
with a graph

MEMORANDUM

TO: Vice President, Marketing

FROM: National Sales Manager

SUBJECT: December sales figures

The sales by region for the month of December are shown in the following table:

Region	Sales
Eastern	$121,400
Northern	72,325
Southern	39,500
Western	85,525

Unfortunately, the strong sales in November in the northern region were not sustained in December. The eastern region, however, has shown significant improvement. The following graph shows the sales trend for the past two months.

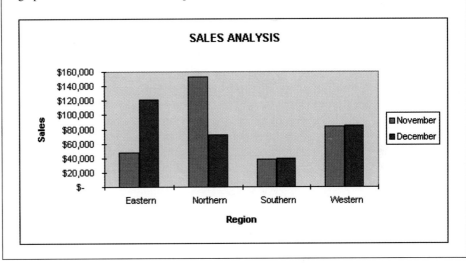

The functions of desktop publishing software are similar to those of word processing programs, except that some capabilities are more sophisticated. A user can enter text using the desktop publishing program in the same way that he or she can enter text with a word processing program. In addition, the user can retrieve text from a file created by another program. For example, the user may enter, edit, and save text using a word processing program and then retrieve the saved text using the desktop publishing program.

In addition to text, the user can retrieve graphic images using the desktop publishing program. Usually, the graphic images are created by another program and may consist of charts, diagrams, drawings, and other nontext data. After text and graphic data are entered, editing can be done, as with a word processing program.

FIGURE 8.27

Transferring data between applications

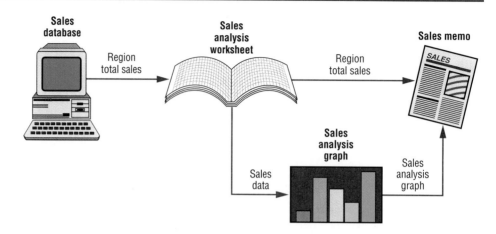

The most powerful function of desktop publishing software, however, is its formatting capabilities. After all the text and graphic data has been entered and edited, it can be formatted in numerous ways. This process is called *page layout* because it involves preparing pages of the document in the format in which they will be printed.

In doing page layout, text can be arranged in one or several columns. Graphic images can be enlarged or reduced to fit with the text, and the text can be rearranged to conform to the shape of the graphics. Horizontal and vertical lines can be included to set off text and graphics; boxes can be drawn around any text or graphic. Practically any formatting feature that you see in a book, newspaper, or magazine can be incorporated into the document. Using the formatting capabilities, documents that appear to be professionally typeset can be prepared. Figure 8.28 shows the screen of a desktop publishing program.

After the document has been formatted, it can be printed. Usually one copy of the document is printed, which is then reproduced using a copier or some other technique.

FIGURE 8.28

Desktop publishing software

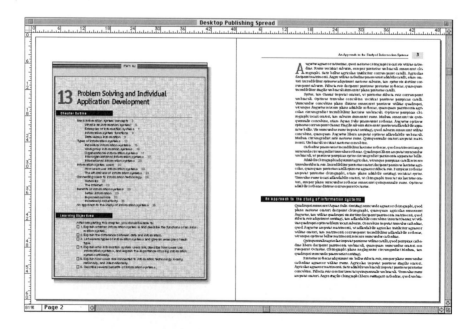

FIGURE 8.29

Multimedia authoring software. This is Macromedia's Director.

Multimedia

Information can be prepared for presentation in a multimedia form. Recall from Chapter 4 that multimedia refers to the use of a computer to present information in more than one way. Word processing software presents information in a text form (sometimes incorporating graphical images), graphics software presents information in a graphical form, and desktop publishing software presents information in a high-quality text and graphical form. Multimedia presentations include text, graphics, animation, video, sounds, voice, music, and other forms.

The parts of a multimedia presentation are prepared using a variety of techniques. Text can be prepared using word processing. Graphic images can be prepared with graphics software or scanned into the computer using a scanner. Video can be converted to a digital form and stored in secondary storage using special hardware and software. Sound can be recorded and stored using other hardware and software.

After all the parts of the multimedia presentation have been prepared, they are brought together using authoring software. This type of software lets the user link together the different parts to create a multimedia presentation. (See Figure 8.29.) After the presentation has been prepared, a person can read, view, or hear the information in the presentation as he or she chooses. Examples of authoring software are Director and Authorware.

Locating Information Using the Internet

The examples presented so far in this chapter have shown how individual application software can be used to manage, analyze, and present business data and information. The data used in these applications often comes from within a business. For example, the sales data entered into the salesperson database described earlier comes from salespeople who work for the business. In some situations, however, a user needs information from outside the business. For example, a sales manager may need to know what products the business's competitors are selling and how they are promoting them.

Internet Use at Art Anderson Associates and Mobius Computer Corporation

The Internet's fun and games are becoming the stuff of serious business. The cutting edge, if you will, is turning into a competitive edge, as up-and-coming small businesses increasingly use on-line resources to get a leg up on market research and customer relations. While many larger companies continue to think of the Internet as a sprawling playground for the young and the wired, enterprising smaller companies are quietly proving that it's also the new frontier for gathering business intelligence. For those companies that take the time to explore the expanding on-line universe of Web sites, the Internet can open up untold worlds of information and opportunity.

Here's a look at how two companies are seeing their on-line time pay off handsomely in critical arenas of business intelligence.

MARKET RESEARCH

The prospect of pinning down accurate international data is what spurred Eric Anderson, CEO of Art Anderson Associates, to take the Internet seriously. A significant portion of his $4 million engineering and architecture business involves designing ferry vessels and port facilities for overseas locations, and it's vital for the firm to obtain reliable geographic surveys. "Lots of coastlines are inaccessible," Anderson points out. "To make them functional, there has to be a ferry service. The Net helps us find information about those sites."

Anderson counts on the Web and newsgroups (on-line discussion groups) run by overseas tourism boards to help his own company "leapfrog into new markets." To get the latest news on development and tourism in Singapore, say, he pulls up the Singapore Web page and checks out which industries are "hot" and who the major players are. "If I see that there's an intensive push to develop industry or tourism in a certain area," he says, "I try to find out who's leading that push." And then he contacts them about building a ferry.

Anderson says that using the Internet is doubly appealing because it cuts his expense budgets. "It allows us to do more preliminary research without the travel expenses we had before." That cost-saving feature is one of the Internet's big attractions. Most companies can justify a $99 software package for getting around on the Net and about $20 a month for an Internet dial-up account for one computer. Compared to what a market research analyst charges for a single report, the Internet looks downright cheap.

COMPETITIVE INTELLIGENCE

Craig Stouffer, CEO of Mobius Computer Corp., used to work the phones feverishly when it came to scouting potential business. The $7.5-million manufacturer of computer systems sells to *Fortune* 1,000 corporations. Keeping close tabs on those companies' annual reports, now available on-line, helps him get an early line on which of them might be in the market for new or upgraded systems.

Stouffer also gathers product information and lists of references from competitors and potential customers by working the Internet. "You can post a question on the newsgroups about products or systems, and 4,500 people respond with their experiences." A slight exaggeration, yes, but there's no question that the number of people you can reach on the Internet is mind-boggling.

Many of the resources that businesspeople like Stouffer are mining on-line— for instance, the inside scoop on competitors from real customers—weren't accessible to them previously in any form. "There's information available now on the Internet that's never been available anywhere," says director of operations Trey Seitz at Competitive Intelligence International in Chicago, a consulting firm that specializes in digging up industry dirt. "The newsgroups are a good place to get information anonymously from experts." Seitz says that exploring the Internet should be a first step for any start-up. "You can pretty much find out what any company in any field is doing. It's a great first step for an entrepreneur—you can evaluate market needs just by posting a message."

QUESTIONS

1. What benefits does Art Anderson Associates receive from using the Internet?
2. What information does Mobius Computer Corp. get from the Internet?

WEB SITES

Art Anderson Associates: www.brainpatch.com
Mobius Computer Corporation: www.mobius.com

Source: Phaedra Hise, "Getting Smart On-Line," *Inc. Technology,* #1, 1996, p.59.

There are a number of sources of external data and information. Databases are available with demographic data, company financial data, and consumer buying-habit data. Information about a company's products is readily available from the company, and data about sales can sometimes be obtained from other sources. Some of this data must be purchased from businesses that specialize in gathering the data, but much data is free.

The Internet makes much of the free data easily accessible. Using a personal computer connected to the Internet, and the appropriate software, an individual can access company World Wide Web sites to search for useful information. A browser is software that lets a user follow links from one Web screen, or page, to another to locate information. (See Fig. 8.30a.) Examples of browsers are Netscape Navigator and Microsoft Internet Explorer. Software on the Web called search engines lets users search for specific types of information. For example, a sales manager can use a search engine to find a competitor's home page, which is a page that is the beginning

FIGURE 8.30

Software for using the World Wide Web

(a) Browser

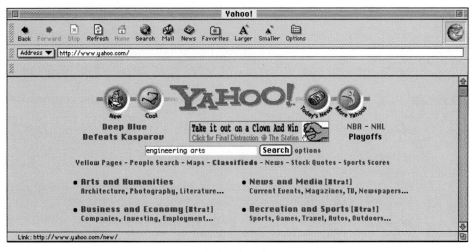

(b) Search Engine

point for information provided by the business. (See Fig. 8.30b.) Then a browser can be used to go from one page to another to locate the desired information. Examples of search engines are Yahoo! and Lycos.

Instead of searching for information using a browser and a search engine, a user can use a special Internet service to have certain types of information sent automatically to his or her computer. This process uses a technique called **push technology** to find information for the user and "push" it to the user's computer. For example, a sales manager may be interested in news articles that refer to products sold by the business's competitors. The manager can use a service to search for appropriate articles periodically, such as every day, and have them sent to the manager's computer. The manager must enter information into the service indicating what types of articles he or she wants, but after that the service identifies and sends articles regularly without the manager having to search for them. An example of a service that uses push technology is PointCast Network.

Although a tremendous amount of information is available on the World Wide Web, it is important for the user to recognize that some information may be inaccurate or misleading. Anyone can put almost anything on the Web. The user must carefully analyze the credibility of the source of the information to ensure that what is received is accurate and relevant.

With this warning in mind, using the World Wide Web can greatly improve a user's productivity in locating information. No longer is it always necessary to go to a library, contact a government agency, or call another business to get information. A user can easily and quickly search for information using a search engine and a browser, or receive information automatically. The information can then be incorporated into other individual application software for storage, analysis, and presentation.

Other Personal Productivity Applications

Database management, spreadsheet, word processing, graphics, and browser software are the most common software used on personal computers. Other software, however, is also used. One example is personal information managers.

A **personal information manager** or **PIM** is multifunction software that provides many capabilities needed for organizing a person's day or helping with desk work. Some of the common functions of this type of software are:

- Scheduling.   The scheduling function lets the user note dates of appointments and other events in a calendar.
- Notepad.   A notepad is a simple word processor for typing quick notes that the user can store and print.
- Task management.   The task management function allows the user to create a list of tasks to be done (to-do lists) and to keep track of the tasks.
- Contact management.   The contact management function lets the user store telephone numbers, addresses, and other information related to customers or clients.

Examples of personal information managers are Sidekick, Lotus Organizer, Claris Organizer, and Microsoft Outlook. Figure 8.31 shows a PIM screen.

Common individual application programs are usually combined and sold together in a software **suite**. A suite often consists of a word processing program, a spreadsheet program, a presentation graphics program, and a database program. A personal information manager may also be included. The programs in the suite usually are designed

FIGURE 8.31

A personal
information
manager

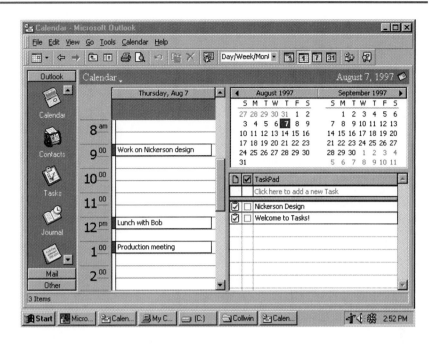

so that data can be transferred between them easily. Examples of suites are Office from Microsoft, WordPerfect Suite from Corel, and SmartSuite from Lotus.

Suites are separate programs packaged and sold together. Another way of combining applications is in integrated software. This type of software may include simplified word processing, spreadsheet, database, graphics, and communications capabilities. These capabilities are not provided by separate programs, but instead by one, integrated program. (See Fig. 8.32.) The program does not provide all the functions of the separate programs, but for less sophisticated applications, it is easier to use. Examples of integrated programs are Claris Works and Microsoft Works.

FIGURE 8.32

Integrated
software

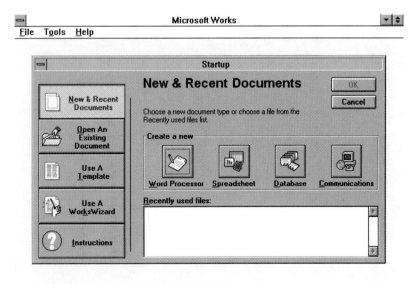

Chapter Summary

☐ Productivity has to do with how much a person contributes to a business. Individual information systems can improve personal productivity by making it easier for individuals to locate, manage, analyze, and present information related to their job. (p. 224)

☐ The main functions that users can perform with **database software** are creating a database, accessing a database, and updating a database. To create a database, a user must first describe the fields and records in the database and then enter data for the database, which is stored in secondary storage. Accessing a database involves retrieving data from the database in secondary storage. Updating a database includes adding new data, deleting old data, and modifying existing data. (pp. 224–231)

☐ Spreadsheet analysis is used to solve problems in which data is organized in rows and columns—that is, in a **spreadsheet**—and calculations are done with the data. **Spreadsheet software** makes spreadsheet analysis easy because the user can create an electronic spreadsheet or **worksheet**. Changes can be made in data in the worksheet, and the computer will automatically recalculate values in the worksheet—a procedure called **what-if analysis**. (pp. 231–234)

☐ The main functions that the user can perform with spreadsheet software are creating a worksheet, changing a worksheet, and printing a worksheet. To create a worksheet, a user enters numbers, text, and **formulas** into **cells** in the worksheet. The formulas use **cell references** and mathematical symbols to indicate how the value of a cell is calculated. A user changes a worksheet because data or calculations change and because he or she wants to do what-if analysis. At any time, the user can print all or part of a worksheet. (pp. 234–239)

☐ Several types of software are used to prepare information for presentation to others. **Word processing software** is used to prepare information in a text document form. **Graphics software** is used to create pictorial or graphical presentations of information. Types of graphics software include **charting software**, **drawing software**, **presentation graphic software**, and **computer-aided design** (**CAD**) software. **Desktop publishing software** is used to prepare information in a high-quality printed form such as a newsletter, pamphlet, or brochure. **Authoring software** is used to create multimedia presentations that include text, graphics, animation, video, sound, and other forms. (pp. 240–251)

☐ Database management, spreadsheet analysis, word processing, and graphics applications can be combined by transferring data from one application to another. The output from one application becomes the input to another application. Data from a database can be transferred to a spreadsheet or a word processing document, or can be used in a graph. Data in a worksheet can be graphed, or transferred to a word processing document or a database. A graph can be transferred to a word processing document. Combining applications improves productivity and increases accuracy. (pp. 247–248)

☐ Much information is available on the Internet. Using the World Wide Web and a **browser**, an individual can access company Web sites to search for useful information. A **search engine** allows a user to search for specific types of information on the Web. Some information may not be correct or useful, but once accurate and relevant information is located, it can be incorporated into other individual application software. (pp. 251–254)

Key Terms

Authoring Software (p. 251)
Browser (p. 253)
Cell (p. 234)
Cell Reference (Address) (p. 234)
Charting Software (p. 245)
Computer-Aided Design (CAD) Software (p. 246)
Database Software (p. 225)
Desktop Publishing (p. 248)
Desktop Publishing Software (p. 248)

Drawing Software (p. 245)
File Manager (p. 224)
Formula (p. 234)
Graphics Software (p. 245)
Home Page (p. 253)
Integrated Software (p. 255)
Page (p. 253)
Personal Information Manager (PIM) (p. 254)
Presentation Graphics Software (p. 245)

Push Technology (p.254)
Search Engine (p. 253)
Spreadsheet (p. 231)
Spreadsheet Software (p. 234)
Suite (p. 254)
What-If Analysis (p. 234)
Word Processing (p. 240)
Word Processing Software (p. 240)
Word Processing System (p. 240)
Worksheet (p. 234)

Assignment Material

Review Questions

Fill-in Questions

1. Two types of data management software are _____ and _____.

2. Three main functions a user can perform with database software are _____, _____, and _____ a database.

3. Three database updating tasks are _____ new data, _____ old data, and _____ existing data.

4. A(n) _____ is an arrangement of data into rows and columns used for data analysis and presentation.

5. When a user changes certain data in a spreadsheet to see the effect on other data in the spreadsheet, the user is performing _____.

6. A spreadsheet created by spreadsheet software is called a(n) _____.

7. A(n) _____ is the intersection of a row and column in a worksheet.

8. The cell reference of the cell in the third row and fifth column of a worksheet is _____.

9. After creating a worksheet using a spreadsheet program, the user must _____ the worksheet in secondary storage before turning off the computer.

10. The process of making corrections or changes in the text of a document is called _____.

11. A graphics program that is used to create charts and graphs from data supplied to the software is called a(n) _____.

12. A graphics program that allows the user to create pictures and diagrams is called a(n) _____.

13. Software used to produce graphic output for a presentation to be given to a group of people is called _____.

14. CAD stands for _____.

15. A group of separate programs that are packaged and sold together is called a(n) _____.

16. A program that combines several common applications such as simple word processing, spreadsheet, database, graphics, and communication capabilities is called _____.

17. A(n) _____ can be used to search for information on the World Wide Web.

18. The beginning screen that a business has on the World Wide Web is called a(n) _____.

Short-answer Questions

1. How can individual information systems improve personal productivity?

2. What two steps are required to create a database?

3. In what situation is spreadsheet analysis used?

4. Why does spreadsheet software make spreadsheet analysis easy?

5. What are the three types of information that a user can put into a cell of a worksheet?

6. What happens when a user enters a formula into a cell of a worksheet?

7. What are the three main functions a user can perform with a spreadsheet program?

8. Give the cell formulas for each of the following cells in the worksheet in Fig. 8.12:

Cell	Formula
B15	= B8 + B9 + B10 + B11 + B12 + B13 + B14
B17	= B5–B15
C15	
C17	
D15	
D17	

9. What are the three main functions a user can perform with word processing software?

10. Why must a user save a word processing document in secondary storage before turning off the computer?

11. Where does a charting program get the data that it uses to create a chart or graph?

12. How can database management, spreadsheet analysis, word processing, and graphics applications be combined?

13. What is desktop publishing?

14. What software is used in preparing multimedia presentations?

15. What capabilities do personal information managers provide?

16. What software is used to locate information on the World Wide Web?

Discussion Questions

1. Sometimes *setting up* computer applications is more time-consuming than actually *using* the applications. The alternative is to do the work some other way. When this happens, is there still an improvement in personal productivity?

2. Most spreadsheet programs have simple "database" capabilities. With these programs you can set up a "database" in a spreadsheet which is actually a table of records and fields. You can then perform certain operations with the data in the table such as searching for specific values. What advantages and disadvantages are there to such "databases" in spreadsheets?

3. What other ways can information be presented besides those discussed in this chapter? What ways might information be presented in the future.

4. This chapter showed how database management, spreadsheet analysis, word processing, and graphics

preparation can be combined in a sales analysis system. Think of another system in which these applications can be combined and describe how it would work.

5. The Internet provides access to information around the world. What problems might be encountered when using World Wide Web information from other countries?

6. Assume that you have been browsing the World Wide Web and you found some information at an obscure site that one of your company's competitors has been involved in sexual harassment of several female employees. You know the women involved and you know that the allegations are completely false. If the information were to become widely known, however, it could damage your competitor. What would you do in this situation?

Problem-solving Projects

1. Using database software, set up the database described in the chapter. Include the Salesperson table and the Region table. You can use the data shown in the figures in the chapter or make up your own data. Then develop the following:

   a. A query giving the names and addresses of salespeople who had sales of $25,000 or more.

   b. A query giving, for each salesperson, the name of the region in which the salesperson works, the number of salespeople in the region, the salesperson's name, and the salesperson's address. The query should display the output in order by region name.

   c. A report giving each salesperson number, name, address, and sales, along with the total sales for all salespeople.

2. Using spreadsheet software, create the sales analysis worksheet described in the chapter. Add another column for the projected sales next month. The projected sales should be the average of the sales last month and the sales this month plus a 15 percent increase. Transfer data from the database you created in project 1 to your worksheet.

3. Using the charting capabilities of your spreadsheet software, develop a graph of the data in the worksheet you created in project 2. The graph should

show the sales last month, the sales this month, and the projected sales next month.

4. Using word processing software, prepare a memo to the purchasing department explaining the projected sales for next month. (The purchasing department needs to purchase adequate stock to meet the projected sales.) Include in your memo the data for all three months from your spreadsheet created in project 2 and your graph created in project 3. Explain how the projected sales were computed in your memo.

5. Assume that you are the national sales manager of an athletic clothing wholesaler, as described in this chapter. Use the World Wide Web to find at least one other company that also sells athletic clothes wholesale. What are the types of products the company sells? Select one product that the company sells and analyze how they promote it on their Web site. Using a word processor, write a summary of what you found.

Real-world Case

Haworth Inc.

Dilbert would not be a fan of Haworth's corporate mission. That's because Haworth manufactures office cubicles. It is a company drowning in a sea of 21 million disparate and untracked inventory parts that make up its products.

The answer for Haworth, based in Holland, Michigan, has been to equip sales representatives with computer-visualization software from Trilogy Development Group, in Austin, Texas. The software lets sales representatives with laptop computers show a customer exactly what's being ordered and how it will look.

Today, the baffling array of possible Haworth furniture combinations is so complex that many customers don't know exactly what they've bought until it's delivered, according to Ward Smith, Haworth's senior sales-automation consultant.

For example, an office chair alone could be assembled in 200 different ways. And the 21 million parts don't even include the many possible color combinations.

Software visualization gives sales representatives the ability to assemble on a laptop's screen the pieces of Haworth's cubicles at the customers' premises. This augments the company's sales process, in which the sales representative must shuttle back and forth between the customer and an office-equipment dealership, allowing a CAD operator at the dealership to create a mock-up based on the parts being ordered, Smith says.

"We can give the laptop to a salesperson who knows nothing about how to configure our product, because the software is programmed to know how our products go together," Smith says.

Smith likes to compare his complicated sales problem to the relatively easy sales approach taken in the automobile industry.

"You can look at a red Corvette, drive it, kick the tires, and then buy it. But with us, you can fly to

Michigan headquarters to look at a close facsimile of our product that is not exactly what you are buying. Then you can work with our dealer on ordering 21 million parts. Then the dealer's CAD operator will try to visualize what you're buying; you'll see a two-dimensional blueprint and maybe a 3-D rendering of one of the several workstations you're probably buying. We make it and deliver it in 15 million parts with instructions on how to put it together. And until you put it together, you will not know if the order is right," Smith says.

Haworth's executives hope that the Trilogy application, called the Sales Builder Engine, will shorten the company's sales cycle, make its huge parts catalog more easily understood, and increase order accuracy. According to Smith, that would be a significant competitive advantage for the 9,000-employee company, which is the world's second-largest seller of office cubicles and had $1.2 billion in sales in 1995. Smith says Haworth spent more than $1 million on the Trilogy software.

The software is expected to speed up Haworth's sales cycle and improve accuracy by eliminating some of the repetitive CAD work and sales representative trips to customers' sites.

The salesperson and CAD operator typically have to go through the CAD mock-up process several times—with the sales representative returning each time to the customer to show the mock-up—to complete an order. Only after the last CAD mock-up is approved is the CAD workstation software used to create a bill of materials that goes to Haworth's factory for manufacturing. What's more, having the sales representative relay information from the customer to the CAD operator sometimes allows errors to creep into the CAD mock-up.

The Trilogy visualization software should eliminate some of the sales representatives' trips back and forth between the customer and CAD operator, while reducing the number of errors, Smith says.

Sales representatives who use the laptops equipped with Trilogy software should be able to configure clusters of as many as 10 cubicles and give the customer approximate prices for what has been created on the laptop screen—all without returning to the dealership.

"The result is that the salesperson can do 'what ifs' with the client all day long," Smith says.

One additional reason the Trilogy software will be useful in eliminating errors is that, besides assembling the Haworth product on-screen, it provides a virtual "walk-through" of a group of assembled work cubicles. The walk-through portion of the application requires laptops with 90-MHz Pentium chips and 16 MB of RAM, Smith says.

"We have a user group that says it now usually takes five discussions between the customer and the dealer before an order goes to manufacturing. I hope to eliminate two of those discussions by collecting the customer requirements accurately the first time," Smith says. "That's important, because the tightest piece of the funnel in the sales process is the CAD-operator design function; for every 10 salespeople there are only two or three CAD operators."

The CAD operator still has a role, however. After the sales representative and customer have agreed on a configuration for the cubicles, the CAD operator takes the configuration file from the laptop, matches it against the architecture of the customer's building, and checks that the parts of the cubicles fit together properly.

But the Trilogy software simplifies the CAD operator's job, Smith says.

"The laptop CAD file has the information about exactly how everything is configured, right down to the fabric and the finish. The CAD operator takes that same file, overlays it on a diagram of the customer's building, then hits the configure button. The CAD system, using the Trilogy model, makes sure that the operator doesn't put workstations in the middle of a wall, and that parts are configured correctly, Smith says.

Smith says that the Trilogy application shouldn't be confused with traditional sales-force automation, which typically means giving a worker a laptop computer and software tools for expense reporting, sales tracking, and e-mail.

With the Trilogy software, Haworth is reengineering its sales by shifting detailed parts-assembly information from the corporate level to the customer level.

"We're going to empower the salesperson with everything the CAD operator could do, in effect, moving those capabilities to the point of sale," Smith says. "We're automating something they couldn't do before, instead of automating what they were doing before."

Questions

1. For what application do Haworth sales representatives use laptop computers?

2. How does the use of a laptop computer improve a sales representative's productivity?

3. How can a Haworth sales representative do what-if analysis?

4. Why is it important to have CAD support at the dealership even though sales representatives have laptop computers?

5. What benefits does Haworth expect to receive from the use of laptop computers by its sales representatives?

Source: Steve Alexander, "Trilogy helps Haworth get through a maze of cubicles," *InfoWorld,* January 27, 1997, p. 92.

9 Group Collaboration

Chapter Outline

Encouraging Group Collaboration   (p. 262)
Characteristics of Group Collaboration   (p. 263)
    Time and Place of Collaboration   (p. 263)
    Form of Communication   (p. 264)
Types of Workgroup Applications   (p. 265)
    Electronic Messaging   (p. 265)
    Information Sharing   (p. 267)
    Document Conferencing   (p. 268)
    Audio Conferencing   (p. 271)
    Videoconferencing   (p. 273)
    Electronic Conferencing   (p. 275)
    Electronic Meeting Support   (p. 276)
    Group Calendaring and Scheduling   (p. 278)
    Workflow Management   (p. 279)
    Summary of Workgroup Applications   (p. 280)
Office Automation Systems   (p. 282)
The Virtual Work Environment   (p. 283)
    Telecommuting   (p. 283)
    Virtual Offices   (p. 284)
    Virtual Meetings   (p. 284)
    Virtual Companies   (p. 284)

Learning Objectives

After completing this chapter, you should be able to:
☐ 1. Explain why group collaboration is difficult in businesses and how workgroup information systems encourage group collaboration.
☐ 2. Describe the main characteristics of group collaboration.
☐ 3. Explain what groupware is.
☐ 4. List and briefly describe the main types of workgroup applications.
☐ 5. Summarize the group collaboration characteristics of the main types of workgroup applications.
☐ 6. Explain what an office automation system is.
☐ 7. Explain the changes in the work environment that can take place as the result of the use of workgroup applications.

Individuals in a business often do not work alone, but rather in teams, committees, departments, and other types of workgroups. To collaborate on common tasks, workgroup members can have meetings, talk on the telephone, send faxes, and distribute memos. Group members can also use *workgroup information systems* to help them collaborate. As you learned in Chapter 1, a workgroup information system is one that affects a group of people who work together. This type of system is also called a group support system or GSS because it supports the work of people in a group. This chapter looks at applications used in workgroup information systems, and shows how these applications affect group collaboration in businesses.

Encouraging Group Collaboration

Businesses use workgroup information systems to encourage group collaboration. Collaborating with others is an essential part of business. People need to discuss ideas, share thoughts, coordinate plans, and comment on the work of others. Employees have to exchange documents, transmit designs, send images, and communicate with different people. Group members need to solve problems together and make collective decisions. When done well, these activities can improve the effectiveness and productivity of the group beyond what individuals can do separately.

The main difficulty with group collaboration is that group members often are not in the same place at the same time. If everyone in a workgroup can get together in one room at one time for a meeting, then much can be accomplished. But often meetings are difficult to arrange, especially when individuals work at distant locations. In addition, meetings be very expensive and time-consuming when people travel significant distances to get together.

Group collaboration is also difficult because groups often change. Individuals come into a workgroup, work for a while, and then leave for another workgroup or job. Some people may be in several workgroups at the same time, and shift between groups from time to time. Workgroups can also cross departmental boundaries. Individuals from several departments, and in some cases several businesses, may be in a workgroup. All these situations make group collaboration complex.

Telephones, of course, play an important role in group collaboration. Much communication takes place between individuals by telephone, and conference calls, which involve three or more people in a group, are common. But when employees have varying schedules or are located across many time zones, finding a time when everyone is available to talk by telephone can be difficult.

Telephones also are deficient because they only provide verbal communication; text, graphics, and images cannot be seen through a telephone. This is the reason fax machines are used so extensively. A fax of a document, diagram, or picture can be sent and received within a few minutes. Then, if necessary, the faxed image can be discussed on the telephone. Still, this approach is not ideal because any time the document, diagram, or picture changes a new fax must be sent.

To solve many of the problems of telephones and faxes, workgroup information systems have been developed. These systems make it easier for members of a group to collaborate over distance and time. They typically use personal computers connected to local area or wide area networks. The Internet and intranets (discussed in Chapter 6) also are used. Workgroup information systems use many types of software, including electronic mail software so that individuals in the group can communicate easily, database software so that the group can share information, and electronic conferencing software so that group members can discuss problems and reach decisions. By making these and other group applications available, a business encourages group collaboration.

Characteristics of Group Collaboration

Group collaboration has several characteristics. One characteristic is *when* the collaboration takes place and another is *where* it takes place. A third characteristic is *what* is communicated during the collaboration. This section examines these characteristics to provide a basis for understanding workgroup information systems.

Time and Place of Collaboration

Two of the basic characteristics of group collaboration are *time* and *place*—the "when" and "where" of collaboration. Figure 9.1 shows these characteristics in two dimensions. If two or more people collaborate, they may do so at the same time or at different times. To work together at the same time, they could be in a room together or talk by telephone. To collaborate at different times, they could leave voice messages, send faxes, use overnight delivery, or send regular mail.

People may also work together at the same place or at different places. They may be in the same room or building, making it possible for them to have direct contact. Alternatively, they may be at widely separated locations, in which case they cannot have direct contact without extensive travel.

Figure 9.1 shows four possible combinations of these characteristics. People working at the same time and place can collaborate directly. A face-to-face meeting is an example of this type of collaboration. People working at the same time but in different places often use the telephone for collaboration. Conference calls also are common in this situation. When people work at different times but at the same place, they collaborate by leaving messages, either on the telephone or by paper

FIGURE 9.1

Time and place of group collaboration

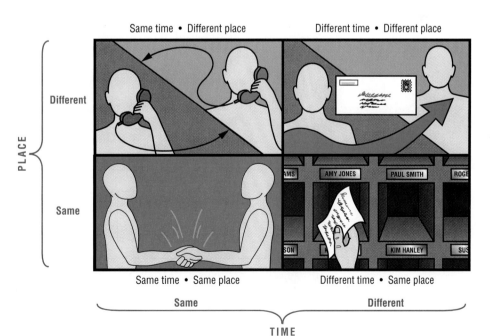

notes. Putting written messages in mailboxes in staff mail rooms is a common way of communicating in this situation. The most complex situation is when people working at different times and places need to collaborate. Voice messages, faxes, overnight deliveries, and regular mail are used in this situation.

Form of Communication

Another way of characterizing group collaboration is by the *form* that the communication between people takes—the "what" of collaboration. Figure 9.2 summarizes some of the forms taken. Perhaps the most often used form of communication in business is *audio communication*; people talk to each other, either in person or on the telephone. Audio communication is not only what is said, but also how it is said. Tone, inflection, and other characteristics of speech often express information. In addition to live, verbal communication, recorded sound is used in group collaboration. Voice mail, taped sound, and other recorded sound are part of audio communication.

A second form of communication in group collaboration is *visual communication*, specifically sights of people or other real things. When groups meet in person, the members of the group can see each other. Their facial expressions and body language give visual clues that provide information about what they are saying and

FIGURE 9.2

Forms of communication in group collaboration

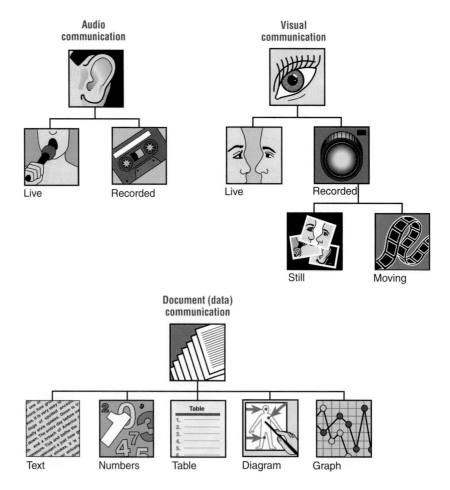

thinking. Recorded sights also are used in some collaborative situations. Still pictures or moving images on video tape may be shown to groups for discussion.

A final form of communication used in group collaboration is *document* (or *data*) *communication*. Documents may contain text, numbers, tables, diagrams, graphs, and other written representations of information. Examples are a report sent to members of a team, a table of data examined by committee members, a diagram of a design examined by several people, and a graph of data discussed by a group.

Types of Workgroup Applications

The previous section discussed the *when*, *where*, and *what* of group collaboration. The *how* has to do with the mechanisms used for group work. Without computers, face-to-face meetings, telephones, faxes, and mail are typically used for collaboration. With networked computers, however, various types of group collaborative software can be used. In general, these types of software are called groupware. The use of groupware by members of a workgroup for collaboration is sometimes referred to as group computing or collaborative computing.

People working in groups can use personal computer software, such as spreadsheet software, to assist in workgroup tasks. For example, a worksheet may be used by several people in a workgroup to analyze data. The worksheet could be stored on a server in a local area network and different individuals, using spreadsheet software on personal computers connected to the network, could use the worksheet at different times.

Although personal computer software can be beneficial in workgroup tasks, these programs are not designed specifically for group work. Groupware, on the other hand, is intended only for workgroup information systems. These programs are used on networks, either local area or wide area, and group members use the programs through personal computers connected to the network.

This section takes a look at the main types of workgroup applications and examines the time (when), place (where), and form (what) characteristics of each type. It also introduces common groupware used for each type of application. It is important to note, however, that many workgroup programs encompass several types of applications.

Electronic Messaging

One of the most common forms of collaboration in workgroups is simple document communication; written notes, memos, task lists, notices, and other messages are commonly sent between members of a group. This form of communication is essential for all aspects of business, and software designed to facilitate it is at the heart of most workgroup information systems. In general, this type of application is called electronic messaging.

Electronic messaging allows document communication to take place between group members at different times from different places. Individuals can send written messages to others at any time of the day or night, and from any place in the world. A disadvantage of electronic messaging, however, is that an important message may not be read immediately. In fact, it could be several days before a message is read. In addition, communication in written form has limitations. Tone, inflection, facial expression, and other nonwritten forms of communication do not come through in an electronic message.

A basic form of electronic messaging is electronic mail or e-mail, in which simple text messages are sent between people. With *electronic mail software*, each user in a network has an *electronic mail address* and an *electronic mailbox*. The address identifies the user's mailbox, which is a space on a disk in the network reserved for the user's electronic mail. When sending electronic mail, the sender identifies the receiver by his or her electronic mail address and the e-mail software stores the mail in the receiver's electronic mailbox. The user can review the mail in the mailbox at any time.

E-mail software provides many useful features including the following:

- Simple word processing capabilities for composing messages. The user also can compose a message with a separate word processing program, and mail the message with the e-mail software.
- The ability to add *attachments* to the e-mail. For example, the user could send a message to someone and attach a separately created document or spreadsheet.
- The ability to send e-mail to a group of individuals. E-mail software usually includes some way of identifying a group by a single name, sometimes called an *alias*. Then the user can send a message to everyone in the group by simply giving the alias to the e-mail software.
- A feature that allows a user to save e-mail for future review. This feature is sometimes called *archiving* and the user may be able to set up separate categories for archiving different types of messages.
- The capability of replying to a message without having to enter an e-mail address. The user can reply to the sender of the message alone, or to everyone to whom the sender originally sent the message.

A number of e-mail programs are in use. Some of the common ones are Lotus cc:Mail, Microsoft Mail, and DaVinci Mail. Figure 9.3 shows the screen of an e-mail program.

FIGURE 9.3

An e-mail program screen. This is Lotus cc:Mail.

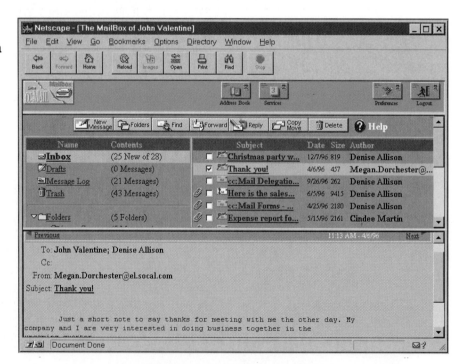

Although electronic mail software is very common, more sophisticated *electronic messaging software* also is available. Such software allows users to send special types of messages to individuals or groups. For example, some electronic messaging software lets a user assign a task to another person or group of people. Thus, a department manager can assign a specific job to an employee in the department. When the employee completes the job, he or she can report this fact to the department manager using the messaging software. Other functions provided by electronic messaging software include the ability to send special notices to others, and to record "while you were out" messages for different people.

An example of a program that includes electronic messaging is Novell GroupWise. GroupWise has electronic mail capabilities plus electronic messaging features such as the ability to assign tasks and send notices. Figure 9.4 shows a GroupWise screen.

Information Sharing

In addition to being able to send messages to each other, members of a workgroup need to be able to share other types of information. Although information to be shared could be sent from one person to another using e-mail, it often is easier to put the shared information in a single location and let each group member access it as needed. One way of accomplishing this is with database software. A database of shared information can be created and each person can use database software to access the database.

The difficulty with using database software to share information is that often the information does not fit the database approach. For example, members of a product design group may wish to share information, including diagrams, graphs, video, and sound, about a new product being developed. Group members may also

FIGURE 9.4

An electronic messaging groupware screen. This is Novell GroupWise.

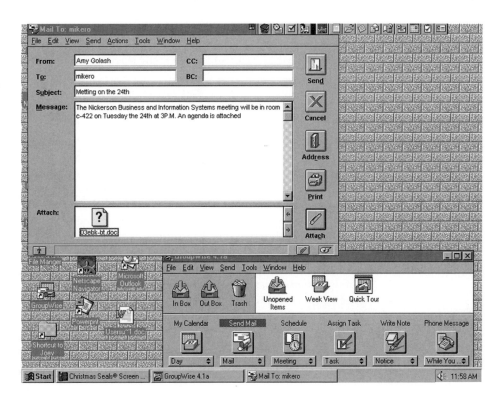

want to share a spreadsheet analysis, a written report, and data extracted from an outside source. Common database software does not provide the capabilities for this type of information sharing.

Information sharing is a workgroup application that involves sharing different types of information among members of a group. With *information sharing software*, many different types of information, including text, graphics, spreadsheets, databases, video, and sound, can be shared. Users can access the information, change it, comment on it, and add new information.

Information sharing allows audio, visual, and document communication to take place between group members at different times from different places. The advantage of information sharing is that individuals in a workgroup can access the shared information at any time from any place. A disadvantage of information sharing is that a person may not access relevant information immediately. Using information sharing effectively requires that all members of a workgroup examine the shared information on a regular basis.

Perhaps the most well-known information sharing program is Lotus Notes. With Notes, users can create "document databases" to share information. Each database can contain text, numbers, graphs, images, sound, and video. Users can comment on information in a database and add new information. Figure 9.5 shows a Notes screen. Other examples of this type of software include Microsoft Exchange and SoftArc's FirstClass.

Although information sharing software provides the ability to share a variety of types of information, its versatility can make this type of program difficult to set up and use. Members of a workgroup sometimes only want to share simple text and graphic documents, and to comment on them. Document sharing is a type of information sharing application that just provides these capabilities. *Document sharing software* usually is simpler to set up and to use than general information sharing programs.

An example of document sharing software is WebFlow's SamePage. With SamePage, users can comment on a document consisting of text, numbers, and graphics. Users also can add items to the document that indicate actions to be done, such as checking a diagram for accuracy. Figure 9.6 shows a SamePage screen. Another example of document sharing software is Radnet's WebShare.

Document Conferencing

Document sharing lets members of a workgroup collaborate on documents at different times. Often, however, group members want to confer on a document *at the same time*. Document conferencing, also called data conferencing, is a workgroup application that provides this form of collaboration. Group members at different locations can simultaneously view a document containing text, numbers, graphs, and other forms of information. Individuals can add comments to the document for others to see and can make changes in the document.

Document conferencing provides for document communication between group members at the same time from different places. It is useful in situations where individuals cannot meet face-to-face to discuss a document. A disadvantage, though, is that group members must be available at the same time to confer on the document.

There are two main types of document conferencing: whiteboard conferencing and application conferencing. With whiteboard conferencing, each user

FIGURE 9.5

An information
sharing groupware
screen. This is
Lotus Notes.

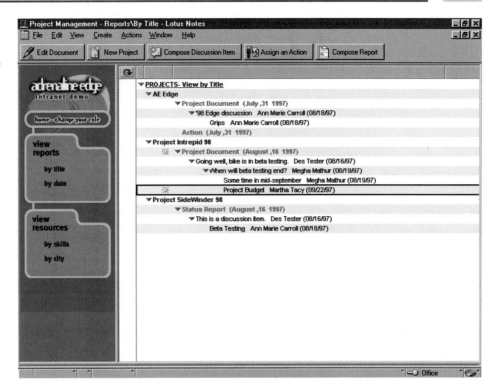

FIGURE 9.6

A document
sharing groupware
screen. This is
WebFlow's
SamePage.

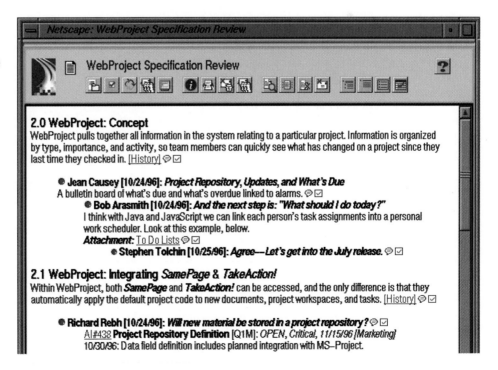

Bookmark

Information Sharing at Jardine Fleming, Hong Kong

Covering investment management, corporate finance, securities broking, capital markets, and banking, Jardine Fleming, one of Asia's leading finance houses, has seen a substantial growth alongside the remarkable transformation and unprecedented growth of the Asian economies. Headquartered in Hong Kong, it is a joint venture, owned equally by London-based investment bank Robert Fleming and international trading house Jardine Matheson.

Employing 3,200 people in its network of offices spanning 29 cities throughout the Asia Pacific region, Jardine Fleming has doubled in size, both in terms of staff and premises, since 1993. This growth has necessitated the installation of a more sophisticated communications infrastructure to accommodate the growing demands of people in the organization.

According to Neil Clapham, Director of the Information Technology Department, Jardine Fleming Management Services Ltd., if the organization hadn't put something in place that allowed people to communicate better, it wouldn't be able to sustain the kind of growth it was experiencing.

A number of different businesses operate within the Robert Fleming and Jardine Matheson operations. Senior management was becoming increasingly aware that it would be highly beneficial if there was a way of leveraging existing client relationships across all the businesses.

"There was a need to know our clients better, understand which clients were doing business with which parts of the organization and who the contact points were," said Clapham. This was only achievable if there was a high-level view of the group's complete client base.

The answer was found in Lotus Notes. A Group Relationship database became the first in a number of Notes-based applications that are being deployed worldwide.

While the Group Relationships database contains top-level company and contact information, individuals need applications underneath to manage their own part of the business, said Clapham. Among other daily activities, they need to track day-to-day information about their products and contact time with clients.

To facilitate this, Jardine Fleming has two main application areas: Corporate Finance, which consists of nine databases and largely holds either company contact information or presentations; and Research, which comprises three databases—the Research Discussion database, Fleming's Asian Broking database, and a Staff Directory.

Both Corporate Finance and Research use Notes as a platform to disseminate information and circulate ideas throughout the offices within the group. The data may be a mix of different types of information. Notes works for the organization more like a reference library, said Clapham. And if there is one common theme across all the applications, it is that of information sharing.

The businesses within Corporate Finance and Research have clear parallels. Both involve small pockets of people distributed across the world. All of them need to exchange information and ideas. With Notes, staff share all manner of documents, including presentations and spreadsheets, across a regional and global network.

This simply didn't happen prior to the implementation of Notes, said Clapham. Previously, a document would have been prepared in one location and either faxed—with the inevitable loss of quality—or couriered, incurring time delays and expense.

Clapham finds the gains that Lotus Notes has made can be seen in the great benefit to client relationships, or what he calls the front end of the business.

QUESTIONS

1. Why did Jardine Fleming have problems with group communication before installing Lotus Notes applications?
2. How does Lotus Notes encourage group collaboration at Jardine Fleming?

WEB SITE
Jardine Fleming: www.jfleming.com

Source: "Jardine Fleming - Connecting People with Lotus Notes," www2.lotus.com/IndustrySpotlight.nsf, Lotus Development Corporation.

sees the same document on an *electronic whiteboard*, which is a white area on the screen containing the document. (See Fig. 9.7.) Any user can write comments on the whiteboard and all users see the comments simultaneously on their whiteboards. Any user can change the document and all users see the changes at the

FIGURE 9.7

A whiteboard conferencing groupware screen. This is DataBeam's FarSite.

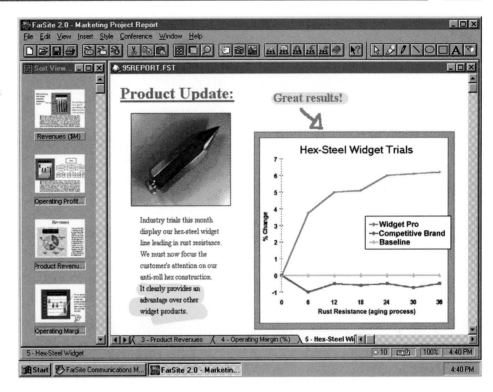

same time. An example of *whiteboard conferencing software* is DataBeam's FarSite. Figure 9.7 shows a FarSite screen. Another example of this type of software is Future Labs' TalkShow.

With application conferencing, each user also sees the same document on his or her screen. But instead of seeing the document on a whiteboard, the user sees it within the actual application program. Thus, users see a text document in a word processing program screen and a worksheet in the spreadsheet software screen. The document is displayed by one user for all users to see, but any user can comment on the document on the screen and make changes in it. Examples of *application conferencing software* are Hewlett-Packard's SharedX, Spectragraphic's TeamConference, and Sun Microsystems's ShowMe SharedApp. Figure 9.8 shows an application conferencing groupware screen.

Although document conferencing is primarily for simultaneous collaboration, it is also possible with some software for a user to work on a document alone and then send the document to other users so that they can work on it at other times. This *store-and-forward* capability makes it unnecessary in some situations for all users to be connected at the same time.

Audio Conferencing

Perhaps the most common way in which people in a workgroup communicate is by telephone. Telephones are universal and easy to use, so people find them very convenient for discussing group work. The telephone can also be used to communicate when working with computers. For example, two people can talk on the telephone about a document that is displayed on both their computer screens. Although not ideal, this form of collaboration is used often.

FIGURE 9.8

An application conferencing groupware screen. This is Sun Microsystems's ShowMe SharedApp.

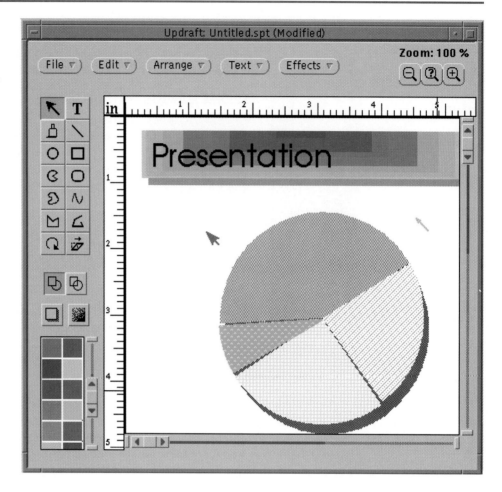

Many personal computers have speakers (or headphones) and a microphone, so it is natural to incorporate telephone capabilities into computers. Some personal computers come with telephone circuitry that allows communication over telephone lines. Another approach, called computer telephony, uses the business's local area or wide area network, or the Internet, for audio communication, thus bypassing the regular telephone lines.

For computer telephony to work, each computer needs special *computer telephony software*, and the appropriate audio input (microphone) and output (speaker or headphone) devices. Examples of computer telephony software include Quarterdeck's WebTalk and VocalTec's Internet Conference. Many computer telephony programs are designed for use over the Internet.

With computer telephony, audio conferencing with computers is possible. In general, audio conferencing is a workgroup application in which two or more members of a group at different locations communicate with each other at the same time by voice over a computer network. It is not necessary to set up a telephone conference call or to use standard telephone lines. All communication takes place using computers and computer networks.

As with telephone communication, audio conferencing provides audio communication between group members at the same time from different places. Its advantage over a telephone is that it uses a computer network for communication, which may be less expensive than a telephone line. Its main disadvantage is the same as that of a telephone: Group members can only communication verbally; visual and document communication is not provided in audio conferencing. In addition, group members must be available at the same time in order to have an audio conference.

Videoconferencing

During an audio conference, people often want to see who they are talking to. Facial expressions and body language can sometimes convey information as much as the words that are spoken. Videoconferencing is a workgroup application in which members of a group at different locations can see each other at the same time that they talk to each other. Videoconferencing always includes audio, although audio conferencing can be done without video.

Videoconferencing allows audio and visual communication between group members at the same time from different places. It overcomes one of the disadvantages of audio conferencing by providing visual communication. It is especially beneficial as a replacement for face-to-face meetings that would require expensive travel by meeting participants. Some businesses use videoconferencing extensively instead of face-to-face meetings in this situation. Still, videoconferencing has some disadvantages. Documents cannot be communicated in a videoconference, and conference participants must be available at the same time.

To have a videoconference, each user location needs a video camera, monitor, microphone, and speaker. Audio and video signals are transmitted from one location to another. Video images are displayed on distant monitors and sound is projected through a speaker. Some videoconferencing systems, called *point-to-point* systems, only allow users at two locations to communicate. Other videoconferencing systems, called *multipoint* systems, allow users at more than two locations to participate in a conference simultaneously.

Two types of videoconferencing systems are room systems and desktop systems. A room (or group) videoconferencing system is designed for use by several people in a room. These systems have a large, special-purpose monitor, often 32 inches across. Some room systems come with several monitors. Room systems also include a high-quality video camera that can be pointed at different parts of the room and can zoom in on the person speaking. Room video conferencing systems can cost up to $50,000. Figure 9.9 shows one of these systems in use.

FIGURE 9.9

A room or group video-conferencing system

Unlike a room system, a <u>desktop videoconferencing system</u> is designed for use by an individual. It uses a personal computer for processing and sending video and audio signals. A desktop system requires a small video camera connected to the computer. Usually the camera is mounted on top of the computer monitor, although a separate camera also may be used. Video images are displayed on computer monitors, not on separate monitors as with room systems. The desktop system also needs a microphone and speaker (or headphone) connected to the computer. Finally, desktop systems need *desktop videoconferencing software* to provide the video and audio processing and transmission. Two examples of desktop videoconferencing systems are Intel's ProShare system and PictureTel's Live system. Figure 9.10 shows a desktop videoconferencing system in use.

One difficulty with videoconferencing is that video signals require a large number of bits when transmitted over a digital channel. Because of this characteristic, special processing called *video compression* is used to code the video signal in such a way that it takes fewer bits for transmission. Then, *video decompression* is used to decode the signal after it is received for display on a monitor. Desktop videoconferencing systems often have a separate circuit board for compression and decompression purposes, although with some high-speed personal computers it is possible to do the required compression and decompression using software in the main computer rather than with a separate board.

Desktop videoconferencing systems are much less expensive than room systems. Typical prices for the hardware and software that must be added to a personal computer for desktop videoconferencing are $1,500 to $3,000, although some systems are less than $1,000. Desktop videoconferencing systems have the disadvantage of being able to show only a small image, such as a single person. The video camera usually can be moved, however, to show someone else in the room or even to show an object. In addition, the video image often is jerky because of the slow speed at which most desktop systems operate. Still, as the price of these systems decreases,

FIGURE 9.10

A desktop video-conferencing system

it is likely that their use will increase. Someday, all personal computers may be equipped with desktop videoconferencing capabilities.

Electronic Conferencing

Videoconferencing systems let members of a workgroup at different locations have audio and visual communication with each other. Combining document conferencing with videoconferencing creates a system with which workgroup members can also have document communication. This combination forms a workgroup application called <u>electronic conferencing</u>.

Some desktop videoconferencing software can be combined with separate whiteboard or application conferencing software to create electronic conferencing systems. More often, however, *electronic conferencing software*, which integrates whiteboard or application conferencing with desktop videoconferencing, is used. Such integrated software offers the most versatility in electronic conferencing.

An example of an electronic conferencing system is Silicon Graphics's InPerson. Figure 9.11 shows an InPerson screen. With InPerson, users at any location can talk to and see each other while sharing images on an electronic whiteboard. Several people can confer at one time, with all their video images showing on each person's screen. Each participant in the conference has a different-shape cursor for marking the whiteboard so that all users know whose comments are appearing on the screen. Electronic conferencing systems such as InPerson let users talk to each other, see each other, view objects held in front of the camera, hear recorded sound, view recorded video, and see and comment on text, graphics, and other images on the whiteboard.

FIGURE 9.11

An electronic conferencing system screen. This is Silicon Graphics's InPerson.

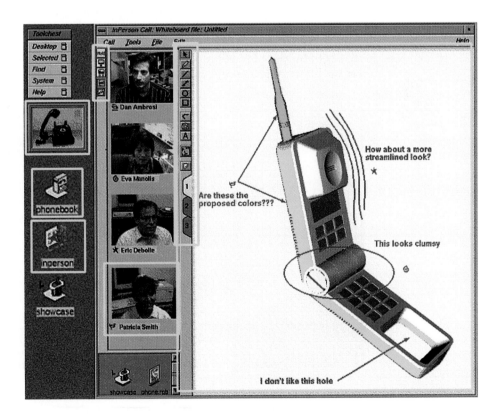

Electronic conferencing is designed primarily for use by users at different locations so that they can confer at the same time. Some systems also let users work at different times, storing information and then forwarding it to other users. For example, a user can work on text or a diagram on his or her whiteboard, record video images and sound, and then send everything to other users for later review and work. Thus, all participants in an electronic conference do not have to be available at the same time.

Electronic conferencing provides all forms of communication—audio, visual, and document—between group members at the same time from different places. Because all forms of communication can be used, it is a very useful tool for group collaboration. It requires powerful computers and networks, however, to handle the software and data, thus making it an expensive form of group computing.

Electronic Meeting Support

Members of a group work together in various ways, some informal and some formal. Informal collaboration includes everything from casual conversations to in-depth discussions. More formal collaboration often takes the form of a meeting, which we usually think of as a group of people discussing specific topics from an agenda and reaching conclusions about those topics. When computer systems are used to facilitate the meeting, the result often is called an electronic meeting. A workgroup application that is designed to support electronic meetings is called an electronic meeting system or EMS.

Electronic meeting systems come in two main forms: room systems and desktop systems. With a room electronic meeting system, a separate *electronic meeting room* is set up with special hardware and software. (See Fig. 9.12.) This type of room also is called a *decision room* because it is used for making group decisions.

An electronic meeting room includes individual workstations for the participants in the meeting. Each workstation has a personal computer which is connected by a network to the other personal computers in the room. In addition, there is a special workstation for the meeting leader or facilitator. This workstation has a per-

FIGURE 9.12

An electronic meeting room

Bookmark

Global Electronic Conferencing at Ford

"The problem is, your shock tower as it stands goes right through my fender. And if I raise the fender, it's going to look super ugly."

"Well, how far above the fender does it go?"

"Here. That's it in blue. I'll circle it for you."

"Oh, yeah. About half an inch too tall. Hmmm."

"You're smiling. Does that mean you can fix it?"

"Sure. Watch this."

This conversation, relaxed and intimate as it sounds, is taking place across nine time zones. Two Ford designers, one working on body design in California, one designing suspensions in Germany, are chatting face-to-face, their eyes on each other and on the same drawing. The miles and kilometers that separate them, and the chilly North Atlantic, do not exist. In the words of Alex Trotman—the Ford CEO who is tearing down the barriers between Ford operations worldwide—they are co-located. What they're doing will inevitably cut Ford's costs, produce better cars, and get cars to market faster. But it is also doing something much more profound: It is changing the way people work.

"This is a cultural change as much as a technological change," says Ford Chief Designer Giuseppe Delena. Silicon Graphics workstations and software such as InPerson, IRIS Annotator, Showcase, and Inventor provide the technological underpinnings for what Ford calls its Global Studio. But the technology is so effective that it seems to step out of the way and let people communicate.

Transoceanic conversations, complete with interactive graphics and live video, are now routine between Ford design centers in Michigan, California, Japan, England, Germany, and Australia. The greatest benefit to Ford, according to Delena, is pure real-time collaboration.

"The ability to work in a collaborative mode internationally is an advantage in itself, because that translates into the ability to operate as a global company—a leaner, faster, company—and produce world cars of higher quality. One fallout of that, we hope, is reduced time to market."

Ford designers have always worked globally, but now the Global Studio has pulled them even closer together. Instead of packing up for a trip to Europe, a designer clicks on a telephone icon on a Silicon Graphics workstation, and is instantly sharing a three-dimensional design with his colleague across the world.

"It's not meant to be a large meeting where we discuss important issues," says Delena. "This is really one-on-one. It's one engineer talking to another, one designer talking to another, discussing a specific problem. It's something you can do right through your workstation and you really get problems resolved faster—much faster—that way. There's an interaction that you just don't get through the phone."

Ford designers received an unexpected bonus from Silicon Graphics technology: the ultimate MediaMail system. If it's too late to reach a colleague in real time, a designer can send a complete multimedia package of work—text, graphics, video clips—and send it overnight digitally with annotations. When the overseas designers come to work in the morning, they just open it up and point and click.

Where is this technology headed? Delena has a broad vision of distant, co-located colleagues and an altered global business culture.

"What do I think? I think this technology may open up new ways to accomplish the job. I think it's possible that in the future people working at home will be able to collaborate on design projects. Geographical locations won't matter. Decision making will be more compressed in time. I think that this technology will work in synergy with others to provide the dynamics for a whole new way of doing business."

QUESTIONS

1. How does Ford use group computing in its Global Studio?
2. How do Ford designers use the store-and-forward capability of their system?
3. What benefits does Ford receive from its Global Studio?

WEB SITE
Ford Motor Company: www.ford.com

Source: Grant Ellis, "Ford's Global Studio Shrinks the World—and Changes the Way It Works," *IRIS Universe*, Number Thirty-Three, Fall 1995, pp. 37, 39.

sonal computer connected to the network and to a large screen, which can be seen by everyone in the room. Finally, special *electronic meeting software* is used to link the workstations and to coordinate the electronic meeting. This software includes a variety of features, including a common whiteboard.

The electronic meeting begins when the leader presents the topic for discussion. Participants in the meeting can key in ideas and comments about the topic at their workstations. The comments are summarized by the meeting leader and displayed on the large screen without identifying who made each comment. For example, the topic of a meeting of the marketing group may be a new advertising campaign. Each participant can enter ideas for the campaign and all participants see the ideas on the large screen. Each participant can enter comments on any idea and again the comments are seen by all on the screen. The fact that the ideas and comments are anonymous means the meeting participants can concentrate on what people write, and not be influenced by who is writing them. The meeting leader can summarize the ideas and then an *electronic vote* can be taken to rank the ideas and decide what actions should be taken.

Room electronic meeting systems are designed for collaboration to take place at the same time and in the same place. Desktop electronic meeting systems, on the other hand, allow collaboration to take place at the same time among users located at different places. These systems provide capabilities similar to room systems but for participants in a geographically dispersed meeting. Users of a desktop electronic meeting system use personal computers connected by a local area or wide area network. An example of electronic meeting software that can be used for both room systems and for desktop systems is Ventana's GroupSystems.

Electronic meeting systems provide document communication between group members at the same time from the same place for room systems, or from different places for desktop systems. They go beyond basic document conferencing by providing special support needed in meetings. Room systems are very expensive, however. In addition, all group members must be available at the same time for an electronic meeting.

Electronic meeting systems often are used to help groups make decisions. In general, any workgroup application that facilitates group decision making is called a group decision support system or GDSS. Chapter 11 will have more to say about information system support for decision making in businesses.

Group Calendaring and Scheduling

When people in a workgroup need to collaborate at the same time, conflicts often arise because of differences in schedules. People work various hours and have numerous time commitments because of work and other responsibilities. Finding a time when everyone can get together for a conference or meeting, whether face-to-face or electronic, can be difficult. The problem is even more complex when members of a workgroup are located in different time zones.

Group calendaring and scheduling is a workgroup application that helps workgroup members coordinate their time. *Group calendaring and scheduling software* includes calendaring capabilities that let users keep individual calendars of appointments and meetings. The software also includes scheduling capabilities to set up meetings. With these capabilities, a user who needs to schedule a meeting indicates to the software who must attend the meeting, and then the software searches the individual calendars for times that would be acceptable to all participants. This application allows group members at different times in different places to coordinate their calendars and schedules.

Users must, however, keep their individual calendars up-to-date. Examples of group calendaring and scheduling software are Campbell Services's OnTime, On Technology's Meeting Maker, and CrossWind Technologies's Synchonize. Figure 9.13 shows the screen of this type of program.

Workflow Management

Group work sometimes involves sequences of tasks that are done by different members of a group. For example, in a marketing department, the design of a new catalog must go through steps such as writing advertising copy, selecting product photographs, laying out the pages in the catalog, proofreading the pages, and so on. Group work may also require that documents be passed from one person in a group to another for processing. For example, in a human resource management department, a prospective employee's application must be passed to several people for review and approval. In both examples, different people are involved in performing tasks or processing documents, with the work flowing from one person to the next. To make the work flow more smoothly, a workgroup application called workflow management can be used.

Workflow management software coordinates the tasks performed by different individuals in a workgroup, and the flow of documents between people. Some workflow software is oriented toward tasks. These programs ensure that each task in the workflow is performed by the right person and in the right sequence. This type of software could be used to coordinate the work of the people designing the new catalog described in the previous paragraph. Other workflow software is oriented toward documents. This type of program ensures that the right documents flow from one person to the next, a process called *document routing*. The processing of the job application described in the previous paragraph could be coordinated by this type of software.

FIGURE 9.13

A group calendaring and scheduling groupware screen. This is CrossWind Technologies's Synchronize.

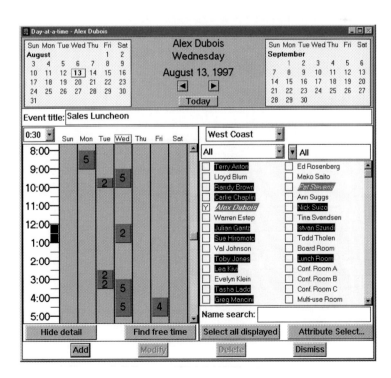

Workflow management is used to coordinate the flow of work between group members working at different times in different places. Users, however, must check the system regularly to see if they have received work. Some examples of this type of software are FileNet's Visual WorkFlo, JetForm Workflow, and Action Technologies's Action Workflow Enterprise Series. Figure 9.14 shows a screen of this type of program. Information sharing software such as Lotus Notes as well as other types of groupware also have workflow capabilities.

Summary of Workgroup Applications

Table 9.1 summarizes the main types of workgroup applications discussed in this section in terms of their time, place, and form characteristics. Some applications are designed for same-time collaboration and some are designed for collaborating at different times. Most group applications are designed for different-place collaboration, although electronic meeting systems are used in the same or different places. Document communication is the main form of communication used in group applications, although some applications provide audio and visual communication. As you

FIGURE 9.14

A workflow management groupware screen. This is FileNet's Visual WorkFlo®.

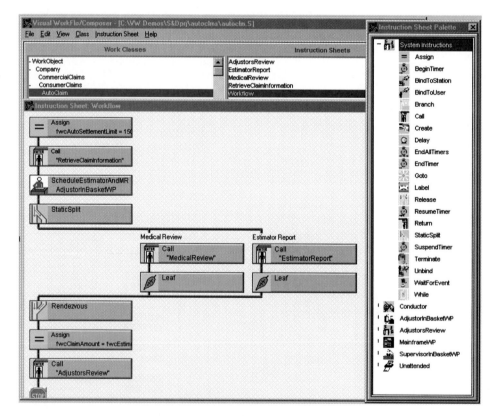

TABLE 9.1   **Summary of types of workgroup applications**

Type of workgroup application	Time of collaboration		Place of collaboration		Form of communication			Example software
	Same	Different	Same	Different	Document	Audio	Visual	
Electronic messaging		X		X	X			Novell GroupWise
Information sharing		X		X	X	X	X	Lotus Notes
Document conferencing	X	X*		X	X			DataBeam FarSite
Audio conferencing	X			X		X		Quarterdeck WebTalk
Video conferencing	X			X		X	X	Intel ProShare
Electronic conferencing	X	X*		X	X	X	X	Silicon Graphics InPerson
Electronic meeting support	X		X	X	X			Ventana GroupSystems
Group calendaring and scheduling		X		X	X			Campbell Services OnTime
Workflow management		X		X	X			FileNet Visual WorkFlo

* With store-and-forward capability.

can see from the table, many combinations of time, place, and form characteristics are found in workgroup applications.

Some groupware provides only the capability of a single type of workgroup application. For example, electronic mail programs only provide simple electronic messaging features. Many programs, however, provide capabilities of several types of workgroup applications. For example, Lotus Notes, although principally an information sharing system, also has electronic messaging and workflow management features. New programs that overlap different categories of workgroup applications or even create new categories are likely to be developed in the future.

Workgroup software often requires customization by the user to create a group application. Some software, such as Lotus Notes, is not ready to use until it has been customized. Programs such as these are really frameworks for developing group applications. Other programs, such as WebFlow's SamePage, are ready to be used as soon as the software is installed on the network. There are many shades between these extremes.

Workgroup applications are designed to be used on networks. Local area networks are used for collaboration among nearby group members, and wide area networks are used for collaboration among group members spread over considerable distances. International wide area networks are used when group members are located in different countries. Many groupware programs are designed to use the Internet or intranets, and in the future, most workgroup applications may use Internet technology for communication.

You can see from the discussion in this section that there are many workgroup applications and many types of groupware. In the future, it is likely that there will be even more applications and software for workgroup collaboration. Personal computer software, such as word processing and spreadsheet software, will take on more groupware characteristics. In the long run, most software used by individual users is likely to be groupware.

Office Automation Systems

Workgroup applications are often combined with individual applications, such as word processing, and other technology to form an office automation system or OAS. In general, an office automation system is an information system that provides support for office functions in an organization. People at all levels of an organization need office support to do their jobs. Secretarial and clerical personnel are not the only ones who do office work. Managers throughout an organization utilize office support to assist in their activities. Office automation systems are used in almost all areas of a business.

Historically, office functions have been performed by secretarial personnel. For example, a manager would dictate a memo to a secretary who would type, copy, mail, and file it. With the introduction of personal computers, managers and other personnel began doing some of their own office work. For example, a manager would use word processing to prepare a memo. Still, a secretary would copy, mail, and file the memo. The next step was to link the office personal computers to a local area network that included other hardware and special software to perform office functions. The result was an office automation system.

An office automation system may include individual applications such as word processing, desktop publishing, presentation graphics, and personal information management. An OAS may also include workgroup applications such as electronic mail, information sharing, calendaring and scheduling, and workflow management. In addition, an OAS may provide other applications such as:

- *Voice processing.* With voice processing, voice messages can be recorded and stored in secondary storage. Then, a stored message can be "sent" to another person who has access to the system. The person can listen to the voice message by "playing" it back.
- *Facsimile.* A fax modem can be connected to the network so that users can fax documents from their personal computers.
- *Electronic filing.* Instead of filing a paper copy of a document in order to save it, a copy can be "filed" electronically in secondary storage. The document can be retrieved in the future and printed if necessary.
- *Image processing.* In image processing, copies of graphs, charts, photographs, and other images can be stored in secondary storage. The images can be viewed by people who have access to the system, or they can be graphed or printed.
- *Document management.* Image processing and electronic filing are often combined to form a document management system that stores and keeps track of documents.

An office automation system can support almost any function found in an office. In the future, the distinction between individual applications, workgroup applications, and applications found in office automation systems may diminish until some day they all converge into one common type of application.

The Virtual Work Environment

Workgroup applications make it possible for people to collaborate in many ways, at any time, and from any place. As a result, it is no longer necessary for everyone in an organization to be at a central office at the same time. People can work in remote offices, at home, in a hotel room, or even in a car. People can work during the day, in the evening, late at night, and in different time zones. The result is that the work environment no longer has to be a real place where everyone comes at the same time. Instead, for many types of work, the work place can be a <u>virtual work environment</u> consisting of wherever and whenever people work.

Telecommuting

The first step toward a virtual work environment came when some employees of businesses began working at home, using personal computers with modems to communicate with their companies' computer systems. This way of working is called <u>telecommuting</u> because instead of commuting by car or by public transit, the employees "commute" over the telephone. (See Fig. 9.15.) Initially, mainly computer professionals such as programmers telecommuted, but now many employees work this way.

Telecommuting offers several advantages to individuals and businesses. Individuals do not have the expense of commuting to work and businesses do not have to provide office space. Employees can work whenever they find it convenient, and can watch after their children while they work. Businesses often find that productivity is increased and absenteeism is decreased. Disadvantages of telecommuting for individuals include the expense of setting up a home office, although some companies provide the necessary computer systems and telephone lines. Another disadvantage for individuals is the lack of face-to-face contact with coworkers and the feeling of isolation. For businesses, disadvantages include difficulty supervising employee work. Despite the disadvantages, telecommuting continues to grow.

FIGURE 9.15

Telecommuting

Virtual Offices

When a large number of employees in a group work at home or at other nontraditional locations, using computers to telecommute and to collaborate with others, the result is a virtual office. Employees may receive work through electronic messaging and information sharing systems. Workflow management systems may be used to coordinate the work. Electronic conferencing systems may be used to allow employees to collaborate on ideas. Employees can work wherever they happen to be; the office exists where the employees are.

Virtual offices compound the advantages and disadvantages of telecommuting because the number of people involved tends to be greater. In addition, more sophisticated software is needed so that electronic conferences and meetings can be held. Still, so many employees telecommute that virtual offices are becoming increasingly common.

Virtual Meetings

Using electronic conferencing and meeting systems allows people at different locations to confer and meet at the same time. Sometimes, however, an electronic meeting occurs in which not everyone is available simultaneously. For example, an electronic meeting may be held between research and development people to discuss a product design, but the participants do not communicate simultaneously. Instead, different people contribute ideas at different times. The meeting may last several days, until all involved have had a chance to comment and a conclusion is reached. This type of meeting is sometimes called a virtual meeting.

Virtual meetings are possible because of the store-and-forward capabilities of some groupware. One participant in a virtual meeting can enter his comments and forward them to another participant who enters her comments and then forwards everything to the next participant. When the meeting participants are located around the world, the virtual meeting can take place during daytime working hours in many time zones. Such international virtual meetings are becoming increasingly common in international businesses.

Virtual Companies

Sometimes a company is set up in such a way that it does not have any regular place of business or an office. Each employee works at his or her home, or uses a rented space near where the employee lives. When an employee is traveling, he or she may work out of a hotel room, or from a client or customer's office. Employees of the company communicate and collaborate using groupware. This type of company is sometimes called a virtual company. Virtual companies are especially common among new, start-up businesses.

Workgroup applications and groupware make it possible for a business to operate in nontraditional ways. Telecommuting, virtual offices, virtual meetings, and virtual companies are the result of workgroup systems. In the future, you can expect even more businesses to have virtual work environments.

Chapter Summary

- [ ] Businesses use workgroup information systems to encourage group collaboration because collaborating with others is an essential part of business. The main difficulty with workgroup collaboration is that people often are not in the same place at the same time. Group collaboration is also difficult because groups often change. Workgroup information systems encourage group collaboration by making it easier for members of a workgroup to communicate, share information, and collaborate over distance and time. (pp. 262–263)

- [ ] Group collaboration has several characteristics. One characteristic is the time when the collaboration takes place. People can collaborate at the same time or at different times. Another characteristic is the place where the collaboration takes place. People can work together at the same place or at different places. A third characteristic is the form that the communication takes. Audio, visual, and document communication may be used between people. (pp. 263–265)

- [ ] In addition to the time, place, and form characteristics of group collaboration, another characteristic is the mechanisms used for the group work. Without computers, people may collaborate in face-to-face meetings, by telephone, by fax, by regular mail, and by other means. With networked computers, people can work together using software that allows users to communicate, share information, and collaborate in other ways. This type of software is called **groupware**. (p. 265)

- [ ] The main types of workgroup applications are:
  Electronic messaging. This application involves sending messages between members of a workgroup. (pp. 265–267)
  Information sharing. This application involves sharing information in different forms between members of a workgroup. (pp. 267–268)
  Document conferencing. This application involves simultaneous collaboration on a document by members of a workgroup. (pp. 268–271)
  Audio conferencing. This application involves voice communication between members of a workgroup using **computer telephony**. (pp. 271–273)
  Video conferencing. This application involves visual and audio communication between members of a workgroup over a network. (pp. 273–275)
  Electronic conferencing. This application involves a combination of video conferencing and document conferencing. (pp. 275–276)
  Electronic meeting support. This application provides computer support for **electronic meetings** of members of a workgroup. (pp. 276–278)
  Group calendaring and scheduling. This application involves coordinating calendars and scheduling meetings of members of a workgroup. (pp. 278–279)
  Workflow management. This application involves coordinating the flow of work between members of a workgroup. (pp. 279–280)

- [ ] Workgroup applications can be distinguished by their time, place, and form characteristics. Some applications are designed for same-time collaboration and some for collaborating at different times. Most applications are designed for different-place collaboration, but electronic meeting systems are used in the same or different places. Document communication is the most common form of communication used in workgroup applications, although some applications provide audio and visual communication. Table 9.1 summarizes these characteristics for the main types of workgroup applications. (pp. 280–282)

- [ ] An **office automation system** or **OAS** is an information system that provides support for a variety of office functions at all levels of an organization. It may include individual applications as well as workgroup applications. In addition, it may provide other applications such as voice processing, facsimile, electronic filing, image processing, and document management. (p. 282)

- [ ] Workgroup applications make it possible for people to collaborate in many ways, at any time, and from any place. As a result, many people no longer always have to work at a central office, but, instead, can have a **virtual work environment** consisting of wherever and whenever they work. The first step toward a virtual work environment came with **telecommuting**. When a large number of employees work in nontraditional locations, and telecommute and collaborate using computers, the result is a **virtual office**. **Virtual meetings**, which can last several days, also take place in the virtual work environment. Some companies, called **virtual companies**, do not have a regular place of work or an office, but exist wherever employees are located. (pp. 283–284)

Key Terms

Application Conferencing (p. 271)
Audio Conferencing (p. 272)
Computer Telephony (p. 272)
Desktop Videoconferencing System (p. 274)
Document (Data) Conferencing (p. 268)
Document Sharing (p. 268)
Electronic Conferencing (p. 275)
Electronic Mail (E-Mail) (p. 266)
Electronic Meeting (p. 276)
Electronic Meeting System (EMS) (p. 276)

Electronic Messaging (p. 265)
Group Calendaring and Scheduling (p. 278)
Group (Collaborative) Computing (p. 265)
Group Decision Support System (GDSS) (p. 278)
Group Support System (GSS) (p. 262)
Groupware (p. 265)
Information Sharing (p. 268)
Office Automation System (OAS) (p. 282)

Room (Group) Videoconferencing System (p. 273)
Telecommuting (p. 283)
Videoconferencing (p. 273)
Virtual Company (p. 284)
Virtual Meeting (p. 284)
Virtual Office (p. 284)
Virtual Work Environment (p. 283)
Whiteboard Conferencing (p. 268)
Workflow Management (p. 279)

Assignment Material

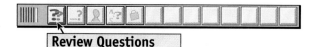

Review Questions

Fill-in Questions

1. Another name for a workgroup information system is _____.

2. Three forms of communication are _____, _____, and _____.

3. Putting a note on a bulletin board for other workgroup members to read is an example of _____ time, _____ place communication.

4. Group collaboration software is called _____.

5. Electronic messaging is used for _____ time, _____ place collaboration.

6. A basic form of electronic messaging is _____.

7. Lotus Notes is an example of a program used for _____.

8. Document conferencing is used for _____ time, _____ place collaboration.

9. Two types of document conferencing are _____ conferencing and _____ conferencing.

10. Videoconferencing provides both _____ and _____ communication.

11. Two types of video conferencing systems are _____ systems and _____ systems.

12. Electronic conferencing combines the applications of _____ and _____.

13. Electronic meeting systems support _____ time, _____ place collaboration.

14. A workgroup application that can be used to schedule meetings between members of a group is _____.

15. A workgroup application that could be used to route a contract through the legal department of a business is _____.

16. A(n) _____ is an information system that provides support for office functions in an organization.

17. When an employee works at home and uses a personal computer with a modem to communicate with the employee's company's computer, the employee is _____.

18. When a number of employees in a group work at home or at other nontraditional locations instead of a central office and use computers to collaborate with others, the result is a(n) _____.

Short-answer Questions

1. Why is group collaboration difficult?

2. How can workgroup information systems encourage group collaboration?

3. What are some of the deficiencies in the use of telephones for group collaboration?

4. What is group computing?

5. What are the disadvantages of electronic messaging?

6. What are some capabilities beyond electronic mail that are provided by electronic messaging software?

7. What is the main advantage of information sharing?

8. What is document sharing?

9. What is the difference between using a telephone and using computer telephony for audio communication?

10. How can videoconferencing save money for a business?

11. How does videoconferencing handle the large number of bits of a video signal that must be transmitted over a digital channel?

12. What is a disadvantage of electronic conferencing?

13. What capabilities other than document communication are provided by an electronic meeting system?

14. What applications are often found in an office automation system?

15. What is a virtual meeting?

16. What is a virtual company?

Discussion Questions

1. Think of a situation in a business or organization with which you are familiar where a workgroup information system would be useful. Describe how that system would work.

2. In the future, most software will be groupware. Do you agree or disagree with this statement? Why?

3. Most of the workgroup applications discussed in this chapter involve document communication. Why do you think this is the case?

4. With electronic conferencing software at international locations in many time zones, it is possible to get 24 hours of work in a day out of knowledge workers without anyone having to work at night. Explain how this can happen.

5. What type of employee, in terms of job function and work habits, would be best suited for telecommuting?

6. Some businesses read their employees' e-mail, arguing that e-mail is like any other correspondence for the business produced by the employee. Other businesses do not read their employees' e-mail, saying that to do so would be a violation of the employee's right to privacy. If you were in a position in a company to make a decision on this issue, what would you do and why?

Problem-solving Projects

1. Find out how an organization or business to which you have access uses groupware. What groupware does the organization use? For what does the organization use the groupware? How has the use of groupware affected group collaboration in the organization? Write a summary of your findings, using word processing software.

2. Using word processing or spreadsheet software, set up a table giving information about groupware.

Have columns for the name of the software, the vendor, and the types of applications found in the software. Start with the software listed in Table 9.1. Remember that many of these programs include several applications. Use the Internet to research these programs and find out what types of applications are in each program. Then locate several more group programs and add information about them to your table.

3. Check the Web sites of the groupware vendors mentioned in this chapter, or of other groupware vendors. Some of these sites have on-line demonstrations of the software. Find a site with a complete demonstration and go through the demonstration until you understand the software and how it is used. Using word processing software, write a memo to your boss (real or hypothetical) evaluating the software. What is good about the program? What is bad about it? Would you recommend it for your organization? Why or why not?

4. Form a team of three or four students and think of a business you would like to start. Once you have had your first face-to-face meeting, agree not to talk in person or over the telephone with your team members about your start-up business. All communications should take place through e-mail and other group software that you have available. Using these methods of communication, prepare a written plan for your new business. The plan should describe the product or service of the business, the potential market for the product or service, how the business will be organized, and how it will be financed. After you have completed the plan, write a summary of the advantages and disadvantages of using groupware alone for this type of activity.

5. Imagine that you have to organize a meeting of three high-ranking executives in a business. One of the executives works where you work and the other two are located in two different parts of the country. The meeting will last three to four hours. You have to decide whether to recommend a face-to-face meeting, with two of the executives flying to the third executive's location, or a videoconference involving all three executives. Assume that your company does not own videoconferencing equipment and would have to use a commercial service that rents room videoconferencing facilities for this purpose. Making whatever other assumptions you need, determine the approximate cost of a face-to-face meeting and a videoconference meeting. Using spreadsheet software, prepare a spreadsheet with your cost figures. Write a memo, using word processing software, summarizing your analysis and stating your conclusion.

Real-world Case

Xerox

For Xerox Corp., the earthquake that rocked Los Angeles in January 1994 was a call to action.

"All of a sudden we had people who had a two- to four-hour drive to get to work, and we needed to find a way for them to be productive without spending all of their time in a car," says Marc Carignan, group program manager at Xerox, in Rochester, N.Y.

Luckily, in the months before the quake struck, Carignan and others at Xerox had been developing a plan to deploy notebook computers to field sales representatives and also to deploy a new client/server system to Xerox's 70 U.S. regional offices. The idea was to create a "virtual office" for Xerox employees and eliminate the need for them to come into an office.

Xerox has 4,000 field sales representatives and another 1,000 employees in administration and management. About 10 percent of the 5,000 field employees are located in the Los Angeles area.

"The original plan was that we would begin rolling out the new system sometime in the next year or so. But then the earthquake made us kick-start the program and get it going sooner," Carignan says. "So we put together a training team and a deployment team and sent them off to Los Angeles."

Come May—five short months later—Xerox had the new system up and running in Los Angeles. In August, the company began deploying it to the rest of the country. By April 1995, the rollout was done.

The deployment was a remarkable feat simply from the perspective of the logistics involved in rolling out so much new technology to so many users in so little time. But the system also has profoundly changed the way Xerox field employees go about their work.

Today, salespeople use a "virtual office" concept in which they share office space with other sales representatives and may occasionally come into the office but do most of their work from home. For those workers, Xerox installed second phone lines into their homes.

With the information system that Xerox used to have, employees in field offices used terminals to connect into mainframes in Rochester. Some employees didn't even have terminals in their offices but had to share a terminal with others. To get information about pricing or product availability, or even to send e-mail, sales representatives in the field had to drive into the office and get onto a terminal.

"The irony is that we had sales reps who were not PC-literate out selling laser printers to customers who typically had LANs and PCs," Carignan says. "Our No. 1 goal was to make our sales force PC-literate."

Having technologically savvy sales representatives wasn't a goal unto itself. Xerox wanted to make its sales force more productive by giving them better access to information. Also, officials believed the company could save money by eliminating office space and allowing sales representatives to work from home.

"Even before the earthquake hit, we thought that we wanted the sales reps to be out in front of customers as much as possible rather than coming into the office," Carignan says.

"Much of the data is still on the mainframe," Carignan continues. "We use remote-access servers to let users dial in and then connect out to the mainframe to retrieve information."

Regional offices are linked around the country. Users can share e-mail seamlessly with users in other regional offices. They also can retrieve files from hard drives in other regional offices just as they can retrieve information from the mainframe system in Rochester.

Carignan declined to say how much Xerox spent on the entire project. But he says Xerox expects to recoup its investment in about three years. Payback comes in three main areas: reduced cost for lease of office space; reduced administrative expenses, since salespeople now can do their own memos, etc.; and increased productivity by the sales force.

Carignan says it's difficult to quantify the productivity gains that can be attributed to the new system.

"It's just impossible to say, 'Well, I gave the salespeople this PC, and, therefore, they made these sales that they wouldn't have made otherwise; and their productivity went up by 1.2 percent, or 10 percent, or whatever,'" Carignan says. "But when we were doing our pilot projects and we looked at areas where we put in the new technology, we could see that they were performing better than the rest of the country."

Recently, Xerox has enhanced the new system with Chameleon, a Web browser from NetManage Inc. In addition, Xerox has deployed a set of Web servers that its employees can use to share information and download forms and notices.

"We've got things like pricing information and the Xerox phone directory posted there," Carignan says.

A more ambitious enhancement involves the reengineering of Xerox's sales and marketing business processes. For example, Xerox plans to streamline the process that sales representatives use when taking an order from a customer. Salespeople will use their notebooks in the field to automatically validate the price that they have quoted to the customer and will also have the ability to submit orders electronically.

"We made a conscious decision to deploy the technology first and get people up to speed and PC-literate before we started changing the underlying business processes," Carignan says. "The main reason was that we didn't want to go through the fairly massive cultural changes that would be involved if we tried to do both at once."

Disruptions have been kept to a minimum, and user response has been largely positive, according to Carignan: "We've had some complaints, but then if we say, 'OK, would you like us to take your PC away and you can go back to the old way of doing it?' they look at us as if we're crazy. So I guess that for me is the litmus test."

Questions

1. Why did the January 1994 Los Angeles earthquake cause Xerox to speed up the implementation of its new system for sales representatives?

2. What is the "virtual office" described in this case and how is it made possible?

3. How does the new system Xerox deployed give sales representatives better access to information?

4. What economic benefits does Xerox expect to receive from the system described in this case?

5. How does Xerox use the Internet to enhance the system described in this case?

Source: Daniel Lyons, "Northridge quake prompts Xerox to take care of its faults," *InfoWorld*, June 3, 1996, p. 74.

10 Business Operations

Chapter Outline

Increasing Business Operations Efficiency (p. 292)
Transaction Processing Systems (p. 293)
    Transaction Processing System Structure (p. 293)
    Transaction Processing System Functions (p. 294)
    Controlling Transaction Processing Systems (p. 298)
    Processing Data in Transaction Processing Systems (p. 299)
Basic Business Information Systems (p. 300)
    Order Entry System (p. 301)
    Billing System (p. 303)
    Accounts Receivable System (p. 304)
    Inventory Control System (p. 305)
    Purchasing System (p. 306)
    Accounts Payable System (p. 307)
    Payroll System (p. 309)
    General Ledger System (p. 310)
Other Business Information Systems (p. 311)
    Accounting Information Systems (p. 311)
    Financial Information Systems (p. 311)
    Marketing Information Systems (p. 312)
    Manufacturing Information Systems (p. 312)
    Human Resource Information Systems (p. 314)
Organizing Information System Functions (p. 315)
    Centralized Systems (p. 315)
    Teleprocessing Systems (p. 315)
    Decentralized Systems (p. 316)
    Distributed Systems (p. 318)

Learning Objectives

After completing this chapter, you should be able to:
- [ ] 1. Give an example of a computer information system increasing the efficiency of business operations.
- [ ] 2. Explain the purpose and structure of transaction processing systems.
- [ ] 3. Describe the functions of transaction processing systems.
- [ ] 4. Describe several ways of controlling transaction processing systems.
- [ ] 5. Explain the difference between batch and on-line transaction processing.
- [ ] 6. Summarize the characteristics of basic business information systems.
- [ ] 7. List several examples of accounting, financial, marketing, manufacturing, and human resource information systems.
- [ ] 8. Describe several ways of organizing the functions of information systems.

The basic operations of a business are those activities that help the business function on a daily basis. These activities provide goods and services for the business's customers; ensure payment for those goods and services; keep track of the business's products; acquire goods and services needed by the business; pay the business's obligations; and report on the business's profitability. Information systems support business operations by processing data related to these activities and by providing information to assist in their management.

This chapter examines the structure and functions of information systems for operational support of a business. It presents the main type of information system used for this purpose. This type of system, called a *transaction processing system,* is essential to all businesses. The chapter also examines examples of information systems that support business operations. Finally, the chapter shows how the functions of an information system may be organized in a business.

Increasing Business Operations Efficiency

Computer information systems increase the efficiency of business operations. Efficiency has to do with how much a system produces relative to the resources, such as people and money, used by the system. For example, consider a system for processing customer orders in a business. (See Fig. 10.1.) Such a system would receive a customer's request for products, check to see if the desired products were available, check the customer's credit, and, if all checks were satisfactory, produce a written sales order describing what is to be sold to the customer.

Customer order processing could be handled entirely manually. The customer request could be written by hand by a salesperson, a warehouse clerk could check the shelves for the desired product's availability, another clerk could look in a credit file or call the customer's bank to check the customer's credit record, and, finally, a typist could type the sales order. This manual approach would require considerable personnel resources to produce the sales order. It would also require a great deal of time to complete the order, with the possible result that the customer could look elsewhere for the product.

FIGURE 10.1

Customer order processing

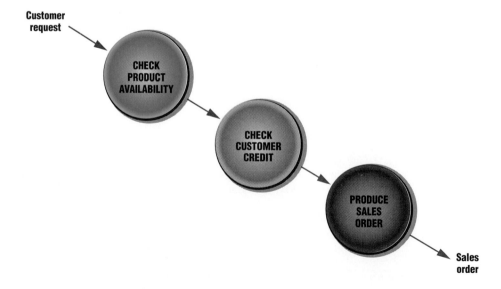

Now consider a computer information system for customer order processing. In such a system the customer's request would be keyed into a computer by a salesperson or, in some cases, by the customer. The system would look up the product availability in an inventory file and the customer's credit rating in a customer file. The system would then produce the sales order without further keying being required. The computer information system would be more efficient than the manual system because it would produce the sales order with fewer resources and in less time.

This example illustrates the idea of increasing the efficiency of business operations. Many information systems that support business operations have a similar benefit for the business. To be competitive today, most businesses require some form of computer information system for their basic operations.

Transaction Processing Systems

The main information systems used for operational support in a business are <u>transaction processing systems (TPS)</u>. This type of system processes data about <u>transactions</u>—events that have occurred that affect the business, such as the sale or purchase of goods. For example, an inventory control system is an information system that processes data about transactions that affect a business's inventory. These transactions are shipments of inventory due to a sale, and receipt of inventory because of a purchase.

Transaction Processing System Structure

The general purpose of a transaction processing system is threefold: (1) to keep records about the state of the organization; (2) to process transactions that affect these records; and (3) to produce outputs that report on transactions that have occurred, that report on the state of the organization, and that cause other transactions to occur. An inventory control system keeps a file of records about the stock of goods that a business has on hand—the inventory—which is one aspect of the state of the business. When items are shipped or received, the state of the business is affected and the inventory control system makes changes in the stored records about the inventory. Periodically, the system prints a list of the shipments and receipts—that is, the transactions—that have occurred. It also prints a report giving the quantity on hand for each item in inventory, which is a characteristic of the state of the business. Finally, when inventory is low, the system produces output that causes more inventory to be ordered, which is another type of business transaction.

Figure 10.2 shows the general structure of a transaction processing system. Users of the system typically are personnel who deal with business transactions, such

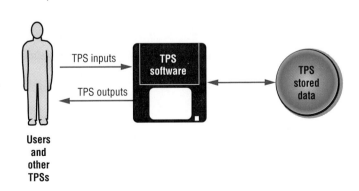

FIGURE 10.2

The structure of a transaction processing system or TPS

as salespeople, accounting clerks, and inventory personnel. Input, which includes data about transactions, comes from users and other transaction processing systems. Output, which includes printed reports, goes to users and to other systems. The transaction processing system stored data consisting of files and databases with data about the state of the organization. The transaction processing system software is application software that accepts the input data about transactions, processes it, makes changes in the stored data, and produces the outputs.

Transaction processing systems exist in all areas of an organization. Examples include systems for entering customer orders, billing customers, keeping track of inventory, and other basic systems discussed later in this chapter. Transaction processing systems exist in all types of businesses. As just one example, a system in a bank for keeping track of customer deposits and withdrawals is a transaction processing system. Transaction processing systems are used for the daily data processing in practically all organizations. As you will see in Chapter 11, they form the foundation for other information systems.

Transaction Processing System Functions

Transaction processing systems, as well as other types of information systems, perform four main functions to accomplish their purposes. As noted in Chapter 1, these are the input function, the storage function, the processing function, and the output function. Figure 10.3 summarizes these functions. The *input function* accepts data from outside the system so that the data can be processed in the system. The *storage function* stores and retrieves data in the system so that it is available for processing. The *processing function* manipulates the input and stored data within the system. The *output function* makes the results of processing available outside the system. Here we discuss the characteristics of these functions in transaction processing systems.

Input Function. Before transaction data can be brought into a transaction processing system it must be acquired from its source—a step called *data capture*. Often, the data is captured by a person who writes the data on a piece of paper or on a form called a <u>source document</u>. Once the data is captured, it must be put into the system—a step called *data entry*. Usually, the data is entered by a person who keys in the data on a keyboard.

An athletic shoe store's inventory control system illustrates data capture and entry. For one part of this system, data about the receipt of merchandise from a supplier must be captured and entered into the system. The data capture occurs when

FIGURE 10.3

The functions of an information system

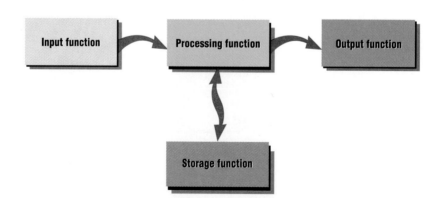

a stock clerk prepares a receiving report, which is a source document indicating that certain items have been received. (See Fig. 10.4a.) This document is then sent to a data-entry person, who keys the data into a computer, thus entering the data into the system. (See Fig. 10.4b.)

As data is entered into the system, a program must check it for errors, a process called <u>data validation</u>. Incorrect data must not be allowed to go beyond the data-entry step. Data validation involves checking input data for all possible errors. Every value entered should be checked. Values that are supposed to be numbers, such as an item number in the inventory control system, should be checked to be sure they contain only digits. Names, such as a customer name, should be checked to be sure they contain only letters. Codes, such as a code indicating the type of payment, should be checked to be sure they are correct. Quantities, such as the quantity sold, should be checked to be sure they are in appropriate ranges. All possible data validation checks should be done to insure that the data is correct.

Output Function.   Much output from a transaction processing system is in the form of <u>reports</u>, which are lists of output data printed on paper or displayed on a screen. Several types of reports are commonly produced by a transaction processing system. A <u>detail report</u> lists detailed information about the results of processing and may contain totals for some of the data. For example, Fig. 10.5a shows a detail report produced by the athletic shoe store's inventory control system that lists inventory transactions for a particular item that have occurred in the last week and gives the total sold and received for the week. A <u>summary report</u> contains totals that summarize groups of data but has no detail data. Figure 10.5b shows a summary report that gives the total inventory value for each line of products stocked by the shoe store. An <u>exception report</u> contains data that is an exception to some rule or standard. Figure 10.5c shows a report about items that have a quantity on hand below a certain level and thus should be reordered. Other items with sufficient quantity are not listed in this report. This last report would cause other transactions to occur, namely the ordering of more stock.

FIGURE 10.4

Data capture and entry

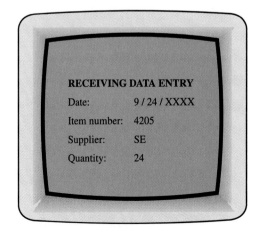

(a) A source document for capturing inventory data

(b) A screen for entering inventory data

INVENTORY TRANSACTIONS

Item number 4205

Week of 9/19/XXXX

DATE	QUANTITY SOLD	QUANTITY RECEIVED
9/19	14	
9/20	16	
9/21	21	120
9/22	18	
9/23	12	
9/24	35	24
9/25	16	
TOTAL	132	144

(a) A detail report

**INVENTORY VALUE
BY PRODUCT LINE**

Week of 9/30/XXXX

PRODUCT LINE	TOTAL VALUE
Running shoes	$24,368.00
Tennis shoes	10,852.00
Sport shoes	8,147.50
Clothing	12,255.75
Accessories	3,604.00
TOTAL	$59,227.25

(b) A summary report

INVENTORY REORDER REPORT

ITEM NUMBER	ITEM DESCRIPTION	QUANTITY ON HAND
1681	RUNNING SHOE	11
1945	TENNIS SHOE	8
3347	TRACK SHOE	3
4205	SOCKS	20
5172	SWEATSHIRT	15

(c) An exception report

FIGURE 10.5

Types of reports

Storage Function. Data in a transaction processing system is stored in data files and databases. Two types of stored data are commonly found in transaction processing systems: master data and transaction data. Master data is the main data used by the system. For example, an inventory control system for an athletic shoe store could have an inventory master file with one record for each item in inventory. Each record would contain fields for the item number, item description, unit cost, unit price, and quantity on hand. Master data usually is permanent data that remains with the system as long as the system is in use.

Transaction data is data about transactions that have occurred. For example, in an inventory control system for an athletic shoe store, an inventory transaction file could be used to store data about additions to and removals from stock. Each record would contain fields for the item number, the quantity added to stock, and the quantity removed from stock. Transaction data usually remains with the system only until the transactions are processed. The transaction data is then replaced with other transaction data for new transactions.

Master and transaction data may be stored in data files or databases. The only difference is the organization of the data; the concept of master data and transaction data is the same no matter how the data is stored. In either case, the data files or databases would form the stored data component of the system.

Before a transaction processing system can do anything with stored data it must *create* the file or database containing the data. That is, it must store initial data in the file or database. Thus, the athletic shoe store must create the inventory master file before it can be used in the inventory control system. To create this file, someone would enter the data for each item currently in inventory, and the system would store the data in the inventory file. Usually, files or databases with master data are created only once. Transaction data, however, is stored in a file or database whenever transactions need to be processed.

After the file or database is created, the transaction processing system can retrieve data from the file or database, a process called accessing the data. The data that is retrieved is processed to produce a report or, sometimes, to create a new file or database. For the inventory control system, the inventory transaction file would have to be accessed to produce the inventory transactions report shown in Fig. 10.5a; the inventory master file would have to be accessed to produce the inventory value report in Fig. 10.5b and the inventory reorder report in Fig. 10.5c.

Sometimes, before a transaction processing system can access stored data, it must arrange the data in a different way. The process of arranging data into a particular order is called sorting. In the inventory control system, sorting would be needed if the records in the inventory master file were not in the order in which a user wished to see them. For example, the user may wish the inventory reorder report to give the items in alphabetical order by their descriptions. If the records were not in this order to begin with, they would have to be sorted into the proper order before preparing the report.

The data put into a file or database when it is created will become out of date over time. Thus, the transaction processing system will have to modify the data periodically, a process called updating the data. Updating may involve *changing* existing data, *adding* new data, or *deleting* old data. In the athletic shoe store's inventory control system, whenever stock is added to or removed from inventory, the quantity on hand for each item affected must be changed in the inventory master file. If a new item—one not currently stocked by the store—is added to the inventory, the number, name, unit cost, unit price, and quantity on hand for that item must be added to the inventory master file. Finally, if an old item is dropped from the inventory, all data about that item must be deleted from the inventory master file.

Updating often is performed by using transaction data to make changes in master data. Thus, the inventory transaction file's data can be used to update the quantity on hand in the inventory master file. After the master file has been updated, it can be processed to produce various reports.

Processing Function. Processing involves manipulating data within the system. In a sense, all the functions already described involve data processing in a transaction processing system. One function that involves just data processing and does not involve any of the other functions is *computation*, which means doing calculations with data. Before a transaction processing system can produce output, the system typically must perform some computations. Input data and stored data are used in the computations to produce the required results that go into the output.

Another processing function is *decision making*. Often, other functions in an information system depend on some condition that needs to be checked during processing. To do so, a decision is made by a program in the system, and processing continues in different ways depending on the result of the decision.

Computation and decision making are needed in the athletic shoe store's inventory control system. For example, to produce the total value in the inventory value report shown in Fig. 10.5b, arithmetic computations must be performed with the inventory data. To determine if an item needs to be reordered so that the item's information can be printed in the inventory reorder report shown in Fig. 10.5c, a decision must be made by the system.

Controlling Transaction Processing Systems

Transaction processing systems must have procedures to ensure the completeness of the data processing and to minimize the chance of errors. In general, these procedures are called controls. Many types of controls are used in information systems. We discuss several types below, but others also are used.

Control Totals. All data may not be processed in a transaction processing system for various reasons. A source document may be misplaced or a data-entry person may forget to key some data. Sometimes hardware fails or a program has an error that causes data to be lost. An information system should have controls to check for these types of errors.

One way that a transaction processing system checks that all data is processed is to use control totals. A control total is a number that is computed when data enters a system and then computed again after the system has processed the data. For example, in the athletic shoe store's inventory control system discussed in the last section, assume that data from the receiving report (Fig. 10.4a) is used to update the inventory master file. Each day a batch of receiving reports is sent in by the stock clerk for entry into the system. The person who receives the receiving reports would count the number of reports sent in. This count would be the control total. As the data was entered and processed, the system would produce a similar count or control total. Then the two control totals would be compared. If the counts were not equal, then not all data was entered and processed by the system. The cause of the error would have to be located and corrected.

This example uses just one type of control total—a count of the number of documents. Other types of control totals are also used, including totals of data on documents. Sometimes, several control totals are calculated and checked in the system to be sure all data has been processed.

Audit Trails. An audit trail is a way of tracing the effect of data through a system. A good audit trail is one in which someone can start with the output and go back through the system to the source document, or vice versa. For example, in the athletic shoe store's inventory control system, one source document is the receiving report prepared by a stock clerk. If one output is a list of all stock received during a month, an audit trail would provide a way of tracing back to the actual receiving report for any shipment listed in the output, or of starting with a receiving report and tracing through the system to a shipment listed in the output. This audit trail would make it possible to randomly check that the system worked correctly, and thus that data was properly processed by the system.

Backup and Recovery Procedures. Computer systems sometimes fail. (We say the system "crashes.") The failure may be because of a malfunction in the hardware or software, or because of some outside factor such as an electric power interruption. When a failure occurs, data stored in the computer can be damaged or lost. In such a circumstance, there must be a way of restoring the data.

The main way of ensuring against loss of stored data is to use a backup procedure. Backing up means that the data is copied periodically to another storage media. For example, in the inventory control system, the inventory master file, which is stored on magnetic disk, would be copied to another disk or to a magnetic tape. How often the data should be backed up depends on how frequently the data is changed. The more often changes are made in the data, the more often it should be backed up. Usually data files and databases are backed up every day or every week, although sometimes backup occurs more or less frequently.

The backup copy of the stored data should be stored away from the computer system in case of fire or other physical disaster. If a system failure occurs, the backup copy can be used to re-create the original stored data by means of a recovery procedure. Without adequate backup and recovery procedures, there is a great risk of losing data permanently.

Processing Data in Transaction Processing Systems

Data in a transaction processing system can be processed using two basic approaches: batch processing and on-line transaction processing. In batch processing, the data for all transactions to be processed is prepared in a form understandable to the computer before the actual processing begins. Then, the batch of data is processed by the computer, and the resulting output is received in a batch. An example of batch processing is the preparation of the weekly payroll for an organization. At the end of the week, each employee turns in a time sheet. The data from each sheet is keyed into the computer and stored in a payroll file. Once all the data is ready, it is processed in a batch by the payroll program to produce the paychecks.

With on-line transaction processing or OLTP, often just called on-line processing, a person uses a keyboard and screen or other I/O device connected to the computer at the time the processing is done. Each set of data for a transaction is entered directly into the computer, where it is processed, and the output is received before the next input data is supplied. Airline reservation processing is an example of this approach. When a customer requests a ticket for a particular flight, the reservation clerk enters the data directly into the computer by using a keyboard. The reservation system checks the data in a flight database and determines if a seat is available on the requested flight. The output goes immediately to the screen so that the customer will know whether the reservation is confirmed.

A transaction processing system may use batch processing, on-line processing, or, most commonly, both. For example, the athletic shoe store's inventory control system, discussed in the previous sections, uses both batch and on-line processing. Batch processing is used to prepare the reports. The data in the inventory file is processed in a batch when each report is printed. On-line processing is used by a salesperson to check inventory availability. The salesperson enters a request for information at a keyboard and receives the response on a screen.

Sometimes you hear the term interactive processing instead of on-line processing. Interactive processing means the user interacts with the computer system while the processing takes place, as opposed to batch processing in which there is no user interaction. For interactive processing, the user must be *on-line*, that is, connected to the computer at the time, so that input can be entered directly into the computer and the output can be received from the computer. Either term can be used, although on-line is heard more frequently than interactive. Sometimes data for batch processing is prepared *off-line*, that is, with the use of equipment not connected to the computer and then transferred to the computer. For example, data may be keyed onto a magnetic disk with the use of special data preparation equipment. The data on the disk then can be processed in a batch by the computer.

Occasionally, people use the term real-time processing instead of on-line processing. *Real-time* means the processing is done immediately after the input is received. This description is not quite accurate for on-line processing. If there are many users of an on-line system, processing may not begin for some time after the input is received. The amount of time, which can be several seconds to several minutes, depends on how many users there are and the type of computer being used. In real-time processing, a delay is not acceptable. Real-time processing is used when an immediate response is essential. An example is a system that monitors a process in a chemical plant. The system must respond immediately—that is, in real time—to any significant change in temperature, pressure, and other critical factors in the chemical process.

Basic Business Information Systems

Chapter 2 introduced eight basic information processing activities found in businesses:

- Entering customer orders
- Billing customers
- Collecting customer payments
- Keeping track of inventory
- Purchasing stock and materials
- Paying bills
- Paying employees
- Reporting financial information

These activities are needed to support the operations of most businesses. They are often performed by computer information systems, which include hardware, software, stored data, personnel, and procedure components. They perform the input, storage, processing, and output functions needed to accomplish these information processing activities. This section describes a computer information system for each of these activities.

Figure 10.6 shows the relationship between the systems described in this section. In the figure, an arrow connects two systems if information flows from one to the

FIGURE 10.6

Basic business information systems

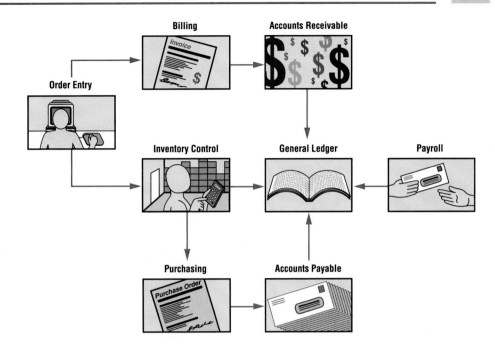

other. These systems are mainly transaction processing systems and the flow of information from one system to another often causes another transaction to take place.

Each of the systems described here processes one or more types of master data. Sometimes the same master data is used by several systems, and sometimes the data is used by only one system. Transaction data is also used by many of these systems. These systems may process master and transaction data stored in data files or in a database.

Each system involves several computer programs and manual procedures performed over a period of time. Each system also includes numerous controls to check for errors and has backup and recovery procedures. Some systems may involve batch processing, some may involve on-line processing, and some involve both types of processing. These details would be needed for a complete understanding of a system.

Although each system is described separately, it is common for several systems to be combined into one, larger system. For example, order entry, billing, and inventory control often form one, integrated information system. It is important to understand each system separately, but it also is important to remember that various combinations of systems are common.

Order Entry System

The purpose of an order entry system is to accept customer orders for goods or services and to prepare the orders in a form that can be used by the business. The functions of this system are summarized in Fig. 10.7. The input to the system is the customer order data, which could be received on an order entry form or over the telephone. The output is the sales order.

In some businesses, customer orders are entered into the system as they are received, and in others, orders are collected and entered periodically in a batch. Orders may also be received electronically using EDI (electronic data interchange). As an order is entered, the data in it is validated by a program. Invalid orders are displayed

FIGURE 10.7

The order entry system

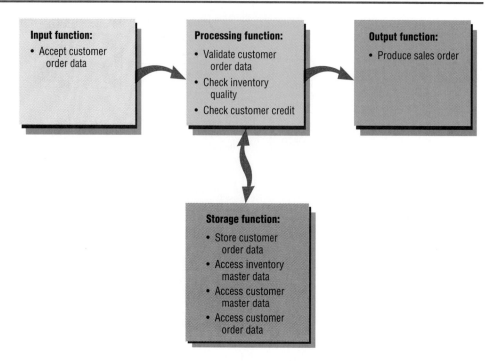

on a screen for manual correction and reentry. Valid orders, which form the transaction data for the system, are stored in a file or database created by the program. This customer order data contains one record for each item ordered by a customer with fields for the customer number, item number, and quantity ordered.

After the customer order data is stored, the orders can be processed. To do so, the following questions must be answered:

1. Does the business have sufficient inventory to fill the order?

2. Should the business extend credit to this customer or require that the customer pay in advance?

To answer the first question, another program accesses a file or database containing inventory master data to determine the quantity on hand for the item ordered. There is one record in the inventory master data for each item stocked by the business with fields for the item number, item description, and quantity on hand. The answer to the second question is found by accessing a file or database containing the customer master data to find the credit rating. There is one record in this stored data for each customer with fields for the customer number, customer name, shipping address, and credit rating.

If sufficient inventory is on hand and the customer's credit rating is acceptable, a sales order, which is the output from the system, is produced by the program. This document contains the customer number, name, and shipping address from the customer master data; the item and the description from the inventory master data; and the quantity ordered from the customer order data.

This system involves two programs and a manual procedure. One program is needed for data entry, data validation, and storage of the customer order data. Another program is needed to access the inventory master data, the customer master data, and the customer order data; and to produce the sales order. These programs are executed in sequence. A manual procedure is needed to correct errors in the customer order.

The data-entry program involves on-line processing. The program interacts with the person entering the data to allow errors to be corrected. The sales order preparation program involves batch processing. The stored customer order data is processed in a batch and the sales orders are printed in a batch.

The customer order data is transaction data used only by this system. It is kept for a time for backup purposes but is deleted eventually. The inventory master and customer master data are permanent stored data that are used repeatedly.

Billing System

The purpose of a <u>billing system</u> is to prepare the customer's bill or invoice. Figure 10.8 summarizes the functions of this system. The sales order data from the order entry system is the input to the billing system. The output is the invoice, which contains the information about how much the customer owes for the items ordered.

To prepare the invoice from the sales order data, two types of master data are needed. The first is the customer master data, which is also used in the order entry system. For the billing system, records in this data must have fields for the customer number, customer name, and billing address so that this information can be printed on the invoice. The second type is the inventory master data, which is also used in the order entry system. For the billing system, the records in this data must have fields for the item number, item description, and unit price. The system looks up the unit price of each item shipped in this data and computes the order amount by multiplying the quantity shipped by the unit price. This information is printed on the invoice along with the item description and the total for all items purchased.

With computerized order entry and billing systems, data can be passed electronically from one system to the other. Data from the sales order, including the customer number, item number, and quantity ordered, could be put in a sales order file by the order entry system. The billing system then could use this transaction file, along with the customer master and inventory master data, to prepare the invoice.

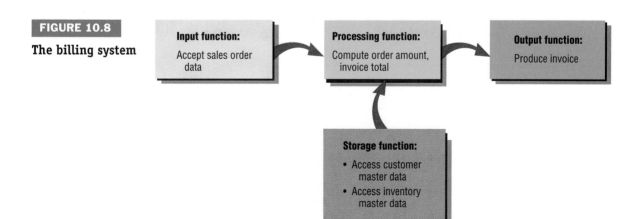

FIGURE 10.8

The billing system

Input function:
Accept sales order data

Processing function:
Compute order amount, invoice total

Output function:
Produce invoice

Storage function:
• Access customer master data
• Access inventory master data

Accounts Receivable System

The purpose of an <u>accounts receivable system</u> is to keep track of money owed to the business by its customers and to record customer payments for invoices. In addition, the system reminds customers of overdue invoices, sends summaries of invoice charges and payments to customers, and provides reports of accounts receivable to other functions of the business.

The functions of the accounts receivable system are summarized in Fig. 10.9. The inputs to the system are the invoice data and data about the customer payment. The outputs include statements which summarize the invoice charges and payments made recently and give the current balance due for each customer; overdue notices which are sent to the customers who have not paid their invoices; and an accounts receivable report summarizing charges and payments for the month. This report contains the total invoice charges and total customer payments for all customers.

To produce the outputs, two types of stored data are used. One is a file or database containing accounts receivable data consisting of one record for each customer with fields for the customer number, previous balance due, invoice date, invoice amount, payment date, and payment amount. The previous balance due is the balance due at the beginning of the current month. The invoice date and amount fields are repeated for each invoice for the current month. The payment date and amount fields are also repeated for each payment made during the current month. The other stored data that is used is the customer master data, which is also used in the order entry and billing systems. For the accounts receivable system, the records of this data need fields for the customer number, customer name, and billing address.

Processing in the accounts receivable system involves several activities. Data from new invoices and customer payments are used to update the accounts receivable data. Each month, statements are printed from this data. The new balance due

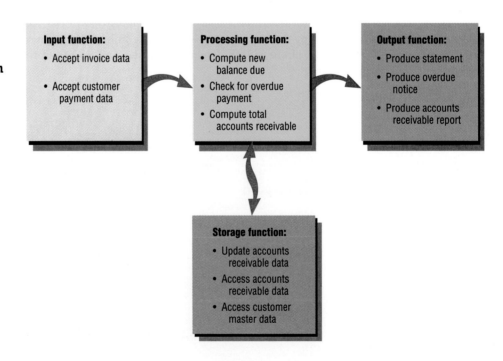

FIGURE 10.9

The accounts receivable system

on each statement is computed by adding the customer's previous balance due and the total of the current month's invoices, and subtracting the total of the current month's payments. The customer name and address on the statements come from the customer master data. Overdue notices are printed for those customers who have not paid their bills recently. Also each month, the total accounts receivable is computed and printed in the accounts receivable report, along with other accounts receivable data.

With computerized billing and accounts receivable systems, data can be passed electronically from one system to the other. Data about each invoice, including the customer number, the invoice date, and the invoice amount, could be put in an invoice file by the billing system. Then the accounts receivable system could use this file to update the accounts receivable data.

Inventory Control System

The purpose of an <u>inventory control system</u> is to keep track of the business's inventory, to indicate when inventory should be reordered, and to compute the value of the inventory. Figure 10.10 summarizes the functions of this system. The inputs to the system are the sales order data and the receiving notice data giving the quantity of items received from suppliers. The outputs from the system are the inventory reorder report, which lists the items that should be reordered, and the inventory value report, which gives the value of the items in stock.

The stored data needed in this system is the inventory master data, which is also used in the order entry and billing systems. For the inventory control system, the fields needed in each record of this data are the item number, item description, unit cost, quantity on hand, reorder point, and reorder quantity. These fields are used to produce the output in the reports. The unit cost, which is the cost per item, and the quantity on hand are multiplied to compute the inventory value for the inventory value report. The reorder point is the quantity below which the business does not want the inventory to fall. If the quantity on hand is less than or equal to the reorder

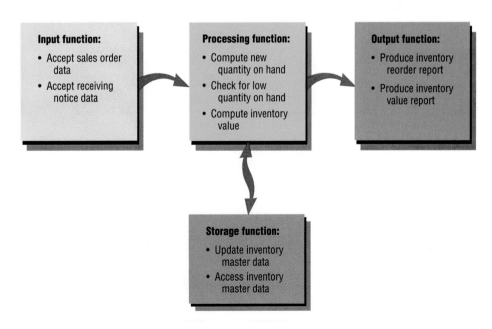

FIGURE 10.10

The inventory control system

Input function:
- Accept sales order data
- Accept receiving notice data

Processing function:
- Compute new quantity on hand
- Check for low quantity on hand
- Compute inventory value

Output function:
- Produce inventory reorder report
- Produce inventory value report

Storage function:
- Update inventory master data
- Access inventory master data

point, the item should be reordered, and this fact is printed in the inventory reorder report. The reorder quantity for the item is also printed in the report and indicates the quantity of the item that should be ordered.

Processing in the inventory control system first involves updating the quantity on hand in the inventory master data from data in the sales orders and receiving notices. The quantity shipped of an item from each sales order is subtracted from the item's quantity on hand, and the quantity received for the item from each receiving notice is added to determine the new quantity on hand. Once a month, or perhaps more often, the inventory reorder report is prepared from the inventory master data, listing all items which should be reordered. Also once a month, the inventory value report is prepared.

With computerized shipping, receiving, and inventory control, updating of the inventory master data can be done by shipping and receiving personnel. As items are shipped, the quantity removed from inventory is entered into the system and subtracted from the quantity on hand at that time. Similarly, as items are received, the quantity added to the inventory is entered and added to the quantity on hand.

Purchasing System

The purpose of a <u>purchasing system</u> is to determine the best suppliers (also called vendors) from which to purchase items and to prepare documents, called purchase orders, which indicate to the supplier what items are wanted. Figure 10.11 shows the functions of the purchasing system. The input is the data from the inventory reorder report indicating what items are to be reordered and what quantity of each should be ordered. The output is the purchase order, which lists the items the business wants to purchase.

To produce the purchase order, the preferred supplier for the item to be purchased must be determined. The inventory master data, which is used in several other systems, provides this information. The fields in the records of this data that are needed for the purchasing system are the item number, item description, and the preferred supplier number. Supplier master data, contained in a file or database, also is needed. There is one record in this data for each supplier, with fields for the sup-

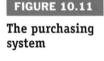

FIGURE 10.11

The purchasing system

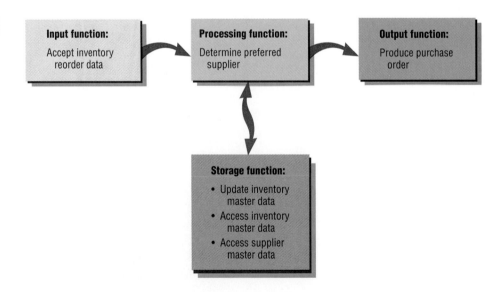

plier number, supplier name, and supplier address. In addition, there may be fields that give information about the supplier's sales policy and performance, such as the payment terms, the average delivery time, the quality of items sold, and so forth.

The supplier's sales policy and performance information is analyzed by the purchasing system to determine the best supplier for each item. The selection of the best supplier may be based on sales terms, delivery time, or other factors that the business considers important. The preferred supplier number is updated in the inventory master data based on the analysis of the suppliers. When purchase orders are to be prepared, the preferred supplier number is determined from the inventory master data, then that supplier's name and address are found in the supplier master data. This information is printed on the purchase order along with the item number, item description, and quantity ordered.

With computerized inventory control and purchasing systems, reordering data can be passed electronically from one system to the other. The data about what items are to be reordered and the quantity to order could be put in an inventory reorder file by the inventory control system. Then the purchasing system could use this file, along with the inventory master and supplier master data, to prepare the purchase orders.

Accounts Payable System

The purpose of an accounts payable system is to keep track of money owed by the business for purchases, to pay suppliers for the items purchased, and to provide reports of accounts payable to other functions of the business. The functions of the accounts payable system are summarized in Fig. 10.12. The inputs to the system are the purchase order data indicating what items were ordered, the invoice data from the supplier showing what items the supplier shipped and the charges for the items, and the receiving notice data indicating what items were received by the business. The outputs from the system include the supplier payment, which is a check sent to

FIGURE 10.12

The accounts payable system

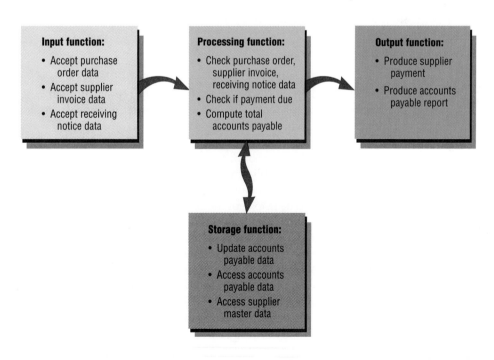

Bookmark

Accounts Payable at Ademco

When Ademco went looking for a new imaging application to help automate its accounts payable process, the best one turned out to be homegrown.

Scott Bernstein, a database applications engineer at Ademco—one of the world's largest security manufacturers—said it took about a year for the company to turn an old, labor-intensive imaging application into one that is more accurate and efficient.

"I would be lost without it," said Mo Coyle, an accounts payable supervisor at Ademco. Coyle can answer questions over the telephone when a vendor calls because all the relevant data can be brought up quickly on screen.

For example, Ademco users can get billing information on their PCs in 10 to 15 seconds. The old billing system would have taken up to a half hour to retrieve an image, Bernstein said.

When a bill comes in, a person in accounts payable working on a PC connects to an IBM System/36 computer.

Besides the basic accounts payable application, there is also a utility on the System/36 that transforms information about the bill and the company sending it into a bar code, which is used to track the bill through the process.

After connecting to the System/36, the user fills out an on-screen form that contains the vendor's name, voucher number, and other information.

Once the process is complete, a dedicated printer issues a cover sheet with the bar-coded information attached.

The user then scans all the supporting information into the accounts payable system through a scanner attached to the PC.

Supporting documentation might include the original bill, a purchase order, and any memos related to the bill. Those images can be retrieved later by anyone who uses the accounts payable system.

Besides retrieving information more quickly, there is another significant benefit to the accounts payable system, Bernstein said. "Now that the data is coming off the bar codes, there's 100% recognition accuracy." He said even with careful checking, hand-filing could result in indexing records in the wrong file about 2% to 4% of the time.

QUESTIONS

1. For what does Ademco use bar codes and imaging in its accounts payable system?
2. What benefits does Ademco receive from its accounts payable system?

WEB SITE
Ademco: www.ademco.com

Source: April Jacobs, "Homemade app pays off," *Computerworld*, May 20, 1996, p. 52.

the supplier, and the accounts payable report summarizing the supplier charges and payments for the month. This report contains the total charges and payments for all suppliers.

To produce the outputs, two types of stored data are used. One is a file or database containing accounts payable data consisting of one record for each supplier with fields for the supplier number, supplier invoice date, supplier invoice amount, supplier payment due date, supplier payment date, and supplier payment amount. All fields in this data, except the supplier number, are repeated for each supplier invoice. The other stored data used is the supplier master data, which is also used in the purchasing system. For the accounts payable system, the fields needed in the records of this data are the supplier number, supplier name, and supplier address.

Processing in the accounts payable system includes several activities. The purchase order is compared with the supplier invoice to determine if the items ordered were shipped by the supplier. The supplier invoice is compared with the receiving notice to see if the items shipped were received. If the supplier invoice correctly states what items were ordered and received, then the data from the invoice is entered into the system and stored in the accounts payable data. Included in this data is the due date for the payment of the invoice sent by the supplier. Frequently, perhaps every day, the accounts payable data is checked to see if any invoice payments are due soon. When a payment is almost due, a check is prepared. The supplier master data is used to find the supplier's name and address. As the checks are prepared, the accounts payable data is updated to indicate that the invoice has been paid. Once a month, the total accounts payable is computed from the accounts payable data and the accounts payable report is printed.

With computerized purchasing and accounts payable, data can be passed electronically from one system to the other. Data about each purchase order, such as the supplier number, item number, and quantity ordered, could be put in a purchase order file by the purchasing system. Then the accounts payable system could use this file to update the accounts payable data.

Payroll System

The purpose of a <u>payroll system</u> is to prepare paychecks for employees and to provide reports of payroll. Figure 10.13 summarizes the functions of the payroll system. The input to the system is the employee work report data, which indicates how much the employee has worked. For an employee who is paid on an hourly basis, this report is a time sheet that shows how many hours the employee has worked each day. For an employee who is paid a fixed salary, the report indicates whether the employee was present for all work days, and, if absent, for what reason. The outputs from the system include the paycheck, giving the amount the employee is paid, and the payroll report, listing for each employee the gross pay, the amount deducted for taxes and for other reasons, and the net pay. The report also gives the total of the gross pay, deductions, and net pay for all employees.

To produce the outputs, the system first creates a file or database with transaction data from the employee work reports. For hourly employees, there is one record in this data for each employee who worked, with fields for the employee number and hours worked. For salaried employees, each record indicates whether the

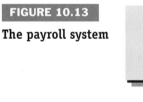

FIGURE 10.13

The payroll system

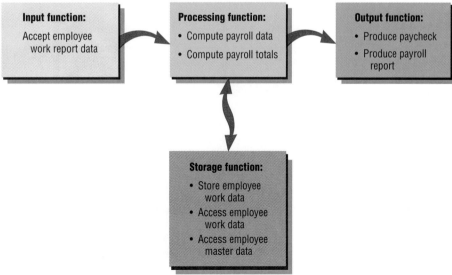

Input function:
Accept employee work report data

Processing function:
• Compute payroll data
• Compute payroll totals

Output function:
• Produce paycheck
• Produce payroll report

Storage function:
• Store employee work data
• Access employee work data
• Access employee master data

employee has worked the entire pay period or only part of the pay period. Also needed by the system is a file or database with employee master data. This data has one record for each employee with fields for the employee number, employee name, employee address, and pay rate or salary.

Payroll processing involves using the employee work data and the employee master data to calculate the payroll data for each employee. If the employee is paid on an hourly basis, the hours worked from the employee work data is multiplied by the pay rate from the employee master data to determine the gross pay. For a salaried employee, the gross pay is the employee's salary from the employee master data unless he or she worked less than a full pay period. Next, the deductions and net pay are calculated and the paycheck is printed with the employee name, address, and net pay. Finally, the total gross pay, deductions, and net pay are calculated and the payroll report is printed.

General Ledger System

The last basic business information system is a general ledger system, the purpose of which is to maintain the business's financial accounts and to prepare financial statements. The functions of the general ledger system are summarized in Fig. 10.14. The inputs are data on revenues, expenses, assets, and liabilities. We have discussed several reports that contain such data, including the accounts receivable report, the inventory value report, the accounts payable report, and the payroll report. The outputs from the general ledger system are financial statements such as the income statement and the balance sheet.

To produce the financial statements, the general ledger system uses a file or database with general ledger data. There is one record in this data for each financial account that the business maintains. Thus, there is a record for sales revenue, for salary expense, for inventory, and for accounts payable, among others. Each record has fields for the account number, account description, and account balance.

Processing in the general ledger system first involves updating the general ledger data with data about current revenues and expenses, and changes in assets

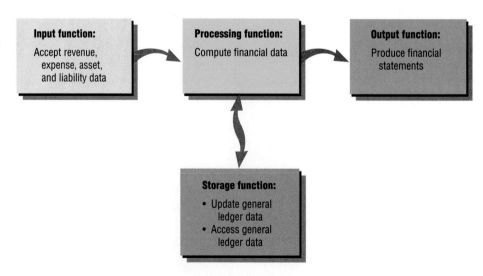

FIGURE 10.14

The general ledger system

and liabilities. After all accounts have been updated, the general ledger data is used in various financial computations and the financial statements are printed.

If other systems are computerized, data can be passed electronically to the general ledger system. For example, the accounts receivable data could be put in a file by the accounts receivable system and payroll expense data could be put in a file by the payroll system. These files and others then could be used to update the general ledger data.

Other Business Information Systems

The eight information systems discussed in the last section are the basic ones found in many businesses. Many other systems, however, are used.

Accounting Information Systems

Recall from Chapter 2 that the accounting function of a business is responsible for recording and reporting financial information about the business. Accounting information systems support the accounting function. Of the information systems discussed previously, billing, accounts receivable, accounts payable, payroll, and general ledger are usually considered to be accounting information systems. In some businesses, order entry, inventory control, and purchasing are also thought of as accounting information systems. Several other common accounting information systems are:

- *Fixed asset accounting.* The purpose of this system is to account for business assets such as buildings, land, and equipment.
- *Budgeting.* This system prepares projections of revenues and expenses, and compares actual figures with the projected ones.
- *Tax accounting.* The purpose of this system is to prepare business tax reports and to pay taxes.

Financial Information Systems

The finance function of a business is responsible for obtaining money needed by the business and for planning the use of that money. Financial information systems provide the necessary support for the finance function. None of the systems discussed previously are considered to be financial information systems (although accounting and financial information systems often are grouped together). Some common financial information systems are:

- *Cash management.* This system balances the needs of the business for cash with the expected cash availability.
- *Capital expenditure analysis.* The purpose of this system is to analyze the effect on the business of large expenditures such as that associated with building a new factory or replacing major equipment.
- *Financial forecasting.* This system forecasts financial information, such as revenues and expenses, for the future. (See Fig. 10.15.)
- *Portfolio management.* This system analyzes alternative investment strategies for the business's cash and keeps track of investments.
- *Credit analysis.* Businesses that extend credit to customers need to determine which customers should receive credit, which is the purpose of this system.

FIGURE 10.15

Financial forecasting

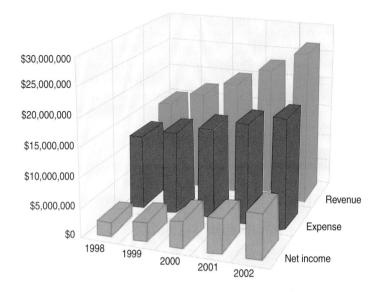

Marketing Information Systems

The marketing function is responsible for selling goods and services for the business. <u>Marketing information systems</u> assist in the marketing function. Of the systems discussed previously, order entry usually is considered to be a marketing information system because customer orders are procured by salespeople working in the marketing function. Billing and inventory control are also sometimes considered to be marketing information systems. Other common marketing information systems are:

- *Sales analysis.* This system determines which products are selling well and poorly, which sales regions have the best and worst sales, which salespeople are selling the most and the least, and so forth.
- *Sales forecasting.* The purpose of this system is to project sales in the future.
- *Marketing research.* This system analyzes information gathered about consumers and products in order to identify trends.
- *Direct mail advertising.* This system prepares advertising pieces for mailing directly to potential customers.
- *Electronic commerce.* This system uses the World Wide Web on the Internet to advertise and sell a business's goods and services.
- *Sales force automation.* This system provides information, usually through notebook computers which can be connected to a central computer, to help sales representatives in their jobs.

Manufacturing Information Systems

The manufacturing function is concerned with the production of goods that the business sells. <u>Manufacturing information systems</u> provide services to support the manufacturing function. Inventory control often is considered to be a manufacturing

Bookmark

Purchasing through the Internet at General Electric

DOUBLE CLICK FOR RESIN

The hype and hoopla over Internet commerce has focused on Web sites selling books, flowers, clothes, and other retail goods. But the real Internet action has been in industrial goods, and that's where a lot of smart people expect it to remain. There are predictions that company-to-company Internet trade will hit $134 billion a year by the end of the decade.

As it is in so many other things, the General Electric Co. has been in the vanguard. Since it was launched, a Web site designed and run by GE's Information Services (GEIS) division has logged $350 million worth of industrial products purchased electronically by GE divisions. This Web site, coupled with its custom software, enables users to zap out requests for bids to thousands of suppliers, who can respond over the Internet. Savings are in time, money, and a lot of paperwork. Here's an example of how it works:

When the machinery at GE Lighting's factory in Cleveland broke down, GE needed custom replacement parts, fast.

In the past, GE would have asked for bids from just four domestic suppliers. There was just too much hassle getting the paperwork and production-line blueprints together and sent out to suppliers. But this time, they posted the specifications and "requests for quotes" on GE's Web site—and drew seven other bidders.

The winner was a Hungarian company. A GE Information Services spokesman says this vendor would not have been contacted in the days of paper purchasing forms. The Hungarian firm's replacement parts arrived quicker, and GE Lighting paid just $320,000, a 20% savings.

To date, all orders made over GE Information Services' Internet purchasing systems have been intra-company. But GE is now offering access to its Web site to outsiders. GEIS has jumped ahead of such companies as IBM, Microsoft, and Netscape to lead the race into business-to-business Internet commerce. The tough part of establishing such a system, says Orville Bailey, who manages GEIS' Internet project, is just getting it

started. Buyers don't want to invest in a system unless suppliers are already on board, and vice versa. "It's the classic chicken-or-the-egg problem," says Bailey.

A clear case where being big is a crucial advantage. GE divisions spend $30 billion a year on other companies' goods and services. So when GE announced that it would be soliciting bids over the Internet, even the smallest, most technophobic of its suppliers listened up. Smiles Bailey: "We could build the critical mass."

GE Information Services claims cost savings of 10% to 15%, thanks to more and lower bids. It also claims a five-day savings in order time, thanks to the immediacy of the Internet.

GEIS' Bailey expects various GE units to be buying goods at the rate of $2 billion a year, and outside firms who purchase the technology from GE to be doing another $3 billion or so. If a $134 billion market for business-to-business Internet commerce by the year 2000 does materialize, as the Boston-based Yankee Group predicts, extrapolating from current volumes means up to $50 billion of that will move over GE's Internet purchasing system.

What of the much-ballyhooed retail Web sites? The Yankee Group figures those sites will do about $10 billion in 2000. That's one-fifth the potential volume of GE's industrial goods Web site alone.

QUESTIONS
1. How does GE do purchasing through the Internet?
2. What specific benefits does GE estimate it receives from its Internet-based purchasing system?
3. What is the difference between electronic commerce on the Internet and the GE Internet-based purchasing system?

WEB SITES
General Electric: www.ge.com
GE Information Services: www.geis.com

Source: Scott Woolley, "Double click for resin," *Forbes*, March 10, 1997, pp. 132, 134.

information system because manufacturing produces the goods for inventory. Purchasing may also be a manufacturing information system in some businesses. Some other common manufacturing information systems are:

- *Production scheduling.* This system schedules the use of manufacturing facilities to produce products most efficiently.

- *Material requirements planning (MRP).* The purpose of this system is to determine what parts and materials will be needed during the manufacturing process and when they will be needed.
- *Manufacturing resource planning (MRP II).* This system is called MRP II to distinguish it from materials requirements planning or MRP. It combines MRP with production scheduling and other functions in a comprehensive manufacturing information system.
- *Just-in-time (JIT) inventory management.* This system is a form of inventory control in which parts and materials are scheduled to arrive from suppliers just before they are needed for the manufacturing process.
- *Computer-aided design (CAD).* This system involves using computers to assist in the design of products to be manufactured.
- *Computer-aided manufacturing (CAM).* This system involves using computers to control machines in the manufacturing process.
- *Robotics.* This system uses computer-controlled robots in the manufacturing process. (See Fig. 10.16.)
- *Computer-integrated manufacturing (CIM).* This system combines many of the other manufacturing systems into a single system.

Human Resource Information Systems

The human resource management function is responsible for hiring, training, compensating, and terminating employees. Human resource information systems (HRIS) support this function. The only system discussed previously that is sometimes considered to be a human resource information system is payroll. Some common human resource information systems are:

- *Performance appraisal.* This system analyzes employee performance on the job.
- *Skills inventory.* This system keeps track of employee skills and matches employees with specific jobs.
- *Benefits administration.* This system manages employee fringe benefit packages.
- *Job applicant tracking.* This system keeps track of applicants for jobs with the business.

FIGURE 10.16

Robotics

Organizing Information System Functions

Transaction processing systems, as well as other information systems, vary in terms of where the functions of the systems are performed. The input, output, processing, and storage functions of the systems may be performed at one location or at several locations. This section describes the main features of four ways of organizing the functions of information systems.

Centralized Systems

Many information systems are centralized systems, which means that all input, output, processing, and storage functions are performed at a single, central location, usually using a mainframe computer. (See Fig. 10.17.) Some centralized systems use batch processing, some use on-line processing, and some use both forms of processing. Centralized systems typically affect several areas within the organization. An example of a centralized system is a payroll system, in which all paychecks are prepared on a central computer.

The advantages of centralized systems are economy and control. One large, central computer for all processing often is the most economical in terms of computer hardware. In addition, with all system functions performed at one location, the computer staff has the most control over what is done and when. The disadvantage of this approach is lack of response to the users. Output may take a long time to be returned to the users. In addition, users must deal with a central computer staff when requesting new systems and changes in existing systems, which can be frustrating. Still, many information systems are centralized.

Teleprocessing Systems

With centralized systems all input data must be sent from the user's location to the central computer location, and all output must be sent back to the user's location. In early systems, data was carried manually from one location to another. With the development of data communications it became possible to transmit input and output data electronically between the user's location and the central location. Systems

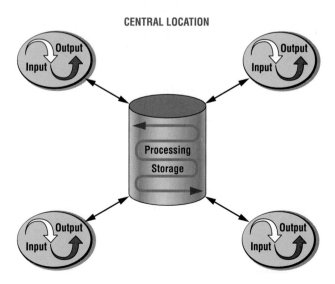

FIGURE 10.17

Centralized systems

CENTRAL LOCATION

that use this approach are called <u>teleprocessing systems</u>. (See Fig. 10.18.) The processing and storage functions are still centralized, often with the use of a mainframe computer; the input and output functions, however, are performed at the users' locations with the use of terminals. Data can be sent to and from the user's location in batches or interactively using data communications. As with centralized systems, teleprocessing systems usually affect a large part of the organization. An example of a teleprocessing system is an airline reservation system in which a central computer keeps all airline data, but reservation data input and output occurs at terminals located throughout the country.

The advantage of teleprocessing systems is quicker input and output response for the user. Generally, users can send in their input and get their output back in a short period of time—sometimes almost instantaneously. Still, the user has to deal with a central computer staff to request new or modified systems.

Decentralized Systems

One of the principal disadvantages of centralized and teleprocessing systems is a lack of response to the user's needs for new and modified systems. To overcome this disadvantage, many information systems are <u>decentralized systems</u>. In this approach, each department or group of users in the organization uses its own computer to perform all input, output, processing, and storage functions for its systems. (See Fig. 10.19.) Furthermore, these separate computers cannot communicate with one another. Thus, the accounting department has a computer that is used for the accounting information systems, the marketing department has one for the marketing information systems, and so on, with no communication between the departmental computers. Often, local area networks or minicomputers are used for the systems. There may also be a central minicomputer or mainframe computer used for company-wide systems.

The advantage of decentralization is better response to the user's needs. Because each group of users has a computer for its systems, the users are more likely to get new systems that meet their needs and quicker changes to existing systems.

FIGURE 10.18

Teleprocessing systems

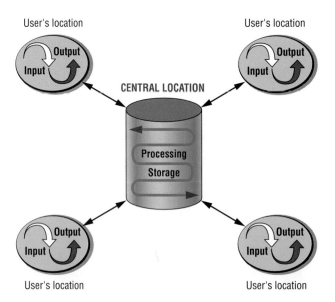

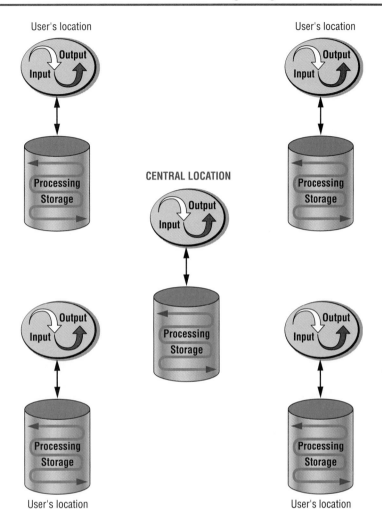

FIGURE 10.19

Decentralized systems

There are several disadvantages to this approach, however. One is hardware cost. Several smaller computers usually cost more than one large computer that is capable of doing all processing. Another disadvantage is lack of control. Each group is responsible for controlling the use of its computer. If the users do not follow appropriate procedures, the system may not perform as desired. Finally, there is often incompatibility between systems in a decentralized approach. One consequence of this is that data from one system may not be transferable to another.

The ultimate form of decentralization is when each user has a personal computer on his or her desk. Then, each user is responsible for input, output, processing, and storage for one or more information systems. If standard procedures for how these systems are to function are not created and enforced, this situation can result in a great deal of incompatibility between systems. Some organizations have set up information centers to deal with this problem. An information center consists of computer professionals who establish hardware, software, data, and procedure standards for personal computers in the organization. The center trains users, sets up hardware and software, and provides other assistance to assure that the use of personal computers is in the best interest of the organization.

Distributed Systems

The three approaches for organizing information systems described so far are used for some types of information systems. Many systems, however, need capabilities that are not available in one of these approaches. For these systems, the <u>distributed systems</u> approach is used.

Distributed systems are similar to decentralized systems in which each user or group of users has its own computer for input, output, processing, and storage. The computers, however, can communicate with one another because they are linked using data communications to form a local area or wide area network. (See Fig. 10.20.) Included in the network may be a centrally located mainframe computer, departmental minicomputers, and personal computers.

With distributed systems, data can be sent from one computer to another by means of data communications. Thus, if one computer needs input data or stored data from another computer, the data can be transferred between the computers. In addition, if a computer does not have the necessary capabilities for a particular processing task, it can send data to another computer where the processing can be

FIGURE 10.20

Distributed systems

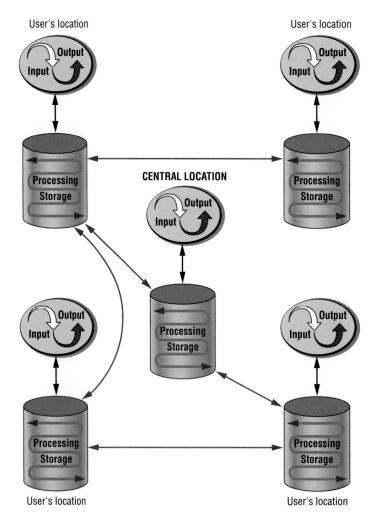

done and then the output can be sent back. Thus, with a distributed system, input, output, or stored data at any location can be transferred to any other location. In addition, processing can be done at any location.

Sometimes, the term cooperative processing is heard in conjunction with distributed systems. This means that two or more computers in a network cooperate in performing the functions of an information system. Usually, one computer performs some of the functions and another computer performs other functions. Thus, a personal computer performing input and output functions may cooperate with another computer performing processing and storage functions.

Client-server computing, discussed in Chapter 6, is a popular form of cooperation processing used in distributed systems. Recall that in client-server computing some computers in a network are clients and some are servers. The client computers provide the user interface and may process data. They cooperate with the server computers, which provide database processing.

There are several advantages to distributed systems. First, they provide the same response to users' needs as do decentralized systems but with more capabilities. Because system functions can be performed on other computers in the network, the functions are not limited to those of the user's computer. Another advantage is more control because to use the distributed system, the user must follow standard procedures. Finally, there is greater compatibility in distributed systems. For example, to transfer data in a network, the data must be compatible with other computers.

The main disadvantage of distributed systems is their complexity. These systems often involve many computers and a sophisticated network. Hardware must be connected in a network; programs must be developed that function in the network; data must be organized so it is compatible with the network; procedures must be devised to ensure proper use of the network; users must be trained in the use of the network. Developing a distributed system and ensuring that it works properly is a difficult task.

Chapter Summary

☐ An example of a computer information system increasing the efficiency of business operations is customer order processing. When done manually, customer orders are written out by hand, shelves are checked for product availability, a credit file is checked for the customer's credit record, and a sales order is typed. With a computer information system, customer orders are keyed into the system, product availability and customer credit rating are looked up by the system, and the sales order is produced by the system. The computer information system is more efficient than the manual system because it produces the sales order with fewer resources and in less time. (pp. 292–293)

☐ The purpose of a **transaction processing system** (**TPS**) is to keep records about the state of the organization, to process **transactions**, which are events that have occurred that affect the organization, and to produce output that reports on transactions, reports on the state of the organization, and causes other transactions to occur. Inputs to a transaction

processing system come from users and other transaction processing systems. Outputs go to users and other transaction processing systems. Transaction processing system files and databases store data about the state of the organization. Transaction processing system software accepts data about transactions, processes it, makes changes in stored data, and produces the outputs. (pp. 293–294)

☐ Transaction processing systems perform input, output, storage, and processing functions. Input functions include capturing data on a **source document** and entering the data into the system. Entered data must be checked for errors, a process called **data validation**. Output functions include producing **reports**, such as **detail reports**, **summary reports**, and **exception reports**. Storage functions include creating files and databases containing stored data, **accessing** stored data, **sorting** stored data, and **updating** stored data. Processing functions involve the manipulation of data, including computation and decision making. (pp. 294–298)

☐ Transaction processing systems use procedures, called **controls**, to ensure the completeness of the data processing and to minimize the chance of errors. One type of control is a **control total**, which is a number used to check for errors in the processing. Another control is an **audit trail**, which is a way of tracing the effect of data through a system. **Backup** and **recovery procedures** are ways of ensuring against loss of data in case of a malfunction of the system. (pp. 298–299)

☐ Two ways of processing data in transaction processing system are **batch processing**, in which data for all transactions to be processed is brought together and processed in a group; and **on-line transaction processing** (**OLTP**), in which a person enters the data for a transaction into a system where it is processed and the output is received before the next input is entered. (pp. 299–300)

☐ An **order entry system** accepts customer order data and accesses stored inventory master data and customer master data to produce sales orders. A **billing system** produces invoices from sales order data and from customer master data and inventory master data. An **accounts receivable system** uses invoice data and customer payment data to update stored accounts receivable data; and accesses this data, along with a customer master data, to produce statements, overdue notices, and accounts receivable reports. An **inventory control system** accepts customer order data and receiving notice data, updates inventory master data, and produces inventory reorder reports and inventory value reports from inventory master data. A **purchasing system** updates inventory master data with the preferred supplier, then uses this data and stored supplier master data, along with inventory reorder data, to produce purchase orders. An **accounts payable system** accepts purchase order, supplier invoice, and receiving notice data; updates stored accounts payable data; and then accesses this data and supplier master data to produce supplier

payments and accounts payable reports. A **payroll system** produces paychecks and payroll reports from employee work data and stored employee master data. A **general ledger system** uses revenue, expense, asset, and liability data to update stored general ledger data, and then accesses this data to produce financial statements. (pp. 300–311)

☐ Examples of **accounting information systems** include billing, accounts receivable, accounts payable, payroll, general ledger, fixed asset accounting, budgeting, and tax accounting. Examples of **financial information systems** include cash management, capital expenditure analysis, financial forecasting, and credit analysis. Some examples of **marketing information systems** are sales analysis, sales forecasting, marketing research, direct mail advertising, electronic commerce, and sales force automation. **Manufacturing information systems** include production scheduling, material requirement planning, manufacturing resource planning, just-in-time inventory management, and computer-integrated manufacturing. Examples of **human resource information systems** (**HRIS**) are performance appraisal, skills inventory, benefits administration, and job applicant tracking. (pp. 311–314)

☐ The input, output, processing, and storage functions of an information system can be organized in different ways. In a **centralized system**, all functions are performed at a single, central location. In a **teleprocessing system**, the processing and storage functions are centralized, but the input and output functions are performed at the users' locations with data transmitted to the central location using data communications. With a **decentralized system**, each group of users has its own computer to perform all functions. A **distributed system** is like a decentralized system but with the computers linked to form a local area or wide area network so that functions can be performed on the user's computer or on other computers in the network. (pp. 315–319)

Key Terms

Accessing (p. 297)
Accounting Information System (p. 311)
Accounts Payable System (p. 307)
Accounts Receivable System (p. 304)
Audit Trail (p. 299)
Backup Procedure (p. 299)
Batch Processing (p. 299)
Billing System (p. 303)
Centralized System (p. 315)

Control (p. 298)
Control Total (p. 298)
Cooperative Processing (p. 319)
Data Validation (p. 295)
Decentralized System (p. 316)
Detail Report (p. 295)
Distributed System (p. 318)
Exception Report (p. 295)
Financial Information System (p. 311)

General Ledger System (p. 310)
Human Resource Information System (HRIS) (p. 314)
Information Center (p. 317)
Interactive Processing (p. 300)
Inventory Control System (p. 305)
Manufacturing Information System (p. 312)
Marketing Information System (p. 312)

Master Data (p. 297)
On-Line Transaction Processing
    (OLTP) (p. 299)
Order Entry System (p. 301)
Payroll System (p. 309)
Purchasing System (p. 306)

Real-Time Processing (p. 300)
Recovery Procedure (p. 299)
Report (p. 295)
Sorting (p. 297)
Source Document (p. 294)
Summary Report (p. 295)

Teleprocessing System (p. 316)
Transaction (p. 293)
Transaction Data (p. 297)
Transaction Processing System
    (TPS) (p. 293)
Updating (p. 297)

Assignment Material

Review Questions

Fill-in Questions

1. A(n) _____ is an event that has occurred that affects an organization or business.

2. A form used to capture data is called a(n) _____.

3. Two steps that must be performed to get data into an information system are _____ and _____.

4. A report that lists totals for groups of data but has no detail data is called a(n) _____.

5. A report that contains data that is an exception to a rule or standard is called a(n) _____.

6. The process of arranging data into a particular order is called _____.

7. Updating a file is a _____ function of a transaction processing system.

8. A(n) _____ is a number computed when data enters an information system and again after the system has processed the data that is used to check for errors in the processing.

9. Important procedures to ensure that stored data is not lost if a computer system fails are _____ and _____.

10. A form of processing in which the processing is done immediately after the input is received, with no delay, is called _____.

11. The sales order is output from the _____ system and input to the _____ system and the _____ system.

12. Data about what items should be purchased by the purchasing system comes from the _____ system.

13. Customer master data is used in the _____ system, the _____ system, and the _____ system.

14. Inventory master data is updated with changes in inventory levels in the _____ system and used to produce invoices in the _____ system.

15. The _____ system and the _____ system print checks.

16. The _____ system receives inputs from several other systems for the purpose of producing financial statements.

17. An information system in which all functions are performed at a single, central location is called a(n) _____.

18. An information system that users use through terminals located some distance away but in which all processing and storage are performed at a central location is a(n) _____.

19. Assume that each department in an organization uses its own computer to perform all functions for its information systems. These information systems are called _____.

20. Some organizations have a(n) _____, which consists of computer professionals who assist personal computer users in the organization.

Short-answer Questions

1. How can a computer information system increase the efficiency of business operations?

2. What is the purpose of a transaction processing system?

3. Where do the inputs for a transaction processing system come from?

4. What do the outputs of a transaction processing system do?

5. Why is data validation important?

6. What is the difference between master data and transaction data?

7. What is an audit trail?

8. Explain the difference between batch processing and on-line transaction processing.

9. What is the input to the order entry system?

10. What is the output from the billing system?

11. What is the purpose of the accounts receivable system?

12. What updating is done in the inventory control system?

13. What is the output from the purchasing system?

14. What stored data is used in the accounts payable system?

15. What computation is done in the payroll system?

16. What is the purpose of the general ledger system?

17. List one accounting information system, one financial information system, one marketing information system, one manufacturing information system, and one human resource information system.

18. What is a distributed system?

19. What is cooperative processing?

20. What information system organizations are usually most responsive to users' needs?

Discussion Questions

1. Think of the course registration system at your college or university. Would a new or changed computer information system improve its efficiency? How would it do so?

2. Identify several transaction processing systems not described in the chapter. What are the input, output, processing, and storage functions of each system?

3. Think of an information system with which you are familiar and identify the controls used in the system.

4. In what types of information systems would batch processing be preferred over on-line transaction processing? Why?

5. Many information systems cannot easily be classified as accounting, financial, marketing, manufacturing, or human resource information systems. Think of several information systems not discussed in the chapter and try to identify in which area or areas they would be classified. Do any fall into several categories?

6. The trend in many businesses is toward client-server computing in distributed systems. Why would a business want to use centralized, teleprocessing, or decentralized systems?

7. What type of information system organization—centralized, teleprocessing, decentralized, or distributed—would be best for an international business? Does the type of business make any difference in the choice?

8. Transaction processing systems, although only supporting the basic operations of a business, can be used unethically. Pick several of the systems discussed in this chapter and describe how they could be used unethically.

Problem-solving Projects

1. The system used by banks with automated teller machines is a transaction processing system. Identify the input, output, processing, and storage functions of the system. Draw a diagram like Fig. 10.7 that shows these functions. If available, use graphics software to draw the diagram.

2. The eight basic business information systems described in the chapter use stored data containing different types of records with many fields in each record. Some types of records are used in only one system and some are used in several systems. In those types of records used in several systems, some fields may be used in one system and others may be used in another system. Prepare a table in which the rows list the fields in each type of record used in the eight basic business information systems. Organize the rows by record; in other words, identify the first type of record, then the fields in that record, then the second type of record, then the fields in that record, and so forth. The columns of the table should list the eight basic business information systems. At the intersection of a row and column put a mark if the field in the row is used in the system identified in the column. Use spreadsheet or word processing software to prepare your table.

3. Using database software, create a simple order entry system like that described in the chapter.

4. Investigate a transaction processing system in an organization or business to which you have access. Find out as much as you can about the system. What are the functions of the system? What controls are used in the system? Is the processing batch or on-line? In what business area does the system fall? How are the functions of the system organized? Using word processing, graphics, and other software, prepare a report of your findings.

5. Locate a World Wide Web site for a mail order company such as L.L. Bean, Lands' End, or REI. Be sure the site has an on-line ordering system that allows the customer to order items using the Internet. How are customer orders entered? In what ways can the customer pay for the order? Does the system tell the customer if the item ordered is available in stock? What special features does the ordering system have? What master data do you think the company is keeping to support the ordering system? What information systems discussed in this chapter are found in the com-

pany's on-line ordering system? Using word processing software, write a summary of what you found.

6. Inventory master data in an inventory control system includes the reorder point and the reorder quantity. These can be calculated as follows:

$$\text{Reorder point} = \text{Demand rate} \times \text{Delivery time}$$

$$\text{Reorder quantity} = \sqrt{\frac{2 \times \text{Demand rate} \times \text{Set-up cost}}{\text{Holding cost}}}$$

Using spreadsheet software, create a spreadsheet to calculate the reorder point and reorder quantity. Test the spreadsheet for the following items:

Item	Demand rate	Delivery time	Set-up cost	Holding cost
1	1025	.25	$ 75	$ 2
2	500	.08	$250	$12
3	2250	.04	$ 35	$ 1
4	125	.17	$450	$50

Real-world Case

Sprint

For a telephone company, communication is everything. When Sprint Corp. realized that its relatively new computer infrastructure inhibited the ability of its sales representatives to communicate effectively with their corporate customers, the irony went unappreciated.

By writing a new order-entry application that communicates with the mainframe in minutes rather than days, Sprint has improved its customer service dramatically. Most commercial customers now get their phones hooked up in a few hours rather than in a week. Not surprisingly, fewer customers cancel their orders after a few days, and Sprint has retained more of its accounts.

The company sped up its order-entry process by moving sales application off the mainframe onto laptops belonging to the Sprint sales force. This new custom application has also decreased errors, and it is object oriented, which Sprint hopes will reduce development time on future applications. Eventually, Sprint hopes to merge its several order-entry applications into the new one, cutting down on maintenance and training.

Before the new system was developed, sales representatives would create orders on paper and fax or mail them to a centralized office. There, they would be logged into an order-tracking system and later—in hours or a day—keyed into Sprint's Customer

Information System, an application and database running on an Amdahl Corp. mainframe. At that point, usually three to five days after the initial order was taken, the customer would receive phone service.

Sprint decided to automate the system at the sales end to eliminate rekeying orders, to cut down on errors, and to speed up the whole process. The sales representatives who sell to corporate accounts frequently visit customers in their offices, so they needed an order-entry program that would run on a laptop.

Sprint developed a custom application called the Automated Order Processing System (AOPS) that ran on a portable and uploaded data to the mainframe when a sales representative dialed in from a remote location. The new application succeeded in cutting down service time from four or five days to one or two days, says Michael Rapken, director of customer acquisition and management systems for Sprint Long Distance, in Dallas.

But the new system had its own problems. The AOPS application uploaded its data to the mainframe via a technique called screen scraping, which in the long run proved cumbersome, Rapken says.

So Sprint decided to create an improved order-entry application. The new program, called Customer Information Systems Extension (CISX), covers Sprint's commercial customer voice products and contains an extensive database of product options so sales representatives can't order services or products that don't work together. The company plans to completely replace AOPS with CISX eventually.

The CISX application runs on IBM laptops. Once a sales representative completes an order, he or she connects to Sprint's Hewlett-Packard (HP) server over the LAN or a telephone. A PC terminal in Atlanta provides access to the company's internal network from the phone line. The server holds the orders where they can be accessed by other sales representatives out in the field before being sent to the mainframe database. This capability is useful when sales representatives have a question and ask a colleague to look at an order. The server also converts the data into a format that the mainframe database can understand. Sprint decided not to run this task on the laptop because it would be too time-consuming.

The new sales system features a drag-and-drop GUI, which makes it easier for users to navigate around an order. In addition, users are no longer restricted to filling out an order line by line. The product database has also made salespeoples' jobs easier, Rapken says.

"We're trying to make it so salespeople can concentrate on what they're doing, which is selling," Rapken says. "So we made it easy to use to cut down on training time and to make it intuitive."

With the new system, users can store an order on the HP server or the laptop without finishing it. On the laptop, an incomplete order is stored in a work-in-progress folder, which contains file objects labeled with the customer's name. The user can click on the folder, complete the order, and, if he or she is connected to the server, drag it onto the "submit" icon to send the information to the server.

The new system has cut down on errors, because the new product database no longer allows users to enter incompatible goods and services. It is also much faster than the old one. Once an order is completed—a process that might take an hour or two at most—the mainframe is updated in 10 or 15 minutes. Once the mainframe receives the order, Sprint contacts the local telephone provider to actually connect the service.

Although customers still don't receive their service instantly, the new application has speeded up delivery. By reusing some of the objects it created for the CISX order-entry system, Sprint plans to take advantage of the new system in future projects such as residential sales order entry, call processing, and switch management applications.

Questions

1. Why did Sprint decide to develop a new customer order entry system?
2. What benefits did Sprint receive from AOPS?
3. Why did Sprint develop CISX to replace AOPS?
4. How is an order entered using CISX?
5. What benefits does Sprint receive from CISX?

Source: Cate T. Corcoran, "Order-entry sales system speeds Sprint phone service," *InfoWorld*, March 25, 1996, p. 76.

11 Management Decision Making

Chapter Outline

Improving Management Decision-Making Effectiveness (p. 326)
Management Decisions (p. 327)
    Levels of Management Decisions (p. 327)
    Characteristics of Management Decisions (p. 327)
    Information Needs for Management Decisions (p. 329)
    Information Systems for Management Support (p. 330)
Management Information Systems (p. 331)
    Management Information System Structure (p. 331)
    Management Information System Functions (p. 332)
    Management Information System Software (p. 336)
Decision Support Systems (p. 337)
    Management Decision Support (p. 337)
    Decision Support System Structure (p. 338)
    Decision Support System Functions (p. 339)
    Decision Support System Software (p. 340)
    Group Decision Support Systems (p. 341)
    Geographic Information Systems (p. 341)
Executive Support Systems (p. 342)
    Executive Information Needs (p. 342)
    Executive Support System Structure (p. 344)
    Executive Support System Functions (p. 346)
    Executive Support System Software (p. 347)
Expert Systems (p. 347)
    Expert Advice (p. 347)
    Expert System Structure (p. 348)
    Expert System Functions (p. 348)
    Expert System Software (p. 350)
    Other Artificial Intelligence Applications (p. 350)

Learning Objectives

After completing this chapter, you should be able to:

☐ 1. Explain how information systems can improve management decision-making effectiveness.

☐ 2. Describe the characteristics of information needed by managers for decision making at different levels of an organization.

☐ 3. Describe the structure of management information systems.

☐ 4. Describe the structure of decision support systems.

☐ 5. Explain the purpose of executive support systems.

☐ 6. Explain how an expert system can provide expert advice.

Information systems support the *operations* and *management* of an organization. Chapter 10 reviewed information systems that assist business operations by providing transaction processing. The current chapter examines systems that provide support for the management of a business. Management involves making decisions and the systems discussed in this chapter provide information to assist in management decision making. As you will see, there are several types of information systems that support management. First, however, you need to understand how information systems can improve the effectiveness of management decision making.

Improving Management Decision-Making Effectiveness

People make decisions all the time. Some decisions are personal and some are business-related. For example, you make a decision when you buy a new car. The decision answers the question, "What car should I buy?" A business manager in an athletic shoe store makes a decision when he or she selects new products to sell. In this case, the question answered by the decision might be, "What style shoes should we stock next winter?"

A *decision* is a selection between several courses of action. For the car-buying decision, you have to decide whether to buy a Ford, a Toyota, a Volkswagen, or some other make of car. For the product-selection decision, the business manager has to decide whether to stock running shoes, tennis shoes, or walking shoes. Almost always, when making a decision, there is uncertainty about what will happen with each alternative. Will the car require a lot of repair? Will customers want to buy the types of shoes stocked by the store?

Information helps reduce uncertainty. With better information, a decision maker is more certain about the outcome from the decision. If you have information about the repair records of the models of cars you are considering, you can be more certain about how reliable the car you buy will be. If the business manager has information about the buying public's interest in athletic shoes, he or she can be more certain about what types of shoes will sell. You cannot eliminate uncertainty entirely, however. Thus, the car you buy may still need repair and the shoes stocked may not sell. With good information, however, uncertainty can be reduced and the outcome from the decision is more likely to be satisfactory.

Information systems improve decision-making effectiveness by providing decision makers with information related to the decisions for which they are responsible. Such information systems can be used for personal as well as business decisions. For example, if you are making a car purchasing decision, you can use a computerized library information system to search for articles and reviews of the cars in which you are interested. A business manager making a product-selection decision can use a sales analysis information system to examine sales trends and a marketing information system to look at marketing research data. In these cases, the effectiveness of the decision making is improved by the information systems.

Chapter 1 explained the difference between data and information. *Data* is a representation of a fact, number, word, image, picture, or sound. *Information*, on the other hand, is data that is meaningful or useful to someone. The purpose of an information system is to accept, store, and process data, and to produce information. The information is used in the management of the business to help in decision making. To be competitive today, businesses must have information systems that provide information to support their management decision making.

Management Decisions

Before examining information systems that support management decision making, you need to know a few things about management decisions. You need to understand the different levels of management decisions, the characteristics of management decisions, and the information needs for management decisions.

Levels of Management Decisions

Management decisions are made at several levels in an organization. Figure 11.1 shows the hierarchy of management decisions. Starting at the bottom, *operational decisions* are day-to-day decisions needed in the operation of the organization. These decisions affect the organization for a short period of time such as several days or weeks. For example, in an athletic shoe store, an operational decision is whether to order more running shoes today. This decision affects the business for the next few weeks. Operational decisions are made by lower-level managers.

At the next level of decisions are *tactical decisions*, which are those that involve implementing policies of the organization. They affect the organization for a longer period of time than operational decisions, usually for several months or years, and are made by middle-level managers. For example, deciding whether to sell running shoes next winter is a tactical decision; it has an effect on the organization for a long period of time.

At the highest level of decisions are *strategic decisions*, which are made by top-level managers. These decisions involve setting organization policies, goals, and long-term plans, and they affect the organization for many years. For example, a strategic decision for an athletic shoe store is whether the store should stop selling athletic shoes and start selling some other product. This decision has a long-term effect on the business.

Characteristics of Management Decisions

Management decisions at different levels have different characteristics, as summarized in Fig. 11.2. The first characteristic, already described, is the time horizon affected by the decision. As shown in Fig. 11.2a, operational decisions affect the business for the short term, tactical decisions affect the business for the intermediate term, and strategic decisions affect the business for the long term.

FIGURE 11.1

The hierarchy of management decisions

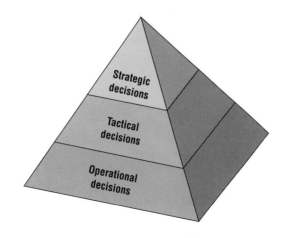

FIGURE 11.2

**Characteristics of
management
decisions**

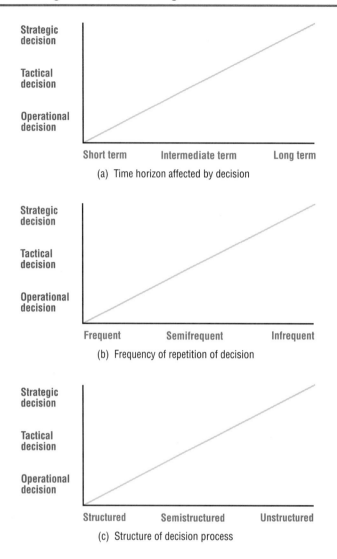

(a) Time horizon affected by decision

(b) Frequency of repetition of decision

(c) Structure of decision process

A second characteristic of management decisions, shown in Fig. 11.2b, is the frequency of repeating the same type of decision. Operational decisions are made frequently. For example, deciding whether to order more running shoes is made every day or every week. Tactical decisions are made less frequently. Thus, deciding whether to sell running shoes next winter is only made once a year. Strategic decisions are made very infrequently. Deciding what business to be in may only be made every 10 or 20 years.

A final characteristic of management decisions, shown in Fig. 11.2c, is the degree of structure in the decision process. By this we mean the degree with which someone can specify a procedure or formula to help make the decision. Operational decisions tend to be very structured. For example, deciding whether to order more stock is a well-structured decision; there are mathematical formulas to help make such a decision. Tactical decisions are semistructured. Thus, the procedure for deciding what to stock next winter is not so well formulated, although there are methods, such as statistical methods, to help in the decision making. Finally, strategic decisions are unstructured. For example, there are few good procedures for deciding what business to be in.

Information Needs for Management Decisions

As you know, information helps reduce uncertainty about the outcome of a decision. The information needs are different, however, for different levels of decision making. Figure 11.3 summarizes two characteristics of information needed for management decision making. The first characteristic is the source of information, which means where the information comes from. As shown in Fig. 11.3a, most information for operational decisions comes from inside the organization, whereas most information for strategic decisions comes from outside the organization. Information for tactical decisions comes from both inside and outside the organization. Thus, to decide whether to order more running shoes today (an operational decision), a manager needs to know the current quantity on hand, which comes from inside the business. To decide whether to sell running shoes next winter (a tactical decision), the manager needs to know how the business's running shoes are selling, which comes from inside the business, and consumer interest in running shoes, which comes from outside the business. Finally, to decide whether to stop selling shoes altogether (a strategic decision), the manager needs to know general trends in shoe sales compared to sales of other products, which is information that comes from outside the business.

The second characteristic of information needed for management decision making, shown in Fig. 11.3b, is the degree of detail or summarization required in the information. Operational decisions require detailed information, tactical decisions

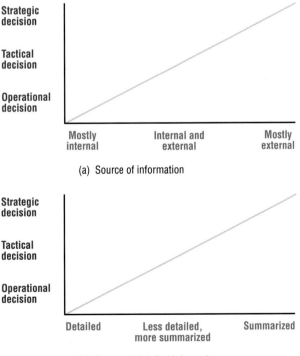

FIGURE 11.3

Characteristics of information for management decisions

(a) Source of information

(b) Degree of detail of information

require less detailed and more summarized information, and strategic decisions need summarized information. Information is detailed if it pertains to individual entities, such as items in inventory, or events, such as sales. Information is summarized if it presents totals or other figures derived from groups of entities or events. For example, to make the operational decision of whether to order running shoes today, a manager needs to know how many pairs of running shoes were sold yesterday, which is very detailed information. To make the tactical decision to stop selling running shoes, the manager may need to know the total sales of running shoes for each month of the past two years, which is less detailed and more summarized information than daily sales. Finally, to make the strategic decision of whether to stop selling shoes altogether, the manager may need to know the total sales of all shoes for each of the past five years, which is even more summarized information.

Information Systems for Management Support

With this background on management decision characteristics and information needs, you can understand how information systems support management. Information systems provide information to help managers make decisions at each of the three levels of decision making. The information is derived from a number of internal and external sources and presented at different levels of detail or summarization. The information helps the manager make decisions but does not make the decision for the manager.

Information systems support management in all the functions of a business and at all levels. (See Fig. 11.4.) Accounting information systems provide accounting information at operational, tactical, and strategic levels. Financial information systems help in financial decision making at all levels. Marketing information systems provide information to marketing managers at different levels. Manufacturing infor-

FIGURE 11.4

**Information
systems support
for management**

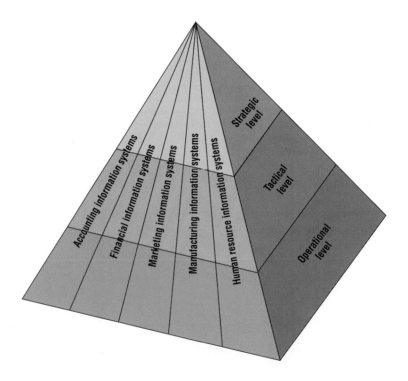

mation systems assist in decisions related to manufacturing and production at all levels. Finally, human resource information systems support personnel decision making at operational, tactical, and strategic levels.

Several general types of information systems for management support are found in organizations. The remainder of this chapter looks at four types. The first, *management information systems*, provide information to managers in the form of reports and query responses. The second, *decision support systems*, provide analysis of information to managers. The third, *executive support* systems, provide special support for the highest level of management. The last, *expert systems*, provide information to managers in the form of expert advice.

Management Information Systems

A **management information system** or **MIS** supports management decision making by providing information in the form of reports and responses to queries to managers at different levels of an organization. This type of system is sometimes called an *information reporting system* or a *management reporting system.* The term *management information system* is also used to refer to all types of information systems including transaction processing systems, although in this book we use it only for the type of system described in this section.

Management Information System Structure

Figure 11.5 shows the general structure of management information systems and their relationship to transaction processing systems. The users of the management information system are managers at each of the three levels of decision making. The users request information from the system and the information is returned in the form of reports and query responses. The MIS database contains data that is processed to

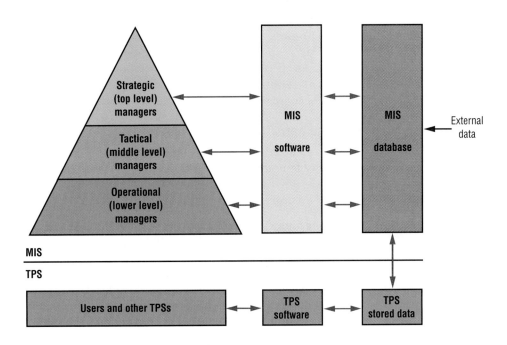

FIGURE 11.5

The structure of management information systems (MIS)

provide the information to the managers. The MIS software consists of application software to manipulate the data in the database. The software accepts requests for information from the managers, accesses data in the database, processes the data, and produces output. The software also updates the data in the database as needed.

The data in the database comes from both inside and outside the organization. Some internal data may be entered by managers, but most comes directly from the stored data of transaction processing systems, as shown in Fig. 11.5. For example, consider a business that has a transaction processing system for inventory control. Assume that this system keeps track of the quantity on hand for each item in inventory in an inventory master file. Each day the quantity data in this file is passed to the management information system database. Then, the software uses the data to help make the operational decision of whether to order more inventory that day. Data at lower levels in the MIS database is passed up through the database where it is summarized for higher-level decisions. Thus, daily inventory quantities used for operational decisions are summarized to get weekly and monthly figures for tactical decisions and summarized again to get yearly figures for strategic decisions.

Data from outside the organization comes from many sources. Periodicals, government publications, and research company reports often contain data that is useful in management decision making. This type of data may be entered into the MIS database by managers or their assistants. Useful data can also be found on the Internet. The data can be copied from the Internet to the MIS database. Another common source of data is *information utilities*, discussed in Chapter 6. Some information utilities, such as Dow Jones News/Retrieval, contain business-related data. The data can be accessed by a personal computer with the use of data communications and downloaded into the MIS database.

As an example of a management information system, consider one that supports inventory decisions at all three levels in an athletic shoe store. This system would contain a database of daily inventory data for each item the store sells. The inventory control system, a transaction processing system, would supply the data. At the operational level, MIS software would produce output with inventory figures for each item. These figures would help a decision maker determine whether to order more of certain items. The inventory data would be summarized by the MIS for the tactical-level decision makers. This data would be used to decide what types of items were overstocked so that appropriate actions, such as dropping them from the product line, could be taken. Finally, inventory data would be summarized further for strategic managers to help determine policies, such as whether another store should be opened.

Management Information System Functions

Management information systems perform the four main functions of an information system: the input function, the output function, the storage function, and the processing function. The functions together provide the capabilities of the system for the user.

Input Function.   Little data entry is required for a management information system. As noted earlier, the internal data for the system comes mainly from transaction processing systems. Those systems provide the data capture, data entry, and data validation steps necessary to get the data into the organization's information systems. External data is often transferred into the management information systems, using data communications techniques. For example, data may be downloaded from an information utility and stored directly in the MIS database.

Once data is in the management information system, a user may want to inquire about the data. A <u>query</u> or <u>inquiry</u> is a request for information from a system. Before a system can respond to a query, the query must be entered into the system. Often, the query is entered directly into a computer by the user. For example, consider the inventory control system for an athletic shoe store. A salesperson may need to inquire about the availability of stock for a particular item. The person enters the query by typing the number of the item for which the available inventory is needed. (See Fig. 11.6.)

Output Function.   The output function of a management information system produces reports and responses to queries. Reports can be *detail reports* or *summary reports*, two types of reports introduced in Chapter 10. Management information systems that support operational decision making require mainly detail reports. Those that support strategic decision making require mostly summary reports. Systems that impact tactical decision making need some detail reports and some summary reports.

Exception reports, described in Chapter 10, are also produced by management information systems. They are very common in management information systems because they provide information for an approach to management, called *management by exception*, which involves taking action only if the business is not functioning as expected. An exception report provides information about exceptions to some rule or standard. A decision maker who receives such a report can then take the necessary steps to correct the situation and return the business to normal functioning.

An inventory reorder report is an example of an exception report. (See Fig. 11.7.) This report gives a list of the items whose inventory on hand has fallen below an acceptable level. Based on this exception information, a manager can decide whether to order more inventory. Note that the manager may, after reviewing the report, decide not to order more stock because of other information the manager has. For example, the manager may know that a new product line is coming out (this is external information from the supplier) and therefore the business

Query entry

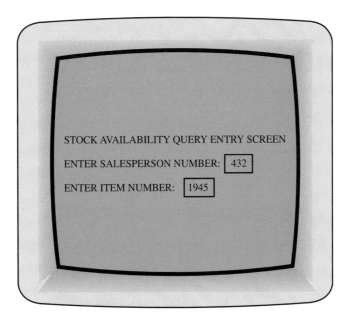

STOCK AVAILABILITY QUERY ENTRY SCREEN

ENTER SALESPERSON NUMBER: 432

ENTER ITEM NUMBER: 1945

FIGURE 11.7

An exception
report

INVENTORY REORDER REPORT

ITEM NUMBER	ITEM DESCRIPTION	QUANTITY ON HAND
1681	RUNNING SHOE	11
1945	TENNIS SHOE	8
3347	TRACK SHOE	3
4205	SOCKS	20
5172	SWEAT SHIRT	15

does not want to replenish stock of the old item. Thus, just because an exception has occurred does not necessarily mean that a certain action should be taken.

Reports are prepared by a management information system at different times. Some reports are prepared periodically and are called <u>scheduled reports</u>. For example, a scheduled report may be prepared every month or every week. Other reports are prepared only when requested. These are called <u>demand reports</u> because someone must request that the report be prepared. A final type of report is one that is prepared only once, for a specific purpose. These are called <u>ad hoc reports</u>.

In addition to report output, a management information system provides responses to queries. The response is an output from the system and is usually displayed on a screen, although it may be printed on paper. The response may be just a few lines, or it could be a lengthy report. For example, in the inventory control system, a salesperson could enter a query about the available stock for a particular item. After determining the stock on hand, the system would respond to the query by displaying the information on the screen. (See Fig. 11.8.)

FIGURE 11.8

Query response

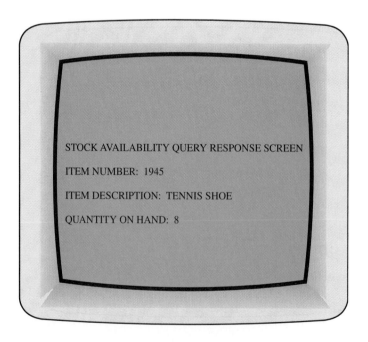

STOCK AVAILABILITY QUERY RESPONSE SCREEN

ITEM NUMBER: 1945

ITEM DESCRIPTION: TENNIS SHOE

QUANTITY ON HAND: 8

Storage Function. Data for a management information system may be stored in files, which are usually master files, but more often the MIS data is stored in a database. Storing data in a database makes it easier to access related data and to produce ad hoc reports and query responses.

The data for the MIS database comes from the transaction processing system and from external sources. This data is used to *create* and *update* the database. The database can then be *accessed* to provide information for the decision makers. The relationships between the data in the database can be used to join together related data to produce reports or responses to the queries. A database management system makes it easy to enter queries, view the responses, and produce ad hoc reports. Other types of reports can also be produced from data in the database.

Processing Function. Processing in a management information system normally involves simple computations. For example, a report may give the value of an item in inventory. This value is found by simply multiplying the quantity on hand by the price per item. Most computations in a management information system are not much more complex than this one.

The main computation that is performed by management information systems involves accumulating totals for reporting at different levels of decision making. Totals of groups of data may be computed for one level and totals of all data may be produced for a higher level. For example, Fig. 11.9a shows a report with group and subgroup totals and Fig. 11.9b shows a report with only main group totals. The latter report, which is more summarized and less detailed than the former report, would be used for higher level decision making.

FIGURE 11.9

Summary reports

**INVENTORY VALUE
BY PRODUCT LINE
9/30/XXXX**

PRODUCT LINE	TOTAL VALUE
Running shoes	$24,368.00
Tennis shoes	10,852.00
Sport shoes	8,147.50
Total shoes	43,367.50*
Running clothing	6,025.00
Tennis clothing	5,410.50
Misc clothing	820.25
Total clothing	12,255.75*
Sport bags	2,268.25
Other items	1,335.75
Total accessories	3,604.00*
TOTAL	$59,227.25**

(a) A report with group and subgroup totals

FIGURE 11.9

Summary reports
(continued)

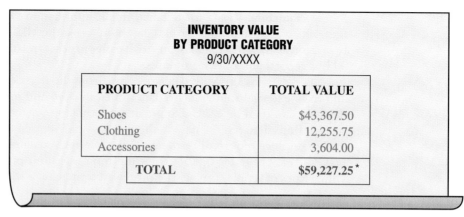

**INVENTORY VALUE
BY PRODUCT CATEGORY**
9/30/XXXX

PRODUCT CATEGORY	TOTAL VALUE
Shoes	$43,367.50
Clothing	12,255.75
Accessories	3,604.00
TOTAL	$59,227.25 *

(b) A report with group totals

Management Information System Software

Software for management information systems is often custom-written using business programming languages. (See Chapter 5.) Such software may use a database management system to provide access to the MIS database. Users may also use a *query language*, such as SQL (discussed in Chapter 7), to access the database for queries and ad hoc reports. Special software called a **report writer** may also be used to prepare reports from data in the database.

When client-server computing is used, the software that provides the report and query response output executes in each user's client computer and the database software executes in the server computer. The client computer software in this case may provide a graphical user interface for easy access to the database. (See Fig. 11.10.)

FIGURE 11.10

Graphical user
interface for client
computer
in a management
information
system

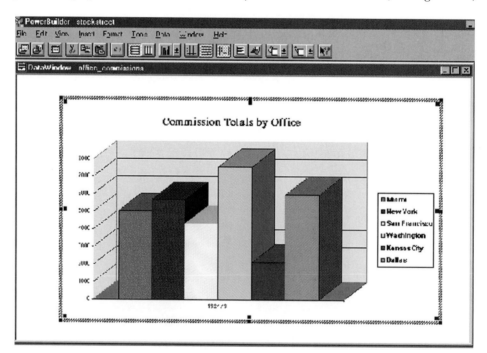

Queries and reports can easily be created in the graphical user interface on the client computer with data for the query response and report output being supplied by the database software on the server.

Decision Support Systems

A management information system helps managers make decisions by providing information from a database with little or no analysis. A decision support system or DSS, on the other hand, helps managers make decisions by analyzing data from a database and providing the results of the analysis to the manager. An MIS supports all three levels of management decision making with reports and query responses. A DSS, on the other hand, usually is best for decisions at the middle and top levels of management. As with an MIS, a DSS helps with making decisions but does not actually make decisions; only managers make decisions.

Management Decision Support

To understand decision support systems you need to know something about how data is analyzed to help in management decisions. A DSS includes several ways of analyzing data. Usually, the manager can select what form of analysis he or she wants. The system performs the calculations required for the analysis, and displays or prints the results.

One form of analysis is *statistical calculations*. In these calculations, data is manipulated to determine characteristics of the data or to draw conclusions from the data. For example, assume that a manager in an athletic clothing store has data about the sales of different types of shoes for each of the last five years. He or she can calculate the average yearly sales for each type, which is one way of characterizing this data. The manager can also use this data to forecast sales in future years. Both of these are types of statistical calculations.

Another form of analysis is *mathematical modeling*. A *model* is a representation of reality. For example, a model airplane is a representation of a real airplane. Models used for decision making are not physical things like airplanes, but sets of mathematical equations. A model can be used to help predict what will happen with different decisions. In effect, the model *simulates*, using mathematical equations, the real world.

An example of a model is one used to simulate inventory flow so that a manager can try different inventory reordering decisions. The following equation is a simple inventory model that might be used to simulate the inventory of running shoes in an athletic shoe store:

Inventory today = Inventory yesterday - 5

This model says, in equation form, that each day the store sells five pairs of running shoes. The manager can also write an equation that calculates the cost of keeping items in inventory. With these equations a manager can compare the cost of ordering a small amount of inventory frequently with the cost of ordering a large amount of inventory less frequently. By trying different strategies, a manager can use the model to determine the least expensive inventory reordering policy.

Decision Support System at Royal Caribbean Cruises

An ocean of archival data is helping Royal Caribbean Cruises Ltd. chart a profitable course to the future.

The Miami-based cruise line uses a decision-support application that culls data gathered over three years to help it make decisions on inventory management, ship deployment, and revenue maximization.

With 11 luxury liners (and two more being built), 1.2 million customers annually, and a planned 675 voyages this year, Royal Caribbean is one of the country's largest cruise lines. In 1996, the company made $150 million in profits on revenue of $1.3 billion.

Much of the company's ability to maintain its profitability depends on how quickly it can spot and analyze trends in fares, capacity, and demand, among other things, said Charles Eubanks, a senior technologist at the company.

"We know for a fact that systematic data analysis can turn into several million dollars of revenue gained, lost, or preserved," Eubanks said.

In the past, executives and sales analysts at the company manually sifted through archived data about itineraries, fares, passenger information, and ship capacity.

By comparing current data with past information, executives decided cruise fares, when and how to promote certain voyages, and whether there was a need to redeploy ships in the fleet.

"A voyage could have revenue opportunity because there is a lot of demand for it [compared to previous years], and we could raise the price. Or it could be the other way, and we would need to do something to stimulate demand," said Bill Martin, manager of revenue management systems at Royal Caribbean.

But the time and effort taken to get to the information was often onerous. "There literally would be a stack of reports about 10 inches high that analysts would

have to wade through" before having enough information to analyze a situation, Martin said.

Royal Caribbean uses a new Revenue Decision Support System to speed up the analysis.

A 100 G byte relational database management system handles the decision-support system and supports analytical models, including a custom on-line analytical processing application.

The system feeds on historical data from multiple servers and looks for trends based on a comparison of past and current data. It then generates forecasts, what-if scenarios, and graphical visualization for executives to act upon.

By looking at just one screen of information, analysts can immediately figure out the revenue status of upcoming voyages and what action needs to be taken. "Red [on the screen] denotes a hot revenue opportunity, yellow a warm opportunity, and blue a cold one," Martin said.

The new applications "give us a lot more information a lot quicker and in a lot more ways than before," he said.

QUESTIONS

1. What types of decisions does the Revenue Decision Support System support at Royal Caribbean?
2. What do the analytical models do in the Revenue Decision Support System?
3. What benefit does Royal Caribbean gain from the Revenue Decision Support System?

WEB SITE
Royal Caribbean Cruises: www.rccl.com

Source: Jaikumar Vijayan, "Royal Caribbean cruises for profit in sea of data," *Computerworld*, May 26, 1997, pp. 63, 64.

Decision Support System Structure

Figure 11.11 shows the general structure of decision support systems. The users of the DSS are managers, usually at the tactical and strategic levels in the organization. The user requests analysis of data from the system and the results of the analysis are displayed on the user's screen or printed in a report. The DSS database contains data that is analyzed to produce the output. The DSS model base (analogous to a database) contains the mathematical models and statistical calculation routines that are used to analyze data from the database.

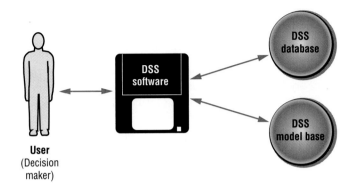

FIGURE 11.11

The structure of decision support systems (DSS)

User
(Decision maker)

The DSS software provides capabilities for the user to access data in the database and to use models from the model base to analyze the data. The software also displays the results of the analysis on the screen or prints it on paper. Often, the output from a DSS is given in a graphic form, although other forms of output are used. Using the software, the user can try different models and data to see what happens.

The data for the DSS database comes from several sources. The user may enter data into the database, or data may be taken from the management information system database or the transaction processing system stored data. In addition, the results of a previous analysis by the DSS may be stored in the database for use in later analysis. External sources, such as information utilities, may also supply data for the DSS database.

An example of a decision support system is one that helps a manager in an athletic shoe store decide what types of shoes to advertise. The system would use data from a database containing past sales of different types of shoes. The sales data would be analyzed by statistical calculation routines to project sales trends. Then, a mathematical model would be used to simulate the effect of advertising on sales. The manager would try different advertising strategies until he or she found the one that was most likely to increase sales.

Decision support systems are best used for situations in which decisions are semistructured or unstructured. The nature of these decisions often involves trying different approaches, asking "what if" questions, finding input values that produce a specific output (a process called *goal seeking*), and checking the result to see how it might change if the input were slightly different (a process called *sensitivity analysis*.) The types of decisions that fit this situation are not made very frequently and often affect the business for some time. All these characteristics point to the use of decision support systems at the tactical and strategic decision-making levels.

Decision Support System Functions

The capabilities of a decision support system are provided by the four information system functions performed by the system.

Input Function.   User input to a decision support system is mainly in the form of requests for analysis of data. The user may enter some input data but, as noted earlier, most of the data used in the DSS comes from the databases and files of other systems. The user may also enter instructions to tell the software to use certain models from the model base or to combine models for different forms of analysis. The main input, however, is in the form of specifying what type of analysis is to be done with what data. For example, the user may request that a particular statistical routine be used to analyze a set of data from the database or that a certain model be used to simulate a decision.

Output Function.   The output function of a decision support system produces the results of analysis on screens and in printed reports. Screens usually display the output in a table or a graphical form. Graphs may be printed on paper or displayed on a large screen using presentation graphics software for group discussion. Reports typically are summary or exception reports. Because of the level of decision making supported by a DSS, detail reports are rarely produced. Reports are usually created on demand or on an ad hoc basis; scheduled reports are not as common in a DSS.

Storage Function.   Data in a decision support system is usually stored in a database. The database may be managed by the decision support system software or by separate database management software. The software allows the database to be created and updated using input data from various sources, both internal and external to the business. The software also allows the data to be accessed for analysis by a model.

The storage function of a DSS also provides capabilities for managing the model base. Software, sometimes called *model base management software*, allows models to be created and modified. This software also lets the user combine models to form more complex models. Finally, with this software the user can use models to analyze data retrieved from the database.

Processing Function.   Processing in a decision support system can be very complex. Some statistical analysis routines require sophisticated computations. Models in decision support systems often involve complex calculations. When several models or statistical procedures are combined, the processing is even more involved. Such processing can be time consuming, and decision support systems can take several minutes or longer to compute the results.

Decision Support System Software

A decision support system usually is developed using general software that is adapted for a specific decision. An example of simple decision support system software is spreadsheet software. This type of software usually includes limited data management capabilities, built-in statistical calculation routines, and simple mathematical models. A user can use the software to access data, do calculations, use and develop models, and display the results in either a table or a graph. The capabilities of spreadsheet software are limited; nevertheless, this type of software can be used to create a DSS for some types of decision problems.

More sophisticated decision support system software is available for personal computers, multiple-user computers, and networks. Some of this DSS software is like spreadsheet software but with more complete database and modeling capabilities. An example is IFPS (Interactive Financial Planning System). Other DSS software is statistical calculation software with limited database capabilities. An example is a statistical package called SPSS. Still other software is modeling software, such as GPSS (General Purpose Simulation Software), which is used to simulate decision situations. Using the appropriate DSS software, a decision support system can be created to help managers make many types of decisions. Figure 11.12 shows the screen of a decision support system.

A decision support system can also be used to analyze the data in a *data warehouse.* Recall from Chapter 7 that a data warehouse is a collection of data drawn from

FIGURE 11.12

Decision support system software

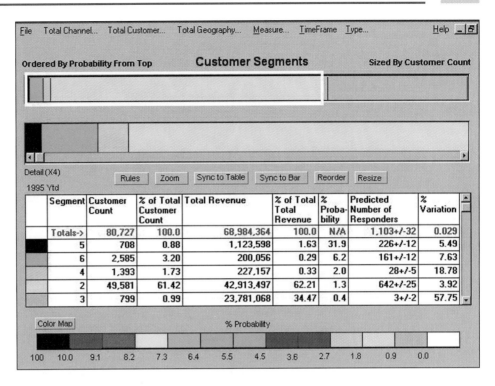

other databases used in a business. Analysis of data in a data warehouse often requires searching for patterns in the data, a process called data mining. For example, a data warehouse of customer purchasing data can be mined to find buying patterns, such as which products are more likely to be purchased on which days. The result of mining of data in a data warehouse can support decision making, such as deciding when certain products should be put on sale or when special advertising should be done.

Group Decision Support Systems

Decision support systems can be used for individual decision making or for group decision making. A group decision support system or GDSS is a system designed to support group decision making. A GDSS is an example of a workgroup information system, discussed in Chapter 9.

A group decision support system typically is used in a network. The GDSS provides information and analysis of data to users at personal computers connected to the network. The users can then collaborate through the network to reach a group decision. Many of the workgroup applications discussed in Chapter 9, such as information sharing and electronic meeting support, are used in group decision support systems.

Geographic Information Systems

A geographic information system or GIS is an information system that provides information for decision making based on geographic location. Certain information depends on where it originates. For example, demographic data, such as population and income levels, is based on geographic location. Similarly, sales data can be gathered by the geographic locations where the sales were made.

A geographic information system includes a database in which all data is organized by geographic location. Thus, a database may contain average household

FIGURE 11.13

A geographic
information
system or GIS

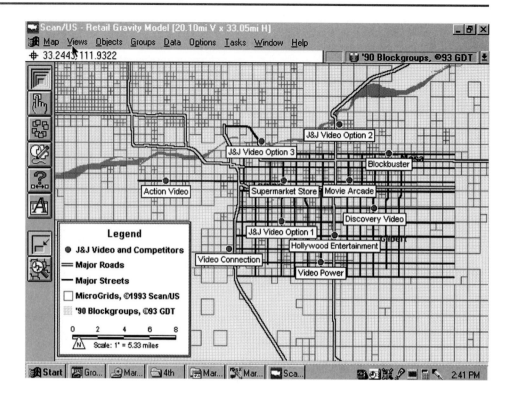

income levels, average age, product sales figures, and similar data organized by location. Almost any type of data can be stored in such a database. You can think of the
data as stored in layers tied together only be geographic location. (See Fig. 11.13.)

Using the data in such a database, a geographic information system can provide
information to support decision making. For example, a database of demographic
and sales data can be used to look for demographic patterns that result in higher
sales. This information can be used to target areas for special advertising and
increased product availability.

Executive Support Systems

The top-level managers of a business have special information system needs that are
different from those of other managers. Although management information and
decision support systems can meet some of those needs, these systems are not commonly used by executives, but rather by managers and staff below the highest level.
An executive support system or ESS, on the other hand, is designed specifically for
the information needs of strategic managers. This type of system, which is also called
an executive information system or EIS, provides information and support that is
most appropriate and useful for top-level managers.

Executive Information Needs

As discussed earlier, managers at the strategic level generally need summarized and
not detailed information. Sometimes, however, a manager needs to focus on the
details of a particular aspect of the information. For example, a manager may notice

that the sales in a certain region have fallen off dramatically. Is the fall off the result of poor sales at a particular sales office or is it a general loss of sales in the region? To answer the question, the manager must get more detailed information through a process called <u>drilling down</u>. The manager starts with the region's sales and drills down to the sales in each sales office in the region trying to locate the source of the lost sales. (See Fig. 11.14). When the source is found (in Fig. 11.14, a problem appears at the Miami office), the manager can drill down even more to try to identify more detailed causes of the problem (in Fig. 11.14, the Miami office sold no shoes or clothing). Once the problem has been fully identified, the manager can concentrate his or her effort to try to correct the problem.

Managers at the highest level need external information as well as internal information. External information provides executives with an understanding of the environment within which the business functions. For example, managers need to know about general economic trends to make decisions about business expansion in the future. Managers need to know about consumer likes and dislikes to decide which products to produce or which services to provide. Managers need to know about financial markets to make decisions about where to borrow or invest money. All this information is external to the organization.

Executives often work in an unstructured way, not knowing in advance what information they will need or what computer functions they will use. They need extremely flexible systems that they can easily adapt to their own requirements. They need to be able to access summarized internal and external information on the spur of the moment and to drill down to more detailed information as needed. All these functions are necessary to support the information needs of top executives.

FIGURE 11.14

Drilling down for detailed information

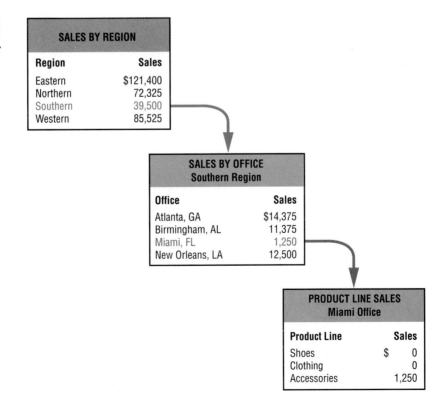

Bookmark

Geographic Information System for the City of Scottsdale, Arizona

One might expect a city where bears and mountain goats roam free, trash collectors carry business cards, and citizens voted 2-1 to increase taxes, to have an unusual information systems culture.

"We have a history of saying, 'We don't have to do it the way the other guy does it,'" said Scottsdale City Manager Richard A. Bowers. "We think the private sector has a lot to learn from us."

That pioneering attitude is paying off. Scottsdale has married a homegrown geographic information system (GIS), one of the most advanced anywhere, to a fiber-optic network. The GIS is lowering costs, improving service to the public, and improving management decision making, according to city workers from the mayor to clerks to police officers.

Recently, the city used its GIS to prove that federal census figures undercounted Scottsdale's population by some 9,000 people. A subsequent correction will result in a $9 million windfall—twice the amount invested in the GIS—in added federal payments over the next five years, according to Scottsdale Mayor Sam Kathryn Campana.

Most city governments, if they have a GIS at all, use it for niche applications such as map making. But Scottsdale has positioned its GIS—really a suite of "map-enabled business applications"—at the center of its IS infrastructure. Virtually everything the city does—including zoning, code enforcement, emergency response, work management, water management, flood control, building permits, and inspections—is supported by the GIS.

"Geographical information is the common denominator," said Greg E. Larson, the city's chief information officer. GIS data supports activities in each of the city's three core areas: resource management, land use, and public safety. And the GIS is the foundation of the city's data warehousing and executive information system architectures, Larson said.

Karen Hatton, a secretary who helps process 15,000 code enforcement complaints per year, said the GIS and related systems have reduced the time required to research and write up a complaint by 60% to 80%.

Previously, she had to go through several paper files just to find the name and address of a property's owner, then fill out a paper complaint sheet and route that to an inspector. That entire process now takes a few keystrokes, she said.

The GIS is used extensively to evaluate the impacts of alternate development strategies in this fast-growing city in the Sonoran Desert. "Of all our systems, the biggest long-term payoff is from our GIS because the city is only one-third built," Bowers said.

The mayor, who taps in to the GIS from a terminal in her office, said City Council members use the GIS at meetings to better understand issues that are before it, including citizen disputes. "It's magic," Campana said. "All I can see is bigger and better applications over time."

The citizens of Scottsdale are politically conservative yet environmentally conscious, Larson said. "The GIS helps balance economic development and environmentalism. It's possible to have that win-win if you have the data to support it," he said.

QUESTIONS

1. What information can be accessed using the geographic information system for the city of Scottsdale?
2. How is the geographic information system used for executive support?

WEB SITE
City of Scottsdale, Arizona: www.ci.scottsdale.az.us

Source: Gary H. Anthes, "City blazes own IS trail," *Computerworld*, September 16, 1996, pp. 81, 85.

Executive Support System Structure

The capabilities of executive support systems vary. Some of the capabilities are similar to those found in management information systems and some are similar to those found in decision support systems. Individual and workgroup applications may also be found in executive support systems. An ESS may include any of the following capabilities:

- On-line access to reports.
- The ability to query the management information system database for information not usually received in reports.

- The ability to access external databases (e.g., information utilities).
- The ability to analyze and summarize data from reports and queries, and to view the results of the analysis graphically.
- The ability to drill down to detailed information.
- Electronic mail to communicate with employees.
- Electronic appointment calendar.
- Basic word processing capabilities for writing notes, memos, and other simple communications.

Figure 11.15 shows the general structure of executive support systems. The users of an ESS are top level, strategic managers. The user uses the ESS software to access a variety of databases, which may include the management information system database (for reports and queries), external databases, special databases created just for the ESS, personal databases created by the user, and electronic mailboxes. The ESS software provides capabilities for analyzing and summarizing data as well as other capabilities listed previously. The user can select the functions to be performed based on his or her needs.

An example of an executive support system is one that helps the owner of an athletic shoe store make top-level decisions. Such a system may provide summarized sales information for different categories of products sold by the store. The system would allow the owner to drill down to detailed sales figures in each category. The system would also provide access to other information stored in various internal databases as well as to external databases containing general economic and consumer trend information. The system would provide electronic mail for

FIGURE 11.15

The structure of executive support systems (ESS)

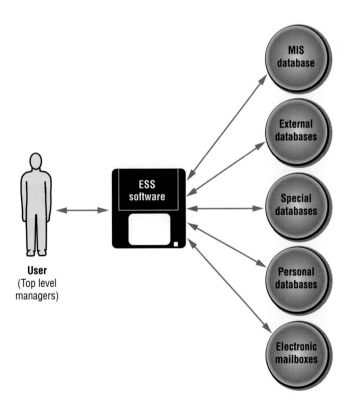

communication with employees and an electronic calendar for keeping track of the owner's appointments.

Executive Support System Functions

An executive support system provides its capabilities through the four information system functions.

Input Function.   Executives usually do not enter input data into an ESS, although they may key in electronic mail, notes and memos, and appointment information. Most of the input to an ESS is in the form of selecting functions for the software to perform. The user can select the reports he or she wishes to see, the data to retrieve from a database, the analysis to perform on the data, and so on. Executive support systems are very flexible so as to allow the executive to select exactly the information needed.

Output Function.   Most of the output produced by an ESS is displayed on a screen, although the user may select to have some output printed on paper. Data usually is displayed in a table or presented in a graphical form. Reports are not scheduled but produced on demand or on an ad hoc basis.

Storage Function.   The principle storage function provided by an ESS is access to various databases. The ESS software or separate database management software provides the database access capabilities. Executives do not normally create or update databases, but they do need to access data in a variety of ways. The ability to drill down to more detailed information in the database is an important storage function provided by the ESS.

FIGURE 11.16

Executive support system software

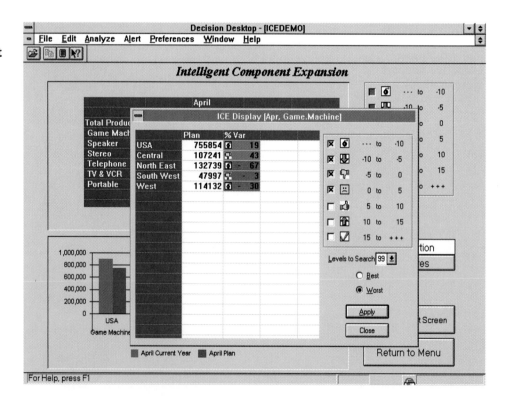

Processing Function. Any processing functions provided by management information and decision support systems may be found in an ESS. Simple total calculations, sophisticated statistical analysis, and complex model calculations may be used in an ESS. The processing functions depend on the capabilities provided by the ESS.

Executive Support System Software

An executive support system is developed using special software that is customized for the specific executive information needs. Some examples of ESS software are Comshare's Commander Decision and Pilot Software's Command Center. Figure 11.16 shows the screen of an executive support system.

Expert Systems

Management information, decision support, and executive support systems help managers make decisions by providing and analyzing information. They do not, however, advise the decision maker on what to do. An expert system or ES, on the other hand, is a type of information system that gives expert advice to the decision maker. An expert system mimics the way a human expert would analyze a situation and then recommends a course of action. The system accomplishes this by incorporating human expert knowledge and by using this knowledge to analyze specific problems. An early example of an expert system is Mycin, which was developed at Stanford University in the 1970s. It was used by doctors to help diagnose certain diseases and to recommend treatment. A recent example is an expert system developed by American Express to decide whether to issue a credit card to a customer.

Expert systems use techniques from the field of artificial intelligence or AI. The goal of artificial intelligence is to mimic human intelligence by using a computer. For example, artificial intelligence programs have been developed to play complex games of strategy such as chess. Expert systems are just one application of artificial intelligence.

Expert Advice

Business managers rely on advice from experts in many situations. Whenever a technical question arises, managers call on engineers or scientists for expert advice. Many financial decisions require the help of an expert in a particular area of finance. The health-care field uses medical experts; the computer field relies on computer experts.

People are experts in a particular area for many reasons. Some are experts because of formal education or specialized training. Others develop expertise through job or other practical experience. Still others become experts by self study. In all cases, the individual can demonstrate his or her expertise in a tangible way.

Expert advice is used in all levels of a business, but is most commonly required for structured problems at the operational and tactical levels. Problems in research and development, engineering, production, finance, computer systems, accounting, and other areas use expert advice. There is practically no area of a business in which experts and expert advice are not used.

Expert System Structure

Figure 11.17 shows the general structure of expert systems. The users are decision makers who are not experts in the types of problems that the expert system is designed to solve. A user uses the system interactively by requesting advice from the expert system and answering questions asked by the system. The expert system responds to the user's request with advice and recommendations.

The knowledge base is like a database of expert knowledge. Different types of expert systems use different techniques for storing knowledge. One technique is to use rules. A rule is an *if-then* structure: *If* something is true, *then* something else is true. For example, Fig. 11.18 shows five rules that might be used in a simple expert system for deciding whether to hire an applicant for a job. All the rules form the knowledge base for the expert system.

The expert system software consists of a user interface and an inference engine. The user interface receives input from the user and displays output. The inference engine analyzes rules in the knowledge base to draw conclusions.

An example of an expert system is one that evaluates a job applicant with the knowledge base given in Fig. 11.18. Figure 11.19 shows how the interaction with the user of this system might appear on the screen. The user enters the applicant's name, education, and work experience. Then, the inference engine uses the knowledge base to evaluate this data. The inference engine does the evaluation by deciding which rules apply and by linking the rules together to draw a conclusion. In this example, the inference engine determines that John Doe has the required education because of Rule 2 and the required experience because of Rule 5. Therefore, because of Rule 1, he should be hired. This recommendation is displayed on the screen.

Expert System Functions

Expert system capabilities are provided by the four information system functions.

Input Function. User input to an expert system is in the form of basic information needed by the system to provide the expert advice. In the example in Fig. 11.19, the input is the applicants name, education, and work experience. Normally, only a small amount of input is required from the user.

Output Function. The output from an expert system is the advice of the system. Thus, in the example in Fig. 11.19, the output is the recommendation about whether the applicant should be hired. Sometimes, several options are given by the system with an indication of the likelihood that each option is best. For example, a financial investment expert system may indicate that one investment has a 60 percent chance of making a particular profit and another investment has a 70 percent chance of making a lesser profit.

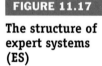

The structure of expert systems (ES)

User

FIGURE 11.18

**Rules in a
knowledge base**

Rule 1: *If* applicant has required education
and applicant has required experience
then hire applicant

Rule 2: *If* applicant has BA in business
then applicant has required education

Rule 3: *If* applicant has BA in non-business field
and applicant has an MBA
then applicant has required education

Rule 4: *If* applicant has 2 or more years experience in sales position
then applicant has required experience

Rule 5: *If* applicant has 4 or more years experience in any position
then applicant has required experience

Storage Function.   The storage function of an expert system involves managing the knowledge base. Although the example in Fig. 11.18 only has five rules, most expert systems have hundreds or even thousands of rules. Storing, updating, and accessing the rules are the main activities of the storage function of an expert system.

Processing Function.   The processing function of an expert system can be very complex. Determining which rules apply and how they interact require very sophisticated processing. This is the role of the inference engine in the expert system. Different techniques are used, depending on the inference engine. When there are many rules, the evaluation of the rules can be time consuming.

FIGURE 11.19

Expert system use

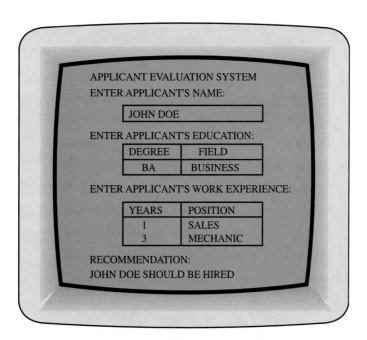

APPLICANT EVALUATION SYSTEM
ENTER APPLICANT'S NAME:

JOHN DOE

ENTER APPLICANT'S EDUCATION:

DEGREE	FIELD
BA	BUSINESS

ENTER APPLICANT'S WORK EXPERIENCE:

YEARS	POSITION
1	SALES
3	MECHANIC

RECOMMENDATION:
JOHN DOE SHOULD BE HIRED

Expert System Software

Expert systems are much more complex than the example shown in Figs. 11.18 and 11.19. Their knowledge base may contain hundreds or thousands of rules, and the inference engine may be very complex. Development of such systems is difficult. Specialists called *knowledge engineers* usually do the development. The knowledge engineer must first contact experts in the problem that the system is trying to solve, and determine what "rules" the experts use. For example, the rules in a personnel expert system would be determined by asking experienced personnel managers in the business how they make hiring decisions. This process can be extremely time consuming.

After the rules have been determined, the knowledge engineer must construct the knowledge base and the inference engine to evaluate the rules. One way of doing this is to prepare a program in a programming language designed for artificial intelligence. Examples of such languages are LISP and PROLOG. Often, however, an existing program is used that provides the skeleton of an expert system. This type of program, called an *expert system shell*, contains an inference engine and a user interface. (See Fig. 11.20.) The knowledge engineer has to enter the rules in the knowledge base into the program to form a complete expert system. Expert system shells are available for all types of computers, including personal computers. Examples of expert system shells are ReSolver,™ VP-Expert, and Guru.

Other Artificial Intelligence Applications

Expert systems are only one application of artificial intelligence in business. Another application is neural networks. A neural network is a program that mimics the way humans learn and think by creating a model of the human brain. The brain is made

FIGURE 11.20

An expert system shell. This is MultiLogic's ReSolver.™

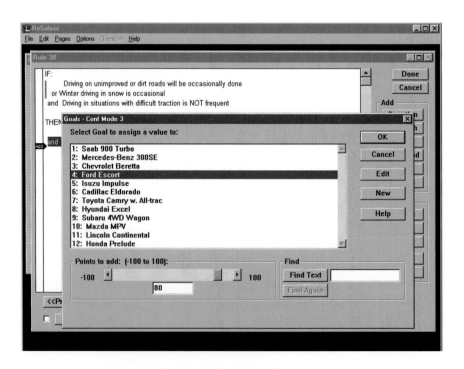

up of cells, called neurons, that are interconnected in complex patterns. (There are about 100 billion neurons in the brain.) A neuron receives signals from other neurons and sends signals to certain other neurons based on those inputs.

A neural network functions in a similar way. It consists of software elements that act like neurons. The elements are interconnected in various patterns. Each neural network neuron receives inputs from other neurons and sends outputs to certain neurons.

A neural network can learn from experience. By entering inputs into the network and having the network compare its outputs with known outputs, the network can modify itself over time to respond correctly. Once the neural network has learned how to respond to different inputs, it can be used for situations where the outputs are not known. Uses of neural networks in business include detecting credit card fraud, making financial forecasts, and identifying trends in the stock market.

Another use of artificial intelligence is for intelligent agents. An intelligent agent is a program that acts on behalf of an individual, based on preferences that are given to the agent. For example, an intelligent agent can be used to identify useful information on the Internet. The user can give the intelligent agent his or her preferences for the types of information the user desires. Then the agent can locate that information on the Internet and return it to the user's computer.

Some intelligent agents use techniques from artificial intelligence to learn the user's preferences. For example, an intelligent agent can keep track of the types of information that a user requests from the Internet. Then the agent can adjust its behavior based on what it has learned. Examples of intelligent agents include agents that find the best prices for products offered for sale on the Internet, ones that put together custom on-line editions of newspapers, and agents that watch for Internet postings for specific types of employment opportunities.

Expert systems, neural networks, and intelligent agents are just three applications of artificial intelligence. A number of other applications are found in business and new uses of artificial intelligence are likely to appear in the future.

Chapter Summary

☐ Information systems improve management decision-making effectiveness by providing decision makers with information related to the decisions for which they are responsible. The information helps reduce the uncertainty about what will happen after the decision is made. Although it is not possible to eliminate all uncertainty, with good information uncertainty can be reduced and the outcome from the decision is more likely to be satisfactory. (p. 326)

☐ A manager needs detailed information, mainly from inside the organization, to make operational decisions related to the day-to-day running of the organization. To make tactical decisions that involve implementing policies of the organization, a manager needs less detailed, more summarized information from both inside and outside the organization. To make strategic decisions that involve setting organizational policies, goals, and long-term plans, a manager needs summarized information, much of which comes from outside the organization. (pp. 327–331)

☐ A **management information system** or **MIS** provides information in the form of reports and query responses to meet managers' needs at different levels of an organization. An MIS maintains a database of internal and external data and processes the data to produce the information at the required level of detail. Transaction processing system stored data provides most of the internal data for the MIS databases. (pp. 331–337)

☐ A **decision support system** or **DSS** helps managers make decisions by analyzing data from a database and providing the results of the analysis to the manager. The data is analyzed using statistical calculations and mathematical models. A DSS consists of a database, a **model base**, and software that lets the user access data in the database and use models from the model base to analyze the data. (pp. 337–342)

☐ An **executive support system** or **ESS** provides top-level managers with support for the functions they perform. This support includes on-line access to reports, the management information system database, and external databases; the ability to analyze and summarize data and view the results graphically; the ability to **drill down** to detailed information; and personal and workgroup applications such as electronic mail, electronic appointment calendar, and basic word processing. (pp. 342–347)

☐ An **expert system** or **ES** provides expert advice by storing human expert knowledge in a **knowledge base** and then using the knowledge to draw conclusions about specific problems. The knowledge is stored as **rules**, which are **if-then** structures. The expert system software consists of a user interface and an **inference engine** which analyzes the rules in the knowledge base to draw conclusions. (pp. 347–350)

Key Terms

Ad Hoc Report (p. 334)
Artificial Intelligence (AI) (p. 347)
Data Mining (p. 341)
Decision Support System (DSS) (p. 337)
Demand Report (p. 334)
Drilling Down (p. 343)
Executive Information System (EIS) (p. 342)

Executive Support System (ESS) (p. 342)
Expert System (ES) (p. 347)
Geographic Information System (GIS) (p. 341)
Group Decision Support System (GDSS) (p. 341)
Inference Engine (p. 348)
Intelligent Agent (p. 351)

Knowledge Base (p. 348)
Management Information System (MIS) (p. 331)
Model Base (p. 338)
Neural Network (p. 350)
Query (Inquiry) (p. 333)
Report Writer (p. 336)
Rule (p. 348)
Scheduled Report (p. 334)

Assignment Material

Review Questions

Fill-in Questions

1. Information used in operational decisions comes mostly from _____ the organization, whereas information for strategic decisions comes mostly from _____ the organization.

2. Detailed information is required for _____ decision making; summarized information is needed for _____ decision making.

3. Most internal data for a management information system comes from _____.

4. Periodic reports produced by an information system are called _____ reports. Reports produced on request are called _____ reports. Reports produced only once for a specific purpose are called _____ reports.

5. A(n) _____ is a collection of mathematical models and statistical routines stored in a computer.

6. Searching for patterns in a data warehouse is called _____.

7. A(n) _____ is a system used to support decision making among members of a workgroup.

8. A(n) _____ is an information system that provides information for decision making based on geographic location.

9. An information system that supports the highest level of managers of an organization is called a(n) _____.

10. The process of finding detailed information that is used to produce summary information is called _____.

11. The use of a computer to mimic human intelligence is called _____.

12. A(n) _____ is a collection of expert knowledge stored in a computer.

13. A(n) _____ is an *if-then* structure that is used in a knowledge base.

14. A program that mimics the way humans learn and think by creating a model of the human brain is called a(n) _____.

Short-answer Questions

1. Why is information important in decision making?
2. How can information systems improve management decision-making effectiveness?
3. Describe the levels of management decisions in an organization.
4. What is meant by the degree of structure of a decision and how does it apply to decisions at different levels of an organization?
5. How does a management information system meet the information needs of managers in an organization?
6. Where does the data in the database of a management information system come from?
7. What is a decision support system?
8. What ways of analyzing data may be included in a decision support system?
9. In what decision-making situations are decision support systems most appropriate?
10. How is the data in the database of a geographic information system organized?
11. What types of databases are used in an executive support system?
12. What is an expert system?
13. Consider an expert system with the knowledge base shown in Fig. 11.18. If Mary Roe is a job applicant with a BA in psychology, an MBA, and three years of experience as a teacher, what would the expert system recommend?
14. What is an intelligent agent?

Discussion Questions

1. What types of management information systems would be found at a college or university?
2. What limitations are there in spreadsheet software that make it difficult to create sophisticated decision support systems?
3. As more computer- and information systems-literate employees move into executive positions, will executive support systems be needed? Why or why not?
4. For an international business, management decision-making styles may be different in different parts of the world. As just one example, in some countries the emphasis is on individual decision making and in others it is on group decision making. What impact would decision-making styles have on the design of information systems that support decision making in international businesses?
5. Will computers ever be able to think like humans do? Why or why not?
6. Assume that you are an expert in some area and the business you work for has decided to create an expert system based on your knowledge. You have been asked to help in creating the expert system, but when it is finished, you may no longer be needed by the business. What ethical problems does this create for you?

Problem-solving Projects

1. Investigate the management of an organization or business to which you have access. Who are the managers of that organization? At what levels of the organization do they make decisions? What types of decisions do they make? What information do they need to make their decisions? Using word processing software, write a summary of your findings.
2. Investigate an information system that supports management decision making in an organization or business to which you have access. (This can be the same organization or business you investigated in Project 1.) Find out as much as you can about the system. Is it an MIS, DSS, ESS, or ES? (Many information systems are combinations of these.) What levels of management decision making does it support? What are its input, output, storage, and processing functions? What software does it use? What database, model base, or knowledge base does it use? Using word processing software, write a summary of your findings.

3. Using database software, create a simple management information system to supply information about different types of cars that a business is considering purchasing for its employees to use. The internal data that goes into the database should be data about employees and their needs for company-supplied cars. (You can use a real business or think of a hypothetical business for this data.) The external data that goes into the database should be data about cars that you gather from the Internet and other sources. Supply data for five to 10 employees and 20 to 30 cars of different makes and models. Develop reports that provide information to management to help in their decision about what cars should be purchased for what employees.

4. This chapter presents the input, output, storage, and processing functions of management information, decision support, executive support, and expert systems. Chapter 10 presented these functions for transaction processing systems. Using word processing software, prepare a table with columns for the four functions and rows for the five types of information systems. Then, fill in the table with brief summaries of each function for each type of system. Identify where the functions of the systems are similar and where they are different. Use the color capabilities of your word processing software to mark common characteristics with the same color.

5. Prepare a spreadsheet to help a business decide how much to charge for a new product it is developing based on the following assumptions:

   a. The business expects to sell 12,000 units per year.

   b. The fixed expenses (the expenses that do not depend on how much is sold) are expected to be $45,000 per year.

   c. The variable expenses (the expenses that depend on how much is sold) are expected to be $8.75 per unit.

   There should be rows in the spreadsheet for the revenue, the fixed expenses, the variable expenses, the total expenses, the net income (revenue minus total expenses), and any other items that might be helpful. The product price, which should be to the nearest cent, should be in a separate cell. Enter different prices into this cell until you find the price for the product, based on the above assumptions, such that the net income is at least 12 percent of the revenue. What would be the price if the business thought it could sell 15,000 units per year?

Real-world Case

Grand & Toy, Canada

As Canada's largest office-supplies company, Grand & Toy sells the pens, the printers, the sticky notes, and the filing cabinets that keep the country's businesses organized and productive. But until recently, Grand & Toy, which has about $257 million in annual sales, had trouble keeping track of its own products' profitability.

In fact, when it came time to figure out which products were selling or bombing, the office-supply giant was relying a little too much on one of its own oldies but goodies: paper. Millions of records boiled down to hundreds of sheets of paper, which somewhere contained the critical information Grand & Toy needed in order to analyze its business.

Toronto-based Grand & Toy is a wholly owned subsidiary of Boise Cascade Office Products. At any given time, the company has about 6,000 active SKUs (merchandise numbers), with a history that includes as many as 20,000. In addition to its own retail stores, Grand & Toy sells to more than 50,000 business clients throughout Canada. Keeping track of product and customer profitability is of critical importance. But before switching its 70 million-line sales history to a database, Grand & Toy's merchandising and marketing departments had little access to information on profitability and cost.

The company's relatively new IBM AS/400 computer meant that there was a good source for data already waiting to be mined. But when department heads went looking for an analysis of how a particular product line was doing, a glacial reporting system didn't give up answers easily. Instead, people had to rely on estimates or a feeling for how something sold in the past. Or they had to search through paper records.

"Lots of data, no information," says John Melodysta, Grand & Toy's director of IT, describing the situation. "Anyone who wanted information had to write a query to the company's AS/400 and hope that it would run some time that month. Some queries could run for a whole weekend to produce data on a category of products. That information is available literally at the click of a mouse now."

Working with Clarity Systems, a Toronto consulting company that specializes in data warehousing, Grand & Toy went looking for a tool that would turn its sales-history data into information.

Essbase, the leading product for on-line analytical processing from Arbor Software, in Sunnyvale, California, soon emerged as a front-runner.

"Essbase seemed to be the most open with the current technology," says Mark Nashman, Clarity Systems' president, and it provided a nice interface for Microsoft Excel, which Grand & Toy already used. Customized spreadsheets for the merchandising department were created for Microsoft Excel.

Currently, Grand & Toy has two Essbase applications: One contains 7 GB of data on profitability for about 20,000 products. The other deals with customer profitability. It contains 4 GB of data about Grand & Toy's 60,000 customers.

Grand & Toy's merchandising department is a key user of the new system, relying on it to decide which products to list or take off the list. With information from Essbase, merchandising can find out which products are selling well in the space of a mouse click.

"Now, in a real-time environment, as the salesperson is sitting there, we can say, 'Oh, yeah, it was a great seller, we sold x number last year. We'll buy a whole bunch more from you this year.' So we use it to make decisions on product," Melodysta says. "With help from Essbase, an individual product manager is able to oversee more than 1,000 SKUs. They've been able to streamline their product offerings so much better by having this tool."

Essbase has also helped Grand & Toy remain flexible and quick on its feet when it comes to sales promotions, Melodysta says. "Throughout a promotion, we want to be able to judge the effectiveness of the item that's being sold. Are we selling a lot of it?" Melodysta says. "If we need to adjust the price downward, we want to know how to react to it quickly."

"The customer-profitability [database] lets Essbase's customer-sales reps identify which customers are doing well and lets them fine-tune product mix for them," Nashman says. "We've taken the dollars per customer, sales dollars, profit dollars, as well as variable costs per customer, to come up with the true contribution of that customer."

Grand & Toy allocates the costs of delivery, selling, and warehousing on an order-by-order basis. That information lets sales representatives know which customers might have to increase order size or find a different mix of products to be profitable.

Although it currently has fewer users, a Sybase database complements Essbase by letting Grand & Toy employees drill down to an even finer level of detail.

"We use Essbase to identify what products are hot or not or what customers are hot or not, then we can look at finer detail in the Sybase world, once you've limited the data that you want to look at," Nashman says.

"Using Cognos Impromptu as a front end, the marketing department can target customers whose profitability is not what it should be. Maybe their mix of products is not that profitable," Nashman says. "You want to drill down and find out what products they're buying and rank those from high-gross profit to low-gross profit."

Grand & Toy plans to add new views of data in the future and expand Essbase access to other departments. A customer-sales view is in the works that Grand & Toy will make available to its branch offices throughout Canada.

Another project is designed primarily for the company's more than 80 retail stores. "That'll be for the district sales managers and eventually right down to the retail-store managers' level," Melodysta says.

A purchasing database has been built that lets Grand & Toy look at product vendors. "We can sort of look at what 3M is doing for us, as opposed to Acco or some of these other vendors," Melodysta says.

With so many people at Grand & Toy gaining access to Essbase, user reaction remains on a high. Of course, this is information that the business community has been dying for, Melodysta adds, so it's embraced very quickly.

Questions

1. Why did Grand & Toy have "lots of data, no information" before developing the applications described in this case?
2. What data does Grand & Toy use in their applications?
3. Why do Grand & Toy employees make use of drilling down?
4. What decisions at Grand & Toy are supported by the applications described in this case?
5. What type of information system is described in this case?

Source: Heather Mackey, "One office-supplies company put an end to its paper trail," *InfoWorld,* March 24, 1997, p. 76

12 Strategic Impact

Chapter Outline

Providing a Strategic Impact   (p. 358)
Strategic Information Systems   (p. 359)
    Characteristics of Strategic Information Systems   (p. 359)
    Identifying Strategic Information System Opportunities   (p. 362)
Interorganizational Information Systems   (p. 364)
    Business Alliances and Interorganizational Systems   (p. 364)
    Characteristics of Interorganizational Systems   (p. 366)
    Electronic Data Interchange Systems   (p. 368)
International Information Systems   (p. 370)
    International Business and International Information Systems   (p. 370)
    International Business Strategies   (p. 371)
    Characteristics of International Information Systems   (p. 373)

Learning Objectives

After completing this chapter, you should be able to:

☐ 1. Describe how information systems can have a strategic impact on a business and give examples of information systems that create a competitive advantage for a business.

☐ 2. Explain what a strategic information system is and what types of information systems are strategic.

☐ 3. Describe how strategic information system opportunities can be identified in a business.

☐ 4. Explain why interorganizational systems are essential for many business alliances to function.

☐ 5. Describe several ways that a business can participate in an interorganizational system.

☐ 6. Explain how an electronic data interchange system functions.

☐ 7. Explain what international information systems are and why they are needed by international businesses.

☐ 8. Describe different forms that international information systems can take and how each form relates to international business strategy.

I nformation systems provide many benefits to an organization. Systems that are used by individuals, such as personal database management and spreadsheet analysis systems, improve personal productivity. Systems that help members of a group work together, such as information sharing and electronic conferencing systems, encourage group collaboration. Systems that support business operations, such as transaction processing systems, increase the efficiency of the operations. Systems that provide information for management decision making, such as management information and decision support systems, improve the effectiveness of the decision making. To be competitive today, businesses must have various computer information systems so that they will be as productive and effective as their competitors.

Even with the necessary computer information systems, some businesses are not as competitive as others because their information systems do not have a *strategic impact* on the businesses. A strategic impact provides a business with an advantage over its competitors. This chapter looks at information systems that can have a strategic impact on a business, including strategic information systems, interorganizational information systems, and international information systems.[1]

Providing a Strategic Impact

Information systems that have a strategic impact on a business help create a competitive advantage for the business. This advantage, which puts the business in a stronger position to compete than other businesses, can be gained in several ways. One way is by *cost leadership*, which means having the lowest production or operating costs among the business's competitors. Computer information systems can help create cost leadership by providing unique operational and managerial support. For example, consider an athletic shoe manufacturer. With innovative uses of manufacturing information systems, such as computer-integrated manufacturing (CIM), the shoe manufacturer could have the lowest production costs in the athletic shoe industry. Its shoes would sell for less than its competitors' shoes, thus giving the business a competitive advantage.

Another way competitive advantage can be gained is by *product differentiation*, which means providing products or services that are unique so that the customer must acquire the product or service from the business. Information systems can help create product differentiation by providing the tools to identify and develop unique products. For example, the athletic shoe manufacturer could use a marketing research information system to identify consumer interests in a new type of shoe, a computer-aided design (CAD) system to design the shoe quickly, and a computer-aided manufacturing (CAM) system to produce the shoe rapidly. If the business could identify and produce a new product before its competitors could, the business would have a competitive advantage at least until other businesses catch up.

A third way competitive advantage can be gained is by *focusing on a niche*, which means providing products or services that are designed for a specific segment of the market. For example, the athletic shoe manufacturer might decide to focus on track shoes and gain a competitive advantage as the main producer of such shoes. Information systems can help a business focus on a niche by providing information to identify niche markets. For example, the athletic shoe manufacturer could use a

---

[1]Much of this chapter is based on ideas presented in Seev Neumann's book, *Strategic Information Systems*, Macmillan College Publishing Company, 1994.

management information system to access external databases that provide information about potential market niches.

Helping a business gain a competitive advantage through cost leadership, product differentiation, or focusing on a niche are just some of the ways that information systems can have a strategic impact on a business. As you read about different types of information systems in this chapter, you will see other ways information systems can have a strategic impact.

Strategic Information Systems

Definition ✱

A strategic information system or SIS is an information system that has a strategic impact on a business. By this we mean that the system affects the way the business competes with other businesses, thus giving it an advantage over its competitors. As explained in the previous section, this advantage can take several forms, including cost leadership, product differentiation, and focusing on a niche.

✳ Characteristics of Strategic Information Systems

Any type of information system can be a strategic information system. Transaction processing, management information, decision support, executive support, and expert systems can all have a strategic impact. Workgroup and individual information systems can also be strategic systems. The word *strategic* in its name does *not* mean that a strategic information system only supports strategic decision making. A strategic information system can provide information for decision making at all levels of an organization. An SIS can also support the basic operations of a business, as well as workgroups and individuals. (See Fig. 12.1).

FIGURE 12.1

Strategic information systems (SIS) support for all levels of a business

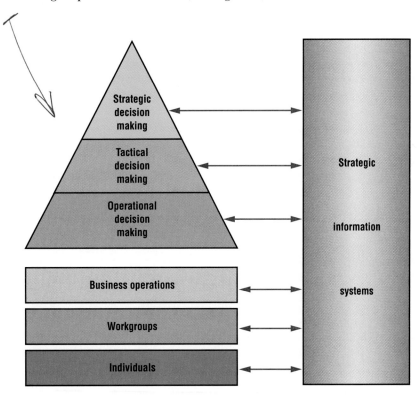

An order entry system, which is a basic transaction processing system, can be a strategic information system for a business if it allows the business to take more orders than its competitors. A management information system that provides marketing information to managers can be a strategic information system if the information is unique to the business. A decision support system that includes a special model for analyzing data is a strategic information system if the model is not used by other businesses. An executive support system can be a strategic information system if the system provides the executives with the ability to make decisions quicker than the business's competitors. An expert system is a strategic information system when it incorporates expert advice available only to the business.

A strategic information system can provide support in all areas of a business. (See Fig. 12.2.) Information systems in accounting, finance, marketing, manufacturing, and human resource management can have a strategic impact. For example, a budgeting system in accounting is a strategic information system when it provides more accurate control over costs than similar systems used by competitors. A credit analysis system in finance is a strategic information system when it reduces credit losses below those of competitors. A marketing research system is a strategic information system if it provides marketing data to the business not available to competitors. A computer-integrated manufacturing system is a strategic information system when it reduces production costs below those of competitors. A job applicant tracking system used in human resource management is a strategic information system if it lets the business hire better employees than its competitors. The point is that any information system in an organization can be a strategic information system *if* it provides an advantage for the business over its competitors.

As described in the previous section, an athletic shoe manufacturer can use various information systems to gain a competitive advantage. These systems are strategic information systems for the shoe manufacturer. Thus, a computer-integrated manufacturing system is a strategic information system because it gives the shoe manufacturer a cost leadership advantage. A marketing research information system is a strategic information system because it allows the shoe manufacturer to differentiate its products. A management information system is a strategic information system because it provides information that helps the shoe manufacturer focus on a niche.

Workgroup information systems can be strategic information systems if they allow employees of a business to collaborate in unique ways. For example, a system that lets engineers in different locations around the world participate in the design of a new product without having to travel can have a strategic impact on the business.

FIGURE 12.2

Strategic information systems support in all areas of a business

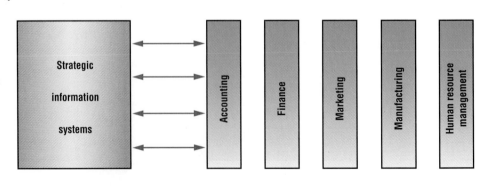

Bookmark

Strategic Web Site at National Semiconductor

It's time to stick a "new and improved" label on the National Semiconductor Corp. home page. Recently, National Semi unveiled a significant Web redesign effort that emphasizes delivery of privileged product information and other special services to a target audience of more than 1 million design engineers through its integrated Internet, intranet, and extranet sites. Most dramatically, engineers now have instant on-line access, via National Semi's extranet, to detailed data sheets for all 27,000 part numbers in the company's catalog. Other new features include a new "pictorial" search engine, icon-driven design, and 24-hour response to technical queries. The site has a stated goal of helping professional design engineers make "faster and better" decisions, company officials said.

"This redesign is about how to change a Web site from a boring information tool to a strategic tool," said Phil Gibson, National Semi's director of interactive marketing in Santa Clara, California. "The expectation when we started was that we could do a much better job of distributing information to our end customers."

Essentially, National Semi's new site is seamlessly "embedded" within customer's intranets by cross-referencing internal part numbers to corresponding National Semi parts. From within their own companies' intranets, users identify themselves with a password, Gibson explained, and gain access to National Semi's site.

"The No. 1 issue, over and over again, was time: time to decision, time to deliver, time to market," Gibson said. "With a consumer site, you want people to get on and stay on. With a business site, you want to get them on, then get them off."

The highlight of the redesign is what National Semi touts as a "groundbreaking" pictorial search engine that allows an engineer to click on a part within a system diagram in order to gain immediate access to detailed information on that part. With interpage hot links and references between pages, "navigating becomes thoughtless," Gibson explained. "You can migrate wherever you want to go."

Altogether, National's site features an array of four ways of finding information: key word search, parametric search, product/category name search, and the new pictorial search. In addition, visitors are now able to download summaries of engineering data books, as well as the data books themselves (40,000 pages in all, updated daily).

Significantly, the new site is icon-driven, owing in large part to exploding numbers of customers from outside the United States, particularly from the Far East, who may have only limited English-language comprehension, Gibson said. Registered users on National Semi's integrated Web site are growing at a rate of 20 percent per month, and nearly half of all new users hail from outside the United States, he said.

One-to-one linking of all 27,000 National Semi part numbers to their corresponding data sheets is welcome news for Bay Networks Inc.'s Don Hardy, a senior engineer in the data administration group at Bay's Billerica, Massachusetts, campus. Hardy is expanding Bay's own intranet to include documents and specifications from all his vendors. The National Semi breakthrough goes a long way toward replacing the traditional data book and other hard-copy materials, he said. "The real key is that we're always going to get the most current information," he added.

Indeed, once he saw what National Semi had accomplished matching part numbers to data sheets, Hardy sent e-mail to other suppliers asking for the same. At least one could comply immediately, although several others have had to ask for time. "National [Semi] is helping me now, not just with their site, but with everyone else's," he said.

QUESTIONS

1. How has National Semiconductor's Web site become a strategic tool?
2. What competitive advantage does National Semiconductor gain from its Web site?
3. When will National Semiconductor's Web site stop being a strategic tool?

WEB SITE
National Semiconductor: www.national.com

Source: Christopher Kenneally, "New and improved," *PC WEEK*, May 12, 1997, pp. 21, 24.

The advantage can come from quicker, less expensive development of new products. In some business, individual information systems may have a strategic impact if they increase personal productivity significantly over that of competitors.

Strategic information systems do not remain strategic forever. Such systems give a business an advantage for a period of time until the competition catches up. For example, the first banks to have automated teller machine systems had an advantage over other banks, and thus these systems were strategic information systems. Eventually, though, all banks implemented ATM systems and so the advantage was lost. Thus, the systems were no longer strategic information systems but a necessary part of the banking business.

A strategic information system is specific to a particular business. A system is not strategic if all competitors use it and it performs the same function in each business. It is not the type of information system that makes it strategic; it is the uniqueness of the use of the system that is strategic.

Some strategic information systems can create *barriers to entry* for competitors. In general, a barrier to entry is something that makes it difficult for a new business to enter the market and compete. A strategic information system can require expensive information technology and costly development. To compete, a new business may have to make such a substantial investment in information technology and systems that it becomes too expensive to enter the market. An example of a barrier to entry provided by a strategic information system is an airline reservation system such as American Airline's SABRE system or United Airline's Apollo system. These systems are so expensive to develop that it is almost impossible for a new business to enter this market.

Strategic information systems can also make it expensive for the customers of a business to change to another business. The expense arises because of high *switching costs*, which are the costs associated with switching to another business. For example, electronic data interchange systems used by some businesses require the customer to make a substantial investment in information technology. Switching to another business becomes too costly for the customer because new technology would be required.

Sometimes a business develops a strategic information system that can provide a source of revenue for the business. When the SIS is sufficiently unique, other businesses may be willing to purchase the system or pay to make use of the system. Airline reservation systems are an example of this situation. American Airlines developed the SABRE system and now it is used by many other airlines. Thus, SABRE has become a major source of revenue for American Airlines.

Identifying Strategic Information System Opportunities

It is sometimes difficult to identify situations in which information systems can have a strategic impact. One approach is to look at the business's <u>value chain</u>. The value chain is the series of activities that add value to the product or service provided by the business.

Figure 12.3 summarizes the activities in the value chain.[2] There are two types of activities: primary activities and support activities. The *primary activities* involve creating, selling, and servicing the business's product. They are:

> *Inbound logistics*: This activity involves acquiring the materials needed for production from suppliers.

> *Operations*: This activity involves manufacturing the product of the firm.

> *Outbound logistics*: This activity involves distributing the finished product to the customers.

---

[2]Michael E. Porter and Victor E. Millar, "How Information Gives You Competitive Advantage," *Harvard Business Review,* July-August 1985, pp. 149–160.

FIGURE 12.3

The activities in the value chain

Primary activities

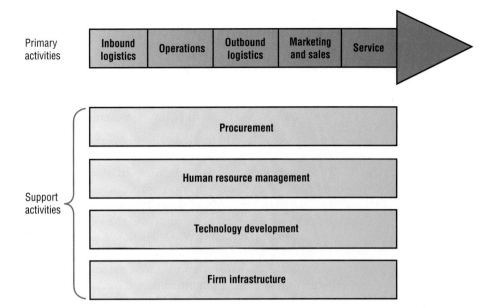

Support activities

Marketing and sales: This activity involves selling the product.

Service: This activity involves servicing the product after sale.

The *support activities* provide the resources and infrastructure needed by the primary activities. They are:

Procurement: This activity involves purchasing resources needed by the business.

Human resource management: This activity involves hiring and training employees.

Technology development: This activity includes improving products and business processes.

Firm infrastructure: This activity supports the entire chain with general management and other functions.

The value chain can be used to identify those information systems that can have a strategic impact on the business. The idea is that a business can gain a competitive advantage when it can perform some activities in the value chain in such a way that the value to the customer of a product or service is increased or the cost of performing the activities is decreased. An information system that adds value or reduces cost can have a strategic impact on the business.

Information systems for all nine of the activities shown in Fig. 12.3 can have an impact. The following are examples of potential strategic information systems for the primary activities in the value chain:

Inbound logistics: just-in-time inventory management system

Operations: computer-integrated manufacturing system

Outbound logistics: delivery scheduling system

Marketing and sales: sales force automation system

Service: problem diagnosis expert system

Some possible strategic information systems for the support activities include:

Procurement: purchasing system

Human resource management: employee skills analysis system

Technology development: computer-aided design system

Firm infrastructure: business planning system

Any of the systems listed here, as well as many others, can have a strategic impact on a business.

The value chain can be useful to help identify strategic information system opportunities. Often, however, strategic information systems are not planned but rather evolve over time. Many times a business develops an information system and enhances it over the years. Eventually, the system has a strategic impact on the business. An example of this phenomenon is airline reservation systems which were not planned as strategic information systems but developed into such systems for the airlines. Thus, although the value chain is a useful way to identify strategic information system opportunities, it is not the only way that such systems are created.

Interorganizational Information Systems

The information systems described so far in this book have mainly been confined to a single business. Such intraorganizational information systems are essential for the proper operation and management of an organization. Increasingly, however, information systems that are shared by two or more businesses are being used. This type of system is called an interorganizational information system, or, for short, an interorganizational system or IOS.

The most familiar example of interorganizational systems are electronic data interchange (EDI) systems, which provide for the transfer of data between businesses, and electronic funds transfer (EFT) systems, which provide for the transfer of funds between financial institutions. Other types of interorganizational systems exist, however. This section takes a look at interorganizational systems and examines their strategic impact on businesses.

Business Alliances and Interorganizational Systems

Businesses compete with other businesses, so it would seem that two businesses, especially if they were direct competitors, would not want to cooperate with each other. This is not always the situation, however, because many businesses find it to their mutual benefit to cooperate with each other. These businesses coordinate some of their operations or link some of their resources to form business alliances, which serve the interests of all businesses in the alliance.

There are several types of business alliances. (See Fig. 12.4.) Some alliances involve businesses that compete directly with each other. For example, computer companies sometimes work together to develop software for use on each companies' hardware. Banks work together to provide automated teller machine access for each other's customers. Insurance companies work together to share the risks of large insurance losses. All these businesses continue to compete; their alliances help them provide their product or service to their customers.

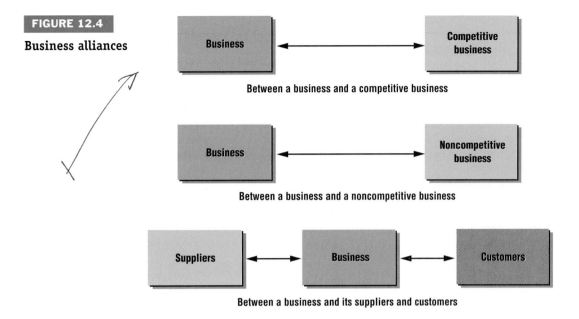

FIGURE 12.4

Business alliances

Between a business and a competitive business

Between a business and a noncompetitive business

Between a business and its suppliers and customers

(handwritten margin notes: — noncompetitive; —Supplier/customer)

Direct competitors are not the only businesses that form alliances. Many alliances are also formed in which the products of two businesses that do not compete directly are promoted and sold together. For example, a bank may form an alliance with an airline company to promote the bank's credit card along with the airline's frequent flyer program. A software company may form an alliance with a publisher to provide software to be packaged with books and manuals. In these situations the businesses in the alliance benefit from promoting and selling their products together.

Alliances also exist between a business and its suppliers and customers. A business may form an alliance with its suppliers to provide for favorable delivery and pricing of raw materials. The business may also form an alliance with its customers to provide for easy ordering of finished products. These alliances are to the benefit of the business as well as to its suppliers and customers.

Interorganizational systems provide for the sharing of information and processing between businesses in a business alliance. Such systems are essential for many alliances to function efficiently. Banks could not provide ATM access for other banks' customers without an extensive interbank network. An airline could not link its frequent flier program to a bank's credit card without the necessary system to provide for the transfer of data between the companies. A business could not provide easy ordering of its products by other businesses without an EDI system. All these are examples of interorganizational systems that make it possible for business alliances to operate smoothly and efficiently.

Interorganizational systems can have a strategic impact on the businesses in an alliance. This impact affects the way the businesses in the alliance compete with other businesses and thus provides them with a competitive advantage. The advantage can come from reduced costs because of the alliance. For example, ordering products electronically with an EDI system is less expensive than ordering other ways. The advantage can also come from unique products or services provided through the alliance, such as when a bank's credit card is linked with products or

(handwritten margin notes: Advantages — reduced costs — unique prod. or services)

Bookmark

Interorganizational System at the National Transportation Exchange

Fill 'er up.

That's the idea behind a new on-line freight shipping service that uses servers and a relational database to make it possible for trucks to carry more cargo as they barrel down the road.

The National Transportation Exchange (NTE) is trying to play electronic matchmaker between shipping companies with partial truckloads and freight carriers that have spare capacity. Based in Downers Grove, Illinois, the exchange automates what has typically been a labor-intensive process of multiple phone calls and price haggling.

Modeling itself after a stock exchange, the NTE collects shipment orders in its database, computes a price for each one, and then matches them to truck routes provided by carriers. The database is updated instantly as new shipments are tendered, and carriers can get a list of loads that meet their route plans in less than 30 seconds, NTE officials said.

"Before, [arranging shipments] was day after day of phone calls and faxes going back and forth between us and carriers. Now it all happens electronically, and the system does the groundwork for us," said Vince Piper, traffic manager at Thrall Car Manufacturing Co. in Chicago Heights, Illinois.

Thrall Car, a maker of railroad freight cars, uses the NTE system to find carriers for about 30 percent of the inbound shipments that go from suppliers to its plants in Illinois and Georgia. That amounts to 20 to 30 shipments per week, and Piper said the reduced phone time frees him to do more shipment planning and other long-term projects that were placed on the back burner before.

Beyond the convenience, the NTE also holds out the potential of tasty financial carrots for both shippers and carriers.

The ability to place a small load in a partially filled truck lets shippers avoid paying the full cost of hiring a carrier. For example, Piper said he has been able to save 5 percent to 40 percent off what he would have had to pay to get a trucking company to carry only his load.

Observers said the NTE concept may be harder to sell to carriers because they already can charge full truckload rates for partial loads. But Greg Rocque, the NTE's president, said carriers could get more aggregate revenue by charging lower prices for multiple shipments in a truck.

The National Private Truck Council, an association that represents 1,100 private fleets, such as corporations with their own trucks, is one large carrier group that is buying in to the NTE approach. It agreed to include the matching service as a recommended option for its members.

For private haulers, filling up unused space in their trucks reduces shipping costs and provides added revenue, according to Gene Bergoffen, president of the Alexandria, Virginia–based council. NTE "is really real time," he added. "Once you're on line, you can see what's available and commit to [carry] something right then and there."

QUESTIONS

1. How does the NTE function as an interorganizational system sponsor?
2. How do IOS participants benefit from the use of the NTE system?

WEB SITE
National Transportation Exchange: www.nte.net

Source: Craig Stedman, "Shipping service keeps users truckin'," *Computerworld*, June 24, 1996, pp. 39,41.

services from other businesses. Without the appropriate interorganizational systems, many business alliances would not function efficiently and no competitive advantage would be gained.

Characteristics of Interorganizational Systems

Businesses are involved in interorganizational systems as either sponsors or participants. An IOS *sponsor* is a business that sets up and maintains an interorganizational system. For example, an airline company that sets up an airline reservation system is an IOS sponsor. So is a communications business that sets up a network to be used by banks for ATM communication. Sponsors develop the interorganizational system and make it available to other businesses.

An IOS *participant* is a business that uses an interorganizational system. For example, a travel agent uses an airline reservation system and thus is a participant in the IOS created by the airline company. A bank attaches its ATMs to a network and thus is a participant in the IOS created by the communications business.

Businesses can participate in an IOS in several ways. (See Fig. 12.5.) In one approach, the business simply enters input and receives output using an IOS sponsored by another business. The example of a travel agent making reservations through an airline reservation system illustrates this approach. EDI systems are also of this type.

In another approach, a business accesses data storage or processing capabilities of another business in the interorganizational system. For example, a supplier may be able to check the inventory levels in the inventory database of its customers through the IOS. With this information, the supplier can automatically restock the customer when inventory levels are too low. Another example is a system that allows a business to check the status of its shipment in a freight company's database.

A third way a business can participate in an IOS is to use capabilities of the IOS received from the sponsor for managing internal operations. The business will also participate in ways described previously but, in addition, will use the IOS for other functions. For example, an IOS for a pharmacy can be used to order drugs from a supplier, manage the pharmacies inventory, and prepare financial statements for the pharmacy. This last function does not require transmitting data to the supplier; it only involves the internal operations of the business.

An athletic shoe manufacturer may be a sponsor or a participant in various interorganizational systems. It may sponsor an EDI system so its customers can order products more easily. It may also use an interorganizational system to check customer inventory levels and automatically resupply certain customers when

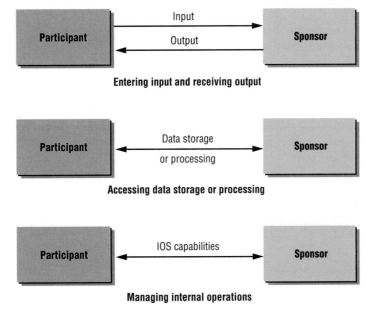

FIGURE 12.5

Participation in interorganizational systems

Entering input and receiving output

Accessing data storage or processing

Managing internal operations

stocks fall too low. The shoe manufacturer may also participate in various interorganizational systems with its suppliers to order raw materials. It may also participate in systems with transportation companies for scheduling shipments of materials or finished products.

Electronic Data Interchange Systems

EDI
fig. 12.7

Because electronic data interchange, or EDI, systems are so common, we will take a separate look at these interorganizational systems. An EDI system provides for electronic communication of data between businesses. Purchase order data, shipping data, invoice data, product description data, price list data, and insurance data are some of the types of data sent using EDI systems.

Often, the data sent by a business using an EDI system represents a transaction. The data is an output of one business's transaction processing systems and an input to another business's transaction processing system. (See Fig. 12.6.) For example, purchase order data may be sent electronically to order products. The purchase order data is an output of one business's purchasing system and an input to the other business's order entry system. As another example, invoice data may be sent to bill for the products sold. The invoice data is produced by the billing system in one business and received by the accounts payable system in the other business. In effect, the transaction processing systems of two businesses communicate with each other using the EDI system.

Not all data sent by EDI systems represent transactions. For example, Fig. 12.7 shows several ways that EDI systems can be used between a business and its suppliers and customers. A business can send specifications for a product to a supplier along with a request for a quotation for supplying the product. The supplier then can send back the requested quotation which the business can use to make a purchasing decision. At that point the business can send a purchase order which the supplier can acknowledge. When the product is ready for shipping, the supplier can send a notification to the business. After shipment, the supplier can send an invoice to the business.

A customer can send a price request to the business and the business can send back a price list. Then the customer can send an order which the business can acknowledge. Eventually, after the order is sent, the business can send a bill to the customer. All this data can be transmitted between the business and its suppliers and customers electronically using EDI.

An EDI system, like all interorganizational systems, requires a data communication link between businesses. This link forms an *interorganizational network* which connects the businesses. (See Chapter 6.) The network may be set up by the business sponsoring the EDI system or by a separate company. The Internet can also be used to provide EDI communication, and it may someday be the main network used for this purpose.

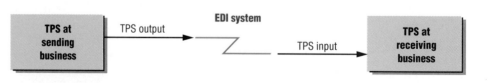

FIGURE 12.6

Transaction processing system communication using EDI

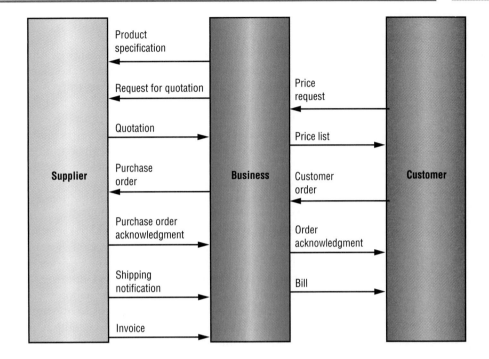

FIGURE 12.7

Electronic data interchange

Each business participating in an EDI system requires computer hardware connected to the network along with EDI software. The software transmits and receives electronic data over the network. The data must be sent in a standardized format agreed to by the businesses participating in the EDI system.

Data sent by EDI is not the same as a fax or electronic mail. A fax document is received and read on paper or on a screen by a person. Similarly, electronic mail is read on a screen by a person. EDI data, on the other hand, is, in general, input to a system used by the receiving businesses. For example, EDI purchase order data is input to an order entry system and starts the process of shipping a product. EDI invoice data is input to an accounts payable system that generates a payment. Some EDI data may be read by people but, for the most part, this data is entered into other systems.

There are several advantages of EDI. One is speed. Electronic data can be transmitted faster than paper documents, so EDI saves time. Another advantage is that data entry errors are reduced. When a paper document, such as a purchase order, is sent from one business to another, the data from the document must be keyed into the system used by the receiving business. Any time data is keyed, errors are possible. With EDI data, however, the data is entered electronically, thus eliminating keying errors at the receiving business. Thus, with EDI, not only is data transmitted faster but also more accurately.

The main difficulties with EDI revolve around organizational and technical problems. First, organizations have to agree to participate in the EDI system. If one business proposes to sponsor an EDI system, other businesses must agree to participate. Second, technical problems must be solved. Appropriate hardware and software must be available to all businesses participating in the system and the necessary interorganizational network must be in place. Once the difficulties associated with an EDI system are resolved, the system can provide significant benefits to the businesses participating in it.

International Information Systems

Some businesses operate entirely within a single country. All the business's product development, production, sales, and management take place in the same country, and all suppliers and customers of the business are located in that country. Increasingly, however, businesses engage in activities that extend beyond national borders. An *international business* may produce its products in several countries and sell them in many countries. Its suppliers and customers may be located anywhere in the world. It may employ engineers and designers in a number of countries to develop new products. The management of the business may be located in a single country or it may be spread out among a number of countries.

The information systems of a business that only operates in a single country are confined to that country. These systems can be called *domestic information systems.* Some of the information systems of an international business may also be confined to a single country and thus are domestic information systems. For example, the payroll system for the business's operations in each country may be specific to the country. Many information systems for international businesses, however, span national borders. These systems, called <u>international</u> or <u>global information systems</u>, provide communication between business locations around the world, transfer of data between international locations, and use of system functions (input, output, processing, and storage) at different locations worldwide. For example, an international order entry system may allow customer orders to be entered in the different countries in which the business sells its products. The orders are then transferred to a single location for storage and processing. After processing, the sales orders are transmitted to distribution points located in other countries for shipment of products to customers.

International Business and International Information Systems

Businesses engage in international activities for several reasons. (See Fig. 12.8.) One is for *international sales.* That is, businesses want to be able to sell their products or

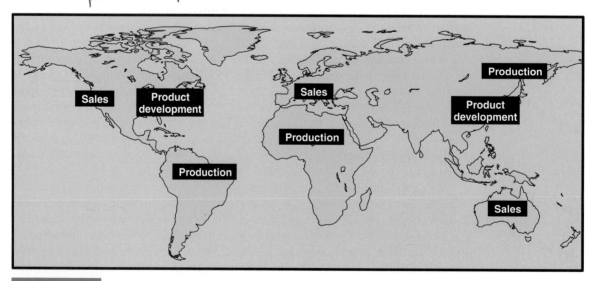

FIGURE 12.8

International business activities

services in many countries. For example, consider an athletic shoe manufacturer. Athletic shoes are sold all over the world, and a shoe manufacturer will want to sell its shoes in many countries so as to increase its sales.

Another reason that businesses engage in international activities is for *international production*. That is, businesses want to be able to produce or manufacture their products in many countries. Thus, the athletic shoe manufacturer will want to produce its shoes in various countries. The decision of where to manufacture a product depends on production costs in different countries and where the product will be sold.

A third reason that businesses engage in international activities is to take advantage of *international product development*. Research and development activities can take place anywhere in the world, depending on where the best development personnel are located. Thus, an athletic shoe manufacturer may use shoe designers in many countries to design its shoes.

International information systems are needed to operate and manage the international activities of a business. Thus, the athletic shoe manufacturer would need an international order entry system to allow its customers around the world to place orders and an international distribution system to plan shipments to the customers. It would need an international manufacturing information system to schedule and coordinate production in a number of countries. Finally, it would need an international product design system to allow designers in a number of locations around the world to work together on shoe design.

International information systems can have a strategic impact on international businesses. This impact comes from several sources. One is the ability of the system to compress time and space. International businesses operate in many different time zones and across considerable distances. International information systems allow distant operations of a business to transmit data nearly instantaneously across any number of time zones and over any distance. The effect is as if the operations of the business were nearby, in the same time zone. This ability of international information systems to compress time and space gives the international business a competitive advantage over businesses without this capability.

Another source of strategic impact from international information systems is the capability for sharing business resources over long distances. With international information systems, business operations and management do not have to be in the same location. For example, engineers working on the design of a new product can be in different locations and share design ideas and details through an international information system. Information for management decision making can come from many locations around the world and be distributed to managers in different locations through an international information system. The business gains a competitive advantage over other businesses without these capabilities because of its international information systems.

International Business Strategies

International businesses may follow one of several basic strategies.[3] (See Fig. 12.9.) In the *multinational* strategy, the business allows its foreign operations to function largely independently of each other and of the central headquarters. In effect, each

---

[3]Jahangir Karimi and Benn R. Konsynski, "Globalization and Information Management Strategies," *Journal of Management Information Systems*, Vol. 4, No. 4 (Spring 1991), pp. 7–26.

FIGURE 12.9

International business strategies

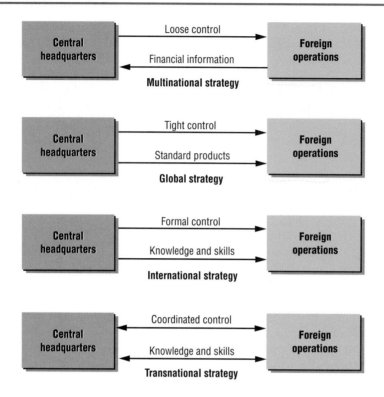

foreign operation is a separate business that makes its own decisions regarding product development, production, and selling. This strategy is very responsive to local needs. The central headquarters exercises only loose control over the foreign operations and the foreign operations mainly just report financial results to the headquarters.

In the *global* strategy, the central headquarters coordinates the activities of the foreign operations closely. The headquarters standardizes products for sale in foreign locations and determines how the products will be sold. Product development takes place at the central location and production may also be centralized. This strategy is less responsive to local needs than the multinational strategy. The central headquarters exercises tight control over the foreign operations.

The *international* strategy involves transferring knowledge and skills from the central headquarters to the foreign operations. Product development is centralized but the foreign operations use the knowledge and skills they receive to determine how best to produce and sell products for their markets. This is different from the global strategy in which the central headquarters determines how products will be produced and sold. Still, formal control of foreign operations is needed in the international strategy.

The *transnational* strategy involves using knowledge and skills from both the central headquarters and the foreign operations. Knowledge and skills flow between different locations of the business, depending on where the greatest expertise lies. Thus, the different parts of the business learn and gain from each other, and coordinate product development, production, and marketing decisions. With this strategy, control must be carefully coordinated between the central headquarters and different foreign operations.

Characteristics of International Information Systems

International information systems differ from domestic information systems in a number of ways. One source of difference is in data communications technology. Domestic information systems generally require shorter distance data communication than international information systems in which data communications between countries is necessary. Long-distance data communications in international information systems may require special technology such as satellites, which may not be needed in domestic information systems. In addition, domestic information systems only have to deal with the telecommunication (telephone) system in a single country. International information systems, on the other hand, must deal with telecommunication systems in many countries that can vary not only in technical details but also in quality. Connecting to these systems as part of an international network can create significant technical problems. Finally, the cost of data communications for domestic information systems is less than for international information systems. Data communications with international information systems is more costly not only because the distances are greater, but also because charges for the use of telecommunication systems for international communications in some countries can be very high.

Another difference between domestic and international information systems is the concern for cultural differences between countries. Domestic information systems only have to be concerned with the culture of a single country whereas international information systems must take into consideration the many differences in culture between countries. These considerations not only involve language differences but also differences in values, norms, and other societal characteristics. For example, a business with an international information system that links operations in many countries must take into consideration such differences as working hours, religious holidays, and the importance of group versus individual work.

Finally, political and legal factors can create differences between domestic and international information systems. Domestic information systems only have to deal with the rules and laws in a single country whereas international information systems must take into consideration the rules and laws in several countries. In addition, many countries have laws that affect transactions that take place over their borders. For international information systems, these laws often affect the flow of data between countries, commonly called transborder data flow or TDF. For example, some countries do not allow personal data about employees to leave the country.

The form that an international information system takes can depend on the basic strategy followed by the business.[4] (See Fig. 12.10.) Businesses that follow a *multinational* strategy tend to have *decentralized* or independent information systems for their central headquarters and different foreign operations. Because the multinational strategy allows foreign operations to function independently, separate information systems usually are used by each operation, with no link between these systems and the systems at the headquarters. Each foreign operation is allowed to select its own hardware and software, and develop its own information systems. In effect, the business does not have an international information system but rather a set of independent domestic systems.

---

[4]Ibid.

FIGURE 12.10

International business strategies and international information systems

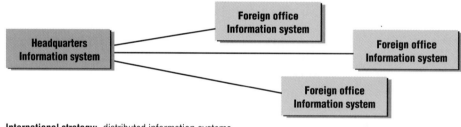

Multinational strategy: decentralized information systems

Global strategy: centralized information systems

International strategy: distributed information systems

Transnational strategy: integrated information systems

Businesses that follow the *global* strategy have a tendency to have highly *centralized* international information systems determined by the central headquarters. The global strategy involves considerable control of foreign operations by the headquarters. Hence, information systems in businesses that use this strategy are centrally developed and controlled. Such systems are located in the central headquarters with the foreign operations having no information systems or minimal systems determined by the headquarters.

③ international ——→ When the *international* strategy is followed, businesses tend to have *distributed* international information systems in which systems in the central headquarters are connected to those in the foreign operations. Because the international strategy involves transferring of information from the central headquarters to the foreign operations, information systems in businesses that use this strategy must have the necessary communication capability. In addition, the systems in the central headquarters and foreign operations must be able to coordinate their processing and databases. The result is information systems in which the systems at the central headquarters are linked to those at the foreign operations.

④ transnational ——→ Finally, businesses that follow the *transnational* strategy require complex, *integrated* international information systems in which the central headquarters and all the foreign operations participate equally. The transnational strategy involves transferring information between all locations of the business and using the best expertise, wherever it lies in the organization. Hence, businesses that follow this strategy must have information systems that communicate between *all* offices and operations of the business, not just between headquarters and foreign operations. These systems must be able to share databases and processing worldwide in a highly cooperative way.

Figure 12.11 summarizes two characteristics of the different forms that international information systems can take. One characteristic is the amount of control of the system exercised by the central headquarters. Distributed and centralized international information systems require the most central control whereas integrated and decentralized systems require the least. The other characteristic is the amount of interconnectivity required by the system. This means how much the systems in the business's different locations must be connected. Centralized and decentralized international information systems require the least interconnectivity, whereas distributed and integrated systems require the most.

International information systems can be almost any type of system. Transaction processing, management information, decision support, executive support, and expert systems can all be international. Workgroup information systems can also be international systems. Business transactions can be transmitted internationally by an international transaction processing system. Information can be made available to managers worldwide with an international management

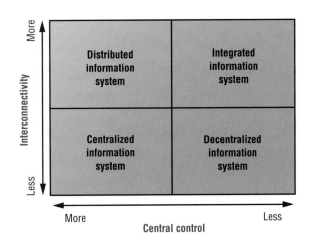

FIGURE 12.11

Characteristics of international information systems

information system. Decision support can be provided for international managers by an international decision support system. Executives can gain access to global information through an international executive support system. Expert advice can be made available throughout the world with an international expert system. Employees around the world can collaborate using an international workgroup information systems.

International information systems are not just *intraorganizational systems* as described so far, but also *interorganizational systems*. Many international businesses use international interorganizational systems for sharing information and processing in international business alliances. For example, international EDI systems link businesses with international suppliers and customers. An international business may be a sponsor or a participant in an international IOS.

Information systems in international businesses can be organized in many ways and provide many different functions for a business. As businesses expand into global sales, production, and product development, international information systems become increasingly important.

Chapter Summary

- [ ] Information systems can have a strategic impact on a business by creating a **competitive advantage** for the business over others. This advantage can be gained by cost leadership, product differentiation, or focusing on a niche. An innovative manufacturing information system can help a business become a cost leader. A marketing research information system can help a business differentiate products. A management information system with access to external databases can provide information to help a business identify market niches. (pp. 358–359)

- [ ] A **strategic information system** or **SIS** is an information system that has a strategic impact on a business. This impact affects the way the business competes with other businesses, thus giving it an advantage over its competitors. Any type of information system can be a strategic information system including transaction processing, management information, decision support, executive support, and expert systems, as well as workgroup and individual information systems. Systems in all areas of a business can be strategic, including accounting information systems, financial information systems, marketing information systems, manufacturing information systems, and human resource information systems. It is not the type of information system that makes it strategic; it is the uniqueness of the use of the system that is strategic. (pp. 359–362)

- [ ] Strategic information system opportunities can be identified by looking at the business's **value chain**. This is the series of activities that add value to the

product or service provided by the business. A business can gain a competitive advantage when it can perform some activities in the value chain in such a way that the value to the customer of the product or service is increased or the cost of performing the activity is decreased. An information system that adds value or reduces cost can have a strategic impact on the business. (pp. 362–364)

- [ ] Many businesses coordinate their operations or link their resources to form **business alliances**. An **interorganizational system** or **IOS** is an information system that is shared by two or more businesses in an alliance. Such systems are essential for many business alliances to function because information or processing needs to be shared between businesses in the alliance. Without the necessary interorganizational systems, many business alliances would not operate smoothly or efficiently. (pp. 364–366)

- [ ] A business can participate in an interorganizational system in several ways. One way is by entering input and receiving output using an IOS sponsored by another business. Another approach is to use an IOS to access data storage or processing capabilities of another business. A third way a business can participate in an IOS is to use capabilities of the IOS received from the sponsor for internal operations. (pp. 366–368)

- [ ] An electronic data interchange or EDI system provides electronic communication of data between businesses. The data often represent transactions that are output from one business's transaction processing system and input to another business's transaction processing system. An EDI system requires an interorganizational network between businesses participating in the system. Each business also requires computer hardware connected to the network and EDI software for transmitting and receiving electronic data in a standardized format over the network. (pp. 368–369)

☐ An international business develops, produces, and sells products in more than one country. Such a business may have domestic information systems confined to a single country in which it operates and **international information systems** that span national borders. The international information systems provide communication between business locations around the world, transfer of data between international locations, and use of system functions at many locations. These capabilities are needed to operate and manage the international activities of the business. (pp. 369–371)

☐ Some international businesses follow a multinational strategy in which foreign operations function largely independently. These businesses tend to have decentralized information systems for their various foreign operations. Other international businesses follow a global strategy in which the central headquarters standardizes products and marketing. These businesses often have centralized international information systems. Still other international businesses follow an international strategy in which knowledge and skills are transferred from the headquarters to the foreign operations. These businesses tend to have distributed international information systems. Finally, some international businesses follow a transnational strategy in which knowledge and skills are transferred between all locations of the business. These businesses usually have complex, integrated international information systems. (pp. 371–376)

Key Terms

Business Alliance (p. 364)
Competitive Advantage (p. 358)
International (Global) Information System (p. 370)
Interorganizational (Information) System (IOS) (p. 364)

Intraorganizational Information System (p. 364)
Strategic Information System (SIS) (p. 359)
Transborder Data Flow (TDF) (p. 373)

Value Chain (p. 362)

Assignment Material

Review Questions

Fill-in Questions

1. An information system that has a strategic impact on a business creates a(n) _____ for the business over other businesses.

2. Three ways that a competitive advantage can be gained are _____, _____, and _____.

3. A(n) _____ is an information system that can have a strategic impact on a business.

4. A strategic information system can create _____, making it difficult for a new business to enter and compete in a market. A strategic information system can also make it expensive for a customer of a business to change to another business because of high _____.

5. The _____ is the series of activities that add value to a product or service provided by a business.

6. An information system that is shared by two or more businesses is called a(n) _____.

7. When several businesses coordinate some of their operations or link some of their resources, they form a(n) _____.

8. An IOS _____ is a business that sets up and maintains an interorganizational system. An IOS _____ is a business that uses an interorganizational system.

9. A(n) _____ is an information system that spans national borders.

10. An international business that allows its foreign operations to operate largely independently of the central headquarters is following the _____ strategy.

11. An international business that transfers knowledge and skills from the central headquarters to the foreign operations is following the _____ strategy.

12. The flow of data between countries is called _____.

13. International businesses that follow the global strategy usually have _____ information systems.

14. International businesses that follow the transnational strategy often have _____ information systems.

Short-answer Questions

1. How can an information system have a strategic impact on a business?

2. Give an example, other than the one in the chapter, of an information system creating a cost leadership advantage for a business.

3. Only certain types of information systems can be strategic systems. True or false? Explain your answer.

4. What types of decisions can a strategic information system support in a business?

5. Do strategic information systems remain strategic forever? Why or why not?

6. How can the value chain be used to identify strategic information system opportunities?

7. Why are interorganizational systems needed for many business alliances to function?

8. How can an interorganizational system have a strategic impact on businesses in an alliance?

9. In what ways can a business participate in an interorganizational system?

10. What type of data is commonly sent using an EDI system?

11. What are the main advantages of EDI?

12. Why are international information systems needed by international businesses?

13. If an international business operates in several countries, must it have an international information system? Why or why not?

14. What are the four basic business strategies followed by international businesses?

15. What are some of the differences between international and domestic information systems?

16. What are the different forms that international information systems can take and how do they relate to international business strategies?

Discussion Questions

1. What information systems could give a college or university a strategic advantage over similar institutions?

2. How can the value chain be used to identify strategic information systems opportunities in a service business?

3. Why is the Internet not used more for interorganizational systems?

4. Some freight companies provide software to businesses so that they can check the status of their shipments. Is this an interorganizational system? Why or why not?

5. What ethical problems might arise in the use of interorganizational information systems?

6. As more and more businesses become international, will all information systems eventually be international systems? Why or why not?

Problem-solving Projects

1. Using the value chain, identify one or more information systems that could have a strategic impact on a business or organization to which you have access. Write an analysis of your conclusions. Use word processing software to prepare your report.

2. Form two teams of three to four students each. One team works for a supplier and the other team works for a customer. Decide on the types of products that the customer buys from the supplier. Then, using database software, the supplier team should develop

a simple order entry system and the customer team should develop a simple purchasing system. During the development of these systems, the teams should not talk to each other. After the systems are developed, develop a simple interorganizational information system that will allow purchase orders from the customer's purchasing system to be entered into the supplier's order entry system. What problems arose in developing the interorganizational system?

3. Investigate an international business to which you have access. Does it follow a multinational, global, international, or transnational strategy? Are its international information systems predominantly decentralized, centralized, distributed, or integrated? Using word processing software, write a summary of your findings.

4. Using the World Wide Web, find information about an international business not headquartered in the United States. What products or services does the business sell and where does it sell them? Where does it develop and produce its products? What problems do you think the business would have setting up international information systems? Using word processing software, write a report answering these questions.

5. A way of selecting between alternatives in a decision is to compute the expected monetary value of each alternative. This calculation involves multiplying the value of each outcome of an alternative by the probability of that outcome, and summing the results. For example, if one alternative has a .6 probability of making $1,000 and a .4 probability of losing $500 (that is, of making -$500), the expected monetary value of that alternative is .6 x 1000 + .4 x (-500) or $400. The best alternative is the one with the greatest expected monetary value.

Assume that a business has to select between two new products—A and B—to develop. The time required to develop the product is critical because the business thinks that its competitors are developing similar products. If the business can get its product to market before its competitors finish their products, then the business can gain a competitive advantage.

The business estimates that it will cost $2 million to develop either product. The development time in years, the probability of taking that amount of time, and the expected revenue in millions of dollars if the product is brought to market in that amount of time for each product are estimated by the business to be as follows:

Development time	Product A		Product B	
	Probability	Expected revenue	Probability	Expected revenue
1	.4	5	.2	10
2	.4	3	.5	3
3	.2	2	.3	0

Prepare a spreadsheet to calculate the expected monetary value of developing each product. Design the spreadsheet so that the development cost, the probabilities, and the expected revenues can be changed easily. Based on the data given so far, which product should be developed? Next, adjust the data to see how sensitive your answer to this question is to different values. What if the product costs $3 million to develop? What if the expected revenue for product B, if the development time is one year, is $12 million? What if the probabilities are different? (Be sure that the probabilities for each product sum to 1.0.) Try different values and combinations of values to see if the preferred alternative changes. What conclusions can you reach?

Real-world Case

Levi Strauss

Employees at jeans giant Levi Strauss & Co. are full of good ideas. But it's not always easy to share them with 37,500 worldwide colleagues. A killer marketing idea developed at a company office in Europe might take weeks or months to reach corporate headquarters in San Francisco—when it might be too late to use it. Those outside the company's financial community might never see or hear about the Chief Financial Officer's recent speech on financial results.

What was missing was a way to quickly and effectively capture and share corporate knowledge across the

globe. When Levi communications executives hit on the idea of using an internal Web site to share best-practices information, they said, "Eureka!" which became the name of the new initiative.

"The goal of the intranet is to empower the organization by cutting down barriers created by different time zones" and disparate computing platforms, says Richard Woo, manager of corporate communications for Levi. Rather than trying to synchronize time zones—not to mention notoriously spotty European telephone service—with a peer half a globe away, or battle unknown e-mail gateways, employees can post their experiences and insights on Eureka to be tapped by someone fishing around for information.

Levi's Information Resources IT group had been using a Web server to share project-status information for a year when corporate communications got an inkling of how Web technology could revolutionize global company communications. Katherine Woodall, director of corporate communications, says her group adopted wholesale a prototype developed by the GAT (Global Architectures & Technology) group. With the help of Craig Lee, director of GAT, Woodall gathered some initial content and put up a pilot, accessible to 25 users at six sites.

The first content was regularly requested information such as product fact sheets, executive biographies, press releases, and copies of speeches. Each document featured links to other useful documents. For example, a press release could contain links to a fact sheet linked to a picture of the product. The Report Card, a twice-monthly report on financial results, is available on line with links to other financial information and a video clip of the chairman's speech of financial results, with his bio also linked. This gives users the ability to use Eureka as a sort of EIS (Executive Information System), says Woodall.

Levi's North American and European organizations recently completed a long re-engineering process focused on improving customer service to retailers. The Asia-Pacific region is undergoing the same re-engineering and will benefit from the experiences of the other two regions. In theory, if the head of operations for the European region needed information, she could pick up the phone and call her U.S. counterpart, but Eureka—Greek for "You found it"—is expected to ease that process considerably. One of the biggest benefits of publishing this type of information is that employees get ideas they might not otherwise have thought of. Eureka is expected to be the cornerstone of continuous improvement.

Along with dissemination of best-practices information, Eureka will soon be used to help Levi employees learn all they can about the business they're in. The global marketing project will collect and publish brand information from around the world. This will include everything from consumer research to information from the external World Wide Web site to data from a company sales kiosk to video clips from Levi's TV commercials from around the world. Users will be able to take a tour of the products, seeing all the information presented to customers.

This will be useful to someone working on an ad campaign or a merchandiser coordinating major accounts. But also it will be used to expand basic business literacy, says Woodall. Any employee could take a "Capitalism 101" tutorial explaining concepts like cash-flow analysis, return on investment, sales and earnings growth, and competitive information, according to Woodall.

Where it might have been too embarrassing for an employee to ask a manager to explain these concepts in the past, when they're posted on the intranet, that person will be able to get educated quickly and efficiently while saving face. After reading a brief explanation of cash flow, for example, a user could click to see the financial data underlying company cash-flow information and see exactly how the numbers were derived.

Does a sewing machine operator really need to be an expert on capitalism's finer points? Probably not, says Woodall, but having all employees gain perspective is what's important. All employees will benefit from learning about emerging markets, which will benefit the company itself. "If you only give employees a narrow focus, it's harder for them to contribute on a global basis," says Woodall.

Also slated is a Chairman's Report Web page, on which Levi's Chairman Bob Haas will create a kind of "virtual fireside chat" in which he'll discuss the view from 60,000 feet. "This will allow much greater intimacy between CEO and employees," says Lee.

Levi's intranauts have been careful not to create layers of red tape on procedural matters. Where the intent is to foster open sharing and employee empowerment, it would be counterintuitive to establish a bureaucratic system for putting up content. Currently, Woodall recommends the communications department of each region act as a content gatekeeper, but the regions are free to disperse their publishing capability. Lee has formed an Editor's Guild, a group of early Web developers that has drafted guidelines on standards for consistent look and feel, appropriate formatting, proper use of logos, and other issues.

Neither the communications department nor the IT department will manage or maintain other divisions' content. "It isn't our intention to control. Our intention is to model clear information," says Woodall.

Questions

1. Based on this case, what type of international business strategy do you think Levi Strauss follows? Explain your reasoning.

2. How does Eureka eliminate time zone barriers for Levi Strauss?

3. How is Eureka used to improve business literacy among Levi Strauss employees around the world?

4. What strategic impact does Eureka have at Levi Strauss?

Source: Lauren Gibbons Paul, "Eureka! Levi finds gold mine of data," *PC Week,* May 13, 1996, pp. 53, 56.

IV

DEVELOPING AND MANAGING INFORMATION SYSTEMS

13 Problem Solving and Individual Application Development

Chapter Outline

End-user Computing   (p. 384)
Problem Solving   (p. 384)
    Solution Procedures   (p. 384)
    Tools for Representing Solution Procedures   (p. 385)
    Basic Procedure Logic   (p. 386)
The Problem-solving Process   (p. 389)
    Problem Definition   (p. 390)
    Solution Procedure Design   (p. 393)
    Software Implementation   (p. 394)
    Implementation Testing   (p. 394)
    Documentation   (p. 396)
Computer Applications   (p. 396)
    User Interface   (p. 397)
    Stored Data   (p. 397)
    Business Rules   (p. 398)
The Individual Application-development Process   (p. 398)
    Application Planning   (p. 400)
    Application Analysis   (p. 400)
    Application Design   (p. 400)
    Application Implementation   (p. 401)
    Application Maintenance   (p. 401)
An Example of Individual Application Development   (p. 402)
    Application Planning   (p. 402)
    Application Analysis   (p. 402)
    Application Design   (p. 403)
    Application Implementation   (p. 404)

Learning Objectives

After completing this chapter, you should be able to:

☐ 1. Explain the meaning of end-user computing.
☐ 2. Explain the role of solution procedures in computer problem solving and describe several tools for representing solution procedures.
☐ 3. Describe the activities in the problem-solving process.
☐ 4. Describe the main parts of a computer application.
☐ 5. Outline the phases and steps in the individual application-development process.

C omputer applications used in individual information systems improve personal productivity. As you saw in Chapter 8, these applications use personal computer software for functions such as database management, spreadsheet analysis, and information presentation. Individual applications are designed to solve one or more problems for the person using the application. These applications do not just "appear," however; they must be carefully developed, often by the individual who will use the application. The application development process involves a number of activities and problem-solving steps. This chapter looks at computer problem solving and the individual application development process.

End-user Computing

Often, people use the term <u>end-user computing</u> when talking about individual applications. This term refers to the development and use of personal computer applications by end-users. In end-user computing, the user decides what applications he or she needs, determines how the applications will function, customizes the software for the applications, and uses the customized software for the processing needed in the applications.

End-users can develop and use computer applications with little formal training other than that required to operate the software. Often, however, untrained users spend considerable time developing an application that does not fully meet their needs. With an understanding of how applications should be developed, end-users can be more effective in their use of computer applications.

Problem Solving

A computer application is designed to solve one or more problems for someone. A <u>problem</u> is a question to which someone does not know the answer, or a statement of something to be done. For example, a problem in sales management could be in the form of a question: What is the commission for each salesperson? A problem in finance could be in the form of a statement: Calculate the expected return on a certain investment. Both these examples are problems because the people involved do not know their *solutions*, which are the answer to the question and the result of the calculation.

Solution Procedures

In business, people want to know the solution to a problem because it helps them do their job. A sales manager needs to know the answer to a commission calculation problem and a finance manager wants to know the result of an investment return calculation. To find the solution requires a sequence of steps that may involve calculations, decision making, and other forms of data manipulation. These steps form a solution procedure for the problem. Finding this procedure is at the core of computer problem solving.

In general, a <u>solution procedure</u> is a set of steps that, if carried out, results in the solution of a problem.[1] For example, consider the "problem" of starting a car. Figure 13.1 shows a solution procedure for this problem. Reading through this procedure, you can see that, if carried out, the problem will be solved; that is, the car will be started. Another example of a solution procedure is a recipe for baking a cake; if

---

[1] Computer professionals often use the term *algorithm* for solution procedure.

FIGURE 13.1

A solution procedure for starting a car

1. **Insert key in ignition**

2. **Put car in neutral**

3. **Repeat the following until car starts or at most 3 times:**
   a. Turn key to start position
   b. Press accelerator pedal
   c. Release key after car starts or after 5 seconds

4. **If car does not start**
   a. Put car in park
   b. Take key out of ignition
   c. Call service station to have car started

a cook follows the solution procedure—the recipe—he or she "solves the problem" of baking a cake.

A computer program is a solution procedure or, more often, several procedures combined together. Each procedure in a program solves a particular problem; the program uses the procedures together to solve a complex problem. For example, a spreadsheet program has many functions for calculating different values. Each function is a procedure that solves a particular problem. A user can create a solution procedure for a complex spreadsheet problem by combining functions in different ways. Similarly, a database program has many solution procedures for manipulating stored data. A user can select individual procedures to create solution procedures for complex problems in database management.

One of the main tasks in computer problem solving is determining the solution procedure needed to solve the problem. This task can be stated as follows: Given a problem, a person must figure out what steps the computer has to go through to solve the problem. Only after these steps have been determined can someone set up the software to solve the problem. This task of developing a solution procedure can be one of the most difficult in computer problem solving; more will be said about it later.

Tools for Representing Solution Procedures

A solution procedure can be represented in many forms. It can be written in English, described in mathematical notation, or drawn in a diagram. The procedure for starting a car, shown in Fig. 13.1, is written in outline form. A procedure for baking a cake is in a form a cook can understand. A computer program written in a programming language is also a representation of a solution procedure.

When someone develops the procedure for solving a problem, he or she must determine the steps in the procedure. These steps should be represented in a form that is clear and easy to understand. For some problems, brief notes or an outline may be sufficient; for other problems, formal tools may be needed. Two tools commonly used to represent solution procedures are *pseudocode* and *flowcharts*.

Pseudocode.   Pseudocode is a written language that uses English and elements that look like a computer programming language to describe a solution procedure. Actually, there are no rules for pseudocode; any written language for showing a solution procedure can be thought of as pseudocode. Many people, however, use a form of pseudocode that resembles a programming language.

As an example, Fig. 13.2 shows the pseudocode for a procedure used to calculate sales commissions and produce a commission report, a problem a sales manager might face. In pseudocode, activities such as input, calculations, and output are

FIGURE 13.2

Pseudocode for a commission-calculation procedure

Write headings for the commission report
DO WHILE there is data for more salespeople
    Get the salesperson's ID number and Sales
    IF Sales are less than $5000 THEN
        Base commission = $500
    ELSE
        Base commission = $500 + 8% of Sales over $5000
    END IF
    Bonus = 25% of Base commission
    Total commission = Base commission + Bonus
    Write the salesperson's ID number, Sales,
        and Total commission on the commission report
END DO

described by short English phrases. The idea is to summarize what is involved in each step without giving all the details. Sequences of these activities are listed in the pseudocode in the order in which they are to be done. To show complex logic in pseudocode, people use special words that look somewhat like a programming language. In Fig. 13.2, the words DO WHILE indicate that the steps that follow, up to the words END DO, are to be repeated as long as a certain condition is true. The words IF, ELSE, and END IF indicate that one step is to be done if a condition is true and another step is to be done if it is false. Reading the pseudocode line by line gives you an understanding of the solution procedure.

Flowcharts. A flowchart (also called a *program flowchart*) is a diagram of a solution procedure. The flowchart is drawn using special symbols such as rectangles and diamonds. Within each symbol is written a phrase describing the activity at that step. The symbols are connected by lines that show the sequence in which the steps take place.

To illustrate, Fig. 13.3 shows the flowchart for a procedure to calculate sales commissions and produce a commission report. This is the same procedure given in pseudocode in Fig. 13.2. The flowchart uses an oval-shape symbol for the beginning and end of the flowchart, a parallelogram for the input and output steps, a rectangle for the calculation steps, and a diamond-shape symbol where decisions are made. Lines with arrowheads, called flowlines, connect the symbols to show the sequence in which the steps are performed. Small circles show where flowlines come together. Reading the flowchart beginning with the symbol marked Start and following the flowlines to the End symbol gives you an understanding of the solution procedure.

Basic Procedure Logic

The *logic* of a solution procedure is the steps in the procedure and the order in which the steps are done. There are three basic ways of arranging the order of the steps in a solution procedure. These ways are called control structures because they control the order of the steps in the procedure. In the first control structure, called a sequence structure, the steps of the procedure are performed in sequence, one after the other. Fig. 13.4 shows the pseudocode and flowchart forms of a sequence structure.

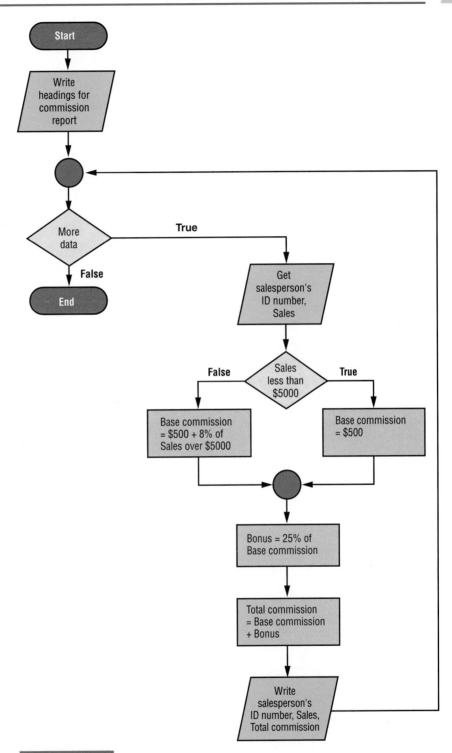

FIGURE 13.3

Flowchart of a commission-calculation procedure

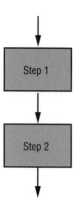

FIGURE 13.4

Sequence structure

Step 1
Step 2

Pseudocode

Step 1

Step 2

Flowchart

The second control structure is called a <u>decision structure</u> because it involves deciding what to do next. The decision is based on a *condition,* which is a phrase that is either true or false, such as whether an employee's sales are less than $5,000. In a decision structure, one group of steps is performed if the condition is true and another group of steps is performed if the condition is false. Figure 13.5 shows the pseudocode and flowchart forms of a decision structure.

FIGURE 13.5

Decision structure

IF condition THEN
  Steps if true
ELSE
  Steps if false
END IF

Pseudocode

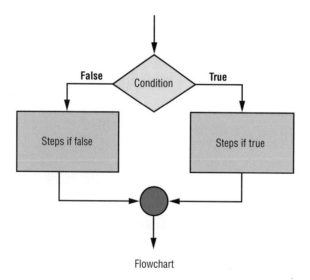

False   Condition   True

Steps if false   Steps if true

Flowchart

FIGURE 13.6

Loop structure

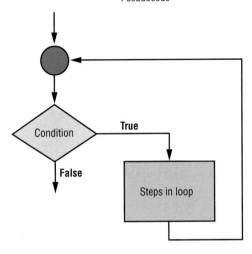

DO WHILE condition
  Steps in loop
END DO

Pseudocode

Flowchart

The third control structure is called a <u>loop structure</u>, or simply a <u>loop</u>. In a loop, a group of steps is repeatedly performed as long as a condition is true. When the condition becomes false, the loop ends. Figure 13.6 shows the pseudocode and flowchart forms of a loop structure.

These control structures can be seen in the sales-commission-calculation procedure in Figs. 13.2 and 13.3. A sequence structure is used for the calculation of the bonus and the total commission. A decision structure is used for the calculation of the base commission. A loop structure is used to repeat the steps as long as there is more data.

There are other control structures besides sequences, decisions, and loops. In fact, there are other forms of decision and loops. *Any* other structure, however, can be created out of these three basic structures. Thus, all someone needs to know to create the logic of a solution procedure is how to sequence steps, make decisions about which steps to perform next, and repeat steps in loops.

In computer programming, these control structures are used extensively. In fact, a computer program written using just these three structures is called a <u>structured program</u> and the systematic process of developing a structured program is called <u>structured programming</u>. These control structures can also appear in other problem-solving situations, such as when using spreadsheet and database software.

The Problem-solving Process

If you need to prepare a computer solution to a problem, you have to perform several tasks. One of them is to set up the software to solve the problem. This task, however, is only one activity in the problem-solving process. In fact, there are five main activities that you must complete:

- Understand and define the problem.
- Design the solution procedure.
- Implement the solution procedure using the selected software.
- Test the software implementation and correct any errors.
- Document the result.

These activities are summarized in Fig. 13.7.

The five activities in the problem-solving process are not necessarily performed in sequence. In fact, several activities usually take place at the same time. For example, documenting begins while you are trying to understand and define the problem. Similarly, you can begin to test part of the solution procedure while you are implementing the rest of it. Often, you have to return to a previous activity. For example, when designing the solution procedure, you may have to go back to the first step to understand more about the problem. The activities are listed not in the order in which they are *started* but in the order in which they are *finished*. For example, you cannot finish designing the solution procedure until you have finished understanding and defining the problem. Nevertheless, you may start the designing activity before you complete the first activity. Similarly, the solution procedure cannot be completely implemented until the design is finished; all testing cannot be completed until implementation is entirely finished; and certain documentation cannot be put into final form until all other activities have been completed.

Problem Definition

In the first activity in the problem-solving process, you must understand completely and define carefully the problem to be solved. Frequently, the most difficult step is recognizing that a problem exists for which a computer solution is appropriate. Since this chapter is about individual applications, the problem solution will be for an individual user. If you are the user, then most likely you will be the one who recognizes the problem.

FIGURE 13.7

The problem-solving process

Problem definition
   Define output
   Define input
   Define calculations
   Define other processing

Solution procedure design
   Design procedure to solve problem

Software implementation
   Implement solution procedure in software

Implementation testing
   Test software implementation
   Debug software implementation

Documentation
   Prepare user documentation
   Prepare developer documentation

Bookmark

Applications Developed by Two Entrepreneurs

Many individuals have recognized technology as a business tool that can take them beyond the charted territories of entrepreneurship. Here are two people who are more expert at business than at technology, but who developed their own computer applications that opened new avenues of opportunity for them.

TRUCKERS TAKE TECHNOLOGY FOR THE LONG HAUL

If you ask truckers to name the device that helps them stay on course over unfamiliar and lonely highways, most will point to a CB radio. But if you pose this question to husband-and-wife team John and Sheila Ewing, they'll tell you that it's software.

The couple, who specialize in long-distance trips, gross about $200,000 a year in revenues. "We travel 6,000 miles a week and we may drive into one state four or five times," says John.

Before buying their big rig, John worked in a metal shop that supplied computer chassis and other metal components to PC manufacturers. He also developed some software for his former employer. This experience came in handy when John realized that he could produce just as much paperwork behind a steering wheel as he had while working behind an office desk. "If your logbooks aren't kept right, you can incur large fines," says John. "It's really time consuming."

John's solution to this paper predicament was to develop a spreadsheet called the Trucker's Helper, which he sells for $50. The template acts as an automated travel report that helps truckers comply with government regulations with a minimum of fuss. Federal and state regulations, for example, require truckers to report how much gas they buy in each state on their itinerary. They also must track other details such as how many miles they travel within each state.

Manually tracking and computing the mileage and gas consumption for each individual trip is a gigantic headache. Fortunately for their fellow truckers, the Ewings came up with a remedy.

BREWER MIXES BEER AND BYTES

By day Marty Johnson is brewmaster and MIS director for Associated Microbreweries in San Diego. By night he markets and sells software designed for the brewing industry.

Johnson gained his programming expertise while employed at a boatyard. "The people writing programs were doing it quite slipshod," he says. "They just about wrote bugs in the programs to ensure they'd keep their jobs." Johnson learned as much as he could about writing programs before deciding to jump ship. He also received a degree in fermentation from the University of California at Berkeley before landing his coveted position as brewmaster.

Johnson not only honed his brewing craft during his six years at Associated Microbreweries, he also developed software to help the business run more efficiently. Johnson now markets The Brew House Records program to other microbrewers. The software stores recipes, records particular beer batches (to aid in quality assurance), and handles tax reporting as required by the Bureau of Alcohol, Tobacco, and Firearms. "It tracks everything, including my caging lots, raw material, past shipments, what's currently in all my tanks, and the status of the beer I've brewed," says Johnson. "The program saves a lot of labor and time. And it cuts record keeping down from hours to minutes." Johnson's fellow beer masters will drink to that.

QUESTIONS

1. Why did John Ewing develop the Trucker's Helper spreadsheet?
2. What benefits does a microbrewer receive from using The Brew House Records program?

WEB SITES
Inc. Magazine: **www.inc.com**
Entrepreneur Magazine: **www.entrepreneurmag.com**

Source: Jenny McCune, "Doing it their way," *Home Office Computing,* February 1996, pp. 53-55.

At first you should try to understand the problem as a whole. What are the requirements of the problem? Usually this involves determining what output is to be produced. What data is available? Answering this question often involves determining what input is to be processed. What calculations and other processing needs to be done? You should try to get a general understanding of the problem as a whole without going into details about the input, output, calculations, and other processing.

After you have a general understanding of the problem, you should refine the problem definition to include specific information about the output, such as its layout; the input, such as how it will be entered; the calculations, such as what formulas are needed; and other processing, such as what conditions affect the results. The refinement of the problem definition should continue until you have sufficient detail to begin designing a solution procedure. At a minimum the problem definition must include the following:

- The output to be produced and its layout.
- The input data available and how it will be entered.
- The calculations to be performed.
- Other processing to be done.

Sometimes you may have difficulty understanding a problem. When this happens, it often helps to isolate parts of the problem and work with each part separately. Another approach is to think of a simpler but similar problem and understand it first. You may get some insight from the simpler problem that helps explain the more complex problem.

Software Selection.   At this stage, or perhaps earlier, you need to determine what type of software you will use for implementing your solution procedure. Chapter 8 discussed a number of types of software used for individual applications, including database, spreadsheet, word processing, and graphics software. Other software is also used by individuals, such as statistical software. Often, the type of software needed for implementing your solution procedure is obvious, but at other times it is not. For example, a problem may require storage and retrieval of data plus analysis of the data. Should database or spreadsheet software be used, or should both be used in combination?

In general, database software is used for situations where there is a large amount of data that needs to be stored, updated, and retrieved. It is especially appropriate when there are several different groups of data that are related. Spreadsheet software is used when data needs to be analyzed using formulas and models. It is very good for "what if" situations, but not appropriate for storage and retrieval of large amounts of data. Word processing, graphics, and desktop publishing software are used for presenting the results of analysis.

Often, an individual application requires the use of several types of software. For example, communication software can be used to download data into a personal database managed by database software. Then selected data from the database can be transferred to a spreadsheet for analysis by spreadsheet software. The results of the analysis can be graphed using the spreadsheet software. The results can also be described in a report using word processing software or prepared in publishable form using desktop publishing software.

The selection of the appropriate software must be based on the characteristics of the problem. You do not have to identify the specific program at this point, only what type of program will be used. The selection is necessary so that you can proceed with the design of the solution procedure.

Solution Procedure Design

With an understanding of the problem, you can begin to design the procedure to solve the problem. The logic of the steps necessary to solve the problem must be carefully planned. As noted earlier, these steps form the solution procedure for the problem. You can express the solution procedure in many ways—in an outline, in pseudocode, in a flowchart, or by using some other technique. This designing activity does *not* involve setting up the software to solve the problem. Before the software can be prepared, you must develop the procedure to solve the problem.

Designing a solution procedure is usually the most difficult task in the problem-solving process, and there are many strategies to help. You should know common solution procedures so that when a problem or a part of a problem requires a known procedure, you can quickly supply it. When you do not know the solution procedure, you must devise one, which can be difficult to do. One approach that may help is to think first of a related problem and develop a procedure to solve it. Another approach is to simplify the problem by discarding some of the conditions and then develop a solution procedure to solve the simpler version. Sometimes it is necessary to return to the problem definition to determine whether anything has been omitted. Any of these approaches may help you think of a procedure for solving the problem.

One technique that you can use to design a solution procedure is called top-down design. In this technique you first design the overall solution procedure. You then break down this procedure into general steps and design the procedure for each of these steps separately. In designing the procedure for a particular step, you may break it down into substeps and design the procedure of each substep separately. This top-down process continues until you have designed all parts of the solution procedure in sufficient detail.

Figure 13.8 illustrates the idea of top-down design for a sales-commission-calculation problem. First you determine that the solution procedure for sales commission calculation requires three main steps:

Get sales data
Compute commission
Produce commission output

FIGURE 13.8

Top-down design

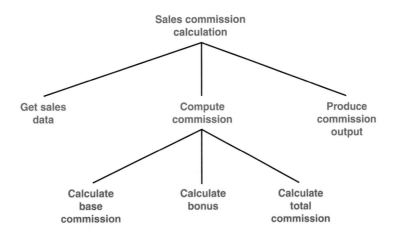

The overall procedure involves performing these three steps in sequence. Then you examine each of these steps separately and design its procedure using a top-down technique. Thus, in Fig. 13.8, you determine that the "Compute commission" step involves three substeps:

> Calculate base commission
> Calculate bonus
> Calculate total commission

You continue to design the solution procedure in a top-down fashion, adding more and more details, until all parts of the procedure have been designed.

Depending on the software selected to implement the solution procedure, there may be more to design than just the procedure logic. If you are using database software, you will have to design the structure of the database, which involves determining what data will be stored in the database and how it will be organized. You may also have to design input data entry forms plus output forms and reports. If you are using spreadsheet software, you will have to determine the layout of the spreadsheet. You will have to decide what will be in the columns and rows, what headings will be used, where input data will be entered, where the output will be shown, and what calculations are needed, among other things. Other types of software will have other special design requirements.

Software Implementation

After you have designed the solution procedure for the problem, you can implement the procedure using the software you have selected. How this is done depends on the software you are using. With spreadsheet software, you enter numbers, text, and formulas into cells in the spreadsheet. With database software, you enter the description of the structure of the database into the software and specify the format of the forms and reports.

To do the implementation, you must know how to use the software. You use your knowledge of the software, an understanding of the problem to be solved, and the design developed previously. You usually have the help of various documents, such as sheets with layouts of the input and output; an outline, pseudocode, or a flowchart of the solution procedure; and formulas to be used in calculations. With this information you set up the software to solve the problem by keying in commands and selecting options with a mouse.

Occasionally during the implementation activity you discover an error in the design, such as steps that are done in the wrong sequence. When this happens, you must redesign part of the solution procedure. It may even be necessary to return to the problem definition and work forward again if a serious error is discovered.

Implementation Testing

Although you may have been very careful in designing the solution procedure and implementing it in the software, the implementation may not be correct. Computer problem solving is a complex activity and it is easy to make mistakes. Thus, the next step in the process is to *test* the software implementation to see if it has any errors.

Three types of errors can occur in a software implementation: syntax errors, execution errors, and logic errors. *Syntax errors* are errors in the form of commands and other entries given to the software. For example, spelling a command incorrectly or entering a formula wrong results in syntax errors. These errors are detected by the software. Usually when such an error is detected, a message describing the error is displayed on the screen. Even though the software has detected a syntax error, it cannot figure out what you want. If there are any syntax errors, the software cannot proceed. You must correct any syntax errors by locating the incorrect entry and changing it.

If there are no syntax errors, the software can execute the commands and instructions you have given it. During execution, other errors may appear. These are called *execution errors*. For example, an attempt to divide a number by zero causes an execution error. These errors are detected by the software as it performs the steps required to solve the problem. When such an error is detected, a message describing the error is displayed on the screen. Still, the software cannot correct the error. You must find the cause of the error and correct it.

The final type of error is detected only after the software has finished processing. If the output is not correct, there is a *logic error*. For example, if the software implementation is supposed to add two numbers and instead you mistakenly used an instruction to subtract, then no syntax or execution error will be detected. The final output will be incorrect, however, because the logic is wrong. The software cannot detect such an error because it does not know what the logic should be. You must determine if there are any logic errors and correct them.

The process used to find logic errors is called **testing**. First you make up input test data. Then you determine by hand what output is expected from the data. Next you run the software implementation with the test data to get the actual output. Finally, you compare the actual output with the expected output. If the outputs are not the same, there is a logic error.

A software implementation must be tested thoroughly before putting it to use. You should test typical sets of input data to be sure the software works in the usual cases, and you should also test unusual sets of data. You might ask someone else to do the testing so that you are not tempted to overlook possible weaknesses just to finish the job. The objective of testing is to reveal as many errors as possible in the software implementation.

After a logic error has been detected through testing, you must locate the error and correct it. An error in a software implementation is called a **bug** and the process of locating and correcting errors is called **debugging**. *Testing* involves determining if errors are present; *debugging* involves finding and correcting errors.

Debugging logic errors can be difficult. People have developed various strategies to try to find the cause of errors. For example, one technique is to step through the logic one instruction at a time, checking the result of each instruction's execution before going on to the next instruction. The idea is to locate any instructions that are causing errors. This technique is very time consuming, however. In fact, testing and debugging often takes as much time as all the other activities of the problem-solving process put together.

Unfortunately, testing only shows the *presence* of errors, not their *absence*. That is, testing can show only whether there are errors, not whether there are no errors. To show that a software implementation is correct, you must demonstrate that under all circumstances it produces the correct result. To do this by using input test data would require executing the software with all possible combinations of data and comparing the output with the expected output calculated by hand. In addition to being an enormous task, this would be senseless, because then you would have all possible outputs calculated by hand and there would be no need for the software (except, perhaps, to check the hand calculations). Thus, you need some other way of showing that the software implementation is correct.

A software implementation is correct because it makes sense logically. There are ways of using a mathematical proof to show that a program is correct, but this approach is very complex and tedious. You can, however, informally "prove" to yourself that your software implementation is correct. This process actually begins with the solution procedure you designed earlier. You need to make sure you understand the reason for each step in the solution procedure and know why, taken together, the steps correctly solve the problem. Then you need to be sure that each step is implemented correctly in the software. The more thought you put into your solution procedure, the better you understand it, and the more carefully you implement it in the software, the more likely the result will be correct.

Documentation

In the last step in the problem-solving process, you bring together all the material that describes the problem, its solution procedure, its software implementation, and the implementation testing. This step results in the <u>documentation</u>, which is a general term that is used for any written description of a computer application. Two types of documentation are user documentation and developer documentation.

User documentation provides information so that the user can understand how to utilize the software implementation. This type of documentation gives instructions for running the software on the computer, including what input to enter and what output to expect. It describes the keys to press to get the software implementation to perform different functions, the meanings of any messages displayed on the screen, and what to do if the software does not work.

Developer documentation is not designed for users but rather for the person who developed the software implementation. It describes how the software implementation works so that it is easier to correct errors and make modifications in the future. This type of documentation includes any written information about the problem definition, the solution procedure design, the software implementation, and the implementation testing. Typically, this documentation contains a brief summary stating the purpose of the software implementation; detailed descriptions of the input and output data; an outline, pseudocode, a flowchart, or any other description of the solution procedure; a list of input test data and the resulting output; and a printed listing of the commands, instructions, and formulas used in the software implementation. Only after all documentation is finished is the problem-solving process complete.

Computer Applications

The first part of this chapter has dealt with computer problem solving and the problem-solving process. The result of the problem-solving process is a solution procedure implemented using computer software. This software implementation may form an entire computer application or it may be just part of an application. For example, a spreadsheet to do financial analysis could be an entire computer application for financial management. A spreadsheet for sales analysis, on the other hand, could be only part of an application that includes other spreadsheet analysis as well as database management. As defined in Chapter 1, a *computer application* is a use of a computer. Any use of a computer, whether it involves a single program or multiple programs, is a computer application.

The software used for a computer application implements the parts of the application. Figure 13.9 shows the three main parts of an application: the user interface, the stored data, and the business rules.

User Interface

The user interface is the part of a computer application that forms the link between the user and the other parts of the application. The user communicates with the software that performs the functions of the application through the interface. Physically, the user interface consists of input and output devices such as screens, printers, keyboards, and mice. Logically, however, the user interface is the interaction the user has with the software through these devices. It is represented by the displays that the user sees on the screen, the printouts the user gets from the printer, the entries the user makes through the keyboard, and the use the user makes of the mouse.

The user performs several main functions through the user interface. One function is *software control*. The user enters instructions or commands, usually through the keyboard or with a mouse, that tell the software what to do. For example, the user tells the software when to do a certain calculation and when to produce a particular output.

Another function the user performs through the user interface is *data entry*, that is, the entry of input data into an application. The software may prompt the user for the required input, often by displaying a data entry form on the screen. The user responds by entering the data, usually through the keyboard.

Still another function the user performs through the user interface is to request information from the software. Such a request is an *inquiry* or *query*. The user enters the request, usually through the keyboard, after being prompted by the software.

Finally, the user receives output through the user interface. This output may be displayed on the screen, printed on paper by a printer, or produced in some other form, such as sound. The output may be the result of processing data entered by the user or retrieved from another source, or may be the response to an inquiry made by the user.

Stored Data

The *stored data* is the part of a computer application that consists of the data used by the application. This data is not the input or output data, but rather the data within the application. The data is used by the application for processing and for responding to inquiries. The stored data is accessed to retrieve data needed by the application. It also is updated as the result of changes entered by the user.

The stored data must be in a form that can be easily accessed and updated. Data may be stored in a spreadsheet, in a file, in a database, or in some other form. In any case, the stored data must be properly organized for ease of use by the software in the application.

FIGURE 13.9

**The parts of a
computer
application**

Business Rules

Between the user interface and the stored data of a computer application is the part that implements the procedures and policies of the business. In general, these procedures and policies are called the <u>business rules</u>. For example, in a sales-commission application a business rule might state that employees who sell more than $5,000 in a month make an 8 percent commission. This rule is implemented in the software of the application.

The business rules form the application logic. The rules state what calculations are done, when data is accessed, how data is updated, which input is entered, and what output is produced. The implementation of the business rules is the main processing performed by the application.

The Individual Application-development Process

If you need to develop an individual computer application, you must do more than just implement a solution procedure using software. As discussed earlier, the problem-solving process includes the activities of problem definition, solution procedure design, software implementation, implementation testing, and documentation. These activities are part of the application-development process, but more is involved in this process than just these activities. In fact, there are four main phases that you must go through in developing an individual application:

- Application planning
- Application analysis
- Application design
- Application implementation

In each phase you must perform several steps, as summarized in Fig. 13.10.

Application planning is the phase in which you decide whether a new application should be developed. During *application analysis*, you determine what the new application must do. Then, during *application design*, you decide how the new application will function. Finally, in the last phase, *application implementation*, you develop the solution procedures that make up the application.

FIGURE 13.10

The application-development process

Application planning
    Need recognition
    Feasibility analysis

Application analysis
    Current procedure analysis
    Requirements analysis

Application design
    User interface design
    Stored data design
    Business rules implementation design

Application implementation
    Solution procedure development
    Application testing
    Application documentation

Bookmark

Creating a Web Site at Archetype

To advertise her Seattle architectural design business, Archetype, Lydia Aldredge used a community newspaper and a women's resource directory. She published photographs of her buildings in the Sunday edition of the *Seattle Times*, and hung signs with her name and phone number at her construction sites. So it made perfect sense to hang her shingle on the World Wide Web as well.

For a long time, Lydia thought the Internet was unnecessary for her small and specialized architectural practice. Why would she want to use a global medium to gain local clients? Then she started talking to friends and colleagues with Internet access who were enthusiastic about the power of the Web, and they convinced her to take the leap. It was time to create her own Web page to promote her business.

She had three goals. First, because her advertising budget allowed only about $500 for creating and maintaining a Web site, she estimated that landing two new jobs from the site would make having the site more than worthwhile. Second, like many architects, she wanted to design her business's promotional materials herself. Finally, she figured that she could spare only about a week's worth of evenings and a weekend for the whole project.

Could she put her business on the Web in a week?

As with any other project, Aldredge started with extensive research. She browsed the Web sites of other small businesses and architecture firms before designing her own home page.

Before she started the actual design, she prepared the contents. Assembling this raw material took time, especially given her mix of graphics—sketches, line drawings, and photographs of her work. She spent a day writing short concise text that describes her business, experience, and the services she provides. Along with a home page, she planned for her Web site to display her résumé, visuals of some recent projects, and her fees.

Gathering up 20 images of architectural sketches, blueprints, and finished photos, she visited a colleague's office to borrow his scanner. It took about an hour to scan, clean up, and crop and fit the images.

She used Claris Home Page to create the Web site. Although Home Page starts with a blank, gray page automatically, she opted for a white background that will make her text more readable.

First, she typed in text for the company logo. She decided on a simple and tasteful text banner rather than a graphic because her Web site would be loaded with images of her work. She chose a conventional blueprint blue, in keeping with the architecture theme, for her company logo. Then she added some scanned images and arranged the text and images on the home page.

Next, she created a new page labeled "Résumé" and imported three images. Then she created a Projects page and a Services and Fees page, bringing her Web site page count to four.

Finally she created links to connect all the pages in the site. Previewing the site to check the links, she found she could easily move among the four pages. She was now ready to upload the files to the subscriber Web site of Earthlink, her Internet service provider.

She organized the Web pages and images in one file and uploaded it to the Earthlink server. Navigating her new site, she discovered some problems with images, but after making a few changes she got her Web site to appear as she had planned. Then, she sent e-mail to the major Web search engines (AltaVista, Web Crawler, Yahoo!) requesting that her new site be placed in their Arts and Architecture links.

Was putting her business on the Web worth the time and effort? Will her Web site deliver new customers to her architectural practice? Although she missed her one-week goal by a few days, she was able to create and post a credible, smoothly functioning, easily downloadable Web site that was ready for business. So far, two potential customers have e-mailed her after visiting her site, and she landed one new project from a company that was impressed with her presence on the Web.

In retrospect, Aldredge is glad she designed her site herself instead of hiring a young computer whiz who knows HTML. As a professional designer, she has strong feelings about how her site looks and how it represents her business. Also, with her new skills, she can update her site in as little as 15 minutes.

QUESTIONS

1. How did Lydia Aldredge evaluate the feasibility of developing a Web site?
2. Which steps in the application-development process did Lydia Aldredge follow in developing a Web site?

WEB SITE
Archetype: home.earthlink.net/~archetype

Source: Lydia Aldredge, "On the Web," *Home Office Computing*, June, 1997, pp. 76-79.

The phases of the application development process are not necessarily completed in sequence. Often, you have to go back to a previous phase when you discover that something you need is missing. For example, during application design you may have to return to the application analysis phase. Thus, application development is an iterative or repetitive process.

Application Planning

In the first phase of the individual application-development process you plan what computer application will be developed. To start the planning phase, someone must recognize the need for a new application. For individual applications, this usually is an individual user. A need exists when the current way of doing things is not working well or when new things need to be done.

After the need for an application has been recognized, you must determine whether it is sensible to develop the application. That is, you analyze the *feasibility* of the application. Many users assume that a computer application is the best alternative, but sometimes a manual procedure is better. A computer application is feasible if it is possible for someone to develop it using existing technology, if the user will use it, and if it makes economic sense. To evaluate the economic feasibility of the application, you should compare the expected costs of developing and using the application with its expected benefits. If the total benefits of the application are greater than the total costs, the application is economically feasible. In analyzing the costs, you must carefully consider the time you will spend developing the application. Application development can be very time consuming, and the time spent developing an application is taken away from other activities.

Application Analysis

After you have decided that a new application is needed and that it is feasible, you must analyze the application to determine *what* it must do. Often, you start by analyzing the current procedures, that is, the way you do things currently. You may gather written descriptions of the current procedures and collect copies of any forms and documents. If there is an existing computer application, you can determine the outputs produced by the application, the data used by the application, the input entered into the application, and the business rules enforced by the application.

Next, you determine what is required in the new application. That is, you analyze the *requirements* for the application. In performing this analysis, you need to think about your needs. You should prepare a written description of the requirements, stating what the application will do. Often, this involves listing the outputs that the application will produce, the inputs that it will accept, and the processing that it will do. The requirements should be such that the need identified earlier is met by the new application. The requirements are the final result of the application analysis phase.

Application Design

Now that you have an understanding of what the new application must do, you can design *how* the application will do it. During this phase you design the main parts of the application. First, you should determine what the *user interface* will be like. You should lay out the arrangement of input and output data on screens and reports, and decide how the user will control the software. After the user interface has been designed, you should determine what *stored data* will be needed in the application and how it will be organized. Finally, you should determine how the *business rules* will be implemented in the application. You should write down any formulas needed for calculations, write a description of any other data processing, and list the conditions under which different processing is done.

To complete the design, you must determine what software will be used for implementation. You may decide to use database software, spreadsheet software, word processing software, or some other software. You may determine that the application will require the use of several types of software. For each program you must describe the outputs, inputs, stored data, and processing. In addition, you must describe how the different programs are related—for example, that the output from one program is the input to another program.

Application Implementation

In the last phase of the application development process you implement the application. This involves developing a solution procedure for each problem that the application must solve. At this point, you use the problem-solving process discussed earlier to solve each problem. Actually, the first step in that process, problem definition, has already been carried out in the earlier application development phases. Now you need to design the solution procedures, implement them using the appropriate software, test the software implementations, and document the results.

The next step is to ensure that the application works as required, which involves testing the application. Before this step is undertaken the individual software implementations in the application are tested separately as they are developed. During the application testing step, these software implementations are brought together, and the application is tested as a whole. All application results should be checked with what is expected; any differences mean that there are errors in the application. When an error is detected, the part of the application that caused the error must be modified and tested again. This process continues until no errors are detected in the application.

The final step in the application implementation phase is documenting the application. Individual software implementations should be documented as described earlier. In addition, the functioning of the application as a whole should be documented. This documentation should describe what the application does, which software is run and when, and how the user interacts with the application. Only after the documentation is complete is the application-development process finished.

Application Maintenance

After a computer application has been in use for a while it may be necessary to make changes in it, a process called <u>maintenance</u>. Maintenance is necessary to correct errors in the application, add new features to the application, and modify the application because of changed requirements. Whenever you have to do maintenance, you must go through the four phases in the application-development process. You must plan the change to be made, analyze what the change will do, design how the change will function, and implement the change. In implementing the change, you need to perform the five activities in the problem-solving process. You must understand and define the change that is needed, design the logic for the change, implement the change, test the software implementation with the change, and document the change. All these steps must be done to complete the application maintenance.

An Example of Individual Application Development

To illustrate the process of developing an individual application, assume that you are the payroll manager of a business. You need a computer application to keep track of the monthly sales of each salesperson in the business, and to compute the commission for each salesperson based on the monthly sales. This section shows how you can develop this application, following the phases of the application-development process described in the previous section.

Application Planning

You start the application-development process by recognizing the need for a computer application. You are having trouble keeping track of the monthly sales of each salesperson. Computing the commission at the end of each month is inaccurate and time consuming. You think that a well-designed sales-commission application could help you with your job.

You can develop a computer application like you want using existing technology and you would make use of it. It makes economic sense because it would save you time on your job. Hence, it is feasible to develop this application.

Application Analysis

Currently you keep track of each salesperson's monthly sales on ledger sheets in a three-ring binder. At the end of the month, the marketing department sends you the total sales for each salesperson, which you record on your ledger sheets. Then you compute the commission for each salesperson based on the monthly sales in the ledger sheets, and prepare a report listing the commissions for all salespeople.

You decide that your new application should meet several requirements, which are summarized in Fig. 13.11. The application should produce a report every month with each salesperson's monthly sales and commission. It should also provide a screen display giving the response to a query about a salesperson's monthly sales so that this figure can easily be looked up at any time. The application should allow you to enter a salesperson's monthly sales. Processing involves updating the monthly sales for a salesperson and calculating the commission, as shown in Fig. 13.11.

FIGURE 13.11

Requirements for the sales-commission application

Outputs.
  The application should produce two outputs:
    1. A printed report giving the monthly sales and the commission for each salesperson.
    2. A screen display giving the monthly sales for any salesperson.

Inputs.
  The application should allow any salesperson's monthly sales to be entered.

Processing.
  The application should perform the following processing:
    1. Update the monthly sales for any salesperson.
    2. Calculate the commission for each salesperson as the sum of the base commission and the bonus. The base commission is determined from the following schedule:

Sales	Base Commission
Less than $5000	$500
$5000 or more	$500 + 8% of sales over $5000

The bonus is 25% of the base commission.

Application Design

You can now determine what software you will use for the application. You decide that the salesperson data will be stored in a database managed by database software. You will enter a salesperson's monthly sales into this software and have the software update the salesperson's sales. You will also use this software to provide a response to the query about the monthly sales for a salesperson.[3] You decide that the commission will be calculated using spreadsheet software, and you will use this software to produce the report of monthly sales and commissions. At the end of the month, the data for each salesperson will be transferred from the salesperson database to the sales commission spreadsheet. (See Fig. 13.12.)

The user interface will include a data entry form for entering a salesperson's monthly sales into the database. You decide that the form will have the layout shown in Fig. 13.13. The user interface will also include a screen that provides a response to a query about a salesperson's monthly sales. Figure 13.14 shows how you decide this output will be laid out. Finally, the user interface will include a printed report of monthly sales and commissions which you determine will be laid out as shown in Fig. 13.15.

The stored data for the application must include each salesperson's monthly sales. In addition, there must be some way of identifying each salesperson, such as a salesperson number. You also need to store each salesperson's name. You conclude that the stored data will consist of the number, name, and monthly sales of each salesperson. You decide that this data can be stored in a single table in the database.

The main business rule that the application will implement involves the calculation of the commission, as shown in the requirements in Fig. 13.11. You decide that this rule can be implemented in formulas in the spreadsheet. The formulas will use a decision structure in the calculation of the commission.

FIGURE 13.12

Software for the sales-commission application

FIGURE 13.13

The data entry form for the sales-commission application

```
┌─────────────────────────────────────────────────────────┐
│ ─ │            Monthly Sales Data Entry           │ ▼ │ ▲ │
├─────────────────────────────────────────────────────────┤
│                                                          │
│         Monthly Sales Data Entry                         │
│                                                          │
│  ▶                                                       │
│        Salesperson Number:        [          234]        │
│                                                          │
│        Enter Monthly Sales:       [             ]        │
│                                                          │
│  │◀ │ ◀ │ Record: 1      │ of 1      │ ▶ │ ▶│ │          │
└─────────────────────────────────────────────────────────┘
```

---

[3]You could store the data in a spreadsheet but it will be easier to manage the data if it is stored in a database.

FIGURE 13.14

The query
response screen
for the sales-
commission
application

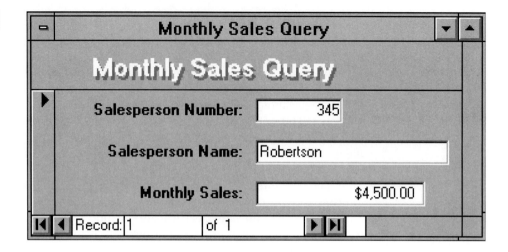

FIGURE 13.15

The commission
report for the
sales-commission
application

Sales Commission Report

Salesperson Number	Salesperson Name	Monthly Sales	Commission
123	Jones	$ 9,000,00	$ 1,025.00
234	Smith	$ 2,000.00	$ 625.00
345	Robertson	$ 4,500.00	$ 625.00
456	Andrews	$ 5,500.00	$ 675.00

Application Implementation

Now you need to implement the application in the software you have selected. You have two problems to solve: a database management problem and a spreadsheet analysis problem. You tackle each problem separately, following the problem-solving process discussed earlier in this chapter, and develop a solution procedure for each problem. You already have defined each problem and selected the software. Now, you design the solution procedure for each problem, implement each procedure in the software, test each implementation, and document the results. In solving the database management problem you design the structure of the database, that is, how the data in the database will be organized. In solving the spreadsheet analysis problem, you decide how the spreadsheet will be laid out. You also determine the logic in the commission calculation, representing it in pseudocode (like Fig. 13.2), in a flowchart (like Fig. 13.3), or using some other technique. You implement and test each solution procedure, using the selected software. After you are finished, you have software solutions for the two main parts of the application.

Next, you test the application as a whole. You have already tested the database and spreadsheet parts separately. Now you enter sample data for several salespeople into the database, transfer the data from the database to the spreadsheet, print the report of monthly sales and commissions, and check the printed output from the spreadsheet against the input entered into the database. You repeat this process several times with different data until you are convinced that the application works correctly.

Finally, you document the application. You already have documentation for the database and the spreadsheet. To this you add documentation on how the application works as a whole. For example, you include notes on how to transfer data from the database to the spreadsheet.

When you are finished with the implementation phase, you can begin using the application. Although the application development process has taken some effort, you are confident that it will work correctly and that it will help you in your job.

Chapter Summary

☐ **End-user computing** is the development and use of personal computer applications by end users. In end-user computing, the user decides what applications he or she needs, determines how the applications will function, customizes the software for the applications, and uses the customized software for the processing needed in the application. (p. 384)

☐ A **solution procedure** is a set of steps that, if carried out, results in the solution of a **problem**. One of the main tasks in computer problem solving is determining the solution procedure needed to solve the problem. Two common tools for representing a solution procedure are pseudocode and flowcharts. **Pseudocode** is a written language that uses English and elements from a programming language to describe the solution procedure. A **flowchart** is a diagram that uses special symbols connected by lines to show the solution procedure. (pp. 384–389)

☐ There are five main activities that you must go through in the problem-solving process. First, you must completely understand and carefully define the problem to be solved. As part of this activity, you may also select the type of software to be used for the implementation. Next, you must design the procedure to solve the problem. Then you can implement the solution procedure using the software you have selected. Next, you must detect and correct any errors in the software implementation. **Testing** involves determining if there are errors in the soft-

ware implementation; **debugging** involves locating and correcting any errors, or **bugs**, that are detected. Finally, you must prepare **documentation** of the result of the process. (pp. 389–396)

☐ A computer application consists of a user interface, stored data, and business rules. The **user interface** is the part of the application that forms the link between the user and the other parts of the application. The stored data is the part of the application that consists of the data used by the application. The **business rules** are the procedures and policies of the business that are implemented in the application. (pp. 396–398)

☐ The first phase of the individual application-development process is application planning. In this phase, you must recognize the need for a computer application and determine if it is feasible to develop the application. The next phase is application analysis in which you analyze the current procedures and determine the requirements for the new application. The third phase is application design. Here you design the parts of the application, including what the user interface will be like, what stored data will be needed, and how the business rules will be implemented. Finally, in the last phase—application implementation—you develop the solution procedures for each problem that the application must solve, test the application, and document the application. (pp. 398–405)

Key Terms

Bug (p. 395)
Business Rule (p. 398)
Control Structure (p. 386)
Debugging (p. 395)
Decision Structure (p. 388)
Documentation (p. 396)
End-user Computing (p. 384)

Flowchart (p. 386)
Loop Structure (p. 389)
Maintenance (p. 401)
Problem (p. 384)
Pseudocode (p. 385)
Sequence Structure (p. 386)
Solution Procedure (p. 384)

Structured Program (p. 389)
Structured Programming (p. 389)
Testing (p. 395)
Top-down Design (p. 393)
User Interface (p. 397)

Review Questions

Fill-in Questions

1. A(n) _____ is a set of steps that, if carried out, results in the solution of a problem.

2. Two common tools used to represent a solution procedure are _____ and _____.

3. A(n) _____ is a way of arranging the steps in a solution procedure.

4. A control structure in which one group of steps is done if a condition is true and another group of steps is done if a condition is false is a(n) _____.

5. A(n) _____ is a group of steps that is repeatedly performed as long as a condition is true.

6. The first step in the problem-solving process is to _____. The last step is to _____.

7. When you start with the overall design of a solution procedure and then successively refine the design until you reach the final solution procedure, you are using a technique called _____.

8. Three types of errors that can appear in a software implementation are _____, _____, and _____.

9. A common term for an error in a software implementation is a(n) _____.

10. Two types of documentation of a computer application are _____ and _____.

11. The part of a computer application that forms the link between the user and the other parts of the application is the _____.

12. The procedures and policies of a business that are implemented in a computer application are called _____.

13. Determining what a new application must do is part of _____. Determining how a new application will function is part of _____.

14. The process of making changes in a computer application is called _____.

Short-answer Questions

1. What is end-user computing?

2. Describe the three basic control structures used in a solution procedure.

3. What is structured programming?

4. In what order are the activities of the problem-solving process performed?

5. What should be included in the problem definition?

6. During which activity of the problem-solving process is the logic of the solution procedure developed?

7. What is the difference between testing and debugging?

8. What are the three main parts of a computer application?

9. What functions can a user perform through the user interface of a computer application.

10. What are the phases of the application-development process?

11. What does it mean to say that a computer application is feasible?

12. During which phase of the application-development process are the requirements for a computer application determined?

Discussion Questions

1. What are some difficulties that an untrained end-user can have in trying to develop a computer application?

2. How can the problem-solving process be adapted for solving problems without using computers, such as problems in a math class or a finance class?

3. What are some examples of business rules in a college or university?

4. As software becomes easier to use, will end-user application development someday be unnecessary? Why or why not?

5. Sometimes an individual application is developed for use by several users on different computers. What additional factors need to be considered in developing such an application?

6. Assume that a co-worker has developed a spreadsheet application for calculating bonuses for employees in your company. You asked him if he tested his spreadsheet and he said he did not have to because he knows it is correct. What would you do in this situation?

Problem-solving Projects

1. Interview several users in a business to which you have access to find out how they developed the computer application they are using. If there are a lot of users, you can develop a questionnaire to ask the same questions of all users. Find out what process the users followed in developing their applications. Which steps in the application-development and problem-solving process did they follow? How successful were they in developing their applications? Using word processing software, write a summary of your findings.

2. Complete the development, including implementation, of the sales-commission application described in the last section of this chapter.

3. Using spreadsheet software, develop a computer application to compare your expenses each month with your budget for various items (for example, rent, food, transportation). Enter amounts that you budget for each item and the amount you actually spent on each item for a recent month. Have the application calculate the difference between each budgeted amount and the amount spent. Also have the application calculate the percent difference.

4. Using database software, develop a computer application to keep track of sales contacts. The data stored in the application should include the customer number, name, address, and phone number; and the date of the last sales contact. The application should produce the following outputs:

   a. A list of the data for all customers.

   b. A display of a specific customer's name, address, and phone number, given that customer's number.

   c. A list of all customers who have not been contacted since a given date.

   Supply data for 15 to 20 customers to test the application.

5. The user interface is a critical part of a computer application. Using the World Wide Web, locate information on how to design a good user interface. Using word processing software, prepare a brief summary of recommendations for user interface design that you found on the Web.

Real-world Case

Cigna

Microsoft Office is the Napoleon of desktop applications: It's ambitious; it can support an empire; and it's getting bloated in its old age.

But the core strength of Office—beyond the functionality of the individual applications such as Excel, Word, and PowerPoint—is that corporate developers can use Office as a foundation for an enterprise-wide platform.

In short, many corporations have turned to Office as a base on which to develop a host of custom applications.

To be sure, Office is fundamentally for individual applications. But for large companies willing to take an innovative approach, a Philadelphia-based division of

the insurance behemoth Cigna shed light on a way to leverage the advantages of Office as a development platform at a very big business.

The consulting division, which accounts for $1.6 billion in revenues out of Cigna's total $96 billion in assets, relies heavily on technology to provide its employees with the reporting tools they require to do their jobs.

Cigna's consultants go to their customers to assess hazardous conditions in client businesses. A typical consultant must quickly arrive at the cost of remedying an industrial accident, assessing the cost of therapy for injured parties, the cost of productivity losses, and a total compensation figure. It typically took three days to produce a report. Although the methodology used by the consultants was formal and well-structured, a lot of time was spent acquiring data.

Until the division decided to migrate its processes to an Office-based system, consultants relied on mainframe sources, which ate time while information-hungry consultants starved in the field.

Cigna decided to bring in someone with the experience to change things quickly: Larry Meador, senior vice president and CIO at Cigna, was successful at overhauling systems at TransAmerica, and he has been on the faculty at MIT.

After all, this division was supposed to be a profit center. But without a major process change, it was losing money. One year, it lost some $530 million. The numbers have turned from red to black with about $100 million in profits recently. Part of this dramatic turnaround can be attributed to the vagaries of the cyclical insurance industry. But the contribution of moving to Office as an efficient developer platform on which to base the division's refocused business processes was also significant, according to Meador.

"The company had no technology strategy before we took over: The division was dying," Meador says.

The current phase of the project is to deploy Office in the field, which will be accomplished by implementing a division-wide intranet.

There is some urgency to this matter. Cigna's consulting business is knowledge-based. This means that when consultants walk out the door, they take Cigna's expertise with them. If a consultant walks permanently away, the very business process with which Cigna makes its bread and butter walks away, too.

Management clearly understood that without codifying Cigna's business processes into something that the company can retain for itself, the company loses expertise with each departure.

"We think of this as a high-level reusable blueprint," Meador says. But "what we have not done is try to replace human judgment. We're developing technology to complement judgment."

Furthermore, the business logic stored in the Office applications can be moved to other areas of Cigna as they come on line.

"We are now prioritizing and 'productizing' our services," Meador says. "We are starting down a path that is providing a way so that our expertise can't walk out the door and leave us out in the cold."

One aspect of Office that made a difference to the company's developers was the more than 600 reusable objects in the applications. Object-based development

can save programmers countless hours of time spent in repetitive programming, though certainly this experience isn't shared by all corporations.

But in Cigna's case, using objects meant development time was crunched into a shorter time period by "using the technology to capture very narrow business domains," Meador says. "Our technology strategy emphasizes reusability, and the 600 objects allow us to get to a new level of integration."

Other components that came in handy, according to Meador, were the intelligent assistants, providing intuitive help models for end-users as well as developers.

"Training costs and customer-service costs are a big issue for us—as I suppose they are for most everybody," Meador says.

In the end, Cigna estimates saving 14,000 hours per year in the amount of consultants' billable time, which directly translates to about $750,000 revenue.

Meador and his staff hope to have Microsoft's desktop Internet Explorer browser deployed to consultants in their home offices, giving direct access to the company intranet and customers by the summer.

End-users have reported satisfaction with the system from the get-go because they were already familiar with Office's individual applications. Help-desk costs are minimal, according to Meador. With the reporting and information-access features in Office, a complicated procedure such as a request for proposal or an evaluation of a client's varying site characteristics is accomplished more quickly and seamlessly at a customer's site. Also, information is made account-specific.

"What all this means is that consultants can take the time to do what they're really paid for," Meador says.

Questions

1. Why would a company use an individual application software suite such as Microsoft Office for an enterprise-wide system?

2. Before using the Office-based system, how did Cigna's consultants acquire data for their reports?

3. Why was there a problem when an employee left Cigna and how did the Office-based system help solve this problem?

4. Who developed the Office-based system at Cigna?

5. What economic benefit did Cigna receive from the Office-based system?

Source: Ilan Greenberg, "Big business takes place using latest Microsoft Office," *InfoWorld*, February 17, 1997, p. 60.

14 Information System Development

Chapter Outline

People in Information System Development   (p. 410)
The System Development Process   (p. 410)
    System Planning   (p. 411)
    System Analysis   (p. 413)
    System Design   (p. 415)
    System Implementation   (p. 416)
    System Maintenance   (p. 418)
System Development Tools   (p. 419)
    Data Flow Diagrams   (p. 419)
    System Flowcharts   (p. 422)
    Entity-relationship Diagrams   (p. 423)
    CASE   (p. 424)
An Example of Information System Development   (p. 425)
    System Planning   (p. 426)
    System Analysis   (p. 427)
    System Design   (p. 429)
    System Implementation   (p. 430)
    System Maintenance   (p. 431)
Other System Development Approaches   (p. 431)
    Prototyping   (p. 431)
    Rapid Application Development   (p. 432)
    Object-oriented Analysis and Design   (p. 432)
Business Process Reengineering   (p. 433)

Learning Objectives

After completing this chapter, you should be able to:

- [ ] 1. Explain the roles of the people who are involved in information system development.
- [ ] 2. Outline the phases and steps in the information system development process.
- [ ] 3. Describe the user's involvement in each phase of the system development process.
- [ ] 4. Explain the purpose of common tools used for system development.
- [ ] 5. Explain the use of prototyping and rapid application development in system development.
- [ ] 6. Describe the purpose of business process reengineering.

C hapter 13 discussed the process that users follow to develop computer applications for *individual information systems*, that is, systems used by a single person. Information systems that involve many users, such as *workgroup, organizational,* and *interorganizational information systems,* are developed following a similar, although more complete, process. This process involves many steps and may take a few days to several years to finish. It may be performed by a single person or by a team of hundreds of specialists. Users also participate in certain steps of the process. This chapter discusses the process of developing multiple-user information systems, emphasizing when and how users will be involved in the process.

People in Information System Development

The people who are primarily responsible for developing information systems are called systems analysts. Systems analysts follow a step-by-step process, described later in this chapter, to develop information systems. Other people, such as computer programmers, also may be involved in the process. Programming, however, is just part of system development.

Users of the system are another important group of people involved in the system development process. An information system is designed to meet the needs of its users. To accomplish this goal, the users must explain their needs to the systems analysts. In addition, the users must determine if the system that is developed meets their needs. As you will see, users are involved in many steps of the system development process.

Often, systems are developed by a group of people who form a project team. The team may consist of several systems analysts and programmers. Users also are included on the team. One person, usually an experienced systems analyst, is the team leader.

The System Development Process

There are many ways of describing the system development process, which is also called the system development life cycle or SDLC. This book divides the process into five main phases:

- System planning
- System analysis
- System design
- System implementation
- System maintenance

Each phase involves several steps, which are summarized in Fig. 14.1 and discussed later. This figure also summarizes the user involvement in each step.

System planning is the phase in which the systems analyst decides whether a new information system should be developed. During system analysis, the analyst studies the existing system and determines what the new system must do. Then, during system design, the analyst specifies how the new system will function. In the next phase, system implementation, the systems analyst acquires the components of the system—such as programs—tests the system, and changes over to the new system. Finally, system maintenance involves modifying the system during its life to meet new requirements.

FIGURE 14.1

The system development process

SYSTEM DEVELOPMENT STEPS	USER INVOLVEMENT
System planning	
Problem recognition and definition	High
Feasibility analysis	Low
System analysis	
Current system analysis	High
User requirements analysis	Very High
System specification	Low
Alternative identification and evaluation	Low
System design	
Input and output design	High
File or database design	None
Program design	None
Procedure design	High
System implementation	
System acquisition	Low
System testing	Moderate
System installation	Very high
System maintenance	Varies

The phases of the system development process are supposed to be performed in sequence. Planning is done before analysis, which comes before design, followed by implementation. Often, however, it is necessary to return to previous phases. For example, during design it may be discovered that further analysis is needed or that the planning was not adequate. Thus, the system development process is really an iterative or repetitive process.

System Planning

In the first phase of the system development process the systems analyst plans what information systems will be developed. To start the planning phase, someone must recognize the need for a new information system. Usually, some type of system already exists in the organization. The existing system may be manual or computerized; it may be formal, with written procedures, or informal, remembered by a few people. In any case, someone must recognize a problem with the existing system and recommend that a new system be developed.

Often, the user of an existing system recognizes the problem. For example, a salesperson using an order entry system may sense a problem with the system when customers complain that orders are being lost. A user may also determine that an entirely new system is needed—one that does things that are not done by any existing system. Even in this case there still is a problem: What is wrong with the existing system that it cannot do everything required? In any case, the user must report the problem to the person responsible for system development.

Next, someone, usually a systems analyst, must carefully define the problem, distinguishing it from its symptoms. For example, lost orders are a symptom of a problem in an order entry system. The actual problem may be inadequate checks for errors in the system, or unreliable hardware. The systems analyst must prepare written documentation of the problem. This documentation establishes the need for the information system.

System Development Lessons from Time Warner Communications

A few years ago, Time Warner Communications in Englewood, Colorado, rolled the dice. It invested almost $1 billion in advanced information systems and networks to break in to the local-access residential telephone business.

The gamble failed, partly because of a bleeding-edge information technology strategy in which Time Warner spent $30 million on a customer service system that couldn't deliver when it was needed most.

Now the company has canceled plans to expand its local residential telephone ventures and is trying to sell the expensive customer service system it developed to support those ventures. Time Warner Communications is the telephony division of Time Warner Cable in Stamford, Connecticut, the cable television subsidiary of New York–based media conglomerate Time Warner, Inc.

The lessons for IS organizations: Don't overspend on the IS infrastructure to support chancy new business; don't mix bleeding-edge technology and bleeding-edge businesses; and test, test, test before you inflict new systems on customers.

Other factors contributed to Time Warner Communication's defeat, including intense competition, regulatory uncertainty, and the company's own financial troubles. But performance lagged in its $30 million Customer Management System (CMS), hobbling Time Warner Cable for nine crucial months as it entered the market.

When Time Warner Communications decided to enter the market, creating an easy-to-adapt customer service application such as CMS seemed the best way to offer less-expensive but better services and features than its competitors.

The company combined customer, account, product, and network data in a data repository. Given the volatile nature of the telecommunications market, the decision was made to select an expert system to implement the business rules. The choice allowed Time Warner Communications to support constant rules changes, such as what type of data is acceptable in ordering and billing forms, without having to rewrite applications.

To cut development time, object-oriented development languages were chosen, even though Time Warner Communications had to build its own software to link applications with its Sybase database. The firm also had to outsource code-writing work to lower-priced developers in Pakistan.

Today, numerous tools effectively link object-based applications and relational databases, but Time Warner Communications' homegrown software slowed response time. The system was so slow that employees were forced to write information such as customer names and the types of service being ordered and later type it into the system.

A mad rush to deploy the system deprived IT personnel of time to perform sufficient testing. Constant "tweaking" of the object-relational database management system link has improved performance substantially.

But in the meantime, other problems bedeviled Time Warner Communications. Regulatory delays prevented it and other carriers from successfully entering local markets. Delays kept the cost of equipment higher than expected. Then there was Time Warner's unfamiliarity with the phone business.

Under the best-case scenario, it would take Time Warner almost a decade to recoup its investment in Time Warner Communications' local telephone bid.

The local telephony business company would need to generate more than $10 billion in revenue to generate enough profit to amortize the costs of building and operating its telephone network and the associated IT infrastructure.

In the end, Teraid Voorhees, former chief operating officer, said, the lesson is that "Trailblazers make mistakes. The idea that we could be a service company as well as a software development house was not working for us."

QUESTIONS

1. What lessons can IS organizations learn from Time Warner Communications' development of CMS?
2. Was the problem with CMS the main reason why Time Warner Communications decided to pull out of the local-access residential telephone business? Explain your answer.

WEB SITE
Time Warner: www.pathfinder.com

Source: Emily Kay, "Failed phone venture show how not to build software," *Computerworld,* May 5, 1997, p. 12.

After the need for an information system has been recognized, the systems analyst must determine if it is feasible to develop the system, a process called feasibility analysis. In this process, the analyst must determine if the system is technically feasible, operationally feasible, and economically feasible. An information system is *technically feasible* if it is possible to develop it using existing technology. For example, a system that requires unrestricted voice input is not yet technically feasible. A system is *operationally feasible* if the people in the business will use it. For example, a system to be used by people who do not want it is not operationally feasible. Finally, an information system is *economically feasible* if it makes sense economically. For example, a system that costs more than it provides in benefits for the organization is not economically feasible. To evaluate the economic feasibility of the system, the expected costs of developing and operating the system are compared with the expected benefits in a process called cost/benefit analysis. If the total benefits over the life of the system are greater than the total costs over its life, then the system is economically feasible.

For an information system to be *feasible*, it must be technically, operationally, and economically feasible. The analyst should prepare written documentation of the feasibility analysis which examines these three forms of feasibility. If the system is not feasible, the development process ends at this point. For a feasible system the analyst goes on to the next phase.

User Involvement in System Planning.   The user often is very involved in the first stages of system planning. As noted, the user is likely to be the one who recognizes the problem. The analyst may talk to the user extensively about the problem to define it completely. The user typically is not involved in feasibility analysis, although the analyst may discuss some aspects of feasibility with the user.

System Analysis

After the systems analyst has decided that a new system is feasible, he or she must analyze the system to determine *what* it must do. The analyst starts by analyzing the current system. He or she gathers any written documentation about the current system and collects copies of all forms and documents used in the system. If the current system is computerized, the analyst determines the output (screens and reports) produced by the system, the files or databases used by the system, the input entered into the system, and the processing done by the system. The systems analyst must interview the user to determine what the system actually does. Finally, the analyst prepares written documentation that describes the current system.

Next, the analyst determines what the user requires in the new system. The analyst talks to the user extensively about the user's needs. He or she prepares written user requirements, which state what the system will do to help the user in his or her job. The requirements should be such that problems identified earlier are solved by the new system. For example, the following is a requirement for an order processing system:

> The system will allow a salesperson to determine the current status of any sales order at any time.

In the user requirements analysis, the analyst determines what the user needs. Next, the analyst determines what the new system must do to meet the user's needs.

The result of this step is called the system specifications[1]. For example, to satisfy the requirement for the order processing system just given, the systems analyst may decide that the system will process a query from the salesperson regarding the status of a sales order. To do so, the system will access stored data about sales orders and will supply a response to the salesperson. The systems analyst determines what functions the system will perform to meet each of the user's requirements, and prepares written documentation of these functions. The analyst may review this documentation with the user.

Now that the analyst has an understanding of the functions of the new system, he or she needs to examine alternatives for performing the functions. The alternatives mainly revolve around the hardware and software components of the system, although the other components (stored data, personnel, and procedures) may be considered. The analyst identifies alternatives and estimates the costs and benefits of each alternative. Then, using cost/benefit analysis, the analyst selects the best alternative for the system and prepares written documentation to justify the choice.

Hardware and Software Alternatives.   Figure 14.2 summarizes the common hardware and software alternatives for an information system. If the organization already has a computer system in-house, then the decision often is to continue to use it. If the decision is to acquire a new computer, then the choice must be made between a personal computer system, a multiple-user computer system, or a networked computer system. An alternative to in-house hardware is to use hardware operated by a separate company that does computer processing for various organizations. This approach is often called outsourcing because it involves using resources outside the organization.

The software alternatives depend on the hardware choice. If in-house hardware is used, the organization can develop custom software using its own in-house programmers. This approach yields software that is designed for the exact needs of the organization, but it can be very time consuming and expensive to develop the software. In addition, the organization must have its own programming staff for this approach. Alternatively, the organization can contract with a separate company for programmers, called *contract programmers*, to develop the software. This approach also provides for highly customized software, but it may be more expensive than using in-house programmers. Still, the organization is not left with a programming staff after the software has been developed.

FIGURE 14.2

Information system hardware and software alternatives

Hardware:
    Use in-house hardware:
        Personal computer system
        Multiple-user computer system
        Networked computer system
    Use outsourced hardware

Software:
    Develop custom software using in-house programmers
    Have custom software developed by contract programmers
    Purchase packaged software
    Purchase packaged software and modify
    Use outsourced software

---

[1] This step is also called *logical system design*. The system design phase later in the process is called *physical system design*.

The next alternative is to purchase packaged software. This alternative is usually the least expensive, but the software may not be exactly what the organization needs. Another alternative is to purchase packaged software and modify the programs to more closely meet the organization's needs. This approach produces software that is closer to the organization's needs than just the packaged programs, but it is more expensive.

If outsourced hardware is used for processing, the company supplying the hardware may also supply the software. Sometimes, however, the organization will provide its own software. Then the software can be acquired by any of the methods discussed previously.

User Involvement in System Analysis.   The user is heavily involved in the first two steps of system analysis. The user likely will provide the analyst with much of the information about the current system. The user's greatest involvement in the entire system development process, however, comes in the user requirements analysis. Because the information system must meet the user's needs, the user must describe in detail those needs to the systems analyst. This process can involve many long hours of meetings with the systems analyst. The user usually is not involved in the remaining two steps of the system analysis phase, although the analyst may discuss the results of these steps with the user.

System Design

Now that the analyst has an understanding of what the new system must do, he or she can design *how* the system will do it. The steps in this process depend on which alternative is selected. If the software will be developed by in-house programmers, one approach is followed. The result of this approach is a system design that specifies how the information system will work. If a different alternative is selected, another approach is needed.

System Design for In-house Development.   When the software will be developed in-house, the first step in the system design process is to decide how the functions of the information system will be performed. At this stage the analyst selects the form of the input and output. For example, the analyst decides how input will be entered—by keyboard, by mouse, or by some other method. He or she decides in what form the output will be returned—on a screen, on paper, or in some other form. The analyst also selects the type of secondary storage—magnetic disk, optical disk, magnetic tape—and decides whether files or a database will be used. Finally, the analyst identifies the programs and manual procedures that will be involved in the processing and the personnel that will be needed.

Next, the analyst specifies the details of the design. These details include the following:

- Layouts of all screens, reports, and forms.
- Organization of all records, files, and databases.
- Descriptions of all programs.
- Descriptions of all manual procedures.
- Specifications for all hardware.
- Descriptions of all personnel.

The systems analyst will consult with the user while designing the system. For example, the analyst will ask the user about screen, report, and form layouts. In addition, the user may be involved in identifying what procedures are needed. The systems analyst, however, develops most of the design and prepares written documentation of the design.

Alternative Approaches.   When an alternative other than in-house software development is selected, the system design phase may be modified. If an external company is to develop the software, then the system design may proceed as described using the organization's analysts, or analysts from the external company may design the system following this process. When packaged software is to be purchased, a detailed system design is not needed because the software usually determines how the system will function. Requirements that specify what the software packages should do, however, are prepared at this time. If packaged software is to be modified, then software requirements are prepared and a system design that specifies what modifications are needed is developed. When the decision is to have an outside company do the processing with its own software, a system design is not necessary. Instead, requirements for processing are prepared so that outside companies can prepare estimates and bids.

User Involvement in System Design.   The user will be involved in those aspects of the system design that affect him or her directly. These include the input and output, or user interface design, and the design of procedures that the user must follow. The user normally will not be involved in other aspects of system design such as file and database design, and program design.

System Implementation

In the next phase of the system development process the analyst puts together the components of the new system, tests them, and changes over to using the new system. The steps in this phase may vary somewhat, depending on which hardware and software alternatives are selected.

The first step is to acquire the components of the new system. Recall from Chapter 3 that an information system has five components: hardware, software, stored data, personnel, and procedures. Some of the components may already exist in the organization, some may have to be acquired from outside the organization, and some are constructed within the organization.

For the hardware component, if the system will use existing in-house hardware, then usually nothing needs to be done. If new hardware is to be purchased, however, then alternative equipment that meets the hardware specifications is evaluated and a selection is made. When outsourced hardware is to be used, different businesses supplying the hardware are evaluated and one is selected.

For the software component, if in-house programmers are to be used to develop the software, then the programming is done at this time. The programming process can be complex, involving many activities, and can take considerable time. When contract programmers will develop the software, the system implementation will be turned over to the company doing the programming. If packaged software is to be purchased, then software alternatives are evaluated and a selection is made at this time. Any modifications to the software are done after the software has been acquired.

The stored data component is not completely constructed at this time. Instead, files or databases are created with sample data that can be used to test the software and the system. The actual data is stored later.

Employees are selected for the personnel component during this step. The personnel may already work for the organization, or they may have to be hired from outside the organization. Training, however, usually takes place later.

Finally, the manual procedures that make up the procedures component are written at this time. Although the type of procedures needed are identified earlier during system design, the detailed writing of these procedures does not take place until implementation. Written documentation of any manual procedures required in the system is prepared by technical writers.

The next step is to make sure that the system works as required, which involves testing the system. Before this step is undertaken the parts of the system are tested individually as they are acquired. For example, all programs are thoroughly tested as they are prepared. During the system testing step, the parts are brought together and the system is tested as a whole. This process involves running the system through all its phases using sample input data and sample data in files and databases. All system functions are checked with what is expected, and any differences mean that there are errors in the system. When an error is detected, the part of the system that caused the error must be modified and tested again. This process continues until no errors are detected in the system.

The last step in the system implementation phase is to install the new system in the business. It is usually at this time that the personnel, including the users, receive their training in the operation and use of the system. In addition, the actual data to be used by the system is stored in the files or databases.

The final activity of this step is to convert from the old system to the new system. The conversion usually is done in one of four ways:

- *Plunge.* The old system is stopped one day and the new system is started the next day.
- *Phased.* The new system is divided into parts, sometimes called modules, and one part is phased in at a time.
- *Pilot.* The new system is installed in part of the organization, such as a single office, as a pilot test before it is used in the rest of the organization.
- *Parallel.* The old and the new systems are used simultaneously for a period of time.

The plunge approach usually is the most dangerous because if the new system fails, there may be no way of returning to the old system. This approach is the least expensive, however, if the new system does not fail. The parallel approach is the safest because if the new system fails, the old system is still operating. This approach is the most expensive, however, because both systems must be in operation at the same time. Between these two extremes are the pilot and phased approaches, which can be effective ways of converting to a new system.

The steps in the implementation phase are performed under the direction of the systems analyst, although other personnel may do much of the work. Hardware specialists may be involved in acquiring any hardware. Programmers develop the software, create files or databases, and assist with the testing. Managers usually hire personnel, and technical writers prepare written procedures. The training staff train personnel including users. After the system is finished, the user usually is asked to compare the system with the user's requirements and accept or reject it.

User Involvement in System Implementation.   The user involvement in system implementation starts off low but ends very high. The user normally is not involved in system acquisition, although the user may be contacted by programmers to clarify aspects of the requirements. During testing, the user may be asked to supply data to test the system, and to check the results produced by the system with what is expected. The user's greatest involvement comes during system installation. It is at this time that the user is trained in the use of the new system. The user will also be heavily involved in the conversion to the new system.

System Maintenance

After an information system has been in use for a while, it may have to be modified, which is the process of system maintenance. Maintenance is required for three reasons. The first is that errors are found that were not detected when the system was tested. Even though the system was thoroughly tested, errors often appear after the system has been in use for a while. The second reason is that a new function is to be added to the system. For example, the preparation of a new report may be needed. The final reason for system maintenance is that requirements change. For example, programs that produce income tax returns have to be modified almost every year because of changing tax laws.

Whenever maintenance is needed, an abbreviated version of the previous four phases is followed. First, the problem that requires system maintenance must be recognized and defined. Then, the feasibility of performing the maintenance must be examined. In some cases, such as in correcting an error in the system or in meeting new legal requirements, feasibility is not an issue, but in other cases, such as when new functions are requested, a feasibility analysis should be done.

Next, the current system needs to be examined to determine how the change should be made. If not already stated, the user's requirements for the change need to be specified and the specific system function affected by the change must be analyzed. Sometimes alternatives to modifying the existing system are examined. For example, it may be less costly to purchase a new program than to modify an existing one.

System design for the modification should be performed. Then, the programming or other activity necessary to make the change is done. Next, the system is tested with the modification. Finally, the modified system is installed.

Any of the people associated with the development of an information system may be involved in system maintenance. Systems analysts and programmers usually do most of the work, but hardware specialists, managers, technical writers, and trainers may also be involved. The user, too, is included in the process to ensure that the modified system meets the user requirements.

Legacy Systems.   Many businesses have older information systems that have been in use for many years. Called legacy systems, these systems often require regular maintenance. For example, a business could have a 20-year-old payroll system that functions well but requires periodic modification because of changes in payroll laws.

When a business has a legacy system that needs maintenance, it has to decide whether to modify the system or develop an entirely new one. The extent of the changes needed often determine which approach the business takes. For example, if only 5 percent of a system needs changing, it usually makes sense to modify it; but if 25 percent of the system must be modified, it may be better to develop an entirely new system. Businesses also may decide to develop a new system rather than modify an old one because of a change in the basic approach to computing in the organization, such as a change from a multiple-user mainframe approach to a networked, client-server approach.

One of the biggest problems in maintaining legacy systems is occurring because of the year 2000. Many older systems store the year in a date as two digits. For example, 1998 is stored as 98. Using this approach, the year 2000 is stored as 00. As a result, any system that relies on the years increasing could no longer function correctly after the year 2000. For example, interest calculation programs in banking systems or accounts receivable systems could fail to calculate interest correctly. Modifying all legacy systems to correct this problem is an enormous job.

System Development Tools

Several tools are used during the system development process to help in the analysis and design of the system. These tools provide a way for the systems analyst to organize his or her thinking about the system and to examine alternative designs. They also serve as documentation of certain steps in the process. The user may have to review some of this documentation during the system development process. A description of several of the more commonly used tools follows.

Data Flow Diagrams

A tool that many analysts use to show the flow of data in an information system is a data flow diagram or DFD. This diagram uses symbols with different shapes to indicate how data flows in the system. Figure 14.3 shows the symbols used in a data flow diagram and Fig. 14.4 gives an example of a DFD using these symbols. In a DFD, a rectangle with rounded corners or a circle is used for a *process*, which is any step that

FIGURE 14.3

Data flow diagram symbols

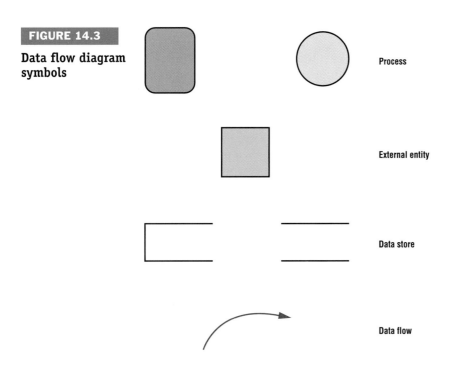

Process

External entity

Data store

Data flow

FIGURE 14.4

A data flow diagram

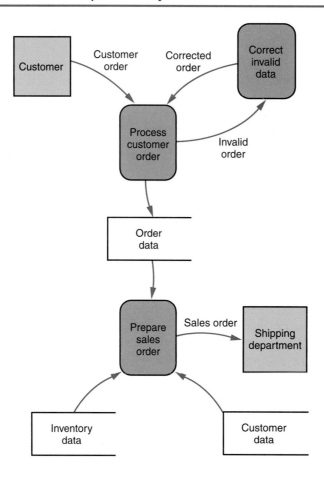

involves manipulating data. The words inside the symbol briefly state what the process does. A square is used for an *external entity*, which is a person, organization, or other system that sends input data (*data source*) or receives output data (*data destination*). A descriptive name for the person, organization, or system is written inside the symbol. A rectangle open at one end or two horizontal lines is used for a *data store*, which is a collection of data kept by the system in any form, such as in a file or database. A name that describes the data store is written in the symbol. Finally, lines with arrowheads are used for *data flows*. Data may flow from an external entity to a process, between processes, from a process to an external entity, and between a process and a data store. The arrowhead indicates the direction of the data flow. Each data flow line has a name written next to it that describes the data that flows, although data that flows to or from a data store does not need a description because the data store's name provides the description.

The data flow diagram in Figure 14.4 is for an order entry system. In this diagram, a customer is an external entity that sends in a customer order. The order is received by a process that checks the order data for errors. This process sends invalid orders to another process for correction and stores valid orders in an order data store. The process to prepare sales orders produces sales orders from data in the order data store, the inventory data store, and the customer data store. The sales order is sent to the shipping department, which is an external entity.

Data flow diagrams are used in several steps of the system development process. They are used in the analysis of the current system to document what the existing system does. In addition, they are used in system specifications to describe the functions of the new system. Finally, they are used in system design to show the design of the new system.

A tool that is used in conjunction with a data flow diagram is the data dictionary. The data dictionary describes the data in each data flow and in each data store in the DFD. Figure 14.5 gives part of the data dictionary for the order entry system. This figure describes the customer-order input, the order data store, and the sales order output. Each description includes the name of the data flow or data store, an equals sign, and the names of the data items or fields that make up the data. The data names are separated by plus signs to indicate that the item on the left of the equals sign is the "sum" of the items on the right.

The data dictionary describes the data in a data flow diagram. To describe the processes in the DFD, the analyst uses process descriptions. There is one process description for each process in the DFD. Several techniques are used for process descriptions, including pseudocode and program flowcharts, which are discussed in Chapter 13. Another technique is *structured English*, which is a simple form of English that uses an outline to describe a process. For example, Fig. 14.6 shows the structured-English

---

FIGURE 14.5

Data dictionary descriptions

Customer order	= Customer name +
	Customer number +
	Customer order date +
	Item number +
	Item description +
	Quantity ordered
Order data	= Customer number +
	Item number +
	Quantity ordered
Sales order	= Customer number +
	Customer name +
	Shipping address +
	Sales order date +
	Item number +
	Item description +
	Quantity ordered

FIGURE 14.6

A process description

PREPARE SALES ORDER PROCESS

For each Customer order in the Order data do the following:

1. Determine the Customer credit rating from the Customer data

2. If the Customer credit rating is satisfactory do the following:

    a. Print the Customer number, Customer name, Shipping address, and Sales order date on the Sales order

    b. For each item ordered, determine the Quantity on hand from the Inventory data

    c. For each item where the Quantity ordered is less than or equal to the Quantity on hand, print the Item number, Item description, and Quantity ordered on the Sales order

description of the process to prepare sales orders in the order entry system. This description is a step-by-step outline that uses simple words and data names from the data dictionary to specify the steps in the process. There would be a similar structured-English description for the other processes in the DFD.

System Flowcharts

Another tool that is used by systems analysts is a <u>system flowchart</u>, which is a graphical representation of the functioning of an information system. It is similar to a data flow diagram in that it shows the flow of data in an information system. In addition, a system flowchart shows what type of input data, output data, stored data, and programs will be used in the system. It is different from a program flowchart (discussed in Chapter 13), which shows the flow of logic in a single program.

In a system flowchart the shapes of symbols provide information about the system. Figure 14.7 shows some of the symbols that are used and Fig. 14.8 gives an example of a system flowchart using these symbols. The *process symbol* is used for any processing function, whether it is done by a computer or manually. If the processing is done by a computer, the symbol corresponds to one or more computer programs. If the processing is done manually, the symbol corresponds to a procedure performed by a person. The *keyboard symbol, screen symbol,* and *document symbol* are used for different types of input and output. The *magnetic disk symbol* and *magnetic tape symbol* are used for different types of data storage. Within each symbol is written a description of the processing, input data, output data, or stored data. The symbols in the flowchart are connected by *flowlines* with arrowheads that show the direction of flow of data within the system. By following the flowlines and reading the symbols in a system flowchart you can get a general understanding of the functioning of an information system.

The system flowchart in Fig. 14.8 is for an order entry system. The flowchart indicates that the customer order data is entered at a keyboard. After processing, invalid order data is displayed on a screen for correction and valid order data is stored in an order file on a magnetic disk. Inventory data also is stored in a magnetic disk file, but customer data is stored in a magnetic tape file. The data files are processed to prepare a sales order, which is a document.

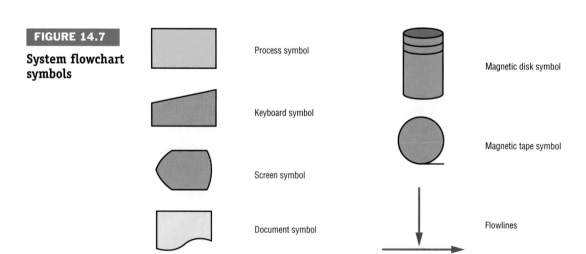

FIGURE 14.7

System flowchart symbols

Process symbol

Keyboard symbol

Screen symbol

Document symbol

Magnetic disk symbol

Magnetic tape symbol

Flowlines

FIGURE 14.8

FIGURE 14.8

A system flowchart

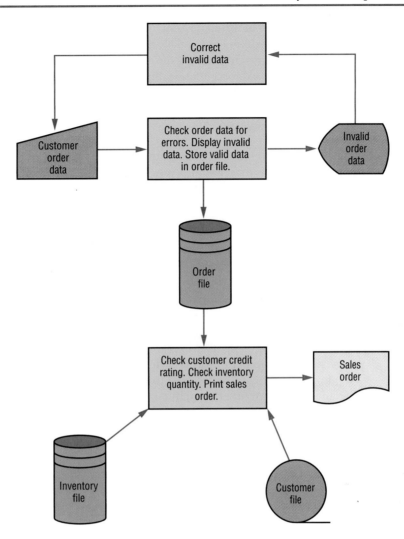

System flowcharts are used in several steps in the system development process. They are used to document the functioning of the current system and also to show the design of a new system. System flowcharts are not as commonly used as data flow diagrams.

Entity-relationship Diagrams

Many information systems process data stored in a database. Recall from Chapter 7 that a database consists of data and relationships between data. To show the design of a database, many systems analysts use a tool called an entity-relationship or ER diagram. An *entity* is something about which data is stored in a database, such as a customer, an item in inventory, or an order.[2] An entity-relationship diagram shows the entities and the relationships between entities in a database.

---

[2] Do not confuse an *entity* in an entity-relationship diagram with an *external entity* in a data flow diagram. The former is something about which data is stored and the latter is a sender or receiver of data.

An entity-relationship diagram uses the symbols shown in Fig. 14.9. Figure 14.10 gives an example of an entity-relationship diagram using these symbols. A rectangle is used for an entity. The name of the entity is written inside the rectangle. A diamond-shape symbol is used for a relationship. A word or phrase that describes the relationship is written inside this symbol. The lines leaving the relationship symbol extend to the entities that are related. The notations on the lines indicate whether the relationship is one-to-one, one-to-many, or many-to-many. (Types of relationships were discussed in Chapter 7.)

The entity-relationship diagram in Fig. 14.10 is for a database used in an order entry system. This diagram indicates that the database stores data about three entities: customers, orders, and items in inventory. Customers are related to orders by a one-to-many relationship. The meaning of this relationship is that each customer places many orders but each order is placed by only one customer. Orders are related to items by a many-to-many relationship. The meaning of this relationship is that each order contains many items from inventory and that each item can be contained in many orders.

Although not shown in Fig. 14.10, an entity-relationship diagram can also list the type of data stored about each entity. Thus, the diagram could show that the customer number, name, and address is stored for each customer. This information could be written on the diagram or on separate paper.

Entity-relationship diagrams are used mainly in the system specification step of the system development process to describe how a database of the new system will be organized. They may also be used to document an existing database design during the analysis of the current system.

CASE

Some of the tools that are used in system development are available in computer software. For example, software is available that allows the systems analyst to draw data flow and entity-relationship diagrams on a screen. (See Fig. 14.11.) The analyst also can develop data dictionaries and process descriptions to accompany data flow diagrams. Using computer-based tools such as these for system development is called CASE, which stands for Computer-Aided Software Engineering. (The term *software engineering* is sometimes used for the process of developing systems of computer programs.) CASE tools are available to help in many other tasks in system development.

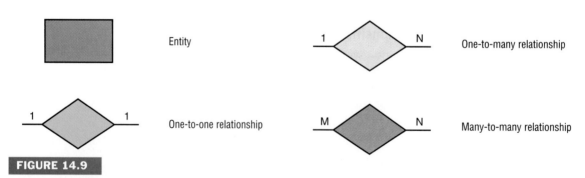

FIGURE 14.9

Entity-relationship diagram symbols

FIGURE 14.10

An entity-
relationship
diagram

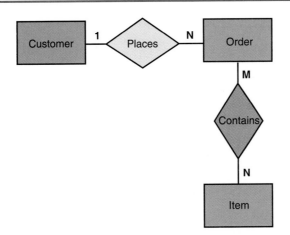

FIGURE 14.11

A data flow
diagram drawn on
a screen using a
CASE tool

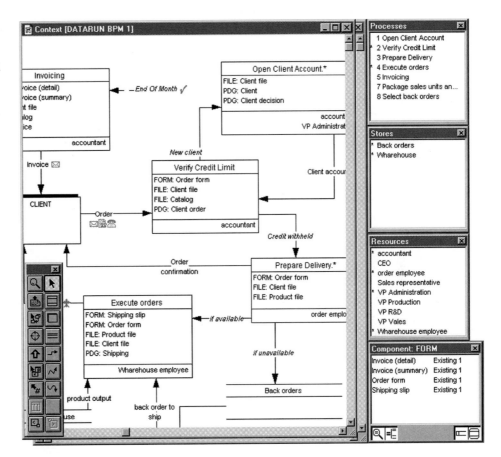

An Example of Information System Development

To illustrate the ideas presented in this chapter, this section examines an example of
the development of an information system. Sportswear Enterprises sells and distributes athletic clothing to retail stores throughout the country. It currently has basic
information systems for order entry, billing, and so forth. The sales manager, Pat

Nichols, feels that the business is not doing the best job it can in selling athletic clothing because she and other sales personnel do not have good information about how well different items are selling and which regions of the country have high sales and which have low sales. Therefore, she has requested a sales analysis system.

System Planning

Pat has started the system development process by recognizing the need for a new system. She has identified a problem with the existing system. The problem, as she

Bookmark

Solving the Year 2000 Problem at The Equitable Life Assurance Society

Bill Born has great credentials for fixing The Equitable Life Assurance Society's year 2000 problem—he helped create the mess 20 years ago.

As a young programmer, Born was assigned to find out why the insurer's Computer Assisted Policyholder Service (CAPS) system continued to report policies dating back to the late 1800s as new business.

Born discovered that the problem was that CAPS, similar to most other systems of the day, used only two-digit year codes, so the system couldn't differentiate between centuries.

Because the oldest policy in the system is from 1893, Born had changed CAPS to regard policies with a date over "92" as old business. That would work until the early 1990s, when "nobody was expecting these systems to still be around," he remembers.

But CAPS is still around, accounts for $1 billion in annual premiums, and hit the wall again. This time, Born says, "it hit me that I had put the problem in."

The wake-up call gave The Equitable a head start in fixing CAPS and other applications that will run into trouble by the year 2000. The firm was also lucky because it still employs information systems veterans who know CAPS and insurance inside out.

The plan for CAPS Millennium, as it came to be called, was developed by a team headed by division manager Jim Fox. The team proposed splitting the year 2000 fix into manageable subtasks and improving CAPS at the same time.

Fox proposed correcting CAPS' 1,500 modules one module at a time, with "bridges" analyzing data streams between corrected and uncorrected modules and doing any needed translation. This means that work on individual modules can proceed without waiting for other modules to be fixed.

Early cost estimates for the fix ran upward of $8 million, a high price just to fix a problem.

The resulting proposal not only included expanding the date fields to four digits, but also expanding other elements such as the face amount on policies, which determines how much the insured can be paid in case of a claim.

Senior Vice President and Chief Information Officer Leon Billis approved the first, or "risk avoidance," phase but ordered that its $2.6 million price be cut. He was already exploring the idea of using offshore programmers to lower information technology costs and drove a hard bargain with HexAware Technologies, Inc. in Princeton, New Jersey, and Bombay, India. HexAware is doing much of the work in Phase 1 for little or no profit to get experience and an inside track on future work.

The year 2000 work "is just a big maintenance project," technical director Ron Johnson says, but that makes it sound easy. The Equitable was in a good position because it understood CAPS, owned the source code, and had proven maintenance methodologies and test suites. When an information technology organization doesn't hold such cards, it must consider other options.

Some critics argue that The Equitable risked failure by overloading the year 2000 conversion with other work. Born admits the team "agonized" over that but points out that the other changes open up new business opportunities.

"We've got 2 million lines of code," Johnson says. "We've got to look at them all . . ." just to change the date elements. "Once we've gone through this, we don't want to look at all that again."

QUESTIONS
1. Why did The Equitable have a year 2000 problem in CAPS?
2. Why was The Equitable successful in solving the year 2000 problem in CAPS?

WEB SITE
The Equitable Companies: www.equitable.com

Source: Robert L. Scheier, "Face up to it," *Computerworld,* March 25, 1996, pp. 83-84.

sees it, is that inadequate sales information is available. She has requested that a new system be developed to help solve the problem. She will be the user of the system, along with other sales personnel.

A systems analyst, Brad Johnson, is then assigned to the project. Brad talks to Pat about the problem and about the idea of a computerized sales analysis system. After a little research into the existing systems, Brad realizes that the problem is not that sales information is unavailable; the necessary data is stored in a database. The real problem is that no system exists for retrieving the data and making it available for use by sales personnel.

Next, Brad does a feasibility analysis of the proposed system. He talks to Pat again and to the sales personnel to get a general idea of their requirements for the new system. He realizes that the system involves retrieving data from an existing database and preparing appropriate reports. The system is within the technical sophistication of the computer personnel in the business, and the people are likely to use the system because the sales manager has requested it and the sales personnel are enthusiastic about it. Brad does a cost/benefit analysis to determine the economic feasibility of the new system. He estimates the costs of developing and operating the system and the benefits from increased sales. Because the benefits exceed the costs, the system is economically feasible and the decision is made to proceed with the development of the system.

System Analysis

Now Brad looks at how sales analysis is currently done. He knows there is no computerized sales analysis system, but there may be a manual system in use. In talking to Pat and the sales personnel, he discovers that sheets are prepared each month listing the best-selling items and the sales regions that have the most sales. (See Fig. 14.12.) No information, however, is kept on poor-selling items or on regions with low sales. The current system is very informal and inaccurate. Each month someone in the sales department goes through copies of sales orders for that month and counts the number of orders on which each item appears. This person also determines from the address on each sales order which sales region the customer is in, and counts the number of sales orders in each region. Finally, he or she prepares a list of the five best-selling items and the three top sales regions.

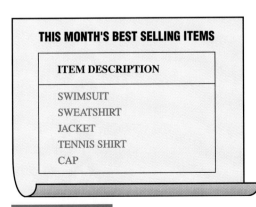
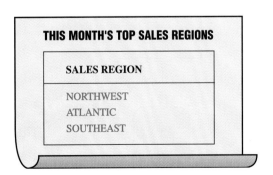

FIGURE 14.12

Sales analysis sheets

Brad notices immediately that these lists do not take into consideration the quantity sold or the selling price and that only the best-selling items and top sales regions are listed. He talks to Pat about the current system. Together they prepare the user requirements for the new system. (See Fig. 14.13.) Brad then discusses these requirements with the other sales personnel to be sure they correctly state what is needed.

Next, Brad prepares the system specifications for the new system. He knows that order data, item data, and customer data are available in a customer order database. This database has the organization shown previously in the entity-relationship diagram in Fig. 14.10. By using the data in this database, the data needed for sales analysis can be produced. Once the sales analysis data is produced, the data can be analyzed in different ways to prepare reports listing the total sales of each item (sales by item) and the total sales for each sales region (sales by region). Brad draws a data flow diagram for the system. (See Fig. 14.14.) He also prepares a data dictionary and process descriptions. He goes over these system specifications with Pat to be sure the new system will meet the users' needs.

FIGURE 14.13

The user requirements for the new system

SALES ANALYSIS SYSTEM USER REQUIREMENTS

1. The system will produce a report each month listing the month's total dollar sales for each item. The items will be listed in decreasing order of sales.

2. The system will produce a report each month listing the month's total dollar sales for each sales region. The regions will be listed in alphabetical order.

FIGURE 14.14

The data flow diagram for the new system

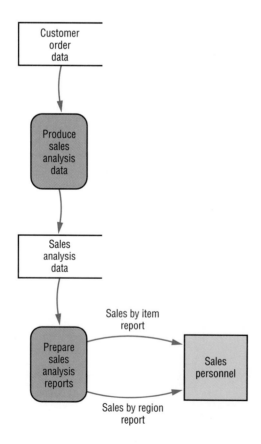

The business has adequate computer hardware for the new system. Brad thinks briefly about packaged software but decides that the system must be customized for the business and that packaged software therefore will not work. The business has in-house programmers who are capable of preparing the programs, so Brad decides to develop the software using the existing programming staff.

System Design

Now Brad prepares the system design. The order data, item data, and customer data already exist in a database on magnetic disk. He decides that the sales analysis data should be a file on magnetic disk. Three programs will be needed in the system: one to produce the sales analysis data from the customer order database, one to prepare the sales by item report, and one to prepare the sales by region report. Brad draws a system flowchart of the system design. (See Fig. 14.15.)

Next, Brad prepares the layout of each report using a form called a *print chart*. (See Fig. 14.16.) This form shows how headings and descriptions will appear in a report, and where variable output (indicated by Xs) will be printed. He shows the layouts on the print charts to Pat for her approval. The organization of the database with the order, item, and customer data is known, but Brad must decide what data will be in the sales analysis file and how the file will be organized. He also documents

FIGURE 14.15

The system flowchart for the new system

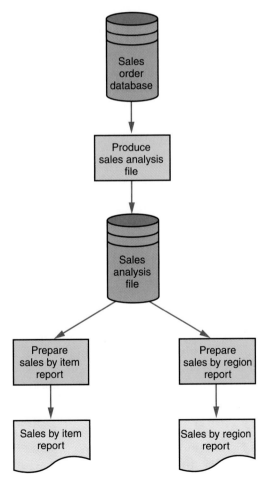

FIGURE 14.16

The print charts for the sales analysis reports

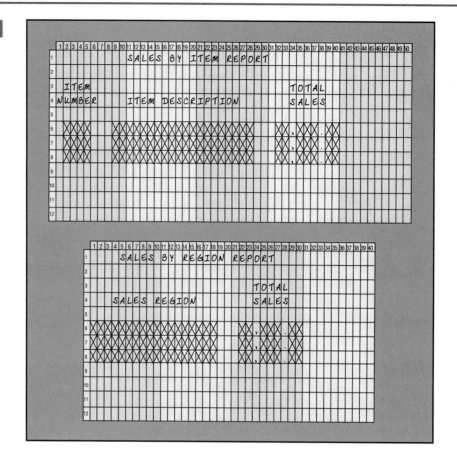

what each program must do and notes that a manual procedure will be needed to tell the computer operator how to run the programs and what to do with the output.

System Implementation

Next, a programmer is assigned to prepare the programs for the system. While the programmer works on the programs, Brad arranges the other components of the system. The hardware is available, so nothing needs to be done about it. The database already exists, but Brad decides to make a copy of part of it for testing purposes. The computer operator who will run the programs and deliver the output is identified. Finally, Brad prepares the operator's procedures.

After the programs and other components have been completed, Brad tests the system with the sample database. He carefully checks the output for errors and has to have some corrections made by the programmer. Once he has determined that the system is working correctly, he takes the sample output to Pat for her approval. (See Fig. 14.17.) Pat brings in sales personnel who will be using the output. After some discussion of the output and of how the system works, she approves the system.

Next, Brad trains the computer operator in the operation of the new system. He also makes sure that all sales personnel understand their role in the system. He replaces the sample database with the actual database. Finally, he decides to phase in the new system. The first month, the system will produce the sales by item report. If all goes well, then during the second month the system will produce both reports.

FIGURE 14.17

The sales analysis reports

SALES BY ITEM REPORT

ITEM NUMBER	ITEM DESCRIPTION	TOTAL SALES
5172	SWEAT SHIRT	15,147.50
6318	SWIM SUIT	12,370.65
1609	JACKET	11,094.00
3804	TENNIS SHIRT	10,755.25
1537	SHORTS	9,208.00
5501	CAP	8,541.75
5173	SWEAT PANTS	6,468.50
3512	TENNIS SHORTS	2,370.40
2719	T-SHIRT	512.00
4205	SOCKS	498.75

SALES BY REGION REPORT

SALES REGION	TOTAL SALES
ATLANTIC	15,342.50
NORTH CENTRAL	6,850.20
NORTHWEST	18,678.00
PACIFIC COAST	12,287.00
SOUTHEAST	14,134.50
SOUTHWEST / CENTRAL	9,674.60

System Maintenance

The conversion goes smoothly, and after several months of operation Brad checks with Pat to see if there are any problems. Pat feels that, for the time being, the system is functioning well, but she thinks that modifications may be needed in the future. Brad assures her that modifications can be handled when requested.

Other System Development Approaches

The system development process described so far in this chapter is the classical approach used for developing information systems. Other approaches are used, however, either alone or along with this classical approach. Here we describe three other approaches: prototyping, rapid application development, and object-oriented analysis and design.

Prototyping

One of the biggest problems in information system development is understanding the user's requirements. Often, the user cannot state clearly what he or she needs. Many times, after a system has been developed, the user says that the system is not what he or she wanted. All the steps that follow the user requirements analysis step depend on accurate requirements. If the requirements are not accurate, the system will not meet the user's needs.

An approach that attempts to solve this problem is called prototyping. In prototyping, the systems analyst obtains informal and incomplete requirements from the user. He or she then develops a prototype of the system, which is a partial version of the system that acts like the real system for the user but that does not perform all the required functions of the system. The prototype is developed very quickly using special prototyping software. The prototype includes sample screens and reports so that the user can see what the system will do. The user then has a chance to change his or her requirements, and the analyst modifies the prototype to reflect the changes. After several such modifications the prototype reaches a point at which the user is happy with it.

Prototyping replaces the user requirements analysis and system specification steps of the system analysis phase of the information system development process. The other steps in the process are still necessary, including identifying and evaluating alternatives, but one of the alternatives now is to continue to develop the prototype into the final system. If this alternative is selected, then prototyping also replaces the system design and part of the implementation phases.

Rapid Application Development

The system development process can take years to complete. After such a time, system requirements may change, new users may be hired, or the system may no longer be justified. Finding ways to shorten the development time has been an ongoing goal of systems analysts.

One approach to shortening system development time is called rapid application development or RAD. This approach uses some of the techniques already discussed. Prototyping is used to determine user requirements. In addition, the prototype is often developed into the final system. CASE tools are used to speed up the analysis and design process. Some of these tools can produce database and program implementations that may be satisfactory for the final system. Other specialized rapid application development software tools may also be used.

Most importantly, rapid application development requires significant user involvement in the development process. The user is involved in requirements analysis, prototype development, system design, and implementation. As a result, the system is more likely to meet the users' needs and require fewer changes because of misunderstandings between users and systems analysts. In addition, the system is developed faster than using other approaches.

Object-oriented Analysis and Design

In the system development process discussed earlier, the data and the methods for processing the data are separated. The data organization is specified in the entity-relationship diagram. The methods for processing the data are given in the descriptions of the processes in the data flow diagram. An alternative approach is to combine the data and processing methods. This approach is called object-oriented analysis and design.

Object-oriented programming was described in Chapter 5 and object-oriented databases were discussed in Chapter 7. Recall that in the object-oriented approaches, data and methods (instructions) for processing the data are com-

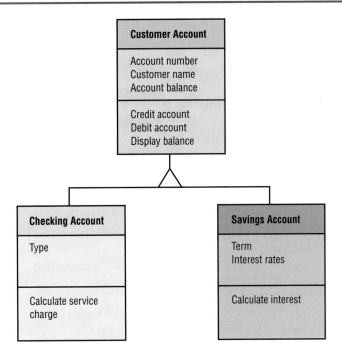

FIGURE 14.18

A diagram used in object-oriented analysis and design

bined to form an *object*. Object-oriented analysis and design involves analyzing the objects that are important in the system and designing the system based on these objects.

Figure 14.18 shows a diagram that could be used in the object-oriented analysis and design of a system in a bank. The boxes represent objects; the name of each object is given above the top line. In the middle of each box are the names of the data items in the object. Below the bottom line are the names of the methods for processing the data in the object. The lines connecting the boxes mean that a customer account is a checking account or a savings account.

Object-oriented analysis and design replaces much of the system development process. System planning, current system analysis, and user requirements analysis are still needed. Object-oriented analysis and design then takes over, replacing the remainder of the system analysis phase and the system design phase. The system is usually implemented using an object-oriented programming language.

Business Process Reengineering

The system development process described in this chapter is a framework for developing information systems. Many of the ideas in this process, along with some of the tools used in it, can be incorporated into the development of other types of systems in an organization. For example, a production system can be developed using some of the ideas presented in this chapter, along with other ideas from production management.

One new approach to business system development that has become common in recent years is called business process reengineering or BPR. (Sometimes it is called *business process redesign*.) The goal of this approach is to completely redesign business processes, which are groups of activities or tasks that accomplish things for the business. For example, completing an order for a customer is a business process. Similarly, authorizing credit, purchasing materials, and developing a new product are business processes.

The goal of business process reengineering is to completely redesign one or more business processes so that it dramatically improves the way the organization functions. For example, reengineering a customer ordering process may result in customers receiving their orders in three days instead of 10. Attempting to achieve such a dramatic improvement is the goal of business process reengineering.

The approach used in business process reengineering often involves starting from scratch. The question is sometimes asked: "If we could design this business process any way we wanted, what would be the result?" This approach is different than starting with the current system and modifying it, as described earlier in this chapter. Business process reengineering is *not* gradual improvement, but rather radical redesign of business processes.

The approach to business process reengineering may involve some of the ideas and tools used in information system development. A team of users and analysts is usually formed to perform the redesign. The team follows a sequence of steps in their efforts. First, the processes in the organization must be identified and those to be redesigned must be selected. Then the existing processes must be understood. Next the new processes must be designed from scratch. Finally, the new processes must be implemented. During the analysis and design, the team may use tools such as data flow diagrams to document their work.

Information technology plays a fundamental role in business process reengineering. Information technology allows business processes to be radically redesigned. For example, an existing process for customer ordering may involve clerks entering customer order data into an ordering system. In this process, the clerks may have to explain prices, credit terms, delivery schedules, and other details to customers. In a reengineered ordering process, the customers can check the business database directly for details such as prices, terms, and schedules, and place orders electronically using electronic data interchange. Thus, information technology provides a way to redesign the process to dramatically improve customer service.

Business process reengineering is a new approach to redesigning business processes. Although it has had many successes, it also has failed at times. Whether it will play a major role in the future of organizations is not certain.

Chapter Summary

☐ The people who are primarily involved in information system development are **systems analysts**. They follow a step-by-step process to develop the system. In addition, programmers are involved because they write the programs that are part of the system. Users are also involved in system development because the system must be designed to meet the needs of its users. Systems analysts, programmers, and users often work together in a **project team** that is responsible for developing the information system. (p. 410)

☐ The first phase in the information system development process, also called the **system development life cycle** or **SDLC**, is **system planning**, in which the systems analyst decides whether a new information system should be developed. In this phase, the analyst defines the problem to be solved by the system and performs **feasibility analysis** to determine if it is feasible to develop a system to solve the problem. The next phase is **system analysis**, in which the analyst determines what the new system must do. In this phase, the analyst analyzes the current system, determines the **user requirements**, prepares the **system specifications**, and identifies and evaluates alternative ways of meeting the requirements. In the next phase, **system design**, the analyst specifies how the new system will function. The result of this phase is the design of the new system. The next phase is **system implementation**, in which the analyst acquires the components of the system, tests the system, and changes over to the new system. The last phase, called **system maintenance**, involves modifying the system during its life to meet new requirements. (pp. 410–419)

☐ The user is often the one who recognizes the need for a new information system by identifying a problem with the existing system. The user should report the problem to the person responsible for system development, thus beginning the system planning phase. During system analysis, the user is interviewed about how the current system functions. In addition, the user provides detailed information about his or her requirements for the new system. The user's involvement in system design is mainly in reviewing screen, report, and form layouts and helping to describe procedures. The user may be involved with system testing during system implementation. When the system is finished, the user is trained in the use of the system and is asked to compare the system with his or her requirements. Finally, the user is involved in system maintenance to ensure

that the modified system meets the user's requirements. (pp. 410–419)

☐ A **data flow diagram**, or **DFD**, shows the flow of data in an information system. A **data dictionary** describes the data in a data flow diagram, and **process descriptions** describe the processes in a data flow diagram. A **system flowchart** shows the flow of data in an information system and the types of input data, output data, stored data, and programs used in the system. An **entity-relationship** or **ER diagram** shows the design of a database. **CASE** (Computer-Aided Software Engineering) tools provide computerized versions of other tools. (pp. 419–424)

☐ **Prototyping** is an alternative approach to system development that attempts to overcome some of the problems of identifying and describing user requirements. In this approach, a **prototype** of the system is developed very quickly using special prototyping software. The prototype is a partial version of the system that acts like the real system for the user but that does not perform all the required functions of the system. The user can change his or her requirements, and the systems analyst can modify the prototype to reflect the changes. **Rapid application development** or **RAD** is an approach to information system development that shortens the development time. It involves significant user involvement along with prototyping, CASE, and other software tools. (pp. 431–433)

☐ The purpose of **business process reengineering** or **BPR** is to completely redesign business processes, which are groups of activities or tasks that accomplish things for the business. In business process reengineering, one or more business processes are redesigned so that the organization realizes a dramatic improvement in the way it functions. (pp. 433–434)

Key Terms

Business Process (p. 434)
Business Process Reengineering (BPR) (p. 433)
CASE (p. 424)
Cost/Benefit Analysis (p. 413)
Data Dictionary (p. 421)
Data Flow Diagram (DFD) (p. 419)
Entity-relationship (ER) Diagram (p. 423)
Feasibility Analysis (p. 413)
Legacy System (p. 418)

Object-oriented Analysis and Design (p. 432)
Outsourcing (p. 414)
Process Description (p. 421)
Project Team (p. 410)
Prototype (p. 432)
Prototyping (p. 432)
Rapid Application Development (RAD) (p. 432)
System Analysis (p. 410)
System Design (p. 410)

System Development Life Cycle (SDLC) (p. 410)
System Flowchart (p. 422)
System Implementation (p. 410)
System Maintenance (p. 410)
System Planning (p. 410)
Systems Analyst (p. 410)
System Specifications (p. 414)
User Requirements (p. 413)

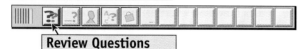

Assignment Material

Review Questions

Fill-in Questions

1. The person primarily responsible for developing an information system is the _____.

2. Determining what a new information system will do is called _____. Determining how the system will function is called _____.

3. The process of modifying a system to meet new requirements is called _____.

4. The process of determining if it is feasible to develop a new information system is called _____.

5. A technique for evaluating the economic feasibility of an information system is _____.

6. Descriptions of what an information system will do to help a user are called _____.

7. Using hardware, software, and personnel resources outside of an organization for an information system is called _____.

8. A(n) _____ is an information system that has been in use in an organization for many years.

9. Each data flow and set of stored data in a data flow diagram is described in the _____. Each process is described by a(n) _____.

10. A(n) _____ is used to show the design of a database in an information system.

11. The use of computer-based tools to help in the development of an information system is called _____.

12. An alternative approach to developing an information system in which a partial version of the system is developed for the user is called _____.

Short-answer Questions

1. Who are the people that are usually on an information system development project team?

2. List the five main phases of the system development process.

3. How is the user involved in system planning?

4. What types of feasibility must the systems analyst evaluate?

5. What steps are involved in system analysis?

6. How is the user involved in system analysis?

7. What are the main software alternatives for an information system?

8. What system details does the systems analyst specify during system design?

9. What steps are involved in system implementation?

10. What approaches can a business use to convert from an old information system to a new one?

11. Explain the difference between a data flow diagram and a system flowchart.

12. In the example in this chapter, why did Pat Nichols want a new information system?

13. During which phases of the system development process in the example in this chapter was Pat Nichols most involved, and during which phase was she least involved?

14. What is business process reengineering?

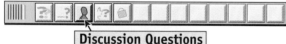

Discussion Questions

1. The users of many information systems in a college or university (e.g., course registration system, library catalog system) are students. Are students ever consulted at your college or university about user requirements? If not, why?

2. Think of an information system that you might use in your career. What would you want that system to do for you? That is, what would be your requirements for the system?

3. As more and more computer-based tools used to develop information systems (such as CASE tools and rapid application development tools) become available in the future, will user involvement in information system development increase or decrease? Why?

4. Workgroup information systems are sometimes developed by members of the group. What steps in the system development process might be different in this situation?

5. What difficulties could arise in developing an information system for an international business?

6. Assume that you use a technique to help you with your job that no one else in the organization knows about. The technique helps you do your work very well and you receive excellent work reports. The organization has decided to develop an information system to assist you and others in the organization. A systems analyst has come to your office and is asking you questions about how you do your job, including the techniques you use. What would you do in this situation?

Problem-solving Projects

1. Interview a systems analyst to find out what he or she does when developing an information system. What steps does the analyst follow in developing an information system? What tools does the analyst use to help in developing a system? Using word processing software, write a summary of your interview.

2. Some departments and offices in your college or university may need new information systems. For example, a computer lab may need an information system to keep track of hardware and software, and an academic department office may need an information system to keep track of its students. Locate a department or office at your college or university that needs a new information system. Identify the users of the system. Then, interview the users to determine their requirements for the new system. Using word processing software, prepare a written description of the requirements. Show the written requirements to the users to get their reaction. Make any changes in the requirements that the users feel are necessary.

3. Think about how the course registration system at your college or university functions. Draw a data flow diagram of how you think the system works. If available, use graphics software to prepare your diagram.

4. A college bookstore has a large inventory of books that are used in many courses taught by many professors. Draw an entity-relationship diagram of how you think a database for such a bookstore would be designed. If available, use graphics software to prepare your diagram.

5. Locate information about several CASE tools on the Internet. What features do the tools offer? How can they be used in developing information systems? Using word processing software, write a summary of your findings.

6. A technique used to analyze a project, such as a new information system, is to find the net present value of the difference between the project's benefits and costs over the life of the project. The net present value can be found using the net present value function in spreadsheet software. Use the help system of your spreadsheet software to find out how to use this function.

Assume that a new information system will cost $500,000 to develop and have an expected life of five years. During the first year the system will cost $150,000 to operate, during the second year it will cost $125,000 to operate, and during the third, fourth, and fifth years it will cost $100,000 per year to operate. The business expects an economic benefit of $50,000 the first year, $100,000 the second year, $250,000 the third year, and $500,000 each of the fourth and fifth years.

Develop a spreadsheet to determine the net present value of the differences between the benefits and operating costs of this information system over its five-year life. Assume a discount rate of 8 percent. If the net present value is greater than the initial development cost, the system is economically feasible. What can you conclude about this information system?

Real-world Case

Inland Steel Industries

Gamblers at the casinos in Northwest Indiana would have blanched at the odds against nearby Inland Steel Industries Inc. A few years ago, Inland started to plan its Order Fulfillment System, a massive systems-development project with 7 million lines of code, a $37 million budget, and a timetable of three years to completion. Such grand projects fail four times in five.

But Inland beat the odds. When it finished the project for its flat-steel operations in Indiana Harbor, the company had added capabilities to provide the best, most consistent customer service in the steel industry. Inland had created a data warehouse to store customer information. It had also built 27 integrated applications, supporting 18 reengineered business processes, and had replaced 60 percent of its legacy code. What's more, Inland did it all on time—and within budget.

"There's absolutely no question in my mind that we have the best system for this purpose in the industry," says William Darnall, CEO of Inland, the nation's sixth-largest steelmaker with 1996 revenue of $4.6 billion.

How did Inland succeed where so many others have failed? Three ways:

- By ensuring that the new systems were aligned across several business processes, not just one—as in Inland's earlier, failed efforts.
- By gaining the unshakable support of the company's top business executives.
- By delivering results in phases, not all at the end. "We wanted early deliverables so we could see the benefits without having to wait for a big bang," says Bill Howard, Inland's VP of IT.

Inland's Order Fulfillment System, known internally as OFS, was designed specifically for both the company's flat-steel production business and its cost- and quality-conscious customers in the automobile and appliance industries. The system provides Inland with a clear view of all activities involved in the business—from sales and marketing, through the plant, and out to the trucks carrying rolls of steel to customers.

Inland's earlier, less ambitious projects to develop order-entry and manufacturing systems were stillborn because they lacked management support. But those failures served as object lessons for VP of IT Howard.

Inland's previous efforts had focused on technology in narrow, vertical functions and were not aligned with the business processes that cut horizontally across those functions. Because management never signed on, adequate funding never materialized.

VP of IT Howard used change management right from the start. He brought in management consultants from one of the top strategy firms, McKinsey & Co., to chart Inland's business and organizational issues. A year later, he retained Andersen Consulting to provide software tools and to help manage the project. Inland then contracted with USX Engineers and Consultants for software skills and business-process design.

Next, Inland assembled a core team of business and technology managers to see the project through from design to implementation. The project was laid out in phases. Early deliverables were assigned to sales, operations planning, manufacturing, and other areas to minimize business risks and deliver value to Inland throughout the three-year effort.

One goal of the project was to eliminate Inland's functional islands of automation. Manufacturing, for example, was doing what it needed to optimize its functions—as was sales—but the departments were not working together.

Yet integrating such systems carries a huge risk, says James Hayes, a partner at Andersen Consulting who worked on the Inland project. "If OFS didn't work," he says, "steel wouldn't go out the door, and that would cost the business millions of dollars a day."

Members of the core team of Inland business and IT leaders were assembled and assigned to one of 18 business processes. Then they regularly reviewed processes under a total quality theme of "plan, do, check, and act."

The regular meetings, reports, and measurements of key criteria such as order-entry cycle times meant that "the business leaders knew both the systems, and the business, and they couldn't be flimflammed," says Timothy Trela, CIO of Inland's flat-steel products unit, which is responsible for 85 percent of Inland's steel-production business.

Like the three branches of the federal government's checks-and-balances system, this core team kept the business units and the technologists on track.

It helped that Inland's business managers fully understood the importance of the OFS project. "I had two of my best management folks involved in the project," says Steven Bowsher, VP of sales and marketing for Inland's flat-steel products unit.

Along the way, the OFS core team fought one of the biggest threats to any big development project: scope creep. This phenomenon happens whenever requirements are continuously added to a systems project, bloating the system until the original deadlines and budgets become an impossible fantasy.

To avoid that, more than 500 requests from the business units for changes and enhancements were carefully reviewed by Inland's core team. In the end, they approved only a couple of dozen, all of them what Howard calls "show-stoppers"—serious problems discovered in the original OFS design.

In all, says Howard Ludwig, program manager for OFS, scope creep expanded the project by less than 10 percent, and most of the changes never threatened the budget or deadlines. In fact, just one addition—a "model factory" environment to train users on the new systems and business processes—extended the schedule, and that by just three months. The core group deemed that delay acceptable because the model factory provided valuable feedback for fine-tuning before OFS systems were deployed.

Now that the system is completed, Inland will implement some of the other noncritical additions and enhancements.

Inland also is assessing the project's impact. OFS already has brought wholesale changes throughout the company's flat-steel business. It has upgraded and expanded some jobs from clerical to professional functions, while automating, consolidating, and eliminating others.

OFS also has integrated information in a relational database that previously had resided in isolated pockets. This integration has improved speed and accuracy throughout the business process. Inland expects those improvements to continue as its business units learn how to use the technology more efficiently.

Questions

1. What were the most important factors that contributed to successful development of Inland's Order Fulfillment System?

2. Why were Inland's earlier system development projects unsuccessful?

3. Who was included in the core project team for Inland's Order Fulfillment System?

4. What risks did Inland face in developing the Order Fulfillment System?

5. How did Inland deal with "scope creep" in the development of the Order Fulfillment System?

Source: Bruce Caldwell, "Taming the beast," *InformationWeek*, March 10, 1997, pp. 38-40.

15 Managing Information Systems and Technology

Chapter Outline

Planning for Information Systems and Technology (p. 442)
    Determining the Planning Horizon (p. 442)
    Evaluating Risk (p. 443)
    Selecting the Application Portfolio (p. 443)
Acquiring Information Technology (p. 444)
    Hardware (p. 445)
    Software (p. 445)
    Network Technology (p. 447)
    Data Management Technology (p. 447)
    Personnel and Training (p. 448)
Organizing Information Systems Activities (p. 448)
    Centralization versus Decentralization (p. 448)
    Information Systems Organizational Structure (p. 449)
Controlling and Securing Information Systems (p. 451)
    Information System Controls (p. 451)
    Information System Security (p. 454)
Social and Ethical Issues (p. 455)
    Privacy (p. 455)
    Employment (p. 456)
    Crime (p. 458)
    Ethics (p. 461)

Learning Objectives

After completing this chapter, you should be able to:
- [ ] 1. Identify several factors that should be considered in planning for information systems and technology.
- [ ] 2. Describe common sources for acquiring information technology.
- [ ] 3. Describe the organizational structure of a typical information systems department.
- [ ] 4. Identify methods used by organizations to control and secure their information systems.
- [ ] 5. Explain some of the social and ethical issues related to information systems and technology.

I nformation systems are an important part of an organization. As you have seen throughout this book, businesses need information systems to support the operations and management of the organization. But like other parts of a business, information systems must themselves be managed. The information systems in an organization must be carefully planned; the technologies used in information systems must be thoughtfully acquired; the development, operation, and use of the information systems must be appropriately organized; and the functioning of the information systems must be precisely controlled. All these activities are part of managing information systems and technology. This chapter looks at these activities in detail so that you will better understand the role and importance of information systems and technology management.

This chapter also examines some of the social and ethical issues related to information systems and technology. It looks at the effect of information technology on privacy and employment, and discusses computer crime and ethics. These issues are an important part of information systems and technology management because they affect many of the decisions that managers make.

Planning for Information Systems and Technology

One of the fundamental activities that managers perform is *planning*. This activity involves determining *what* should be done. For example, a manager plans when he or she determines what products a business will produce or what form an advertising campaign will take. Planning is always future directed: What will the business do next month? next year? in five years?

Planning for information systems and technology involves determining what systems will be developed and what technology will be used in the future. Will the business develop a new order entry system or will it develop a new customer support system? Will the new system involve transaction processing or will it provide expert advice? Will it use keyboard input and screen output, or will it have voice input and multimedia output? These are the types of questions that managers ask as part of information systems and technology planning.

Determining the Planning Horizon

Planning can involve varying amounts of *time* in the future, called <u>planning horizons</u>. (See Fig. 15.1.) *Operational planning* involves a planning horizon of a few weeks to a few months. For example, planning what system modification will be done in the next three months is operational planning. In *tactical planning*, the planning horizon is several months to a few years. For example, planning what new systems will be developed and what technology will be used with those systems in the next two years is tactical planning. Finally, *strategic planning* involves a planning horizon of several years to 10 years or more. For example, planning the use of interorganizational and international information systems in five years is strategic planning.

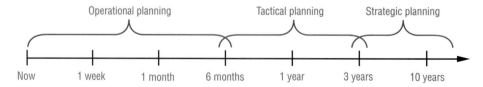

FIGURE 15.1

Planning horizons

Determining the planning horizon is an important part of planning for information systems and technology. How far into the future do we plan? Information *technology* changes rapidly, so it is often difficult to plan for specific technology more than a few years into the future. But information *systems* often stay with a business for many years. For example, some businesses have legacy systems that are more than 20 years old. These older systems most likely use updated information technology, but they still function essentially the same as when they were first developed. Thus, the planning horizon for information systems can be many years, but the planning horizon for information technology is usually only a few years.

Evaluating Risk

Planning can involve varying amounts of *risk*. Whenever you make plans for the future, you cannot be certain of the result or outcome. For example, you may plan to take a vacation in August because the weather is likely to be best that time of year, but then it rains for your entire trip. There are many risks in information systems and technology. A system may take longer to develop than was planned or not work correctly when completed. New technology that is less expensive and better than current technology may become available soon after the current technology is implemented. Another business may develop a better system that reduces that business's costs, thus giving it a competitive advantage, just as your business installs its new system. All these risks make information systems and technology planning difficult.

Risk is often related to three factors which should be considered when planning new information systems.[1] The first is the size of the system development project. In general, larger projects have more risk than smaller projects. Developing a new on-line inventory control system is riskier than developing a spreadsheet application. The second factor is the familiarity of the business with the information technology used in the new system. Systems that use low technology relative to the business, that is, technology with which the business is already familiar, are less risky than those that use high, or unfamiliar, technology. The final factor is the amount of structure in the system development project, which means how accurately the system's characteristics, such as its outputs, can be described in advance. Projects with high structure are, in general, less risky than those with low structure.

Figure 15.2 summarizes the risk associated with information system development when these three factors are combined. The most risky systems to develop involve large projects that have low structure and use high technology. An example might be an expert system for financial analysis in a national stock brokerage. The least risky systems to develop involve small projects that have high structure and use low technology. An example might be a spreadsheet application used for simple budgeting. In between are many other types of systems with varying degrees of risk.

Selecting the Application Portfolio

Planning what information systems should be developed and what technology should be used involves selecting an application portfolio. Such a portfolio is a description of what systems will be developed and when, plus an assessment of the risk associated with each system. For example, Fig. 15.3 shows an application portfolio for planning information systems in a hypothetical business. The portfolio allows the business to balance

---

[1] Lynda A. Applegate, F. Warren McFarlan, and James L. McKenney, *Corporate Information Systems Management* (Chicago: Irwin, 1996), pp. 266-267.

FIGURE 15.2

Information system and technology risk

		Low Structure	High Structure
Low Technology	Large Project	Low risk	Low risk
	Small Project	Very low risk	Very low risk
High Technology	Large Project	Very high risk	Medium risk
	Small Project	High risk	Medium low risk

FIGURE 15.3

An information system planning portfolio

PROJECT	DEVELOPMENT TIMEFRAME	SIZE	TECHNOLOGY	STRUCTURE	RISK
Budgeting	2001	Small	Low	High	Very low
Order entry	2001–02	Large	Low	High	Low
Workgroup support	2002–03	Large	High	High	Medium
Delivery routing	2003–05	Large	High	Low	Very high
Executive support	2004	Small	High	Low	High

the risks associated with different projects. For example, if the portfolio contains only low-risk projects, then consideration should be given to higher-risk projects that might provide a strategic impact for the business. Similarly, a portfolio of primarily high-risk projects may cause problems for the business if too many projects fail.

In summary, a business needs to plan for information systems and technology with varying time horizons and risk levels. A business needs to consider all types of systems, from short-term, low-risk transaction processing systems, to long-term, high-risk management information systems. The factors discussed in this section need to be taken into consideration in developing an application portfolio for information systems planning in a business.

Acquiring Information Technology

Managers often need to make decisions about how to acquire the technology used in information systems. Hardware needs to be purchased; software needs to be developed or bought; networks need to be acquired; and data management systems need to be selected. In addition, managers need to make decisions about hiring and training personnel to operate and use the information systems. All these decisions are part of managing information systems and technology. Figure 15.4 summarizes some of the sources of information technology.

Hardware

Computer hardware can be purchased from a number of sources. Multiple-user computer systems—minicomputers, mainframe computers, and supercomputers—are usually purchased directly from computer manufacturers. Companies such as IBM, Digital Equipment Corporation, Unisys, Hewlett Packard, and Cray Research sell their computers directly to businesses. Sometimes multiple-user computer systems are not purchased but rather leased from the manufacturers.

Personal computer systems are sometimes purchased directly from manufacturers. IBM, Apple, Compaq, Dell, and many other companies sell their microcomputers directly to businesses. Alternatively, many microcomputer manufacturers sell their computers to distributors, computer stores, or other businesses that resell them to businesses and individuals. Businesses called value added resellers or VARs purchase computers from manufacturers, add other hardware, software, and services, and then resell the complete package to businesses and individuals. IBM clones can be purchased from numerous businesses and computer stores that assemble the computers from parts purchased from other sources.

Software

As discussed in Chapter 14, computer software can be developed from scratch, purchased as a package, or purchased and then modified. Often, one of the biggest management decisions that a business must make is whether to custom develop software

FIGURE 15.4

Sources of information technology

Hardware:
  Computer manufacturers
  Distributors/retail stores
  Value added resellers

Software:
  Developed or modified
    In-house programmers
    Contract programmers
  Purchased
    Computer manufacturers
    Software companies
    Retail stores
    Value added resellers

Networks:
  Network companies
  Computer manufacturers
  Software companies
  Value added resellers
  Telecommunications companies
  Value added network companies

Data management:
  Computer manufacturers
  Software companies
  Database companies

Bookmark

Outsourcing Information Systems at Esprit

Many companies fail to appreciate the complexities of switching from centralized mainframe to client/server computing until they're hip-deep in these projects.

At Esprit de Corp., however, midcourse correction in its ambitious client/server plans led to a selective outsourcing deal that is expected to save money and a good deal of staff angst.

"Esprit is not a technology-driven company, and I was not able to afford an MIS staff with significant depth at different skill sets," said Peter Hanelt, chief operating officer at the $300 million apparel maker.

The missing skill sets included distributed database management and UNIX expertise. So Esprit decided to expand its outsourcing arrangement with Software Maintenance Specialists (SMS) in Santa Ana, California.

With the estimated $15 million, five-year extension, the SMS contract now includes installation of client/server hardware and software, network management, and application development.

SMS will now support a select group of Esprit's information systems operations in several client/server initiatives over the next few years. That support includes the rollout of an electronic data interchange order fulfillment system with retailers and a retail management system from Montreal-based Richter & Associates.

The San Francisco–based women's and children's clothing wholesaler began working with SMS several years ago to outsource its legacy processing.

By expanding the outsourcing deal, Esprit expects to reduce its client/server initiation costs by several hundred thousand dollars over the next five years.

"The outsourcing arrangement gives us the ability to ramp up and ramp down on [personnel] resources when needed," explained Chuck Bell, director of systems applications at Esprit.

The move also should enable Esprit to meet its original four-year plan, which the company wasn't meeting on its own. In addition, the outsourcing relationship should enable Esprit to tackle its client/server projects faster than if it hired outside contractors to handle each independent phase, Hanelt said.

Esprit's 25 IS staffers were picked up by SMS to support the selective outsourcing functions.

The deal makes sense for Esprit because it allows the company to retain strategic control over its client/server migration while enabling it to off-load nonessential activities such as equipment installation to SMS.

Esprit's approach also agrees with industry trends. "It's a great strategy. User companies can shorten their time of implementation and get accountability from these vendors," said Allie Young, a senior analyst at Dataquest Worldwide Services Group in Westboro, Massachusetts.

Efficiency is particularly important for Esprit and other players in the women's apparel industry, where profit margins continue to get squeezed.

"In these difficult times, retailers are looking for greater performance from their wholesalers," Hanelt said. "Therefore, we have to continue to focus our attention on our customers' needs and outsource where it makes sense."

QUESTIONS

1. Why did Esprit change from in-house development to outsourcing for its client/server computing?
2. What benefits does Esprit receive from outsourcing its client/server computing?

WEB SITE
Esprit: www.esprit.com

Source: Thomas Hoffman, "Esprit alters the fit of its outsourcing," *Computerworld*, January 22, 1996, p. 62.

or purchase a software package. Sometimes this is called the "make or buy" decision. Custom-developed software usually fits the organization's requirements better than packaged software but it is also usually much more expensive. Purchasing software and then modifying it is sometimes a good compromise between custom-developed software and packaged software. For personal computers, software usually is purchased; for multiple-user and networked computer systems, software may be purchased, purchased and modified, or developed from scratch.

If software is going to be developed from scratch, or purchased and modified, then managers must decide whether to use in-house programmers or to use contract programmers from an outside source. The advantage of using in-house programmers is that they usually are less expensive than contract programmers and they may be more loyal to the business. Contract programmers, on the other hand, may be more experienced in developing the type of software needed by the business or have specializations not found in in-house programmers, and they do not remain on the business's payroll after the work is completed.

Software can be purchased from a variety of sources. Computer manufacturers sell many software packages directly to businesses, as do general software companies such as Microsoft. Many specialty software companies also sell software packages to businesses. For example, a company may develop an accounting package for the hospitality industry that it sells directly to hotels. Individuals and some businesses purchase software packages from retail stores. Value added resellers usually sell software with hardware.

An alternative to operating its own hardware and software for its information systems is for a business to contract with an outside company to handle some or all processing. This approach is *outsourcing*, which was discussed in Chapter 14. The advantage of outsourcing is that the business can sometimes reduce expenses and get specialized services. One disadvantage is that the contracts for outsourcing are often very long—as much as 10 years. Not only will technology change significantly during the contract, but also the business's needs will often change considerably.

Network Technology

Technology for networks can be acquired from a number of sources. Local area network hardware and software can be purchased from companies specializing in network technology, such as Novell and 3COM; from computer manufacturers, such as IBM; or from software companies, such as Microsoft. Value added resellers also provide complete LANs constructed from hardware and software from several sources.

Much of the hardware and software for wide area networks can be acquired from companies specializing in communications technology. Long-distance channels, however, are often provided by telecommunications companies such as AT&T, Sprint, and MCI. These companies are called *common carriers* because anyone who pays their fees can use them. They provide two types of telephone lines. The first, called *switched* or *dial-up* lines, are the standard lines used by business and residential telephone customers for everyday telephone calls. The second, called *leased* or *dedicated* lines, can be used only by customers who lease them. These lines are better quality and provide faster and more accurate transmission. Another alternative for wide area network communication is a value added network or VAN. This is a network provided by a company that leases communications lines from common carriers and adds special services for long-distance data communication.

Data Management Technology

Acquiring data management technology first requires that a decision be made about the basic approach to data management: Will databases be stored on multiple-user computers? Will client-server computing be used with databases stored on a server in a network? Will data be distributed among different computers in a network? Once this decision has been made, the necessary software can be selected. Many companies supply database software including computer manufacturers such as IBM, general software companies such as Microsoft, and specialized database companies such as Oracle, Sybase, and Informix.

Personnel and Training

Although not a form of information technology, personnel are needed to operate and use an information system. Managers can select the personnel from inside the organization or hire them from outside. In either case, the personnel must be trained. Some businesses have training departments with full-time instructors to provide courses and other forms of computer and information systems training. Other businesses use outside services to provide training on a contract basis. In any case, personnel must be carefully trained before they can use and operate the system.

Organizing Information Systems Activities

The activities associated with developing, operating, and using information systems must be carefully organized in a business. Personnel who work in these activities need to be part of an organizational structure that provides appropriate direction and control. Businesses use a variety of organizational structures for their information systems activities. This section takes a look at some of the common elements of these structures.

Centralization versus Decentralization

One of the fundamental questions in information systems management is whether to have a centralized or decentralized management structure. (See Fig. 15.5.) In a *centralized* management structure, decisions related to information systems and technology are made for the entire organization by a single, centrally located group of managers. Information systems are developed by specialists working at a central location, and then deployed throughout the organization. Often, the resulting systems use centralized computers connected by networks to computers at other locations. For example, a business using a centralized information systems management structure may decide to develop a new sales reporting system which, after development, is distributed to its sales offices around the country.

In a *decentralized* management structure, information systems and technology decisions are made by managers working in local departments or groups. Systems are developed by specialists in those groups. The resulting systems use computers and networks that are located at the local site. For example, in a business using a decentralized information systems management structure, a regional office may decide to develop a new information system to keep track of its own sales. The system is developed and implemented at the regional office.

Both of these management structures have advantages. Centralized information systems management is often more economical than decentralized management because there is less duplication of personnel. With the decentralized approach, information systems specialists are needed throughout the organization, possibly resulting in duplication of effort. Centralized management also provides more control of system development than the decentralized approach. Managers can keep track of systems development projects more easily when the development effort is centralized, and costs can be controlled more closely.

FIGURE 15.5

Centralized versus decentralized information system management structure

Centralized

Decentralized

Decentralized information systems management provides better response to user needs than centralized management. When information system decisions are made at the department or workgroup level, the users' needs usually are more carefully considered. The system development effort is closer to the users and the users feel more a part of the process, often resulting in greater satisfaction with the system.

The debate over centralized versus decentralized information systems management has gone on for years. The pendulum swings back and forth between these approaches. Both have their advantages and disadvantages. Some businesses may find the centralized approach better for their needs, while others may prefer the decentralized approach.

Information Systems Organizational Structure

Many organizations and businesses have a department that is responsible for the development and operation of computer information systems. This department may be called information systems (IS), management information systems (MIS), information technology (IT), or something similar. It is headed by an <u>information systems manager</u> who is responsible for the management of the department. A business that follows the centralized information systems management approach will have a single such department for the entire business. In a business that follows the decentralized approach, information systems departments or similar groups may exist in a number of areas throughout the organization. Some organizations have a single person, called the <u>chief information officer</u> or <u>CIO</u>, who is responsible for all information systems and technology in the organization, not just that done by a single information systems department. The CIO usually reports to the chief executive officer of the company.

Figure 15.6 shows how a typical information systems department might be organized. This department has four areas: systems development, operations, technical support, and end-user support. Each area has its own manager.

Systems Development.   The systems development area is concerned with developing and maintaining information systems. *Systems analysts*, discussed in Chapter 14, and *programmers*, discussed in Chapter 5, work in this area. The programmers are often called <u>application programmers</u> because they develop application programs. Sometimes a person does both system analysis and application programming and is called a <u>programmer/analyst</u>.

Operations.   The operations area is concerned with operating the computers and related equipment needed in information systems. <u>Computer operators</u> run the computers. They put disks and tapes into the appropriate drives, load paper in printers, start and stop programs, remove output from printers, and monitor the hardware and software for errors and malfunctions. <u>Data entry operators</u> key input data, verify that data has been correctly keyed, and correct errors.

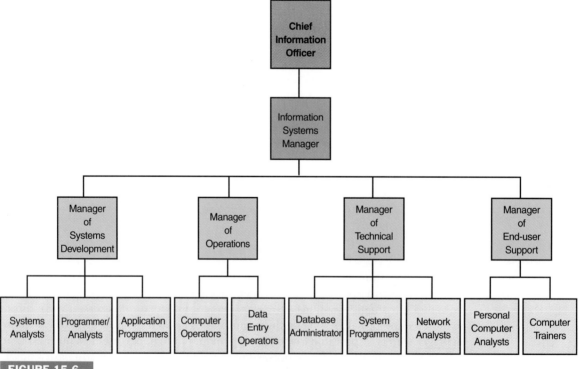

FIGURE 15.6

Organization of an information systems department

Technical Support.   The technical support area provides assistance in technical specialties to the other areas. The *database administrator* or *DBA*, discussed in Chapter 7, is responsible for managing the organization's databases. This person (or group of people) designs databases for the organization, selects database management software, and controls the use of databases by giving permission to specific users to access data in the databases. System programmers are responsible for setting up and maintaining system software such as operating systems and compilers. Network analysts are responsible for the organization's data communications hardware and software used in local area and wide area networks.

End-user Support.   Many organizations have an *information center*, discussed in Chapter 10, to help end-users develop and use computer applications, mainly on personal computers. The information center is usually part of the information systems department, but in some organizations it is a separate department.

The end-user support area has personal computer analysts who are responsible for evaluating and selecting personal computer hardware and software for use in the organization. In addition, they help users set up personal computers, they develop applications for end-users, and they assist users in utilizing application software. For example, a personal computer analyst may help a user select and install a personal computer or set up a graphics application on the user's personal computer. The analyst also may show a user how to access data in a company database or may develop a spreadsheet application for several users. Often, personal computer assistance is provided over the telephone from a help desk, which is staffed by personal computer analysts. The end-user support area also has computer trainers who provide users with in-house training courses on personal computer hardware and software.

Controlling and Securing Information Systems

One of the biggest concerns that managers have with information systems is ensuring that the systems function properly and securely. Many questions arise related to these concerns. Is all data being processed correctly? What will happen if the hardware malfunctions? Is the system secure from damage or failure? Answering these questions and more is part of controlling and securing information systems.

Information System Controls

Information system controls deal with ensuring that the system functions correctly. These controls fall into three main categories: application controls, hardware controls, and failure recovery procedures.

Application Controls.   Application controls are designed to ensure that the application processes all data correctly and produces the desired output. These controls are implemented in the software and procedures of the information system. They involve the four main functions of the system: input, output, storage, and processing.

Input controls are concerned with ensuring that input data is correctly entered into the system. As discussed in Chapter 10, a common technique used for this is *data validation*, which involves checking input data for possible errors. All input data should be validated as it is entered into the system. Invalid data must not be allowed into an information system.

Output controls deal with ensuring that all required output is produced. One form of output control is a *control total*, described in Chapter 10. An example of a control total is a count of the number of output documents. This control total can be compared with a similar total produced from the input data to indicate whether all output has been produced.

Storage controls are designed to ensure that the correct data is stored and accessed. Stored data should be under the control of the database administrator of the organization. Then anyone needing access to the data must go through the DBA. The DBA provides information on how to access the data, including file or database names and any special access codes. The file or database software checks the names and codes to be sure the correct data is being accessed.

Processing controls ensure that computations are performed correctly. One approach is to perform a particular computation several ways and to compare the results. In critical systems, where it is essential that the results are correct, computations sometimes are done differently on different computers and then the results are compared on another computer. For example, computer systems that control the flight of airplanes and space craft often work this way.

Hardware Controls. Hardware controls are features built into the hardware that reduce the chance of failure. One form of hardware control is to use *parity bits*, discussed in Chapter 4, to check for errors in the primary storage of the computer. This technique, called *parity checking*, is a common feature of business computers.

Another form of hardware control is to have duplicate or redundant hardware. For example, some businesses use a *RAID* (redundant array of inexpensive disks) system, discussed in Chapter 4, with their computers. This system includes multiple magnetic disks with data duplicated on different disks. Thus, if one disk is damaged, the data is not lost. Sometimes many components of a computer system are duplicated to create a fault-tolerant computer system. All input, output, storage, and processing is done on two systems simultaneously. If any component fails, the computer continues processing using other components.

So that hardware will not stop when power is interrupted, many organizations use an *uninterrupted power supply* or UPS. A UPS is a device that includes a battery that takes over when the main power is cut off. The programs running on the computer at the time can then be terminated and the computer turned off without damaging the system. Alternatively, the UPS can take over until a generator is started to supply continuous power and keep the computer running. A UPS is essential for a fault-tolerant computer system.

Failure Recovery Procedures. Information systems do not always work correctly. Hardware can fail, software can have bugs, people can make mistakes. Control procedures need to be in place to recover the system in case of a failure.

One of the most common system failures is loss of data on a magnetic disk or other secondary storage medium. Data can be accidentally erased; a disk drive can fail; a magnetic tape can be damaged; many things can happen to lose data. The most common procedures for dealing with this situation are *backup* and *recovery procedures*, discussed in Chapter 10. Secondary storage data needs to be backed up periodically and stored at a safe location. A procedure needs to be in place to recover the stored data if the original is lost.

A computer system can fail completely, or it can be damaged by a natural or other disaster. In this case, the business needs a *disaster recovery plan*, which is a plan

Bookmark

Disaster Recovery Plan at Options Clearing Corporation

If ever an organization needed foolproof data security and backup, it's Options Clearing Corp. The Chicago issuer, clearing agency, and guarantor for securities options clears more than 280 million contracts worth nearly $4 trillion annually.

With this kind of money on the line, OCC goes to great lengths to ensure data integrity and accessibility. It uses not one, but three emergency backup facilities.

The result may well be the envy of even the most secure and protected government data facilities. If disaster strikes and the production system goes down, first VP of information technology Len Neuzil says it can be restored within 30 minutes to three hours, depending on the type of disaster and the time of day it occurs.

Under the plan, financial data is automatically backed up and transmitted each day from mainframes and midrange systems at OCC's Chicago data center to a site operated by disaster-recovery vendor Comdisco Inc. in North Bergen, New Jersey. The data travels over Comdisco's high-speed nationwide network. When the final transmission is complete, a series of checks and balances ensures data integrity.

Neuzil says the recovery program is worth the expense. "The benefits make it well worth it," he says. "With our financial liability, we can't afford to lose data."

The OCC's five member exchanges appreciate its efforts to protect critical data. "We couldn't survive without the OCC being operational or without that data," says Edward Joyce, executive VP of the Chicago Board Options Exchange. "That's as sophisticated a backup process as there is." The other OCC member exchanges are the American Stock Exchange, the New York Stock Exchange, the Pacific Stock Exchange, and the Philadelphia Stock Exchange.

A typical day in the life of OCC's backup efforts starts before sunrise. Between 4 a.m. and 6 a.m., IT staffers at OCC transmit all current data to Comdisco's disaster-recovery systems. This ensures that the data in North Bergen is identical to databases in Chicago. During the workday, OCC employees go about their business, accessing on-line systems to determine current stock prices, editing prices, and processing matched trades provided by OCC's member exchanges.

Between 7 p.m. and 11 p.m., OCC uses its private network to retrieve trade data from its member exchanges. Once that data is in and edited, the network is shut down. At that time, OCC begins night processing

using a relational database, with parallel processing at North Bergen as backup. This is completed at about 2 a.m. This data is transmitted to North Bergen, and the process begins all over again.

In case of a disaster, IS staff at OCC's data center in Chicago would relocate to a Comdisco facility in nearby Rosemont, Illinois. From workstations in Rosemont, Neuzil says, they'd be able to access up-to-date OCC data from the North Bergen site, which would become OCC's temporary production center.

While a lot of organizations would consider this to be adequate backup, OCC goes a step further. A second Comdisco facility, in Woodale, Illinois, serves as a backup data center to the North Bergen site. If Chicago is out for longer than a week, or if North Bergen goes down, the Woodale facility would become the production center. And if for some reason all of its facilities in Illinois were incapacitated, a Comdisco facility in New York would take over.

"We try to avoid flying on one engine," Neuzil says. "Our disaster-recovery planning means there is a backup for our backup."

OCC also keeps its recovery staff sharp. At least once every three months, as many as 100 employees take part in "fire drills" to make sure they are familiar with recovery procedures. The staff visits the Rosemont facility, and North Bergen is activated to simulate disasters. "We want to make sure everyone always knows where to go and how to run the systems," Neuzil says.

The biggest challenge in the entire process is keeping the systems at the various locations in sync. "We have to constantly make sure we have the correct versions of all data files, and that takes an extended effort," Neuzil says. So far, the effort seems to be well worth it.

QUESTIONS

1. Why is it important that OCC have an extensive disaster recovery plan?
2. What would OCC do in case of a disaster?

WEB SITE
Options Clearing Corporation:
www.optionsclearing.com

Source: Bob Violino, "Serious security," *InformationWeek*, November 25, 1996, pp. 107–108.

for dealing with a disaster. Businesses often contract with special companies that provide computer services in case of a complete system failure. Sometimes these companies have computer systems in trucks that they can take to the business's location and use to continue the business's processing. (See Fig. 15.7.)

Information System Security

Information systems must be secure from damage due to unauthorized access or use. Security for information systems falls into two categories: physical security and electronic security.

Physical Security. Physical security involves methods that prevent physical access or damage to components of an information system. Major hardware systems, such as multiple-user computers and network database servers, often are isolated with limited access. Employees may require special identification cards or codes to gain entry to computer rooms. (See Fig. 15.8). Secondary storage data is secured by storing backup copies in a fireproof vault or at a site away from the business.

Electronic Security. More complex than physical security is electronic security, which involves preventing access to the information system or system components through communications lines. With the extensive use of networks and data communications, electronic security has become very important. Data sent over a communications channel can be intercepted, unauthorized access to a system can be gained through a terminal or a personal computer, and even the Internet can be used for intercepting data or accessing a business's computer system.

Data encryption, discussed in Chapter 6, is a common technique for preventing intercepted data from being interpreted. Encrypted data is unintelligible unless a special number called a *key* is known. Unauthorized access to a system can be reduced by having account numbers and passwords for all authorized users. Some systems are designed so that once a user connects to the system, the computer breaks the connection and then calls the user back to reestablish the connection.

The Internet causes special security problems for businesses. Many businesses have one or more computers connected to the Internet to provide information and advertising. These businesses want potential customers to gain access to the information through the Internet. Once the contact is made, however, it may be possible

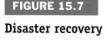

Disaster recovery

FIGURE 15.8

**Computer room
access control**

to access other business information in the computer. To prevent this from happening a *firewall*, discussed in Chapter 6, is used. The firewall consists of special hardware and software that creates an electronic barrier between the Internet site and the rest of the business's computer systems.

Social and Ethical Issues

Information systems and technology have an impact that goes beyond the organization or business. This impact is felt in many aspects of society, including privacy, employment, and crime. Society must pay some costs for the benefits gained from information technology. Information system managers must weigh these costs against the system benefits in making their decisions. This section examines some of the social issues of information systems and technology.

Along with the social issues go ethical issues. Managers and others in the information systems function of an organization must consider these issues in their actions and decision making. This section looks at some of the ethical questions faced by individuals and businesses in their use of information systems and technology.

Privacy

One of the main costs of information systems and technology to society is a reduction in people's privacy. Privacy has to do with keeping information about oneself to oneself. People need privacy so that they feel free to do what they want. If people do not have privacy and the things they do are recorded somewhere, they may feel threatened and inhibited. (Read George Orwell's *1984* for some idea about what the world would be like without privacy.)

Information Systems and Privacy.   Information systems reduce people's privacy by recording information about people. Many government agencies have computer files and databases with personal information. For example, the Social Security Administration has files on practically everyone who has worked in the United States. The Internal Revenue Service has computerized versions of tax returns.

Nongovernment organizations and businesses also have computerized information about people. For example, TRW, the largest credit reporting company in the United States, has computerized credit histories for over 120 million people. Firms that sell mailing lists have large files listing personal characteristics and preferences so that mailing lists can be targeted at certain types of individuals.

There are legitimate uses and benefits of computerized information about people. No one would receive social security checks without the Social Security Administration's system. Credit would be harder to get without computerized credit bureaus. But such information can also be abused. For example, should social security information about you be available to any business that wants to check on your work history? Should credit information about you be available to anyone without your permission? To many people, the answer to questions such as these is "No."

One way that computerized information can be abused is through matching This is a process in which data in one file or database is compared with data in another. Computers can match data in large files or databases very rapidly. Matching can be useful; for example, matching welfare recipient data with social security data can detect welfare fraud. But it can also be used to further reduce people's privacy. For example, matching credit files, mailing list files, work history files, and medical databases would provide detailed descriptions of people.

As information systems become larger and more comprehensive and as information technology becomes more sophisticated, it becomes easier for government agencies and businesses to match information about people from many sources. How would you feel if all the computerized information about you were stored in one central computer and made available to anyone who requested it? This is a far-fetched idea, but it does show the abuse that is possible with large computerized files and databases.

Protection of Privacy.   Fortunately, there are safeguards that help prevent the misuse of computerized information. These safeguards are in the form of legislation that limits the use and access of computerized information about individuals. Some of the major laws in the United States are listed in Fig. 15.9. Other countries have their own privacy laws. Although laws cannot prevent all misuses of computerized information, they can help minimize the problem and thus provide more assurance of privacy to people.

Employment

Another social cost of information systems and technology is changes in employment. Some people have lost their jobs to computers, and others have obtained new jobs as a result of computerization. Many, if not most, people's jobs have changed because of information technology. Overall, people's work lives have been affected by information systems and technology.

The Effect of Information Technology on Employment.   Information technology sometimes replaces employees. When an organization installs a computer system for some function, the people who previously performed the function are displaced. Some of these people may lose their jobs, and others may be shifted to other jobs in the organization.

FIGURE 15.9

Major U.S. privacy
laws

- **Freedom of Information Act of 1970.**
  Lets people find out what information government agencies store about them.

- **Fair Credit Reporting Act of 1970.**
  Allows people to inspect and challenge information in their credit records.

- **Privacy Act of 1974.**
  Prohibits government agencies from collecting information about individuals
  for illegitimate purposes.

- **Right to Financial Privacy Act of 1978.**
  Gives procedures that the government must follow to examine information
  about individuals in financial institutions.

- **Electronic Communications Privacy Act of 1986.**
  Provides protection from unauthorized interception of electronic communications.

- **Computer Matching and Privacy Act of 1988.**
  Regulates the use of matching of files and databases by the government.

What should be done with workers who are displaced by computers? If people lose their jobs because of information technology, they just add to society's social and economic problems. Many organizations offer the option of retraining to the affected workers. People have to adapt in a changing society, and retraining should be expected in one's life. Retrained employees continue as productive members of the organization and of society. Another option is early retirement for older employees. Some workers who are close to retirement may prefer this option to retraining.

It may seem like many jobs have been lost to computers. Some studies have shown, however, that overall this is not the case. While some jobs have been lost, new jobs have been created. Many of these new jobs have been in the computer industry, including jobs in the manufacturing, sales, and repair of computers. Other new jobs have resulted from new functions not performed before computerization. For example, programming and information systems analysis were not needed before computers, but are common jobs today.

Changing Patterns of Work.   What is clear is that many people's jobs have changed as a result of information technology. The typist now uses a computer for word processing rather than a typewriter for typing. The office manager now communicates with electronic mail rather than with paper memos. The factory worker now checks on the operation of computerized robots rather than working on the assembly line. The jobs are still there; what the employees do is different.

Where and when people work also has changed. With personal computers, data communications, and workgroup applications, it is possible for some people to work regularly away from their office or business. Many people *telecommute*, a topic discussed in Chapter 9. They use computers in their home or elsewhere to communicate with their organization's central computer system. In addition, people can work at almost any time of the day or night on almost any day of the week because the central computer system operates 24 hours a day, seven days a week. Thus, some employees may choose to work in the evenings or on weekends rather than during the regular nine-to-five workday. The effect is to create a *virtual office* of employees, another topic discussed in Chapter 9.

Employee Health. In addition to changes in employment patterns, information technology may affect the physical and mental health of employees. In the past, people have thought that prolonged use of CRT screens may cause cataracts, birth defects, miscarriages, and other serious problems. Most of these concerns have not proven to be true, although the evidence is not conclusive in all cases. Until final proof of safety has been established, some people recommend against prolonged use of CRT screens, especially by pregnant women.

Other physical problems, however, definitely occur in some computer users. Eyestrain, headaches, backaches, neck pain, wrist pain, and similar conditions are common among people who use computers extensively. One way of reducing these problems is through good ergonomic design of both the computer and the employee's work environment. (*Ergonomics* was discussed in Chapter 4.) Some communities have enacted legislation requiring employers to provide ergonomically sound environments.

In addition to physical health, there is concern that computer use can affect employees' mental health. Because computers work fast, some people feel pressured to work faster than normal just to "keep up" with the computer. This situation can create stress for the employee. In addition, people who work with computers often work alone, creating a feeling of isolation. One potential problem with telecommuting is that the employee does not have the social interaction common in an office environment, again contributing to a feeling of isolation. These concerns are real and need to be considered by employers when determining how employees will work.

Crime

A third cost of information systems and technology to society is the emergence of new forms of crime. With computers and other technology, many criminal activities are possible that could not be done before. To guard against these activities new forms of security are needed.

Theft of Money. Information technology can be used to steal money from organizations and businesses. Computers are used extensively in banks and other financial institutions. Networks are used to transfer billions of dollars electronically all over the world every day using electronic funds transfer. There are many opportunities for electronic theft of money in the complex systems needed by financial institutions.

Some examples of the use of computers to steal money are:

- A consultant taps into the electronic funds transfer system of a bank and transfers money to a secret account.
- A computer programmer modifies the interest calculation program for a savings and loan so that fractions of a cent are not rounded correctly but instead are put into a special account. Over time, the fractions build up to thousands of dollars.
- A manager at a credit union modifies computer records of loans to a friend so that the loans appear to have been repaid.

To prevent such crimes, organizations need procedures that detect discrepancies in transactions and files. Financial records should be audited regularly for any inconsistencies. Software should be checked to be sure it performs correctly. Some organizations have one programmer develop a program and another programmer test it. The programmers would have to be in collusion to illegally modify the program. Most important of all, the organization should hire trustworthy employees.

Theft of Data. Data is a valuable resource of an organization. Businesses store data about their operations in computer systems, and the data often is of interest to competitors. For example, a business may store data about prices of a new product. A competitor would be interested in the prices so that it would know what to charge in order to undersell the business. This type of data must be protected so that others cannot obtain it.

To prevent the improper use of data, data security measures need to be taken. One measure is to use passwords to access the computer system. Whenever someone attempts to retrieve or change data, the system asks for the person's password. If the person cannot supply the correct password, the system does not perform the requested processing. Passwords should be changed frequently to prevent a person with an old password from using the system without authorization. In addition, passwords must be kept secret so that an unauthorized person cannot discover a password.

Some people enjoy gaining access to computer systems not to steal data, but just for the challenge of breaking in. Sometimes the term hacker is used for this type of person, although this term is also used for computer programmers in general. Many hackers use personal computers at home to gain access to remote computers operated by businesses and organizations. Most hackers are not interested in doing anything malicious, but just want to investigate other computer systems. To prevent hackers from accessing their computers, many organizations use sophisticated security procedures. In addition, various laws provide penalties for illegally accessing a computer system.

Another data security measure is to use data encryption to change the data on a disk to an unintelligible form. Then, even if someone knows the password, he or she cannot understand the data because it is encrypted. Data encryption is also used when data is sent over a communications channel. Because channels can be tapped for illegal purposes, data can be intercepted as it is transmitted. If the data is encrypted, however, the person intercepting the data cannot interpret it without the encryption key.

Data stored on floppy disks poses an especially difficult security problem for a business or organization. Often, important data is stored on floppy disks. If the disks are left on a desk, they can be taken by someone with little chance of detection. Many organizations have a policy that no floppy disk may be removed from the organization's property and that all disks must be stored in a locked case when not in use. Also, data encryption can be used for data stored on a floppy disk so that only the person with the key can understand the data.

Theft and Destruction of Hardware. Hardware can be physically damaged or stolen. An unhappy former employee or other person may try to destroy hardware. An unscrupulous employee may steal equipment to use elsewhere or to sell. Security procedures need to be taken to prevent occurrences such as these.

Multiple-user computer systems and network equipment usually are kept in locked rooms and only authorized personnel are allowed access. Computer rooms often have special fire-extinguishing equipment to protect the hardware in case of fire. Precautions such as these are necessary to protect the equipment from physical damage.

Personal computers in an office environment are sometimes easy to steal. To prevent theft, personal computers are often bolted or chained to the desk. Use by unauthorized personnel is also a potential problem with personal computers. Consequently, some personal computers have keys that must be used before they can be turned on. Security procedures such as these are used to protect personal computer equipment.

Illegal Copying of Software.   Most software is *copyrighted*, just as books, movies, and recordings are copyrighted. This means that it is illegal to make a copy of the software without the permission of the owner of the copyright. When someone works hard developing a program, he or she should be rewarded for the effort. Just as you should not make a copy of someone else's book, movie, or recording, you should also not make a copy of someone else's software.

When you purchase a program, you purchase the right to use the program but not the right to give away or sell copies of it. Most programs come with a written software license agreement, which states what the purchaser can legally do with the software. Most software license agreements allow the purchaser to use the program on only one computer at a time and to make copies only for backup purposes.

When a business or organization purchases a program, it purchases the right for its employees to use the program. Usually, however, only one employee can legally use the program at a time. Making copies of the program so that more than one employee in the organization can use it usually is illegal. If several people need to use the program, multiple copies must be purchased. Alternatively, some software vendors sell a site license for an additional fee, which allows more than one person in the organization to use the program at a time.

To prevent the illegal copying of software, many organizations have policies stating that employees who copy software illegally will be disciplined or fired. As an additional measure, employees are usually not allowed to take software disks away from the organization's property.

Some software is not copyrighted. This software, called public domain software, can be legally copied and used by anyone. Another kind of software, called shareware, is copyrighted but is given away or sold for a small fee and includes permission to use the software and to make copies for others for evaluation purposes. If, after evaluating the software, the business or individual decides to continue to use it, the full price for the software must be paid. If the business or individual decides not to use the software, however, nothing is owed. Because shareware is copyrighted and is not public domain software, the terms specified by the developer must be followed. The shareware concept is, however, an inexpensive way of evaluating many programs to decide which is the best for the business's or individual's needs.

Occasionally an individual or a business will make an illegal copy of a program and try to sell it. This is called software piracy, and software developers sue the individual or the business. You should always be sure you are buying a legal copy of any program.

Destruction of Data and Software.   Some people do not wish to steal data or illegally copy software, but instead destroy or otherwise vandalize it. A disgruntled employee may try to physically damage disks or tapes. A hacker may try to erase programs or data electronically. In addition, data may be destroyed by fire or natural disaster. To help prevent the permanent destruction of data and programs, backup copies are made and stored in a fireproof vault or at a location away from the organization.

A particularly dangerous form of data and program destruction is caused by a computer program called a <u>virus</u>. A virus is created by a hacker who puts the virus on floppy disks or on a hard disk on a computer used by several people. Usually, the virus does not do any damage for some period of time, such as several months. During this time people may unknowingly copy the virus to other disks, or the virus may copy itself. At a certain time all the copies of the virus activate themselves and destroy programs and data in many computers.

Sometimes a hacker will put a virus on a computer in a local area or wide area network. Then the virus will copy itself to other computers in the network. This type of virus is sometimes called a *worm* because of the way it moves through the network. After a while, all the copies of the virus in the network begin destroying programs or data in the network.

To prevent viruses, no one should copy a disk from an unreliable source. Backup copies of original software disks should always be kept in case of a virus attack. Virus checking programs can be used to search disks for the presence of viruses. (See Fig. 15.10.) Some of these programs are designed so that they check for viruses whenever a new program is executed. Detecting viruses in a network is especially difficult because there are many computers in the network.

Ethics

The social issues discussed in this section involve ethical questions often faced by employees and managers of a business. *Ethics* has to do with the standards of behavior that we follow: what is right and what is wrong. Information system professionals and users must be ethical in their use of systems and technology.

Balancing an individual's right to privacy with a business's legitimate need for information about people raises complex ethical issues. Under what circumstances

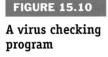

FIGURE 15.10

A virus checking program

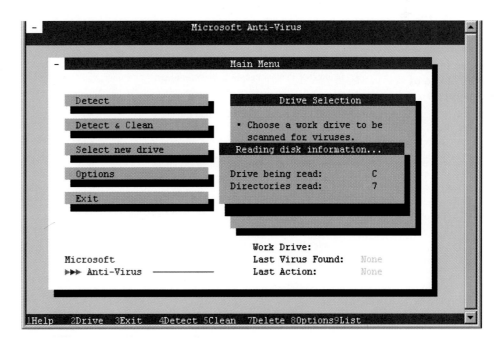

should a business access a potential employee's driving record? Should a business read an employee's e-mail? What should a business do to protect an employee's personnel records?

Evaluating the effect of information technology on employment in a business requires careful thinking about ethical questions. What obligations does a business have to employees who are displaced by information technology? What special responsibilities does telecommuting impose on employees? Who is responsible for health issues related to computer use, the employee or the company?

Maintaining security from computer crime requires ethical behavior. The security measures described in this chapter will not prevent all computer crimes. Ultimately, the behavior of the individual determines the security of an information system. Without ethical behavior, security measures would be so strict that the use of information systems would be almost impossible except by a very few people.

You may confront a number of ethical questions in your life revolving around information systems and technology. For example, a friend may ask you to make a copy of a program you bought so that he or she can try it out. You may find out that a co-worker has accessed the company's database and has learned management salary data. Another co-worker, you may discover, has put a seemingly harmless virus on the company's local area network that causes every computer on the network to play a song at a certain time each day. What would you do in each of these situations? Although these may seem like harmless acts, they involve questions of ethics that you would have to deal with.

There are common rules for the ethical use of computers. Figure 15.11 shows one list of rules. In addition, many professional organizations have a code of ethics that describes ethical behavior in a particular profession. You may someday belong to such an organization and should adhere to its code of ethics. But ethical behavior goes beyond lists of rules and professional codes. Individuals must decide for themselves what is ethical. Businesses and their employees must understand and address ethical questions in the use and management of information systems and technology.

FIGURE 15.11

Rules for the ethical use of computers

1. Do not use a computer to harm other people.

2. Do not interfere with other people's computer work.

3. Do not look in other people's computer files.

4. Do not use a computer to steal.

5. Do not use a computer to bear false witness.

6. Do not copy or use proprietary software for which you have not paid.

7. Do not use other people's computer resources without authorization or proper compensation.

8. Do not appropriate other people's intellectual output.

9. Think about the social consequences of the program you are writing or the system you are designing.

10. Always use a computer in ways that ensure consideration and respect for your fellow humans.

Chapter Summary

- [ ] Factors that should be considered in planning for information systems and technology include **planning horizon** and risk. Operational planning involves a planning horizon of a few weeks to a few months. In tactical planning, the planning horizon is several months to a few years. Strategic planning involves a planning horizon of several years to 10 years or more. Risk in information systems and technology often is related to three factors. The first factor is the size of the system development project; smaller projects are less risky than larger projects. The second factor is the familiarity of the business with the information technology; low (familiar) technology is less risky than high (unfamiliar) technology. The third factor is the amount of structure in the system development project; high structure projects are less risky than low structure projects. An **application portfolio** should be prepared, describing what systems should be developed and when, plus an assessment of the risk associated with each system. (pp. 442–444)

- [ ] Information technology can be acquired from a number of sources. Computer hardware can be purchased from computer manufacturers, distributors, retail stores, and **value added resellers** (**VAR**). Software can be developed using in-house programmers or contract programmers, or purchased from computer manufacturers, software companies, retail stores, and value added resellers. Network technology can be acquired from network companies, computer manufacturers, software companies, value added resellers, telecommunications companies, and **value added network** (**VAN**) companies. Data management technology can be acquired from computer manufacturers, general software companies, and database software companies. (pp. 444–448)

- [ ] A typical information systems department is organized into four areas: systems development, operations, technical support, and end-user support. The systems development area includes systems analysts, **application programmers**, and **programmer/analysts**. The operations area includes **computer operators** and **data entry operators**. The technical support area consists of a database administrator, **system programmers**, and **network analysts**. The end-user support area includes **personal computer analysts** and **computer trainers**. The information systems department is headed by an **information systems manager**. There may also be a **chief information officer** or **CIO** who

is responsible for all information systems and technology in the organization. (pp. 448–451)

- [ ] Information systems controls include application controls, hardware controls, and failure recovery procedures. Application controls are designed to ensure that all data is correctly processed and that the desired output is produced. They include input controls, output controls, storage controls, and processing controls. Hardware controls are features built into hardware to reduce the chance of failure. They include parity checks and duplicate or redundant hardware. Failure recovery procedures are designed to recover the system in case of failure. They include backup and recovery procedures, and a disaster recovery plan. Information system security includes physical security and electronic security. Physical security involves methods that prevent physical access and damage to components of an information system. It includes computer room access control and off-site storage of backup data. Electronic security involves preventing access to the information system or system components through communication links. It includes data encryption and firewalls. (pp. 451–455)

- [ ] One of the social costs of information systems and technology is a reduction of people's privacy. Information is recorded about people in files and databases, and **matching** can be used to compare personal data in several files or databases. Another social cost is changes in employment. Information technology sometimes replaces employees in an organization, and many people's jobs have changed because of the technology. The physical and mental health of employees also can be affected by computer use. A third social cost of information systems and technology is the emergence of new forms of crime. Information technology can be used to steal money and organizational data, hardware can be stolen or destroyed, software can be illegally copied, and data and software can be destroyed by **viruses**. A number of ethical issues arise in the use of information systems and technology including balancing individuals' rights to privacy with a business's legitimate need for information, evaluating the effect of information technology on employment, and providing security measures to prevent computer crime that may infringe on individual rights. (pp. 455–462)

Key Terms

Application Portfolio (p. 443)
Application Programmer (p. 450)
Chief Information Officer (CIO)
    (p. 450)
Computer Operator (p. 450)
Computer Trainer (p. 451)
Data Entry Operator (p. 450)
Fault-tolerant Computer System
    (p. 452)
Hacker (p. 459)

Help Desk (p. 451)
Information Systems Manager
    (p. 449)
Matching (p. 456)
Network Analyst (p. 451)
Personal Computer Analyst (p. 451)
Planning Horizon (p. 442)
Programmer/Analyst (p. 450)
Public Domain Software (p. 460)
Shareware (p. 460)

Site License (p. 460)
Software License Agreement
    (p. 460)
Software Piracy (p. 460)
System Programmer (p. 451)
UPS (p. 452)
Value Added Network (VAN)
    (p. 447)
Value Added Reseller (VAR) (p. 445)
Virus (p. 461)

Assignment Material

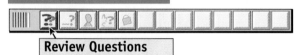

Review Questions

Fill-in Questions

1. The time span for which planning is done is the
   _____.

2. A business should prepare a(n) _____
   describing what information systems will be developed and when.

3. A(n) _____ purchases computers from
   manufacturers, adds other hardware, software, and
   services, and resells the complete package to businesses and individuals.

4. A(n) _____ is a network provided by a
   company that leases communications lines from
   common carriers and adds special services for long
   distance data communications.

5. The head of the information systems department in
   an organization or business is called the
   _____. The person responsible for all
   information systems and technology in an organization or business is called the _____.

6. A(n) _____ does both computer programming and system analysis.

7. A(n) _____ runs the computer equipment used in an information system.

8. The person responsible for an organization's data
   communications hardware and software is called
   a(n) _____.

9. Personal computer assistance is often provided over
   the telephone from a(n) _____.

10. A(n) _____ computer system has duplicate components designed so that the system will
    continue to function if any component fails.

11. A device with a battery that takes over supplying
    power to a computer system when the main power
    is cut off is a(n) _____.

12. The process of comparing data in several computer
    files or databases for the purpose of locating common data is called _____.

13. A(n) _____ is a person who enjoys gaining access to a computer system for the challenge of
    breaking in and for the purpose of investigating the
    system.

14. Software that is not copyrighted is called
    _____.

15. Making illegal copies of software for sale to other
    people is called _____.

16. A(n) _____ is a computer program that
    copies itself from one computer system to another and
    activates itself after a period of time, usually destroying
    programs and data in many computer systems.

Short-answer Questions

1. Explain the difference in the planning horizon of
   operational, tactical, and strategic planning.

2. What factors affect the risk associated with a new
   information system?

3. What are the main sources for acquiring computer hardware and software for an information system?

4. Give the advantages of centralized information system management and of decentralized information system management.

5. How is an information system department typically organized?

6. What are application controls?

7. What are some forms of hardware controls?

8. How can an information system be secured from damage due to unauthorized access or use?

9. How can information systems and technology reduce people's privacy?

10. Identify several U.S. laws that help prevent the misuse of computerized information about individuals.

11. What are some of the effects of information systems and technology on employment?

12. What can be done to help prevent the theft of money using information technology?

13. What is a software license agreement. What is a site license?

14. What is shareware?

15. What can be done to help prevent the permanent destruction of data and programs?

16. What are some of the ethical issues that arise in the use of information systems and technology?

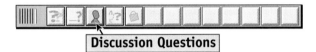

Discussion Questions

1. Think of several new information systems for your college or university. How much risk would be involved in developing each system?

2. What additional factors, besides those given in the chapter, should an international business consider in planning its international information systems?

3. Consider the course registration system at your college or university. What controls should be included in that system to assure that students are enrolled in the classes they request? What security should be included in the system to prevent inappropriate use of it?

4. A fellow employee has printed out information about a celebrity client of your company and is handing out copies in the lunchroom. What would you do in this situation?

5. A new information system has been installed in the department that you manage in your business. The system is such that 20 percent fewer employees will be needed in your department. You have been told by your superior to determine which employees will be terminated. How will you make this decision?

6. Some viruses do not do any damage to a computer system. They may play a song on a speaker, display an image on a screen, or do some other benign thing that is simply a nuisance. Why would a business be concerned about these viruses?

Problem-solving Projects

1. Develop an application portfolio for information system projects for a business with which you are familiar. Use spreadsheet software to prepare the portfolio. Design the spreadsheet so that the projects can be sorted by different factors. Sort the projects by development time frame. Also sort the projects by risk.

2. Investigate the organization of the information systems department of a business with which you are familiar. Draw a diagram, similar to Fig. 15.6, that shows the organization. If available, use graphics software to prepare your diagram.

3. Interview a computer professional about his or her career in the computer field. How did the person get started? What education does the person have? What was his or her first job in the computer field? What promotions has the person had in his or her career? What does the person do now? Using word processing software, write a summary of your interview.

4. This chapter lists several U.S. privacy laws. Using the Internet, find out more about these laws. Also, locate information about other privacy laws in the United States. Using word processing software, pre-

pare a brief summary of the privacy laws that you found. You may wish to prepare your summary in the form of a table. Determine the effects of the laws on businesses and incorporate this information into your summary.

Real-world Case

Malden Mills

The fire that engulfed the Malden Mills complex in Lawrence, Massachusetts, in December 1995—causing more than $300 million in damage—could have shut down the Polartec fabric maker for good. Instead, it invigorated the mill's workers and accelerated a previously planned $10 million to $15 million information and automation systems overhaul.

The day after the fire, Aaron Feuerstein, president and co-owner of Malden Mills Industries, Inc., wowed observers by pledging to rebuild locally and promising to pay idled workers. His bold directive inspired his top managers, who immediately made the massive system redesign their top priority.

In an unusual move, a top business executive—not an IS manager—was put in charge of the system redesign. Michael Backler, corporate director of planning and operations, got the call. He said the company hopes that using a top business manager instead of an IS manager to run the so-called Merrimack project will "Help give customers what they want: timely information about their orders and an ability to deal with the company electronically."

Separately, automation experts were dispatched around the globe. Their mission was to find the best textile manufacturing innovations in the world. The goal was to replace aging information technology in order to gain better control of production, inventory, and automation processes.

William L. Baggeroer, Malden's vice president of IS, hadn't even reported for his first day of work when the fire hit. "The [11 p.m. news] report said Malden Mills just blew up, and I saw this blaze that looked like Hades and thought, 'My God, it's gone,'" he said.

When a worried Baggeroer called in, he was told to help set up a new IT system. The idea behind the system modernization plan was to fundamentally change the company "to make it more customer-focused instead of only manufacturing-focused," he said.

A bold undertaking, to be sure. But Feuerstein and his financial managers expect a huge return on what could be a $15 million investment. "It will come back many times in coming years by having customers give us preference," Feuerstein said. The investment is also expected to position the mill well ahead of its competitors.

The mill's IT vision is even more impressive, considering that the company, which was already struggling to rebuild its physical structure, could have held off on the systems revamp. Although flames swept through three century-old mill buildings and seriously injured 12 workers, the IS infrastructure was mostly spared.

Indeed, the day after the fire, the Hewlett-Packard Co. HP 3000 mainframe system was running, churning out the next week's payroll and staffing information. Only 10 percent of Malden's systems were lost, but that included some irreplaceable screenprint patterns.

At one point during the blaze, however, the wind shifted and put the data center at risk.

Data center manager Al Autieri Jr. recalled driving to work, ordering the center closed, and sending the overnight IS workers home. He decided to rescue hundreds of data storage tapes himself. "I grabbed them up any way I could in a panic and loaded them into a van," he said. He drove the van to his home until everything was settled several hours later.

As it turned out, the data center was spared, and it took hours to return the tapes to their proper order. Nearly all the vital corporate records were regularly backed up and stored by a contractor miles away, but "saving the most up-to-the-minute data somehow seemed vital at the time," Autieri recalled with a smile.

The fire destroyed half a fiber-optic loop on the 29-acre campus, half the phones, about 300 PCs in remote locations, 160 printers, and part or all of 300 large dye and finishing machines.

The company's research and development and design studios lost some vital data that contained formulas and designs for printing fabric. Some of the fabric designs had to be recreated even though data backup procedures were in place. In one case, data backup tapes for designs were kept in a separate building, but both that building and the one that contained the design PCs were destroyed.

Some data was recovered, thanks to users who had taken PC floppy disks home.

One upside to the fire is that in the aftermath, managers seized the opportunity to reform business practices with technology as soon as Feuerstein decided to rebuild.

"To the credit of the executive group, they didn't lose sight of long-term goals," Baggeroer said. "They took advantage of the fire to speed up [these projects]." He was referring to the fact that Merrimack, the new systems project, was in its infancy prior to this. The fire gave the program its legs.

"Merrimack will give us many, many things, but one critical thing is it will give customers service and deliveries on time," Feuerstein said.

Merrimack "brings Malden Mills closer to a just-in-time production process," agreed Bruce Richardson, an analyst at Advanced Manufacturing Research in Boston. Such a change means fabric is manufactured to each customer's order instead of being placed in inventory at the mill's expense.

"Sometimes it takes a cataclysmic event like a major fire to bring about profound change in an organization, and that's clearly what's working here," Richardson said. "Left to their own devices, people usually don't make such sweeping changes."

Questions

1. What data security precautions did Malden Mills take before the fire?

2. What could Malden Mills have done better in terms of data security?

3. What effect did the fire have on Malden Mills' information systems planning?

4. What ethical problem did the Malden Mills president face after the fire and what did he decide to do?

Source: Matt Hamblen, "Mill disaster fires up planned IS overhaul," *Computerworld*, January 20, 1997, pp. 1, 28-29.

GLOSSARY

The number following each entry indicates the chapter in which the term is defined.

Accessing The process of retrieving stored data. (10)

Accounting The function of a business that records and reports financial information about the business. (2)

Accounting information system An information system that supports the accounting function of a business. (10)

Accounts payable system A system that keeps track of money owed by the business, pays the business's bills, and provides reports of money owed by the business. (10)

Accounts receivable system A system that keeps track of money owed to the business by its customers, records customer payments, and provides reports of money owed to the business. (10)

Address A unique number that identifies a storage location in primary storage. (4)

Ad hoc report A report that is prepared only once, for a specific purpose. (11)

AI Artificial intelligence. (11)

ALU Arithmetic-logic unit. (4)

Analog signal A signal that transmits data by a wave pattern that varies continuously. (6)

Application conferencing A form of document conferencing in which each user sees the same document within an application program. (9)

Application generator A program that is used to develop a computer application including input and output forms, reports, menus, calculations, and database queries. (7)

Application portfolio A description of what information systems an organization should develop and when, and an assessment of the risk associated with each system. (15)

Application programmer A programmer who develops application programs. (15)

Application software Programs designed for specific computer applications. (3)

Arithmetic-logic unit (ALU) The unit of the CPU that does arithmetic and performs logical operations. (4)

Artificial intelligence (AI) The use of computers to mimic human intelligence. (11)

ASCII An industry standard code for representing characters using seven bits per character although commonly extended to eight bits per character. Stands for American Standard Code for Information Interchange. (4)

Assembler A program that translates assembly language programs into equivalent machine language programs. (5)

Assembly language A programming language in which each instruction consists of a symbolic operation code and one or more symbolic operands. (5)

Asynchronous transmission Transmission of data in a channel one character at a time. (6)

Audio conferencing A workgroup application that involves voice communication by members of a group located at different places using a computer network. (9)

Audit trail A way of tracing the effect of data through an information system. (10)

Authoring software Software used to create multimedia presentations. (8)

Auxiliary storage Secondary storage. (3)

Backup copy A copy of data stored separately in case the original data is lost or destroyed. (4)

Backup procedure A procedure for making a copy of stored data in order to ensure against loss. (10)

Bandwidth The capacity of a channel to transmit data. (6)

Bar code scanner A device that recognizes a bar code, which is a series of bars of different widths. (4)

BASIC A programming language used mainly for simple programs. Stands for Beginner's All-purpose Symbolic Instruction Code. (5)

Batch processing A form of data processing in which all the data to be processed is prepared in a form understandable to the computer before processing, then processed in a batch to produce the output. (10)

Baud rate The rate at which a signal on a communications channel changes. (6)

Billing system A system that prepares customer bills or invoices. (10)

Binary digit A 1 or 0. (4)

Bit Binary digit. (4)

Booting The process of loading the supervisor of an operating system. (5)

BPR Business process reengineering. (14)

Browser A program which lets a user locate information on the World Wide Web by following links between Web pages. (5,8)

Bug An error in software. (13)

Bus network A network in which each node is connected to a single, common communications channel. (6)

Business alliance A group of businesses that coordinate some of their operations or link some of their resources. (12)

Business process A group of activities or tasks that accomplishes something for a business. (14)

Business process reengineering (BPR) The complete redesign of one or more business processes in an organization. (14)

Business rule A procedure or policy of a business. (13)

Button An icon or other symbol on a screen enclosed in a shape that looks like a key on a keyboard. (5)

Byte A group of bits used to store a character. (4)

C A programming language used extensively for system programs and for complex application programs. (5)

CAD Computer-aided design. (8)

CASE The use of computer-based tools to help in the development of an information system. Stands for Computer-Aided Software Engineering. (14)

CD Compact disk. (4)

CD-ROM A type of optical disk system that can only retrieve data from compact disks but cannot store data on disks. Stands for Compact Disk-Read Only Memory. (4)

Cell The intersection of a row and a column in a worksheet. (8)

Cell address Cell reference. (8)

Cell reference The identifier for a cell in a worksheet. Consists of a column letter followed by a row number. (8)

Centralized system An information system in which all functions are performed at a single, central location. (10)

Central processing unit (CPU) The central component of a computer that carries out instructions in the program. Sometimes called the processor. (3)

Character A symbol such as a digit, letter, or special symbol. (3)

Charting software Software used to create charts and graphs. (8)

Chief information officer (CIO) The person responsible for all information systems and technology in an organization. (15)

Chip A common term for an integrated circuit which is a piece of silicon containing millions of electronic circuits. (4)

CIO Chief information officer. (15)

CIS Computer information system. (1)

Client A computer in a network with which the user interacts and that provides access to a server in the network. (3)

Client-server computing The use of a network in which some computers are client computers running application software that provides data processing and a user interface, and one or more other computers are database servers providing database storage and database software. (3, 6)

COBOL A programming language used mainly for business application programs. Stands for COmmon Business Oriented Language. (5)

Collaborative computing Group computing. (9)

Command A word or phrase entered into a computer that tells a program to perform a function. (5)

Communications channel A link between computer devices used for data communications. (6)

Communications control unit A device that controls communications traffic over a channel. Includes multiplexors, controllers, and front-end processors. (6)

Communications device A device that provides communication processing capabilities, usually between a computer and a communications channel. (6)

Communications hardware Hardware that provides for communication between computers. (3)

Communications software Software used to control communications between computers. (3, 6)

Compact disk (CD) A small optical disk. (4)

Competitive advantage An advantage that puts a business in a stronger position to compete than other businesses. Can be gained through cost leadership, product differentiation, or focusing on a niche. (12)

Compiler A program that translates third-generation language programs into equivalent machine language programs. (5)

Computer An electronic device that stores and processes data by following the instructions in a program. (3)

Computer-aided design (CAD) software Software used to design objects such as buildings and machines. (8)

Computer application A use of a computer. (1)

Computer information system (CIS) An information system that includes one or more computers. (1)

Computer operator A person who operates computer equipment. (15)

Computer telephony The use of a computer network for audio communication. (9)

Computer trainer A person who trains end-users in the use of personal computer hardware and software. (15)

Control A procedure for ensuring the completeness of data processing and for minimizing errors in an information system. (10)

Control structure A way of arranging the steps in a solution procedure. (13)

Control total A number, computed when data enters a system and again after the system has processed the data, that is used to check for errors during the processing. (10)

Control unit The unit of the CPU that analyzes and executes instructions. (4)

Cooperative processing Computer processing in which two or more computers in a network cooperate in performing the functions of an information system. (10)

Cost/benefit analysis The process of comparing the expected costs and benefits of an information system to determine its economic feasibility. (14)

C++ A version of the programming language C with additional features for object-oriented programming. (5)

CPU Central processing unit. (3)

CRT A tube similar to that used in a television. Stands for Cathode Ray Tube. (4)

Cursor A mark on a screen that indicates where the next output will be displayed or the next input will be entered. (4)

Custom software Programs that are prepared from scratch for a specific person, business, or organization. (3)

Data A representation of a fact, number, word, image, picture, or sound. (1)

Database A collection of data and relationships between the data, stored in secondary storage. (3, 7)

Database administrator (DBA) A person responsible for managing an organization's databases. (7)

Database management system (DBMS) Software that provides capabilities for creating, accessing, and updating data in a database. (7)

Database server A server with a secondary storage device, usually a large hard disk drive, that is used for database processing by other computers in the network. (6)

Database software Software used to create, access, and update a database. (5, 8)

Data conferencing Document conferencing. (9)

Data dictionary A description of the data in a data flow diagram. (14)

Data encryption The process of changing data to a form that is unintelligible unless a special key is known. (6)

Data entry operator A person who keys input data into an information system. (15)

Data file A collection of related records stored in secondary storage. Also just called a file. (3)

Data flow diagram (DFD) A diagram of the flow of data in an information system. (14)

Data mart A part of a data warehouse containing just the data needed by a group of users. (7)

Data mining The process of searching for patterns in the data of a data warehouse. (11)

Data validation The process of checking data entered into a system for errors. (7, 10)

Data warehouse A collection of current and historical data extracted from databases used in an organization. (7)

DBA Database administrator. (7)

DBMS Database management system. (7)

Debugging The process of locating and correcting errors in software. (13)

Decentralized system An information system in which each user or group of users in an organization uses its own computer to perform all input, output, processing, and storage functions for its applications. (10)

Decision structure A control structure in which one of two groups of steps in a solution procedure is performed based on a condition. (13)

Decision support system (DSS) An information system that helps managers make decisions by analyzing data from a database and providing the results of the analysis to the manager. (11)

Demand report A report that is prepared only when requested. (11)

Department A group of people in a business who have specific responsibilities related to a business function. (2)

Desktop computer A microcomputer designed to sit on a desk and not be moved. (3)

Desktop publishing The use of a personal computer to prepare high-quality printed output similar to that produced by a printing company. (8)

Desktop publishing software Software used for desktop publishing. (8)

Desktop videoconferencing system A videoconferencing system designed for use by individuals with personal computers. (9)

Detail report A report that lists detailed information about the results of processing. (10)

DFD Data flow diagram. (14)

Dialog box A box on a screen in which the user provides input requested by software. (5)

Digital signal A signal that transmits bits as high and low pulses. (6)

Direct access Random access. (4)

Direct file A data file in which each record is stored at a location determined directly from the record's key field. (7)

Disk Magnetic disk, Optical disk. (3)

Disk drive A device for recording data on and retrieving data from magnetic disks. (3)

Disk pack A stack of several hard disks with spaces between the disks. (4)

Distributed database A database that is divided into parts with each part stored on a different computer in a network. (7)

Distributed system An information system in which each user or group of users performs input, output, processing, and storage functions on its own or other computers in a network. (10)

Distributor Wholesaler. (2)

Documentation Written descriptions of an information system or computer application. (3, 13)

Document conferencing A workgroup application that involves simultaneous collaboration on a document by members of a group. (9)

Document sharing A workgroup application that involves sharing text and graphic documents among members of a group. (9)

Dot-matrix printer A printer that prints each character by striking a ribbon and the paper with a group of pins that cause dots, arranged in a rectangular pattern or matrix, to be printed on the paper. (4)

Downloading Transferring data from a remote computer to a local computer. (6)

Draft-quality printer A printer that produces output that is of low to medium quality. (4)

Drawing software Software used to draw pictures and diagrams. (8)

Drilling down The process of finding detailed information that is used to produce summary information. (11)

DSS Decision support system. (11)

EBCDIC A code developed by IBM for representing characters using eight bits per character. Stands for Extended Binary Coded Decimal Interchange Code. (4)

EDI Electronic data interchange. (1)

EFT Electronic funds transfer. (1)

EIS Executive information system. (11)

Electronic commerce The use of the World Wide Web and related technologies to promote and sell products. (6)

Electronic conferencing A workgroup application which combines video and document conferencing. (9)

Electronic conferencing software Software that lets members of a group talk to and see each other while also viewing a common document on a computer screen. (5)

Electronic data interchange (EDI) The use of computers to exchange data electronically between businesses. (1)

Electronic funds transfer (EFT) The use of computers to transfer funds electronically between financial institutions. (1)

Electronic mail (E-mail) A computer application that involves transmitting messages electronically between users. Also refers to the messages that are transmitted. (1, 8)

Electronic meeting The use of a computer system to facilitate a meeting among members of a group. (9)

Electronic meeting system (EMS) A workgroup application designed to support electronic meetings. (9)

Electronic messaging A workgroup application that involves sending different types of messages between members of a group. (9)

Electronic messaging software Software used to send different types of messages between members of a group. (5)

E-mail Electronic mail. (1, 9)

EMS Electronic meeting system. (9)

End-user User. (1)

End-user computing The development and use of personal computer applications by end-users. (13)

Enterprise information system Organizational information system. (1)

Entity-relationship (ER) diagram A diagram of the design of a database. (14)

ER diagram Entity-relationship diagram. (14)

Erasable optical disk A form of secondary storage consisting of a disk on which data is recorded magnetically with the aid of a laser. The recorded data can be erased and changed. (4)

Ergonomics The study of how to design machines for effective human use. (4)

ES Expert system. (11)

ESS Executive support system. (11)

Exception report A report that contains data that is an exception to some rule or standard. (10)

Executive information system (EIS) Executive support system. (11)

Executive support system (ESS) An information system that provides support for the information needs of strategic managers. (11)

Expert system (ES) An information system that provides expert advice. (11)

Extranet An intranet that is accessible from outside the organization by companies or individuals that have special codes or passwords. (6)

Fault-tolerant computer system A computer system with duplicate components designed so that if any component fails, the system will continue to function. (15)

Feasibility analysis The process of determining if it is feasible to develop an information system. (14)

Field A group of related characters. (3)

File A collection of related items stored in secondary storage. Also refers specifically to a data file. (3)

File manager A program that allows the user to process the data in one file at a time. (8)

File server A server with a secondary storage device, usually a hard disk drive, that is used for file storage by other computers in the network. (6)

File transfer A function provided by communications software that allows files to be transferred between computers. (6)

File-transfer protocol Protocols that specify how files of data will be transferred between computers and how error-checking will be provided. (6)

Finance The function of a business that obtains money needed by a business and plans the use of that money. (2)

Financial information system An information system that supports the finance function of a business. (10)

Firewall A hardware and software system to prevent access to an organization's private computer data from outside the organization. (6)

Flat panel screen A screen that is thin and light weight. (4)

Floppy disk A magnetic disk made of flexible plastic with a metallic coating. (3)

Flowchart A diagram that uses special symbols connected by lines to show a solution procedure. Also called a program flowchart. (13)

Formula An expression entered into a cell in a worksheet that describes how the value of the cell is to be computed. (8)

FORTRAN A programming language used mainly for scientific application programs. Stands for FORmula TRANslation. (5)

4GL Fourth-generation language. (5)

Fourth-generation language (4GL) A programming language that requires significantly fewer instructions to accomplish a particular task than a third-generation language. (5)

Full-duplex transmission Transmission of data in a channel in both directions simultaneously. (6)

GB Gigabyte. (4)

G byte Gigabyte. (4)

GDSS Group decision support system. (9, 11)

General ledger system A system that maintains the business's financial accounts and prepares financial statements. (10)

Geographic information system (GIS) An information system that provides information based on geographic location. (11)

Gigabyte (G byte, GB) 2^{30} bytes. Commonly thought of as one billion bytes. (4)

GIS Geographic information system. (11)

Global information system International information system. (1, 12)

Graphical user interface (GUI) A user interface that usually includes icons, menus, and windows. (5)

Graphics software Software used to create graphic output. (8)

Group calendaring and scheduling A workgroup application that involves coordinating appointment calendars and scheduling meetings of members of a group. (9)

Group computing The use of groupware by members of a workgroup for collaboration. (9)

Group decision support system (GDSS) A workgroup information system that supports decision making among members of a group. (9, 11)

Group information system Workgroup information system. (1)

Group support system (GSS) Workgroup information system. (9)

Group videoconferencing system Room videoconferencing system. (9)

Groupware Software used for group collaboration. (5, 9)

GSS Group support system. (9)

GUI Graphical user interface. (5)

Hacker A person who gains access to a computer system mainly for the challenge of breaking in and investigating the system. Also a term for a computer programmer. (15)

Half-duplex transmission Transmission of data in a channel in both directions but only in one direction at a time. (6)

Hard disk A magnetic disk made of rigid metal. (3)

Hardware The computer and related equipment used in an information system. (3)

Help desk A group in an organization that provides personal computer assistance to end-users, usually over the telephone. (15)

Hierarchical database A database in which all relationships are one-to-one or one-to-many, but no group of data can be on the "many" side of more that one relationship. (7)

Hierarchical network A network in which the nodes are organized in a hierarchical fashion, like a family tree. (6)

Home page A page on the World Wide Web that is the beginning point for information provided by a business, organization, or individual. (8)

Host language A programming language for preparing application programs in which commands from a query language are embedded. (7)

HRIS Human resource information system. (10)

HTML A language used to create pages on the World Wide Web. Stands for Hypertext Markup Language. (5)

Human resource information system (HRIS) An information system that supports the human resource management function of a business. (10)

Human resource management The function of a business that hires, trains, compensates, and terminates employees. (2)

Hybrid network A network that is a combination of star, hierarchical, bus, ring, and other network organizations. (6)

Icon A small picture, displayed on a screen, that represents a function that a program can perform. (5)

Impact printer A printer that makes an image by striking paper with a metal or plastic mechanism. (4)

Indexed file A system of two files, one a sequential data file and the other an index file containing the key field of each record in the data file and the location of the corresponding record in the data file. (7)

Indexed sequential file Indexed file. (7)

Individual information system An information system that affects a single person. (1)

Inference engine Software that analyzes rules in a knowledge base to draw conclusions. (11)

Information Data that is meaningful or useful to someone. (1)

Information center A department or group in an organization that helps end-users develop and use computer applications, mainly on personal computers. (10)

Information services The function of a business that provides computer information system support for the business. (2)

Information sharing A workgroup application that involves sharing different types of information among members of a group. (9)

Information sharing software Software used to sharing different types of information among members of a group. (5)

Information superhighway A concept for allowing any computer to be connected to a national or international network. (6)

Information system (IS) A collection of components that work together to provide information to help in the operation and management of an organization. (1)

Information systems manager The person responsible for the management of the information systems department in an organization. (15)

Information technology (IT) Computers and technology used in information systems. (1)

Information utility A company that supplies access to information stored in a computer for a variety of users using data communications. (6)

Ink-jet printer A printer that prints each character by spraying drops of ink on paper. (4)

Input data Data that goes into an information system. (1)

Input device A device that accepts data from outside the computer and converts it into an electronic form that the computer can understand. (3)

Input function The actions of an information system that accept data from outside the system. (1)

Inquiry Query. (11)

Integrated software Software that provides multiple applications. (8)

Intelligent agent A program that acts on behalf of an individual, based on preferences given to it. (11)

Interactive processing A form of data processing in which the user interacts with the computer as the processing takes place. (10)

Internal storage Primary storage. (3)

International information system An information system that spans national borders. (1, 12)

Internet A public, international collection of interconnected wide area and local area networks offering a variety of services for users. (1, 6)

Internet service provider (ISP) A company that provides Internet access and e-mail. (6)

Internetwork A collection of networks that are interconnected. (6)

Interorganizational information system An information system that functions between several organizations. (1,12)

Interorganizational system (IOS) Interorganizational information system. (12)

Interpreter A program that translates and immediately executes program instructions. (5)

Intranet An Internet-type network only accessible from within an organization. (6)

Intraorganizational information system An information system that is confined to a single business. (12)

Inventory control system A system that keeps track of a business's inventory, indicates when inventory should be reordered, and computes the value of the inventory. (10)

IOS Interorganizational system. (12)

IS Information system. (1)

ISDN A digital telephone communications system. Stands for Integrated Services Digital Network. (6)

ISDN terminal adapter A device used to connect a computer to an ISDN telephone line. (6)

ISP Internet service provider. (6)

IT Information technology (1)

Java A programming language that allows a World Wide Web page developer to create programs for applications that can be used through a browser. (5)

KB Kilobyte. (4)

K byte Kilobyte. (4)

Keyboard An input device that accepts keyed data. (3)

Key field A field that uniquely identifies a record in a data file. (7)

Kilobyte (K byte, KB) 1,024 bytes. Commonly thought of as one thousand bytes. (4)

Knowledge base A collection of expert knowledge stored in a computer. (11)

LAN Local area network. (3)

LAN adapter A device for connecting a computer to a local area network (LAN) channel. (6)

Laser printer A printer that prints each page by recording an image of the page on the surface of a metal drum with a laser, then transferring the image to paper. (4)

Legacy system An information system that has been used in an organization for many years. (14)

Letter-quality printer A printer that produces output that is the quality expected in a business letter. (4)

Line printer A printer that prints one line at a time. (4)

Local area network (LAN) A network that covers a small area such as a single building or several nearby buildings. (3)

Loop structure A control structure in which a group of steps in a solution procedure is performed repeatedly. (13)

Machine language The basic language of a computer. (4)

Magnetic disk A form of secondary storage that consists of a disk with a metallic coating on which data is recorded magnetically. (3)

Magnetic disk drive Disk drive. (3)

Magnetic ink character recognition (MICR) A technique used by the banking industry for processing checks imprinted with special characters. (4)

Magnetic strip reader A device that can recognize data recorded in a magnetic strip. (4)

Magnetic tape A form of secondary storage that consists of a tape similar to audio recording tape on which data is recorded magnetically. (3)

Magnetic tape drive Tape drive. (3)

Mainframe computer A large, multiple-user computer. (3)

Maintenance The process of making changes in a computer application. (13)

Management information system (MIS) An information system that supports management decision making by providing information to managers at different levels of an organization. (11)

Manufacturer A business that produces goods sold to other businesses or to individual customers. (2)

Manufacturing The function of a business that produces the goods sold by the business. (2)

Manufacturing information system An information system that supports the manufacturing function of a business. (10)

Many-to-many relationship A relationship in which many groups of data are related to many other groups of data. (7)

Marketing The function of a business that sells the goods and services of the business. (2)

Marketing information system An information system that supports the marketing function of a business. (10)

Massively parallel processing The use of hundreds to thousands of CPUs in a computer simultaneously to increase speed. (4)

Master data The main data used by an information system. Usually permanent data that stays with the system. (10)

Matching The process of comparing data in several files or databases for the purpose of locating common data. (15)

MB Megabyte. (4)

M byte Megabyte. (4)

Megabyte (M byte, MB) 1,048,576 bytes. Commonly thought of as one million bytes. (4)

Megahertz (MHz) The units used to measure the internal clock speed of a computer. One megahertz is one million cycles per second. (4)

Menu A list of options for a program displayed on a screen. (5)

MHz Megahertz. (4)

MICR Magnetic ink character recognition. (4)

Microcomputer A small, single-user computer. Also called a personal computer or PC. (3)

Microprocessor A CPU contained on a single chip. (4)

Microsecond One millionth of a second. (4)

Millisecond One thousandth of a second. (4)

Minicomputer A medium-sized, multiple-user computer. (3)

MIS Management information system. (11)

Model base A collection of mathematical models and statistical calculation routines stored in a computer. (11)

Modem A device that converts digital signals to analog signals (modulation) and analog signals to digital signals (demodulation). (3, 6)

Monitor A CRT designed for computer use. (4)

Mouse A hand-held device that is rolled on a tabletop and that is used to enter input by pressing buttons on its top. (3)

Multimedia The use of a computer to store data and present information in more than one form. (3, 4)

Multiprocessing The use of several CPUs simultaneously in a computer to increase speed. (4)

Multitasking The process of executing more than one program at a time by switching between programs. (5)

Nanosecond One billionth of a second. (4)

Near-letter-quality printer A printer that produces output nearly as good as that of a letter-quality printer. (4)

Network A collection of computers and related equipment connected electronically so that they can communicate with each other. (1)

Network analyst A person who is responsible for an organization's local area and wide area networks. (15)

Network computer An inexpensive computer with capabilities limited to Internet access. (6)

Network database A database in which any type of relationship is allowed. (7)

Network operating system (NOS) Software used on server computers in a network that manage multiple client computers, and provide communication between clients and servers. (5)

Neural network A program that mimics the way humans learn and think by creating a model of the human brain. (11)

Nonimpact printer A printer that makes an image in some way other than by striking the paper. (4)

Nonvolatile storage A storage medium that does not lose its contents when the power to the computer is turned off. (4)

NOS Network operating system. (5)

Notebook computer A small microcomputer that folds to the size of a notebook. (3)

OAS Office automation system. (9)

Object A combination of data and instructions for processing the data. (5)

Object-oriented analysis and design The analysis and design of information systems based on objects. (14)

Object-oriented database A database that stores objects. (7)

Object-oriented programming A form of programming that uses programming languages in which the data and the instructions for processing the data are combined to form an object. (5)

Object-relational database A database that includes object-oriented and relational database capabilities. (7)

Office automation system (OAS) An information system that provides support for a variety of office functions at all levels of an organization. (9)

OLTP On-line transaction processing. (10)

One-to-many relationship A relationship in which one group of data is related to many other groups of data, but not vice versa. (7)

One-to-one relationship A relationship in which one group of data is related to only one other group of data. (7)

On-line transaction processing (OLTP) A form of data processing in which a person enters the data for a transaction into a computer where it is processed and the output is received before the next input is entered. (10)

Operating environment A program that provides a special interface between the user and the operating system. (5)

Operating system A set of programs that controls the basic operation of a computer. (3)

Operations The function of a business that performs the main activities of the business. (2)

Optical disk A form of secondary storage in which data is recorded and retrieved using a laser. (3)

Optical disk drive A device for recording data on and retrieving data from an optical disk. (3)

Order entry system A system that accepts customer orders for goods and services, and prepares them in a form that can be used by the business. (10)

Organizational information system An information system that affects people throughout a business or organization. (1)

Organization chart A diagram that shows the arrangement of people who work for a business. (2)

Output data Data that comes out of an information system. (1)

Output device A device that converts data from an electronic form inside the computer to a form that can be used outside the computer. (3)

Output function The actions of an information system that produce information resulting from processing. (1)

Outsourcing Using hardware, software, and personnel resources from an outside company for information systems. (14)

Packaged software Programs that are purchased. (3)

Page A screen on the World Wide Web. (5, 8)

Page printer A printer that prints one page at a time. (4)

Payroll system A system that prepares paychecks for employees and provides reports of payroll. (10)

PC Personal computer. Also used to refer specifically to an IBM-type personal computer. (3)

PDA Personal digital assistant. (3)

Pen input An input method involving a screen that is sensitive to the touch of a special pen. (4)

Peripheral equipment A device used with a computer other than primary storage and the CPU, such as secondary storage and input and output devices. (3)

Personal computer (PC) A computer used by one person at a time. (3)

Personal computer analyst A person responsible for evaluating and selecting personal computer hardware and software in an organization, and helping end-users utilize personal computers. (15)

Personal database A database used by only one user. (7)

Personal digital assistant (PDA) A handheld microcomputer with capabilities to assist an individual in his or her work. (3)

Personal information manager (PIM) Multifunction software that provides capabilities needed for organizing a person's day or helping with desk work. (8)

Personal information system Individual information system. (1)

Personnel People who use and operate an information system. (3)

PIM Personal information manager. (8)

Pixel The smallest mark or dot on a screen. Short for picture element. (4)

Planning horizon The time span for which planning is done. (15)

Platform The hardware and operating system upon which the application software of an information system runs. (5)

Plotter A device that creates graphic output on paper. (4)

Presentation graphics software Software used to create graphic output for presentations. (8)

Primary key An column or combination of columns that uniquely identifies a row in a table of a relational database. (7)

Primary storage The part of a computer that stores data currently being processed and instructions in the program currently being performed. (3)

Print server A server with a printer that can be used for printing by other computers in the network. (6)

Printer An output device that produces output data on paper. (3)

Problem An unanswered question or statement of something to be done. (13)

Procedures Instructions that tell personnel how to use and operate an information system. (3)

Process description A description of a process in a data flow diagram. (14)

Processing function The actions of an information system that manipulate the data in the system. (1)

Processor Central processing unit (3)

Production Manufacturing. (2)

Program A set of instructions that tells a computer what to do. (3)

Program file A file containing a program stored in secondary storage. (3)

Programmer A person who prepares computer programs. (5)

Programmer/analyst A person who functions as both a systems analyst and an application programmer. (15)

Programming The process of preparing a computer program. (5)

Programming language A set of rules for the form and meaning of instructions in computer programs. (5)

Project team A group of systems analysts, programmers, and users that work together to develop an information system. (14)

Prompt A word or symbol, displayed on a screen, indicating that the software is ready for input. (5)

Protocol Rules that describe how computer devices communicate. (6)

Protocol converter A device that converts the protocols of one computer device to those of another computer device. (6)

Prototype A partial version of an information system that acts like the system for the user but does not perform all the system's functions. (14)

Prototyping The process of developing a prototype of an information system. (14)

Pseudocode A written language that uses English and elements that look like a computer programming language to describe a solution procedure. (13)

Public domain software Software that is not copyrighted. (15)

Purchasing system A system that determines the best suppliers from which to purchase items and prepares purchase orders. (10)

Push technology A technique for identifying on-line information that is of interest to a user and sending the information to the user's computer. (8)

Query A request for information from an information system. (11)

Query language A language that is used to query a database, that is, to retrieve data from a database. May also be used to update a database. (7)

RAD Rapid application development. (14)

RAID A system of magnetic disks on which data is duplicated or stored in a way that data can be recovered if a disk is damaged. Stands for Redundant Array of Inexpensive Disks. (4)

RAM Random access memory. (4)

Random access The process of reading or writing data in secondary storage in any order. (4)

Random access memory (RAM) A type of primary storage in which programs and data can be stored and retrieved in any order. (4)

Random file Direct file. (7)

Rapid application development (RAD) An approach to the development of information systems that involves significant user involvement, prototyping, and the use of CASE and other tools in order to reduce the development time. (14)

Read only memory (ROM) A type of primary storage in which programs and data, stored once by the manufacturer, can be retrieved as many times as needed, but in which new programs and data cannot be stored. (4)

Real-time processing A form of data processing in which the processing is done immediately after the input is received rather than possibly being delayed while other processing is completed. (10)

Record A group of related fields. (3)

Recovery procedure A procedure for recreating original stored data from a backup copy. (10)

Relational database A database that consists of one or more related tables. (7)

Relationship A way in which groups of data in a database are related. (7)

Report A list of output data printed on paper or displayed on a screen. (10)

Report writer Software used to prepare reports from data in a database. (11)

Research and development The function of a business that develops new products to be manufactured by the business. (2)

Retailer A business that purchases quantities of goods from wholesalers or manufacturers and resells them one at a time or in small quantities to individual customers. (2)

Ring network A network in which the nodes are connected to form a loop. (6)

ROM Read only memory. (4)

Room videoconferencing A videoconferencing system designed for use in a room with several people. (9)

RPG A programming language used mainly for programs that produce business reports from data in secondary storage files. Stands for Report Program Generator. (5)

Rule An *if-then* structure that is used in a knowledge base. (11)

Scanner A device that senses the image on a page for input to a computer. Also called an image scanner or a page scanner. (4)

Scheduled report A report that is prepared periodically. (11)

Screen An output device that displays output data as video images. (3)

Screen resolution The number of pixels that can be displayed on a screen at one time. (4)

SDLC System development life cycle. (14)

Search engine A program on the World Wide Web that lets a user search for specific types of information. (8)

Secondary storage A device that stores data not currently being processed by the computer and programs not currently being performed. (3)

Sequence structure A control structure in which the steps of a solution procedure are performed in sequence, one after the other. (13)

Sequential access The process of reading or writing data in secondary storage in sequence. (4)

Sequential file A data file in which the records are organized in sequence one after the other in the order in which they are stored in the file. (7)

Serial printer A printer that prints one character at a time. (4)

Server A computer in a network that provides services, such as data storage and printing, to other computers in the network. (3)

Service business A business that provides services to other businesses or to individuals. (2)

Shared database A database used by many users. (7)

Shareware Inexpensive or free copyrighted software that comes with permission to use and make copies for evaluation purposes, but that must be paid for in full if the user wishes to use it after evaluating it. (15)

Simplex transmission Transmission of data in a channel in one direction only. (6)

SIS Strategic information system. (12)

Site license A software license agreement that allows the use of software by more than one person at a time within an organization. (15)

Software Instructions that tell computer hardware what to do. (3)

Software license agreement A written statement of what the purchaser of certain software can legally do with the software. (15)

Software piracy The process of making illegal copies of software in order to sell the copies. (15)

Solution procedure A set of steps that, if carried out, results in the solution of a problem. (13)

Sorting The process of arranging data into a particular order. (10)

Source document A document in which data is captured at its source. (10)

Spreadsheet An arrangement of data into rows and columns used for data analysis. (8)

Spreadsheet software Software used to create, modify, and print electronic spreadsheets. (5, 8)

SQL A commonly used query language. Stands for Structured Query Language. (7)

Star network A network in which each node is connected to a central computer. (6)

Storage function The actions of an information system that store and retrieve data in the system. (1)

Storage location A group of bits in primary storage used to store a certain amount of data. (4)

Stored data Data that is kept in an information system. (1, 3)

Strategic information system (SIS) An information system that has a strategic impact on a business. (12)

Structured program A computer program that uses only sequence, decision, and loop structures. (13)

Structured programming A systematic process for developing computer programs that are well structured, easily understood and modified, and correct. (13)

Suite A group of programs sold together as a package. (8)

Summary report A report that contains totals that summarize groups of data but that has no detail data. (10)

Supercomputer A computer designed for very fast processing. (3)

Synchronous transmission Transmission of data in a channel in blocks of characters. (6)

System analysis The phase in the system development process in which the systems analyst studies the existing system and determines what the new system must do. (14)

System design The phase in the system development process in which the systems analyst specifies how the new system will function. (14)

System development life cycle (SDLC) The process of developing an information system. (14)

System flowchart A diagram that uses special symbols connected by lines to show the functioning of an information system. (14)

System implementation The phase in the system development process in which the systems analyst acquires the system components, tests the system, and changes over to the new system. (14)

System maintenance The process of modifying an information system. (14)

System planning The phase in the system development process in which the systems analyst decides whether a new information system should be developed. (14)

System programmer A programmer who sets up and maintains system software. (15)

Systems analyst A person who develops an information system. (14)

System software General programs designed to make a computer usable. (3)

System specifications A description of what a new system must do to satisfy the user's requirements. (14)

Tape Magnetic tape. (3)

Tape drive A device for storing data on and retrieving data from a magnetic tape. (3)

TDF Transborder data flow. (12)

Telecommuting Working with a computer away from an office or business and communicating with the organization's computer systems electronically. (9)

Teleprocessing system An information system in which processing and storage functions are performed at a central location, input and output functions are performed at the users' locations, and data is sent between locations using data communications. (10)

Terabyte 2^{40} bytes. Commonly thought of as one trillion bytes. (4)

Terminal A device that is a combination of an input device and an output device. Often a keyboard combined with a screen. (3)

Terminal emulation A function provided by communications software that makes a personal computer appear to another computer as if it is a terminal. (6)

Testing The process of determining if there are any errors in software by executing the software with test data and comparing the result with what was expected. (13)

Time-sharing A technique used by an operating system for allowing multiple users to use a computer by giving each user a small amount of time to execute his or her program before going on to the next user. (5)

Top-down design A problem-solving technique for designing a solution procedure which involves starting with the overall procedure and then successively refine the steps in it until the final design of the solution procedure is reached. (13)

Touch screen A screen that can sense where it is touched by a person's finger. (4)

TPS Transaction processing system. (10)

Track A concentric circle on a magnetic disk, spiral line on an optical disk, or straight line on a magnetic tape, along which bits are recorded. (4)

Trackball A device with a ball on top to move the cursor on the screen and buttons to select program functions. (4)

Transaction An event that has occurred that affects a business. (10)

Transaction data Data about transactions that have occurred. (10)

Transaction processing system (TPS) An information system that keeps records of the state of an organization, processes transactions, and produces outputs that report on transactions, report on the state of the organization, and cause other transactions to occur. (10)

Transborder data flow (TDF) The flow of data between countries. (12)

Updating The process of modifying data. Includes changing existing data, adding new data, and deleting old data. (10)

Uploading Transferring data from a local computer to a remote computer. (6)

UPS A device containing a battery that takes over supplying power to a computer system when the main power is cut. Stands for Uninterrupted Power Supply. (15)

User A person who gains some benefit from using a computer information system in his or her personal or work life. (1)

User interface The part of a computer application that forms the link between the user and the other parts of the application. (5, 13)

User requirements A description of what an information system will do to help a user in his or her job. (14)

Utility program A program that provides additional capabilities beyond those of an operating system, such as sorting and merging. (5)

Value added network (VAN) A network provided by a company that leases communications lines from common carriers and adds special services for long distance data communication. (15)

Value added reseller (VAR) A business that purchases computers from manufacturers; adds other hardware, software, and services; and resells the complete package to businesses and individuals. (15)

Value chain The series of activities in a business that add value to the business's product or service. (12)

VAN Value added network. (15)

VAR Value added reseller. (15)

VDT Video display terminal. (4)

Videoconferencing A workgroup application that involves visual and audio communication between members of a group at different locations. (9)

Video display terminal (VDT) A terminal consisting of a keyboard and a screen. (4)

View Part of a database to which a user has access. (7)

Virtual company A company that does not have a regular place of business or an office, and in which employees work at home or other places not operated by the company. (9)

Virtual meeting An electronic meeting between members of a workgroup that does not involve simultaneous communication, and typically takes place over several days. (9)

Virtual memory The memory that a computer appears to have, consisting of primary storage and some secondary storage. It is created by the operating system so that programs that are too large for primary storage can be executed. (5)

Virtual office A group of employees who work at different locations and use computers to collaborate with other employees. (9)

Virtual reality The use of a computer to produce realistic images and sounds in such a way that the user senses that he or she is part of the scene. (4)

Virtual work environment A work environment consisting of wherever people are at whatever time they work. (9)

Virus A computer program that copies itself from one disk to another and that activates itself after a period of time, usually destroying programs and data in many computer systems. (15)

Volatile storage A storage medium that loses its contents when the power to the computer is turned off. (4)

WAN Wide area network. (3)

Web server A server used to store an organization's World Wide Web pages. (6)

What-if analysis The process of changing certain data in a spreadsheet to see the effect on other data in the spreadsheet. (8)

Whiteboard conferencing A form of document conferencing in which each user sees the same document on an electronic whiteboard on a screen. (9)

Wholesaler A business that purchases large quantities of goods, then sells smaller quantities to retailers, and ships or distributes the goods to the retailers. (2)

Wide area network (WAN) A network that covers a large geographic area. (3)

Window A section of a screen surrounded by a border and containing one type of display. (5)

Wireless LAN A local area network (LAN) that uses a wireless system such as radio waves or infrared beams for communication. (6)

Word processing The use of a computer to prepare documents containing text. (8)

Word processing software Software used to enter, edit, and print documents. (5, 8)

Word processing system A personal computer with word processing software. (8)

Workflow management A workgroup application that involves coordinating the flow of work between members of a group. (9)

Workgroup A group of people working together in a business to perform specific tasks or activities. (2)

Workgroup information system An information system that affects a group of people who work together in a business or organization. (1)

Worksheet A spreadsheet created by spreadsheet software. (8)

Workstation A powerful microcomputer. (3)

World Wide Web (WWW) A service on the Internet that links information so that the user can easily go from one piece of information to another, related piece. (1, 6)

WWW World Wide Web. (1, 6)

PHOTO CREDITS

1.1a   Courtesy of International Business Machines Corporation. Unauthorized use not permitted.

1.1b   Tony Stone Images/Mitch Kezar

1.2b   Photo Researchers/David R. Frazier

1.7   Courtesy of International Business Machines Corporation. Unauthorized use not permitted.

1.8   Courtesy of Microsoft

1.9   Courtesy of Microsoft

1.11   Courtesy of QUALCOMM Incorporated

1.12   Courtesy of WebFlow Corporation

1.13   Courtesy of International Business Machines Corporation. Unauthorized use not permitted.

1.15   FPG International/Steven Gottlieb

2.2c   Comstock

2.2d   FPG International/Richard Laird

3.3a   Courtesy of International Business Machines Corporation. Unauthorized use not permitted.

3.3b   PhotoTake/Phil Matt

3.3c   Courtesy of International Business Machines Corporation. Unauthorized use not permitted.

3.3d   Courtesy of Hewlett Packard

3.4   Courtesy of International Business Machines Corporation. Unauthorized use not permitted.

3.6a   PhotoTake/David A. Wagner

3.6b   Photo Researchers/Vanessa Vick

3.6c   Courtesy of International Business Machines Corporation. Unauthorized use not permitted.

3.8a   Courtesy of International Business Machines Corporation. Unauthorized use not permitted.

3.8b   Courtesy of Apple Computer Inc.

3.9   Courtesy of International Business Machines Corporation. Unauthorized use not permitted.

3.10   Courtesy of Apple Computer Inc.

3.11   Courtesy of Sun Microsystems Computer Company

3.12a   Courtesy of DEC

3.12b   Courtesy of International Business Machines Corporation. Unauthorized use not permitted.

3.12c   Courtesy of Cray Research, a Silicon Graphics Company

3.13   Courtesy of Hewlett Packard

4.1   Courtesy of Microsoft

4.2a   FPG International/Gary Buss

4.2b   Courtesy of International Business Machines Corporation. Unauthorized use not permitted.

4.2c   Image Bank/Nicolas Russell

4.3a   FPG International/R. Rathe

4.3b   Courtesy of Apple Computer, Inc.

4.4a   Photo Researchers/George Haling

4.4b   FPG International/Gary Buss

4.5a   Tony Stone Images/Shaun Egan

4.7   Courtesy of International Business Machines Corporation. Unauthorized use not permitted.

4.8a   Courtesy of Hewlett Packard

4.8b   PhotoTake/Yoav Levy

4.8c   Image Bank/Andy Caulfield

4.9a   Courtesy of International Business Machines Corporation. Unauthorized use not permitted.

4.9b   Courtesy of Xerox

4.10   Courtesy of Hewlett Packard

4.11   Science Source/Hank Morgen

4.12   Image Bank/Ted Kawalerski

4.13   Photo Researchers/James King-Holmes

4.14   Rainbow/T.J. Florain

4.18   Danny McCoy

4.20   Uniphoto/David Mallory Jones

4.25   Comstock

5.6   Courtesy of I.S.T., Inc.

6.6a   Comstock

6.6b   Comstock/Bob Pizaro

6.7   FPG International/Michael A. Keller

6.20   Courtesy of Sun Microsystems, Inc.

8.24   Courtesty of Microsoft

8.29   Courtesy of Macromedia

8.30a Courtesy of Engineering Arts

8.30b Courtesy of Yahoo! Inc.

8.31   Courtesy of Microsoft

9.3   © 1977 Lotus Development Corporation. Used with permission of Lotus Development Corporation. Lotus and Lotus Notes are registered trademarks of Lotus Development Corporation.

9.4   Courtesy of Novell

9.5   © 1977 Lotus Development Corporation. Used with permission of Lotus Development Corporation. Lotus and Lotus Notes are registered trademarks of Lotus Development Corporation.

9.6   Courtesy of WebFlow Corporation

9.7   Courtesy of DataBeam Corporation

9.8   Courtesy of Sun Microsystem, Inc.

9.9   Courtesy of Hewlett Packard

9.10   FPG International, Spencer Grant

9.11   Image courtesy of Silicon Graphics, Inc.

9.12   Photos courtesy of Ventana Corporation. Group Systems is a registered trademark of Ventana

9.13   Courtesy of Crosswind Technologies

9.14   Courtesy of Filenet Corporation

9.15   Image Bank

10.16 FPG International/Jean Kugler

11.10 Courtesy of Sybase Inc.

11.12 Courtesy of Pilot Software

11.13 Courtesy of MicroGrids, © 1993 Scan/US

11.16 Reproduced with permission. Copyright 1997 Comshare, Inc.

11.20 Courtesy of MultiLogic

14.11 Courtesy of Silverrun Technologies, Inc.

15.7   Courtesy of Sungard Recovery Services Inc.

15.8   PhotoEdit/Michael Newman

15.10 Courtesy of Microsoft

ACKNOWLEDGMENTS

Chapter 1

Bookmark: *Inventory control at Guess?* From "Buying More Time" by Candee Wilde, *Information Week*, September 23, 1996. Copyright © 1996 by CMP Media Inc., 600 Community Drive, Manhasset, NY 11030. Reprinted from *Information Week* with permission.

Bookmark: *International information system at Timberland* from "Timberland Gets Global Boost from New Software" by Tom Stein, *Information Week*, November 4, 1996. Copyright © 1996 by CMP Media Inc. Reprinted from *Information Week* with permission.

Real-world Case: *The Benetton Group.* Website information from www.benetton.com/benetton-web/benetton/companyintro.html. and "The Network: Information Technology," www.benetton.com/benetton-web/benetton/it.html. Copyright © 1996 by Benetton Group S.p.A. Reprinted by permission.

Chapter 2

Bookmark: *Information systems at American Red Cross and Nature Conservancy* from "Nonprofits Rely on IS Innovation" by Tim Ouellette, *Computerworld*, December 16, 1996. Copyright 1996 by *Computerworld*, Framingham, MA 01701. Reprinted by permission of *Computerworld*.

Bookmark: *Custom jeans order entry at Levi Strauss* from "Business and Related Services" by Stefanie McCann, *Computerworld*, June 3, 1996. Copyright 1996 by *Computerworld*. Reprinted by permission of *Computerworld*.

Real-world Case: *Daka International* from "Daka Freshens its Restaurants' Information Relay Systems" by Rambir Sidhu, *Infoworld*, November 25, 1996. Reprinted by permission of *Infoworld*.

Chapter 3

Bookmark: *Wearable computers from Carnegie Mellon University* from "The Ultimate in Portability" by Alice LaPlante, *Computerworld Client/Server Journal*, August 1995. Copyright 1995 by *Computerworld*. Reprinted by permission of *Computerworld*.

Bookmark: *Linking railroads at the Association of American Railroads* from "Working on the Railroad" by Candee Wilde, *Computerworld Client/Server Journal*, February 1996. Copyright 1996 by *Computerworld*. Reprinted by permission of *Computerworld*.

Real-world Case: *Beamscope Canada* from "Beamscope Canada, Inc." by Chris Staiti, *Computerworld Client/Server Journal,* August 1996. Copyright 1996 by *Computerworld.* Reprinted by permission of *Computerworld.*

Chapter 4

Bookmark: *Voice recognition at Boeing* from "Speech Replaces Point and Click" by Dan Richman, *Information Week,* July 3,1995. Copyright © 1995 by CMP Media Inc. Reprinted from *Information Week* with permission.

Bookmark: *Supercomputers by Alcoa, AAA, and Best Western* from "More Power, Lower Cost" by Willie Schatz, *Information Week,* February 26, 1996. Copyright © 1996 by CMP Media Inc. Reprinted from *Information Week* with permission.

Real-world Case: *United Parcal Service* from "Data is Part of the Package" by Eric R. Chabrow, *Information Week,* December 25, 1995. Copyright © 1995 by CMP Media Inc. Reprinted from *Information Week* with permission.

Chapter 5

Figure 5.19: from Addison Wesley Longman website that supplements Building Business Applications Using C—by Lucy Garnett. © 1997 Addison-Wesley Longman Inc. Reprinted by permission. For additional information visit http://www.awl.com/cp/garnett.htm. All rights reserved.

Figure 5.21: "HTML for part of a World Wide Web page" from part of the HTML for the Addison-Wesley Longman Information Systems home page, www.awl.com/he/is. Reprinted by permission of Addison-Wesley Longman.

Bookmark: *Operating systems choices at Gap, LG&E Energy, and Chevron* from "How Does Windows NT Fit into Your Company?" by Robert L. Scheier, *Computerworld,* March 24, 1997. Copyright 1997 by *Computerworld.* Reprinted by permission of *Computerworld.*

Bookmark: *Java Internet application at CERA Bank, Belgium* from "Java's on the Job at Belgian Bank" by Martin LaMonica, *Infoworld,* March 10, 1997. Reprinted by permission of *Infoworld.*

Real-world Case: *Oakland Housing Authority* from "Client/Server System Puts Housing Agency into Overdrive" by Rachel Parker, *Infoworld,* January 8, 1996. Reprinted by permission of *Infoworld.*

Chapter 6

Bookmark: *Wireless communications at the Internal Revenue Service* from "IRS Goes Wireless to Fight Diesel Fuel Tax Fraud" by Mindy Blodgett, *Computerworld,* February 10, 1997. Copyright 1997 by *Computerworld.* Reprinted by permission of *Computerworld.*

Bookmark: *Internetwork at Scientific-Atlanta* from "Networking Around the Globe" by Kristina B. Sullivan. Reprinted from *PC Week,* May 13, 1996. Copyright © 1996 by Ziff-Davis Inc. Reprinted by permission.

Real-world Case: *Geffen Records* from "Intranet Solution Makes Geffen Shake, Rattle, and Roll" by Paul Karon, *Infoworld,* February 12, 1996. Reprinted by permission of *Infoworld.*

Chapter 7

Bookmark: *Object-oriented database at Air France* from "Object Project Files" by Craig Stedman, *Computerworld,* February 10, 1997. Copyright 1997 by *Computerworld.* Reprinted by permission of *Computerworld.*

Bookmark: *Data warehouse at PacificCare Health Systems* from "Data 'Carehouse'" by Charles Babock, *Computerworld,* November 4, 1996. Copyright 1996 by *Computerworld.* Reprinted by permission of *Computerworld.*

Real-world Case: *Environmental Protection Agency* from "Saved by the Web" by Richard Adhikari, *Information Week,* March 17, 1997. Copyright © 1997 by CMP Media Inc. Reprinted from *Information Week* with permission.

Chapter 8

Bookmark: *Overcoming spreadsheet limitations at MTV* from "MTV Rocks on Again with TM1 Perspectives" by Grant Faulkner, *Infoworld,* December 16, 1996. Reprinted by permission of *Infoworld.*

Bookmark: *Internet use at Art Anderson Associates and Mobius Computer Corporation* from "Getting Smart On-Line" by Phaedra Hise. Adapted with permission from *INC. Magazine* #1, 1996. Copyright 1996 by Goldhirsh Group, Inc., 38 Commercial Wharf, Boston, MA 02110.

Real-world Case: *Haworth Inc.* from "Trilogy Helps Haworth Get Through A Maze of Cubicles" by Steve Alexander, *Infoworld,* January 27, 1997. Reprinted by permission of *Infoworld.*

Chapter 9

Bookmark: *Information sharing at Jardine Fleming, Hong Kong* from "Jardine Fleming—Connecting People with Lotus Notes" www2.lotus.com/ IndustrySpotlight.nsf, Lotus Development Corp. Reprinted by permission of Lotus Development Corporation.

Bookmark: *Global electronic conferencing at Ford* from "Ford's Global Studio Shrinks the World— and Changes the Way It Works" by Grant Ellis, *Iris Universe,* Number Thirty-Three, Fall 1995, now *Innovation*[3]. Copyright © 1995 Silicon Graphics, Inc. Reprinted courtesy of *Innovation*[3].

Real-world Case: *Xerox* from "Northridge Quake Prompts Xerox to Take Care of its Faults" by Daniel Lyons, *Infoworld,* June 3, 1996. Reprinted by permission of *Infoworld.*

Chapter 10

Bookmark: *Accounts payable at Ademco* from "Homemade app Pays Off" by April Jacobs, *Computerworld,* May 20, 1996. Copyright 1996 by *Computerworld.* Reprinted by permission of *Computerworld.*

Bookmark: From "Double Click for Resin" by Scott Woolley in *Forbes,* March 10, 1997. Copyright © 1997 by Forbes Inc. Reprinted by permission of *Forbes* Magazine.

Real-world Case: *Sprint* from "Order-Entry Sales System Speeds Sprint Phone Service" by Cate T. Corcoran, *Infoworld,* March 25, 1996. Reprinted by permission of *Infoworld.*

Chapter 11

Bookmark: *Decision support system at Royal Caribbean Cruises* from "Royal Caribbean Cruises for Profit in Sea of Data" by Jaikumar Vijayan, *Computerworld,* May 26, 1997. Copyright 1997 by *Computerworld.* Reprinted by permission of *Computerworld.*

Bookmark: *Geographic information system for the city of Scottsdale, Arizona* from "City Blazes Own IS Trail" by Gary H. Anthes, *Computerworld,* September 16, 1996. Copyright 1996 by *Computerworld.* Reprinted by permission of *Computerworld.*

Real-world Case: *Grand & Toy, Canada* from "One Office-Supplies Company Put an End to its Paper Trail" by Heather Mackey, *Infoworld,* March 24, 1997. Reprinted by permission of *Infoworld.*

Chapter 12

Bookmark: *Strategic Web site at National Semiconductor* from "New and Improved: National Semi Remarks home page" by Christopher Kenneally. Reprinted from *PC Week,* May 12, 1997. Copyright © 1997 Ziff-Davis Inc. Reprinted by permission of Ziff-Davis Inc..

Bookmark: *International system at the National Transportation Exchange* from "Shaping Service Keeps Users Truckin'" by Craig Stedman, *Computerworld,* June 24, 1996. Copyright 1996 by *Computerworld.* Reprinted by permission of *Computerworld.*

Real-world Case: *Levi Strauss* from "Eureka! Levi Finds Gold Mine of Data" by Lauren Gibbons Paul. Reprinted from *PC Week,* May 12, 1997. Copyright © 1997 Ziff-Davis Inc. Reprinted by permission of Ziff-Davis Inc.

Chapter 13

Bookmark: *Applications developed by two entrepreneurs* from "Doing it Their Way" by Jenny McCune, *Home Office Computing*, February 1996. Copyright © 1996 by Scholastic Inc. Reprinted by permission of Scholastic Inc.

Bookmark: *Creating a web site at Archetype* from "On the Web" by Lydia Aldredge, *Home Office Computing*, June 1997. Copyright © 1997 by Scholastic Inc. Reprinted by permission of Scholastic Inc.

Real-world Case: *Cigna* from "Big Business Takes Place Using Latest Microsoft Office" by Ilan Greenberg, *Infoworld*, February 17, 1997. Reprinted by permission of Infoworld.

Chapter 14

Bookmark: *System development lessons from Time Warner Communications* from "Failed Phone Venture Shows How Not to Build Software" by Emily Kay, *Computerworld*, May 5, 1997. Copyright 1997 by *Computerworld*. Reprinted by permission of *Computerworld*.

Bookmark: *Solving the year 2000 problem at The Equitable Life Assurance Society* from "Face Up to it" by Robert L. Scheier, *Computerworld*, March 25, 1996. Copyright 1996 by *Computerworld*. Reprinted by permission of *Computerworld*.

Real-world Case: *Inland Steel Industries* from "Taming the Beast" by Bruce Caldwell, *Information Week*, March 10, 1997. Copyright © 1997 by CMP Media Inc. Reprinted from *Information Week* with permission.

Chapter 15

Figure 15.2: "Information System and Technology Risk" from *Corporate Information Systems Management* by Linda M. Applegate, F. Warren McFarlen, and James L. McKenny (Richard D. Irwin, Chicao 1996). Reprinted by permission of McGraw-Hill Inc.

Figure 15.11: "Rules for the Ethical Use of Computers" based on "Ten Commandments of Computer Ethics." Reprinted by permission of Computer Ethics Institute, Washington DC.

Bookmark: *Outsourcing information systems at Esprit* from "Esprit Alters the Fit of its Outsourcing" by Thomas Hoffman, *Computerworld*, January 22, 1996. Copyright 1996 by *Computerworld*. Reprinted by permission of *Computerworld*.

Bookmark: *Disaster recovery plan at Options Clearing Corporation* from "Serious Security" by Bob Violino, *Information Week*, November 25, 1996. Copyright © 1996 by CMP Media Inc. Reprinted from *Information Week* with permission.

Real-world Case: *Maiden Mills* from "Mills Disaster Fires Up Planned IS Overhaul" by Matt Hamblen, *Computerworld*, January 20, 1997. Copyright 1997 by *Computerworld*. Reprinted by permission of *Computerworld*.

INDEX

Access. *See* Microsoft Access; Random
   access; Sequential access
Accessing data, 227, 297
Accounting, 34–35
Accounting information system, 311
Accounts payable, 50
   data, 308
   report, 50, 308
   system, 307–309
Accounts receivable, 46
   data, 304
   report, 46, 304
   system, 304–305
Action Technologies Action Workflow, 280
Address, 106–107
Ad hoc report, 334
AI. *See* Artificial intelligence
Algorithm, 384*n*
ALU. *See* Arithmetic logic unit
Amdahl Corporation, 73
American Standard Code for
   Information Interchange. *See* ASCII
Analog signal, 159
Apple Computer, Inc., 69, 445
Apple Macintosh, 69, 110, 208
Applet, 148
Apple II, 69
Application. *See* Computer application
Application analysis, 398, 400
   example, 402
Application conferencing, 271
   software, 271
Application control, 451–452
Application design, 398, 400–401
   example, 403
Application development. *See* Individual
   application development; System
   development

Application generator, 143, 212
Application implementation, 398, 401
   example, 404–405
Application maintenance, 401
Application planning, 398, 400
   example, 402
Application portfolio, 443–444
Application program, 75, 212
Application programmer, 450
Application software, 75, 126
   individual, 127–128
   interorganizational, 129
   organizational, 128–129
   workgroup, 128
Archiving, 266
Arithmetic-logic unit (ALU), 108
Artificial intelligence (AI), 347, 350
ASCII, 105–106
Assembler, 141
Assembly, 141
Assembly language, 141–142
Asynchronous transmission, 161
AT&T, 447
ATM. *See* Automated teller machine system
Attachment, 266
Audio communication, 204
Audio conferencing, 271–273
Audit trail, 299
Authoring software, 251
AutoCAD, 247
Automated teller machine (ATM)
   system, 17
Auxiliary storage. *See* Secondary storage

Backbone, 179
Backup copy, 119
Backup procedure, 299, 452
Balance sheet, 52–53, 310

Bandwidth, 160
Bar code, 94
Bar code scanner, 94
BASIC, 144
Batch operating system, 135
Batch processing, 299
Baud rate, 160
Beginner's All-purpose Symbolic
   Instruction Code. *See* BASIC
Benefits administration, 314
Billing, 44–45
   system, 303
Binary digit, 105
Binary representation, 105
Bit, 105
Bits per second (bps), 159–160
Booting, 132
BPR. *See* Business process reengineering
Bps. *See* Bits per second
Bridge, 178
Browser, 128, 180, 213
Budgeting, 311
Bug, 395
Business
   basic information processing, 43–53
   environment, 30
   functions, 34–37
   organization, 37–38
   purpose, 30–31
   types, 31–34
Business alliance, 364–366
Business process, 434
Business process reengineering (BPR),
   433–434
Business rule, 398
Bus network, 174
Button, 132
Byte, 106

C, 142, 143, 146, 212
CAD. *See* Computer-aided design
CAM. *See* Computer-aided manufacturing
Campbell Services OnTime, 279
Capital expenditure analysis, 311
Carpal tunnel syndrome, 91
CASE, 424
Cash management, 311
Cathode Ray Tube. *See* CRT
CD. *See* Compact disk
CD-ROM, 116
Cell, 234
Cell address. *See* Cell reference
Cell reference, 234
Centralized information system, 315
    international, 374
    management, 448–449
Central processing unit (CPU), 65–66,
    107–108
    common, 109–112
    compatibility, 108–109
    speed, 109
    structure, 108
Channel. *See* Communications channel
Character, 78, 90, 224
Characters per second (cps), 98
Chart, 244–245
Charting software, 245
Chief information officer (CIO), 450
Chip, 104
CIM. *See* Computer-integrated manufac-
    turing
CIO. *See* Chief information officer
CIS. *See* Computer information system
Claris Organizer, 254
Claris Works, 255
Client, 74, 137, 176
Client-server computing, 74, 176–177,
    208, 319
Clock speed, 109
Clone. *See* IBM clone
Coaxial cable, 162
COBOL, 142, 143, 144, 212
Codec, 163
Collaboration. *See* Group collaboration
Collaborative computing, 265
Command, 132
Command processor, 131
COmmon Business Oriented Language.
    See COBOL
Common carrier, 165, 447
Communications channel, 158–159
    characteristics, 159–162
    media, 162–164
    sources, 164–166
Communications control unit, 167–168
Communications device, 159, 166–169
Communications hardware, 68, 158–169
Communications software, 76, 139, 169
    multiple-user computer, 170

network, 170
    personal computer, 169–170
Compact disk (CD), 116
Compact Disk-Read Only Memory. *See*
    CD-ROM
Compaq Computer Corporation, 69, 445
Competitive advantage, 358
Compilation, 142
Compiler, 142
Compiler language, 142
Components
    of a computer, 62–67
    of an information system, 60–62
Computation, 298
Computer, 5, 62
Computer-aided design (CAD), 314
    software, 246–247
Computer-aided manufacturer (CAM),
    314
Computer-Aided Software Engineering.
    See CASE
Computer application, 6, 396–397
    business rule, 398
    stored data, 397
    user interface, 397
Computer art, 245
Computer information system (CIS), 6
Computer-integrated manufacturing
    (CIM), 314
Computer operator, 450
Computer system, 68
    multiple-user, 71–73
    networked, 73–74
    personal, 69–71
Computer telephony, 272
    software, 272
Computer trainer, 451
Comshare Commander Decision, 347
Condition, 388
Contract programmer, 414
Control, 298, 451
    application, 451–452
    failure recovery procedure, 452–454
    hardware, 452
Controller, 167
Control structure, 386–389
Control total, 298, 452
Control unit, 108
Cooperative processing, 319
Copy utility, 139
Corel Chart, 245
Corel Draw, 245
Corel WordPerfect Suite, 255
Cost/benefit analysis, 413
Cost leadership, 358
C++, 143, 146–148
Cps. *See* Characters per second
CPU. *See* Central processing unit
Cray Research, 73, 445
Credit analysis, 311

Crime, 458–461
CrossWind Technologies Synchronize,
    279
CRT, 96–97
Cursor, 92
Customer master data, 302, 303, 304
Customer order, 8, 44, 301
Custom software, 77

Data, 5, 10–11, 196. *See also* Stored data
    organization, 78–79
    representation, 105–106
    versus information, 10
Database, 13, 78, 128, 195, 196, 224
    object-oriented, 206
    organization, 199–202
    types, 202–206
    use, 213
Database administrator (DBA), 216, 451
Database management, 197–198,
    224–231
    combining with spreadsheet analysis,
    239
Database management software, 206–207
    multiple-user computer, 208
    networked computer, 208
    personal computer, 207–208
Database management system (DBMS),
    139, 195, 225
Database processing, 195
    advantages, 198–199
    disadvantages, 199
Database server, 175
Database software, 13, 128, 225
    functions, 226–227
    using, 209–212
DataBeam FarSite, 271
Data capture, 294
Data communications, 158, 265
Data conferencing. *See* Document confer-
    encing
Data destination, 420
Data dictionary, 421
Data encryption, 169, 454
Data entry, 294, 397
Data entry operator, 450
Data file, 66, 78, 190, 193, 224. *See also*
    File
Data flow, 420
Data flow diagram (DFD), 419–422
Data management
    acquiring technology for, 447–448
    in information systems, 191
    operating system function, 131
Data mart, 215
Data mining, 341
Data source, 420
Data store, 420
Data validation, 194, 295, 451
Data warehouse, 214–215, 340–341

DaVinci Mail, 266
DBA. *See* Database administrator
dBASE, 208, 225
DBMS. *See* Database management system
DB2, 208
Debugging, 395
DEC, 72, 110, 137, 445
DEC Alpha, 110
Decentralized information system, 316–317
 international, 373
 management, 448–449
Decision, 326. *See also* Management decision
Decision making, 41–43, 298, 326
Decision room, 276
Decision structure, 388
Decision support system (DSS), 331, 337
 functions, 339–340
 group, 278, 341
 software, 340–341
 structure, 338–339
Dedicated line, 447
Dell Computer Corporation, 69, 445
Demand report, 334
Demodulation, 166
Department, 37
Desktop computer, 69
Desktop printer, 97, 98–99
Desktop publishing, 248
 software, 248
Desktop videoconferencing
 software, 274
 system, 274–275
Detail report, 295, 333
Developer documentation, 396
DFD. *See* Data flow diagram
Diagram, 245
Dialog box, 132
Dial-up line, 447
Digital Equipment Corporation. *See* DEC
Digital signal, 159
Digitizer tablet, 93
Direct access. *See* Random access
Direct file, 193
Direct mail advertising, 312
Disaster recovery plan, 452–454
Disk. *See* Magnetic disk
Disk drive. *See* Magnetic disk drive
Disk operating system. *See* DOS
Disk pack, 113
Distributed database, 208
Distributed database management system, 208
Distributed information system, 318–319
 international, 375
Distributor, 31
Documentation, 80, 396
Document communication, 265
Document conferencing, 268–271

Document management, 283
Document routing, 279
Document sharing, 268
 software, 268
Domestic information system, 370
DOS, 136
Dot-matrix printer, 99
Downloading data, 170
Draft-quality printer, 98
Drawing software, 245
Drilling down, 343
DSS. *See* Decision support system
Dumb terminal, 101

EBCDIC, 105, 106
Economic feasibility, 413
EDI. *See* Electronic data interchange
Editing, 240–241
Efficiency, 292–293
EFT. *See* Electronic funds transfer
EIS. *See* Executive information system
Electronic commerce, 180, 312
Electronic conferencing, 275–276
 software, 128, 275
Electronic data interchange (EDI), 18, 129, 368–369
Electronic filing, 282
Electronic funds transfer (EFT), 18
Electronic mail, 15, 180, 266
 software, 266
Electronic mail address, 266
Electronic mailbox, 266
Electronic meeting, 276–278
 software, 278
Electronic meeting room, 276
Electronic meeting system (EMS), 276
Electronic messaging, 265–267
 software, 128, 267
Electronic spreadsheet, 127, 234
Electronic vote, 278
Electronic whiteboard, 270
E-mail. *See* Electronic mail
Employee master data, 310
Employment, 456–458
EMS. *See* Electronic meeting system
Encryption. *See* Data encryption
End-user. *See* User
End-user computing, 384
Enterprise information system. *See* Organizational information system
Entity, 423
Entity-relationship (ER) diagram, 423–424
Erasable optical disk, 117
ER diagram. *See* Entity-relationship diagram
Ergonomics, 91, 97, 458
ES. *See* Expert system
ESS. *See* Executive support system
Ethernet, 175

Ethics, 20, 461–464
Excel. *See* Microsoft Excel
Exception report, 295, 333
Executing a program, 74–75
Execution error, 395
Executive, 131
Executive information system (EIS), 342
Executive support system (ESS), 331, 342
 functions, 346–347
 software, 347
 structure, 344–346
Expense, 30
Expert system (ES), 331, 347
 functions, 348–349
 software, 350
 structure, 348
Expert system shell, 350
Explorer. *See* Microsoft Internet Explorer
Exporter, 31
Extended Binary Code Decimal Interchange Code. *See* EBCDIC
External entity, 420
Extranet, 182

Facsimile, 282
Failure recovery procedures, 452–454
Fault tolerant computer system, 452
Feasibility analysis, 400, 413
Fiber-optic cable, 162–163
Field, 78, 190, 224
Fifth-generation language, 143
File, 66, 78, 190, 224
 management, 193–194
 organization, 191–193
FileMaker Pro, 225
File manager, 224–225
FileNet Visual WorkFlo, 280
File processing, 190–191
 advantages, 194
 disadvantages, 194–195
File server, 175
File transfer, 170
File-transfer protocol, 170
File Transfer Protocol. *See* FTP
Finance, 35
Financial analysis system, 12–13
Financial forecasting, 311
Financial information system, 311
Financial statement, 52–53, 310–311
Finished goods inventory, 48
Firewall, 181, 455
Firm infrastructure, 363, 364
First-generation language, 140
Fixed asset accounting, 311
Flat-file manager, 224
Flat panel screen, 97
Floppy disk, 66
Flowchart, 386. *See also* System flowchart
Focusing on a niche, 358
Font, 240

Forms designer, 143
Formula, 234–236
FORmula TRANslation. *See* FORTRAN
FORTRAN, 142, 143, 144

4GL. *See* Fourth-generation language
Fourth Dimension, 208, 225
Fourth-generation language (4GL), 143
FoxPro, 208, 225
Front-end processor, 167
FTP, 181
Full-duplex transmission, 160
Functional area, 34
Future Lab Talk Show, 271

Gateway, 178
GB. *See* gigabyte
G byte, 107
GDSS. *See* Group decision support system
GemStone, 208
General ledger
    data, 310
    system, 310–311
Generations of programming languages,
    140–143
Geographic information system (GIS),
    341–342
Gigabyte (GB), 107
GIS. *See* Geographic information system
Global information system. *See*
    International information system
Global strategy, 372, 374
Goal seeking, 339
Gopher, 181
Government, 34
GPSS, 340
Graph, 244–245
Graphical user interface (GUI), 132
Graphic design, 245
Graphics, 244
    combining with other applications,
        247–248
    software, 13, 245
    system, 13
Group calendaring and scheduling,
    278–279
    software, 278
Group collaboration, 262–263
    characteristics, 263–265
Group computing, 265
Group decision support system (GDSS),
    278, 341
Group information system. *See*
    Workgroup information system
Group support system (GSS), 262
Group videoconferencing system, 273
Groupware, 128, 265
GSS. *See* Group support system
GUI. *See* Graphical user interface
Guru, 350

Hacker, 459
Half-duplex transmission, 160
Hard disk, 66
Hardware, 5, 60, 90
    acquiring, 445
    alternatives, 414
    central processing unit, 65–66,
        107–112
    communications, 68
    input device, 62–63, 91–95
    need for, 90–91
    output device, 63, 95–101
    primary storage, 65, 103–107
    secondary storage, 66–67, 112–119
Hardware control, 452
Harvard Graphics, 246
Health, 458
Help desk, 451
Hewlett-Packard Company (HP), 72, 445
Hewlett-Packard SharedX, 271
Hierarchical database, 202
Hierarchical database management sys-
    tem, 205–206
Hierarchical network, 173–174
High-volume printer, 97, 99–100
Home page, 180, 253–254
Host language, 212
HP. *See* Hewlett-Packard Company
HRIS. *See* Human resource information
    system
HTML, 148
Human resource information system
    (HRIS), 314
Human resource management, 37, 363,
    364
Hybrid network, 175
Hyperlink, 148
Hypertext, 180
Hypertext Markup Language. *See* HTML
IBM, 69, 72, 73, 137, 208, 445, 447
IBM clone, 69, 110
IBM PC, 69, 109
IBM Personal Computer. *See* IBM PC
IBM System/390, 110
Icon, 132
IDMS, 208
IFPS, 340
Image processing, 282
Image scanner, 94
Impact printer, 97
Importer, 31
IMS, 208
Inbound logistics, 362, 363
Income statement, 52–53, 310
Indexed file, 193
Indexed sequential file, 193
Index file, 193
Individual application development
    example, 402–405
    process, 398–401

Individual information system, 12–13,
    224, 384, 410
Inference engine, 348
Information, 4, 10, 11, 22, 326
    and business management, 41–43
    and business operations, 39–41
    versus data, 10–11
Information center, 317, 451
Information reporting system, 331
Information services, 37
Information sharing, 158, 267–268
    software, 128, 268
    system, 15
Information superhighway, 178
Information system (IS), 5–6, 54, 60
    benefits, 22–23
    components, 5, 60–62
    control, 451–454
    development. *See* System develop-
        ment
    examples, 6–9
    functions, 9–10
    organizational structure, 449–451
    security, 454–455
    types, 12–18
    users, 18–19
Information systems manager, 449–450
Information technology (IT), 6
    acquiring, 444–448
Information utility, 172, 332
Informix, 208, 448
Ink-jet printer, 98
Input control, 451
Input data, 10
Input device, 62–63
    keyboard, 91
    magnetic scanning, 94–95
    optical scanning, 93–94
    pointing, 92
    touch, 92–93
    voice, 95
Input function, 10
    decision support system, 339–340
    executive support system, 346
    expert system, 348
    management information system,
        332–333
    transaction processing system,
        294–295
Inquiry, 333, 397
Integrated international information sys-
    tem, 375
Integrated Services Digital Network. *See*
    ISDN
Integrated software, 255
Intel Corporation, 109–110
Intelligent agent, 351
Intelligent terminal, 101
Intel ProShare, 274
Interactive operating system, 135

Interactive processing, 300
Internal storage. *See* Primary storage
International business, 18, 31, 370
    and international information systems, 370–371, 373–376
    strategies, 371–372
International Business Machines Corporation. *See* IBM
International information system, 18, 370
    characteristics, 373–376
International network, 178
International product development, 371
International production, 371
International sales, 370–371
International strategy, 372, 375
Internet, 21, 178–182. *See also* World Wide Web
    locating information on, 251–254
Internet Explorer. *See* Microsoft Internet Explorer
Internet Protocol. *See* TCP/IP
Internet service provider (ISP), 173
Internetwork, 178
Interorganizational communication, 158
Interorganizational information system, 17–18, 364, 376, 410. *See also* Interorganizational system
Interorganizational network, 18, 178, 368
Interorganizational system (IOS), 364
    business alliance and, 364–366
    characteristics, 366–368
    participant, 367
    sponsor, 366–367
Interpretation, 142
Interpreter, 142
Intranet, 181–182
Intraorganizational information system, 364, 376
Inventory, 6
Inventory control, 46–48
    information flow in, 39
    system, 5, 6–8, 305–306
Inventory master data, 302, 303, 305, 306
Inventory reorder report, 47–48, 305
Inventory value report, 47–48, 305
Invoice, 45, 303
I/O device, 63
IOS. *See* Interorganizational system
IP. *See* TCP/IP
IS. *See* Information system
ISDN, 166
ISDN terminal adapter, 167
ISP. *See* Internet service provider
IT. *See* Information technology

Java, 148
JetForm Workflow, 280
JIT. *See* Just-in-time inventory management

Job applicant tracking, 314
Just-in-time (JIT) inventory management, 314

KB. *See* Kilobyte
K byte, 107
Kernel, 131
Key, 169, 191, 454. *See also* Key field; Primary key
Keyboard, 63, 91
Key field, 191
Kilobyte (KB), 107
Knowledge base, 348

LAN. *See* Local area network
LAN adapter, 169
Laser printer, 98–99, 100
LCD, 97
Leased line, 447
Legacy system, 418–419
Letter-quality printer, 98
Light pen, 93
Line printer, 98, 99
Lines per minute (lpm), 98
Liquid crystal display. *See* LCD
LISP, 350
Loading a program, 74
Local area network (LAN), 13, 21, 68, 175–176
Logging in, 132
Logging out, 132
Logical system design, 414n
Logic error, 395
Loop, 389
Loop structure, 389
Lotus cc:Mail, 266
Lotus Notes, 268, 280, 281
Lotus 1-2-3, 234
Lotus Organizer, 254
Lotus SmartSuite, 254
Lpm. *See* Lines per minute
Lycos, 254

Machine dependent language, 141
Machine independent language, 142
Machine language, 108, 140–141
Macintosh. *See* Apple Macintosh
Mac OS, 76, 137
Mainframe computer, 15, 72–73
    CPU, 110
Magnetic disk, 66, 112–113
    access, 114–115
    drive, 66, 113–114
    usage, 115
Magnetic ink character recognition (MICR), 94–95
Magneto-optical (MO) disk, 117
Magnetic scanning input device, 94–95
Magnetic strip reader, 94
Magnetic tape, 66, 117–118

access, 119
    drive, 67, 118–119
    usage, 119
Maintenance, 401. *See also* System maintenance
MAN. *See* Metropolitan area network
Management, 41, 326
Management decision. *See also* Decision making
    characteristics, 327–329
    information needs for, 329–330
    levels, 327
    support, 337
Management by exception, 333
Management information system (MIS), 331
    functions, 332–335
    software, 336–337
    structure, 331–332
Management reporting system, 331
Manufacturer, 31
Manufacturing, 36–37
Manufacturing information system, 312–314
Manufacturing resource planning (MRP II), 314
Many-to-many relationship, 200–202
Marketing, 35–36, 363
Marketing information system, 312
Marketing research, 312
Mark-sense reader, 94
Massively parallel processing, 112
Master data, 297
Matching, 456
Material requirements planning (MRP), 314
Mathematical modeling, 337
MB. *See* Megabyte
M byte, 107
MCI, 447
Megabyte (MB), 107
Megahertz (MHz), 109
Memory. *See* Primary storage
Menu, 132
Merge utility, 139
Metropolitan area network (MAN), 177
MHz. *See* Megahertz
MICR. *See* Magnetic ink character recognition
Microcomputer, 69. *See also* Personal computer
    CPU, 109–110
Microprocessor, 109–110
Microsecond, 109
Microsoft Access, 208, 225
Microsoft Corporation, 447, 448
Microsoft Excel, 234
Microsoft Exchange, 268
Microsoft Internet Explorer, 253
Microsoft Mail, 266

Microsoft Office, 255
Microsoft Outlook, 254
Microsoft PowerPoint, 246
Microsoft Publisher, 248
Microsoft Word, 240
Microsoft Works, 255
Microwave, 163–164
Mid-range computer, 72
Millisecond, 109
Minicomputer, 72
    CPU, 110
MIS. *See* Management information
    system
MO. *See* Magneto-optical disk
Model, 337
Model base, 338
Modem, 68, 166
Modulation, 166
Monitor, 96, 131
Monochrome monitor, 96
Motorola, Inc., 69, 110
Mouse, 63, 92
MRP. *See* Material requirements planning
MRP II. *See* Manufacturing resource
    planning
MultiLogic ReSolver, 350
Multimedia, 79, 101–102, 251
Multinational strategy, 371–372, 373
Multiple-user computer system, 71–73
Multiple-user operating system, 134–135
Multiplexor, 167
Multipoint videoconferencing, 273
Multiprocessing, 112
Multitasking, 134

Nanosecond, 109
Natural language, 143
Navigator. *See* Netscape Navigator
Near-letter quality printer, 98
Net income, 30
NetNews, 181
Netscape Navigator, 253
NetWare. *See* Novell NetWare
Network, 21, 68. *See also* Local area
    network; Wide area network
    acquiring technology, 447
    organization, 173–175
Network analyst, 451
Network computer, 182
Network database, 203
Network database management system,
    206
Networked computer system, 73–74
Network operating system (NOS), 137,
    170
Neural network, 350–351
Niche, 358
Nonimpact printer, 97
Nonvolatile storage, 204
NOS. *See* Network operating system

Notebook computer, 70
Notes. *See* Lotus Notes
Not-for-profit organization, 30, 34
Novell GroupWise, 267
Novell, Inc., 447
Novell NetWare, 137

OAS. *See* Office automation system
Object, 146, 433
Object-oriented analysis and design,
    432–433
Object-oriented database, 206
Object-oriented database management
    system, 206
Object-oriented programming, 146, 432
Object-relational database, 206
ObjectStore, 208
OCR. *See* Optical character recognition
    device
Office automation system (OAS), 282
Off-line, 300
OLTP. *See* On-line transaction processing
One-to-many relationship, 200
One-to-one relationship, 199–200
On-line, 300
On-line processing, 299
On-line transaction processing (OLTP),
    299–300
On Technology Meeting Maker, 279
Operand, 140
Operating environment, 136
Operating personnel, 80
Operating system, 76, 130
    characteristics, 132–135
    common, 135–137
    functions, 131
    organization, 131–132
    using, 132
Operational decision, 327
Operational feasibility, 413
Operational planning, 442
Operation code, 140
Operations, 39, 292, 326, 362, 363
Optical character recognition (OCR)
    device, 94
Optical disk, 66, 116
    access, 117
    drive, 66, 116–117
    erasable, 117
    usage, 117
Optical scanning input device, 93–94
Oracle, 208, 448
Order entry, 44
    system, 8–9, 301–303
Organizational information system,
    15–17, 410
Organization chart, 38
OS/2, 136–137
Outbound logistics, 362, 363
Output control, 452

Output data, 10
Output device, 63
    plotter, 100
    printer, 63, 97–100
    screen, 63, 95–97
    sound, 101
    voice, 100–101
Output function, 10
    decision support system, 340
    executive support system, 346
    expert system, 348
    management information system,
        333–334
    transaction processing system, 295
Outsourcing, 414, 447

Packaged software, 77
Packard Bell, 69
Page, 128, 180, 253
Pagemaker, 248
Page printer, 98, 100
Page scanner, 94
Pages per minute (ppm), 98
Paradox, 208, 225
Parallel conversion, 417
Parallel processing. *See* Massively parallel
    processing
Parity bit, 106, 452
Parity check, 452
Payroll, 51
    system, 16, 309–310
PC. *See* IBM clone; IBM PC; Personal
    computer
PDA. *See* Personal digital assistant
Pen input, 93
Pentium, 110
Performance appraisal, 314
Peripheral equipment, 67
Personal computer, 12. *See also* Apple
    Macintosh; IBM clone; IBM PC
    communication, 172–173
Personal computer analyst, 451
Personal computer system, 69
Personal database, 213
Personal digital assistant (PDA), 70
Personal information manager (PIM),
    254
Personal information system. *See*
    Individual information system
Personnel, 62, 80, 448
Physical system design, 414*n*
PictureTel Live, 274
Pilot conversion, 417
Pilot Software Command Center, 347
PIM. *See* Personal information manager
Pixel, 95
Planning, 442
Planning horizon, 442–443
Platform, 126
Plotter, 100

Plunge conversion, 317
PointCast Network, 254
Pointing device, 92
Point-of-sale (POS) system, 5
Point-to-point videoconferencing, 273
Portfolio management, 311
POS. *See* Point-of-sale system
Powerbuilder, 208
PowerPC, 110
PowerPoint. *See* Microsoft PowerPoint
Ppm. *See* Pages per minute
Presentation graphics software, 13, 245–246
Primary key, 204
Primary storage, 65, 103
    capacity, 107
    data representation, 105–106
    organization, 106–107
    structure, 104–105
Print chart, 429
Printer, 63, 97
    classifications, 97–98
    desktop, 98–99
    high-volume, 99–100
Print server, 175
Print utility, 139
Privacy, 455–456
    laws, 457 (fig.)
Private communications system, 164–165
Problem, 384
Problem definition, 390–392
Problem solving, 384
    process, 389–396
    solution procedure, 384–389
Procedures, 5, 62, 80
Process, 419–420
Process description, 421–422
Processing control, 452
Processing function, 10
    decision support system, 340
    execution support system, 347
    expert system, 349
    management information system, 335
    transaction processing system, 298
Process management, 131
Processor, 65. *See also* Central processing unit
Procurement, 363, 364
Product differentiation, 358
Production. *See* Manufacturing
Production scheduling system, 9, 18, 313
Productivity, 23, 224
Program, 62. *See also* Software
    execution, 74–75
    loading, 74
Program file, 66
Program flowchart, 386, 422
Programmer, 139, 450
Programmer/analyst, 450

Programming, 139
Programming language, 139
    generators, 140–143
    Internet, 148
    object-oriented, 146–148
    selection, 140
    traditional, 143–146
    types, 140–143
Project team, 410
PROLOG, 350
Prompt, 132
Protocol, 168–169
Protocol converter, 169
Prototype, 432
Prototyping, 431–432
Pseudocode, 385–386
Public communications system, 164–165
Public domain software, 460
Purchase order, 49
Purchasing, 48–50
    information flow in, 39
    system, 306–307
Push technology, 254

Q&A, 225
QBasic, 144
QBE. *See* Query-by-example
Quarterdeck WebTalk, 272
Quattro Pro, 234
Query, 209, 333, 397
Query-by-example (QBE), 211
Query language, 143, 209, 336
QuickBASIC, 144

RAD. *See* Rapid application development
Radnet WebShare, 268
RAID, 114, 452
RAM. *See* Random access memory
Random access, 115, 193
Random access memory (RAM), 104
Random file. *See* Direct file
Rapid application development (RAD), 432
Raw materials inventory, 48
Read only memory (ROM), 104
Realistic image, 245
Real memory, 135
Real-time operating system, 135
Real-time processing, 300
Receiving notice, 47
Record, 78, 190, 224
Recovery procedure, 299, 452
Reduced Instruction Set Computer. *See* RISC
Redundant array of inexpensive disks. *See* RAID
Relational database, 203–205
Relational database management system, 206
Relationship, 196, 199–202, 224, 424

Remote access, 158, 171–173
Repetitive strain injury, 91
Report, 295
Report generator, 143
Report Program Generator. *See* RPG
Report writer, 336
Requirements, 400. *See also* User requirements
Research and development, 37
Resolution. *See* Screen resolution
Resource management, 131
Resource sharing, 158
Retailer, 32–33
Revenue, 30
Ring network, 174–175
RISC, 109
Risk, 443
Robotics, 314
ROM. *See* Read only memory
Room videoconferencing system, 273
Router, 178
RPG, 146
Rule, 348

Sales, 363. *See also* Marketing
    information flow in, 39
Sales analysis, 312
    system, 5
Sales force automation, 312
Sales forecasting, 312
Sales order, 44, 301
Scanner, 94
Scheduled report, 334
Screen, 63, 95–97
    resolution, 96
SDLC. *See* System development life cycle
Search engine, 253
Secondary storage, 66–67, 112
    magnetic disk, 112–115
    magnetic tape, 117–119
    optical disk, 115–117
Second-generation language, 141–142
Security, 454
    electronic, 454–455
    physical, 454
Sensitivity analysis, 339
Sequence structure, 386
Sequential access, 115, 191–193
Sequential file, 191
Serial printer, 98
Server, 73–74, 137, 175, 176
Service, 23, 363
Service business, 33–34
Shared database, 213
Shareware, 460
Sidekick, 254
Silicon Graphics InPerson, 275
Simplex transmission, 160
Single-tasking, 134
Single-user operating system, 134

SIS. *See* Strategic information system
Site license, 460
Skills inventory, 314
Smalltalk, 146
Social issue
    crime, 458–461
    employment, 456–458
    privacy, 455–456
SoftArc FirstClass, 268
Software, 5, 60–61, 74
    acquiring, 445–447
    alternatives, 414–415
    application, 75
    debugging, 395
    implementation, 394
    selection, 392
    sources, 77–78
    system, 75–76
    testing, 394–396
    types, 75–76
Software control, 397
Software engineering, 424
Software license agreement, 460
Software piracy, 460
Solution, 384
Solution procedure, 384–385
    basic logic, 386–389
    design, 393–394
    tools for representing, 385–386
Sorting, 297
Sort utility, 139
Sound output device, 101
Source document, 294
Spectragraphic TeamConference, 271
Spreadsheet, 12, 231–232
    concepts, 234–236
Spreadsheet analysis, 231–239
    combining with database management, 239
Spreadsheet software, 12, 127, 234
    functions, 236–239
Sprint, 447
SPSS, 340
SQL, 143, 209–211, 212, 336
Star network, 173
Statement, 46, 304
Statistical calculation, 337
Storage control, 452
Storage function, 10
    decision support system, 340
    executive support system, 346
    expert system, 349
    management information system, 335
    transaction processing system, 297–298
Storage location, 106
Store-and-forward, 271
Stored data, 10, 61, 78–79, 397, 400–401
Strategic advantage. *See* Strategic impact

Strategic decision, 327
Strategic impact, 358–359
Strategic information system (SIS), 359
    characteristics, 359–362
    opportunities, 362–364
Strategic planning, 442
Structured English, 421–422
Structured program, 389
Structured programming, 389
Structured Query Language. *See* SQL
Suite, 254–255
Summary report, 295, 333
Sun Microsystems, Inc., 71
Sun Microsystems ShowMe SharedApp, 271
Supercomputer, 73
    CPU, 110–112
Supervisor, 131
Supplier master data, 306–307, 308
Switched line, 447
Sybase, 208, 448
Synchronous transmission, 161
Syntax, 139
Syntax error, 394–395
System analysis, 410, 413–415
    example, 427–429
    user involvement in, 415
System design, 410, 415–416
    example, 429–430
    user involvement in, 416
System development
    example, 425–431
    other approaches, 431–433
    people in, 410
    process, 410–419
    tools, 419–425
System development life cycle (SDLC), 410
System flowchart, 422–423
System implementation, 410, 416–418
    example, 430
    user involvement in, 418
System maintenance, 410, 418, 431
System planning, 410, 411–413
    example, 426–427
    user involvement in, 413
System program, 75–76
System programmer, 451
Systems analyst, 410, 450
System software, 75–76, 126, 130
System specifications, 414

Tactical decision, 327
Tactical planning, 442
Tag, 148
Tape. *See* Magnetic tape
Tape drive. *See* Magnetic tape drive
Tax accounting, 311
TCP/IP, 179–180
TDF. *See* Transborder data flow
Technical feasibility, 413

Technology development, 363, 364
Telecommunications, 158
Telecommunications monitor, 170
Telecommuting, 283, 457
Teleprocessing system, 315–316
Telnet, 180
Terabyte, 107
Terminal, 63, 101
    communications, 171–172
    video display, 101
Terminal emulation, 169
Testing, 394–396
Text file, 66
Third-generation language, 142–143

3Com Corporation, 447
Time-sharing, 135
Time sheet, 51
Token Ring, 175
Top-down design, 393–394
Touch input device, 92–93
Touchpad, 92, 93
Touch screen, 92–93
TPS. *See* Transaction processing system
Track, 112, 116, 117
Trackball, 92
Trackpoint, 92
Training, 448
Transaction, 293
Transaction data, 297
Transaction processing system (TPS), 292, 293, 332
    controlling, 298–299
    functions, 294–298
    processing data in, 299
    structure, 293–294
Transborder data flow (TDF), 373
Transmission Control Protocol. *See* TCP/IP
Transnational strategy, 373, 375
Twisted-pair wiring, 162

Uninterrupted power supply. *See* UPS
Unisys Corporation, 73, 445
Universal Product Code (UPC), 94
UNIX, 136
UPC. *See* Universal Product Code
Updating data, 227, 297
Uploading data, 170
UPS, 452
Usenet, 181
User, 5, 19–20, 80
    application development, 384
    in decision support systems, 338
    direct versus indirect, 20
    effective, 24
    in executive support systems, 345
    in expert systems, 348
    involvement in system development, 410, 413, 415, 416, 418

in management information systems, 331

in transaction processing systems, 293–294

User documentation, 396

User interface, 132, 397, 400

User requirements, 413

Utility program, 139

Value added network (VAN), 447

Value added reseller (VAR), 445, 447

Value chain, 362–364

VAN. *See* Value added network

VAR. *See* Value added reseller

VDT. *See* Video display terminal

Ventana GroupSystems, 278

Versant ODBMS, 208

Video compression, 274

Videoconferencing, 273–275

Video decompression, 275

Video display terminal (VDT), 101

View, 213

Virtual company, 284

Virtual meeting, 284

Virtual memory, 135

Virtual office, 284, 458

Virtual reality, 102–103

Virtual work environment, 283

Virus, 461

Visio, 245

Visual Basic, 143, 144, 148

Visual communication, 264–265

Visual programming language, 148

VocalTec Internet Conference, 272

Voice input, 95

Voice output, 100–101

Voice processing, 282

Voice recognition, 95

Volatile storage, 104

VP-Expert, 350

WAN. *See* Wide area network

WebFlow SamePage, 268, 281

Web server, 180

What-if-analysis, 234

Whiteboard conferencing, 268–271

software, 271

Wholesaler, 31–32

Wide area network (WAN), 15, 21, 68, 177–178

global, 18

Window, 132

Windows, 136

Windows 95, 76, 136, 137

Windows NT server, 137

Windows NT workstation, 136, 137

Wireless LAN, 164

Word. *See* Microsoft Word

WordPerfect, 240

Word Pro, 240

Word processing, 240

combining with other applications, 244

system, 12, 240

Word processing software, 12, 147, 240

functions, 240–242

Workflow management, 279–280

software 279

Workgroup, 37

Workgroup application

summary, 280–282

types, 265–280

Workgroup information system, 13–15, 262, 410

Work-in-process inventory, 48

Worksheet, 234. *See also* Spreadsheet

Worksheet file, 66

Workstation, 70–71

World Wide Web (WWW), 21, 148, 180, 253–254

Worm, 461

WORM drive, 117

Write Once, Read Many drive. *See* WORM drive

WWW. *See* World Wide Web

Yahoo!, 254

Year 2000 problem, 419